VISIONS IN PSYCHOTHERAPY RESEARCH AND PRACTICE

The Society for Psychotherapy Research (SPR) is devoted to the development and dissemination of research, as well as the integration of empirical, theoretical, and clinical knowledge in psychotherapy. A highlight of the SPR Annual Meeting is the presidential address, wherein the president delivers what many view as the most important presentation of their career. In *Visions of Psychotherapy Research and Practice*, Bernhard Strauss, Jacques Barber, and Louis Castonguay, three recent past presidents, compile their own and the preceding 17 presidential addresses from SPR into a single volume. Then the presidents comment on how the visions they described in their addresses have developed over time.

Bernhard M. Strauss, PhD, is full professor of medical psychology and psychotherapy and head of the Institute of Psychosocial Medicine and Psychotherapy at the University Hospital Jena, Germany.

Jacques P. Barber, PhD, ABPP, is professor and dean of the Derner Institute of Advanced Studies in Psychology at Adelphi University.

Louis G. Castonguay, PhD, is professor at the department of psychology at Penn State University.

VISIONS IN PSYCHOTHERAPY RESEARCH AND PRACTICE

Reflections from Presidents of the Society for Psychotherapy Research

Edited by Bernhard M. Strauss, Jacques P. Barber, and Louis G. Castonguay

Routledge
Taylor & Francis Group
NEW YORK AND LONDON

First published 2015
by Routledge
605 Third Avenue, New York, NY 10017

and by Routledge
2 Park Square, Milton Park, Abingdon, Oxon, OX14 4RN

Routledge is an imprint of the Taylor & Francis Group, an informa business

Library of Congress Cataloging-in-Publication Data
Visions in psychotherapy research and practice : reflections from presidents of the Society for Psychotherapy Research / edited by Bernhard M. Strauss, Jacques P. Barber, and Louis G. Castonguay.
p. ; cm.
Includes bibliographical references and index.
I. Strauss, Bernhard, 1956- , editor. II. Barber, Jacques P., 1954- , editor. III. Castonguay, Louis Georges, editor. IV. Society for Psychotherapy Research.
[DNLM: 1. Biomedical Research—trends—Addresses. 2. Biomedical Research—trends—Collected Works. 3. Psychotherapy—trends—Addresses. 4. Psychotherapy—trends—Collected Works. 5. Psychological Theory—Addresses. 6. Psychological Theory—Collected Works. WM 420]
RC337
616.89'140072—dc23
2014029234

ISBN: 978-0-415-50679-3 (hbk)
ISBN: 978-0-415-50680-9 (pbk)
ISBN: 978-0-203-12671-4 (ebk)

Typeset in Bembo
by Apex CoVantage, LLC

CONTENTS

LIST OF ILLUSTRATIONS

Figures

Tables

PREFACE

For more than 40 years, the Society for Psychotherapy Research (SPR) has been devoted to the development and dissemination of research, as well as the integration of empirical, theoretical, and clinical knowledge in psychotherapy. As such, SPR has played a significant role in the mental health field around the world with regard to the understanding, application, and refinements of psychosocial interventions. In particular, the work and voices of the presidents of the organization has been of great influence in shaping the field. Recognized internationally as leaders in psychotherapy research and psychotherapy in general, the presidents of SPR include innovative scholars and investigators from different theoretical orientations (psychodynamic, humanistic, cognitive-behavioral, integrative therapies) who have developed research programs and treatment interventions for common clinical problems.

As part of the SPR tradition, each president presents a presidential address at the Annual Meeting of the organization. These addresses not only represent the highlight of a presidential mandate, but they are often perceived as the most important presentation of their entire career.

Since the foundation of the official journal of the society (*Psychotherapy Research*) in 1991, the presidential addresses have been published as articles in the journal. They are also very visible papers, which are highly regarded by other researchers and clinicians. As recent past presidents (2008–2010), we have shared the idea of bringing together the SPR presidential addresses of the last 20 years into this one book.

Primarily, the book provides a collection of the written versions of the addresses that have been published in *Psychotherapy Research*, from its first issue in 1991 until 2011. Two of the addresses included in the book (those of Karla Moras and Bernhard Strauss) have not been published before.

Although we are admittedly biased, the presidential addresses contain a variety of important visions, ideas, and thoughts that do not deserve to be forgotten and would benefit from being collected in one location/book. Because they have shaped the foundations and are still at the forefront of our current understanding and practice of psychotherapy, it is very likely that these papers will be of high interest to researchers, scholars, clinicians, educators, and students in the mental health field.

In order to go beyond an aggregated reprinting of presidential addresses, we have also asked the living presidents to comment on how the ideas and visions they described in their respective addresses have developed since their publications. Specifically, we asked each past president to provide a comment addressing the following three questions: 1) From your current perspective, what (if any) would you change in your address? 2) Have you observed changes in the field that you predicted in your talk, and/or that have been consistent with, perhaps even influenced by your talk? and 3) What are your predictions for psychotherapy research in the near future, including issues raised in your talk that you wish the field will pay attention to in the future?

The presidential addresses from the pre-journal era (before 1991) were not available in their entire format. Therefore, to complete the historical picture of the SPR and its presidents, we invited two past presidents who were involved in the creation of SPR, David Orlinsky and Irene Elkin, to provide an introductory chapter summarizing the 40 years history of SPR and the ideas developed by its presidents in the years before 1991.

In addition to this introductory chapter, we have closed the book with a summary of the visionary thoughts expressed in main chapters and an outline of some perspectives for the future of psychotherapy research, theory, and practice.

We would like to thank all colleagues who supported our project and contributed to this book. We thank Paolo Machado and J. Chris Muran, the editors of *Psychotherapy Research*, for their encouragement. Last but not least we want to express our appreciative thanks to the Routledge staff for their positive response and support.

We hope that this book will stimulate the discussion about the future of psychotherapy research and that it will help to preserve 20 years of "visions in psychotherapy research and practice."

Fall 2014
Jena, Garden City, University Park
Bernhard M. Strauss
Jacques P. Barber
Louis G. Castonguay

ABOUT THE EDITORS AND CONTRIBUTORS

Mark Aveline, MD, FRCPsych, retired from his clinical and teaching position in Nottingham in 2002. He is an Emeritus Consultant Psychiatrist and Psychotherapist for Nottinghamshire Healthcare NHS Trust and Honorary Professor of Counselling and Psychotherapy at the University of Leicester. He was President of the British Association for Counselling and Psychotherapy 1994–2000, and of the Society for Psychotherapy Research (SPR) 2003–2004, having previously been President of the UK Chapter. Author of over 80 publications and three edited books, he has long been an advocate for more science in clinical practice and more clinical wisdom in research design and interpretation. Training, integrated clinical service, time-limited group and individual psychotherapy and researching ways to increment effectiveness have been his passion. He lives in the UK near Cirencester in the Cotswolds and in mid-Wales, enjoying planting trees, walking the dog, and the arts.

Jacques P. Barber, PhD, ABPP is Professor and Dean, Derner Institute of Advanced Studies in Psychology, Adelphi University. He is Professor Emeritus at University of Pennsylvania Perelman School of Medicine. He is past president of the society for psychotherapy research and was a recipient of its early career award in 1996. His research and scholarship focus broadly on the outcome and process of psychodynamic and cognitive therapies for depression, panic disorder, PTSD, substance dependence, and personality disorders. Most of this has been funded by the NIMH and NIDA. He has published more than 180 papers, chapters, and books in those areas.

Lorna Smith Benjamin studied with Harry Harlow and had postdoctoral training at the University of Wisconsin's Department of Psychiatry. Leaving in 1988 to go to the University of Utah, she now is retired. She created Structural Analysis of

Social Behavior (SASB), an interpersonal model that has been incorporated in many assessment methods, including the CCRT, CMP, and OPD-2. Her first book used SASB for interpersonal diagnosis of personality disorder. Her second applied SASB to psychotherapy (IRT). A draft book proposes "natural biology" to understand mechanisms of change. She continues to offer workshops, consultations for clinicians learning IRT, and private practice.

Franz Caspar is Professor for Clinical Psychology and Psychotherapy, University of Bern (Switzerland), after having served as professor at the universities of Freiburg (Germany) and Geneva (Switzerland). He is also director of a psychotherapy outpatient clinic and of two psychotherapy training programs. Currently he is also dean of the faculty of human sciences at the University of Bern, president of the International Federation for Psychotherapy (IFP), and Steering Committee member of the Society for the Exploration of Psychotherapy Integration (SEPI). His research interests include the use of concepts of basic psychology and neurobiology for psychotherapy, the therapeutic relationship, hypothesis generation and decision making of psychotherapists, and the training of psychotherapists.

Louis G. Castonguay, PhD, is Professor at the Department of Psychology at Penn State University. With more than 140 publications (including five co-edited books), his scholarly work and research focus on different aspects of the process of change and training, the investigation of new integrative treatments for generalized anxiety disorder and depression, and the development of Practice Research Networks aimed at facilitating the collaboration between clinicians and researchers. He has received several awards, including the Distinguished Psychologist Award for his lifetime contributions to the field of psychotherapy from the American Psychological Association Division of Psychotherapy. He also served as President of the North American Society for Psychotherapy Research and the International Society for Psychotherapy Research.

Paul Crits-Christoph, PhD, is director of the Center for Psychotherapy Research at the University of Pennsylvania, where he is also a Professor of Psychology in Psychiatry. He has published 180 journal articles, 63 chapters, and 5 books. He has conducted a wide range of studies of the process and outcome of psychotherapy for depression, generalized anxiety disorder, and substance use disorders. Most recently, his focus has been on the treatment of depression and substance use disorders in community-based agencies. He was president of the International Society for Psychotherapy Research during 1996–1997.

John F. Clarkin, PhD, is Clinical Professor of Psychology in Psychiatry and co-director of the Personality Disorders Institute at the Weill Medical College of Cornell University, New York. He is a past president of the international Society for Psychotherapy Research. Dr. Clarkin's research activities have focused on the phenomenology of the personality disorders and the treatment of patients with borderline personality disorder and bipolar disorder. He is the author of numerous articles and books on psychopathology, differential treatment planning, and the personality disorders.

Irene Elkin, PhD (formerly Waskow), is Professor Emerita, School of Social Service Administration, University of Chicago. She held a number of successive positions at the National Institute of Mental Health, where she spent most of her professional career. These included Research Psychologist in the Psychopharmacology Research Branch and the Clinical Research Branch, Head of the Section on Treatment Development and Process Research in the Psychosocial Treatments Research Branch, Head of the Psychosocial Treatment Program in the Affective and Anxiety Disorders Research Branch, and chair of the NIMH Psychotherapy and Rehabilitation Research Consortium. She is best known for co-editing the volume on Psychotherapy Change Measures and for her role in designing and coordinating the NIMH Treatment of Depression Collaborative Research Program, the first multi-site collaborative study initiated by the NIMH in the field of psychotherapy. The last 10 years of her career were at the University of Chicago, where she directed the NIMH Mental Health Services Research Training Program, taught clinical research methods to social work doctoral students, and conducted psychotherapy research under an NIMH Research Scientist Award. Her honors include a U.S. Public Health Service Special Recognition Award, an Alcohol, Drug Abuse and Mental Health Administration Award for Meritorious Achievement, and the SPR Distinguished Research Career Award. She was President of SPR in 1978–1979.

Robert Elliott, PhD, is Professor of Counselling in the Counselling Unit at the University of Strathclyde. Professor Emeritus of Psychology at the University of Toledo (Ohio), he is co-author of four books, including *Learning Process—Experiential Psychotherapy* (2004), and *Research Methods in Clinical Psychology* (2002), as well as more than 120 journal articles and book chapters. He previously co-edited *Psychotherapy Research* and *Person-Centered Counseling and Psychotherapies.* He has received the Distinguished Research Career Award of the Society for Psychotherapy Research, and the Carl Rogers Award from the Division of Humanistic Psychology of the American Psychological Association.

Marvin R. Goldfried, PhD, is Distinguished Professor of Psychology at Stony Brook University. He is the recipient of numerous awards from various psychological associations, past president of the Society for Psychotherapy Research and the Society of Clinical Psychology, and current president of the Psychotherapy Division of APA. He is founder of the journal *In Session* and author of numerous articles and books. Dr. Goldfried is co-founder of the Society for the Exploration of Psychotherapy Integration (SEPI), and founder of AFFIRM: Psychologists Affirming Their Lesbian, Gay, Bisexual and Transgender Family.

Leslie Greenberg, PhD is Distinguished Research Professor of Psychology at York University in Toronto, Ontario. He is a leading authority on working with emotion in psychotherapy and the developer of an evidence-based approach/emotion-focused therapy. He has authored the major texts on emotion-focused approaches to treatment of individuals and couples. These include: *Emotion in Psychotherapy* (1986), *Emotionally Focused Therapy for Couples* (1988), and *Facilitating Emotional Change* (1993). More recently he has published *Emotion-Focused Couples Therapy: The Dynamics of Emotion, Love and Power* (2008), *Emotion-Focused Therapy: Theory and Practice* (2010), *Working with Narrative in Emotion-Focused Therapy: Changing Stories, Healing Lives* (2011), and *Therapeutic Presence* (2011). Dr. Greenberg has published extensively on research on the process of change. He has received the Distinguished Research Career award of the International Society for Psychotherapy Research, as well as the Carl Rogers Award and the Distinguished Professional Contribution to Applied Research of the American Psychological Association. He also has received the Canadian Council of Professional Psychology Program Award for Excellence in Professional Training and the Canadian Psychological Association Professional Award for Distinguished Contributions to Psychology as a Profession. He conducts a private practice for individuals and couples and trains people in emotion-focused approaches.

Clara E. Hill earned her PhD at Southern Illinois University in 1974. She started her career in 1974 as an assistant professor in the Department of Psychology, University of Maryland, and is currently still there as a professor. She has been the president of the Society for Psychotherapy Research, the editor of the *Journal of Counseling Psychology*, and the editor of *Psychotherapy Research*. She was awarded the Leona Tyler Award from Division 17 (Society of Counseling Psychology), the Distinguished Psychologist Award from Division 29 (Psychotherapy) of the American Psychological Association, the Distinguished Research Career Award from the Society for Psychotherapy Research, and the Outstanding Lifetime Achievement Award from the Section on Counseling and Psychotherapy Process and Outcome Research of the Society for Counseling Psychology. Her major research interests are helping skills, psychotherapy process and outcome, training therapists, dream work, and qualitative research. She has published more than 180 journal articles, 65 chapters in books, and 10 books (including *Therapist Techniques and Client Outcomes: Eight Cases of Brief Psychotherapy*; *Helping Skills: Facilitating Exploration, Insight, and Action*; and *Dream Work in Therapy: Facilitating Exploration, Insight, and Action*).

Leonard M. Horowitz is Professor of Psychology Emeritus at Stanford University and a Fellow of the American Psychological Association. He is a past president of the SPR and of the Society for Interpersonal Theory and Research (SITAR). His research has focused on interpersonal processes in the study of psychotherapy, psychopathology, and personality; he also received SPR's Distinguished Research Career Award in 2010. His test, the *Inventory of Interpersonal Problems* (*IIP*), is now published by Mind Garden, Inc. Prof. Horowitz's books include (with Hans Strupp and Michael Lambert) *Measuring Patient Changes in Mood, Anxiety, and Personality Disorders* (American Psychological Association, 1997); *Interpersonal Foundations of Psychopathology* (American Psychological Association, 2004); and (with Stephen Strack) *Handbook of Interpersonal Psychology* (2010). He has been a Woodrow Wilson Fellow and a Social Science Research Council Fellow (at Johns Hopkins University); a Fulbright Fellow (at University College, University of London); a Special Fellow of the National Institute of Mental Health (at Mt. Zion Psychiatric Clinic, San Francisco), and a James McKeen Cattell Awardee for Scholarship (at University of California, Berkeley).

Horst Kächele, MD, PhD, is at present Professor at the International Psychoanalytic University in Berlin, after having chaired the Department of Psychosomatic Medicine and Psychotherapy at Ulm University. His clinical work as psychoanalyst has inspired his research interest in process and outcome, in psychosocial aspects of bone-marrow transplantation, and in clinical attachment research. Besides numerous publications in journals and books, he co-authored the Um textbook on psychoanalytic therapy that has been translated into many languages. He has received the M. Sigourney Award of the American Psychoanalytic Association and was honored recently for his lifetime achievements by the Society for Psychotherapy Research.

Michael J. Lambert, PhD, is a Professor of Psychology holds the Susa Young Gates University Professorship at Brigham Young University, teaching in the Clinical Psychology Program. He is an honorary professor, Queensland University, Brisbane, Australia. He has been in private practice as a psychotherapist throughout his career. He was the recipient of the Distinguished Psychologist Award from Division 29 (psychotherapy) of the American Psychological Association, and the Academic Excellence Award from the Utah Psychological Association. In 2003, he was the recipient of the Distinguished Career Research award by the Society of Psychotherapy Research for his lifetime contributions to professional practice. His research spans 40 years and has emphasized psychotherapy outcome, process, and the measurement of change. He has edited, authored, or co-authored 9 academic research-based books, and 50 book chapters, while publishing over 150 scientific articles on treatment outcome. He is the editor of *Bergin and Garfield's Handbook of Psychotherapy and Behavior Change* (5th and 6th editions), the most authoritative summary of the effects of psychological treatments. His current program of research focuses on reducing treatment failure and non response through the use of advanced statistical methods and computer applications outlined in *Prevention of Treatment Failure: Measuring, Monitoring, and Feedback in Clinical Practice.*

Erhard Mergenthaler is a retired professor from the University of Ulm, Germany, where he was director of the Section of Informatics in Psychotherapy. His educational background is computer science and linguistics and he has been engaged in psychotherapy research since 1975. His scholarly work and research focuses on theoretical aspects of the process of change and its empirical assessment, with special attention to computer-assisted analysis of written-language-like transcripts from therapy sessions and a focus on practice orientation. He is also an expert in text bank management and drug information systems. He was Visiting Professor at the University of California, San Francisco; Adelphi University, New York; University College London; Universidad Belgrano, Buenos Aires; PUC Campinas, Brasil. He has also taught in Moscow, Salamanca, Milan, and other places in Italy. He has received several awards and major funding from the German Research Foundation and the German government. During his term as President of the International Society for Psychotherapy Research, he was chair of the international meeting in Edinburgh in 2006, with its largest attendance to date.

Karla Moras, PhD, was the 32nd President of the SPR (2003). She received SPR's Early Career Contribution Award (1994), served as an Associate Editor of SPR's journal, *Psychotherapy Research* (1991–1996), and also was President of SPR's North American Regional Chapter. Main foci of her research have been depression and anxiety in adults, the relationship between depression and anxiety, refining efficacious treatments for both, and treatment development for medication-resistant depression. She received grants from the U.S. National Institute of Mental Health and the National Alliance for Research on Schizophrenia and Depression for research on the topics. She is now an independent consultant in Merion, Pennsylvania, USA.

David Orlinsky, PhD, is Professor of Comparative Human Development at the University of Chicago. In 1968, with Ken Howard, he founded the SPR; served as first president-elect, and as founding president of the North American SPR; and organized the SPR interest sections on Culture and Psychotherapy and on Therapist Training and Development. Through more than 100 articles, chapters, and books, his pioneering research focused on studies of psychotherapy process as experienced by patients and therapists, both during their sessions and the times between sessions (e.g., Orlinsky and Howard, *Varieties of Psychotherapeutic Experience*, 1975), and also focused on studies of the professional and personal characteristics, experiences, and development of psychotherapists in many countries (e.g., Orlinsky and Rønnestad, *How Psychotherapists Develop*, 2005; Geller, Norcross and Orlinsky, *The Psychotherapists' Own Psychotherapy*, 2005). His critical scholarship on research relating therapeutic process to outcome exerted a major influence on the field (via chapters in four successive editions of Bergin and Garfield's *Handbook of Psychotherapy and Behavior Change*) and formed the basis for the theoretical model known as the "Generic Model of Psychotherapy." The professional recognition he has received include the Distinguished Psychologist Award of the American Psychological Association Division of Psychotherapy, the Senior Distinguished Career Award from the

Society for Psychotherapy Research, and an honorary doctorate from the University of Oslo on its 200th anniversary.

William E. Piper, PhD, is Professor Emeritus in Psychiatry at the University of British Columbia. He has over 200 publications (including six co-edited books). His research and publications focused upon the process and outcome of different forms of individual and group psychotherapies. Since 1974, he has been funded continuously from external research grants. He has served as President of the Canadian Group Psychotherapy Association and President of the International Society for Psychotherapy Research, and is a Distinguished Fellow of the American Group Psychotherapy Association. He also received the Group Psychologist of the Year award from the American Psychological Association in 2010.

David A. Shapiro, PhD, led a psychotherapy research group at Sheffield and Leeds for over 20 years, authoring some 200 publications, many of which reported on the programmatic, landmark Sheffield Psychotherapy Projects, process–outcome studies of contrasting treatments of depression conducted in a research clinic. He established a UK chapter of the Society for Psychotherapy Research, before serving as President of the international organisation and as founding managing editor of its journal, *Psychotherapy Research.* He also edited the *British Journal of Clinical Psychology*. Following a career downshift occasioned by his daughter's severe ME, he pursued research consultancy and service development projects for several years, before retraining as a (part-time) professional photographer, specializing in community projects and creative arts.

William B. Stiles is Professor Emeritus of Psychology, Miami University, Oxford, Ohio, USA. He has also taught at the University of North Carolina at Chapel Hill, and he has held visiting positions at the Universities of Sheffield and Leeds in the United Kingdom, at Massey University in New Zealand, and at the University of Joensuu in Finland. He received his PhD from UCLA in 1972. He is president-elect of Division 29 (Psychotherapy) of the American Psychological Association and a past president of the Society for Psychotherapy Research. He has served as editor of *Psychotherapy Research* and *Person-Centered and Experiential Psychotherapies* and associate editor of *British Journal of Clinical Psychology.* He has published over 250 journal articles and book chapters, most dealing with psychotherapy theory, research, and practice, verbal interaction, and research methods.

Bernhard M. Strauss, PhD, is full Professor of Medical Psychology and Psychotherapy and head of the Institute of Psychosocial Medicine and Psychotherapy at the University Hospital Jena, Germany. His work in the field of psychotherapy research is focused on group psychotherapy, attachment, psychotherapy training and process–outcome studies related to different psychological disorders. Other research activities of his research group relate to health psychology, psychosomatic medicine, and sex research. He has published more than 300 journal articles, more than 230 chapters, and edited or (co-)authored 50 books. He is editor emeritus of *Psychotherapy Research* and *Gruppenpsychotherapie & Gruppendynamik*, and is currently co-editing major German journals of psychotherapy and sex research. He is past president of the German College of Psychosomatic Medicine, the German Society for Medical Psychology, as well as the Society for Psychotherapy Research (SPR).

INTRODUCTION

Forty Years of Research and Relationships: A Personal Perspective on the Past, Present, and Future of SPR[1]

David Orlinsky

INCLUDING RECOLLECTIONS AND COMMENTS BY IRENE ELKIN

Hello. I'm here to introduce this book. Allow me to introduce myself first—David Orlinsky, one of the founders of the Society for Psychotherapy Research (SPR), its first president-elect, and second president following my friend, colleague, and SPR co-founder, Kenneth Howard. As it happened, I was also the first to give a presidential address at our third annual international conference in Nashville, Tennessee, in 1972. No presidential addresses were given at previous meetings and there was no plan to have one at this meeting, but a prominent "invited speaker" withdrew at the last minute and the "presidential address" was invented as a replacement. As I was president then, it fell to me to fill the time, which I did with a lecture titled "Person, Praxis and Process in Psychotherapy"[2]—but that was before personal computers allowed everyone to preserve everything they had written, and the talk I gave then has long since disappeared. Possibly that is why the editors invited me to write the introduction for this book, which is a collection of SPR presidential addresses that have been preserved, since 1991, through their annual publication in the SPR journal *Psychotherapy Research.*[3]

One might guess that a collection of past presidential addresses from any source would as exciting to read as a book composed of ceremonial "graduation day" addresses, which is to say "very little to nil"—but, as it turns out (and those will see who read on), you would be wrong to guess that in this case. The list of SPR presidents (shown in Table I.1) is a veritable "Who's Who" of distinguished colleagues that have contributed much to the field of psychotherapy research, and their reflections on their work, and on the field we all work in, are important and well worth preserving. Our field—the scientific study of psychotherapy—has acquired a "history," since it began as a continuous enterprise in the late 1940s. This history needs to be recorded and remembered, so that those who joined the field lately, and will join in years to come, do not waste

TABLE I.1 Annual Conferences and Presidents of the Society for Psychotherapy Research

Year	*Conference Site*	*President*	*Term*
1968	San Francisco, California (pre–SPR meeting)	[D. Orlinsky and K. Howard, hosts]	
1969	Highland Park, Illinois (SPR founded)	[K. Howard and D. Orlinsky, hosts]	
1970	Chicago, Illinois (SPR constitution adopted)	[D. Orlinsky and K. Howard, hosts]	
1971	Saddle Brook, New Jersey	Kenneth Howard	1970–1971
1972	Nashville, Tennessee	David Orlinsky	1971–1972
1973	Philadelphia, Pennsylvania	Hans Strupp	1972–1973
1974	Denver, Colorado	Lester Luborsky	1973–1974
1975	Boston, Massachusetts, and London, England	Allen Bergin	1974–1975
1976	Coronado Beach, San Diego, California	Sol Garfield	1975–1976
1977	Madison, Wisconsin	Aaron T. Beck	1976–1977
1978	Toronto, Canada	Morris Parloff	1977–1978
1979	Oxford, England	Irene Elkin Waskow	1978–1979
1980	Asilomar State Park, Pacific Grove, California	Edward Bordin	1979–1980
1981	Aspen, Colorado	Mardi Horowitz	1980–1981
1982	Smugglers' Notch, Vermont	Stanley Imber	1981–1982
1983	Sheffield, England	Alan Gurman	1982–1983
1984	Lake Louise, Canada	Arthur Auerbach	1983–1984
1985	Evanston, Illinois	A. John Rush	1984–1985
1986	Wellesley, Massachusetts	Jim Mintz	1985–1986
1987	Ulm, Germany	Larry Beutler	1986–1987
1988	Santa Fe, New Mexico	Larry Beutler	1987–1988
1989	Toronto, Canada	Charles Marmar	1988–1989
1990	Wintergreen, Virginia	Leslie Greenberg	1989–1990
1991	Lyon, France	Horst Kächele	1990–1991
1992	Berkeley, California	Lorna Benjamin	1991–1992

1993	Pittsburgh, Pennsylvania	Leonard Horowitz	1992–19931
1994	York, England	David Shapiro	1993–1994
1995	Vancouver, Canada	Clara Hill	1994–1995
1996	Amelia Island, Florida	Klaus Grawe	1995–1996
1997	Geilo, Norway	Paul Crits-Christoph	1996–1997
1998	Snowbird, Utah	William Stiles	1997–1998
1999	Braga, Portugal	Marvin Goldfried	1998–1999
2000	Bloomingdale, Illinois	William Piper	1999–2001
2001	Montevideo, Uruguay	Robert Elliott	2000–2001
2002	Santa Barbara, California	Franz Caspar	2001–2002
2003	Weimar, Germany	Karla Moras	2002–2003
2004	Rome, Italy	Mark Aveline	2003–2004
2005	Montreal, Canada	John Clarkin	2004–2005
2006	Edinburgh, Scotland	Michael Lambert	2005–2006
2007	Madison, Wisconsin	Erhard Mergenthaler	2006–2007
2008	Barcelona, Spain	Jacques Barber	2007–2008
2009	Santiago de Chile	Bernhard Strauss	2008–2009
2010	Asilomar State Park, Pacific Grove, California	Louis Castonguay	2009–2010
2011	Bern, Switzerland	Lynne Angus	2010–2011
2012	Virginia Beach, Virginia	Guillermo de la Parra	2011–2012
2013	Brisbane, Australia	George Silberschatz	2012–2013
2014	Copenhagen, Denmark	Hadas Wiseman	2013–2014

time "reinventing the wheel"; for, as Santayana (1905/1998) said, "Those who cannot remember the past are condemned to repeat it."

The presidential addresses collected in this book are a significant part of the history of psychotherapy research. They typically review the state of research at the time they were written, summarize the main achievements of the speaker's career, and focus on future challenges faced by the field. Taken together, they provide an incisive conceptual introduction to scientific research on psychotherapy as well as a unique historical record of its growth and development over the past two decades. They also provide a valuable companion to the volume of biographical chapters collected in *Bringing Psychotherapy Research to Life* (Castonguay, Muran, Angus et al., 2010) that describe the lives and achievements of many whose addresses are included in the present volume.

In this context, then, may I say what a pleasure and privilege it is for me to introduce readers to the Society for Psychotherapy Research (SPR), which—due in large part to the spirit instilled in it and sustained by its successive presidents—has become not merely a "society" (*gesellschaft*), but a true scientific "community" (*gemeinschaft*) in the best and fullest sense: not merely an interest group (it is that) or convenient association (that, too), but a set of mutually supportive and loyal *personal relationships*, not unlike an extended family or kinship network. Annual SPR conferences have a distinct flavor of "family reunion" about them, a happily anticipated and exciting gathering to greet old friends and meet young and newly added colleagues to the fold. The proceedings at SPR conferences are congenial and informal, and the sometimes bitter rivalries one hears about at meetings of other scientific societies are not found—although jocular exchanges and *kibbitzing* frequently are. This devoted, personal, and playful spirit runs deep in the culture of SPR, infused by the mutual warmth and respect its founders felt for one another. Like Ken's and mine, their names—Strupp, Luborsky, Garfield, Bergin, Parloff, Elkin, Bordin—are among the earliest listed in the Table I.1; many (sadly) now deceased and sorely missed, others (thankfully) still alive and kicking. Along with others not listed, they were and are dear friends and comrades-in-research. Yet they would not begrudge my saying that first and foremost among them for me was Ken Howard, my fellow student in graduate school, my long-time research collaborator, co-author, and lifelong friend.

SPR might well have been started by other people because, in the late 1960s, the times were ripe for starting such a group; but, as it happened, it fell to us (to me and to Ken)—accidentally or otherwise—to take the initial steps that led to the founding of SPR, to infuse it with the spirit of our friendship, and to serve it for years in various capacities. In a recent letter, Allen Bergin described his memory of us at the first conference in 1969: "I was surprised that most of the people were so young. I wondered where the senior people were . . . As for Howard and Orlinsky, I wondered: 'Who are these guys? What gives them the authority or *chutzpah* to be doing this instead of the famous establishment people?'"

As the first and second presidents, Ken and I wrote the bylaws and constitution for SPR, which years later I helped twice revise—in 1986 with Winfred Huber, John Rush, and David Shapiro, and in 1999 with Mark Aveline, Franz Caspar, and Bill Stiles—as the organization grew and its requirements changed. From the mid-1980s through the early 1990s, Ken served as SPR's first executive officer, and I had a role in broadening SPR from its origins as a basically North American group into a society with international chapters, and members in many countries around the world. Ken was present in 1993 with Horst Kächele (our 20th president) to bless the first South American chapter meeting in

Mendoza, Argentina, and the next year Horst and I were privileged to attend the chapter's second meeting in Santiago de Chile.[4]

Here I wish to write briefly (and, of necessity, very selectively) about the past, present, and future of SPR. I will start with a reference to the situation in our field prior to SPR, the situation that led to the formation of SPR. Psychotherapy research had begun as a continuous undertaking in the late 1940s and early 1950s, pioneered by teams of investigators at the University of Chicago under the leadership of Carl Rogers (1954), and at Johns Hopkins University in Baltimore Maryland under the leadership of Jerome Frank (Stone, 1978), and at the Menninger Foundation in Topeka, Kansas (Wallerstein, 1989). By the end of the 1950s, the field of psychotherapy research had become large enough to have a cadre of well-established investigators, and the first of three major invitational conferences was called in 1958, jointly sponsored by the American Psychological Association's Division of Clinical Psychology and the U.S. National Institute of Mental Health. A second conference was held three years later in 1961, and a third was held five years after that, in 1966.

This last meeting was held at the University of Chicago, where I was an assistant professor who had begun to do research on psychotherapy but had not yet published in this field. When I heard that the conference would be held at my own university, I called the organizers to ask permission to attend—but was repeatedly told that I could not, because admission was by invitation only, and I (an unknown) had not been invited. Being a faculty member of the university where the conference was to be held made no difference; neither I nor my co-worker, Ken Howard, would be admitted.

My first experience with the psychotherapy research "establishment," therefore, was one of exclusion, frustration, and not a small measure of anger. From this experience, a determination arose within me to organize a conference that would be open and inclusive, a conference to which all who were actively interested in therapy research might come. With the quiet support of Hans Strupp, who met with us while on a personal visit with his wife to Chicago in 1967, we arranged to have a day-long conference on therapy research held prior to the 1968 American Psychological Association meeting in San Francisco, sponsored jointly by the American Academy of Psychotherapists (of which I was treasurer) and the then newly formed APA Division of Psychotherapy. We did this by sending letters of invitation to everyone we found listed in the journal *Psychological Abstracts* who had published an article on psychotherapy in any journal during the preceding five years—and many people came to that first session!

Our experience provided several lessons that were influential in shaping the culture of SPR. The first lesson was to resist any temptations to elitism and "establishment" thinking; to be inclusive rather than exclusive; and especially to welcome young researchers to the field, and to make them feel "part of the family."

The second enduring lesson was to step forward and dare to take initiative when that seems called for; to make one's voice heard; and to constructively challenge rather than accept the status quo when that seemed needed and worthwhile. Ken and I might never have done this separately as individuals, but together we complemented and completed each other in a way that made us each capable of doing more than we otherwise would have attempted. Together we felt like Butch Cassidy and the Sundance Kid, the title characters in the classic Newman/Redford movie. Together we possessed what Allen Bergin (using vernacular more likely learned at Columbia than at Brigham Young)[5] called *chutzpah*—the audacity, daring, conspicuous boldness, even as "unknown nobodies" to take action, based on a passionate wish to share in a quest for knowledge, and take part in a conversation with others who felt the same passion.

The third lesson learned in the process of forming SPR was drawn mainly from the experience of the initial "proto-SPR" meeting in 1968, where the people who came spent the day talking together and asking one another about the research they had published and were doing. Recurrently, one heard a colleague say, "Oh, so that's what you meant!" in a tone of surprise and sudden understanding. We discovered more vividly there what should have already been clear: that journal articles generally communicate rather poorly what their authors meant and hoped to convey about their ideas, their procedures, and findings.

A consensus developed there that opportunity for extended conversation was crucial to mutual understanding and further development in our field, and the conference organizers (Ken and I) were requested to arrange for another meeting in 1969, at a different time than the APA conference so that the field of psychotherapy research could recognize and welcome colleagues from the disciplines of psychiatry, social work, and related fields as well as from psychology. Thus, extended and informal person-to-person communication became, and still remains, the raison d'être and hallmark of SPR meetings. That was the intended purpose, and the rewarding achievement, of the multi-day meeting for all interested psychotherapy researchers that Ken and I organized in 1969. It was the group of colleagues who attended that second conference who decided to establish an independent scientific society, and to name it the Society for Psychotherapy Research.

Irene Elkin, who was present at the meeting in 1969, contributed the following memory of that conference:

> The first "formal" meeting of SPR in 1969 came at an especially propitious time for me. I had just moved from the Psychopharmacology Research Branch at NIMH to the Clinical Research Branch, where I could turn again to my real professional love: psychotherapy research. I found it incredibly exciting to attend a meeting with researchers in this field, across a broad age range, with different theoretical views and different approaches to research. But, despite these differences, there was an atmosphere not

> only of collegiality, but almost of camaraderie. I was especially excited about meeting people like Hans Strupp, whose work I had known and admired from my graduate school days. And I was surprised to find that Hans remembered the article based on my dissertation research. I later decided that he and Allen Bergin, who had recently, together, compiled a bibliography of research on individual psychotherapy, must remember everything in the literature! In the small groups we broke into, there was a lot of stimulating discussion and an impressive openness to others' views. That, for me, has been a major characteristic of SPR throughout the years.

The greatest challenge that our Society confronts, given its growing membership and geographical expanse, is how to achieve this same intimacy of communication and reciprocity of understanding. Attendance at SPR meetings is five, six, or seven times what it was in the early days, and those who attend come to present their work to interested colleagues as well as hear what others have been doing. At this point annual conferences often require 10 or more parallel tracks on topics of competing interest, and allow little if any time for plenary sessions. In the early years, when there were closer to 100 members at conferences, we used to start our meetings with the kindergarten practice called "Show and Tell," when each person stood and briefly said what they working on, and what they wanted to hear from and talk about with others. In that way everyone was able to find the people they most wanted to talk with during the conference days. Sadly, in growing big, we have lost the genius of this childlike practice.

While we ponder that vexing question, let me turn again to Irene Elkin to show why it is worthwhile to search for an answer. She wrote:

> The SPR annual meeting was generally the professional highlight of my year: I always looked forward, not only to the presentations that I would hear, but also to the informal stimulating conversations and to the personal friendships that were formed . . . One of the outstanding aspects of our meetings was the effort made by everyone to be inclusive, e.g., by introducing students and young researchers to established researchers whose work they had read. I remember early presentations of work that I sensed would point us in new fruitful directions, e.g., the initial presentation by Laura [Rice] and Les [Greenberg] of "A Method of Studying Active Ingredients of Psychotherapy."[6] . . . I also remember meeting young researchers whom I recognized from early on as future leaders in the field . . . SPR also provided me with the opportunity to organize sessions in areas that were not yet common in the literature, e.g., panels on issues related to women and psychotherapy; and (partly due to my position at NIMH) I was able to invite speakers to our conferences from outside of our own research world . . . Those of us in the area of psychotherapy at NIMH felt especially

> connected to SPR and took an active role in the conferences. In addition to organizing symposia and panels, we often consulted informally with grantees and prospective grantees, and we reported on NIMH workshops, conferences, and program directions. Being at NIMH, we were also aware of much that was going on in the field and so could help to "network," connecting people with similar interests.

From my own memories, I recall Robert Elliott (our 30th president) addressing one of the informal plenary sessions we used to have at our conferences, where he said that coming to SPR meetings was like attending a family reunion; an extended family of brothers and sisters, parents and grandparents, uncles and aunts and cousins galore, and eventually our own offspring, nephews, and nieces. And as at these sometimes indecorous but warmly connected and personal events, the rule was to have fun! There was camaraderie, good humor, and no great formality in sessions, with open joking and friendly heckling or teasing often coming from the back of the room—an art of *kibbitzing* often practiced to perfection by such eminent colleagues as Sol Garfield, Morris Parloff, and Alan Gurman. In the same vein, here is another of Irene Elkin's recollections:

> I can't conclude an account of my memories without mentioning all the fun we had. Our wonderful dinner dances, for instance. And our generally jocular spirit. I particularly remember the "roast" for David and Ken . . . [at the 1985 conference]. Art Auerbach's straight-faced, low-keyed hilarious contribution. The study I did, having people rate David and Ken, separately, on semantic differential scales, including items such as sweet-tart. I was told later that David hadn't believed that I had actually done the "study" (I had; during the days at the meeting preceding the dinner), that it was all a joke[;] while Ken spent part of the night poring over the raw data I gave them! And we did dance! So my memories of SPR meetings include not only an incredible amount of intellectual stimulation, but also a lot of fun!

I may add from my own recollections that I often had the pleasure of having the first dance at our banquets, when I would invite Ken Howard to waltz, then Hans Strupp to foxtrot, and then Lester Luborsky to tango (or at least two-step)! I also remember waltzing around the deck of a rocking sailboat on Lake Ontario with Edward Bordin at the 1989 meeting in Toronto; and, year after year at meetings, when Les Greenberg and I would race toward each other, with our ample abdomens thrust forward, to renew our friendly tradition of bumping bellies.

Members of SPR who meet together have also often collaborated to create new projects and programs of research. I mention here just the examples I know best due to my own involvement. In 1989, at the SPR European Chapter conference in Bern Switzerland hosted by Klaus Grawe (our 25th president) and

Franz Caspar (our 31st president), a group of members formed the SPR Collaborative Research Network to design and conduct an international study of the development of psychotherapists. This project has thrived for 25 years based on the voluntary efforts of dozens of members in countries on every continent, and has amassed wide-ranging data on nearly 12,000 psychotherapists worldwide, most recently in Australia, India, Mexico, and Chile. The success of this "research co-op" has been made possible by the combined efforts of many individuals, who each had relatively little money or professional time to devote to research, but who cared enough about enlarging our knowledge and understanding of psychotherapists—of how they work and grow—to invest personally in a long-term, large-scale collaboration.

Another example is the development within SPR of a special interest section on Culture and Psychotherapy, which has not only sponsored numerous sessions at SPR conferences but initiated and conducted collaborative research by members such as investigating the impact of multilingualism in therapy, comparing the status and prospects of the psychotherapeutic professions in many countries, and collecting critical incident narratives of the ways that social, economic, political, and cultural factors and conflicts have impacted the lives and work of patients and therapists. Another, more recent collaborative achievement within SPR was the formation in 2011 during the months leading up to the 42nd annual SPR of the SPR Interest Section on Therapist Training and Development, which was held once again in the Swiss federal capital city of Bern.

I know that initiatives have been taken by other groups of SPR members to organize special interest sections for research on child and adolescent therapy, and for research on psychotherapy training and supervision. And I know that many other research collaborations have arisen over the years, stimulated by conversations that began at SPR meetings and that were shaped and implemented through the leadership skills that SPR members have exercised. But I know that my space is limited, so I will end with a final quote from Irene Elkin's notes:

> In answer to David Orlinsky's questions about what we "old-timers" would say to present leaders of SPR and to those who will be future leaders, I would simply suggest that the spirit that has over the years pervaded SPR be maintained: the spirit of openness to various theoretical views, various approaches to research, and a spirit, indeed, of camaraderie based on our shared desire to learn more about the processes and outcomes of psychotherapy. At times throughout our history, people have been concerned that we may be a "dying field," but those dire predictions have never been realized. And they won't be, as long as there are researchers who are dedicated to understanding what makes psychotherapy work when it does work, and how to make it work better in order to help more people. It is both our intellectual curiosity and our interest in applying the fruits of

our scientific endeavors to real patients and real therapists that keeps this field alive and thriving.

I suppose I must be counted as one of the "old-timers" that Irene referred to, as I have become an old man over the 40-plus years since SPR was founded; but I want to say that the young man of 40 years ago is still alive inside, and still wants to learn and create and is searching for friends, new and old, with whom to work. As you look within and around yourself, may you find the energy and companionship to do the same. And if you seek models and paradigms of how to go forward, read herein the presidential addresses of 20 of those who have led SPR, preserved its spirit, and enhanced the field of psychotherapy research.

Notes

1 This chapter is a revised version of an invited address presented at the 40th annual international meeting of the Society for Psychotherapy Research, Santiago de Chile, June 2009.

2 Some years later, in 1988, Ken Howard did, however, give the first "catch-up" presidential address (at the SPR conference in Santa Fe, New Mexico), when Larry Beutler, serving a second term as president, had already given his address at the 1987 conference in Ulm, Germany. With a characteristic flourish, Ken began his "presidential address" by projecting a photo of a well-known building at "1600 Pennsylvania Avenue."

3 Unfortunately, we have no formal record of the fate of the presidential addresses prior to 1991, although some may have appeared in other publications.

4 Horst Kächele, the first European colleague to serve as SPR president, deserves special recognition for helping SPR expand internationally, especially in South America and Eastern Europe.

5 Columbia University in New York City and Brigham Young University in Provo, Utah.

6 A paper that was subsequently expanded into the important book by Rice and Greenberg.

1

RESEARCH ON THE PROCESS OF CHANGE (1991)

Leslie S. Greenberg

There are many unanswered questions in the field of psychotherapy research, including: How does therapy work or how does change occur, and how can we best study the process of change? There are also some unquestioned answers, which assume that psychotherapy research is aimed at evaluating or comparing treatment efficacy, and that the effects of all therapies are equivalent. This paper will focus on the methodological shifts needed to engage in a new style of process research to investigate unanswered questions and thereby explain how change occurs.

Psychotherapy research, for a variety of reasons, initially adopted a defensive position to prove that therapy works, rather than attempting to discover how it works and *what leads to change*. In most sciences the reverse is true, discovery generally precedes proof. Our goal for the next decade is to establish how change occurs; we no longer wish to justify that therapy works nor to support the assumption that one particular dogma or approach is superior to another. In the more conciliatory and enlightened period we are entering, we will advance by improving our understanding of different approaches, rather than by trying to demonstrate the superiority of one approach over another.

Science makes its greatest leaps forward when researchers are able to discover new phenomena and to grow with their data. A science that cannot discover new phenomena by intensive investigation is on its way down. If a research program is sufficiently intensive and discovery-oriented, it will reach a point at which both old conceptions begin to crumble and new techniques become necessary for the investigation of variables that were previously unrecognized. My hope is that the next generation of researchers will be speaking a sufficiently different language, one that past generations would have difficulty understanding. Already on the horizon we have new concepts such as fuzzy sets and prototype measurement (Horowitz, Weckler, & Doren, 1983) to capture the ambiguity inherent in the classifying of behavior. Researchers are beginning to talk about transportability in addition to reliability of measures, and we have new tools such as interpersonal process recall (Elliott, 1986), intention lists (Hill & O'Grady, 1985), and textbanks (Mergenthaler & Kaechele, 1985).

Now that we have faced Eysenck's challenge and established that therapy is more effective than no treatment at all ("all have won and all shall have prizes"), we must stop and confront the fact that a field which relies for its scientific respectability on establishing that certain magnitudes of differences in therapeutic outcomes are not due to chance alone is a rather flimsy science. Rather than treating our present findings as answers to questions, we need, instead, to view them as raising questions which beg for answers. Answers which will eventually explain the causal processes or mechanisms that produce those effects which appear to be due to more than chance alone.

The World of Scientism

On entering graduate school in psychology at the end of the 1960s from doctoral studies in engineering, I was troubled by finding in psychology a predominance of "scientism" rather than true science. A type of "methodolatory" culture prevailed, one with which I was unfamiliar and which emphasized method over the understanding of phenomena. Psychology was dominated by a logical-empiricist view of hypothesis testing rather than by the spirit of scientific exploration and discovery. This positivist cult of fact translated in psychotherapy research into worshiping group designs, and a set of methodological rules for constructing the individual evaluation study and generalizing from the results. There was little concern with strategies of how to proceed from study to study, or with programmatic research oriented toward *understanding* of phenomena. Two worlds existed: the world of testing and the world of understanding.

In the world of logical positivism, one predominant "fiction" is propagated—*the hypothesis testing fiction* (McGuire, 1986). According to this testing fiction a scientist derives, from some theory, a hypothesized relationship between a dependent and an independent variable, and designs a situation in which to objectively measure the variables and test the hypothesis. According to this fiction, if evidence for the predicted relationship is found, confidence is increased in the truth of the hypothesis and in the theory. If evidence for the predicted relationship is not found, these formulations are rejected.

On the other hand, in the world of "Understanding," the doctrine of *exploratory actuality* (McGuire, 1986) is offered as an alternative to the hypothesis testing fiction. In this view the typical scientist (even the adherent of logical empiricism) is seen as being guided by theoretical presuppositions which point to problems worth studying. He or she does not simply receive facts through direct sense data. The scientist proceeds by selecting a phenomenon for study (a crucial act), observing it, carrying out thought experiments about appropriate variables, measures, contexts, and hypotheses, and then cogitating on how validity might be empirically demonstrated. Having explored alternative manipulations, tested the sensitivity of measures, and believing a promising study has been devised, the investigator carries out a final empirical confrontation and inspects the data. In the view of the doctrine of exploratory actuality, however, the data often are unfriendly and fail to confirm the hypothesis. But does this outcome lead the experienced investigator to reject the hypothesis in accordance with the logical empiricist rule? No. Rather, this leads to the potential discovery of what has actually occurred and what went wrong in the experiment in actuality. The experiment is rejected, not the hypothesis.

The seasoned scientist may also tinker with the unfriendly data using more powerful tests, or may deal with oddities, control another variable, transform measures, and so on. If this doesn't help, more drastic action is taken, such as analyzing if the relationship holds for some special subgroup. If none of this works, the investigator, based on what has been learned, designs a new, better study, with better measures, different population controls, additional variables, and so forth. In the world of understanding, this is all appropriate scientific behavior; such exploratory searchings are proper procedure and should not be suppressed (Kaplan, 1964; McGuire, 1986; Toulmin, 1961; Tukey, 1977).

The claim by those in the world of understanding is that it is only in writing up a study, and not in conducting research, that even the adherents of logical empiricism obey the canons of logical empiricism (McGuire, 1986). While doing research all good scientists adopt an exploratory style of discovery-oriented, empirical confrontation. The real work of science occurs in the thought experiments, observations, prestudies, and unsuccessful initial experiments by which the scientist discovers the fuller meaning of the initial insight and the contexts in which the hypothesized relationship does and does not hold. It is just this contextual information (Rosnow & Georgoudi, 1986) that is eliminated when the scientist adopts a logical empiricist stance to write up a study as a confirmation. In fact, all hypotheses are probably true—a dedicated scientist with sufficient resources can always create or find a special context in which the hypothesized relationship holds.

Process Research in the New Image of Science: A Process Analytic Approach

In psychological research there have been, to date, two predominant research traditions: correlational and experimental. One attempts to study individual differences (how different people vary in response to similar situations); the other, to establish general laws of behavior (how different people respond similarly across situations). I suggest we need a third, *process analytic* approach to research which transcends these two opposing approaches in a study of in-situation conduct. This third approach involves a study of in-situation performance; a study of how people perform and experience similarly in similar situations. This is often best done by comparing occurrence and non-occurrence instances of a change performance in similar situations. In this approach, *change performances in specific behavioral contexts which are similar as behavior are studied to isolate common features and processes.* This type of investigation is undertaken to establish specific laws that will help explain the in-situation performances.

In this framework, we at York University have, for example, studied and developed specific models of how people resolve conflict in the context of two-chair dialogue, unfinished business in the context of empty chair work, and problematic reactions in the context of evocative unfolding (Greenberg, 1984a; Greenberg, Elliott, & Foerster, 1990; Rice & Greenberg, 1984). Others at other centers have studied interpretation of core conflictual relationship themes (Luborsky, Crits-Cristoph, Mintz, & Auerbach, 1988), interpersonal cycles (Strupp & Binder, 1984), and proplan interpretations (Silberschatz, Curtis, & Fretter, 1985). The fundamental assumption in these endeavors is that in *highly specified in-therapy contexts,* behavior and experience are lawfully explainable, and valid, specific models or micro-theory can be developed to help explain therapeutic change processes.

General Laws or Specific Models?

With regard to the value of the development of specific models that apply to specific contexts, as opposed to the development of general laws of behavior, it is interesting to note that so-called general laws of physics, such as the *laws of thermodynamics* or the *laws of motion*, are actually context-specific laws. No scientist worth his or her salt would drop a billiard ball and ping-pong ball and expect to see them accelerate at the same rate, and neither would disconfirming results in a comparative study on the differential time to impact of ping-pong and billiard balls lead the hypothesis to be refuted. Rather, the investigator would conduct other studies to discover the highly restrictive and, I might add, possibly nonexistent context of a total vacuum, in which the hypothesis does and does not hold. Thus, if we determine context-specific laws or microtheories, we will not be falling short of a scientific ideal, but, rather, we will take a major leap forward in developing a true science of psychotherapy.

Cronbach (1975, 1982) has suggested that generalization has not stood up well in the sciences. Instead of making generalization the ruling consideration in our research, we should instead describe what was controlled and uncontrolled, and move from situation to situation interpreting effects anew in each new situation. The development of context specific models will help greatly in this task.

In addition to problems inherent in the application of the concept of generalizability to psychotherapy research, are problems in our view with ideas of *control* and *random sampling*. One of the methodological difficulties in psychotherapy research is that we do not have control of many of the influencing variables. We inappropriately attempt to cover our ignorance of so-called *extraneous* influencing variables with random sampling logic, treating extraneous influences as randomly distributed. Behavior and experience, however, are not random, nor do I believe are their causes randomly distributed. The assumption that randomization takes care of all the uncontrolled variables, even if it is true in experimental designs, is just not tenable in clinical trials. The possible influencing variables are too numerous and the sample sizes are not large enough.

In addition to the problems involved in relying on random sampling in clinical trials, the actuality of an unfolding treatment is far better captured by the images provided by chaos theory than by those provided by experimental design. In chaos theory small perturbations of initial conditions are seen as having large, complexly determined effects at a distance. Chaos theory's image of patterned complexity offers a far better picture theory (Hansen, 1958) to guide our research efforts than does experimental design's billiard ball determinism image of direct and linear causality. An alternative to experimental studies in psychotherapy is a research approach which recognizes the complexity of the psychotherapeutic process and attempts to analyze the complex unfolding of moment by moment performance of people in specific states and contexts.

The Specification of Context: Process Diagnosis and Measurement

Adoption of a process analytic view to study the unfolding performances in therapy, in order to build specific models, has certain immediate implications for research activity, the most urgent being the need to specify intermediate level therapeutic contexts such as change episodes (Greenberg, 1986), and to construct classification systems (Greenberg & Pinsof, 1986) to measure the complex in-therapy states and in-therapy performances that occur in these contexts. First generation process research measured in-therapy process but did not identify meaningful in-therapy episodes and characteristic in-session states, and did not focus on understanding the process of change in these contexts. In terms of measuring in-therapy states, we need to think in terms of process diagnoses (Greenberg, 1986; Rice & Greenberg, 1984). These types of process diagnoses (as opposed to person diagnoses) are essentially definitions of person-situation interaction states in therapy that are problematic and need intervention. They are very concrete in-therapy manifestations of problem determinants (Goldfried, Greenberg, & Marmor, 1990). We need definitions and measures of in-therapy states such as experiencing conflict, engaged in transference or in self critical thoughts, or being in interactional patterns such as pursue/withdraw or attack/defend. Defining such in-session phenomena will lead to their investigation. These will become the phenomena to understand.

A Rational/Empirical Methodology

In order to engage in the process analytic alternative to correlational and experimental work, we need to adopt a combined *rational/empirical methodology,* as opposed to a purely rational or purely empirical approach. Investigation of the swamp of process requires that we approach the phenomena with an idea as a light to guide our way, as well as immersing ourselves in the data. We (Greenberg, 1975; Rice & Greenberg, 1984) have spelled out the steps of a rational/empirical discovery oriented approach of task analysis adapted from cognitive developmental psychology and the study of problem solving (Newell & Simon, 1972; Pascual-Leone, 1984; Pascual-Leone & Goodman, 1979).

Steps of task analysis

Perhaps the most basic difference in task analysis from either an experimental or correlational paradigm is that a substantial part of the research effort is discovery oriented and is invested in strategies for making extensive *rigorous observations* of single individuals performing tasks. From these observation resolution strategies and components of competence that characterize successful change performances are identified. Note the important shift in this approach is toward observation based research of the process of change, and away from the controlled experiment to establish outcome effect sizes. The steps of this approach are outlined and described in Table 1.1.

1. Explicate the intuitive map of the expert clinician

We begin with an expert clinician/investigator who, in addition to an explicit general model of therapy possesses, based on clinical experience, an implicit, cognitive map of some of the specific important events of therapy. The first step

TABLE 1.1 Steps of Task Analysis

Discovery-oriented steps
1. Explicate implicit map of expert clinician
2. Select and describe the task and task environment
3. Verify the significance of the task
4. Rational analysis of performance—possible performance diagrams
5. Empirical analysis of performance—description of actual performance
6. Comparison of actual and possible performances—construct a specific model
Verification-oriented steps
7. Validation of model
8. Relating complex process to outcome

involves the explication of this map to provide a framework to study therapeutic change.

For example, in studying splits and unfinished business within a Gestalt framework, explication of implicit theory suggested that (a) resolving splits between shoulds and wants was therapeutic and was facilitated by creating a dialogue between those aspects of the personality which embodied them, and (b) lingering bad feelings toward significant others interfered with functioning, and therapeutic dialogues with imagined significant others helped to resolve unfinished business.

2. Select and describe the task and task environment

The most basic assumption underlying this research approach is that psychotherapy can be broken down into a series of events or episodes, the resolution of which advance the course of therapy and lead to change (Rice & Greenberg, 1984). Working in this framework, and guided by my implicit understanding of the process of change in this therapy, I selected for study two change tasks: the resolution of splits and of unfinished business. Each task begins with an in-therapy statement or marker of the problem. For example, a marker of unfinished business is constituted by the presence of four measurable features: (a) a lingering unresolved feeling, (b) toward a significant other, (c) in which the emotion is experienced in the present, (d) but the emotional expression is interrupted or constricted. Similarly, split markers were defined and measured. Splits contain four identifiable features: the two opposing aspects of self, a juxtaposition indicator pitting the two parts against each other, and an indicator of a current struggle between the parts (Greenberg, 1979, 1984a). These markers constitute *process diagnoses* of states in need of, and currently amenable to, specific types of intervention.

In studying change it is important to recognize that the client is the site of change, and therefore we must put our investigatory emphasis on the client rather than on the therapist. We initially treat the intervention as a controlled background variable defining the therapeutic environment as a constant task environment in which the client task performance will be studied. Our emphasis is then focused on the client change performance. The task environment eventually becomes more and more specified, and can result in an intervention manual.

3. Verify significance of the task to be studied

The investigator may wish to, or need to, demonstrate the presence of active ingredients of change in the episode or task to be studied before proceeding on an intensive analytic research program. This was done by demonstrating the efficacy of two-chair dialogue for resolving splits (Greenberg, 1984a), and empty chair dialogue for resolving unfinished business (King, 1989; Maslove, 1990).

4. The rational analysis—constructing performance diagrams of possible performances

Having selected and defined a task and the task environment, and having shown its significance, the investigator now begins the intensive analysis of the client's task performance. The investigator first draws on his or her implicit map and on some intensive scrutiny of a few tape-recorded interviews to generate possible resolution performance paths, and to *diagram* these. The investigator thus conducts a kind of "thought experiment" (Husserl, 1973) in which possible resolution performances are varied freely in imagination to extract the essential nature of the performances and the fundamental strategy underlying the performance.

Having constructed an initial rational model, the investigator then needs to consider how the different performance components can be measured. This step of constructing a rational model is essentially a disciplined form of creative clinical thinking stated in some kind of precise process language.

5. Empirical analysis—description of actual performance

Having developed a diagram of a possible performance, the investigator now makes a detailed sequential description of the actual performance of one or more single individuals engaged in the therapeutic process under study. These sequential descriptions should use performance categories which are minimally inferential, and yet serve to reduce the complexities involved to manageable proportions. It is important that the descriptions of possible task performances in Step 4 above, and the description of actual performance here in Step 5, be stated in the *same* process language, or at least that the language of Step 5 can be translated into the language of Step 4.

In this step the investigator analyzes the performance intensively and attempts to draw pictures of the data. This was most helpful in our study of split resolution in the graph of depth of experiencing (Klein, Mathieu, Kiesler, & Gendlin, 1969) in each chair, which showed that each chair operated at different experiencing levels, until some critical point, when the levels converge and then both increase. This point, which we initially called the merging point, came to signal the beginning of a key change process in the resolution of conflict: that of the softening of the previously harsh critic.

Since temporal patterns are, however, notoriously easy to impose on sequential data, we need simple rules for verifying that certain performances patterns are in fact appearing across subjects. For example, in split resolution performances we found statistically significant differences both on Depth of Experiencing and Client Vocal Quality for stages of the dialogue before and after merging, as well as different frequencies of occurrence of specific performance configurations of experiencing, voice, and structural analysis of social behavior (Greenberg, 1984a).

6. Comparison of actual and possible performances—construct a specific model

The investigator compares the actual performance with the possible performances (Steps 5 and 4), and from this comparison begins to construct a specific model, consistent with the general model, of the kind of performances that could have generated the observed performance. In building a specific model, the investigator is able to progressively correct, expand, and make more explicit his or her understanding of the processes involved in generating resolution performances. It is at this stage that the clinician-scientist attempts to conceptualize the mechanisms that enable the process of therapeutic change. The construction of a detailed, specific model of the components of resolution involving successive repetitions of Steps 4 to 6 is the long-range goal of the model-building effort.

A refined model of the resolution of Unfinished Business obtained by this procedure was built. The resolution process was found first to involve the client expressing blame, complaint, or hurt to a negative other in the empty chair. The client then differentiates these feelings, often recalling and reliving a related episodic memory. Resolution involves the intense expression of a specific emotion (generally anger or sadness), and the mobilization and expression of an associated previously unmet need. In the enactment, in the empty chair, of the significant other, resolution performances move through the expression of specific negative aspects by the other to a shift to the expression of more positive to personal aspects by the other. Finally, resolution occurs in the self chair either by the expression of self-affirmation and self-assertion in which the other is held accountable for his or her damaging actions, or by the development by the client of a new view of the other, in which the client understands and/or forgives the other. These components were measured using Depth of Experiencing (Klein et al., 1969), Structural Analysis of Social Behavior (Benjamin, 1981), an Emotional Arousal Scale (Daldrup, Beutler, Engle, & Greenberg, 1988), and a measure of needs.

This step provides a model of change that can now be subjected to testing and ends the discovery-oriented phase of the task analysis.

(Verification Phase) *7. Validation*

Making use of the newly constructed specific model, hypotheses concerning client performance on the task are advanced. Resolution and nonresolution performances are now rigorously compared to validate that specified components discriminate between resolvers and nonresolvers. This validates the model. In a recent study of unfinished business, 11 resolved and 11 unresolved events were compared, and the resolution components described above were validated (Foerster, 1990). A similar type of study of conflict resolution demonstrated differences between components of resolved and unresolved conflict resolution performances (Greenberg, 1984a).

8. Relating process to outcome

As a final step in this program, complex client process patterns, viewed as a causal chain of change processes, are related to short- and longer-term outcomes. The advantage of this type of study, coming at this stage of the research program, is that hypothesized causal links between highly specified client process steps and outcome provide increased control over client performance variance.

One of the problems with treatment efficacy studies is that, in comparing or evaluating the assumed direct effects on outcome of different treatment interventions, there is a hidden, intervening variable, which is not accounted for. This variable can be thought of as *absorption of the treatment* by the client. I may deliver the treatment, but does it take? It's all very well that I invite a client to experiment with expressing feelings to a Significant Other, but if a treatment group contains some clients who become involved in the process, some who do so only intellectually, and others who refuse, we are not getting a true test of the active ingredient of the treatment. Probably what is being tapped in most outcome studies is an overall measure of the effectiveness of therapists in building alliances, getting people to agree on the goal, and to engage in the therapeutic tasks, rather than a measure of the effectiveness of the *resolution* of therapeutic tasks themselves. Current outcome studies predominantly capture the effects of therapists' ability in creating an alliance, and dealing with any interpersonal difficulties that arise in maintaining the alliance. If, however, in a specified treatment we studied those clients who went through the process steps in the required manner to see if they changed more than those who didn't, we would then truly be testing for causal change processes. The controlled experiment and the control group are not the most preferred way of gathering evidence on causal processes in therapeutic change. Rather, I suggest we compare the outcomes of those clients who engage in treatment in the hypothesized change process with those who don't. We need to study the client change process/outcome link and demonstrate that particular processes lead to particular types of change.

For example, in a study of the resolution of decisional conflict in 31 clients, we demonstrated that a differential, complex chain of process predicted outcome. Those clients who engaged in the predicted process steps had superior outcomes at termination and follow-up on anxiety, target complaints, degree of indecision, and on a behavioral index of decision making to those who did not engage in the steps. We are currently planning a study to see if those patients who resolve unfinished business in the course of treatment according to our model show better outcomes than those who do not.

Research Programs

The steps of task analysis described above represent a strategy for a research program which at different times emphasizes discovery and hypothesis generation, and at other times hypothesis testing. A research program of this sort probably involves 5–10 years of study on one phenomenon in which a large-scale group study is a final product. The field needs to recognize the steps along the way as good science. Hypothesis testing should be the final step in a rigorous program of discovery and understanding. We shouldn't try to prove something until we are confident of success; otherwise, much effort is wasted.

Conclusion

A true science aims at understanding and specifying causal processes. To this end I have suggested the need for a rational/empirical, process analytic methodology which focuses on change processes in a context-sensitive, discovery-oriented fashion, and aims at building explanatory models which will ultimately allow us to relate complex sequences of change process to outcome.

COMMENTARY

STUDYING WHAT PEOPLE ACTUALLY DO IN SESSIONS: "DREAM NO SMALL DREAMS FOR THEY HAVE NO POWER TO MOVE THE HEARTS OF MEN" (GOETHE)

In my address I suggested that psychotherapy research would benefit greatly by studying the process of change in psychotherapy and that this is best done by adopting a discovery-oriented process analytic approach to psychotherapy research as an alternative to the experimental or correlational approaches that dominate scientific psychology and evidence based approaches to treatment. A process analytic approach emphasizes the study of in-situation *performance*, comparing occurrences and nonoccurrences of phenomena of interest in specific contexts (change events in-session of psychotherapy to discover how people change). Psychotherapy research then would involve studying change performances, which are similar as behavior, in specified contexts, to identify common features and processes in the performances.

This, I proposed, would offer psychotherapy the opportunity of becoming a true investigative field of study in its own right rather than utilizing experimental and natural science methods of study. Rather than engaging in experiments comparing treatments and performing correlations on self-reports, I proposed a combined rational empirical task analytic, bottom-up approach, to help study what people actually do in psychotherapy. In this approach a map is provided by the rational analysis to guide the empirical analysis to avoid getting lost in the swamp of process. I also proposed an ultimate integration of observationally based discovery-oriented methods with more conventional statistically based, hypothesis testing, falsification-oriented methods in a *research program*. A research program would lead to the progressive understanding and explanation of phenomena of interest in multiple, cumulative, studies as opposed to single studies, and to prediction as a final, rather than initial, endeavor.

This suggested approach working as it was against a dominant paradigm has not had the significant influence I would have hoped it would but knew it would not. One reason why it hasn't succeeded in influencing the field probably is that the programmatic nature of the research may be too daunting in a field that rewards a single study approach to investigation. It therefore is hard to obtain funding, publish, and build a career for young scholars based on an authentic program of research based on initial small, often exploratory studies, that only later lead to larger validation oriented studies. A research program approach, however, is consistent with the view that science progresses best through the development of research programs rather than by falsification in single studies (Lakatos, 1970). Another reason for the lack of influence of the proposed task analytic view is that the exemplification of the method was initially limited to studies of mechanisms of change in single significant in-sessions events and the episodic nature of this did not catch the more dynamic aspect of change over the course of therapy.

Despite its lack of success, I remain committed to all these ideas. The approach has been expanded to address the study of change over sessions giving more sense of how change occurs across treatment (Greenberg, 2007; Pascual-Leone, 2009; Pascual-Leone & Greenberg, 2007). A further expansion to my original proposal is that I have come to see large N mediational studies, that relate process to outcome, as more worthwhile. Although these were proposed as part of the validation phase of the task analytic research program, they were not emphasized and I now see them as more necessary, if nothing else, because they are more convincing to those embedded in the traditional model of science. In these designs, investigating the active ingredients of a treatment essentially requires that statistical relationships be established between the client process and outcome, between therapist actions and outcome, and finally between the therapist actions and the client process. When all three links are established, we can say that a path to outcome has been found. Ideally, this design logic would also specify differential links between different interventions, processes, and outcomes. To do this, measures of different interventions, different processes, and different outcomes, are needed. This would result in an evidence based explanations of treatment (EBET).

Although the type of study of process that I proposed has had some effect, especially among European researchers, I would say that the current focus on evidence based treatment (EBT) and randomized clinical trials as their main arbiter has pushed the field in the opposite direction. RCTs basically have informed us that most clients find psychotherapy useful, and that *many treatments work possibly because of the relationship and general factors and some specific unknown factors.* This research, however, has not illuminated the active ingredients of specific forms of treatment, nor has it had much success in identifying which treatment works best for which client. For psychotherapy research to become a true applied science, it needs to specify the processes of change that produce psychotherapeutic effects. Because of Eysenck's challenge, psychotherapy research got off on the wrong foot, to show that it did work, and because of school wars it continued in this vein trying to prove mine is better or bigger than yours!

My argument is that change process research can reveal the actual mechanisms of change. Although process research has been given a little more credence, and a current discussion of moderators and mediators pays lip service to the complexity of the change process, there is still no major effort to study what people actually do in therapy, especially from an observationally based discovery-oriented perspective. Qualitative research has made an impact, but generally it still does not study what people actually do but rather their reported experience. Task analysis utilizing qualitative methods to describe and form categories of performance has indirectly gained support from and has supported qualitative research efforts, but it differs from these methods by highlighting that no observation is theory-free and therefore calls for the explication of the investigator's implicit assumptions and theory by building a rational model to frame the empirical analysis.

Treatment Effectiveness

For a convincing scientific argument that a treatment is effective, we need evidence that both what the therapist does (the distal variable) and the processes he or she induces in clients (the proximal variable) relate to outcome. Without knowing the specific processes and causal paths to the outcome, we do not have a scientific understanding of the treatment. Manuals specify how therapists implement specific treatments, but they are not clear on what constitutes competent delivery, nor do they specify the clients' contributions to the process. For a true science, we need to specify client and therapist processes as well as their interaction.

Reports of overall treatment effects that ignore the important role of the client's process of change fail to recognize the two distinct groups in any treatment: those who fully engage in the change processes and those who don't. This factor has a major influence on outcome. For example, intensive analyses of the client's change process in the empty chair dialogue led to studies that demonstrated that those who engaged fully in the change processes specified by the developed model of change benefited more than those who did not, and they benefited more than those who experienced the more general effects of a good alliance. If, however, when we deliver a treatment, we do not know the active ingredients, we are not able to assess whether the clients fully engaged in the process or not.

This is similar to not knowing whether a person in a drug treatment absorbs the medication. In a clinical trial, we have only the crudest index of the treatment's effects because we are lumping together people who absorb the treatment with those who do not.

Note that this is a complex path to resolution not the relationship of a few variables in a regression analysis, to outcome. More complex statistical procedures like hierarchical linear modeling, although promising, still put a veil between us and what is actually happening and often represent a situation akin to using a nuclear-powered engine (powerful statistics) to drive a rickety sail boat (weak measures and constructs) and still cannot catch the complex patterns involved in a human change process.

Honest Reflections

Retiring from my efforts to build a research program, I feel more inclined to say what I most honestly believe. I think that the current approach to the scientific study of psychotherapy is fundamentally flawed. Psychotherapy in my view should be approached as a human science and needs to develop its own methods of studying human experience and behavior. It should not be bound by the straitjacket of positivist and experimental methods of natural science. It currently should be an observational and measurement construction approach. Currently, however, the pressure is for researchers essentially to emulate natural and experimental sciences for legitimacy. Experimental design and the logic of hypothesis testing in my view are inadequate for dealing with issues of how to study human concerns, mainly because of the complexity of human change and agency. I find the application of experimental methods of natural science, based as they are on linear determinism, highly misplaced in studying non-linear dynamic self-organizing systems in interaction. Application of RCTs adapted from medicine, as though psychotherapy is the application of a drug, rather than a meaning-making task in which two agents interact, is fraught with difficulties that have been explicated frequently elsewhere.

As I said in my original address, psychology suffers from methodolatory rather than investigative authenticity. It needs methods true to its subject matter. For example, in the applied science of engineering one does not see RCTs in the modeling of phenomena such as the airflow in a wind tunnel, or the flow of fluid through a nozzle, or, more recently in the basic science of physics, the study of the "God particle" does not rest on comparative trials to understand and explain the nature of physical reality. A human science approach with its own methods suited to its phenomena will always be necessary to study how people change in psychotherapy. In my view this will need to include a study of what people actually do in treatment—both their performance and their experience. In the future my hope is that this research will incorporate findings from basic science, such as understandings from affective neuroscience of anger or trauma.

The Social Psychology of Knowledge

There appear to be two fundamental issues in the field that need to be addressed if we are to make real progress. The first is the problem of social/political/economic power in which the whole issue of treatment research is embedded. The second, more epistemologically based issue is the logic of science as applied to psychotherapy. The political issues center on a conflict between a dominant objectivist narrative and the attempts of disempowered groups to have their voices heard around evidence-based treatment. The dominant group, believing in the correctness of their view, claims superior understanding of the issues but lacks true understanding of the effects of their power position on minority groups. The dynamics of oppression lead to the marginalization of dissenting voices. In psychotherapy research, power involves privileged access to and controls of resources (grants), communication (publications), and positions (tenure). The power group essentially suppresses diversity and the promise of innovation by extremely conservative criteria of what constitutes science. It is in the nature of science to be conservative but dominant paradigms have endlessly proven to be wrong, and my hope is that the existing paradigm will undergo a sea change. Until such time as all proposed treatments are given a fair test, to claim the superiority of some approaches that happen, through preparedness as well the exercise of power and influence, to have been tested, is tantamount to oppressive control. It is this lack of a level playing field that is the main problem, not arguments about the logic of causation. Although the logic of experimental procedures is impeccable, in my view it is not applicable to evaluating the effectiveness of psychotherapy. The arguments for the best designs for making causal inferences, although sound, lack wisdom. Wisdom implies the ability to use knowledge to make sensible decisions by applying knowledge in appropriate contexts. Arguments for RCTs as the gold standard of treatment outcome research, in that that they offer the best way to make causal inferences, do not deal with the issue of whether we are in a domain in which this logic applies. The concern at this stage of psychotherapy research is not on how best to infer cause, but on how applicable, at this early stage of development of psychotherapy, causal inference logic is to the question of what treatments work and work best.

I am strongly in favor of empirically *investigated* treatments but we are at a preliminary state of knowledge in psychotherapy research and we need to start bottom up to learn what is effective. RCT proponents apply the right logic prematurely, wanting to run before we can walk. Over my career I have witnessed too many proclamations of truth in the name of science. These claims ranged from: Psychotherapy is no more effective than spontaneous remission—no, it's not; Behavioral change is superior to insight—no, cognition is important; The necessary and sufficient conditions of helping have been found—no, they haven't. This was followed by: CBT is the treatment of choice for depression, then no, it isn't. Each proclamation comes in the name of science by groups with an axe to grind. Changes in fads based on RCTs in psychotherapy should make all thoughtful people skeptical. Let us not support the power dynamics involved by calling it science. Psychotherapy research needs, rather, to study how people change by observing sequences or patterns of events. The moment-by-moment change process needs to be studied in innovative ways with methods of pattern identification with attention to in what context a particular kind of process occurs.

2

NARRATION AND OBSERVATION IN PSYCHOTHERAPY RESEARCH

Reporting on a 20-Year-Long Journey from Qualitative Case Reports to Quantitative Studies on the Psychoanalytic Process[1] (1992)

Horst Kächele

Psychotherapy Research as a field of institutionalized research activity has been made visible by establishing the Society for Psychotherapy Research (SPR) in 1968. For many years it was tied up to the Anglo-American world. With the establishment of a European-continental chapter, a growing awareness of research activities outside led to the 1987 meeting in Ulm which paved the way to integrate the European continent into the self-concept of SPR. Reporting on the work of the Ulm group allows for an overview on a 20-year-long journey from qualitative case reports to quantitative studies on the psychoanalytic process, which entails the notion of narration versus observation.

When the Ulm group began its work in the early 1970s, first focusing on the extensive analysis of a single case treated by H. Thomä, it seemed promising in many ways. It would help us to bridge the gap between the clinical and the scientific approach and it would enable us to keep qualitative and quantitative avenues in touch with one another. Therefore it has been our strategy first to investigate within the single case where narrative accounts of the therapists were available, and then to aggregate the cases only when we felt safe enough not to violate the specifics of the single case.

Studying the psychoanalytic process involved other strategic decisions as well. As we all know, out there is a multiplicity of meaning of the notion "psychoanalytic process"; so many theories, so many models of the analytic process (Compton, 1990). There is no shared opinion whether models have to be tested or are but language games useful for those who use them. Our investigations have been guided by a working model of the process which encompasses all of the steps along the way from the start of a patient/analyst contact to its termination. The methodological specificity of the psychoanalytic process is produced by the analytic method which prescribes a specific discourse—with evenly hovering attention and free association as functional units. The impact of these rules on both parts sets in motion a process which transforms covered processes within the patient (transference dispositions) into relationship patterns between patient and the analyst.

So our task was defined mainly as a descriptive enterprise, as a job to develop tools with which to describe the vast number of verbal transactions that make up a psychoanalytic treatment. In terms of a well-known distinction of how to proceed in setting up a research program, we used both the so-called bottom-up approach and the top-down approaches, where one sets out to test a piece of theory which serves as a guiding tool of what data to select.

Bottom-up approaches start with very low-level theories, everyday theory so to speak, first establishing descriptive worlds. This may be seen as something like going out and catching butterflies in the wilderness. Indeed, confronted with a long-term psychoanalytic treatment it is not an easy choice to decide what part of the material deserves careful descriptive work. The bottom-up methods are defining observables not all of which have clear relationship to the clinical theory of psychoanalysis. However, we thought careful observational work supported by systematized narrative knowledge would have reverberations on our theorizing of the process.

Our leading idea was to use descriptive data of different quality to examine clinical process hypotheses. Our methodological conception was inspired by Helen Sargent's (1961) recommendations for the Topeka project—consisting of a four-level approach; on each level different methods with appropriate material representing different levels of conceptualization had to be worked on:

1. clinical case study
2. systematic clinical description
3. guided clinical judgment procedure
4. computer-assisted and linguistic text analysis.

This multi-level multi-method approach reflected our understanding that the tension between clinical meaningfulness and objectivation could not creatively be solved by using one approach only. Up to now this approach has been applied to a total of four cases varying in amount of work performed in the different domains.

1. Clinical case study

I already have made clear that we highly appreciate the research-based case study approach; it does fulfill an important function in orienting about the total picture, it provides an overview that might be helpful when interpretation of results of more stringent methods are called for. Anyone interested in this traditional way of reporting can fulfill his curiosity by peeping in the second volume of our textbook on psychoanalytic practice (Thomä & Kächele, 1994). So I may continue by discussing the method of systematic clinical descriptions.

2. Systematic clinical description

Systematic clinical descriptions import quite a different way of approaching the material. The complex array of interactions of a treatment process are considered with the help of preset points of view; they clearly represent the researcher's interest. They might vary from case to case. For example, for patient Christian Y[2] "anxiety and transference" were the key notions; for Amalia X it was the hirsutism (male type of hairiness) and the development of her heterosexual relations that were of prominent interest. All treatments were completely tape-recorded; one case (Christian Y) was completely transcribed; the others, due to restricted financial means, only partially. The material basis of these systematic descriptions was based on verbatim transcripts of different samples:

Sampling strategies

a. sessions 1–5, 26–30, 51–55, 76–80, 101–105, 126–130, . . .
   a.1. sessions 1–5, 51–55, 101–105, 151–155, . . .
   a.2. sessions 26–30, 76–80, 126–130, 176–180, . . .
b. sessions 1, 11, 21, 31, 41, 51, 61, 71, 81, 91, 101, . . .
c. blocks of eight sessions drawn in random distance from one another out of the total population
d. all items (like dreams) within the first 100 sessions versus all items in the last 100 sessions.

The task of systematically reading the verbatim records of the sessions and then writing up condensed summaries of the content and transactions of the sessions still moves very close to clinical narration. In producing these descriptions by third, uninvolved persons, we feel that they can procure a fairly reliable perspective of what has happened. This clinical-descriptive step permits an evaluation that is under some formal constraints: no longer the report is dictated by the narrator's epic perspective which characterizes the traditional case study approach. Instead, by using a systematic sample the assumption is made that the repeated description in fixed time intervalls captures the decisive processes of change that have occurred.

The material available after such an effort looks like a little book; the voluminous collected verbatim records—thousands of pages—have been elegantly compressed to 100 pages of a readable account. This booklet can serve many purposes besides its being a valuable achievement in itself. It helps for an easy access to an orientation on the whole case, being more detailed and more systematic as a traditional case history which tends to be more novella-like, whereas the systematic description record marks out the orderly progress of things. One can rearrange the qualitative data, concatenating all transference descriptions one after the other and by doing so gain a good view on the development of major transference issues.

It is not by chance that these descriptions remind one of titles of fairy tales. At any given point in treatment the relationship between patient and analyst is organized in a narrative pattern which clinicians are very able to spot. Systematic clinical descriptions thus rely on the very capacity of narrative accounting, but using the systematic sampling technique these accounts change in their nature. Systematic clinical description is a way to recount the treatment in a mixed mode. In order to introduce some objectivity to the narrative accounts based on verbatim records, we recommend two readers and impose on them to agree upon their account.

An even more condensed version of a systematic clinical description can be achieved by using a so-called topic index (Simon, Fink, Endicott & Gill, 1968). A long list of items (like father, mother, body, friends—the more direct, the better) is scanned for presence or absence in a session. There are elegant graphical means to represent these yes/no decisions, which lead to a topographical description of the treatment process (Thomä, 1975).

3. Guided clinical judgement procedures

In order to get more control over the descriptive reliability, one has to narrow down the window of observation. This is achieved by selecting theoretical concepts for which observational referents can be specified. Concepts are unlike the ingrediants of a compound, though we might think of it that way; they are imposed on the material and help us to abstract the material. Our favourite concepts for which manual guided clinical judgment procedures were developed and applied were the following:

1. "Transference, Anxiety and Working Alliance" (Grünzig, Kächele & Thomä, 1978; Kächele, Thomä & Schaumburg, 1975)
2. "Changes in self-esteem" (Neudert, Grünzig & Thomä, 1987)
3. "Suffering" (Neudert & Hohage, 1988)
4. "Emotional insight" (Hohage & Kübler, 1988)
5. "Cognitives changes during psychoanalysis" (Leuzinger-Bohleber & Kächele, 1988).

Study 1 was done on the case Christian Y; studies 2–4, on the case Amalia X; and study 5 used two additional cases, Franziska X and Gustav Y, from which also larger samples in verbatim form are available.

The results of these guided procedures are graphical representations like linear or non-linear curves, replacing the rich fabric of narratives by unidimensional series of values which mark the transition from a qualitative to a quantitative view of things. By this very procedure we suddenly are able to speak of high and low transference, of little change or great changes along a continuum mapped out by the investigator. The loss in descriptive richness is balanced by a gain in greater control of the phenomena under discussion.

Such seductive charts induce the illusion to have mastered the complex dimension. However, we have to keep in mind that these standardized evaluations are built on the working rule to freeze in the process of interpretation in a way that reliable judgments can be made. Everyone who has worked in this rating business is aware that training of raters often means depriving them of their natural tendency to increase information by interpreting data but instead reducing information by selective attention.

A main research question on this level of description was: Can we use these this kind of dimensional descriptions in order to identify "phases of process" that would support our theoretical notion of the psychoanalytic process (Kächele, 1988)? As described in more detail elsewhere, "we conceptualize psychoanalytic therapy as an *ongoing, temporally unlimited focal therapy with a changing focus*" (Thomä & Kächele, 1994, p. 347).

4. Computer-assisted and linguistic text analysis

Our way to handle the complexities of treatment processes had begun with improving on the traditional case study by introducing the systematic time-sampled clinical description, then turning to rating approaches, thus reducing the interpretative excess in order to get better control. One step further along the continuum between narration and observation consisted in directing our attention to the very raw material that was provided by the verbatim records.

It is more than appropriate to acknowledge on this special occasion that the discovery of this approach was directly influenced by Hartvig Dahl and Donald Spence, whose seminal papers (Dahl, 1972, 1974; Spence, 1968, 1969; Spence & Lugo, 1972) opened my eyes to the possibilities of the computer as a tool to considerably increase the descriptive power.[3]

We got started by implementing the program described by Spence (1969) and found it useful for dealing with small amount of text material (Kächele, Thomä, & Schaumburg, 1975). In 1975, we got hold of the program EVA ("Elektronische Verbalanalyse," developed by K. Holzscheck), which had been devised for the analysis of newspaper headlines. The amount to be processed with psychoanalytic material made a revision necessary, which was performed by E. Mergenthaler in the following years (so called EVA-Ulm & TAS). Since then, the use of the computer as tool has been broadened to include not only dictionary-based content analysis, but to refer to text analysis in a more general sense (Mergenthaler and Kächele, 1988, 1991). The concept to develop a formal institution called "Ulm Textbank" arose out of the pure necessity to handle the growing data corpus of our own. It was only after a while that we realized that this in itself was a valuable objective to serve the field, by providing textual material on many different forms of therapy and providing various forms of textanalyses (Mergenthaler, 1985).

We have used computer-aided text analyses in quite a few investigations, most of them exploratory-oriented, to find out what descriptive powers of this easy-to-do strict observational methods would be producing results that evoke narrative efforts to make sense out of them:

1. Verbal activity (Kächele, 1983)
2. Long-term transference trends (Kächele, 1976, 1990)
3. Personal pronouns (Schaumburg, 1980)
4. Redundancy in patient's and therapist's language (Kächele & Mergenthaler, 1984)
5. Classification of anxiety themes (Grünzig, 1983; Grünzig & Kächele, 1978)
6. Emotive aspects of therapeutic language (Wirtz & Kächele, 1983)
7. Change of body concepts (Schors & Kächele, 1982)
8. Cognitive changes during psychoanalysis (Leuzinger-Bohleber & Kächele, 1988)
9. Changes of latent meaning structures (Mergenthaler & Kächele, 1985)
10. Affective Dictionary (Hölzer, Scheytt, Pokorny, & Kächele, 1989)
11. Parts of speech (Mergenthaler, 1990; Parra, Mergenthaler, & Kächele, 1988)
12. Core conflictual words (Kächele, 1991).

To illustrate my point that the more observational one´s approach is, the more narrative interpretation is needed, I summarize our data on the verbal activity in two psychoanalytic treatments (Kächele, 1983).

Verbal activity is easily measured by the computer; either one uses the one-off patterns analysis by direct recording, as developed by Feldstein and Jaffe (1963) or, if verbatim transcripts are stored in a computer, counting words is all you need.

Our figures for the overall verbal activity in the two dyads of psychoanalytic cases showed that the total ratio varies between 1:1.1 to 1:4.0. This way of looking at verbal activity was not yet very informative, so we analyzed the distribution of verbal activity by forming classes of sessions of varying verbal activity and focused on the patients Christian Y and Amalia X treated by the same analyst Amalia displayed a wide spectrum of verbal activity in different hours; the analyst, in contrast, was fairly restricted in his verbal activity, role specific as a textbook perspective of psychoanalysis would prescribe.

However, in the other case, where the patient Christian exhibited an extremely restricted range, the analyst clearly shifted to more verbal activity. These data gave only a static view about a characteristic of the verbal exchange system. And we did not know what role silence plays. So E. Mergenthaler suggested

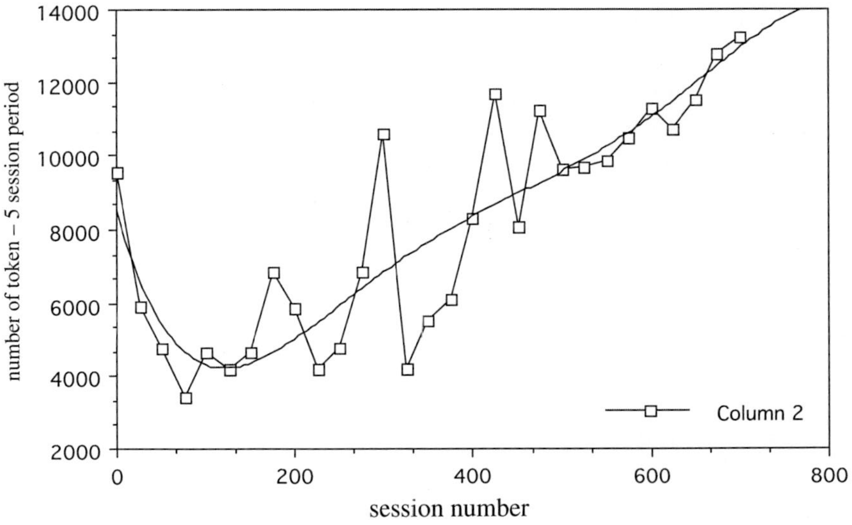

FIGURE 2.1 Verbal Activity of Patient Christian (Number of Tokens) Sessions 1–700

and constructed a three-dimensional graph neglecting the times when both speaker overlapped and calculated the relative proportions of both speakers and silence of the total session time.

Amalia's graph shows a wide variation of the patient from nearly zero to 100 percent, with the analyst moving around an average of 15 percent participation and a varying amount of silence. Correlation between patient's and analyst's activity was practically zero (0.04).

In the other treatment, we found both patient and analyst at a rather low verbal activity, with a lot of silence. The correlation of the two verbal activities based on 110 sessions was +0.30, which is highly significant. Studying verbal activity along the temporal axis of the treatments, we learned of another feature of the process. Patient Amalia was developing nicely her capacity to vary verbal activity over the course of treatment and her analyst behaved unobtrusively, even reducing his participation more and more as the analysis came to an end.

Patient Christian and the same analyst remained intertwined throughout session 1 to session 450, represented by every tenth session, which formed the basis of this measurement.

Being clinically well aware of what happened, we knew that these data described a very difficult analysis, with a patient who was most of the time silent, with an analyst who most of the time initiated verbal interaction, who tried to get the patient involved in the analytic task of using the space provided for him. At the end of this observational period one could discern a slow development of the patient's capacity to become a more active participant. It was only from session 500 onward that he developed the same verbal activity features that I

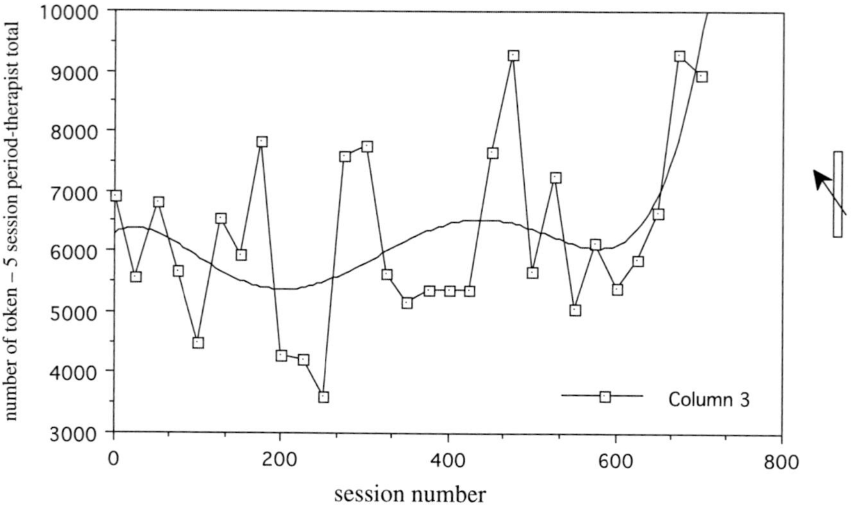

FIGURE 2.2 Verbal Activity of Therapist of Patient Christian (Number of Tokens) Sessions 1–700

could demonstrate of the other patient. At a later time, when after 700 sessions the treatment had ended, the remaining sessions also had been transcribed and we repeated the measurement for patient Christian's verbal activity. This time we used another sample, taking five sessions in an even distance of 25 sessions for each data point.

To interpret the data from our clinical knowledge of the treatment it was fairly obvious that the patient went into a long regressive state characterized by a decrease in talking. The therapist stayed close to the patient's verbal activity without falling into the hole of regression but instead tried to verbally activate the patient. The correlation of verbal activity over the total treatment length was even larger in this larger sample (+0.43 Spearman rank).

The observational possibilities of the textbank system also allow for even a more detailed diagnostic of the way verbal activity is deployed. Instead of categorizing with Strupp´s intervention catalogue, we used the empirically demonstrable correlation between types of intervention and length of intervention (Kitzmann, Kächele, & Thomä,. 1974a, 1974b).

By analyzing the distribution of length of interventions using large sample of interventions (N = 14,000) we were able to point out that the analyst in the Amalia case transported his verbal activity by relying on short interventions, whereas with Christian he showed a shift in his spectrogram toward using a much higher proportion of medium and more lengthy interventions. We may be seduced to think from our clinical experience that good effective

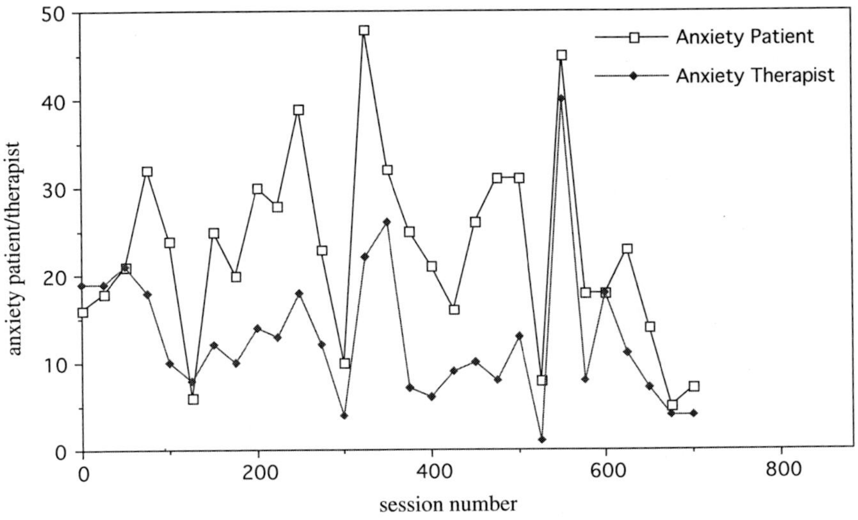

FIGURE 2.3 "Anxiety" Frequency

psychotherapeutic work does indeed take place through short remarks instead of bulky interpretations.

In order to better understand this treatment, we studied in detail the use of "Core Conflictual Words" (Kächele, 1991)—to paraphrase Luborsky's CCRT—in the analysis of patient Christian Y. This patient suffered from such severe anxiety neurosis that he was unable to leave the hospital for three years and was treated on an inpatient basis five times a week. His most frequent noun was the word "anxiety." Looking at the course of this word over the treatment for both patient and therapist displays a remarkable synchrony:

Now, it is a firm conviction in the psychoanalytic world that such severe states of anxiety have to do with repressed aggressive feelings toward the primary love object. We therefore selected the word "anger" and mapped its relative frequency over treatment.

A first inspection of the graphical representations underlines a very important feature: there is a striking covariance of these central concepts. Balint's thesis, that the patient has to learn the language of the analyst, can just as well be turned round by saying that both partners have to establish a constructive mixture of similarity and dissimilarity in talking about the inner world of the patient. The use of the word "anxiety" correlates between patient and analyst with +0.60; the use of the word "anger" even correlates +0.81 over the whole course of treatment. Though positive correlation of content are usual features of conversations, the figures for these two nouns were extremely high.

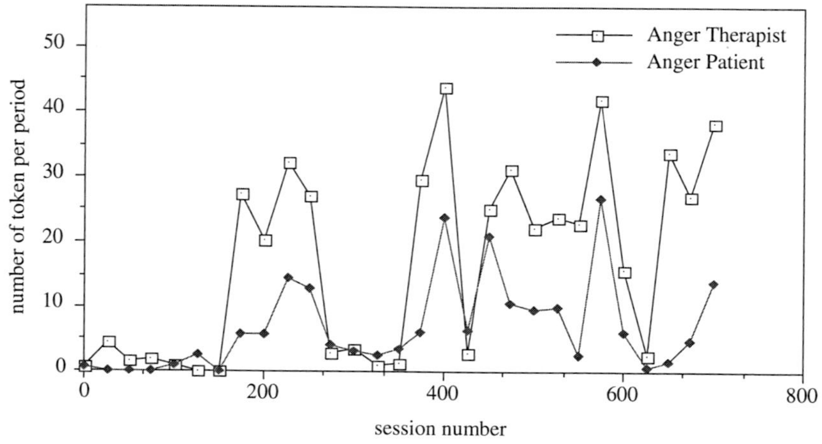

FIGURE 2.4 "Anger" Frequency—Patient/Therapist

However, the similarity with regard to the use of the word "anxiety" only refers to the process aspect. The degree of intensity of usage shows a striking difference. The analyst, through taking up this main complaint by the patient, is reluctant in its use. The word "anger," barely used as a element in the dialogue for more than 150 sessions, is heavily imported the first time into the dialogue by the analyst from sessions 175–255. It is in this phase of the treatment where the analyst tries for the first time to focus on the theoretically relevant connection of anxiety and anger.

There are quite a few other approaches of text analysis we have tried on our research cases. Analyzing the use of personal pronouns, we found quite different relationships in each of the four analytic cases that we have worked with. Impressive contingencies between the pronouns "I" and "you" in one case alternate, with insignificant relations of the same variables in the other (Schaumburg, 1980). As the analysis of personal pronouns was once introduced by Daniel Jaffe as a promising measure for the "language of the dyad" (Jaffe, 1958), with exciting "tracking phenomena" observed in a series of nine interviews, I may make the point that our experience with large series of sessions does not support this early enthusiasm. Generalizations are not warranted. The same holds true for the grammatical aspect of the dyadic language system in psychoanalysis. Analyzing the use of passive constructions Beermann (1983) could demonstrate on our four analytic cases that each patient preferred special ways of constructing the passive voice; change in direction to more active forms took place in all four treatments.

Going back to the organizing notions of this talk—narration and observation—this approach clearly is naked observation of elements: generating only *data bruta*—which are but the letters of the therapeutic alphabet. In order to make sense out of them we have to find the words and sentences which built up to narratives of interaction. These data would be meaningless if measured only as a single instance; they approach meaning by the repeated measurement. But looking at them as a series of events, they are easily placed into a frame of understanding this specific case. These data show shifts in patterns of language; by looking at them from this holistic view brings them into the horizon of representing a new language game. The manifold bottom-up approaches convinced us that careful descriptive work on the microprocesses is necessary to understand the working of the macroprocesses grasped by our clinical notions.

All results on psychoanalytic dialogues studied by these techniques underscore the dyadic nature of the process. Whatever microsystem is analyzed, one finds dyadic dependencies and specifics within dyads. This has been one of the reasons why the Ulm research paradigm has been so intrigued by the study of singular cases. This kind of work may seem not to be in the mainstream of the work done in SPR for various reasons. One seems to be our tenacious stand with investigating long-term cases in their full length and richness. This is connected to the maybe unique German situation that the societal perspective on psychotherapy research as represented by the agencies responsible for the funding of psychotherapy is still convinced that long-term treatment within the psychoanalytic frame of reference for a certain share of patients is the proper thing to do. Another reason lies in a strong support for basic research provided by the German Research Foundation. We therefore could concentrate on basic research since 1970, having received continuous funding since then for diverse projects all focused on the issues I have dealt with in this presentation.

COMMENTARY

FROM NARRATION TO OBSERVATION AND BACK TO NARRATION IN PSYCHOTHERAPY RESEARCH

From today I would have to add that my initial discussion of selecting a single-case approach was rather narrow. In the last decades single-case research has developed in many sophisticated ways, especially in the fields of social science. We encounter now titles like "Five misunderstandings about case-study research" (Flyvbjerg, 2006) that summarize its message with the Kuhnian insight "that a scientific discipline without systematic production of thoroughly executed case studies is a discipline without systematic production of exemplars" (p. 219). Besides being too narrow in reasoning why the Ulm program decided to study one psychoanalytic case extensively, I also was too short in describing the clinical insights gained by studying this one case so extensively.

The second level of our methodology – the "systematic clinical description" – stands up the test of time, although we have not seen an overwhelmingly number of cases reported in such a systematic and detailed way.

Level three in my lecture dealt with such measures that Lester Luborsky has aptly named "guided clinical judgments" and which make up the bulk of present treatment research.

These clinical concepts are—by necessity of such a method—narrowed down and will lose some of the rich clinical connotations which have been criticized by psychoanalysts working on conceptual research (Dreher, 2005).

In the two decades that followed, further studies have been performed on the German specimen case Amalia X, as reported in a recent volume (Kächele et al., 2009). Also, the role or position of the researcher is given greater critical attention. Single case research offers a rich opportunity for this process of putting findings back in the clinical context. Looking back on my lecture, I did miss this aspect. It is this interaction between clinical work and scientific study that should become standard in our field.

Notes

1 Revised version of the presidential address to the annual meeting of the Society for Psychotherapy Research, Lyon, July 1991. Correspondence to the author: International Psychoanalytic University, Berlin.

2 Throughout this text the patients are named in concordance with our procedure explained in Thomä and Kächele (1994).

3 Since this address was delivered in France, it seems useful to mention that the French word for computer, *ordinateur*, is much more suitable to catch the specific use of this tool in text analysis, which is "ordering symbols."

3

EVERY PSYCHOPATHOLOGY IS A GIFT OF LOVE (1993)[1]

Lorna Smith Benjamin

There are so many different perspectives on psychotherapy that it is easy to find cartoons about it in the popular press. Their pervasiveness provides testimony to the importance of psychotherapy within Western culture. From an array of more than 50 therapy approaches, the cognitive and behavioral perspectives seem to be most often taught in graduate schools and medical centers. Today's students are less likely to be taught dynamic psychotherapies, probably because their efficacy has not been so well documented. Yet, many members of the Society for Psychotherapy Research (SPR) seek to address the problem of how to apply methods of science to study dynamic reconstructive psychotherapy. It is that version of therapy, the one that seeks to change the underlying structure of personality, that I would like to discuss. In the process, I will sketch a generic theory of psychotherapy that presumes to pinpoint the "heart of darkness," the point where personality change ultimately does or does not occur.

Efficacy Revisited

Current funding for providers of psychotherapy services or for psychotherapy research studies is given mostly for approaches that have demonstrated *efficacy*. Antidepressants and antipsychotic and anxiolytic drugs have less than perfect but nonetheless unquestioned efficacy in the management of the symptoms of depression, thought disorder, and anxiety. In the eyes of third-party payers, this means that biochemical interventions have priority in the treatment of mental disorders. The same view prevails in research funding. Psychotherapy researchers often compete unsuccessfully with "drug" protocols that involve, at a minimum, comparing a control group to an experimental group that has a "biological" (that is, chemical or physical) treatment.

But psychotherapy does have demonstrated efficacy, albeit less dramatic. Efficacy was shown in the collaborative study at NIMH that sought to compare and contrast psychosocial (Klerman & Weissman's [1986] interpersonal), the Beck, Rush, Shaw, and Emery (1979) cognitive, and a drug (Imipramine) treatment. However, findings were controversial. Conclusions about efficacy varied according to the initial level of severity, the site at which the treatments were implemented, the stage at which measurements were taken, and the measures of efficacy (Elkin et al., 1989; Shea et al., 1992). For many of the contrasts, Imipramine was effective in treating depression. The arguing was mainly over identification of which psychosocial intervention was also effective, whether the effect was additive, under what conditions, and for what reasons.

Other studies, not necessarily involving contrasts with drugs, also have shown that psychotherapy is effective. Results repeatedly suggest that one school of therapy is no better than another (Luborsky, Singer, & Luborsky, 1975). The generic effectiveness of psychotherapy is sometimes interpreted as evidence that the various theories and techniques have not correctly identified the underlying change agents. A widely accepted hypothesis is that general or nonspecific factors may be the critical change agents. Examples of general factors proposed to account in the main for therapy effects include attention, support, and relaxation. This interpretation raises the challenge to show whether therapy is truly more effective than whatever is offered by friendly bartenders and sympathetic friends.

Years ago, Allen Bergin introduced the topic of deterioration to the psychotherapy research literature. Occasional subsequent studies were reviewed by Lambert, Shapiro and Bergin (1986). Some variables relevant to deterioration in psychotherapy are patient diagnosis, degree of disturbance, style of group leader, therapist maladjustment, exploitativeness, and immaturity. Selected other factors on the list include therapist failure to structure or focus the session, to address negative attitudes; therapist tendency to passively accept problem behaviors, or to make poorly timed, inaccurate interpretations. Therapists with a poor self-concept have worse outcomes (Henry, Schacht, & Strupp, 1990).

Clearly it is important to worry about deterioration in psychotherapy as a part of tests of effectiveness. And yet, psychological "folk wisdom" has long recognized that in psychotherapy "things may get worse before they get better." It is vital, therefore, to be able to distinguish deterioration that is necessary to the therapy process from deterioration that is simply destructive. Later, I will suggest a framework that helps make that differential. Meanwhile, present funding patterns give preferential treatment to approaches that offer simple evidence of efficacy for symptom relief and these do not permit acceptance of episodes of worsening that might be related to profound change. This emphasis on short-term outcome severely compromises the processes of scientific inquiry, and the discovery or enhancement of methods that are potentially more effective in the long run.

Studies of Variables: The Hall of Mirrors

Many members of this Society have been instrumental in the identification of issues central to psychotherapy, and in the development of methods to study those issues. Goldfried (1991) offered a convenient summary of the state of the art: "The absence of research findings that consistently point to the superiority of one school of therapy over another suggests that we begin to investigate more closely the change processes associated with each of these approaches, so as to determine which are common to all and which are unique to some." Orlinsky and Howard (1986) have made significant contributions to that challenging task. They have been instrumental in identifying generic factors that are relevant to therapy process and outcome. Examples include therapy contract, role, interpretation, confrontation, support, affective arousal, therapeutic bond, patient motivation, therapist expressiveness, empathy, and focus. Beutler (1991) has offered lists of variables that inhere in therapists, in patients, and in the therapy orientation. Such lists are very long. Selected examples from Beutler illustrate some factors that need further study. Patient variables include defensiveness, problem severity, affectivity, neuroticism, dependency, reactance, diagnosis, goals, and expectations.

Therapist variables include facilitative skills, experience, credibility, maturity, emotional well-being, and expectancies. Therapy variables include orientation, whether there is to be insight or action, whether the therapy is directive or evocative, whether it is systemic or person centered, whether it is group or individual, whether it is short- or long-term, and whether it is oriented on growth or treatment.

Beutler cited studies that showed these sorts of variables interact with one and another and cannot be studied in isolation. He observed: "There are nearly one and one-half million potential combinations of therapy, therapist, phase, and patient types that must be studied to rule out relevant differences among treatment types." Criticizing the purely empirical approach to this problem, Beutler concluded: "Given the enormity of the task of exploring potential interactions among the many patient, therapist, and psychotherapy types, a guiding model is needed by which to narrow our search for variables that mediate between treatment type and outcome."

The Need for Organizing Testable Theory

SPR has traditionally been dedicated to the value of staying close to a reliable, replicable database. Some members share the view I have also heard from graduate students, who equate theory with "bias." These people hold that a theoretical framework causes investigators to see only what they want to see, and to miss seeing what they do not want to see. But the need to retreat from the "Dustbowl of Empiricism" in psychotherapy research is supported by a coexisting chorus of criticism of the pure empiricism of the DSM (American Psychiatric

Association, 1987). The DSM has come under fire for lack of theoretical coherence. Millon (1991), Carson (1991), Morey (1991), and Skinner (1981) have all argued that hypothetical constructs must be invoked to develop effective understanding of mental disorder and its associated treatments. Psychotherapy researchers must rise to the same issue. The challenge of identlfying and testing effective theories of psychotherapy must be confronted. The purely empirical approach is unlikely to be effective in the long run, either in defining mental disorder or psychosocial therapy interventions.

Use of well-constructed and validated theory does not necessarily introduce observational bias, and it certainly is not equivalent to "no data." To the contrary: use of theory can sharpen observational skills and generate highly relevant data. The classical view is that there must be an interaction between theory and data. Theory guides the gathering of data, and the gathering of data informs and shapes theory. The iteration reverberates infinitely. Data are vital to theory, and theory informs data gathering.

Available Theories

Several prominent members of SPR have already responded to the call. They have offered specific theories that mark the essence of therapeutic change. They have studied therapy using research measures that reflect their respective theories of change. For example, Lester Luborsky has translated key concepts from psychoanalysis into Core Conflictual Relational Themes (CCRT) (Luborsky, 1984; Luborsky & Mark, 1991). Weiss and Sampson (1986) have translated psychoanalysis into a study of Plan Formulations. Mardi Horowitz (1979) describes ideas from psychoanalysis with his Configural Analysis of States of Mind. Strupp and Binder (1984) focus on Cyclical Maladaptive Patterns, while Greenberg and Rice emphasize Task Analysis (Greenberg, 1984b). All these theoretical approaches share the goal of operationally defining the key issue for the patient, the point upon which the therapist should focus most sharply, and around which research measures should be organized.

I have worked for almost *25* years on an operationally defined, testable, and refutable theory of interpersonal and intrapsychic interactions. Structural Analysis of Social Behavior (SASB) is a model of social and intrapsychic process that has generated questionnaires, a coding system, and software that can be used to study psychotherapy (Benjamin, 1974, 1984). Rather than focusing much on SASB now, I choose instead to sketch a "generic" theory of psychotherapy that I think is also testable and refutable. The proposed generic interpretation of therapy is responsive to the demand that psychotherapy research be organized by overarching theoretical concepts that permit identification of change processes independently of school of therapy. It happens that the SASB methods and concepts are very useful in detailing, implementing and testing the proposed generic theory of therapy.[2] SASB is to the generic theory of therapy as, say, French is to Proust's

Remembrance of Things Past. The storyline can be told in any number of languages. SASB is a language that conveys the story very well, but the reader need not necessarily "speak SASB" to use the generic theory. He or she must, however, have some language that permits effective description of what is going on in the therapy.

A Theory of Psychopathology

A useful theory of psychotherapy must begin with an understanding of psychopathology. One cannot discuss corrective processes without first understanding what has gone wrong. Diagnosis is a worthy tradition. Six hypotheses about psychopathology are required by the proposed generic theory of psychotherapy. They have clear implications for what needs to be done in psychotherapy. The ability to prescribe interventions, according to what has gone wrong, provides a frame for therapist decision rules for defining "errors."

Assumption 1

Most mental disorders are an adaptation rather than a breakdown. They are not the result of inherent imbalances or defects as, for example, in Down's Syndrome. They also are not the result of externally induced insult as, for example, in syphilis or head injury. Instead, the symptoms of mental disorder are the result of efforts to adapt, to restore interpersonal and intrapsychic balance.

Assumption 2

Each person has genetically based, biochemically implemented vulnerabilities and strengths. These predispositions very much affect the shape of a disorder and the response to psychotherapy. I think that Bob Carson (Carson & Butcher, 1992) has offered an appropriate perspective on the proverbial nature-nurture question about mental disorder. He invokes the model of the computer. The hardware compares to the genetic or innate factors, while the software corresponds to the developmental or environmental factors. A programmer must, for example, be aware of constraints like memory size that are imposed by the hardware. An engineer who develops hardware must be ever sensitive to the preferences of the programmer and users. By analogy, the biochemists study the "hardware" of mental disorder, while psychotherapists study the "software." Eventually electron microscopes or comparable technologies may clearly identify and replicate findings of a genetic process that accounts for a definitive portion of the variance in mental disorders. Even then, it is likely that most disorders will be found to be significantly affected by the interface of environment and predisposition. Learning and experience have a tremendous impact on human development. The SPR studies mostly the consequences of experience, the psychosocial "software." Nonetheless, SPR members can and should stay aware of current developments in valid and replicated research on "hardware." Questions about the interface between a given disorder and temperament, for example, should be given increased attention by SPR.

Assumption 3

Specific experiences shape specific symptoms. In other words, for every interpersonal and intrapsychic pattern, there are specific antecedent or concurrent social inputs that relate in meaningful ways to the symptom, given the requisite temperament.

Assumption 4

Empathic viewing from inside the person makes sense of the symptoms. If the therapist can truly see the world as does the patient, the adaptive significance of the "problem" patterns can be seen and understood.

Assumption 5

Mental processes "replay" original object relations. Thoughts and their associated feelings and actions relate rather directly in form and purpose to prior or concurrent important social interactions.

Assumption 6

Attachment, or security, is a primary need. Primates have evolved as group animals, and bonding to the group is essential for survival. When attachment fails, the predispositions set by the process of evolution fail to be realized. My major professor, Harry Harlow, summarized succinctly: "A lone monkey is a dead monkey." If the acts of nurturance and trust that have been programmed into the genetic makeup of the species do not or cannot take place, attachment atrophies or assumes a deviant form. The consequences are monumental. Complete attachment failure results in death of the infant. But there are many ways to interfere with attachment, and each has different consequences. Health problems, including the need for psychotherapy, could be dramatically reduced if more skillful ways of childrearing could be articulated and implemented. As we seek to better our understanding of what it is we treat, members of SPR could also contribute to that idealistic goal of prevention.

These hypotheses have been reviewed elsewhere (Benjamin, 2003) and related to their sources. Key predecessors include B. F. Skinner (1981), H. F. Harlow (e.g., Harlow & Harlow, 1962), H. Murray (1938), H. S. Sullivan (1953), Freud (1905/1959), and various latterday object relations theorists.

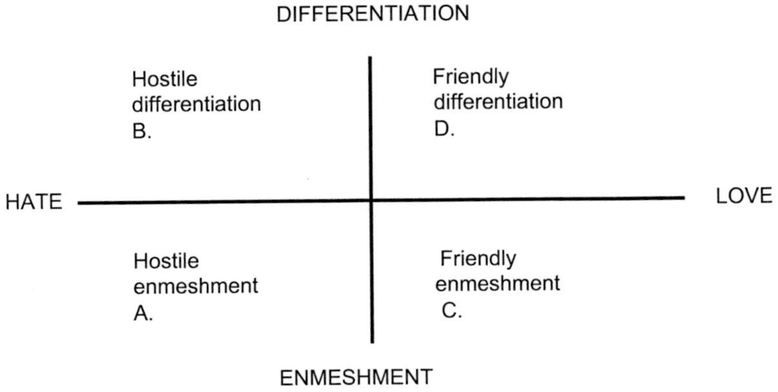

FIGURE 3.1 The Four Types of Relationship Defined in Terms of Enmeshment and Differentiation

The SASB model provides a convenient way to operationalize the object relations concepts inherent in the basic assumptions, and the generic therapy of therapy drawn below. The SASB model describes interpersonal and intrapsychic relationships with three underlying dimensions: focus (other, self, internalized), affiliation (love-hate), interdependence (enmeshment-differentiation). Figure 3.1 shows how the various combinations of the dimensions of affiliation (+ or –) and independence (+ or –) can describe four types of relationship: friendly differentiation (+ , +), friendly enmeshment (+ , –), hostile enmeshment (–, –), and hostile differentiation (-,+). Figure 3.1 includes only four patterns, and they can encompass large groups of "disorders" and variations on "normality."

Hostile differentiation is an important baseline position for a number of mental disorders, like antisocial, schizotypal, schizoid, avoidant personality disorders; and certain types or phases of schizophrenia, or psychotic depressions. Hostile enmeshment is an important baseline position for several mental disorders, like borderline, obsessive-compulsive, passive-aggressive, self-defeating personality disorders; and certain types or phases of schizophrenia, anxiety disorders, and depressive disorders. Friendly enmeshment is characteristic of normative infants and parents, new lovers, and successful variants of the "traditional" marriage. Friendly differentiation is rare in Western culture. It reflects the idea invoked by concepts like "harmoniousness," and, perhaps, by descriptions of higher levels of morality (Kohlberg's [1969] stages 5 and 6; see also Berlin & Johnson, 1989).

The underlying dimensions of the SASB model can be combined to describe more than the four basic groups just reviewed. In fact, it can describe any number of ways of relating to others. Infinity is the theoretical limit to number of subdivisions that could be made on each of the axes of the model. A more complex, but still relatively simple, version of the SASB model appears in Figure 3.2. There,

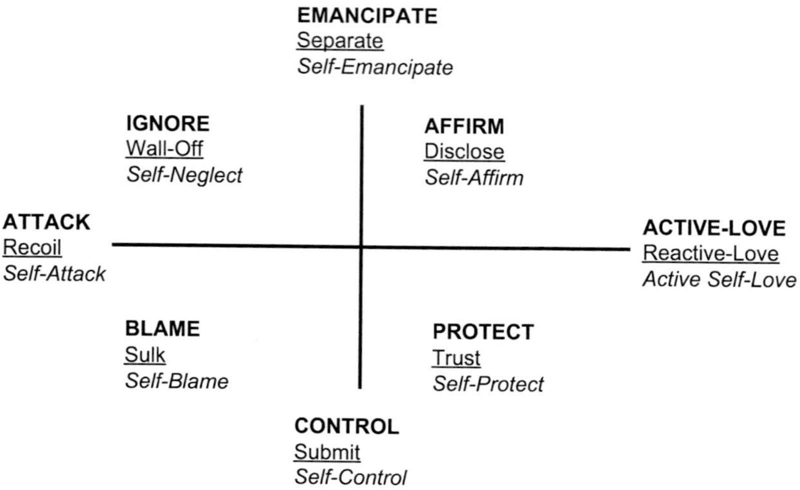

FIGURE 3.2 The Simplified SASB Cluster Model

Note: The horizontal axis runs from hate to love, and the vertical axis, from enmeshment to differentiation. The three types of focus are represented by different styles of print. Complementarity is shown by adjacent **BOLD** and UNDERLINED points. Introjection is shown by adjacent **BOLD** and *ITALICIZED* points. From L. S. Benjamin (1993) *Interpersonal diagnosis and treatment of personality disorders*. New York: Guilford Press.

the dimension of focus is added to the picture, and is represented by three kinds of print. The first category of focus (**bold type**) describes patterns that are actively directed toward others (transitive focus on other). The second (*underlined type*) describes actual or anticipated reactions on behalf of the self (intransitive focus on self). The third (*italicized type*) involves actions that are directed actively and internally upon the self (introjection or internalization of focus on other).

The topography of Figures 3.1 and 3.2 is the same. Hostile enmeshment, shown in Figure 3.1, also appears in the lower lefthand corner of Figure 3.2. In the more complicated figure, the center of this region of hostile enmeshed space includes the points: **BLAME**, Sulk and *Self-Blame*. The three differ only in focus and all are composed of equal amounts of the underlying elements represented by the axes of the model. There is a mixture of pure interdependence on the one side (to the right), and pure hostility on the other (to the left).

The eight subdivisions of Figure 3.2 show that for any given type of focus, it is possible to define eight different positions merely by shifting the underlying components of affiliation and independence. Starting at point under discussion, **BLAME**, one can progress clockwise, adding hostility and increasing independence, to reach **ATTACK**. Continuing in the same direction, other points will follow in succession: **IGNORE, EMANCIPATE, AFFIRM, ACTIVE-LOVE, PROTECT, CONTROL**. The circle is completed when there is a return to **BLAME**.

The geometric, circumplexial arrangements of Figure 3.2 summarize important connections among interpersonal positions. They show that a qualitatively broad range of behaviors can be accounted for by just two underlying dimensions.[3] They also generate a number of useful predictive principles. Three principles that can be used to connect early patterns with the patterns characteristic of a given mental disorder are *complementarity, similarity,* and *introjection.*

The eight points appearing in **bold face** in Figure 3.2, and their adjacent points that are underlined, describe eight different forms of *complementarity.* These are likely pairings of interpersonal positions that are often seen within a dyad, like parent and child. For example, in a relationship characterized by hostile enmeshment, one person will usually Blame, while the other will usually Sulk. One position draws for the other. Sulking elicits blaming and blaming elicits sulking. Therapists can often see that a patient's problem position preserves the original position that was complementary to the parent's baseline offering. The chronically blaming family shapes the child to assuming a position of hostile compliance, called *Sulk* in Figure 3.2. Therapists who encounter patients who are oppressed and miserable can assume that these people have been exposed to much hostile control or **BLAME**.

The principle of *similarity* describes what is otherwise known as identification. The child who acts like the parent or other important figures is *similar* to them. Therapists who come across patients who angrily oppress and blame others can assume that these people, too, have been exposed to much hostile control or **BLAME**. Some variables that determine whether a child maintains complementarity as an adult, or identifies with the oppressor, can be suggested (Benjamin, 1993a), but extensive research is needed.

The principle of *introjection* comes from Sullivan's (1953) idea that self-concept is the result of treating the self as have important others. In Figure 3.2, introjection is shown by pairings of **bold** points and adjacent *italicized* points. If a child is raised in an environment pervaded by **BLAME**, he or she will be very likely to internalize it and engage in *Self-Blame.* Eight different types of self-concept, and their social antecedents are described in Figure 3.2. Therapists who meet with patients who are guilty and constantly blame themselves can assume that these people have been exposed to a lot of hostile control or **BLAME**.

The usefulness of these principles can be illustrated by a brief consideration of the so-called "Helplessness paradox" noted by Abramson and Sackein (1977). The puzzle is in the thought: *If depressed people feel so worthless and helpless, why do they believe they are responsible for eveything that goes wrong? How can people who feel so weak and powerless feel they are responsible for so much that is bad?* The SASB model offers a parsimonious resolution of the paradox. These individuals are simply manifesting the principles of complementarity and introjection. People who engage in behaviors described by the paradox are predicted to have been raised in a blaming environment. By the principle of complementarity, they remain submissive and helpless. By the principle of introjection, they blame themselves. Both are *natural* consequences of being raised in an environment characterized by hostile control. Linear logic has nothing to do with it.

Symptoms Involving Affect and Cognition Will Correlate with Social Perceptions

The SASB model's emphasis on behavioral interaction with the self or others does not rule out consideration of affect or cognition. Elsewhere (Benjamin, 1986), I offered first-draft proposals for parallel models of affect, and of cognition. The idea is simple: If a behavior, like dominance, has adaptive value, there should be an affect that enhances its likelihood. There also should be a cognitive style that is consistent with and helps maintain the adaptive behavior. The parallel model for affect proposes that the SASB point, **CONTROL** is accompanied by an affect called Forceful (or victorious). This, in turn, is accompanied by a cognitive style called Sharp Focus on Detail. For another example, the point **BLAME** shown in Figure 3.2 is paralleled by **Arrogance** in the affect model. The associated point on the cognitive model might be **Judgmental**.

Studies of any one of these domains—social behavior, affect, or cognition—should have clear and direct implications for another. I have chosen to emphasize the social domain first. In psychotherapy, the interpersonal and intrapsychic perceptions described by the dimensions of love-hate and enmeshment-differentiation serve to focus the dialogue. But it is important that the therapist remember also to ask, "How do you *feel?*" and "What and how do you *think* (about the social or intrapsychic pattern under discussion)? Constant focus on specific interactions, the associated affect, and the cognitive style keep therapy high in "the white heat of relevance."

The hypothesis that there are parallels among social perceptions, affects, and cognitions provides a link between changes in object relations and symptom changes. Interpersonally, I think that *anxiety* is a natural affect that accompanies a perception that one is threatened with harm, with the blocking of plans or wishes, or with major loss of someone (including the self) or something. The anxious person *intends* to cope with the threat, but is afraid that it cannot be mastered. A depressed person has the same perceptions, but feels helpless, unable to cope with the threats. In other words, anxiety appears at moments the person thinks he or she might try to cope with the situation, depression prevails when he or she is sure that things are hopeless and nothing can be done.[4] The idea of parallel models permits symptoms like anxiety and depression to be interpreted in terms of the patient's prevailing interpersonal beliefs.

A Generic View of Psychotherapy

If mental disorder is an adaptation to perceived social situations, and if affects, cognitions, and behaviors are reliable correlates, it is important to understand clearly what the patient is adapting *to.* Present patterns in the patient's life are likely to have links to the past. The therapy should develop the patient's understanding of the patterns, where they came from, and what they are for (i.e., the associated wishes and fears). Correlated affects and cognitive styles should be noted. It also is important to assess the impact of the patient's expectations for the future. It is likely that the patient's (unconscious) hopes and fears drive and organize the present patterns. These hopes and fears arise from the original situation to which an adaptation had to be made. The wishes and fears that grew out of the original learning experiences lock in the present patterns of the disorder. Until they are transformed, purely behavioral or other here-and-now therapy interventions will only have a small chance of making lasting impact.

The interviewing process that is needed to implement this algorithm must be interpersonally specific about perceived input, response, and internalizations. It must track parallel affects and cognitions. The interviewer and interviewee must collaborate, and it is helpful to allow the process to be directed by the patient's unconscious. The interviewer assumes the patient makes sense and accepts the challenge to find the meaning, the internally consistent connections between the present and past and wishes and fears.

In therapy, the patient learns to recognize his or her interpersonal and intrapsychic patterns, their associated affects and cognitions.[5] The patient comes to understand where these patterns came from and *what they are for:* At some point, the patient must consider whether the old adaptations are still worth it. If the answer is no, then the process of learning new patterns that are now more adaptive can begin. Attempts to help the patient learn new patterns are likely to fail if the patient has not in one way or another *decided* to give up the underlying (usually unconscious) hopes and fears.

This dynamic learning interpretation of psychotherapy permits correct interventions to be defined. A given intervention is correct if it:

1. enhances collaboration to work on the problem
2. helps the patient learn about his or her interpersonal, cognitive, or affective patterns
3. blocks patterns that are presently maladaptive
4. enhances the will to change
5. effectively teaches new interpersonal, cognitive, or affective patterns.

These five categories of correct modes of intervention also are arranged approximately in hierarchy, and reflect stages of progress through therapy. Like any description of stages, there is considerable variability in progress through them.

But, on the whole, a therapy will progress from the development of collaboration, through learning about patterns, and mobilizing the will and the courage to change. The first priority is to keep the therapy relationship collaborative. If it is not, it must be repaired immediately. Learning and reliably using new patterns characterizes the later stages of the therapy process. The categories can be applied to patient-therapist interactions in many therapies, including psychoanalytic, client centered, existential, cognitive, behavioral, interpersonal, and others.

The listing of correct interventions permits definition of therapist errors. An error occurs whenever the intervention is not correct, and correctness is assessed on the basis of the patient's response, not the therapist's intention. If, for example, the therapist intends to block a pattern, but instead enables the pattern, the intervention is an error. Perhaps it was not properly timed or framed.

In the domain of individual therapy, there is a long list of interventions that are regarded as generically good. Many therapists believe that catharsis, especially the expression of anger, is categorically helpful. Most hold that enhancing self-esteem is unequivocally good. It is widely accepted that deep experiencing is a desirable therapy process goal. Most assume that providing support for the patient is a "safe bet." Interpreting or "pointing out" is an important therapy process that is often invoked to generate change. These, and other such categories of therapist behavior, are tallied and related to therapy outcome to study change processes (Garfield & Bergin, 1986). Some other categories include therapist silence, approval, reassurance, reflection, asking questions, interpretation, and therapist self-disclosure. Tallies of the frequency of these therapist behaviors serve to compare and contrast different therapy approaches (e.g., Hill, 1986).

Although the time-honored interventions included on these research lists often are correct, they also are often wrong. Counting such therapist behaviors independently of the context may obscure important information. For example, in some contexts, silence may contribute to growth. In other contexts, therapist's silence may reinforce a patient's destructive beliefs. The categories of intervention can enable as well as challenge maladaptive patterns. By making errors, therapists fail to maximize psychotherapy's tremendous potential for effectively treating mental disorder.

Consider the summary that appears in Table 3.1 of selected therapy techniques commonly assumed to be correct regardless of context. The examples in Table 3.1 rely on the reader's understanding of personality disorders as defined in the current DSM. The first line of Table 3.1 suggests that it is effective to encourage the expression of anger in a person summarized by the DSM label, Dependent Personality Disorder (DPD). On the other hand, the table shows it is more likely to be iatrogenic to encourage the expression on anger in someone whose patterns are summarized by the label, Histrionic Personality Disorder (HPD). The definition of correct and erroneous uses of a technique depends on the definition and understanding of the problem pattern. Consider the SASB-based interpersonal translations of DSM definitions of these two disorders (Benjamin, 1993):

Dependent Personality Disorder (DPD)

The baseline position is of marked submissiveness to a dominant other person who is supposed to provide unending nurturance and guidance. The wish is to maintain connection to that person even if it means tolerating abuse. The DPD believes he or she is instrumentally incompetent, and this means that he or she cannot survive without the dominant other person.

Histrionic Personality Disorder (HPD)

There is strong fear of being ignored, and a wish to be loved and taken care of by someone powerful. The person is controlled through use of charm and skills in entertaining. The baseline position is of friendly trust that is accompanied by a secretly disrespectful agenda of forcing delivery of the desired nurturance and love. Inappropriate seductive behaviors, and manipulative suicidal attempts, are examples of such coercions.

These interpersonal definitions suggest that if a DPD were to express anger to or about a dominant other, the potential for constructive change of the DPD patterns would be enhanced. On the other hand, the HPD's baseline problem pattern of trying to coerce nurturance would likely be enhanced by expression of anger. The same intervention, encouraging expression of anger to or about a dominant other, is correct in one context and an error in another. It corrects the DPD's problem patterns, but enhances the HPD's.

The second line of Table 3.1 considers the popular therapy intervention of "enhancing self-esteem." Exercises in self-esteem can be very helpful with someone who oppresses him- or herself. For example, a subgroup of depressed individuals that is characterized by inordinate self-criticism (Blatt, 1974) might benefit from self-esteem exercises. On the other hand, interventions that encourage self-approval can be iatrogenic with someone who does not hold him- or herself to appropriate normative standards, like a person with Narcissistic Personality Disorder.

Narcissistic Personality Disorder (NPD)

There is extreme vulnerability to criticism or being ignored, and a strong wish for love, support, and admiring deference from others. The baseline position involves noncontingent love of self and presumptive control of others. If the support is withdrawn, or if there is any evidence of lack of perfection, the self-concept degrades to severe self-criticism. Totally lacking in empathy, these persons treat others with contempt, and hold the self above and beyond the fray.

The idea that deep experiencing is essential to good psychotherapy is widely accepted both in practice and research (e.g., Klein, Mathieu-Coughlan, & Kiesler, 1986). Indeed, deep experiencing often is an important part of constructive therapy process. Deep experiencing is very likely to be helpful to a person with Obsessive Compulsive Personality Disorder (OCD).

Obsessive Compulsive Personality Disorder (OCD)

The OCD fears he or she will make a mistake or be accused of being imperfect. The quest for order yields a baseline interpersonal position of blaming, inconsiderate control of others. The OCD's control alternates with blind obedience to authority or principle. There is excessive self-discipline, restraint of feelings, harsh criticism of and neglect of the self.

Clearly the OCD, who is characterized by restraint of feeling, could profit by learning to experience affect deeply. But it is not categorically true that deep experiencing enhances needed learning. Consider the idea of deepening the experience of anger in an individual with Borderline Personality Disorder (BPD).

Borderline Personality Disorder

There is a morbid fear of abandonment and a wish for protective nurturance, preferably by constant physical proximity to the rescuer (lover or caregiver). The baseline position is friendly dependency on a nurturer, which becomes hostile control if the caregiver or lover fails to deliver enough (and there is never enough). There is a belief that the provider secretly, if not overtly, likes dependency and neediness, and a vicious introject attacks the self if there are signs of happiness or success.

Very intense feelings of rage typically emerge in the BPD when there is perceived abandonment by a caregiver or lover. It is usually expressed without restraint and serves the destructive purpose of trying to coerce more caregiving from the "negligent" caregiver or lover.

The fourth line of the table addresses correct and incorrect uses of interpretation, or "pointing out." These activities often are tabulated in research studies of therapy process independently of context. Again, the success of the intervention will depend on the nature of the underlying problem, and the stage of the therapy at the moment. For example, a therapist who "points out" early in therapy with the NPD is likely to destroy the therapy relationship. The NPD will terminate at this hint of anything other than therapist approval. Usually such confrontations are better accepted after a therapy relationship has developed, and the patient has indicated that he or she is willing and able to collaborate against "it," the problem patterns.

Even after there is a contract to work on the problem patterns, there will be times when the patient will regress and be defensive in response to interpretation. Those moments are not the time for confrontation. Making interpretations when the therapeutic relationship is in trouble is more likely to represent therapist defensiveness than helpfulness. For example, *if* the patient is angry at the therapist, "interpretation" is very likely to sound like invalidation of the patient's possibly legitimate view. It may blame or appear to blame the patient. One likely consequence of perceived blaming from the therapist is patient *self-blame.* Depending on the character of the patient, another consequence would be to counter-blame, and to escalate problems in the therapy relationship. Neither outcome is good for the therapy learning process.

The next line of the table considers interventions that attempt to teach alternative responses to problem situations. Workshops or groups that teach skills in communication, assertiveness, expression of affect, negotiation, mediation, and the like can be enormously helpful. The chances of having a positive effect on young normal participants are quite good. However, informal observations suggest that these interventions often do not have lasting effects in clinical populations. For example, "trust fall" games will not affect a person with paranoid personality disorder. Assertiveness training is unlikely to change the expressive paralysis of those with dependent personality. If it does, they are likely to get flattened the first time they try asserting with their significant other person.[6] And so on. Such skill-teaching is effective in normals or, alternatively, at the fifth and last stage of therapy outlined above. The chances for improvement for severely disordered patients are increased after underlying wishes and fears have been elucidated in the light of earlier adaptations, and the decision has been made to change things.

The final line of Table 3.1 addresses therapist support, a feature of psychotherapy that is suspected to be a potent nonspecific, or general, therapy change agent. Support is always appropriate for individuals who are in crisis, whether that be due to a loss of someone or something loved, to a crushing burden, or other such severe life stresses. On the other hand, there are situations when support encourages problem patterns. For example, the individual with passive-aggressive personality disorder desperately wants support. He or she should not receive support, however, when it serves the unconscious agenda of conspicuously suffering to indict a negligent caregiver as hypothesized for individuals with Passive Aggressive Personality disorder (Klein et al., 1986: ch. 11).

TABLE 3.1 Different Views of Standard Techniques

Technique	*Effective Use*	*Ineffective Use*
Encourage expression of anger	DPD	HPD's dramatic
Enhance self-esteem	Depressed self-critic	NPD's self-love
Encourage deep experiencing	OC Personality Disorder	BPD's rage
Interpret (point out)	Collaborative moments	Moments of resistance
Teach alternative responses	Counseling situation	Personality disorders
Support	Moments of crisis	Enable ongoing dependency

Summary of Passive-Aggressive Personality Disorder (PAG)

The PAG sees any form of power as inconsiderate and neglectful. He or she believes authorities or caregivers are incompetent, unfair, and cruel. PAG agrees to comply with perceived demands or suggestions, but fails to perform. He or she often complains of unfair treatment, and envies and resents others who fare better. His or her suffering indicts the allegedly negligent caregivers or authorities. PAG fears control in any form and wishes for nurturant restitution.

The therapist's decision about whether the interventions (like those listed in Table 3.1) will be correct depends on therapist understanding of the disorder. In other words, choice of intervention depends on the diagnosis and implicit or explicit theory associated with the diagnosis.

But the proposed guidelines are not easy to invoke. Sometimes one of these guidelines will contradict another. For example, support may sometimes be correct, even if it temporarily encourages the problem patterns. Resolution of such conflicts usually is possible by thinking of the categories in hierarchy. The therapy relationship has priority over everything else. If the therapist needs temporarily to support maladaptive patterns to preserve the therapy relationship, the intervention is correct. This often happens in therapy with individuals with narcissistic or passive-aggressive personality disorder, for example. Failing to provide adequate support for the NPD's present ways of doing things may "injure" him or her too greatly. Similarly, the PAG is likely to take failure to support as further evidence of inadequate care and enjoin the battle with unsurpassed vigor. For maximal efficiency, the therapist must constantly judge when the relationship will bear the strain of growth, and when it will not.

A Case Showing Things May Get Worse Before They Get Better

The generic theory of therapy will be applied to an illustrative case selected from a series in which the chief complaint must have lasted for more than 10 years, and at least two previous therapies have failed. In this case, there had been five previous failed therapies. She qualified for the DSM label Avoidant Personality Disorder. My interpersonal view of this pattern is: There is intense fear of humiliation and rejection. To avoid expected embarrassment, the AVD (Avoidant Personality Disorder) withdraws and carefully restrains him or herself. He or she intensely wishes for love and acceptance, and will become very intimate with those few who pass highly stringent tests for safety. Occasionally, AVD loses control and explodes with rageful indignation.

At the time of this SPR meeting, one and one-half years into therapy, the SCL-90R (Derogatis, 1977) measures suggested there had been decreases in some symptoms (anxiety) and increases in others (anger). The MCMI (Millon, 1982) measures of depression remained at the 100th percentile, as they had been at the start of therapy. Tellegen's (1982) trait measures also showed no change. SASB measures suggested that, in her best state, the patient was somewhat less self-critical and improved in her ability to do nice things for herself. However, in her worst state, she remained very self-blaming and attacking, and her tendency to neglect herself had increased. In short, objective measures would not suggest this therapy had been effective.

However, measures of the patient's view of the therapist and the therapy suggested that collaboration was intact, and that something important was happening. She wrote in response to a question about therapy on Strupp's RATE questionnaire: "There is a different quality to my pain. Was sharpened, and more panic-inspiring. Now duller but deeper—more my own. Have started to think of my life as more real than malleability of words. The balance has shifted: more searching mixed in with the blind fighting against being me, being female." Later she wrote, "I believe I am on a therapy-track that will prove significant for real change . . . From where I stand, it looks like part-way therapy can make things worse, so a commitment seems necessary . . . I hurt more in focus. Escapes don't work as well as before. Things feel worse (and it feels better that it feels worse??) So I assign patience to the process of therapy."

It is, as mentioned above, necessary to make the differential between deterioration that is a part of the reconstructive process, and simple deterioration that serves no constructive purpose. It is not true that increase in symptoms necessarily means that there is deterioration. Measures of symptoms must be interpreted in the light of the definition of the problem, and its associated treatment plan. If there is a clear theory of therapy change, then symptomatic changes can be evaluated dynamically because changes in external and internal object relations covary sensibly with changes in symptoms.

To the extent reconstructive therapy uncovers unpleasant memories, correlated undesirable affects also will increase. As the person in the illustrative case reflected on herself and her role in the family, her perceptions changed. So did her affect. An increase in anger accompanied changes in her memory of her relationship with her mother. The SASB Intrex questionnaires showed that she shifted from high ratings for maternal **AFFIRM, ACTIVE-LOVE** and **PROTECT** to high ratings for **CONTROL, BLAME,** and **ATTACK**).[7] Their correlated affects, depression and anxiety also were present. It was only later in therapy that the antecedent social input (maternal **CONTROL, BLAME,** and **ATTACK**) was remembered. This finding is consistent with classical clinical wisdom that would argue that it is necessary to uncover those associated inputs (parental hostility) before the problem position (resentful compliance) and associated affects (depression, anxiety) can be transformed. It is also true, however, that remembering alone does not change the problem. The relationship with the internalized significant objects must be transformed before behaviors, cognitions, and affects can change.

In the illustrative case, the father was warm to the patient, but not to his wife. As therapy continued, the patient came to *see* that her father had exerted substantial hostile control over her mother. This attitude of male dominance had been sanctioned in the family in particular, and in their culture at large. The patient had unconsciously internalized these views, and consequently she hated her assignment to the female gender.

Every Psychopathology is a Gift of Love

Ultimately, the task is to move on, to differentiate from destructive internalizations and take up, with full awareness, one's own choice of ways of being. As the patient in the illustrative case gains a broader perspective on family relations in individual psychotherapy, she may become less likely to see the given patterns as reflections of ultimate truth. Representations of the self that represent incorporation or identification with important others must be modified. This does not necessarily mean that a patient needs to become alienated from family. The ideal outcome is that internal differentiation becomes so secure that the patient can maintain cordial relations with family as it is in the present, while no longer being vulnerable.

This particular patient is remarkably insightful and evocative in her imagery. She offered a wonderful description of the crossroads of change during a session after she had completed an especially challenging and frightening task.

> I told him that for a while I had been feeling this big need. To—to tell him goodbye. Because I wanted—I wanted a life. I wanted—I wanted Some*thing*. He, he was holding himself back. From enjoying his life. And I told him that it was really sad to be leaving him alone back there with that. I actually told him, I—(this is kind of, I mean this is just so weird to me that I actually told him in, in real words)—that, I had to —I had to leave him, in a sense, in order to go ahead. And he told me that he, um—how—he waved goodbye to me on my journey. I mean, this is so—this is really bizarre to have a conversation like—as if it were a physical journey. Like going—going across the ocean. Only, we knew perfectly well that we were talking about our emotional states. (It is really bizarre to have a conversation with another human being, metaphorically like this, and to have him tell me "goodbye," and "have a good journey" and—and all this stuff. And to be—and to tell me that he was glad for me. To be going to do that.)

I call this session "Father Says Bon Voyage." It is not easy to say what contributes to that vital step. The process of separating from old destructive beliefs about the self and others can be facilitated if the patient can get permission from the "real object" to separate. Unfortunately, this rarely happens. In addition, people usually respond more to internalizations of parents than to the "real thing." A conversation like this one can help transform the internal representation of father, but the result is not guaranteed.

I believe that the primary attachment to early objects (parents, siblings, or others) is an important basis of psychopathology. The effect interacts with given temperament but, beyond that, is transmitted by simple learning: the patient either maintains the early childhood position or identifies with the parent. The wishes and fears that arise from these old patterns organize the problem patterns of adulthood. To achieve reconstructive change, psychosocial therapy must therefore strike effectively at the destructive aspects of this bond. *Every psychopathology is a gift of love.* In my book on personality disorders (Benjamin, 1993a), this thesis that problem patterns are driven by attachment is addressed at greater length. Here is a brief excerpt:

> The first level of expression of wishes often is hostile. For example revenge is a common organizing wish. Passive-Aggressive, Borderline, Avoidant, Narcissistic, Paranoid, [and] Antisocial personalities all can verbalize the hope that they can punish, inflict pain, wreak revenge, or torture selected others. Nonetheless, the love beneath the hostility can be uncovered if the therapist looks for it. Consider the patient who contemplates murdering his father. The therapist can ask: "And then what," looking for the love beneath. The nature of the answer will vary depending on the structure of the disorder. Maybe the patient hopes for a fantasied scene of reconciliation in heaven or hell. Maybe he or she envisions a rescued and grateful mother as she sees father fallen in a bloody heap. Maybe the murder will realize father's lifelong demands that the patient be a "man." The present thesis is that underneath statements like: "I hate him," there is a residual of attachment to someone important.

Unfortunately, such glimpses at the problem of will have found their way into clinical practice largely in the form of blaming the patient when he or she fails to change. It is possible to acknowledge the important role of will, and still to assign substantial responsibility for the therapy process to the therapist. Elsewhere (Benjamin, 1993), I have tried to make a list of interventions that can be used to try to engage the patient's will to change. My observations represent little more than clinical hunches. Therapy researchers and clinicians need to learn a lot more about how to mobilize the will to change. There is a nascent literature on the subject of will or choice (Sappington, 1990). Psychotherapy researchers might profitably focus more on the problem of assessing the will to give up destructive attachments and their associated patterns.

Outcome Should be Measured by Stages of Change

Therapy is a staged process that involves learning about problem patterns, their origins and purposes. The attachments that underlay the organizing wishes and fears can be transformed if the patient decides to give them up. Then new patterns can be learned. If therapy occurs in stages, then outcome should be assessed in stages rather than in terms of simple increases or decreases in symptom change or social attitudes. There is a precedent for this idea. Prochaska, a behavioral psychologist who has had some success in helping people break addiction to substances like tobacco, identifies four stages of change (Prochaska, Rossi, & Wilcox, 1991). They are precontemplation, contemplation, action, and maintenance. Prochaska's analysis of change in addicts is compatible with the present analysis of generic psychotherapy. *To compare object relations psychotherapy to this behavioral change literature, one need only view the underlying attachment to the bad objects* as *an addiction.*

I would not propose that psychotherapy be assessed exactly in terms of Prochaska's stages. Rather I would like to count progress in psychotherapy according to movement through the hierarchical list of five correct interventions. If, after treatment, collaboration is present when it was not there before, that should be counted as a success on the ladder of change. For example, an inpatient hospitalization might serve to engage a patient with his or her problems, so that he or she becomes willing to collaborate and work earnestly in outpatient therapy. This should count as a (limited form of) success.

The staging method of assessing efficacy would suggest that the illustrative case has made progress even though the therapy is not complete and the traditional outcome measures are not good. The first two or three stages are well underway. There is good collaboration and considerable learning about patterns and their origins. A few maladaptive patterns have been blocked (e.g., avoiding femininity by trying to "look dreadful"), and tiny new ones (e.g., little steps in better self-care) have been learned. As the patient learns more about how she is trapped in, rather than defiant of, her family beliefs about females and "the way things are," she may mobilize the will to change. Now, as she haltingly dares to remember how it really was and how she felt, she seems to prepare to let go of loyalty to old beliefs. She might soon move on to claim her right to happiness and success.

COMMENTARY

EVERY PSYCHOPATHOLOGY IS STILL A GIFT OF LOVE

In 1993, I wrote "Every psychopathology is a gift of love" (GOL; Benjamin, 1993a), and GOL was described this way:

> I believe that the primary attachment to early objects (parents, siblings, or others) is an important basis of psychopathology. The effect interacts with given temperament, but beyond that, is transmitted by simple learning: the patient either maintains the early childhood position, or identifies with the parent. The wishes and fears that arise from these old patterns organize the problem patterns of adulthood. To achieve reconstructive change,

psychosocial therapy must therefore strike effectively at the destructive aspects of this bond.

In that paper, I also reviewed: 1) difficulties using the drug protocol (Randomized Control Trials, RCT) to establish effectiveness of psychotherapy; 2) the need to embrace the fact that during structural change patients often get worse before they get better and it should be possible to distinguish necessary regression from harmful deterioration; 3) the need to heed calls to provide integrative theory to make sense of the growing lists of variables related to psychopathology and therapy process; and 4) the problem of engaging the will to change.

My attempt to pull things together included a demonstration of how to use Structural Analysis of Social Behavior (SASB; Benjamin 1979, 1996) and its predictive principles to link current patterns of personality disorder to early interactions with attachment figures. Comparing present interactive patterns to relationships with attachment figures made sense in the light of the ever-growing literature on the impact of attachment on adult characteristics. The key to therapy change was illustrated by an example of "friendly differentiation" from (the internalized representation of) an attachment figure. Another way of saying that is that therapy change follows relinquishing GOLs. I sketched a five-step therapy model and suggested therapy outcome might be described by these stages: 1) collaboration working toward therapy goals; 2) learning about patterns and where they came from; 3) blocking problem patterns; 4) engaging the will to change; and 5) learning new patterns. Resistance to change is based on Gifts of Love, and the will to confront and let go of them (step 4) must be engaged before new patterns can be learned (step 5).

In the intervening 20 years, the RCT paradigm in therapy research has become dominant, illustrated by a resolution issued by the American Psychological Association: "The effects produced by psychotherapy, including the effects for different age groups (i.e., children, adults, and older adults) and for many mental disorders, exceed or are comparable to the size of effects produced by many pharmacological treatments and procedures for the same condition" (APA, 2013, p. 103).

Aside from clearly establishing that psychotherapy is effective, not a lot else has changed with respect to the issues mentioned in my 1993 paper:

1. It is still true that no one therapy approach is consistently better than others ("All have won and all must have prizes").
2. It is still true that raw empiricism prevails over testable theory about mechanisms of change that can explain how therapy works. Calls for integrative theory continue (Castonguay, 2011; Magnavita, 2008). Some might counter that lists of variables and their interactions already are integrated by "theory" represented by Structural Equation Modeling or comparable forms of multivariate analysis. But that claim would overlook the fact that the same methods

used to create the theory are used to test its "validity." Taking replication as validation confuses reliability testing with establishing construct validity.

3. The problem of distinguishing harmful deterioration from "things get worse before they get better" in reconstructive work has not been solved. In fact, if a patient starts to deteriorate, concurrent outcome measures can trigger an administrative response to the effect the treatment approach needs to change, just as one would change medications that are not working after a while (Lambert, 2013).
4. The subject of will has been approached in the literature by W. R. Miller's "motivational interviewing (e.g., Moyers, Miller, & Hendrickson, 2005) and is promising. But in its present form I believe motivational interviewing emphasizes common factors more than underlying motivations related to pathology or the change process.

Most of the points I made about therapy in 1993 have been confirmed and further developed. But there is one that was wrong. Discussing the nature-nurture problem, I endorsed Carson's analogy that inheritance compares to computer hardware while environmental effects are reflected in software. The comparison was not valid. Although sequences of DNA don't change, epigenetic mechanisms reflect the impact of environment on genes (e.g., by shape of the DNA molecule, or piRNA-based signaling). Further, epigenetic changes are heritable because they affect transcription. I also overlooked mainstream biology's demonstrations that genes are expressed and silenced by interactions with the environment. So genes are changed by at least two environmental mechanisms: expression/silencing and epigenetic process. La Mark had a valid point. Among other things, this shows that research that correlates features of a gene in an adult to an attribute of the brain does not necessarily show that attribute is inherited. And a virus can spin a hard drive into self-destruction, permanently changing it.

Argument, by analogy, is dangerous. Correlational research and statistical comparisons of groups are suggestive at best. Real science studies the nature of nature, describes mechanisms, and systematically seeks to eliminate alternative explanations. Psychotherapy research in particular and psychology in general does little of that kind of research. An outstanding exception is the work of Michael Meany (e.g., Bagot & Meaney, 2010), who has showed in careful work spanning more than two decades that mother/pup interactions affect anxiety in the rats as adults, and in succeeding generations! His exploration of alternative explanations was impressive, as are his detailed, credible descriptions of mechanisms to explain these effects. He described his work in an honorary lecture at the 2012 meetings of American Psychologists and almost nobody came. Is the material too intimidating for psychologists? Are the implications too unwelcome? Is the idea that studies of rats can generalize to humans too preposterous? Is psychology a life science? I am totally puzzled by the lack of impact of this breathtakingly important work showing lasting effects of parenting behavior on psychopathology.

Believing in the continuity of life forms, and in the wisdom of trying to emulate the methods of the physical sciences, for the past 10 years I have been writing and rewriting a third book that centers on what I call a "natural biology" of psychopathology and mechanisms of symptom change (Benjamin, draft). In it, I draw upon mainstream biological descriptions of the structure and function of the nervous system and relate it to the IRT case formulation and treatment models. The IRT models backed by this version of natural biology work have been well received when practicing, teaching, supervising, and demonstrating IRT.

The arguments are radically simple. Very briefly: anger, anxiety, and depression are controlled by the threat (sympathetic nervous) system. In nature, they predispose adaptive behavioral responses to threat such as freeze, fight, flight, hide, camouflage, and surrender. In opposition to threat, the behaviors of resting, relaxing, complex learning, bonding are predisposed by parasympathetic nervous system chemistry which is triggered by perception of safe conditions. Children learn about what is threatening and how to find safety from caregivers. These rules about safety and threat (e.g., don't touch the hot stove) are long-lasting and transmitted by internalized representations of attachment figures (family in the head). Adaptive lessons in safety and threat enhance survival and are internalized as a secure base. Inappropriate lessons in safety and threat sponsor symptoms of mental illness. Attachment figures normally activate safety system chemistry by virtue of frequent proximity, offers of contact comfort, and showing some responsiveness to the young one. If abusive, attachment figures also activate the threat system. There are two important consequences of having a threatening "safe base": 1) affects are "dysregulated," and 2) because of frequent proximity to the abusive attachment figure, the child's stress system is activated chronically. Pathological brain changes and symptoms follow.

For example, suppose a child frequently is told he/she will not be with the family in heaven if he/she does not keep everything in perfect order. Because separation from caregivers is the most severe threat for a young primate, and because perception rather than reality drives affects and behavior, such a child is likely to become very anxious if things are not in exact order, whether or not circumstances pose an objective threat. Devotion to order compromises reality testing and functioning; the resulting self-sabotage through obsession with neatness is that child's GOL to the sponsoring attachment figure.

My very talented and greatly valued colleague, Ken Critchfield, and I work at the University of Utah Neuropsychiatric hospital with a population we call CORDS (Comorbid, Often Rehospitalized, Dysfunctional and Suicidal). We choose to work with them because of the great need and the important conceptual challenges they present. It is unlikely that the observed pre-post decreases in suicidal attempts, rehospitalizations, and days in hospital are achieved by "common factors," alone because this population already has had so many treatments with medications, psychotherapies, and more. They are referred as inpatients for assessment of personality disorder and treatment planning. I write a consultative report and the inpatient and outpatient treatments that follow (if our resources permit) are supervised by Ken. Treatments are organized by principles from an SASB-based description of DSM5 personality disorders[8] (Benjamin 2003a) and from Interpersonal Reconstructive Therapy (IRT; Benjamin, 2003a). The latter developed the assumptions about psychopathology and model of therapy sketched in the 1993 paper in much greater detail.

Ken Critchfield is director of Interpersonal Reconstructive Therapy (IRT) research, as well as director of the IRT clinic. He did most of the work on two publications using normal and inpatient samples already collected by me. With N greater than 100 in each sample, we tested and confirmed the existence of the IRT concept of copy processes. These can be tracked by the SASB predictive principles and they are the natural biological mechanisms that link current problem patterns and the associated symptoms to lessons in threat and safety from attachment figures (Critchfield & Benjamin, 2008, 2010). With the help of our colleague Kathleen Levenick, Ken also established that the IRT case formulations that identify copy processes associated with specific attachment figures are highly reliable when developed by independent viewers at different sites. With graduate student Matt Davis, Ken created detailed adherence scales for IRT based on descriptions of the treatment model in the IRT book. These scales are unusual in the specificity with which concepts are defined, and in their ability to identify therapist errors. For example, if a trainee shows extended empathy for behavior that is classified as maladaptive (e.g., the patient's yearning that mother would have been different), that is an error. If the trainee shows empathy for behavior consistent with the treatment plan (e.g., the patient's resolve to stop trying to change the past and explore his own preferences for lifestyle), that is adherent. The more clearly the conversation is related to optimal descriptions of a therapy step (e.g., collaboration with therapy goal), the greater the adherence. With help from graduate students and hospital psych tech volunteers, reliable ratings of therapy session adherence to the IRT case formulation and treatment models were gathered. Early results show that adherent focus that increases the patient's will to relinquish the GOLs is followed directly by decreases in depression.

Our samples are necessarily small and we value effects that are large enough that we can see them at the level of N = 1. We could demonstrate that more exact uses of the IRT model has better effects, while therapy errors are associated with no change or increase of symptoms. We propose that this method of linking assessments of proposed mechanisms to change to symptom change is a valid method of showing effectiveness. Moreover, the method permits examination of which components of the model are more important. We already see that if collaboration is intact, the outcome is more likely to be good than if it is not. In my new book, I break the action stage of engaging the will to change into five subphases that theoretically are critical to letting go of GOLs, and therefore are core to change in psychotherapy. It is at this point that it is expected "things will get worse before they get better." And it is at this stage that dropout is most likely. I believe we will find that long-lasting reconstructive change will be observed *if and only if* the symptom-relevant GOLs are relinquished and the associated nearly unbearable losses are grieved. Every psychopathology truly is a Gift of Love.

Notes

1 Conflict of interest disclosure as author of two books (and one in press) that draw on SASB and refer briefly to IRT research: I receive royalties from sales of these books (except for international sales). I give workshops for a fee teaching practicing clinicians how to use IRT concepts. Sometimes I talk briefly about IRT or SASB research. Author of the following assessment instruments: SCID-II (renamed SCID-PD) ©American Psychiatric Press and WISPI (Wisconsin Personality Disorders Inventory) ©Marjorie H. Klein. I have no financial interest in SCID or WISPI. Author of SASB models and technology ©University of Utah. I do have potential interest in SASB. These are university author's benefit if UU sells SASB to a testing company or if I ever lease it from UU to use in an LLC.

2 There are SASB rating scales (Intrex questionnaires) that allow patients or others to code interpersonal and intrapsychic patterns. There is a formal coding system that permits objective observers of video of key interactions (as in psychotherapy) to codify both process, content and outcome. PC software creates parameters that can be used at both the individual and the group levels.

3 A nearly infinite number descriptions is possible because SASB coding rules permit description of complex interactions in terms of more than one point of the model. For example, the "classic" double bind is described by warmth (**ACTIVE-LOVE**) plus coercion (**CONTROL**), while denying that what is happening is happening (**IGNORE**). See Humphrey and Benjamin (1986).

4 Recently ideas similar to these have received some support by laboratory studies (Zinbarg, Barlow, Brown, & Hertz, 1992).

5 Many have suggested that dynamic psychotherapy can be described in terms of learning theory favor the process of identifying social cognitions or input first, and then tracking the responses, internalizations, and affects. This sequencing is consistent with the practices of cognitive therapy (Beck et al., 1979), and Rational Emotive Therapy (Ellis, 1973). But one could begin with affects, and track the social cognitions and internalizations. Whatever mode of entry is chosen, the therapist should realize that much of what is important is unconscious, at least initially. I believe that affects (e.g., anxiety, depression) are more likely to be conscious initially than the associated social cognitions.

6 SASB complementarity theory describes the tendency of dependent individuals to pair with dominant others. The DSM indicates that their need to be taken care of is so strong that they will tolerate abuse rather than challenge the dominant other.

7 The picture was not entirely positive at the beginning: there also were high ratings for maternal **IGNORE** and **EMANCIPATE.**

8 DSM5 descriptions of personality disorder are identical to those in DSM-IV.

4

PSCHEMAS, PSYCHOPATHOLOGY, AND PSYCHOTHERAPY RESEARCH (1994)

Leonard M. Horowitz

A wealthy Boston matron, whom I shall call Abigail Cogsworth, had always lived in Boston and regarded Boston as the hub of her universe. One day a friend gave Abigail some advice: "Abigail, you have plenty of money and you have the time to travel. It might be nice if you traveled and saw a bit of the world." "My dear," Abigail replied, "Why should I travel? I'm already here!" We psychotherapy researchers sometimes resemble Abigail in our complacence: We have no need to expose ourselves to the methods or findings of other disciplines, since we are, after all, "already here." In my view, one important function of the Society for Psychotherapy Research is to broaden ourselves with occasional excursions into other domains. In this paper, I take two excursions—one into the arts and one into cognitive psychology—in order to explore a psychological phenomenon that is relevant to psychotherapy research.

During the past year I had an opportunity to review a book edited by John Clarkin, Elsa Marziali, and Heather Monroe-Blum (1992), on the borderline personality disorder (BPD). The book is informative, interesting, and thought-provoking, a balanced and up-to-date summary of research on the assessment, etiology, and treatment of BPD. As the reviewer, I read the book carefully and became aware of an ambiguity in the literature that I would like to describe.

DSM-III-R states, "the essential [characteristic of BPD] . . . is a pervasive pattern of instability"—in self-image, in interpersonal relationships, or in affect. This instability is said to be related to an *identity disturbance*, a term that is never defined. In fact, DSM-III-R (1987) seems to use two different terms interchangeably. One is a rapid shift between contrasting, or even contradictory, identities. Therapists are familiar with patients who are sometimes intensely dominant and strong and other times equally submissive and helpless. Or sometimes clearly proud and self-respecting, other times equally unworthy and contemptible. I call shifts of this type an "identity confusion" to emphasize the shift between intense states that alternate.

The term *identity disturbance* is also used to denote a general vagueness in self-definition—a diffuse, foggy conception of the self. A well-functioning histrionic patient of mine once said that she felt as though she had no "core me." She was a vegetarian, she said, to be like her sister; a Democrat to be like her boyfriend; a travel agent because her brother-in-law found a job for her in a travel agency. She noticed that whenever someone made a recommendation to her, she liked the idea and wished that she had thought of it. But then she inferred that she had no ideas or convictions of her own—and felt like an empty shell.

I call this kind of vagueness about the self *identity diffusion*. When people complain about feeling empty inside or lacking a core self, they are not talking about a shift in identity. Yet DSM-III-R does not differentiate between these two forms of identity disorder, *confusion* and *diffusion*. Conceptually, though, they are very different. A person who shifts abruptly from one clear set of behaviors, traits, values, or mood to another shows two or more clear identities. A person with a diffuse (vague) identity would seem more likely to feel empty or vulnerable to being overtaken by a dominant person. The two forms of identity disturbance, in my view, call for quite different therapeutic strategies and goals: In one, therapy needs to integrate two contrasting images; in the other, therapy needs to help the person gain one clearer image by articulating values, motives, and associated characteristics. Both refer to ambiguous identities, but the term *ambiguous* is itself ambiguous: A stimulus may be ambiguous because we cannot discern a single sharp image—or because two clear but contrasting images are in competition.

The Arts and Psychopathology

Colleagues in the arts have examined identity disturbances as revealed in creative works of art. Let us begin with the work (and writing) of Edvard Munch (1863–1944), a Norwegian artist associated with the school of German Expressionism. In letters and diaries Munch described his own diffuse sense of self (identity *diffusion*) and his conviction that other stronger people could impose their ideas, feelings, and mental states onto him, thereby displacing his own self with theirs. As a result, he had good reason to remain aloof, isolated, and separate from other people. This isolation, however, left him feeling intensely lonely, producing a dilemma—to connect, producing severe anxiety versus to stay isolated, producing severe loneliness. As one biographer wrote: "Closeness, whether it involved friendship with a man, sexual intimacy with a woman, or even looking at a person, was frightening to him . . . His concept of closeness between two individuals was of a destructive incorporation of one by the other" (Steinberg & Weiss, 1954, p. 410). He deliberately represented these disturbing cognitions in such famous works as *The Scream*, where he portrayed his own severe fear of annihilation, and in *The Kiss*, which portrays his preoccupation with being incorporated by, or merging with, a partner. Biographers have reported the many dreadful experiences in Munch's early life that apparently gave rise to his sense of helplessness to resists negative impacts beyond his control.

Let us also consider an illustration of *identity confusion*. The phenomenon can be illustrated visually with the type of perceptual phenomenon known as reversible figures. One example is the familiar "old hag vs. young woman," which can be seen either as a young woman wearing a hat or as an old woman with a big nose and a protruding chin. Each perception is clear, and we can shift—all-or-none—between the two. However, we cannot perceive the two images simultaneously. Similarly, identity confusion implies an all-or-none property—one or the other, but not both simultaneously. The composer Robert Schumann recognized and wrote about his two contrasting "selves," assigning separate names to each (Ostwald, 1985). Florestan (F) named a powerful, fiery, upbeat, aggressive character; and Eusebius (E), a soft, gentle, sensitive, depressive character. Schuman's composition *Die Davidsbündler-Tänze* contains 18 pieces, with a dedication ". . . from Robert Schumann (Florestan and Eusebius)." The pieces alternate in mood. Some were allegedly written by Florestan and display an F at the end; the others, by Eusebius, display an E at the end. Thus, a piece with "ungeduldig" (impatient) in the instructions is loud, bold, and impatient; it credits F at the end. Another, with the instructions "not fast and with extremely strong feeling", credits E at the end. Schumann himself has discussed these contrasting selves, and biographers have described the origins of his identity confusion (e.g., Ostwald, 1985). Thus, identity diffusion and identity confusion have been portrayed clearly in the arts. It is up to psychologists, however, to clarify the origins of each and their role in psychopathology and necessary therapeutic interventions.

Schema as a Psychological Concept

The concept of a schema lends itself well to psychotherapy research and may help us think about people's conceptions of self and other people. When a schema characterizes a person (self or someone else), we call it a person schema, or, in this paper, a "pschema" (with a silent p), which is particularly apt for psychotherapy research.

Definition of a Schema

The term *schema* has never been clearly defined. We define it as a collection of mental representations that are inter-associated and function together as a unit. This definition contains three important properties. First, the elements (mental representations) are neural traces that reside in the nervous system due to prior

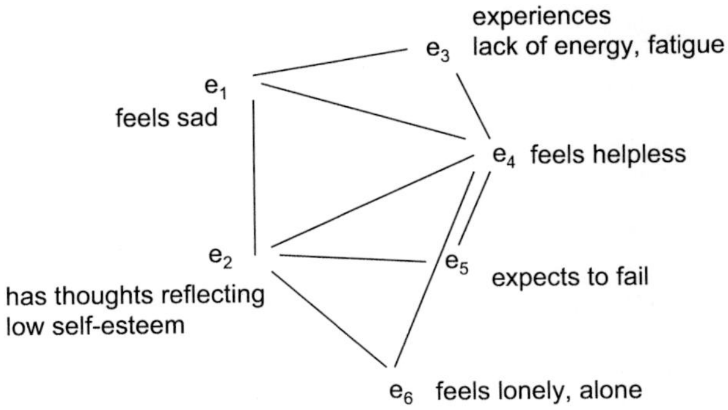

FIGURE 4.1 A Hypothetical Example of Some Elements of One Person's Schema for his or her Depression

behaviors and internal states (thoughts, feelings, bodily sensations, expectancies, etc.). The pschema of one's mother is a complex set of representations that have accrued over many years: witnessed and imagined behaviors and thoughts of the mother; observed and inferred feelings; perceived traits. Similarly, the schema of one's experience of depression contains representations of bodily sensations, associated sadness and other feelings; thoughts that typically arise when depressed; and so on. Figure 4.1 shows a simplified representation of elements—feeling sad, lacking energy, feeling low self-esteem, expecting to fail, feeling helpless, and many, many others.

Second, the ingredients (elements) of a schema are inter-associated. Elements that have frequently been experienced together generally have a stronger associative link than those that have co-occurred less often. If "sad feeling" often co-occurs with "drop in self-esteem," an occurrence of sadness, however generated, would tend to activate "low self-esteem." Figure 4.1 depicts these connections (inter-associations) between pairs of mental representations.

Third, the elements function as a unit because the connection among elements is relatively stable over time. Whenever some elements are activated, they call forth the entire network (schema). If a small number of elements is activated, the entire network is activated: A substantial part of the schema, when activated, re-arouses the whole schema. In this way, a relatively simple event (e.g., a sad memory) can activate a drop in self-esteem, a drop in energy, and so on, thereby producing a full experience of depression.

Not all ingredient elements would be equally effective in activating depression. Different people have different learning histories, so the elements are differently associated for different individuals. For some people, a failure in performance might activate enough elements to induce depression. For other people, a personal rejection or an experience of isolation might induce depression. Recent research (Beck, 1983; Blatt, 1974; Blatt & Schichman, 1983; Hammen,

Marks, Mayol, & deMayo, 1985; Robins, Block, Peselow, & Klein, 1986; Zuroff & Monagrain, 1987) supports this view. Let us now examine three implications of the schema concept, with implications for psychotherapy research. Then we return to identity diffusion and confusion.

Three Implications of a Person's Schema for Depression

Incidental Activation of Irrelevant Elements

When one or two elements of a depression schema are activated, they activate other elements as well, even though those other elements may have nothing to do with the original stimulus event. Lopata (1969) examined the reactions of widows shortly after their husbands died. Naturally, the women felt alone, isolated, and sad about their loss; those reactions followed from the loss itself. But Lopata noticed that a subset of the women also reported a drop in self-esteem, though a drop in self-esteem would not seem to follow necessarily from the death of her spouse. Other elements (e.g., chronic fatigue) might also get activated that do not in themselves follow directly from the husband's death. Miranda and Persons (1988) reported a similar phenomenon more elegantly. They identified women who were vulnerable to depression, but were not currently depressed. The women completed the Dysfunctional Attitudes Scale (Weissman, 1979), a measure of negative thinking. Despite their vulnerability, the women (not depressed at that time) did not differ from non-depressed women in negative thinking at that time. Then Miranda and Persons (1988) induced a sad mood in each group. They used the Velten (1968) Mood Induction procedure to make each person feel sad. Theoretically, this procedure activated the negative schema in the vulnerable women, but the non-vulnerable women did not have an established schema for depression to be activated. Following the sad mood induction, the vulnerable women then endorsed negative thoughts on the Dysfunctional Attitudes Scale, whereas the non-vulnerable group did not. Thus, the mood induction induced negative thoughts only in women who had a depression schema. If psychotherapy is successful in treating depression, the person, after treatment, should no longer be as vulnerable to a reactivation of depression through a simple mood-induction. Such implications need to be tested.

There Are Psychological Advantages and Disadvantages to Schemas

People who have a particular schema perceive elements of that schema more quickly than other people, and they are better able to recall those elements after they have genuinely occurred. Many studies have demonstrated quicker perception of and superior memory for content that is part of a well-developed schema (e.g., Bruner, 1957; Dunbar & Lishman, 1984). Therefore, depression-prone people should more rapidly detect bodily sensations, feelings, and thoughts that are part of a depression schema and better recall those details at a later time than non-depressed people.

On the other hand, research has shown that depression-prone people are also more likely to misperceive and misremember because of the schema. As one example, Zuroff, Colussy, and Wielgus (1983) compared depressed and non-depressed women recalling a list of depressive and neutral words. A week after the presentation of the word lists, the women were asked to recall words that they had previously seen. The depressed women recalled more negative words, but they also "recalled" more negative words that they had not seen. In addition, on a recognition task, the original words were mixed with a set of depressive and neutral distractor words, and they were asked to indicate which words they had seen before and which were brand-new. The depressed women endorsed more negative words overall, so they were more often correct in their responses. However, many of their responses to depressive words were false alarms—and a statistical correction for this bias eliminated their superior recognition. The recognition bias is important for psychotherapy researchers. A successfully treated depressed person should no longer show the bias after he or she is successfully treated. If so, the result would provide a subtle outcome measure that was independent of self-reported improvement.

The Activation of a Schema Can Impede Performance on an Unrelated Task

Consider the Stroop color-naming word test (Stroop, 1935): Words are presented in different colors, and the person is asked to ignore each word's meaning and simply name its color as quickly as possible. When the word "car" appears in blue letters, for example, people on average respond "blue" in about half a second. The task becomes harder, however, when the stimulus word "red" appears in blue letters. When set to name colors, people have trouble ignoring the meaning of the word and simply naming its color. A well-developed schema for the physical color gets activated by the stimulus word, and it competes with the actual color of the word.

A variation of the procedure has been used to differentiate between depressed and non-depressed people. In one variation Gotlib and McCann (1984) presented words one by one in different colors. Some of the words were elements of a depression schema (e.g., "sad," "lonely," "hopeless") and other words were neutral in meaning but comparable in other ways (e.g., "son," "lively," "harmless"). The person was instructed to ignore the meaning of each word and name its color as quickly as possible. Words that activated the depressive schema (e.g., "sad") distracted depressed people, so it took them longer to name the color of the word. In a recent variation of our own, we found that currently depressed and non-depressed people named the color of neutral words equally fast (553 vs. 552 msec.), but depressed people took significantly longer to name the color of words with a depressive meaning (594 vs. 562 msec.). This result also raises a question for psychotherapy researchers: Does the effect disappear after depression is successfully treated? If so, can this test also provide a subtle objective outcome measure that is independent of self-reported improvement?

Schema for Describing Persons

Attachment Styles and Pschemas

We now turn to the problem of pschemas (*person*-schemas) in order to characterize (and distinguish between) a diffuse and a confused image. We assume that an individual's image of the self or of someone else is derived in part from his or her attachment history: Through generalization, severely frustrating early experiences with caretakers lead some people to distrust others and avoid intimate contact. Owing to their reduced contact, their descriptions of others should be shallow or vague. On the other hand, some people have had such mixed experiences (positive and negative) that they have acquired contradictory schemas of the very same person—sometimes hurtfully rejecting, other times supportively accepting. Their descriptions should reflect evidence of contrasting (or even contradictory) schemas.

I have collaborated with Constance Milbrath, Edward Bein, and Nicole Wordlaw in studying the attachment styles of women who were mourning the loss of a loved one. The women were interviewed shortly after the loved one had died. The interviews were tape-recorded, and trained raters classified each woman as to her attachment style—detached, enmeshed, or secure. We expected detached individuals to provide the vaguest, most superficial (diffuse) descriptions, and the enmeshed individuals to provide internally contradictory (confused) descriptions. The sample consisted of 30 women who had recently lost a mother, a father, or a husband. They ranged in age from 26 to 52. They were interviewed about their grief reactions and about their prior interpersonal relationships with the deceased. Every interview was transcribed verbatim, and computerized procedures were used to identify every statement that mentioned specific persons—self, mother, father, or husband.

On average, the women's descriptions of the deceased person during the interview contained 37.3 statements. The three attachment groups did not differ significantly in the length of their descriptions. However, they did differ in content: Judges evaluated and rated each statement in each woman's description to tell how well it helped a listener know the person in depth as a person. The statement "My mother couldn't trust anybody" was judged more helpful, whereas the statements "My mother and I were completely different" and "My mother grew up in South Dakota" were judged less helpful. Also, the descriptions by *detached* women contained a smaller proportion of "helpful" ideas. Less than a fourth of the ideas were judged to be helpful in getting to know the person better, whereas about half of the statements generated by *secure* and *enmeshed* women were judged that way. Thus, the women classified as detached had more diffuse descriptions, and we believe that their self-descriptions, if assessed, would have been similarly diffuse. In future research, we expected to confirm this hypothesis.

The text describing each deceased person was recorded and presented to nine listeners. Listeners were undergraduate or graduate students at Stanford University. After hearing a description, they immediately wrote down whatever they could remember. Here is an example showing the recall of a detached patient describing her late husband. It contains the students' most commonly recalled statements.

> When I first met my husband, he was married. He and I were super dancers and avid jazz fans. [After we married] we did everything together, which was wrong. We tried to have kids right away. He's a kind of troubleshooter type of person. He was very family-oriented, much more so even than me. He once had his own business but had to declare bankruptcy. In the 1960s he worked for a government agency.

Contrast those statements with ones from a secure patient's description of her late husband:

> Tom and I were old to get married for the first time when we got married. All his friends had been married and divorced, and he was skeptical about getting married. He felt that, if he was going to get married, he was going to be sure. One thing that isn't as much fun for me about winning prizes at work nowadays is that Tom was almost like a proud parent. He had very close friends, people he had known for years. He was the kind of person that always went to see friends. He never wrote, but he telephoned all the time.

A therapist, hearing a description by a dismissing patient, might find it hard to imagine the patient's significant others. That limitation, of course, could hinder the therapeutic process.

Now consider descriptions by enmeshed individuals, where confused (internally contrasting or contradictory) schemas of self and others are thought to be found. The following descriptions were recorded verbatim from a woman's statements about her mother.

> Mother was stoic. She rarely cried. She was the guiding force in the family. She was strong. She was always a good mother and homemaker, the one who made me practice my piano. Education, education, education; that was the kind of thing she valued. I don't see anything negative about her at all. She was the one you could always turn to. She was always there

> when you needed her. She would have done anything for me. Mother was smart. She was savvy. She was very perceptive about people. She was the hub; everybody would come around her. She drew people. She'd sit down, and they'd all come around her.

From these statements one gets an image of an unambiguously strong, competent, and caring mother. On the other hand, later in the interview, the very same patient also made the following remarks about her mother.

> We had a total role-reversal, where I was the parent. My mother and father wouldn't do a thing without me. Mother was alone. It was like isolation. If I didn't take her out to do something with her, she'd be by herself; she was miserable and unhappy. After my brother's death, they never went anywhere without me. They would really cry and carry on. I once asked her if she loved me, because she wasn't affectionate. She said, "There was no room. I was too drained to show more affection. I just couldn't show more." When I was in labor, I said to her, "Come with me;" she said, "I have to go to the bank." She really couldn't face it; she was so terrified. She must have been reliving her own horrors in having a child. I felt sorry for her.

These statements convey a very different schema, an image of an unhappy, needy, and helpless mother. Some patients find a way to integrate contrasting views of a person that contains both positive and negative aspects. But the descriptions of this mother are not integrated. One is entirely positive, the other, entirely negative, like the perceptions in a reversible figure. Apparently, one is activated on some occasions; the other, on other occasions. About half of the enmeshed patients in our sample showed contradictory images in their description of the deceased person. Such descriptions never occurred in the descriptions by secure or detached patients.

Interpersonal Problems

Contrasting schemas also manifest themselves in other ways, and this section shows how contrasting views of the self sometimes manifest themselves through contrasting sets of interpersonal problems identified using the Inventory of Interpersonal Problems (IIP; Horowitz, Rosenberg, Baer, Ureño, & Villaseñor, 1988). The IIP contains statements describing common interpersonal difficulties. Some begin "It is hard for me to . . ." (say "no" to other people, join groups, disclose personal things), and other statements have the form "These are things I do too much" (I fight with other people too much; I disclose personal things too much).

Problem behaviors vary along two principal dimensions. As shown in Figure 4.2, the X-axis represents a dimension of communion (or affiliation), ranging

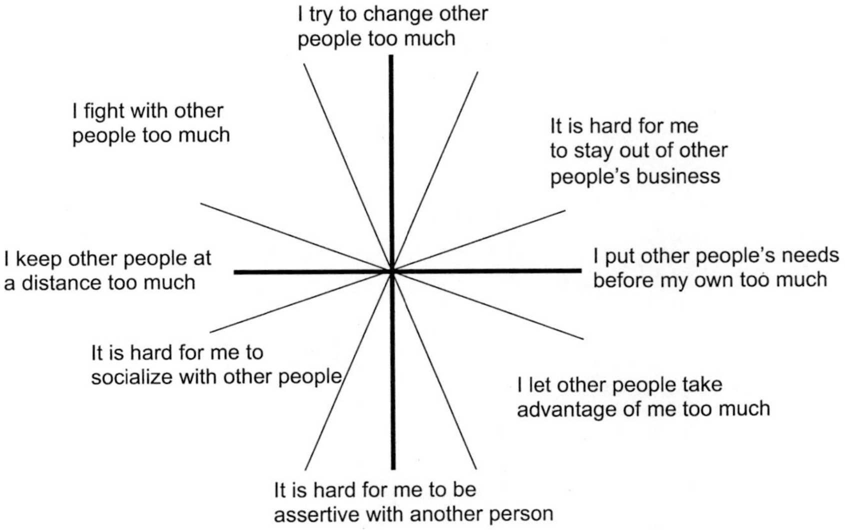

FIGURE 4.2 Typical Problems of the IIP Placed along the Two Principal Dimensions

from being *too cold or disconnected* to being *too warm or connected.* An item at the cold end is "I keep other people at a distance too much"; one at the warm end is "I put other people's needs before my own too much." The Y-axis represents a dimension of agency (control, influence) that ranges from being *too domineering* to being *too submissive.* An item at the dominating end is "I try to change other people too much;" one at the submissive end is "It is hard for me to be assertive with another person." The various problems may be plotted in this two-dimensional space. For example, the problem "I fight with other people too much" implies being *too cold* and *too domineering.* "I let other people take advantage of me too much" implies being *too friendly* and *too submissive.*

The graph in Figure 4.2 is divided into eight octants. Each octant contains related problems that characterize behavioral difficulties associated with that region of the graph. Eight subscales have been formed, corresponding to each of the eight octants (Alden, Wiggins, & Pincus, 1990). Each subscale then describes a specific type of interpersonal problem. Problems in one region, for example, concern difficulties being too domineering; those in another region describe problems being too exploitable; and so on. When a patient completes the inventory, we can determine the amount of distress reported from problems in each region and then draw a profile showing which octants describe the most distressing problems for that patient.

Figure 4.3 shows the location of interpersonal problems for a 28-year-old woman who had difficulty being assertive; she was much too accommodating to other people and had always been "the good girl." The problems that she

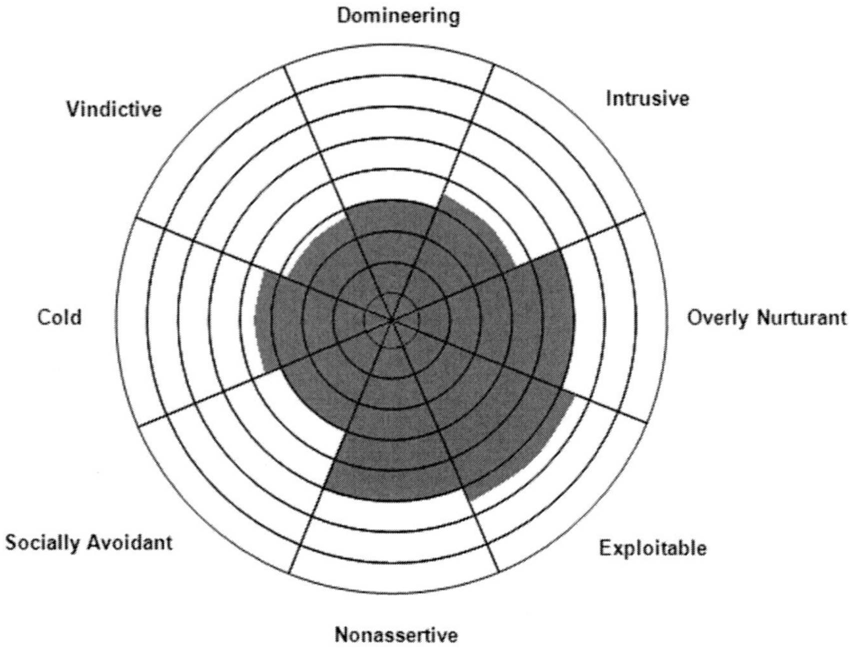

FIGURE 4.3 The Distribution of Self-Reported Problems for a Woman who Had Difficulty Asserting Herself

reported were primarily from the lower right-hand region: too nonassertive, too exploitable, too nurturant—schematically coherent content. Figure 4.4 shows the major interpersonal problems of another patient, a 38-year-old woman who was unable to establish a long-term relationship with a man. She described herself as dominating and aggressive in relationships. Specifically, as shown by the figure, she described herself as too bossy, too dominating, and too hostile—again, schematically coherent content.

These two profiles are unimodal; they each show one continuous region of the graph containing the person's most distressing problems. Sometimes, however, a patient's profile is not unimodal. Figure 4.5 describes the problems of a patient with two contrasting modes. The patient reports being *too cold and dominant* (too competitive, too vengeful), on the one hand, and also being *too cold and submissive* (too asocial, too readily intimidated by others). She was a depressed, 23-year-old woman who complained that she found herself provoking her boyfriend to hit her. She would provoke others to react aggressively, and then she would view herself as the downtrodden victim of abuse and sadistic attacks. The profile shows a contrast between her two distinct octants—the aggressor at times and the victim at other times. Bimodalities, such as this one, may help expose a single person's contrasting (confused) identities described earlier.

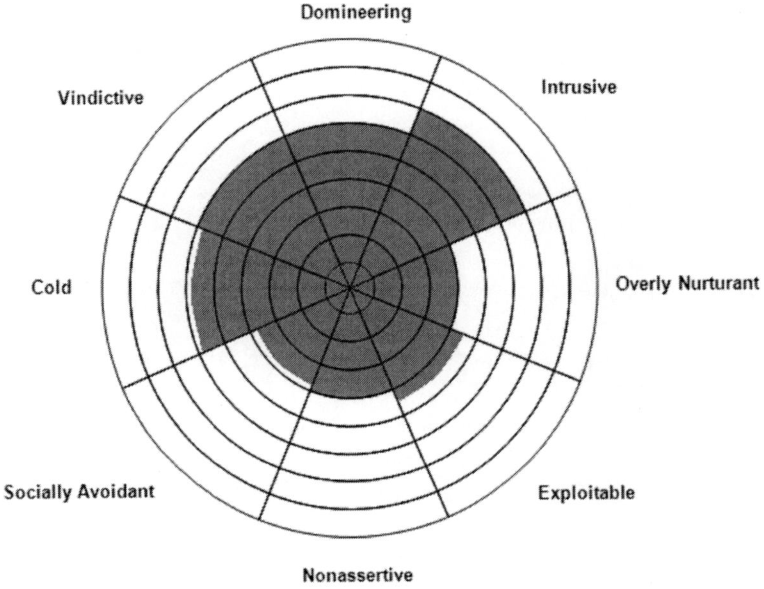

FIGURE 4.4 The Distribution of Self-Reported Problems for a Woman who Could Not Establish a Long-Term Relationship

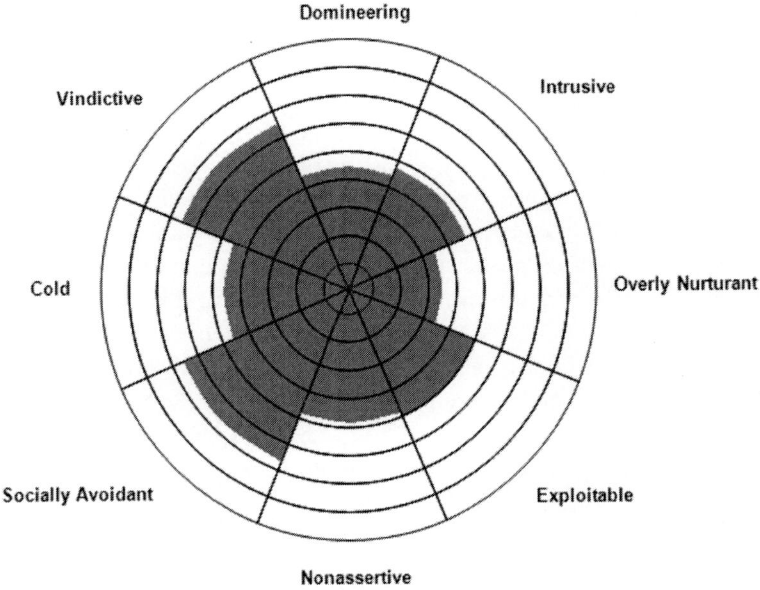

FIGURE 4.5 The Distribution of Self-Reported Interpersonal Problems for a Woman with Contrasting Sets of Modal Problems

The Privilege of Psychotherapy Researchers

This paper has had several concurrent agendas. First, I have tried to advance the concept of a schema as a theoretical construct that is relevant to our goals as psychotherapy researchers. Second, I have argued that we need to cast our sights beyond the usual and familiar paradigms of psychotherapy research. We need to keep challenging ourselves with the contributions of colleagues in the arts and in other areas of academic psychology because their contributions are very relevant to our own work.

Third, I have tried to convey a meta-communication: We who do psychotherapy research are in a truly privileged position. In no field do researchers have access to a more sincerely motivated participant population. Our patients, in all earnestness, open their hearts and, in a spirit of trust and optimism, reveal what is most private and personal. When we then divide ourselves into narrow theoretical fiefdoms at odds with one another and rigidly align ourselves with this or that extremist theory or brand name, I believe we do an injustice to our patients. I think we are better off integrating our understandings and building upon the best that previous efforts have yielded. One reason I find the schema concept appealing is that it integrates the teachings from the cognitive-behavioral perspective with teachings from the psychodynamic perspective. And that kind of integration, in my opinion, is the best way to repay our patients for their generosity, goodwill, and trust.

COMMENTARY

A COMMENTARY 20 YEARS LATER

Why, exactly, do people seek psychotherapy? Whatever theory we adopt, our answer to this question should help us discover new and useful interventions for improving a treatment's effectiveness. My presidential address 20 years ago emphasized a class of problematic cognitions that I had hoped might clarify particular types of interpersonal problems. The type of cognition that I examined in that talk was the *schema* for operationalizing self and significant others. However, today I consider the schema to be too imprecise a construct to add much to our understanding of the work of treatment. Instead, I would now replace that type of cognition with a more precise cognition, namely, that of a *prototype*. A prototype is a knowledge structure, and I shall propose that some types of knowledge structures can help a person think more clearly about satisfying interpersonal needs and resolving problems.

Despite my continued emphasis on cognitions, my approach should not be confused with a cognitive-behavioral theory of treatment. An interpersonal approach emphasizes more than cognitions and behavior; it heavily emphasizes frustrated interpersonal motives and distressing affect. Moreover, knowledge structures may specifically help satisfy interpersonal motives and reduce distressing affect. For this reason, I begin my commentary by stating four propositions that I consider basic to any rational account of therapy.

Four Propositions that Relate Interpersonal Cognitions to Interpersonal Motives and Affect

Interpersonal Interactions

Generally speaking, all human beings, as social organisms, exhibit a need to interact with one another in order to satisfy basic requirements for sustaining a comfortable life. These interpersonal behaviors may be organized graphically in a two-dimensional space. One dimension, *communion*, describes the degree to which a behavior bonds two people, leading them to feel close; the negative pole of communion concerns a complete separation between them. The other dimension, *agency*, describes the degree to which a behavior reflects one person's attempt to influence or control the partner; the negative pole of agency represents a person's yielding fully to the partner's influence or control.

Interpersonal Cognitions

From everyday interactions, people acquire cognitions about the self, other people, and relationships. The term *cognition* covers beliefs, knowledge, expectancies, hypotheses, etc. Cognitions organize, summarize, and explain behavior. They also affect incoming observations: Thus, a person's beliefs about a partner affect that person's interpretation of the partner's behavior.

Interpersonal Motives

The human organism, from birth, possesses innate sources of *motivation*—including a communal motive to feel connected to or bonded with familiar others. Over time, as cognitions become more complex, the person comes to acquire additional interpersonal motives, for example, motives to feel a) superior to others, b) protected by a strong partner, or c) free of demands by others. Like behaviors, interpersonal motives may be located graphically along the dimensions of *communion* and *agency* (Horowitz et al., 2006).

Affect

When interpersonal motives involving self and other are satisfied, positive affect results (e.g., pride, love). When those motives are frustrated, they produce negative affect (e.g., anger, sadness). Subjective distress arising from interpersonal problems implies that corresponding interpersonal motives are being frustrated.

Concept of Schema and Its Limitations

My earlier talk tried to describe a dysfunctional schema as a way to characterize the self or significant others. Twenty years ago, the *person-schema* was a popular construct for psychotherapy researchers, a construct that seemed to hold promise for operationalizing and investigating problems requiring therapeutic work. We had hoped to be able to describe, as crisply as possible, a client's image of self and significant others in order to expose and explain the resulting interpersonal problems. Our results did expose one type of dysfunctional schema—a very vague schema of significant others. The client's vague descriptions suggested that cognitions about significant others were so spare, unelaborated, and/or poorly integrated that the client apparently did not possess vivid imagery and salient memories involving significant others. This result suggested a relatively meager connection, bond, or feeling of closeness with important others, frustrating a very basic human motive. In contrast, most clients described a significant other with richer, more accessible, and cohesive content, suggesting that they have known the experience of intimacy. But, even among those people, a subset existed for which the content contained glaring internal contradictions—and therefore seemed poorly integrated. One woman, for example, described her mother in glowing terms throughout the interview (e.g., "My mother was the force in the family, the one who was always there when you needed her"). But, elsewhere in her description, she noted in passing that her mother "was not affectionate" or available (e.g., "when I was in labor, she told me she had to go to the bank").

Thus, by using the concept of a *schema* to document a client's descriptions of a significant other, we could judge the depth and quality of that relationship—as well as the degree of interpersonal satisfaction obtained from the relationship. Generally speaking, however, empirical procedures for describing a *schema* had significant limitations. Operationalizing a schema does not take us far beyond what was already known from the earlier observations of wise therapists. Nor have novel interventions emerged for producing therapeutic change. Furthermore, in operationalizing a schema, the information obtained about a significant other was not systematic—a diverse set of words, phrases, and themes that varied considerably from one client's schema to the next—including impressions, false beliefs, perceptions, memories, inferences, and so on. There was no objective way to cross-validate the person's description of a significant other.

Today, I prefer the concept of a prototype, which is methodologically more sophisticated and easily replicated. Like the schema, it refers to a type of cognition. A prototype is an idealized knowledge structure aggregated from a very large group of contributors that tells, for example, "how-to-attain-some-interpersonal-goal." This aggregated knowledge then becomes a standard against which a client's own knowledge may be evaluated. Deficits in knowledge may then be identified, and the consequence for interpersonal functioning may be studied. In the remainder of this paper, I shall illustrate the approach with two examples of an interpersonal prototype. One describes knowledge about ways to attain a feeling of intimacy with a partner. The other describes cues that reflect whether a partner can be counted on to provide social support. Both rely on the "wisdom of the crowd" principle (see summary by Horowitz & Turan, 2008) to expose the knowledge empirically. Each client's own actual knowledge can then be assessed against the group-generated standard.

Two Illustrative Interpersonal Prototypes

Concept of a Prototype

Consider any familiar interpersonal motive. One example might be a desire to experience intimacy with a partner. Another might be a desire to form a friendship with a partner whom you could count on to be supportive when you want support. Special knowledge is needed to satisfy each of these motives. For attaining intimacy, people have to know some good strategies or situations for generating a feeling of intimacy. For selecting a supportive partner, people have to know how to identify a partner who "can be counted on to be there for me when I want support." These types of special knowledge are contained in the two prototypes that I shall call: (a) *good ways to produce a feeling of intimacy with a partner*; and (b) *cues that a partner can be counted on to provide social support.*

To construct a prototype, we need two separate groups of informants—*nominators*, who are asked to name important instances of the concept (e.g., ways to experience intimacy); and *raters*, who then rate each nominated instance to tell how good it is as an instance of the concept (its prototypicality). The instances are then ordered according to the mean of all raters' ratings. The final set, ordered from best to worst, constitutes the prototype of the concept. Thus, the prototype of "good ways to get intimate" would provide a list of elements (ways to experience intimacy with a partner). For more details, see Horowitz and Turan (2008).

Prototype 1: Ways to Get Intimate

To derive the "Ways to Get Intimate" Prototype, 72 nominators were asked to think of good ways (strategies, situations) that would help them feel close, connected, or intimate with another person. From the listing that they produced, we selected as potential elements ways or strategies that were cited by two or more contributors; 48 strategies met this criterion and constituted the elements of the prototype. Examples included "recall shared memories together," "share a secret together," and "mourn a tragedy together". Then the 48 elements were presented to an independent group of 73 raters, who were asked to rate each strategy on an eight-point scale from "1" (not a useful way) to "8" (an extremely useful way). The instructions stated: "Here is a list of behaviors that might help a person to feel close, connected, or intimate with another person (O). In your opinion, how good is each one for inducing a feeling of closeness, connectedness, or intimacy with O?" The mean ratings were averaged, and the items were listed in descending order of prototypicality.

The seven elements with the highest prototypicalities are shown in Table 4.1. For each element, the table also shows the range of ratings across all raters. The full prototype, like other prototypes generated in this way, has interesting properties (see Horowitz & Turan, 2008). First, the 48 elements contained in the prototype vary considerably in their prototypicalities from 7.0 to 3.2. Consider the seven elements in the upper part of Table 4.1. They are distinctly different; yet, abstractly, they seem conceptually coherent. That is, they have the following theme in common: In each of these seven elements, the mental content of one partner—a feeling, thought, attitude, value, memory, etc.—that is usually kept private gets disclosed in this situation so that the partner witnesses the disclosure firsthand. In addition to the seven elements shown in Table 4.1, many other elements in the full prototype conform to the same abstract principle.

In contrast, some elements near the bottom of the prototype (Table 4.1, lower section) do not conform to this abstract principle. For example, the lowest seven elements in the prototype are quite disparate. They do not concern private mental content at all; instead, they involve such activities as gossiping, joking, playing practical jokes, and complaining. In fact, it is difficult to find any comparable abstract rule or principle that makes these low-rated entries seem

TABLE 4.1 Fragment of "Ways to Get Intimate" Prototype

Way to Get Intimate	*M Rating*	*Range*
Listen as O tells you his/her private feelings and thoughts	**7.0**	4–8
Come across evidence that O trusts you	**6.9**	4–8
Recall shared memories with O	6.8	2–8
Tell private feelings and thoughts to O	6.8	1–8
Survive a disaster or trauma together	**6.4**	1–8
Empathize with O	**6.4**	3–8
Mourn a tragedy together	**6.1**	2–8
Complain to each other about some third person or situation	**4.4**	1–8
Gossip with O	**4.2**	1–7
Have a drink or use drugs together	**4.1**	1–8
Tell a good joke to O	**3.6**	1–8
Go to a party together	**3.6**	1–7
Get O to tell you a good joke	**3.4**	1–7
Play a joke on a victim together	**3.2**	1–7

coherent. Because a large majority of elements in the full prototype do conform to the abstract principle described, one feels confident that the "Ways to Get Intimate" Prototype, schematically shown in Table 4.1, is indeed a meaningful knowledge structure. A person who possesses this knowledge a) should better understand the concept of intimacy, and b) should be better able to use that knowledge to find good ways to satisfy an intimacy motive.

How might we measure *the degree to which* a person (e.g., a client) possesses the knowledge contained in the prototype? Before we answer the question, notice another property of the prototype depicted in Table 4.1. For every element, notice the range of ratings made by different raters: Raters differed considerably from each other on every element in Table 4.1. Even in the top group of elements, some raters assigned quite low ratings (1, 2, or 3). For example, *some* raters considered the element "Tell private feelings and thoughts to the partner" to be a poor way to feel close or connected to a partner (1, 2, or 3)—even though most raters gave quite high ratings to that element.

Therefore, we might consider the *prototypicality* of each element to reflect a kind of wisdom—the wisdom of the group—and then determine, for any one client (say), how that person's own ratings of the elements would correlate with the corresponding (group-generated) prototypicalities. In other words, a client would be asked to rate each of the 48 elements, and we would then correlate that one person's responses with the corresponding prototypicalities. If this correlation coefficient is .86 (say), reflecting a good match to the prototype, we would infer that he or she is knowledgeable about ways to attain intimacy. But if the correlation coefficient were .11 or –.06, we would infer that the person lacked familiarity with ways to get intimate.

To summarize, the "Ways to Get Intimate" Prototype provides 48 ways to experience intimacy, ordered according to their quality. Using the wisdom of a large and representative group of raters, the prototypicalities estimate the quality of each element in the prototype for producing an experience of intimacy. By correlating a client's own ratings of each element with the corresponding prototypicalities, we can assess a client's degree of knowledge. In this way, we might ultimately detect cognitive deficits in "know-how" and determine whether such deficits a) impair interpersonal functioning, b) frustrate interpersonal motives, and c) relate to interpersonal problems and distress.

Prototype 2: Cues of a Supportive Partner

As a second example, we now consider elements of another knowledge structure in the form of a prototype. This prototype contains good cues or indicators that an acquaintance can be counted on "to be there for me" at times of stress. As discussed by Turan and Horowitz (2007) and by Horowitz and Turan (2008), a prototype seems to contain the best available predictors of behaviors that meet a particular criterion. In this case, the best cues help satisfy a person's motive to obtain social support from suitable others at times of stress. Empirical data will also be reported to show that people who do possess the knowledge contained in the prototype are better able than other people to analyze and correctly understand a relationship problem that is described.

The phrase "to be there for [someone]" means "to be available to provide help and support for someone" (Cambridge Dictionaries Online, 2007). According to attachment theory and theories of social support, an innate human motive is evident early in life; and throughout the lifespan we continue to turn to others for comfort and support at times of stress (Ainsworth, Blehar, Waters, & Wall, 1978; Bowlby, 1979; Sarason, Shearin, Pierce, & Sarason, 1987).

The question therefore arises: How do people come to believe that a friend or partner "will be there for me" at times of stress? What cues enable a person to make that judgment? Prototype methodology enables us to identify many cues that people use and then order those cues for their value as predictors. The prototype should also help identify clients who systematically use poor cues in making such judgments and later feel disappointed that their friend or partner was not "there for me when I needed support." Therapy patients who lack this knowledge would seem to have a social handicap, and the elements of the prototype may help a person re-examine his or her decision-making in selecting a friend or partner.

To identify these cues, Turan and Horowitz (2007) constructed a prototype (some of the cues are shown in Table 4.2). About 200 nominators were asked to think of cues that would help them decide whether they "could count on someone to be there for me emotionally at difficult times when the chips are down." They generated 55 indicators that had been mentioned by at least 2 nominators. A group of raters then rated, on a scale from 1 to 8, how good each one seemed to be. The ratings of each cue were averaged to yield that particular cue's prototypicality, and the cues were ordered from highest to lowest.

Like the "Ways to Get Intimate" Prototype, the "Cues of a Supportive Partner" Prototype reveals a coherent theme among the top-rated cues. As shown in Table 4.2, cues with the highest prototypicalities have the following theme in common: In the past the partner in question (friend, acquaintance), without any prompting, has a) detected an uncomfortable internal state in the person, b) relayed the observation by word or deed, and c), implicitly or explicitly, offered to help resolve the problem. Cues low in prototypicality are generally unrelated to this theme and conceptually more diverse. The low-rated cues describe a supportive partner as self-disclosing; not irritating; organized and goal-oriented; and unlikely to ignore others.

If a person's own ratings of the various cues resemble the corresponding raters' means (prototypicalities), the person would seem to possess good knowledge of the most predictive cues for deciding whether a person can be counted on to be there. Such people should be able to discriminate easily between good and poor cues in everyday life. To create an easy-to-score test (the "KNOWI

TABLE 4.2 Sample Elements from "Cues of a Supportive Partner" Prototype

Cue that Partner Will Be There for Me at Times of Stress	*Mean Rating*
Sacrifices his/her own plans to provide support	6.85
Stops by or calls when I am sick	6.56
Sticks up for me if someone gives me a hard time	6.55
Notices changes in my mood and asks if anything is wrong	6.31
Offers to help me with something without my asking	6.26
Asks me if I'm OK when getting the feeling that I'm not	6.11
Knows something is wrong even though I haven't said anything	6.08
Knows how I feel about something even if I haven't explained it explicitly	6.07
.	.
Makes an effort to stay in touch with his/her own family	5.66
Does not pass judgment on my concerns	5.56
.	.
Freely discloses information about self	5.27
.	.
.	.
Is friendly to everyone	4.32
Has interests in common with me	4.32
Has a nice personality	4.29
Does not ignore others on the street	4.25
Does not do things that are irritating to me	3.91
Does not get on my nerves	3.87
Is organized and goal-oriented	3.64

Scale," for "Knowledge of Indicators"), Turan and Horowitz (2007) selected a set of 11 highly prototypic (G, for "good") cues and, separately, a set of 11 much less prototypic (P, for "poor") cues. To these two sets they added a larger set of other cues ("filler items") that simply camouflaged the difference between the G and P cues. The resulting collection of cues were intermixed and presented to participants, who rated the quality of each as a predictor of a partner's "being there." Each participant's ratings of the G items were averaged, as were the ratings of the P items. The difference between the two means assessed that particular person's ability to discriminate good from poor cues. Let us call that difference-score the "G–P Difference." If it is small (or negative), the person would seem to lack the knowledge contained in the original prototype. A person with a high score, on the other hand, should be better able to make informed judgments about the supportiveness of potential partners. The following study tested this hypothesis, thereby validating the KNOWI Scale.

Fifty-six participants each interacted with a confederate. In order for the experimental conditions to be standardized across all participants, the participants and confederates were all women. During the interaction, the confederate (who seemed to be another participant) was asked to describe a personal problem to her partner, the participant. Each participant was asked to listen and react naturally to the confederate's problem. The problem the confederate described concerned a recent difficulty with her roommate, who had become distant and moody lately for reasons that the confederate did not understand. The confederate went on to describe some recent negative events in her roommate's life. She also mentioned that her roommate was in a new relationship with a boyfriend who was described in generally positive terms (e.g., he is fun to be with). She also mentioned, casually and without value-judgment, three brief vignettes in which the boyfriend behaved in ways that happened to violate highly prototypic cues. A person sensitive to the support issue could interpret the boyfriend's behavior to mean that he could not be counted on for support, thereby distressing the roommate.

When the interaction ended, a separate interviewer (blind to the participant's score on the KNOWI Scale) interviewed each participant individually about her interaction. The semi-structured interview was designed to show whether the participant was sensitive to incidentally mentioned details concerning another person's supportiveness. Successive questions led to details about the problem, the roommate's relationship with her boyfriend, and the boyfriend's characteristics. Eventually it made sense for the interviewer to ask the participant what she thought of the roommate's relationship with her boyfriend and what kind of a person he seemed to be. She was also asked what she would do if she were in the roommate's shoes.

The interview was tape-recorded, and coders (blind to the participant's score on the KNOWI Scale) later rated the participant's apparent sensitivity to the supportiveness issue. For example, they noted, from the interview, whether the participant mentioned the three vignettes and remembered them correctly. The coders also rated the participant's overall understanding of the roommate's situation. Three coders each performed the ratings for each participant. Their judgments showed excellent interrater reliability. Finally, these "sensitivity ratings" were averaged. The final ratings ranged from 1.0 to 7.0. They were then correlated with the participants' "G–P Difference Score" on the KNOWI Scale. The value of r between the two measures was highly significant; $r = .45, p < .001$. Interestingly, participants with the highest sensitivity ratings recalled all three vignettes and cited them as possible evidence that the boyfriend could not be counted on. They had had no advance warning that they would be asked about the boyfriend or his "being there when needed," yet they were able to provide many relevant details. For them, the knowledge structure was accessible, like a process operating in the background that enables a person to notice particular kinds of detail and later answer questions about them.

Conclusion

In my view, people often seek psychotherapy for the following reason: Interpersonal cognitions affect the person's interactions with other people, and those interactions either satisfy or frustrate basic interpersonal motives. If interpersonal motives are chronically frustrated, the person experiences subjective distress. To help reduce a client's distress, we psychotherapists try to alter self-handicapping cognitions by identifying them and then challenging unfounded beliefs and tactfully exposing faulty "knowledge or know-how." Part of our task is to persuade a client that good ways do exist for attaining one's interpersonal goals. The advantage of the prototype construct is its simplicity, objectivity, and credibility: The prototype provides a way of summarizing and presenting wisdom contained in the judgments of a large, representative normative sample. It orders elements for their judged quality so that a client can see at a glance ways judged best-to-worst in attaining particular goals. If a particular knowledge structure is relevant to a client's own situation, it can impress the client as stimulating and plausible—testimony that simple time-honored ways do exist for solving personal problems and achieving satisfaction. In time, I think we can incorporate prototypes into a treatment and use them to deepen patient-therapist conversation and increase a client's interest in and commitment to self-exploration, interpersonal change, and rational decision-making.

5

FINDING OUT HOW PSYCHOTHERAPIES HELP PEOPLE CHANGE (1995)

David A. Shapiro

Our purposes as psychotherapy researchers are twofold. First, we seek to establish an empirical basis for the provision of psychological treatments, to find out what is helpful, for whom, under what circumstances. Second we seek to describe and understand the mechanisms of change, to find out how psychotherapies in general, and specific forms of psychotherapy in particular, achieve their effects. These two purposes are, of course, linked. Ultimately the first goal depends upon the realization of the second, which is the more intellectually challenging and exciting one.

Understanding treatment mechanisms requires us to chart the relationships between the transactions of therapy and the changes experienced by clients in their lives outside the consulting room. This has proved no easy task. Stiles, Shapiro, and Elliott (1986; Elliott, Stiles, & Shapiro, 1993) described the "equivalence paradox" of similar apparent effectiveness of treatments whose constituent therapist-patient transactions are demonstrably dissimilar. Until this paradox is resolved, our understanding of treatment mechanisms will remain severely limited.

This will be a personal and selective overview of work by the Sheffield group,[1] acknowledging the formative influences on this of the work of other groups of SPR members. The presentation will be organized in terms of the four approaches to resolving the equivalence paradox outlined by Stiles et al. (1986), with a view to highlighting the synergy between these approaches. It will end with some recommendations for the development of the field.

Resolution I: Limitations of Outcome Research

The randomized, controlled trial and psychotherapy research

Psychotherapy researchers have sometimes questioned the status of the randomized, controlled trial (RCT) as setting the "gold standard" for establishing treatment efficacy. Limitations identified by Howard, Orlinsky, and Lueger (1995), for example, are that: (1) random assignment does not ensure generalizability; (2) the sample size is never sufficient to ensure that random assignment will equate groups with regard to all the multitude of possible confounds; and (3), in research with patients, failure to complete treatment regimens and supply information (attrition) compromises random assignment.

Alternative or supplementary methodologies will be described below. At the outset, however, two points should be noted. First, psychotherapy researchers are in some respects ahead of other areas of medicine in the development of RCT methodology. Because psychological processes are the focus, rather than nuisance variables to be eliminated from a trial, they are relatively sophisticated in their approach to relevant aspects of RCT design (e.g., in considering the nature of control groups, they cannot dismiss as placebo effects all psychological mediators of change, as do pharmacotherapy researchers).

Second, the ideological origins of the RCT should not be forgotten. Its recent status as orthodoxy makes it appear to some a reactionary, Procrustean inhibitor of innovation that would outlaw investment by practitioners, treatment developers, or researchers in methods not supported by RCT data. However, from a public health or patient advocacy standpoint, the RCT ensures the accountability of clinicians—including clinician/researchers.

Design a Stronger RCT

Resolution I attributes apparently equivalent outcomes to limitations of outcome research itself. The methodology of outcome research has gained in precision over recent years. The Second Sheffield Psychotherapy Project (SPP2; Shapiro, Barkham, Rees, Hardy, Reynolds, & Startup, 1994a, 1995) was designed to overcome limitations of many prior studies.

The substantive questions of the outcome phase of this study were concerned with (i) the comparative efficacy of cognitive-behavioral (CB) and psychodynamic-interpersonal (PI) psychotherapies of depression, (ii) the incremental benefit of 16 weekly sessions as contrasted with just 8 sessions; and (iii) differential effects of treatment method or duration in relation to the severity of depression at intake.

The PI therapy is based on Hobson's (1985; Goldberg et al., 1984) Conversational Model. Using psychodynamic, interpersonal, and experiential concepts, it focuses on the therapist-client relationship as a vehicle for revealing and resolving interpersonal difficulties viewed as primary in the origins of depression. The method emphasizes negotiation (therapist's views expressed as tentative statements, open to correction, inviting elaboration and feedback), a language of mutuality, the use of statements rather than questions, and the offering of hypotheses about the client's experiences and their interconnections.

The CB therapy is a multimodal method somewhat more behavioral in emphasis than is Beck, Rush, Shaw, and Emery's (1979) Cognitive Therapy. It emphasizes the provision by the therapist of cognitive and behavioral strategies for application by the client. A wide range of techniques is available to the therapist, including anxiety-control training, self-management procedures, cognitive restructuring, and a job-strain package.

Clients were stratified into three levels of severity of depression on the Beck Depression Inventory (BDI; Beck, Ward, Mendelson, Mock, & Erbaugh, 1961)—low severity, 16–20; moderate severity, 21–26; high severity, 27+—prior to randomization to one of the four cells of the treatment X duration design. The 16-week interval between Assessments 1 and 2 was due to time required for assignment and scheduling at the outset of treatment. The outcome methodology is fully described in Shapiro et al. (1994a); Shapiro, Barkham, Rees, Hardy, Reynolds, and Startup (1995) outline the rationale of key decisions made in designing this study. The present account highlights features designed to enhance the study's sensitivity to treatment differences.

Client Selection

Uncontrolled heterogeneity in clients and their problems prevent treatment differences from being detected. Clients were required to meet criteria for a DSM-III Major Depressive Episode within the three months prior to intake, to present current symptomatology attaining an Index of Definition of 5 or more on the Present State Examination (PSE; Wing, Cooper, & Sartorius, 1974), and to return a BDI score of 16 or above. Stratification into three levels of BDI severity prior to randomization served to reduce severity-related variance in error terms. Clients were excluded if the PSE was scored for psychotic, manic, or obsessional symptoms, or if depression was attributable to organic illness. Clients were also excluded if there was evidence of a continuous history of depression extending beyond two years, or if they had received substantial psychological treatment (defined as three or more sessions) over the previous five years.

Recruitment, Attrition, and Bias

Attrition was limited quite successfully, in that 138 clients entered treatment, and 117 of these completed treatment and sufficient outcome measures for inclusion in the study. Similar numbers were lost from each of the four treatment conditions. An initial pool of 540 potential clients yielded 169 meeting all objective inclusion and exclusion criteria. Comparisons revealed that those completing treatment were somewhat older, were less likely to be single, and had received more education, than those excluded or failing to complete therapy.

Several differences occurred between treatment conditions prior to randomization. In particular, within the High Severity group, clients subsequently assigned to 16 sessions of treatment were more depressed than those subsequently assigned to 8 sessions. Statistical control and disaggregation of data were therefore required to minimize bias.

Statistical Power

Kazdin and Bass (1989) show that the majority of comparative outcome studies are vitiated by inadequate sample sizes. Samples upwards of 60 per group are required to detect an effect equal to the median effect size of .47 of a standard deviation obtained in comparisons between alternative treatments, if the conventional levels of significance (.05) and power (.80) are adopted.

The SPP2 design called for 60 clients to complete each of the two treatments (CB and PI), and for 60 clients to receive each of the two durations of treatment (8 and 16 sessions). As noted by Norcross and Rossi (1994), the study's power to detect interactions between treatment method and duration fell short of the ideal, although this did not materially compromise our conclusions, given the precaution against Type II error whereby no findings yielding a liberal *p* value of .15 were overlooked (Shapiro, Barkham, Rees, Hardy, Reynolds, & Startup, 1994b).

Therapists

It is preferable from an experimental design standpoint to have all therapists conduct all treatments within a study, to separate variance due to individual therapists from that due to the treatment technique. This design was chosen, with each of five qualified clinical psychologists working in all four treatment conditions.

Therapist Adherence to Treatment Manuals

If treatments lack integrity (i.e., they are not delivered in accordance with an explicit specification), then comparative outcome data cannot be expected to show differential effects. Our CB and PI treatments had been manualized for a previous study (Shapiro & Firth, 1987). All therapists treated at least two training cases in each of the four treatment conditions of the study, prior to treating project cases. Training cases were supported by audiotape-based supervision after every session, and each new therapist was admitted to the project team only when established therapists were satisfied of their competence in each condition. For all five therapists to attain this competence required a total of 64 training cases.

Adherence ratings (Shapiro & Startup, 1992; Startup & Shapiro, 1993a) were obtained on 220 sessions sampled at random, and 97 percent of these were correctly classified in a discriminant function analysis (Startup & Shapiro, 1993b). This demonstration of adherence would ideally be supplemented by independent, expert, ratings of competence (Waltz, Addis, Koerner, & Jacobson, 1993).

Outcome Measures

The apparently equivalent outcomes of contrasting treatments could reflect the use of measures insufficiently precise to measure specific effects. Two depression measures were included, the BDI and the Depression subscale of the SCL-90-R (Derogatis, 1983), together with a measure of the conceptually related dimension of self-esteem. Measures should also reflect the goals of treatment. We included the Social subscale of the self-report Social Adjustment Scale (Cooper, Osborn, Gath, &, Fegetter, 1982) and the Inventory of Interpersonal Problems (IIP; Horowitz, Rosenberg, Baer, Ureño, & Villaseñor, 1988), to tap putatively specific effects of the PI treatment.

Outcome Findings

If the equivalence paradox is indeed attributable to limitations in outcome research design, how successful were we in revealing treatment effects? Results on the BDI will be highlighted here. They indicated an advantage to 16-session treatment over eight-session treatment, and also to CB over PI. However, at one-year follow-up, eight-session PI treatment appeared less effective than the other three conditions. Analyses of covariance (Shapiro et al., 1994a, 1995) confirmed these findings, except that short-term superiority of 16- over eight-session treatment was confined to the High severity group This finding has important implications for the provision of psychotherapy services, suggesting that just eight sessions may be sufficient for the treatment of less severe depressions.

Findings at one year (Shapiro et al., 1995) were somewhat different from the immediate post-treatment results. Not only was eight-session PI treatment now less effective than the other three conditions, all of which appeared equivalent, but also the advantage of 16- session over eight-session treatment in the treatment of severe depression had disappeared.

To summarize the results on the other outcome measures, these were broadly similar to those on the BDI, except that there was no evidence whatever for differences in immediate effects of treatment between CB and PI on any other measure than the BDI (Shapiro et al., 1994a).

Our findings give restricted support to the first resolution of the equivalence paradox. Our efforts to increase the study's sensitivity to treatment effects yielded quite modest differences between CB and PI therapies of depression. These results suggest that treatment method alone is not a powerful determinant of outcome.

Resolution II: Highlight Common Factors

The second resolution of the equivalence paradox attributes the benefits of psychotherapies to factors other than those specified in manuals or highlighted by the theories on which these are based (Stiles, Shapiro, & Elliott, 1986). Arguably, such common factors vary independently of, and are more significant psychologically than, treatment methods and models. This resolution holds that different treatments yield equivalent outcomes because methods are outweighed by such factors as the quality of the relationship formed between client and therapist.

This is an intuitively appealing idea, with strong empirical support (Orlinsky, Grawe, & Parks, 1994). However, conceptual problems are legion, although the field is making good progress with dealing with these. For example, measures of alliance that include overt reference to the client's progress in dealing with problems are contaminated with "early outcome." And even if the measures makes no reference to early outcome, it is hard for any judge not to observe indicators of treatment benefits in evaluating the client-therapist relationship. We developed a relationship measure minimizing reference to the client's progress (Agnew, Harper, Shapiro, & Barkham, 1994). Parallel client and therapist forms comprise 28 items measuring four factors—Involvement; Confidence; Empowerment; and Openness. Client characteristics (Garfield, 1994), such as comorbid personality disorders, may also outweigh factors specific to treatments. In SPP2 we found that 39 of 114 treatment completers who had completed an abbreviated version of the Personality Disorders Examination (Loranger et al., 1991) at intake received one or more of three Cluster C personality disorders (Avoidant, Obsessive-Compulsive, or Dependent). Controlling for pretreatment severity of depression, personality disordered clients returned significantly higher BDI scores after treatment (Hardy, Barkham, Shapiro, Rees, Reynolds, & Stiles, 1994).

The comparative process-outcome design exemplified by SPP2 can show whether the impact of client characteristics or process variables is indeed common across treatments. If client and process variables are differentially related to outcome in the two treatments, that suggests differing modes of action. In SPP2, the effect of personality disorders proved largely confined to those receiving PI therapy.

Frank (1968, 1973) highlighted the importance of the client's belief or faith in the treatment and remoralization as common factors in treatment response. Again, however, it is important to establish just how common such factors really are across treatments. Within SPP2, every client's endorsement of both PI and CB treatment principles was assessed before they had been informed of the treatments available at the clinic. Subsequently, the credibility of the treatment to which each individual client had been assigned was also measured Hardy, Barkham, Shapiro, Reynolds, Rees, and Stiles (1995) found that CB principles were more strongly endorsed than were PI principles in advance of treatment assignment; after assignment, however, clients in all treatment groups returned similar credibility ratings of the treatment to which they had been assigned. Improvement in CB therapy was unaffected by clients' endorsement of either CB or PI principles. In contrast, improvement in PI therapy was predicted by endorsement of CB principles. PI improvement was also predicted by endorsement of PI principles, but only with respect to interpersonal problems. Symptom change was not predicted by endorsement of PI principles.

Thus, the benefits of PI treatment appear more dependent than are those of CB upon client characteristics, ranging from freedom from comorbid personality disorder to the "psychological mindedness" yielding endorsement of psychological treatment principles. This is consistent with PI therapists' concern with clients' treatment suitability.

The second resolution's emphasis on factors other than treatment method that help to determine outcome clearly warrants more research. Not only may such factors as therapeutic relationship quality outweigh the specific methods used, but also these factors may interact with treatment method, suggsting different change mechanisms in contrasting treatments.

Resolution III: Encompassing framework

Perhaps the equivalence paradox can be resolved by the development of integrative or overarching theory to account for the effects of each method within an overall story (Stiles, Shapiro, & Barkham, 1993). This is Resolution III, an intuitively appealing approach which has developed considerably in recent years. This has two objectives. Its theoretical objective is to explain equivalent outcomes in terms of different pathways to similar effects, building overarching theories of how people may be helped to achieve change, within which specific treatment methods can be subsumed; its practical objective is to develop new therapies based on such theorizing.

In common with other investigators, our pursuit of Resolution III has also invoked the fourth resolution of the equivalence paradox, which challenges the paradigm followed by research giving rise to the paradox, and proposes alternative or supplementary methodologies. Accordingly, this account of Resolution III will address conceptual and clinical issues, with empirical examples presented after reviewing Resolution IV.

Encompassing and Integrative Theory

In building encompassing frameworks, there is a strategic choice between simplification on the one hand, and recognition of complexity and diversity on the other. There is much in favor of simplification, the big idea that transcends seemingly uninterpretable contingencies and complication. We are often taught that science is about the formulation of general principles, "laws of nature," that explain many observations. On the other hand, the complexity of the phenomena and their interrelationships in the field of psychotherapy has—thus far at least—defied cogent simplification (Elliott & Anderson, 1994). The equivalence paradox argues against the simplifications attempted by mainstream research over several decades.

In seeking to understand how psychotherapies help people change, there would seem to be an inescapable dialectic between the "big idea" and the "minute particulars"; our efforts need to be guided by general principles, and yet these principles must prove their worth in relation to diverse specific observations.

Encompassing frameworks import explanatory constructs from elsewhere in psychology (Horowitz, 1994). For example, the assimilation model draws on work by Piaget (1970). It posits a sequence of characteristic stages (Warded Off, Unwanted Thoughts, Vague Awareness, Problem Statement/Clarification, Understanding/Insight, Application/Working Through, Problem Solution, and Mastery) through which a problematic experience is assimilated into a schema that is developed in the client-therapist interaction (Stiles, Elliott, Llewelyn, Firth-Cozens, Margison, Shapiro, & Hardy, 1990). The model posits that different psychotherapies are apt to enable clients to move through different portions of the assimilation continuum (Stiles, Barkham, Shapiro, & Firth-Cozens, 1992).

Further theoretical work with Mark Williams and William B. Stiles is currently exploring the contributions of cognitive scientists' recent work on memory to the development and evaluation of the assimilation model. For example, parasuicidal and PTSD patients report predominantly generic rather than specific autobiographical memories (see Williams, 1992, for a review). Such generic memories could serve as evidence that a problematic experience has been warded off, which is not otherwise observable. Another relevant area of memory research concerns prospective memory: the intrusive effects of unfulfilled intentions may help us understand the intrusive impact of unassimilated experiences characteristic of posttraumatic states, the importance of which may well extend beyond PTSD to such problems as depression and borderline personality disorder.

Another approach to understanding the process of warding off is to consider what the client might have to fear in relation to that experience For example, the client might fear rejection, humiliation, or loss of status in the relationship with the therapist (Gilbert, 1984). Such fears are disconfirmed by the therapist's continuing acceptance of, and continuing constructive work with, the client despite hearing about such an experience. The accompanying emotions may in time be extinguished through repeated exposure.

The proposition that such processes are common to many forms of psychotherapy is reminiscent of the seminal integrationist thinking of Murray and Jacobson (1971). CB therapists enlist the client's problem-solving competencies to overcome negative beliefs and assumptions, whereas experiential therapists' unconditional empathic acceptance also disconfirms the client's negative sense of self.

Within PI therapies (Henry, Strupp, Schacht, & Gaston, 1994), the control-mastery theory of the Mount Zion Psychotherapy Research Group hinges upon the importance of the therapist's disconfirmation of the client's pathogenic beliefs (Silberschatz, Curtis, & Nathan, 1989; Silberschatz, Fretter, & Curtis, 1986). Meanwhile, work at Vanderbilt (Henry, Schacht, & Strupp, 1990; Strupp, 1993) has highlighted the negative impacts of therapist responses and strategies experienced as punitive, hostile, or rejecting (i.e., confirmatory of pathogenic beliefs). Within the Sheffield program, Agnew, Harper, Shapiro, and Barkham (1994) have considered how to repair the damage done by critical or punitive therapist interventions. If the client has the courage to complain (and offer a "confrontation challenge"), this sets the stage for resolution, in which the therapist acknowledges the client's feelings and their own role in giving rise to these. The study of moments in which therapists get things wrong, failing to be "good enough" figures, may cut across therapies to highlight pitfalls and improve effectiveness.

This suggests the possibility of an encompassing framework describing how, across treatment models, the therapist embodies disconfirmation, and both contains and responds to the client's demands. The framework would then have to embrace the effects of sharing problematic experiences with the therapist in enabling the client to mobilize social support in other relationships; the balance between containment and structure on the one hand, and responsiveness on the other, may be central to the understanding and enhancement of psychotherapy's effectiveness. Such emerging encompassing frameworks often highlight factors that are common to several therapies, thus bridging Resolutions II and III.

Integrative Therapies

The second (practical) objective is to develop new therapies. The pressure to develop more effective methods to tackle pressing clinical problems will lead integrative theory to be, possibly prematurely, translated into "cookbook" manuals striving to combine effective elements from several approaches. Ryle's Cognitive-Analytic Therapy (CAT; Ryle, 1990) integrates psychoanalytic, personal construct and CB ideas. Theoretically, its Procedural Sequence Model describes mental and behavioral processes. In practice, the method begins with prose and diagrammatic reformulations in which the therapist describes to the patient their target problems and associated target problematic procedures. Subsequent sessions use specific techniques drawn from PI and CB approaches to revise the target problematic procedures. Close attention is paid to problematic procedures manifest within the session (transference).

Meanwhile, the Sheffield group developed an integration of PI and CB techniques based on the assimilation model (Shapiro, Barkham, Reynolds, Hardy, & Stiles, 1992). The underlying theoretical assumption was that the goal of therapy is to help clients assimilate their problems. Accordingly, PI interventions were offered in relation to unassimilated problems, and CB interventions in relation to more full assimilated problems. But do we need more therapies, or should we rather work to understand better the ones we already have? There is a danger of yesterday's integrative framework becoming tomorrow's umpteenth brand-name therapy.

This treatment of conceptual and clinical issues supports the third resolution of the equivalence paradox. Failure to demonstrate large differences in efficacy among existing treatment methods suggests we need better ways of understanding the psychotherapeutic process than are offered by traditional therapy models; these are at least prospectively on offer from current and emerging theories integrating insights from several such models or applicable across models. Our efforts to evaluate these ways of understanding psychotherapies will be reviewed after outlining the fourth resolution of the equivalence paradox.

Resolution IV: Challenge the Research Paradigm

Most of the Sheffield group's work on encompassing frameworks has also embraced the final resolution of the equivalence paradox. This attributes the paradox to deficiencies in the predominant research paradigm, and suggests that new research paradigms will yield less paradoxical results. Resolutions III and IV, taken together, form a paradigm shift. Resolution IV incorporates two components. First, it criticizes the "old" paradigm. Orthodox research methods are considered inappropriate to understanding how psychotherapies help people change. For example, Stiles and Shapiro (1989) critique much process-outcome research as following an oversimplified and overextended analogy with drugs. For example, Stiles (1988) demonstrated that process-outcome correlations are invalid indices of the efficacy of process elements, and Stiles and Shapiro (1994) found few correlations between theoretically relevant, reliably measured verbal process components and symptomatic change. Other problematic assumptions of the drug metaphor include the passive role of the client, the dispensing of "active ingredients" by the therapist without regard to client requirements, and an oversimplified distinction between process and outcome (Stiles & Shapiro, 1989). A meta-analytic review by Shapiro, Harper, Startup, Reynolds, Bird, and Suokas (1994) demonstrated the low yield of conventional process-outcome research seeking to identify therapist interventions yielding favorable outcomes.

The constructive element of Resolution IV is the proposal and realization of alternative research strategies. Among psychotherapy researchers themselves, the battle for methodological pluralism would appear to have been won (Bergin & Garfield, 1994; Kazdin, 1994). Funders of research and services may still, however, balk at such methods, or dismiss programs that do not include the randomized, controlled trial design.

Quantitative methods can be used to describe responsive client-therapist processes within psychotherapy sessions (e.g., Stiles & Shapiro, 1995), or to detail the shape of change over time in the multiple problems presented by individual clients (Barkham, Stiles, & Shapiro, 1993; Stiles, Shapiro, & Barkham, 1993). They can also be used to study phenomena at a level of abstraction between the specific techniques used by the therapist and the higher-order theoretical constructs that explain why these procedures are likely to be effective. Goldfried (1980) argued for the empirical investigation of general strategies of intervention. Kerr, Goldfried, Hayes, Castonguay, and Goldsamt (1992) applied a coding system of therapist feedback to excerpts of the Sheffield CB and PI therapies. Results suggested that therapists' intrapersonal links (between components of the client's functioning) were associated with good outcome of CB therapy, whereas therapists' interpersonal links (between the client's emotion and the action of another person) were associated with good outcome of PI therapy.

The events paradigm (Greenberg, 1991; Rice & Greenberg, 1984) substitutes analysis of specific classes of significant event occurring within therapy for evaluation of the effectiveness of entire treatments. More generally, qualitative methods, with appropriate quality standards (e.g., Stiles, 1993), are increasingly accepted as of value in the explication of change processes in psychotherapy. Meanwhile, the facile notion that only quantitative research can refute hypotheses was falsified by case history narratives within the Menninger study (Wallerstein, 1986, 1989), which revealed that psychoanalyses achieved lesser outcomes than predicted, whereas supportive psychotherapies often achieved more than predicted.

In sum, Resolution IV makes a strong case that to advance our understanding of how psychotherapies help people change requires innovative research methods going beyond the RCT and process-outcome correlations (Stiles, 1988). Some applications of these methods within the Sheffield program will be described next.

Resolutions III and IV: Examples

The following examples are of lines of work that are currently in progress rather than completed, although preliminary results are available from each.

Content-Impact-Outcome Strategy

To understand change processes, we advocate analysis of relationships between the contents of treatment sessions, the states in which participants enter and leave those sessions, and those longer-term changes in participants' states that are described, in the case of the client, as "outcomes" In collaboration with William B. Stiles, we have examined the impact or immediate subjective effects of the session, including clients' evaluations of the session, their assessment of its specific character, and their post-session affective state. Measures of impact are concerned with clients' internal reactions to sessions which, logically, must intervene between in-session events and the long-term effects of treatment. Such measures could be considered "mini-outcomes" and their quantitative analysis merely a refinement of Resolution I. However, our content-impact-outcome strategy goes further, describing change processes and testing models thereof. Although predominantly evaluative rather than descriptive attributes, our chosen measures also yielded a transitory Arousal Index tapping the energizing impact of sessions, and a single-item Unwanted Thoughts index that was more highly and more variably rated by clients with more severe depression (Reynolds, Stiles, Barkham, Shapiro, Hardy, & Rees, 1993; Stiles, Reynolds, Hardy, Rees, Barkham, & Shapiro, 1994).

Analyses relating session contents to the impact measures, and impacts to outcomes, are under way. For example, Reynolds et al. (1993) related session impact to treatment method and to the duration of treatment. As predicted, CB sessions were smoother than PI sessions, and CB clients left their sessions in a more positive mood than did PI clients. PI sessions were experienced as more variable than were CB sessions. Ratings of the PI therapeutic relationship improved more markedly over time than did ratings of the relationship by CB clients. As predicted from the assimilation model, problem-solving was low in early sessions of PI and increased in later sessions. In CB sessions the mean level of problem solving was higher and the increase over the course of therapy was less marked.

Common vs. Specific Processes in the Facilitation of Insight

Most, if not all, psychotherapies involve the client learning something new about him- or herself. Insight is a key type of change sought by psychotherapists, and an encompassing framework that described how this is achieved would be useful. Enhanced insight may be accomplished by different means in different treatment models. On the other hand, there may be features common to several treatment methods in the processes giving rise to insight.

Elliott, Shapiro, Firth-Cozens, Stiles, Hardy, Llewelyn, and Margison (1994) examined insight events in both CB and PI therapies. Both CB and PI therapists used interpretation, well grounded in client material, exemplifying the treatment model and delivered in a firm, persistent but interactive style. All events involved what Rice and Saperia (1984) called a "meaning bridge," linking the client's reaction to its context, so that the reaction comes to make sense. Features common to all events were embodied in a five-step sequential model to describe the attainment of insight:

1. contextual priming (earlier sessions provide therapist with relevant thematic information and develop alliance; client's recent problematic life event narrated to the therapist)
2. novel information (therapist interpretation links recent painful event with general themes)
3. initial distanced processing (client mulls over information acquiescently and unemotionally)
4. insight (client conveys connection or reconnection, with surprise)
5. elaboration (client elaborates emotional or other implications of insight).

There were also sharp differences between CB and PI insight events. For example, only PI events were characterized by painful awareness. CB and PI insights differed in their contents: CB events were primarily reattributional, whereas PI events involved connection to an earlier conflict theme. Thus, commonalities and divergences among insight events from two contrasting therapies exist side-by-side.

Tracking Assimilation of Problematic Experiences

Building on earlier, qualitative work (e.g., Stiles, Shapiro, & Harper, 1994), Field, Barkham, Shapiro, and Stiles (1994) applied a methodology for evaluating the assimilation model combining experimental rigor with clinical sensitivity to a good-outcome PI case within SPP2. The method comprised (a) identifying a problematic content domain, (b) defining a problematic experience within that domain, and (c) rating the experience's changing level of assimilation across randomly ordered passages from selected sessions. Independent sets of raters carried out the tasks of each phase. Results supported the assimilation model's hypothesized progression by which a problematic experience is successfully incorporated into a schema, and highlighted one session in which much of the clinical progress on one problem was achieved

This research needs to be developed in several ways. It should contrast series of successful and unsuccessful cases. Only after failing to observe similar in-session progress in poor-outcome cases will we be able to assert with confidence that the assimilation observed is productive of favorable outcome. Other types of therapy should also be observed, to ascertain the extent to which progress from vague awareness to insight is specific, as hypothesized, to PI therapy. The content-impact-outcome strategy described above should be applied to demonstrate the relationship between in-session assimilation (content), assimilation-related impacts ranging from awareness to problem solution, and long-term change in problems and symptoms. Finally, the relationship of assimilation to other in-session events, notably to therapist interventions, needs to be studied in order to show how therapists help clients assimilate problematic experiences.

These examples illustrate the current state of development of research using innovative methods to study encompassing frameworks. By way of overall evaluation, it is fair to say that this is promising and provocative rather than—as yet—definitive.

Conclusions and Recommendations

This is an exciting time for psychotherapy research. Psychotherapy is high on the public and policy agenda, whether in relation to the debate about false memory syndrome vs. early abuse, or to policy issues concerning the provision of psychological services. Meanwhile, our science is coming of age. Building on the relatively secure base of evidential support for psychological treatments now available, the basic question of the field has shifted from "Does it (psychotherapy) work?" to "How do they (the several psychotherapies) work?" An increasingly broad, robust, and yet sensitive range of investigative methods has borne fruit. There are promising findings and clear ways forward. We are closer than ever before to achieving an understanding of how psychotherapies help people change.

To take this process forward, we should exploit public interest in psychotherapy by demonstrating the need for research to answer questions of public concern, and the utility of the answers already available from existing research. We should recruit the support of diverse stakeholders, including users, commissioners, and providers of psychological treatments, so that research becomes a routine and integral part of the delivery of psychotherapy (Aveline, Shapiro, Parry, & Freeman, 1995). For example, user satisfaction and clinical audit are both so closely related to research methods (client ratings and outcome evaluation, respectively) that research can easily "piggy-back" on these policy-driven activities. Increased convergence between researcher and practitioner objectives will in turn make research more useful to clinicians (Morrow-Bradley & Elliott, 1986; Talley, Strupp, & Butler, 1994).

In terms of methodology, the Sheffield program described here illustrates the power of multi-level, multi-method research (e.g., qualitative and quantitative analysis of change processes within an RCT) to address central questions concerning the mechanisms of change within treatments. A useful strategic framework for these questions is one that identifies change processes that are common to several treatment methods, and contrasts these with others that are specific to a given method. This paper has been organized in terms of four resolutions of the equivalence paradox. However, the development of multi-method research programs such as the one reviewed here, and advances in our understanding of change processes, may be bringing about a coalescing of what 10 years ago appeared to be quite distinct approaches to the paradox. The Sheffield program also illustrates the importance of collaboration between investigators. Methodological pluralism requires a range of expertise that is unlikely to be encompassed by a single individual or group. Collaborations integral to the Sheffield program have been forged in contacts made at meetings of the Society for Psychotherapy Research. Furthermore, the thrust of the entire program reflects interests developed through participation in those meetings. The special qualities of the meetings include mutual support, intellectual challenge, and shared commitment in equal measure to both scientific and clinical advance. As the Society flourishes, so too will the field. Collaborative research will play an increasingly central role in our progress toward understanding how psychotherapies help people change.

COMMENTARY

HOW, NOW, TO FIND OUT HOW PSYCHOTHERAPIES HELP PEOPLE CHANGE? REFLECTIONS OF A RETIRED PSYCHOTHERAPY RESEARCHER

By way of a disclaimer, I retired in 2006. Prior to that, from 1999 onward I had worked mainly as a clinician, in service development, and in consultancy, with diminishing involvement in research per se. Thus I write as an ex-researcher.

Values, Politics, and Strategy

Since my 1994 Society for Psychotherapy Research (SPR) presidential address, the context in which we do psychotherapy research has become much more challenging, although hindsight suggests that this process was already underway back then. I remain of the view, reflected in the title of my address alongside central themes of the proceedings of SPR since its inception, that establishing an empirical basis for psychological treatment services requires scientific understanding of change mechanisms. Such understanding remains unlikely to flow solely or directly from higher-order, general psychological principles, but to require systematic study of the psychotherapeutic process itself. However, it appears ever more difficult to secure the resources required to pursue this basic science of psychotherapy.

My working life has been informed by progressive or left-wing political values. My purpose as a psychotherapy researcher was to use scientific methods to improve services. My primary self-identification was as a scientist-practitioner rather than as a proponent of one brand of therapy over another. I consider brand loyalties inimical to scientific progress.

I grew up in a Britain, whose National Health Service (NHS), through which governments exercised a responsibility to deliver healthcare according to need, was nationally treasured, and internationally respected for its effectiveness and efficiency. Similarly, I received education and training within a state-funded, meritocratic system. Accordingly, my work was driven by a collectivist appreciation of rights and responsibilities: I do not own the skills and knowledge I have been privileged to receive; I owe a duty to give back to society by investing these skills for the common good. As a health professional, I owe that duty to work for the collectively financed and delivered NHS rather than in a private sector which is inescapably parasitic upon the state-funded system (for example, for training its professionals, for unbiased research and development, and for picking up the pieces when things go wrong), with its primary goal that of shareholder advantage, and in consequence preferentially serving advantaged over disadvantaged members of society. In Britain, most psychological therapy has been provided by the NHS, although this has been underresourced relative to population-based assessments of need.

Throughout my career, I considered it important to pay attention to strategic issues. Psychotherapy is a complex activity addressing complex and challenging human problems. Progress has been slow, and knowledge has not cumulated to a satisfying extent. In Kuhnian terms, we have not enjoyed a settled period of consensual, normal, scientific progress free of disagreement and controversy about how to move forward. I drew from my undergraduate philosophy studies, in particular the later work of Wittgenstein, an abiding preoccupation with the interdependence of findings with research methods.

Bill Stiles, Robert Elliott, and I described the equivalence paradox of broadly similar outcomes of demonstrably diverse therapeutic methods (Stiles, Shapiro, & Elliott, 1986). The quotation marks of that paper's title, "Are all psychotherapies equivalent?," were key. It emerged that some readers did not appreciate this. We were not asking whether all psychotherapies are equivalent but, rather, characterizing diverse research approaches in terms of four possible answers to that question. Correspondingly, my 1994 presidential address conceptualized the work of the Sheffield group and its collaborators in terms of four equivalence-paradox resolution strategies.

Narrative Context of Presidential Address

The Sheffield group was in a productive phase at the time of my presidential address. The primary report of the outcomes of the Second Sheffield Psychotherapy Project (SPP2) appeared that year. Further reports, including a 12-month follow-up and numerous process analyses, were forthcoming over several years. Other, related projects were completed through the late 1990s.

The research I presented in 1994 was made possible by substantial and continuous funding from the UK Medical Research Council (MRC) from 1977 to 1995. Our group formed a team within a research unit jointly funded by MRC and the UK Economic and Social Research Council (ESRC). Our programmatic approach, modeled upon those of some of our most distinguished seniors and contemporaries within SPR, both required and served to justify the support we received. Our team's primary purpose was, as reflected in my presidential address title, to find out how psychotherapies help people change. While our task was intellectual, the means to accomplish it were that and more: to build and maintain a cohesive team of scientist-practitioners whose individual and collective goals and ambitions could be realized synergistically, through a research clinic. That mode of operation is one that others have followed, in a variety of ways, both before and since. My presidential address came towards the end of a period of uncertainty for our group. Our funding was about to end following a periodic review in 1992–3. The reason given for this termination was that the research was not judged to be of internationally competitive quality. We naturally found this judgment narcissistically injurious, especially since we were publishing key papers in the *Journal of Consulting and Clinical Psychology* (JCCP). Our studies had been designed and implemented expressly to meet the known, exacting standards of JCCP and thus satisfy our funders by appearing in the premier journal of clinical psychology worldwide. Naively, perhaps, we had considered publication therein an operational criterion of the required international competitiveness.

Alongside this overt judgment concerning scientific quality, however, we also understood that the decision to end our funding flowed from strategic priorities: cognitive neuroscience was favored for major funding over other kinds of psychological research. However, the culture and practice of research resource allocation required such strategic choices to be dressed in the clothes of competitive evaluation. With hindsight, we might have made more effort to align our work with those strategic choices.

Our response was to take up a joint investment by the University of Leeds and its local NHS to strengthen clinical psychology research and practice. In Leeds, our research became less programmatic, more pragmatic in its objectives, more embedded in the practice of collaborating services, and more piecemeal and opportunistic in responding to policy-based funding initiatives. This work is now taken forward at the University of Sheffield by key members of the original Sheffield team: Michael Barkham, Gillian Hardy, and Glenys Parry.

Current and Future Contexts

The more pragmatic approach we adopted in Leeds was in tune with contemporaneous national developments toward evidence-based practice and policy, notably during the period of Labour (left-of-center) government (1997–2010).

The National Institute for Health and Clinical Excellence (NICE) develops evidence-based guidelines for the management of a range of physical and mental health conditions, alongside appraisals of specific interventions. NICE was established to maximize the cost-effectiveness with which finite resources are allocated. The aim was to arbitrate among the competing demands of different patient groups, each of which is supported by a corresponding group of professionals who work with them, not to mention the commercial interests of pharmaceutical and other companies who naturally seek returns on their investments. Despite imperfections, this represents an internationally unprecedented attempt at rational allocation of resources, and has much to commend it. Appropriately enough, the requirements of NICE have increasingly defined research funding priorities.

Several years ago, the economist Richard Layard persuaded the UK government of the economic benefits that would result from increased provision of psychological therapies for common mental health problems. At a time of relative prosperity, much of the argument was based on the potential to help the long-term unemployed get work. The resulting Improving Access to Psychological Therapies (IAPT, www.iapt.nhs.uk/) program (Clark, 2011) trains therapists to deliver NICE-approved psychological treatments of depression and anxiety disorders across the country. The programme began with cognitive-behavioral therapy, but has now broadened, in accordance with the evidence base, to encompass interpersonal and dynamic therapies, as well as counseling, for the treatment of depression. The competences required of IAPT therapists include generic competences that draw upon common factors of research familiar to SPR members.

Meanwhile, however, by 1994, the postwar consensus underpinning Britain's welfare state and education system was already under strain. Today in 2013, this process is accelerating rapidly. The Conservative-led government is breaking up the NHS, using a populist rhetoric of patient choice and clinician-led commissioning to admit private interests to the management and delivery of health care on an unprecedented scale. The predictable outcome of this will be widening inequalities in access to care, alongside growing inefficiencies as resources are diverted to transaction costs, overpayment of corporate leaders, and shareholder profit. Private companies will cherry-pick profitable services, leaving a rump NHS to carry the remainder, ranging from accident and emergency to mental health. A relatively small number of wealthy and well-insured individuals will throw vast resources at receiving the best treatments, when that same expenditure could transform the lives of many poorer people with relatively commonplace conditions whose treatment will receive dwindling resources. The government willfully ignores the motivating benefits of the public service ethos that is undermined once an organization is governed by the competitive pursuit of shareholder value and/or the personal enrichment of its directors.

Meanwhile, our universities must follow the American model whereby students pay large fees, becoming "customers" entitled to own outright the fruits of their education, identified as a private rather than a public good. While this might in time be mitigated by an American-style philanthropic tradition, that is no substitute for the model of democratically accountable public service. Furthermore, the capacity of academics to critique government policy or corporate interests—to speak truth to power—has been progressively eroded by straitened finances. Universities must think and act commercially, rendering ever more salient their reliance on funds from vested interests, that inevitably come with strings attached. The public service ethos and autonomy of the research community are thereby undermined. Who pays the piper calls the tune; questions addressed by researchers are framed by others; science is for sale. Even when the priorities of those commissioning research are congenial, autonomy is lost; the focus of scientific activity may be shifted too far towards the immediately applicable to allow coherent development of generalizable principles.

The UK Conservative Party, when seeking election by "detoxifying its brand," affected to listen to Wilkinson and Pickett's (2010) evidence that inequality damages a nation's health, but now in office uses the pretext of an economic crisis of falling demand—and hence tax revenues—brought about by self-serving speculative activity in the financial sector, to pursue counterproductively pre-Keynesian policies whose effects are to increase rather than reduce inequality, without reducing the indebtedness they purport to target. A massive transfer of resources is underway, from the majority to a tiny minority. Academia is infected by the ideology of personal enrichment when vice-chancellors, the chief executives of universities, are paid £300,000 a year and thereby insulated from the realities of everyday life for the majority.

Epidemiological evidence shows the devastating impact of these societal changes on public health (Stuckler & Basu, 2013): austerity kills. Needs for mental health services in general, and psychotherapy in particular, are set to increase. Consider, for example, the lost generation of young people from many of whom educational and employment opportunities have been stolen. As is reminiscent of the 1980s, our energies might be more effectively spent challenging such damaging societal priorities and political decisions—prime causes of psychological ill-health—rather than seeking to mitigate their effects by research-based enhancements to psychotherapeutic services, increasingly resembling a sticking plaster, albeit one improved by the addition of empirically supported ingredients.

I would now say in a presidential address that pragmatic adaptations to the changing environment will be key to the future of psychotherapy research. I would revisit a theme of David Orlinsky: doing research without a grant. Low-cost research may be more limited in scope or quality, but it gains autonomy by not relying on paymasters. However, much of this non-funded work is likely to require collaboration with practitioners. As our NHS is dismembered and resources are transferred to the privateers, it will become ever more difficult to secure this.

Research opportunities will increasingly depend upon the requirements of service development priorities. It is no longer realistic—if it ever was—to hope that the psychotherapy research community can secure funds to pursue its scientific agenda except in harness to priorities and objectives set by others. This presents a huge strategic challenge. The research upon which the IAPT program draws in defining generic competences would not get funded in today's climate.

Methodological Advances

Methodologically, my presidential address advocated a multi-level, multi-method approach to the analysis of change mechanisms. I was by no means alone in calling for methodological pluralism, and others before and since have included process analyses within randomized trial protocols. My address may have contributed to a developing consensus in support of this approach.

I remain convinced of the central importance of scientific understanding of change mechanisms. Without this, we will be left with a confusing babel of claims and counterclaims for the effectiveness of one brand of treatment over another, supported only by a tenuous balance of empirical support from pragmatic trials devoid of evidence identifying mechanisms to account for the outcomes achieved. This understanding will not be advanced until resources are made available for the basic science of psychotherapy.

One respect in which my presidential address is outdated concerns the methodology of clinical trials. As scientist-practitioners, we were content, 20 years ago, to design and implement our studies with little or no involvement of outside experts. Nowadays, that would not do. For example, we would not now have randomization carried out by a team member, albeit with safeguards against contamination, but would contract out this task. Had we known then what we know now about the impact of investigator allegiance on comparative outcome research, we would have involved external consultants in the design of our studies.

In conclusion, my presidential address sought to express a vision derived from, and in turn contributing to, a shared set of values, objectives, and beliefs emblematic of the work of SPR. These remain of lasting importance. However, shifts since 1994 in the economic, political, and societal contexts have made it harder to work toward realization of that vision. Accordingly, if written today, my presidential address would have been more modest and pragmatic, and less programmatically ambitious, in its approach.

Note

1 The work of the Sheffield group is a team effort involving Michael Barkham, Susan Field, Gillian Hardy, Heather Harper, Anna Madill, Anne Rees, Shirley Reynolds, and Mike Startup, together with our National Health Service collaborators Roxane Agnew, Alison Culverwell, Jeremy Halstead, and the late Veronica Harrington, and American co-investigators Robert Elliott, Marv Goldfried, Bill Stiles, and their students.

6

DREAMS AND THERAPY (1997)

Clara E. Hill[1]

Let me begin by telling you a recurrent dream that one of our research clients presented in the fifth session of brief therapy. She was a 46-year-old woman who had been sexually abused as a child, and then served as a nurse in two tours of duty in Vietnam.

She is at the Vietnam Veteran's Wall in Washington, DC. She is carrying her scrapbook in which she had kept photos of different patients, evacuation rosters, military pay certificates, and poems from her first tour in Vietnam. She is feeling distraught, hopeless, alone, and that life is worthless. She feels engulfed by her memories and by all the horrible things that went on in Vietnam. She takes the scrapbook and throws it at the Wall, saying, "Take this, take back the memories, I don't want them anymore." After throwing the book at the Wall, she says, "Now take the rest of me," and pulls out a gun and shoots herself through the heart.

This dream illustrates the type of troubling and vivid dream that clients often bring into therapy. It also shows why therapists need to work with dreams in therapy.

The first form of psychotherapy might have been dream interpretation. The earliest written records, from about 3000–4000 BC, indicate that people have long been intrigued by their dreams and have tried to understand their meaning. In this article, I will explore why people have been so intrigued by their dreams and talk about how we ought to be paying more attention to dreams in psychotherapy and psychotherapy research. First, I will give some historical perspective on how dreams have been viewed and the implications of these views for therapy. Then I will describe what we know about dreaming and the effects of this knowledge for therapy. Next I will present an overview of my model for how dreams are formed, because that lays the foundation for my model for working with dreams. Then I will question why therapists have not been using dreams in therapy and discuss some common misconceptions that therapists have about dreams. That leads directly to the model that I have developed for working with dreams in psychotherapy. Finally, I will describe a little about our research program on dream interpretation, using a model that we have developed, and then present some ideas for future research.

History

In this section I discuss how dreams have been viewed down through the ages (van de Castle, 1994) and discuss the implications of these views for dream interpretation.

Dreams as Messages from External Sources

Positive Dreams

On the positive side, people throughout the ages have viewed dreams as prophetic, as messages that foretell the future. The Old Testament of the Bible and the Talmud have many references to dreams. The Pharaoh's dream, reported in the Old Testament, about the seven fat cows and the seven lean cows, is an example of a prophetic dream. Joseph interpreted this dream for the Pharaoh as predicting seven years of good harvest followed by seven years of famine. Because the Pharaoh heeded Joseph's dream interpretation, the country stored up grain during the good years and thus was able to survive during the lean years.

In ancient Mesopotamia and Greece, people often went to special temples to have their dreams incubated. They went through elaborate rituals to gain access to dreams from the gods that forecast the future or that diagnosed or prescribed cures for illnesses. The idea was that the gods spoke to people through dreams, although these dreams often needed to be interpreted by qualified people. Dream interpretation influenced the most serious of all personal, political, and economic decisions.

In several cultures, people thought that their souls left their bodies during sleep and went to talk with the spirits or gods. It was considered dangerous to waken people during sleep, because their souls might not be able to return to their bodies.

Negative/Evil Dreams

Another view of dreams was that they came from devils or demons. From time immemorial, people have been nervous about what they do in their dreams. In dreams, people have been known to murder, have sexual relations with someone other than their spouse, or be involved in incredible and often illicit adventures. People in ancient times, and even in present times, have had a difficult time separating out what was dreaming and what was reality, so they thought that they were responsible for what they did in their dreams. If they dreamed about having a sexual affair, that was tantamount to having the affair. The ancients thus considered some dreams dangerous and did not discuss them for fear of increasing their potency. They used amulets or charms to protect themselves from bad dreams. Rituals were used to ward off the evil consequences of dreams.

An example of the consequences of the belief that dreams are evil is an incident that occurred in Europe in about 300 AD. A Catholic priest named Jerome, who had very troubling dreams, declared dreams to be from the devil. In translating the Hebrew Bible into the Latin Vulgate, he apparently deliberately misinterpreted a few times the Hebrew word for "witchcraft" into "observing dreams." Hence, instead of warning against witchcraft, he warned readers against observing dreams. Because the Vulgate was used until the 20th century, this translation had an incredible impact on how dreams were viewed for the next 15 centuries. As if that were not enough, a contemporary of Jerome's, a man by the name of Macrobius, believed that demons sexually possessed dreamers during dreams; his book became the most important and well-known book on dreams in medieval Europe. After this time, demons and devils became an obsessive concern for European Christians. Dreams became a hunting ground for inquisitors seeking evidence of demons. Needless to say, not many people during these times were willing to reveal their dreams, and many tried to suppress having dreams.

Implications

If dreams are from external sources, the implication is that people better pay attention to the message. If the message is positive, the person needs to act on the message. If the message is negative, people need to protect themselves from the consequences.

Another implication is that, if dreams come from external sources, they are not personal and thus can be interpreted through a dream dictionary. Indeed, dream dictionaries have been found in almost every culture. For example, in India, riding an elephant in your dream was considered to be lucky, whereas riding a donkey was unlucky. In China, if one dreamed about the sun or moon rising, one's family would prosper, whereas dreaming about teeth falling out signified that one's parents were in danger.

Dreams as Physical Manifestations

Throughout the centuries there have been people who believed that dreams are purely physiological entities. In ancient Greece, Aristotle believed that dreams were merely due to sensory sensations and somatic disturbances. Cicero, a Roman, argued that if the gods were truly trying to help people, they would send messages when people were awake and better able to receive the information rather than when they were asleep and prone to forget what they had experienced. In 1690, Locke proposed that dreams were determined by sensory inputs. In the first American psychiatry book, published in 1812, Rush considered dreams a transient paroxysm of delirium, arising from changes in cerebral bloodflow, signifying imperfect sleep and often indicating an impending illness. Wundt, who founded the world's first psychological laboratory in Germany, held that dreams arose mainly from sensory stimuli. Most recently, Hobson and McCarley (1977) have proposed that dreams arise from random activation of the brain, with the forebrain making the best of a bad job to integrate all the pieces into a cohesive whole. Crick and Mitchison (1983) proposed that too much goes on during the day to store it all. They postulated that the dream's function is to clear the brain of these unneeded, meaningless connections, so dreaming is essentially the wastebasket of the brain.

Implications

If one believes that dreams are merely psychosomatic sensations, there is certainly no need to interpret dreams or try to understand them. At best, if dreams are random bursts of energy, and hence meaningless from a psychological perspective, it is a waste of time to interpret them. At worst, recalling one's dreams might strengthen neural connections that should be purged.

Psychological Origins

Others have viewed dreams as expressions of our personalities and thus have believed that dreams are very personal and individual. Plato suggested that our reasoning ability is suspended during sleep and thus passions and desires reveal themselves with full force. Artemedorius, in about 100 AD, felt that images in dreams vary, depending on the dreamer, and urged flexibility in interpreting particular dreams. In 1865, Seafield wrote an extensive treatise on dreams, in which he stated that dreams were comprehensible, reflected the dreamer's personality, could be compensatory, were capable of problem-solving, and led to a better balanced personality if interpreted.

Following in this tradition, Freud developed his approach to dream interpretation, based on the notion that dreams are unconscious wish fulfillments. He thought that dreams are a compromise between allowing the person to sleep and allowing unconscious desires to be expressed, albeit through distorted means, hence making the content acceptable to the dreamer. Freud considered his book *The Interpretation of Dreams* (1900) to be his greatest work. Many of the major theorists about psychotherapy since Freud (Jung, Adler, Perls, Boss, and Binswanger) have developed their own theories about dreams, all maintaining that dreams are psychologically important.

Implications

The implication of the belief that dreams are important personal psychological events is that dreams should be interpreted to lead to greater self-understanding. Furthermore, because dreams reveal important psychological material, another implication is that therapists should work with dreams in therapy.

Source of Creativity and Problem-Solving

Another way that dreams have been viewed is as a source of creativity and problem-solving. Examples abound in science and technology, art, sports, and history. The design for the sewing machine, the understanding of carbon chains, the circular structure of the benzene ring, and the periodic table were all discovered during dreams. The artist Salvador Dalí referred to his work as "hand-painted dream photographs." Ingmar Bergman said that all his films were dreams. The inspiration for both *Frankenstein* and *Dr. Jekyll and Mr. Hyde* came through dreams. During a bad slump in his golf game, Jack Nicklaus had a dream in which he held his golf club differently and swung perfectly. When he tried it the next day, it worked. Harriet Tubman claimed that dreams helped her find safe pathways to lead slaves to freedom on the Underground Railroad.

Implications

The implication for viewing dreams as sources of creativity and problem-solving is that there is not a major need to interpret the dream, but rather the person should just use the dream directly. Not surprisingly, when someone needs to make a decision or solve a problem, we often encourage him or her to "sleep on it." Other implications are that we could teach people to incubate their dreams and to recall their dreams more, so that this source of creativity and problem-solving would be more readily available to them.

What Do We Know about Dreams?

Scientific interest was sparked in physiological aspects of sleep and dreaming beginning with Aserinsky's discovery of rapid eye movements (REM) around 1950 (Aserinsky & Kleitman, 1953, 1955). We now know a great deal about the physiology of sleep and dreaming, dream recall, and dream content.

1. The average person spends about two hours a night in REM sleep, which is the stage of sleep where most dreaming seems to occur.
2. Most people have four or five dreams per night, but the average person remembers only one to two dreams per week.

3. Dreams are more likely to be remembered if they are highly salient (novel, bizarre, vivid, active, long, and emotionally charged), if they are the last dreams of the night, if one is sleeping lightly, if one is not suddenly aroused (e.g., by an alarm clock), or if one gets more sleep than usual (e.g., on weekends).
4. Most current dream researchers agree that dreams reflect waking concerns. Rather than being an attempt to disguise concerns, as Freud indicated, substantial evidence now shows that waking concerns, particularly negative ones, are incorporated into dream content either directly or indirectly. For example, Garfield (1991) found that dreams of being buried alive or lost at sea were common for women anticipating or undergoing divorce.
5. The characters in dreams are usually people with whom the dreamer is emotionally and often conflictually involved. The settings are generally commonplace and familiar. Affect in dreams is negative about two-thirds of the time.
6. Dream content reflects gender, race/ethnicity, socioeconomic status, marital status, developmental level, personality, and pathology. For example, depressed people's dreams are full of masochism, dependency needs, and self-defeating thoughts and ideas. In contrast, schizophrenics' dreams are filled with feelings of loneliness, a lack of human contact, sterility, limited and/or bizarre imagery, danger, morbidity, a sense of emergency or stress, and feelings of hopelessness and helplessness. Hence, the pathology is carried on in dreams.
7. Most college students report having had a recurrent dream sometime during their lives. Recurrent dreams are more likely than regular dreams to involve only the dreamer and to involve being chased or attacked. Recurrent dreams appear to be metaphorical representations of traumatic events. Recurrent dreams seem to reflect longstanding unresolved problems.
8. Nightmares are one of the features of post-traumatic stress disorder (PTSD). People suffering from PTSD often dream the exact sequence of events from the traumatic event over and over, making sleep quite unpleasant and difficult. Vivid nightmares of combat have been reported for years after the actual event, sometimes after a delay with no nightmares. Fortunately, when nightmares are discussed extensively and worked on in therapy, they tend to dissipate, although they often return when another stressful event occurs.

Hence, from the research we can conclude that dreams are meaningful, organized, and non-random events that reflect personality and waking life rather than disguise waking concerns. Nobody yet knows for sure what the functions of dreams are. There appear to be many types of dreams and many functions of dreams. But, perhaps serendipitously, dream interpretation can be useful, even if dreams have no psychological function, because dreams reflect waking issues so well.

Cognitive-Experiential Model of Dreams

Let me give you a hypothetical example of how dreams are formed. This might have been the dream I would have had the night before I gave this Presidential Address, had I been able to sleep. The example begins on the day prior to the dream. When I first get to Vancouver for the SPR conference, I go and practice my Presidential Address in the room where I will give it the next day. I remember other Presidential Addresses that I have heard, as well as other speeches that I have heard and given. Then I go for a walk down to Wreck Beach. I see cruise ships off in the distance and remember nostalgically the wonderful cruise I had with my husband for our 20th anniversary. When I get ready to sleep that night, I am still worrying about my Presidential Address and wondering whether people will like it. When I go into non-REM sleep, I go over lines of the speech and practice how to say them. When I go into REM sleep, I make up a story that combines the elements of waking experience with my past memories. I first dream that I am on a cruise ship relaxing before I have to give my Presidential Address. All of a sudden I realize that I am five minutes late. I rush over to the room and get in front of the audience, and all of a sudden realize that . . . I forgot my Presidential *dress*.

I postulate that dreams help us incorporate waking events into memory. Let me explain how this works. When something happens in waking life, the event triggers the activation of the relevant schemata (defined as clusters of associated thoughts, feelings, and memories stored in the mind). During the day, of course, other events occur that activate other schemata. As new schemata get activated, others tend to lose activation, unless they are very salient. Thus we remember only the salient events that we attend to, rather than all the details that occur during the day.

When we go to sleep, some of the schemata are still activated. During non-REM sleep, we think about these issues in much the same way we do during waking thought. During REM sleep, however, we weave the memories from the activated schemata into a story, using images that are powerful expressions of these schemata.

Dreams appear to be metaphorical and imagistic. Some have likened dreams to our "theater of the night," where we create, direct, and star in a production about what is currently important to us. Dreams appear to be a way to help us place the waking events into the relevant schemata. However, our dreams cannot always help us assimilate events into the schemata. No other similar events might exist in our schemata or the experience might be discrepant from the schemata. Then we are more likely to have troubling dreams, recurrent dreams, or nightmares.

Need to Focus on Dreams in Therapy

Because dreams reflect waking conflicts and touch us emotionally in very deep ways, and because some people have frightening and troubling dreams, one would think that dreams would be focused on in therapy. One would also think that therapists would be trained in how to work with dreams.

Despite the emphasis of dream interpretation by the early psychoanalytic theorists, however, there was a dearth of interest in dream interpretation outside of psychoanalytic circles for much of the middle and latter parts of the twentieth century. Mahrer (1990) estimated that only 10–15 percent of therapists work with dreams.

Erikson (1954) suggested that dreams went out of fashion in psychiatry in the 1930s because they did not fit well with the emphasis on speed and practicality in U.S. culture. He thought that many therapists felt that it took too long to unravel all the associations for even one dream and that working with dreams took them too far away from everyday life. Cartwright (1993) additionally postulated that the U.S. love affair with science and the mistrust of anything subjective militated against using dreams. She also noted that the newly found ability to control abnormal behavior with drugs and behavioral-management programs further caused psychotherapy training programs to discard dream interpretation as archaic.

Unfortunately, there are still many misconceptions about dreams that prevent therapists from working with dreams in therapy. Many therapists dismiss dreams as being "just dreams" and consider them to be trivial and meaningless. Others feel that dreams are unscientific, or associated with the Occult. In fact, books on dreams are often in the New Age section of bookstores, rather than in the psychology section. Many feel that dream interpretation can be used only by psychoanalysts in long-term therapy, because it takes so long to uncover all the unconscious determinants of the dream.

My rebuttal to these misconceptions is largely based on clinical evidence. Indeed, dream interpretation seems to play an important role in long-term therapy, providing therapists and clients an excellent opportunity to delve into series of dreams in great detail. Themes can be derived from dream series and changes in dream content can be charted to reflect changes through therapy. However, dream interpretation also has an important place in brief therapy, because it can help to establish a focus of what is troubling clients. Dreams provide a stimulus that often enables clients to express themselves more quickly than they would otherwise. In our research on dream interpretation (Cogar & Hill, 1992; Falk & Hill, 1995), therapists have reported that using dreams in early sessions opened up material that would otherwise have taken much longer to surface. Similarly, Weiss (1986) and Rosenthal (1980) indicated that dream analysis can help clients reach core issues in psychotherapy quickly, thereby shortening the therapeutic process.

Dream interpretation often leads directly to a person's central conflicts, even though the person previously could not articulate what was making him or her unhappy. Often clients are out of touch with what is truly troubling them, but quickly come to troubling issues when they associate to images in their dreams. Dreams seem to be particularly powerful, because they deal in images and metaphors. Hence, working with dreams might actually speed therapy or help to develop a focus in the therapy, especially if therapists use a dream interpretation approach that emphasizes the connection of dreams to waking life, and helps the dreamer develop some action based on the dream.

Cartwright (1993) noted that interest in dreams has revived in recent years. She attributed the increased interest to the revolutionary discoveries about sleep and dreaming and the development of sleep disorder clinics that help people with sleep disturbances. In addition, interest in internal phenomena has once again become acceptable since the advent of the cognitive revolution around 1970 (see Hill & Corbett, 1993).

Research on Dream Interpretation

As surprising as the lack of attention to dreams in therapy is the lack of attention to dream interpretation in the psychotherapy research literature. In *PsycLit*, for journal articles between 1974 and 1994, I found 2,353 references to dreams and 817 references to dream interpretation or dream analysis. But I could find only six empirical studies on the process or outcome of dream interpretation, although a few additional empirical studies used changes in dream structure or content as a measure of change in therapy.

Why are there so few empirical studies on dream interpretation? Perhaps therapists who believe in dream interpretation feel no need to study it because they "know" it works. Instead they write about how to do dream interpretation. Perhaps the more "scientific" therapists have avoided studying dreams because there is still a stigma against dreams. I believe that dream interpretation is a powerful therapeutic strategy that deserves our empirical attention. In the next section I propose my model of dream interpretation and provide examples of the program of research that we have begun on dream interpretation in the hopes of encouraging more people to work with dreams in therapy and to do research on dream interpretation.

Model of Dream Interpretation

The assumptions underlying our model of dream interpretation are:

- Dreams are personal and unique to the individual; hence dreams cannot be interpreted through a dream dictionary or standard symbolic interpretations.

- The best way to approach dream interpretation is through a collaborative method, in which therapists act as guides to help clients construct the personal meaning of the dream, rather than being experts who know the meanings of dreams.
- Dreams reflect waking life, rather than being disguised messages from the unconscious.
- Both cognitions and emotions are important in dream interpretation.

To understand the dreams, we need to reverse the process of dream formation. The relevant schemata need to be reactivated and then changed.

I propose a three-stage model of dream interpretation: exploration, insight, and action. In the exploration stage, the therapist helps the client re-experience the dream by first retelling the dream, sequentially describing each of the images, and then associating to each of the images. The therapist then helps the client find the links to waking life and works with uncovered conflicts if necessary. The exploration leads directly to the insight stage, in which the therapist and client work together to put it all together and figure out the meaning of the dream for the dreamer. The insight leads to new schematic organization or accommodation of the schemata to fit the new information. Exploration and insight lead directly to the action stage, in which the therapist and client figure out what the client could do differently based on what he or she learned about himself or herself. Action is important because it helps the client to consolidate new schematic connections and sets the behavior-change process in motion.

Description of Four Studies

Cogar and Hill (1992) examined whether dream interpretation was effective in increasing self-esteem and decreasing symptomatology. Undergraduate volunteers were randomly assigned to one of three conditions. In one condition, participants monitored their dreams (through keeping a dream diary) and participated in six weekly individual dream sessions. In the second condition, participants monitored their dreams for six weeks. The third condition was a wait list control. Dream interpretation was not significantly better than the other two conditions in terms of changes in symptomatology and self-esteem. In open-ended questions at post-testing about increases in understanding, clients in the dream interpretation condition did, however, report increased self-understanding.

In Hill, Diemer, Hess, Hillyer, and Seeman (1993), undergraduate volunteers were randomly assigned to discuss, with a therapist for a single session, *either* a recent dream of their own, another person's dream, or a recent troubling event of their own. Results indicated that clients who received dream interpretation rated their sessions as *deeper* and indicated that they achieved *more insight* than did clients who participated in the conditions in which they worked on another person's dream or a recent personal troubling event. These results provide preliminary evidence that dream interpretation is more effective than other similar techniques and that the effects of dream interpretation cannot be attributed solely to projection or to the interpretation process. Dreams seem to provide a unique stimulus that helps people gain self-understanding.

As a follow-up to the Hill et al. (1993) study, Diemer, Hill, Lobell, and Vivino (1996) studied the effects of dream interpretation compared with event interpretation within the context of brief therapy. We recruited people who wanted individual therapy (rather than dream interpretation) but only selected people as clients who reported that they remembered and were willing to work on dreams and troubling events in therapy. Clients received 12 sessions of therapy from trained therapists. Of the eight middle sessions, two were dream interpretation and two were event interpretation. The results indicated that the overall treatment involving dream interpretation, event interpretation, and unstructured sessions reduced symptomatology and increased interpersonal functioning. The test of the primary hypothesis, however, revealed no differences on post-session measures for dream interpretation, event interpretation, and unstructured sessions. These results suggest that, although dream interpretation might not be the "royal road" to greater self-understanding, it is probably as good a path as any other.

Falk and Hill (1995) investigated the efficacy of dream groups for women who were separating or divorcing. One member presented a dream during each group session, with the rest of the members projecting onto the person's dream as if it were their own. This projection is thought to be helpful, both for giving the dreamer additional ideas about his or her dream, and for allowing all group members to get something from the interpretation process for themselves. The results indicated that women in the dream groups increased more in self-esteem and insight than did women in a wait list control. The collaboration and energy generated in the groups was very positive.

In summary, the conclusions of the research are contradictory at this time, with two studies indicating that dream interpretation using this model is helpful compared with other conditions, and two indicating that it is not more helpful than other conditions. We obviously need more studies to partial out the effects of client pathology and motivation for dream interpretation, therapist skill, therapist training, and context issues, such as whether dream interpretation is presented alone or in the context of ongoing therapy.

Recommendations for Future Studies

We know so little about the efficacy of dream interpretation that the field is wide open for investigation. From our preliminary work, several areas seem promising:

1. We need to focus more on working with troubling dreams. People who have recurrent dreams, nightmares, and/or sleep terrors are often very much in need of help.

2. We need to investigate who is responsive to dream interpretation. Clearly, some people do not recall or value their dreams, so it is difficult, if not impossible, to work with dreams in therapy with these people. Others recall their dreams but are very literal in their associations and insights, and are not as rewarding to work with, doing dream interpretation. A third group seems to profit from working with dreams, and is able to associate and play with the dream in a cognitively complex manner (Diemer et al., 1996). We need to better determine what characterizes this third group.
3. We should also develop methods for training clients to work with dreams. Cartwright, Tipton, and Wicklund (1980) have done some interesting work using dreams as preparation for therapy for people who are at risk for dropping out of therapy. This application of dreamwork seems promising as a method for teaching people to look inward and examine their dreams and waking events in a systematic way, much as is required for any type of therapy.
4. We need to study the process of dream interpretation. Although I have proposed a three-stage model, we do not know if all stages are necessary, nor do we know the best techniques within each stage. We also need to compare the steps of our model with other methods of doing dream interpretation.
5. We need to study the effects of therapist expectations about dream interpretation on the process. It is notable in the clinical literature that many therapists seem to believe fervently in dream interpretation. It may be the fervent belief rather than the actual method that produces the effects.

Conclusions

In conclusion, I hope I have corrected a number of misconceptions about dreams. I hoped to show that dream interpretation is not similar to reading palms or tea leaves, and that dreams cannot be interpreted with a dream dictionary or standard interpretations. Furthermore, I hope I have relieved some of you who feel that therapists must understand what a dream means when the client first tells it. Dreams come from the individual, and interpretation can lead directly to an examination of personal issues and waking conflicts, sometimes more quickly than dealing with the problematic situations more directly. Also, dreams can be fun to work with in therapy, because they can be so imaginative, creative, and expressive. I hope I have persuaded some of you to work with dreams in therapy and to train therapists to work with dreams. Furthermore, I hope I have encouraged some to think about investigating dream interpretation, so that a more scientific basis for the practice of dream interpretation can be developed.

COMMENTARY IN 2015

DREAMS AND THERAPY: REVISITED 18 YEARS LATER

In my Presidential Address and journal article (Hill, 1996a), as well as in two books (Hill, 1996b, 2004), I have asserted that dreams are psychologically meaningful expressions of personality and thus can be used in psychotherapy to lead to greater self-understanding. I proposed a model for working with dreams that involves a three-stage collaborative model of exploration of the major images, overall insight into the meaning of the dream, and action based on understanding the meaning of the dream. I described four studies that examined the effects of this model. I noted that the results were "contradictory, with two studies indicating that dream interpretation using this model is helpful compared with other conditions, and two indicating that it is not more helpful than other conditions" (Hill, 1996a, p. 13).

Since this article was published in 1996, my students and I have conducted more than 25 studies on this model. Along the way, we have modified and improved the model based on training therapists and incorporating research findings. At this point, we have convincing evidence that the model is effective. In this section of the chapter, I briefly review the extant research on the effectiveness of the model and what makes the model effective. I also describe our current work, describe future possibilities for research on dreams in psychotherapy, and draw conclusions about the role of dream work in psychotherapy.

Is Dream Work Effective?

In a recent review of our work (Hill & Knox, 2010), several findings stand out. After dream sessions (most typically, single sessions with volunteer clients), clients have consistently evaluated single dream sessions much higher in depth (i.e., quality, satisfaction), working alliance, and session impact than did clients in regular psychotherapy sessions. In addition, those clients who participated in dream work as compared with loss work using the same model gave higher ratings of depth throughout the course of brief psychotherapy when clients had both troubling dreams and recent loss. We speculated that clients evaluated dream sessions so highly because they came in with specific dreams that they wanted to understand and left feeling good that they had gotten what they came for.

In addition, we found substantial evidence that dream work led to the specific changes that are the focus of the model. Thus, as would be predicted, clients reported gaining insight, ideas for action, major gains in the target problem represented in their dreams, and more positive attitudes toward dreams. In terms of more standard measures of symptomatology and interpersonal functioning, there were mixed findings, which is not surprising given that these concerns were not necessarily reflected in the dreams. It makes more sense to assess outcomes more directly related to dream work than to general functioning.

In conclusion, we can solidly assert that dream work using the Hill model is effective. Clients reported liking working with dreams; they gained insight and ideas for action; they made improvements in their target complaints; and they became more positive in their attitudes toward dreams.

What Makes Dream Work Effective?

In a number of studies involving both qualitative and quantitative methods, we found evidence for the effectiveness of the components of the model. Specifically, we found that both description and associations were helpful aspects of the exploration stage. In the insight stage, we found that focusing on waking life, parts of self, relationship insight, and spiritual insight were all helpful. We also found that inclusion of the action stage was important for the client to gain ideas for action and that the quality of the action stage predicted implementation of action. Clients consistently reported that the most helpful aspects of dream work were gaining insight, associations, links to waking life, catharsis, having an objective perspective, and working with a therapist. They did not consistently report anything as unhelpful.

In terms of therapist variables, working with a therapist as compared with working alone (using paper-and-pencil or computer prompts) was preferred and led to better outcome. Furthermore, therapist probes for insight were found to be the most consistently effective intervention.

In terms of client variables, only about 20–30 percent of undergraduates volunteer for dream sessions. Those who volunteered had very positive attitudes toward dreams and high dream recall. Once people volunteered for dream sessions, client involvement in the sessions was crucial in predicting outcome.

In sum, all of the components of the model that have been examined thus far have been found to be helpful.

Recent Research

All of the above research was conducted in a laboratory where therapists adhered closely to the dream model. Although these findings provide convincing evidence for the model when delivered in its controlled state, the findings offer little for the practicing clinician. As one example, the typical session in the research was 90 minutes, whereas most therapists offer 45- to 50-minute sessions. Furthermore, volunteer research clients only discussed dreams, whereas clients in ongoing psychotherapy focus mostly on other topics and might only occasionally bring up dreams.

Our recent efforts were thus involved in assessing what therapists who have been trained in the Hill dream model do in open-ended psychodynamic psychotherapy (Hill et al., 2013). Therapists were randomly assigned to indicate or not to indicate in the first session that they like to work with dreams. Interestingly, this manipulation made no difference in whether dreams were discussed or in the process or outcome of therapy. In terms of the extent of dream work, we found that half of the clients presented at least one dream, with an average of 13 minutes spent discussing the dream. The clients who discussed dreams had more positive attitudes about dreams and lower attachment anxiety than their counterparts. In terms of therapist activities in working with the dreams, therapists mostly listened and asked for description of the images. Clients who talked about dreams did so because they wanted insight or had troubling dreams; they found the dream work to be helpful. Clients who did not talk about dreams did not remember dreams and thought other issues were more important to discuss in therapy.

Of 13 therapists in our clinic, nine had dreams about their clients (Hill et al., 2014). These therapists had higher dream recall than did their counterparts. The clients who were dreamed about had higher pre-therapy interpersonal distress, higher therapist-rated session evaluation, and more therapist-rated transference and countertransference than their counterparts. Therapists found that examining these dreams helped them work better with the clients. Interestingly, only two of the 67 clients, both of whom had high attachment anxiety, had dreams about their therapists.

Implications

Implications for Practice

Given the compelling evidence for the effectiveness of working with dreams, I suggest that therapists work with dreams either in single sessions or in ongoing psychotherapy. Dream work seems particularly appropriate when clients bring in troubling dreams or nightmares and when they like to work with dreams.

I do not advocate that therapists should work with dreams with all clients. Not all clients remember their dreams, and some are not interested in working with dreams. It makes sense for therapists to mention early in treatment that it is possible to discuss dreams and also to ask about dreams during impasses, plateaus, when clients mention dreams, and when clients indicate an interest in learning more about themselves. Furthermore, given that dreams are a hallmark of post-traumatic stress disorder, it makes sense to ask about nightmares when clients have experienced trauma.

I also strongly believe that therapists need to be trained in how to work with dreams. They do not need to follow my model, but they do need to listen to dreams and help client gain insight and ideas for action. Given that graduate programs may not prepare students for working with dreams, therapists may need to train themselves by reading books and attending workshops.

In summary, dream work can be a powerful tool in psychotherapy when therapists are trained to do such work and clients are amenable to such work. As one of my students noted, dreams are a way of going in the back door and allowing the client to talk about thoughts and feelings that they might not otherwise address in psychotherapy. It is also sometimes fun and engaging to work with dreams and help therapists get to know clients in a different way.

Implications for Research

Although I started investigating dream work as a stand-alone intervention, I think that the cutting edge of research is now in the integration of emotionally evocative events such as dream work into ongoing psychotherapy. We need to ask the who, what, when, and where questions to provide evidence to guide practitioners in the judicious use of such events in psychotherapy.

Furthermore, we need to know more about how such emotionally evocative events ultimately lead to change. In other words, it may be that, once a therapeutic alliance is established, the therapist engages the client in a series of emotionally evocative events that cumulatively build toward reconstructive change. This sequence could be studied.

Note

1 The first part of this chapter is a condensation and modification of my presidential address, and the resulting journal article (1996a). The second part is taken from two books on dream work (Hill 1996b, 2004) and a review of the literature (Hill & Knox, 2010).

7

THE INTERPERSONAL INTERIOR OF PSYCHOTHERAPY (1998)[1]

Paul Crits-Christoph

From Freud's (1912/1958) discussion of the concept of transference through the object relations theories of Klein (1948) and Winnicott (1958) and the interpersonal psychoanalytic perspective of Sullivan (1953), psychodynamic theories have focused on the interpersonal world of the psychotherapy participants as central to the treatment process. Modern schools of brief psychodynamic therapy (Benjamin, 1991; Luborsky, 1984; Strupp & Binder, 1984) have continued this focus and added explicit methods of identifying interpersonal themes during psychotherapy sessions. The interest in interpersonal processes, however, is not unique to psychodynamic schools, with other treatments such as Klerman, Weissman, Rounsaville, and Chevron's (1984) interpersonal therapy for depression and Safran and Segal's (1990) cognitive-interpersonal perspective also placing interpersonal processes in one form or another as central to the psychotherapy model.

Interpersonal processes in psychotherapy in terms of the quality of the patient-therapist relationship (the therapeutic alliance) have been a major focus within psychotherapy research over the past 15 years, and, indeed, the alliance has been found to be a consistent predictor of treatment outcome across a wide range of different psychotherapies (Horvath & Symonds, 1991). There has also been renewed interest in interpersonal diagnosis and interpersonal factors in psychopathology (Benjamin, 1993b; Horowitz & Vitkus, 1986). Research in personality and social psychology has also evidenced substantial interest in interpersonal themes and "schemas" (Singer & Salovey, 1991).

There are a variety of ways to investigate interpersonal processes in psychotherapy. Research can focus on patient's interpersonal problems and the extent to which these problems change over treatment or predict changes in symptoms (e.g., Davies-Osterkamp, Strauss, & Schmitz, 1996; Horowitz, Rosenberg, Bauer, Ureño, & Villaseñor, 1988). The efficacy of treatment approaches that have an interpersonal emphasis can be investigated (e.g., Elkin et al., 1989; Frank, Kupfer, Perel, & Comes, 1990). Studies have coded how patients and therapists are behaving towards each other during sessions (e.g., Henry, Schacht, & Strupp, 1986). As mentioned, investigations of the quality of the therapeutic alliance have yielded important data about psychotherapy.

An additional window into patients' interpersonal worlds and the therapy process is the examination of the stories or narratives that patients tell during sessions. One of the programs of research at the Center for Psychotherapy Research at the University of Pennsylvania has focused on narratives told during psychotherapy sessions. The purpose of this article is to review this program of research, with attention to three questions: (1) How consistent are interpersonal themes across different narratives told by patients in psychotherapy? (2) What can narratives reveal about the patient-therapist relationship? and (3) What is the impact of therapist interventions as they relate to interpersonal themes apparent in narratives? In the original version of this article (Crits-Christoph, 1998), I also reviewed data on the reliability of identifying narratives in sessions and the frequency and quality of narratives (see the original article for information on these topics).

The Content of Narratives: Consistency of Themes

The primary system that we have employed in our research on the interpersonal themes contained in narratives is the CCRT method (Luborsky, 1977). Details of this method and a compilation of early studies using the instrument have been presented elsewhere (Luborsky & Crits-Christoph, 1990). These studies, among others, include investigations of the reliability of scoring CCRT patterns in narratives (Crits-Christoph, Luborsky, Dahl, Popp, Mellon, & Mark, 1988), changes in CCRT patterns over the course of dynamic psychotherapy (Crits-Christoph & Luborsky, 1990), and CCRT patterns in dreams versus narratives (Popp, Diguer, Luborsky, & Faude, 1996). Here I will briefly describe the essence of the CCRT method and then review some of the more recent studies involving a variant of the CCRT.

The CCRT method uses clinical judges to formulate three main components of interpersonal patterns: the patient's wishes or needs in interpersonal situations, the perceived responses of others toward the patient, and the consequent responses of the patient (responses of self). Judges independently read the relationship episodes located in sessions for each patient (usually a minimum of 10 episodes per patient contained in each episode). After reading all episodes for a particular patient, judges reread episodes and modify their scoring of each based upon their understanding of the material obtained from reading all episodes. The final CCRT is derived by listing the highest-frequency wishes, responses from other, and responses of self across all episodes for a patient.

A modification of the CCRT method, termed the Quantitative Assessment of Interpersonal Themes (QUAINT; Crits-Christoph, Demorest, & Connolly,

1990) was used in some of the more recent studies. The QUAINT method modified the original CCRT system in three ways: (1) relationship episodes with identifying information deleted or modified are extracted from transcripts and episodes from different patients are randomly sorted (so that judges cannot identify which episodes come from the same patient and each episode is scored independently from others); (2) a well-validated standard vocabulary, the Structural Analysis of Social Behavior system (SASB; Benjamin, 1974), is used for coding wishes, responses of the other, and responses of the self; and (3) each episode is rated (on a 1 to 5 scale) on all categories, revealing a detailed picture of the full breadth of possible contents of each episode. These refinements to the CCRT method were made so that more objective studies of the patterns of interpersonal elements across different narratives within an individual could be performed. Moreover, the use of SASB categories provides an anchoring of the research method to a theoretically derived model of interpersonal behavior, rather than relying on the empirical categories that evolved within the context of the original CCRT method.

An example of two relationship episodes rated using the QUAINT system is displayed in Figure 7.1. Although the full QUAINT rating system utilizes 104 different categories (32 wishes, 32 responses from other, 40 responses of self), our studies have typically found 29 to 38 of these items are rated with sufficient reliability (i.e., greater than .65 interjudge reliability) to retain for analysis. Figure 7.1 depicts the mean ratings (averaged across three judges) for 12 wishes, 12 responses from other, and 14 responses of self for a relationship episode about

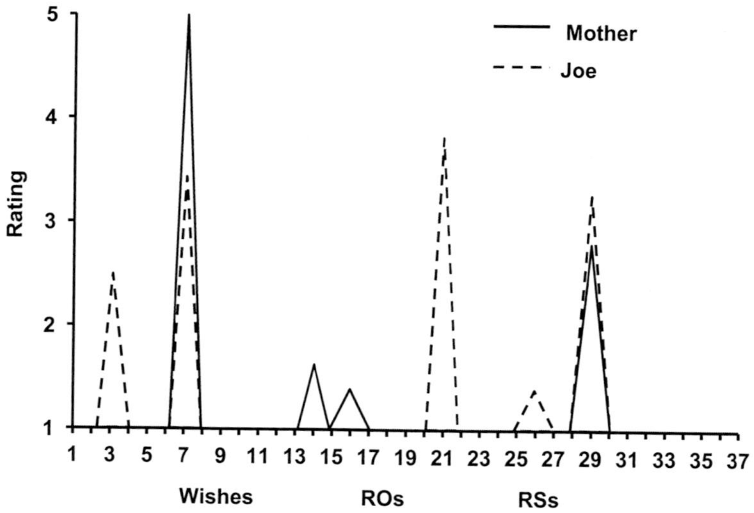

FIGURE 7.1 Ratings of Wishes, Responses from Other (ROs), and Responses of Self (RSs) on Two Narratives

a friend Joe and another episode from the same patient about the patient's mother. The episode about Joe was characterized by high ratings on the wish "to be nurturing and protecting" and the wish "to be asserting and separating." The main response from other was "is trusting and relying," and the highest rated response of self was "feels constrained and helpless." The episode about mother was also characterized by the wish "to be asserting and separating" and the response of self "feels constrained and helpless." No response from other was rated highly on the episode about mother. The profile of ratings on the episode about Joe can be compared to the profile of ratings on the episode about mother by computing a Pearson correlation across the two profiles. In this case, the correlation was .64, indicating a high degree of similarity of the profiles, as was evident from the inspection of the individual items.

This method of comparison of profiles within individual episodes was used by Crits-Christoph, Demorest, Muenz, and Baranackie (1994) to examine the consistency of interpersonal themes across all episodes told by patients during three early-in-treatment therapy sessions. About 10 narratives from each of 60 patients from the Woody et al. (1983) study of cognitive therapy and psychodynamic therapy for opiate addiction were rated by three independent judges using the QUAINT system. For each patient, the 38-item QUAINT profiles for every relationship episode were correlated with all other episodes for that patient and the average correlation between narratives was computed. Because these average correlations were computed between profiles within each patient, standard statistical significance tests were not likely to be appropriate. In order to control for chance levels of correlations among profiles, we conducted permutational tests (Gibbons, 1985). The permutational tests provided a baseline level of correlation that would occur by chance. This approach involved comparing the correct average correlation among profiles to an average correlation obtained from randomly rearranging (permuting) the items for each profile being compared (i.e., item 1 on narrative 1 matches up randomly with for example item 17 from narrative 2, and so on). The random permutations were performed 1,000 times for the profile on each narrative, and the correct average correlation was compared to the distribution of average correlations obtained from the permutations.

The major finding revealed from this analysis was that there was a typically small average correlation of narrative profiles within a patient. Patients' average correlations ranged from .00 to .44, with a median .13 (Crits-Christoph et al., 1994). Based upon the permutational tests, consistency of interpersonal themes across narratives was found for 49 of the 60 patients. Thus, although the results showed low consistency of interpersonal themes on average across patients, there was wide variability in the pervasiveness of interpersonal themes and most patients demonstrated consistency that was greater than would be expected by chance. No patients, however, demonstrated a single theme that cut across all narratives.

These findings have led us to reject the notion that the same interpersonal theme is likely to be apparent in all narratives. In subsequent research (described below), we have moved on to methods that permit a multiplicity of themes across a set of narratives for a patient. The fact that some degree of repetitiveness of interpersonal themes is discernible in narratives, however, is an important step in validating an aspect of the concept of transference as a mental representation that is applied to ongoing and new relationships in a patient's life. In the next section, I describe how we have used narratives to investigate more specifically the clinical phenomena of transference in the therapeutic relationship in particular.

The Content of Narratives About the Therapist

Patients often tell narratives about their therapist. For example, patients will sometimes recount in sessions something the therapist had previously said to them and how they reacted to it. Relationship episodes that are "enactments," occurring in real time between the patient and therapist, also occur. The CCRT method provides an opportunity to study the content of these relationship episodes involving the therapist. Of primary interest is whether the patterns that are played out with the therapist are similar or different from the patterns that are evident in patients' other relationships outside of therapy (i.e., the clinical notion of transference in the therapeutic relationship). We have performed three studies to date attempting to examine this fundamental clinical notion.

The first of these studies (Fried, Crits-Christoph, & Luborsky, 1992) used the original CCRT method as applied to relationship episodes involving the therapist versus all other relationship episodes. For 35 patients in dynamic psychotherapy, a set of three judges rated the similarity of the CCRT patterns in therapist episodes versus CCRT patterns in "other people" episodes. For each patient, the judges also rated the similarity of the therapist episode CCRT patterns to CCRTs derived from other patients, in order to control for chance levels of similarity. The results indicated a beyond chance level of similarity for the wish and response of self components of the CCRT, but not for the response from other component. Further exploratory analyses revealed that the level of similarity increased when more relationship episodes involving the therapist were available, probably as a result of a more reliable therapist CCRT pattern emerging as the number of episodes about the therapist increased.

Since this first study (Fried et al., 1992) used the original CCRT method, it was limited by the fact that the CCRT judges scored the therapist relationship episodes and other person episodes together as a set (i.e., they were aware of which narratives were about the therapist and which were about other people for each patient, and in fact revised their scorings of each after reading the entire set). In our next study of relationship episodes involving the therapist, we employed the QUAINT method that keeps judges unaware of which narratives come from which patient. Moreover, the QUAINT method provides a more complete profile of wishes, responses from other, and responses of self on each narrative. In this second study (Connolly, Crits-Christoph, Demorest, Azarian, Muenz, & Chittams, 1996), 35 of the 60 opiate-dependent patients examined in the study by Crits-Christoph et al. (1994) were selected based on the occurrence of at least one narrative told about the therapist. Based upon the Crits-Christoph et al. (1994) results showing only a small degree of consistency of themes across all relationship episodes, we rejected the concept that the CCRT pattern would apply to all episodes.

Rather than relying on the CCRT pattern that emerges as highest in frequency across all narratives, for the Connolly et al. (1996) study we implemented a methodology involving cluster analyses of themes for each patient. The 38-item QUAINT profiles for each patient's narratives were intercorrelated and cluster-analyzed. A median inter-narrative correlation of at least .30 was selected to define a cluster. Figure 7.2 shows an example of a cluster analysis of the full set of narratives told by the patient who related the two narratives displayed in Figure 7.1. As can be seen, the two highly intercorrelated narratives about Joe and mother form one cluster, another cluster is defined by similar episodes about a girlfriend and father, a third cluster contains narratives about a probation officer and a friend, Pete, and a fourth cluster involves stories about a landlord, parents, a friend's (Karen's) parents, and a doctor. The distinct themes contained in each of these clusters of narratives can then be examined in terms of their degree of similarity to therapist narratives.

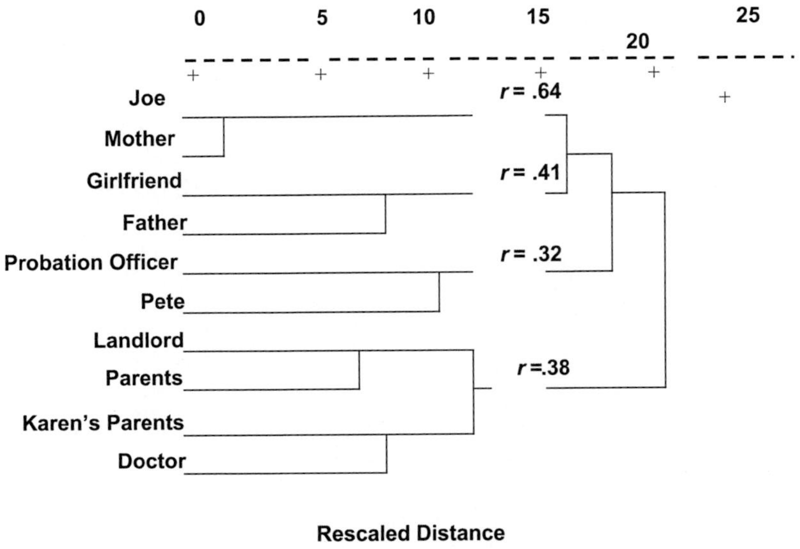

FIGURE 7.2 Cluster Analysis of One Patient's Narratives Based upon Interpersonal Content

We obtained a similar set of clusters of narratives for each of the 35 patients in the study. For each cluster, a mean profile was computed by averaging across the narratives in that cluster. The cluster that contained the greatest number of narrative profiles was labeled the *main cluster*. All cluster profiles were then correlated with the narrative profile about the therapist for each patient. Permutational tests were once again employed to evaluate statistical significance.

The results of the Connolly et al. (1996) investigation revealed that all patients in the sample had at least one cluster that contained multiple relationship episodes, supporting the hypothesis that patients demonstrate similar interpersonal themes across at least some relationships in their lives. Furthermore, the majority of patients had more than one cluster of narratives, indicating that several themes are often apparent. The comparison of "other-person" narratives with the therapist relationship episodes revealed a significant correlation between some cluster profile and the therapist profile for 60 percent of the patients. The main cluster showed a significant correlation with the therapist profile for 34 percent of patients.

One alternative explanation for the similarity found between therapist relationship episodes and other episodes is that therapists might create the existence of a pattern. There are several ways this might happen. First, a given therapist might be a stimulus for creating a particular interpersonal theme in the patient-therapist relationship. For example, a patient who has problems with dependency might elicit rejecting behaviors from a therapist who is uncomfortable with the dependency that the patient is displaying. The patient then tells a narrative about how he or she felt rejected by the therapist last session, the same way he or she feels rejected by others. In this case there is still a transferential element (the patient brings pre-existing schemas to the problematic relationship transaction), but the other person also contributes (i.e., countertransference response by therapist). In a variant of this possibility, a given therapist might have a subtle rejecting (or at least disaffiliative) stance with all patients, and this leads to the activation of a *transference* pattern in the therapeutic relationship for those patients who have a sensitivity about rejection (this would be an example of a poor patient-therapist "fit").

Another way in which similarity between therapist episodes and other episodes might occur is when the patient does have a repetitive interpersonal theme displayed in outside-of-therapy relationships, and the therapist interprets this theme as relevant to the therapeutic relationship, although in fact there was no evidence for this theme in the patient-therapist relationship (i.e., no transference to the therapist has occurred). Psychodynamic therapists who are prone to overinterpret transference to the therapist might display this type of inaccurate formulation of the nature of the patient-therapist relationship, and may convince the patient of this formulation. The patient might then be prompted to tell a story about the therapist that appears to fit the therapist's conclusion, thereby producing similarity of the outside of therapy narratives to the therapist relationship episodes. In another extreme example, a therapist might elicit a whole series of narratives about other people that contain material that appear to confirm the therapist's inaccurate formulation. Neither the theme in the patient-therapist narratives nor the theme in the other-person narratives is accurate in this scenario, but the themes resemble each other due to the persuasive powers of the therapist in convincing the patient that the formulation is correct.

In the Connolly et al. (1996) investigation, an equal degree of correlation of main cluster profiles with therapist profiles occurred for cognitive therapy and psychodynamic therapy. However, dynamic therapy did reveal significantly higher correlations of secondary clusters with therapist narratives, while cognitive therapy revealed significantly higher correlations between single narratives (unrelated to other narratives in their content) and the therapist relationship episodes. The extent to which these findings reflect the therapist inaccurately formulating what is going on in the patient-therapist relationship, and subsequently eliciting narratives from the patient that appear to be in line with this formulation, versus differential skills of dynamic and cognitive therapists at examination of repetitive themes (dynamic) or situational specificity (cognitive-behavioral), cannot be unraveled from the data, but raises intriguing possibilities for further investigations.

While none of these alternative explanations is easy to rule out, we have conducted a third study of the similarity of therapist narratives and other person narratives in an attempt to disentangle the influence of the therapist. In this study (Connolly, Crits-Christoph, Barber, & Luborsky, 1997), narratives about other people were obtained from patients before therapy began through the use of a semi-structured interview, and therapist narratives were obtained from treatment sessions. These data were part of a larger study (Diguer, Barber, & Luborsky, 1993) of brief dynamic therapy for major depression. For 18 patients that had at least one therapist relationship episode, QUAINT ratings were made of the narratives obtained pre-therapy, and a second set of QUAINT judges rated therapist narratives obtained from the treatment sessions. The results were very consistent with the previous study (Connolly et al., 1996), with 50 percent of patients showing a moderate or greater degree of similarity between a multiple narrative cluster and the therapist thematic profile, and the main cluster displaying such similarity for 33 percent of the patients.

The general findings from these three studies of the therapeutic relationship as revealed in narratives are: (1) transference to the therapist does occur, but it is not detectable with our methods for all patients (only about half); (2) the theme "transferred" to the relationship with the therapist is not always the most pervasive interpersonal theme; and (3) the therapist does not appear to "create" the themes in the therapeutic relationship. These studies, however, are all limited by the use of early-in-treatment sessions (usually sessions 3–6) to examine the patient-therapist relationship. Early-in-treatment sessions were used in these investigations because of the emphasis in brief therapy on rapid formulation and intervention. However, a study (Crits-Christoph, Demorest, & Connolly, 1990) of a single patient using a preliminary version of the QUAINT method found that, in fact, similarity of other person and therapist themes did not occur during the first half of a 31-session treatment, but did emerge during the second half.

Therapists' Interventions Based upon Formulations from Narratives

If transference to the therapist does occur, does this suggest that the often recommended psychodynamic technique of interpretation of the transference themes in the patient-therapist relationship is the most effective way to induce change over the course of treatment? Literature on the frequency of transference interpretations has been reviewed by Henry, Strupp, Schacht, & Gaston (1994), who found little support for the notion that relatively more interpretation of the patient-therapist relationship produced better outcomes. In fact, several more recent studies (Connolly, Crits-Christoph, Shappell, Barber, & Luborsky, 1997; Høglend, 1993; Piper, Joyce, McCallum, & Azim, 1993) have actually found that high rates of interpretation of the patient-therapist relationship actually is associated with poor outcome, at least for some meaningful subgroups of patients. These negative findings are perhaps not surprising in light of our data indicating that about half of patients in brief therapy do not show a marked *transference-to-the-therapist* effect, at least during early-in-treatment sessions. Therapists who focus to a large extent on the therapeutic relationship, when in fact there is not much evidence for transference in the therapeutic relationship, probably elicit negative or at least perplexed reactions about therapy. However, despite the lack of transference effects found in the therapeutic relationship, and the emerging literature on the negative effects of high rates of transference interpretation, there are a number of reasons why it is premature to abandon research attention on the role of transference in the therapeutic relationship. It may be that attention to such transference is particularly relevant to a subgroup of patients (e.g., patients with borderline personality disorder), although less relevant to many other patients. It may also be that, while high rates of transference interpretation are problematic, a single, well-timed interpretation about the therapeutic relationship might have an important impact.

Rather than focusing on the frequency of a certain kind of intervention (e.g., those relating to the patient-therapist relationship), our research on interpersonal themes in narratives has oriented us toward the examination of the accuracy of therapists' interventions. Accuracy is assessed as the extent to which a therapist addressed the interpersonal themes that are contained within narratives. The assessment of accuracy mirrors the process in which therapists engage while conducting Luborsky's (1984) supportive-expressive dynamic therapy: therapists first listen to patients' descriptions of their interactions with others, then formulate a CCRT pattern, and interpret this pattern to the patient, maintaining this focus in a brief dynamic therapy. Note that accuracy refers to the therapist's response to the patient's general interpersonal themes (i.e., outside of therapy relationships), not specifically to themes in the relationship with the therapist.

Our research method for assessing accuracy involves the following steps: (1) locating narratives in sessions; (2) rating interpersonal themes in these narratives using either the original CCRT method or the QUAINT method; (3) identifying and extracting the main therapist interventions during sessions (e.g., interpretations); and (4) rating the extent to which each intervention addresses each component of the CCRT (i.e., wishes, responses from other, responses of self). Each of these rating tasks is performed by separate sets of judges working independently.

An example, taken from Crits-Christoph, Barber, and Kurcias (1993), can serve to illustrate our concept of accuracy. The CCRT (using the original method) formulated by clinical judges on one patient contained one wish (to make contact with others, to be close), two negative responses from other (critical, unhelpful), and two responses of self (uninvolved with people, anxious). This patient's therapist made the following interpretation in one session:

> My thought about it runs as follows: if you get close to somebody else, your perception is that they can then control you and make you do things and tell you to do things and . . . not wanting to be controlled would make a distance between you and others.

This therapist statement was rated as accurate on the wish (to be close) and on the first response of self (uninvolved with people), but not accurate on the responses from other or the second response of self (anxious).

Using this methodology, we have examined the relation of accuracy to outcome, attrition, and the alliance. In the first study of accuracy, Crits-Christoph, Cooper, and Luborsky (1988) assessed accuracy of interpretations drawn from two early-in-treatment sessions for 43 patients seen in moderate length (about one year) dynamic psychotherapy. It was found that accuracy on the main wishes and the responses from others was significantly related ($r = .44$, $p < .011$) to treatment outcome, even after controlling for the effects of general errors in technique and the quality of the therapeutic alliance. Accuracy relative to negative responses of self was not related to outcome. These findings suggest that when therapists accurately address the interpersonal aspects of patient material (i.e., the wishes towards others and their expected or actual responses), rather than on patients' feeling states (i.e., the response of self component of the CCRT), greater progress results.

A subsequent study investigated the relation of accuracy of intervention to the development of the therapeutic alliance (Crits-Christoph, Barber, & Kurcias, 1993). The results of the study indicated that a composite accuracy on the wish and response from other dimensions of the CCRT correlated significantly with the change in the alliance from early to later (about nine months) in treatment. This finding was independent of the impact of psychological health-sickness on the alliance. When accuracy was low, initially positive alliance deteriorated and poor initial alliances did not improve. Thus, the quality of the relationship with the therapist is not simply a function of what the patient brings to therapy, but appears to be influenced by the technical interventions made by the therapist.

The concept of accuracy of intervention has also been examined by other investigators. Piper, Joyce, McCallum, and Azim (1993) found that the correspondence of interpretations with the therapist's initial dynamic formulation was significantly related to outcome in a sample of 64 patients treated with brief dynamic therapy. Silberschatz, Fretter, and Curtis (1986) found that, for each of three patients, the extent to which therapists' interpretations accurately addressed an independently derived patient formulation predicted a more positive immediate response to interpretations. Following up on the Silberschatz et al. (1986) study, Norville, Sampson, and Weiss (1996) added four more patients for a total sample of seven and found that average therapist accuracy was highly correlated with treatment outcome.

Although the concept of accuracy emerged from a psychodynamic tradition, we were also interested in the extent to which it applied to other forms of therapy. It may be, for example, that effective cognitive-behavioral therapists also focus on the repetitive maladaptive relationship themes of their patients, albeit using the models and language of a cognitive-behavioral perspective. We examined accuracy in relation to dropping out of therapy in a sample of 34 opiate-dependent patients treated with cognitive therapy drawn from the Woody et al. (1983) clinical trial. The results indicated that accuracy of interpretation related significantly to treatment duration in cognitive therapy (Crits-Christoph & Baranackie, 1991). Among the cases where there was a low level of accuracy (below the median), none of the patients had stayed in treatment longer than 10 sessions. Where there was a higher level of accuracy, 39 percent of the patients stayed in treatment longer than 10 sessions. Ongoing research will examine the relation of accuracy to outcome, including relapse and recurrence of symptoms, following both cognitive and interpersonal therapies.

The possibility that accuracy of addressing interpersonal themes is a cross-theoretical idea raises the question of whether it is similar to the clinical concept of empathy that is important to many schools of psychotherapy. However, our measure of accuracy refers more specifically to an interpersonal pattern, the elements of the CCRT (wishes, responses from other, responses of self), rather than referring to an understanding of what the patient is expressing or feeling at the moment. We have examined this relation directly, correlating a measure of Rogerian qualities (the Facilitative Conditions subscale of the Collaborative Study Psychotherapy Rating Scale; Hill, O'Grady, & Elkin, 1992) with accuracy of intervention. For patients in both dynamic ($r = .08$, $p > .10$) and cognitive ($r = -.26$, $p > .10$) therapies, no statistically significant relationship between these measures was apparent (Crits-Christoph, 1991).

Conclusions and Recommendations

Narratives about interactions with other people provide one window into understanding repetitive interpersonal themes. Our approach to the study of narratives has combined an idiographic method (cluster analyses of individual patient's data) with a nomothetic method (standard categories of interpersonal behavior based upon SASB). This combined idiographic and nomothetic method has potential for capturing clinically relevant phenomena at the individual level, but in terms that are generalizable to larger group of patients. Thus, this methodological contribution can serve to advance research on interpersonal processes in psychotherapy.

At a substantive level, the findings from our studies on the nature of interpersonal themes in psychotherapy are more consistent with models that emphasize multiple patterns, rather than one theme. The extent to which each of a patient's themes are differentially related to the process of therapy (e.g., the alliance) and treatment outcome remain interesting questions for further research. Studies of therapist accuracy in addressing interpersonal themes in therapy will need to take into account the multiplicity of themes that are apparent.

We can also speculate on several implications of our findings for clinical practice. If a therapist is interested in focusing on interpersonal processes in therapy, our data suggest that by modifying his or her treatment model and attending to the quality of the alliance the therapist can encourage the articulation of more and better-quality narratives by patients, thereby providing ample clinical material for formulating interpersonal dynamics. Another implication of our findings for practice relates to the degree of focus on the patient-therapist relationship. While our studies suggest that transference to the therapist does occur, it is not apparent in all patients (at least, early in treatment). The implication for the practice of brief therapy is that a high level of focus on therapeutic relationship is probably not indicated for many patients. Therapeutic attention to interpersonal themes in outside-of-therapy relationships (i.e., transference in everyday life) may be a sufficient, if not superior, method of inducing change.

The study of interpersonal processes in psychotherapy is an inherently arduous and complex task, and definitive causal connections are difficult to establish. Nevertheless, the research by our group and others to date suggests that it is possible to study these phenomena and that some of the therapeutic action of psychodynamic as well as cognitive-behavioral treatments is likely to involve in-session and out-of-session interpersonal processes. Unraveling the interpersonal mechanisms of change in psychotherapy may help us to construct more efficacious treatments, teach psychotherapy more effectively, and perhaps reveal information about the nature of psychopathology and human interaction in general.

COMMENTARY

THE INTERPERSONAL INTERIOR OF PSYCHOTHERAPY, REVISITED

My SPR Presidential address article (Crits-Christoph, 1998) focused on our ongoing research that used interpersonal narratives as a basic unit of analysis in psychotherapy research. In my article, I reviewed our studies on the reliability of locating interpersonal narratives in psychotherapy and then presented studies of the frequency and correlates of narratives in sessions. Further studies presented included investigations that used interpersonal narratives as a window into the patient–therapist relationship, particularly as an assessment of transference themes enacted with the therapist. Finally, I described the use of interpersonal narratives as a method to uncover core conflictual relationship themes and then assess therapists' ability to formulate and accurately interpret the relationship themes that are apparent in narratives.

As a review of a narrow field of research, I can't say there is anything I would now change in the article, with one exception: I would change the title. Although I thought the title ("The interpersonal interior of psychotherapy') was a compelling one, it was too broad a descriptor. Concepts like the therapeutic alliance, not specifically reviewed in my article, would be included in this description and therefore a more specific title that addresses the use of interpersonal narratives in psychotherapy research would have been better.

My goal here is to provide a brief update of research related to the topics I discussed in my Presidential Address article. Although my Address article was largely constrained to the program of research that myself and my colleagues had conducted, in the current article I will also describe research conducted by others on this topic. However, I do not view my Presidential Address article as likely influencing these other research efforts, particularly since many of these efforts had origins that predated my Address. Following the update of research on the topics that I touched upon in my Presidential Address article, I conclude with some speculations on the future of research on psychotherapy.

New Research on Interpersonal Themes within Patient Narratives

The importance of narratives in psychotherapy and psychotherapy research has received substantial attention in the years before and following my Presidential Address. There are clinical approaches that focus on narratives in psychotherapy (see Angus & McLeod, 2004; Lieblich, McAdams, & Josselson, 2004). Two special issues of journals have been devoted to research on narratives in psychotherapy (Gonçalves & Stiles, 2011; Machado & Gonçalves, 1999). Most of the other approaches to narratives in psychotherapy, however, take a somewhat different approach than the approach that guided the research I presented in my

Presidential Address article. Specifically, many of the other approaches to narratives have a primary interest in the patient's life-narrative or self-narrative, i.e., the story that patients tell themselves about their lives in order to construct meaning out of their experiences. Our use of the concept of narratives centers on the stories that patients tell in psychotherapy sessions about their interactions with other people. Such narratives, labeled "relationship episodes" in our research, are of interest in their own right but primarily also as a part of a method to identify patients' core conflictual relationship themes (CCRT; Luborsky & Crits-Christoph, 1998).

Subsequent to the publication of my article, there have been a number of studies that used our method of identifying relationship episodes in psychotherapy sessions. A search of PsycInfo reveals 114 articles since 1998 that address core conflictual relationship themes. However, many of these articles were single case studies or relied upon narratives told by patients outside of psychotherapy (i.e., in an interview). A selected few examples of studies that used narratives obtained within psychotherapy sessions are described below.

The relationship between CCRTs in therapy and defensive functioning was examined by de Roten, Drapeau, Stigler, and Despland (2004). Using 60 patients assessed early in brief therapy, the authors found many significant correlations between CCRT components and aspects of defenses. This study is particularly useful because the concept of defenses was largely ignored in the development of the CCRT method. Rather than being a completely distinct aspect of patient functioning, defenses are apparently intimately connected to CCRT patterns. Further theoretical development of the CCRT would be useful to better incorporate how defenses are involved in CCRTs.

In an attempt to replicate the findings of one of the studies (i.e., Crits-Christoph & Luborsky, 1990) that I reviewed in my Presidential Address article, Lunnen, Ogles, Anderson, and Barnes (2006) examined changes in the pervasiveness of CCRT patterns over the course of brief dynamic therapy. The authors found little change in the pervasiveness of CCRT patterns using one early session (session 3) and one later session (between 11 and 16) to measure change. In addition, unlike the findings of Crits-Christoph and Luborsky (1990), Lunnen et al. (2006) failed to find significant relationships between change in the CCRT and symptom improvement. The lack of findings in the Lunnen et al. (2006) study are likely due to the short timespan between the early and late sessions, the use of only one session's relationship episodes to score the CCRT at each point in time, and/or the type of treatment examined (the treatment had a very high focus on the relationship with the therapist rather than broader interpersonal themes). Another study (Bressi et al., 2000) reported findings replicating the Crits-Christoph and Luborsky (1990) study, further suggesting that the lack of findings in the Lunnen et al. (2006) study is likely due to the methods of that study.

A study by Sommerfeld et al. (2008) explored the relationship between the occurrence of ruptures in the working alliance and the emergence of CCRTs.

A total of 151 sessions from five therapies were included in the study. The main finding of the study was that alliance ruptures were positively related to the emergence of patients' CCRT during the session, but only when the therapist was addressed as the "other" in a relationship episode. The potential convergence of these two approaches (alliance ruptures and CCRT) appears to be a ripe area for further investigation.

Two studies specifically used interpersonal narratives in therapy to examine relationship themes transferred to the therapist. Beretta et al. (2007) examined the CCRT patterns of 40 patients in brief psychodynamic therapy. CCRTs in the relationship episodes with significant others were compared with relationship episodes with their therapist. The results indicated that 60 percent of patients displayed similar CCRT patterns with their therapist and with significant others. Interestingly, the CCRT patterns that were reenacted with the therapist were not necessarily the most pervasive patterns but were the patterns similar to those found in relationship episodes involving parents or romantic partners. These findings add to the earlier study by Fried, Crits-Christoph, and Luborsky (1992) reviewed in my Presidential Address article, and provide further support for the clinical concept of transference of repetitive relationship themes to the therapist.

In a second study of transference, Tellides et al. (2008) used the CCRT method to examine the manifestation of therapeutic transference in the first three sessions of therapy for 22 high-functioning individuals. Focusing on the "wish" and "response from other" components of the CCRT, the authors found a complementary pattern of relating in which the therapist is idealized and others are devalued by the patient. It is not clear if the failure to find more evidence for transference in this study was a function of only using the first three treatment sessions or perhaps a function of focusing only high-functioning patients. With high-functioning patients, it may be that transference patterns are more subtle and become evident only later in treatment.

Also bearing on the concept of transference was a study by Hamilton and Kivlighan (2009), who had therapists identify the CCRTs in relationship episodes taken from multiple patients. In addition, the therapists' own CCRTs were identified from narratives told by the therapists in an interview. This study then examined the degree to which therapists' views of the content of patient narratives was influenced by their own CCRT patterns. This is the first study to show that therapists' formulations of patient interpersonal themes may reflect, to some degree, a projection of their own issues.

New Research on the Interpretation of Relationship Themes

After the publication of my Presidential Address, there have been two studies that have used narratives told by patients during therapy to identify patients' central relationship problems and then rate the accuracy of therapists' interventions. The first was a study by Stigler et al. (2007). This study extended our original work on the accuracy of therapists' interventions in psychodynamic therapy by measuring therapist accuracy (related to the CCRT) and also the amount and type of conflict addressed in psychotherapeutic interpretations. Stigler et al. (2007) used transcribed texts from brief psychodynamic intervention interviews in 29 outpatients to rate for accuracy and for conflictuality. The results of the investigation were that the sum of accuracy and conflictuality scores, but neither one alone, was significantly related to the alliance. No significant relationships with outcome were found. Treatment, however, was very brief (four sessions) in this study. This study follows an earlier one by the same group in which a similar method of assessing the accuracy of therapists' interpretations was used to examine the accuracy relative to patient's defenses, as measured in therapy sessions (Junod et al., 2005).

The second study was conducted by our research group. While previous studies had focused on psychodynamic therapy, in this investigation (Crits-Christoph, Gibbons, Temes, Elkin, & Gallop, 2010) we sought to examine the role of interpersonally accurate interventions in cognitive therapy and interpersonal therapy. The interpersonal accuracy of interventions was rated using transcripts of treatment sessions for 72 patients who were being treated with cognitive or interpersonal therapy for major depressive disorder through the NIMH Treatment of Depression Collaborative Research Program (TDCRP; Elkin et al., 1989). A total of 288 early sessions and 260 late sessions were transcribed from the TDCRP archives of taped sessions and scored for the presence of relationship episodes. The CCRT patterns in these relationship episodes were then identified. In addition, all therapist statements were coded for type of statement and extracted from the transcripts. In a final step, specific therapist statements were rated for the extent to which the statement addressed the CCRT content unique to each patient.

Results of the study were that statistically significant interactions of interpersonal accuracy of interventions and treatment group (cognitive vs. interpersonal therapy) in relation to outcome were evident. Significant interaction effects were found for the prediction of change of depressive symptoms and social adjustment, with higher levels of interpersonal accuracy associated with relatively poorer outcomes for patients receiving cognitive therapy but relatively better outcomes for patients in interpersonal therapy. The reasons why interpersonally accurate interventions were not helpful in the context of cognitive therapy are not clear. One reason may be when cognitive therapists focus more on interpersonal issues, they have relatively less available time in sessions to implement standard cognitive therapy techniques. Implementing a range of different techniques within the context of a brief therapy may not be as effective as staying focused on a smaller set of interrelated techniques. Regardless of the reasons why interpersonally accurate intervention were helpful in interpersonal therapy but not helpful in cognitive therapy, this study illustrated that the use of patient narratives (relationship episodes) in psychotherapy sessions can shed useful light on the mechanisms of change of diverse psychotherapies.

The Future of Psychotherapy Research

The future of psychotherapy research is difficult to forecast. Certainly, as with real estate, the future of psychotherapy research depends on "location, location, location." By this, I mean that trends in the nature and focus of psychotherapy research will to some degree vary by country.

Within the United States, large-scale research on psychotherapy is shaped by funding priorities at the National Institutes of Health (NIH). Over the past decade, there have been several clear trends in priorities at two NIH institutes, the National Institute on Mental Health and the National Institute on Drug Abuse, that fund much of the larger-scale research of psychosocial treatments in the US.

One clear trend has been towards effectiveness research done in "real-world" community settings. This trend was initiated because of the view that much research conducted in academic settings (i.e., tightly controlled studies using carefully selected and trained therapists and homogeneous patient populations) would have little generalizability to the real world of clinical practice (Norquist, Lebowitz, & Hyman, 1999). Although this trend towards community-based effectiveness research started more than a decade ago, the time lag in studies receiving funding and being conducted would suggest that there will be publications on such studies emerging for a number of years to come. Along these lines, the National Institute on Drug Abuse created a national Clinical Trials Network to conduct many large-scale community-based clinical trials of treatments for substance use disorders (see http://drugabuse.gov/CTN). Over 30 large-scale studies have been conducted to date, though more recent studies have focused more on pharmacological interventions rather than psychosocial interventions. At the National Institute of Mental Health, recent priorities have shifted beyond simply testing the effectiveness of treatments in clinical settings towards research that informs the dissemination and implementation of evidence-based treatments in real-world settings.

These trends in funding priorities suggest that controlled efficacy studies and larger-scale studies of the process of psychotherapy, such as the ones that generated much of the research I covered in my Presidential Address article, will not be common, at least in the United States. However, there is one exception to this trend: In order to adequately disseminate treatments to community settings, it is necessary to train therapists and evaluate the adequacy of their training. Typically, this is done through rating tapes of psychotherapy sessions for therapist fidelity to a treatment model. A Funding Opportunity Announcement (see http://grants.nih.gov/grants/guide/rfa-files/RFA-MH-12-050.html) in 2011 called for studies designed to develop and test methods for improving the fidelity, and ultimately the effectiveness, of empirically supported psychosocial treatments implemented by frontline therapists in community practice settings. Studies funded through this announcement will emerge in the literature over the coming decade. We can anticipate a series of studies that help identify the most effective therapist techniques within evidence-based therapy packages.

Of course, much psychotherapy research will be conducted in the coming decade that is not influenced by funding priorities at NIH. The direction of such unfunded research is more difficult to predict. However, the nature of academia is that new investigators are rewarded for new ideas that go substantially beyond existing approaches. Therefore, I anticipate that, rather than sticking within the confines of current psychotherapy treatment models, there will be efforts to develop new treatment methods that likely incorporate developments from basic cognitive, social, and neuroscience research. Other approaches to improving patient outcomes, such as the use of outcomes assessments and feedback, will also likely continue to be a fruitful area for investigation in the coming years. Not knowing which, if any, of these various lines of research will ultimately pay off in terms of a noticeable improvement in treatment response rates is what continues to keep psychotherapy research a stimulating and challenging field of inquiry.

Note

1 Research reviewed in this manuscript was supported by grants P50-MH-45178, K02-MH00756., and R01-MH40472 funded by the National Institute of Mental Health. Correspondence concerning this chapter should be addressed to Paul Crits-Christoph, Ph.D., Department of Psychiatry, University of Pennsylvania, Room 650, 3535 Market St., Philadelphia, PA 19104; e-mail: crits@mail.med.upenn.edu

8

SIGNS AND VOICES IN PSYCHOTHERAPY (1999)

William B. Stiles

Psychotherapy is a laboratory as well as a treatment (Greenberg, 1991; Kvale, 1997; Thompson, 1987). It offers a more intimate access to human experience than does almost any other arena. As Len Horowitz (1994) pointed out, psychotherapy researchers have the truly privileged position of working with people who "open their hearts and, in a spirit of trust and optimism, reveal what is most private and personal" (p. 18). I think that from studying psychotherapy we can draw concepts and understandings about human thoughts, feelings, communication, and relationships that have a far wider application.

The phenomena with which psychotherapy researchers are most concerned, particularly significant psychological change, are not rare or unfamiliar. They occur in our offices every day—or at least on good days. Consequently, in psychotherapy research, our search is not so much for new discoveries as for clear ways to understand what we have already seen and heard.

I'll begin by outlining some simple but, I think, powerful ideas I am currently researching. The ideas are not original. I say this not from modesty, but from a theoretical position that will become clear shortly. As you read, many of you will recognize your own ideas or ideas borrowed from others you know. Then I will offer a retrospective, to show you how I got here, before I return to my newer interests.

The powerful ideas are *sign* and *voice* (Honos-Webb & Stiles, 1998; Leiman, 1992, 1997; Stiles, 1997b). Much of the work I am doing in this area is qualitative, and part of the retrospective is aimed at showing why I find myself relying increasingly on qualitative data. Space restrictions required that this article be condensed by 25 percent for this book; I have done this mainly by deleting a few sections and paragraphs and pruning references rather than rewriting.

Signs

Sign is a very general concept; examples include words, gestures, tokens, pictures, and stories. Signs represent reality. They point to something besides themselves. They also are part of reality. They are tangible and observable. Psychotherapy is conducted almost entirely as sign-mediated communication.

Signs are a means by which events reproduce themselves across time and place. For example, events that occurred previously in my laboratory and in other laboratories and in other talks and conversations are being reproduced here and now—in part and in flavor—as you read the words I have written. I and this journal are vectors carrying the signs that are reproducing those events.

How do signs convey the effects of events? Signs carry the experience of one person to another. The fundamental phenomenon is illustrated by my telling you about something I did or thought and you having some aspects of my experience, as you are doing right now. Put another way, we are sharing an experience, mediated by signs.

We can say that the experience carried by a sign is the sign's meaning. But in speaking of meaning, it is important not to suppose that sign meanings are fixed. The meaning to the speaker is never exactly the same as the meaning to the hearer. And each sign's meaning changes continually, reflecting the experience of each speaker and the audience and context in which the sign is used.

Signs accumulate these meanings. Each use adds another layer. That is, the meaning changes on each use, but the sign also retains the meaning of previous uses. For example, the next time you speak of signs or voices, there will be a bit of my experience tucked in. In this way, signs convey not only the experience of the speaker but also something of the experience of previous speakers who have used those signs. The quality of accumulating meaning was described by Bakhtin (e.g., 1981), and is sometimes called the historicity of signs. The many layers of meaning need not be consciously understood by the speakers. Thus, clients and therapists can, and normally do, say far more than they know. As Roy Hattersley (1991/1976), a British politician and author, said, writing about a conversation with author John Braine: "I remember him explaining to me the true message and real moral of *Room at the Top* and discovering how much better was the novel I had read than the one he had written" (p. 120).

Thus, we live in an ocean of signs—words and images and objects that were created by other people and convey other people's experience. Much of our experience is distilled from other people's experience and passed to us by signs. And not just by words. Gestures and facial expressions can speak volumes. Red stop signs without the word "Stop" still tell us to stop. A wealth of cultural meaning is conveyed by simple household objects; contrast, for example, the meaning of a knife and fork with the meaning of chopsticks. Even natural objects, such as the sun and the moon, have acquired manifold meanings by being invested with other people's experiences.[1]

Voices

The other powerful idea is voice. An emerging understanding considers people not as separate, unitary individuals, but rather as mosaics or communities of different voices. This understanding encompasses the possibility of internal conversations, and the observation that people's statements or other actions often contradict each other. Each of us seems to carry many voices, representing people, ideas, or events that we've encountered or that have been passed to us by signs. These include voices of our parents, our friends, our therapists, our favorite authors, our goals and ambitions, and our fears and resentments.

Some voices, such as belief systems, psychological theories, or group identities, may transcend individuals, so that the same voice speaks within many of us. For example, to some degree all members of the Society for Psychotherapy Research can speak for the society.

By the same token, most of what we say and think comes from other people. This is what I had in mind when I said that virtually none of what I'm saying here is original. Most of it comes from other people's voices in me, passed to me by signs.

As discussed in the closing plenary session at the 1997 SPR meeting in Geilo, Norway, many theoretical orientations describe psychotherapy clients as bringing multiple, often conflicting perspectives to treatment. Internal multiplicity is represented, for example, (a) in such cognitive-behavioral concepts as automatic thoughts, intrusive thoughts, self talk, and self statements, (b) in such psychodynamic concepts as internal objects, introjects, and states of mind, and (c) in the humanistic focus on contradictory aspects of self and unrealized potentials. Multiple internal voices are central in dialogue accounts of the self, and in archetypal psychology, and they may be dramatically apparent in dissociative phenomena and borderline states. Multiple "I" positions are deliberately used in the service of therapy and personal growth, in the facilitation of reflective thinking, in the analysis of reciprocal role procedures in cognitive analytic therapy, and in empty chair and two chair work in Gestalt and process-experiential therapy (see Stiles, 1997a, for illustrative references).

Multiple voices within people can represent depth of resources and flexibility, or they can represent fragmentation and dissociation. The difference is the strength of the meaning bridges—the sign-mediated links between the voices. (The term "meaning bridge" was used in a related sense by Rice & Saperia, 1984.) In many psychopathological conditions, meaning bridges are weak or absent; internal communication is painful, poor, or, in the extreme, nonexistent. Movement between self-states tends to be abrupt and discontinuous. Some voices may be warded off and silent.

The concepts of active voices and meaning-accumulating signs can help to overcome the misleading notion, promoted by library and computer metaphors, that information in people is passive (Stiles, 1997b). I'm suggesting that there is a formal similarity between interpersonal communication and intrapersonal communication. Both are mediated by signs, and both become easier, smoother, and less painful as understanding grows, that is, as the signs become more meaningful. We can say that the meaning bridges grow stronger. In successful therapy, this is something that happens both between therapist and client and within clients by the exchange of signs. I'll return to this theme later.

The Equivalence Paradox

First, however, I will review some of my own history in psychotherapy research, to show how I became interested in signs and voices. To a large extent, this retrospective is a story of frustrations.

When I entered psychotherapy research, I found it on the horns of the dilemma that David Shapiro, Robert Elliott, and I have called the equivalence paradox—the apparently equivalent effectiveness of different therapies in contrast to the apparent nonequivalence of their processes (Stiles, Shapiro, & Elliott, 1986). The equivalent effectiveness is often described (notably by Luborsky, Singer, & Luborsky, 1975) in terms of the verdict of the Dodo in the 19th-century children's story of *Alice's Adventures in Wonderland* regarding the winner of a race in which the competitors ran around in a circle: "*Everybody* has won and *all* must have prizes" (Carroll, 1946/1865, p. 28; italics in original). This venerable null result cannot really be true, of course; no two things are exactly alike in psychology or psychotherapy (Meehl, 1978). Nevertheless, more than 60 years after it was first quoted to describe the similar outcomes of different psychotherapies (Rosenzweig, 1936), the Dodo's verdict remains a plausible summary. Effect sizes (ES) found in meta-analyses (see Lambert & Bergin, 1994; Wampold et al., 1997) show that psychotherapy is substantially better than no psychotherapy (mean ES = .82) and somewhat better than a placebo (mean ES = .48), and the placebos have done better than no therapy (mean ES = .42). But the small-to-negligible differences found among the bona fide therapies suggest that they are more or less equivalent (.00 < ES < .21).

My starting point was on the other horn of the dilemma—the nonequivalence of the process. I spent several years building on work by Jerry Goodman (Goodman & Dooley, 1976) to develop a classification of verbal response modes. Each utterance—roughly, each simple sentence or independent clause—can be classified into one of eight modes following theoretical principles, including source of experience and frame of reference (Stiles, 1979, 1992a). For example, therapist self-disclosures and advisements (directives) concern the therapist's experience, whereas therapist's questions and interpretations concern the client's experience. Interpretations put the client's experience into the therapist's frame of reference, as Rogers (1951) emphasized, whereas reflections express the client's experience in the client's own frame of reference (see Table 8.1).

TABLE 8.1 Mean Percentage of Therapist Utterances in Client-Centered, Gestalt, and Psychoanalytic Therapy

Principles (Verbal Response Mode)	*Theoretical Approach*		
	Client-Centered	*Gestalt*	*Psychoanalytic*
Using therapist's frame of reference			
Concerning therapist's experience			
Disclosure	1.9	4.8*	1.9
Advisement	0.6	36.7*	2.8
Concerning client's experience			
Question	2.7	19.9*	12.2*
Interpretation	0.4	26.2*	48.7*
Using client's frame of reference			
Concerning therapist's experience			
Edification	1.9*	0.2	2.1
Confirmation	0.2*	0.0	0.2
Concerning client's experience			
Acknowledgment	46.1*	5.2	17.9*
Reflection	45.4*	3.7	9.9*
Coder disagreement	0.6	0.2	0.3
Total	*100.0*	*100.0*	*100.0*

Note: Based on transcripts of therapy conducted by leading proponents of their respective theoretical approaches. Adapted from Stiles (1979). Principles for coding verbal response mode intent, including frame of reference and source of experience are explained in Stiles (1992).

*Theoretically prescribed modes.

Coding what therapists of contrasting schools actually did yielded clear evidence of technical nonequivalence (Stiles, 1979; see Table 8.1). Importantly, the differences corresponded to the theories. Client-centered therapists used verbal response modes that were in the client's frame of reference-reflections and acknowledgments. Gestalt therapists, who were instructed by Perls (1969) to stay in the now and not listen to "the content of the bullshit the patient produces" (p. 53), used modes that were in their own frame of reference, such as advisements and disclosures. Psychoanalytic therapists, instructed by Freud (1913/1958) to be like a mirror, used modes from both frames of reference, but restricted themselves to modes that concerned the client's experience—questions, interpretations, acknowledgments, and reflections—avoiding those that would have revealed or imposed their own experience. Similar demonstrations of large, theoretically consistent differences have been made in many other studies of contrasting therapies, using a variety of coding systems and treatments (e.g., Brunink &

Schroeder, 1979; DeRubeis, Hollon, Evans, & Bemis, 1982; Elliott et al., 1987; Hill, O'Grady, & Elkin, 1992; Stiles, Shapiro, & Firth-Cozens, 1988; Strupp, 1955, 1957).[2] The nonequivalence of process is at least as robust as the equivalence of outcomes.

Disabuse of the Drug Metaphor

The systematic differences among treatments seem consistent with understanding alternative psychotherapies in terms of the drug metaphor (Stiles & Shapiro, 1989, 1994; cf. Yeaton & Sechrest, 1981). Each therapy specifies a set of supposedly active psychological or interpersonal ingredients, analogous to a drug's chemical ingredients, which can be coded in the therapist behavior.

Are the theoretically specified interventions really the active ingredients? A reasonable person might suppose that this could be tested straightforwardly. If interpretation, for example, is an active ingredient, then clients who get more interpretations should do better than those who receive fewer, and interpretations should be correlated with outcome across clients. That is, according to the more is better drug metaphor logic, by coding the process and correlating process components with outcomes, investigators should be able to tell which are the active ingredients (indicated by positive correlations), and which are flavors and fillers (indicated by null correlations). This more is better characterization is, of course, an oversimplification of the effects of actual pharmacological agents (which typically have optimal levels, curvilinear dose-response curves, or more complex relations to outcomes), but it has been powerful and pervasive in psychotherapy research (Stiles & Shapiro, 1989).

I spent 10 years and a good deal of several governments' money exploring this logic. I now think it is misleading, for reasons I will discuss shortly. Empirically, outcome was not reliably correlated with the theoretically important process components, at least not with in-session behaviors that can be classified and counted. For example, we coded the verbal response mode of each therapist and client utterance in half of the sessions delivered in the first Sheffield Psychotherapy Project, a clinical trial of brief therapies for depression (Shapiro & Firth, 1987), including over 330,000 utterances (Stiles et al., 1988). We selected as process measures the percentages of theoretically-important verbal response modes—therapist interpretations, questions, exploratory reflections, general advisements, and client disclosures—which together accounted for a large proportion of what therapists and clients did in these sessions. None showed any hint of correlating with improvement on standard outcome measures. We analyzed these data in many ways, with the same null results (Stiles & Shapiro, 1994).

Of course, not every process-outcome study has had such uniformly null results. Investigators have reported significant correlations with some measures, though most have not been consistent across studies. The biggest exception is evaluative measures, such as the alliance (a discussion of which has been removed to save space, but see Stiles & Wolfe, 2006). What we don't find is the pattern one would expect from the drug metaphor logic-strong process-outcome correlations for theoretically important ingredients and weak or negligible correlations for the supposed flavors and fillers.

In retrospect, we can see that the null process-outcome correlations are the equivalence paradox writ small. If the different treatments, with their huge process differences, have equivalent outcomes, then it's not *so* surprising that particular treatments varying in particular process components also have equivalent outcomes. Of course, one could argue from the drug metaphor that we simply haven't considered the true active ingredients yet. This argument implies, however, that the theories and clinical intuition are wrong about what is important in the process.

Responsiveness

I now think that the problem was not the choice of measures but rather the statistical logic. The drug metaphor reasoning overlooks, or at least oversimplifies, the dynamic relations between process and outcome. This dynamic relation can be described as responsiveness (Stiles, Honos-Webb, & Surko, 1998). Responsiveness refers to behavior that is affected by emerging context, particularly including client requirements. For example, therapists are being responsive when they assign a client to a treatment based on the presenting problems, design a homework assignment taking into account a client's abilities and circumstances, or rephrase an explanation that a client seemed not to understand the first time.

Appropriate responsiveness in therapy means responding to emerging context in a way that advances the goals of treatment. Clients differ in their requirements for each process component, and these requirements may change from moment to moment. Therapists try to respond appropriately to these requirements. They're not perfect, of course, but I suggest that they do far better than the random (noncontingent) emission of techniques implicit in the process-outcome correlation logic.

Responsiveness can occur on a timescale as long as months (e.g., treatment selection and planning) or as small as a few tens or hundreds of milliseconds. To illustrate the latter, in a qualitative Comprehensive Process Analysis of insight events, we found that therapists made adjustments in the course of giving interpretations, in response to client's ongoing reactions (Elliott et al., 1994). For example, a therapist might begin an interpretation and then pause before proceeding, to provide support when the client seemed to have trouble tolerating the emotional pain.

To the extent that therapists adjust their interventions to indications of client's changing requirements, outcome is reciprocally affecting process. In such a feedback system, small fluctuations can be amplified, leading to a cascade of effects that is unpredictable in advance. For example, remarking on some small nonverbal behavior may trigger a productive line of work and send the session off in some unexpected direction. The relations among variables in such a system are likely to be complex or chaotic, rather than linear (Barton, 1994; Gleick, 1987).

If therapists respond appropriately to client requirements for a particular process component (e.g., interpretations), then each client will tend to get the optimum amount at the optimum time. It wouldn't help to get more or less. In one study, clients were classified as overinvolved or as underinvolved in relationships or as balanced in their involvement, on the basis of pretreatment measures. Therapists tended to use more affective and relationship-oriented interventions with the overinvolved clients and more cognitive interventions with the underinvolved clients, and the clients with these different interpersonal styles had roughly equivalent outcomes (Hardy, Stiles, Barkham, & Startup, 1998). A responsiveness interpretation is that the different interventions represented appropriate responsiveness to differing client requirements, so that all groups benefited more or less optimally from their treatment.

If a component is always delivered at an optimum level, outcome will tend to be the same across clients insofar as it depends on that component. The level of the process component might vary across clients, but it would not predict outcome unless, by coincidence, client requirements happened to predict outcome. That is, important therapeutic ingredients may be uncorrelated with outcome (Stiles, 1988; Stiles & Shapiro, 1989, 1994). Reviewers seeing reports of null correlations are likely to conclude, mistakenly, that the component is useless.

If essential ingredients may be uncorrelated with outcome, then, conversely, a null correlation does not imply that a process component is ineffective or useless. Note that this is not a measurement problem. This problem with the process-outcome correlation logic holds even for perfect measures of key ingredients.

Even formal treatment manuals recommend responsiveness, rather than standardized application of techniques. For example, the last three of five considerations for selecting targets and techniques offered in the manual for cognitive therapy of depression (Beck, Rush, Shaw, & Emery, 1979) specify responsiveness.

3. The therapist should attempt to gear his approach to the patient's level of sophistication, personal style, and typical coping techniques.
4. The relative urgency and severity of the various problems and symptoms may dictate the priorities; that is, which problem(s) to deal with first.
5. A certain amount of "trial and error" is usually necessary. The patient should be told: "We have a number of approaches that have been shown to be successful for various problems. We may have to try out several before we find the one that really fits you. Thus, if one method is not particularly helpful, it will provide us with valuable information regarding which method is likely to succeed" (p. 169).

The Attractions of Qualitative Approaches

The failure of the process-outcome correlation logic, and recognizing the importance of responsiveness, pointed me toward qualitative methods (Stiles, 1993). Qualitative observations, in the form of case histories, have always been used to support theories of psychotherapy and psychopathology; this is what we used to call anecdotal evidence and now call narrative research.

In any scientific research, investigators try to simultaneously maximize generality, precision, and realism. Unfortunately, gains in one of these desirable qualities generally entail losses in another one (Levins, 1968). In comparison with hypothesis testing using ratings or verbal coding, the thick descriptions produced by intensive case studies of psychotherapy seem to me to yield gains in realism but a loss of generality.

Narrative discourse (for example, a case history) has advantages for presenting empirical observations of therapy process (Stiles, 1993). Narratives are linguistic. Narratives facilitate empathy with the protagonist, in effect making direct use of our ability to understand the experience of others. Narratives supply the context as part of the story. And narratives can deal with chaos in the technical sense, with human behavior that is like the weather, deterministic but unpredictable in the long term. In short, a narrative understanding incorporates responsiveness.

To summarize my retrospective: I've argued that the drug metaphor process-outcome correlation problem is a product of responsiveness, and that responsiveness can be dealt with in qualitative research.

The Assimilation Model

One alternative to the drug metaphor is the assimilation model (Stiles et al., 1990). Psychotherapy process is typically measured across seconds or minutes, whereas outcome is measured across months or years. Process observations are typically focused on a narrow aspect or topic, whereas outcome is typically considered in relation to the whole person. The assimilation model attempts to reconcile the time scale and scope of process and outcome by identifying particular problematic experiences and tracking them across sessions in the therapy dialogue. In effect, it breaks outcome into smaller pieces and studies how the pieces change.

According to the first formulation of the model (Stiles et al., 1997, in successful therapy the problematic experience is gradually assimilated into a schema. A problematic experience might be a traumatic memory, an unacceptable wish, an overwhelming feeling, or any other idea, attitude, or intention that is threatening or painful to the client. Schema is a broad concept that might be a frame of reference, a way of living, a narrative, a metaphor, or a theme. Consistent with Piaget's (1970) conception, the model suggests that assimilating a problematic experience requires accommodations in existing schemas or the development of new schemas within the therapist-client relationship. In successful therapy, the client schemas change to assimilate the problematic experience. Thus, the formerly problematic experience becomes part of the schema.

More recently, we have formulated the assimilation model in terms of voices (Honos-Webb & Stiles, 1998). In this complementary formulation, the problematic experience is considered to be an active voice within the person. Instead of being considered a passive piece of information, a problematic experience is considered to speak for itself. For example, a traumatic experience has a voice that strives for expression. By speaking and by being heard and understood—that is, by exchanging signs—a problematic voice can gradually build meaning bridges and be assimilated into the community of voices. It can become part of the self.

In either of these formulations, the assimilation model recognizes that the problematic experience changes as therapy proceeds. This change in the client's problem has previously created a problem for process researchers, which we have called the metamorphosis problem (Stiles, 1992b). The client's problem changes form as it develops, so that later versions may not be recognizable from earlier versions, just as a 50-year-old man may not be easily recognizable as the 5-year-old boy he once was. Of course, you wouldn't have the problem if you saw him every few weeks. Analogously, the assimilation methodology deals with the metamorphosis problem by longitudinal study of problems and by narrative presentation of results. Briefly, we extract passages dealing with selected problematic topics or themes, and observe how the expressions change from session to session (Stiles, et al., 1992; Stiles, et al., 1991).

As a problematic voice is assimilated, it seems to pass through predictable stages or levels, summarized in the Assimilation of Problematic Experiences Scale (APES; Stiles, et al., 1991). Our current names for the stages are: warded off, unwanted thoughts, vague awareness or emergence, problem statement or clarification, understanding or insight, working through or application, problem solution, and mastery. This scale represents an approximation to what we think are common formal features of the process of change. That is, we hypothesize that in some ways the process of psychological change is similar across cases, even though the problematic experiences may vary a great deal. Clients may enter therapy with problems anywhere along this continuum, and any progress along it could be considered as positive.

Although I have focused on qualitative assimilation research in this article, we have also done quantitative research on the model (Field, Barkham, Shapiro, & Stiles, 1994; Reynolds et al., 1996; Stiles, Barkham, Shapiro, & Firth-Cozens, 1992; Stiles, Shankland, Wright, & Field, 1997a, 1997b). Recently, we developed a marker-driven rating system based on the voices formulation (Honos-Webb, 1998; Honos-Webb, Surko, & Stiles, 1998; Honos-Webb, Surko, Stiles, & Greenberg, 1999). This will make it possible to obtain reliable independent ratings of assimilation in passages of therapy.

We've done quite a few intensive case studies of assimilation in various types of therapy (Honos-Webb, Stiles, Greenberg, & Goldman, 1998, 2006; Honos-Webb,

Surko, Stiles, & Greenberg, 1999; Shapiro, Barkham, Reynolds, Hardy, & Stiles, 1992; Stiles, Meshot, et al., 1992; Stiles, Morrison, et al., 1991; Stiles, Shapiro, & Harper, 1994; Stiles, Shapiro, Harper, & Morrison, 1995; Varvin & Stiles, 1999). We find assimilation everywhere we look, but of course we would. Such case reports can show others how to look with our eyes and hear with our ears—how to understand psychotherapy as a process of assimilation.

Intrusion of a Problematic Voice

A client's different internal voices are sometimes made salient by the intrusion of material that not only expresses distinct material but does so in a distinctive-sounding voice. The following qualitative example was drawn from the case of Debbie (a pseudonym), who has given permission for use of her materials in research and scholarly presentation (Stiles, 1999b). An additional example of assimilation was deleted from this reprinted article to save space, but is included the original version (Stiles, 1999a) and presented in greater detail elsewhere (Varvin & Stiles, 1999).

Debbie was a 29-year-old mother of two who sought treatment for depression at a clinic in London, England, where she was considered to have borderline characteristics. She was seen for 16 sessions of Cognitive Analytic Therapy (CAT) (Ryle, 1990) as part of a research project on borderline personality disordered clients (Ryle, 1997). She was considered a successful case according to standard measures, as well as in her own and her therapist's judgment.

Debbie's husband of 12 years was alcoholic and had been in and out of the home for several years. He had announced during his last extended visit, three months previously, that from the beginning of their relationship he had never wanted to be with her. This, she said, rang true and had precipitated a severe depressive episode. In her first session, she said she could not stand to see him because it reminded her of the rejection. She said she had lost control and physically attacked him the last time he had shown up unannounced. She also said she felt "paranoid" about his mother, who had never approved of the match. The following passage was taken from about eight minutes into the first session. Debbie was explaining that her and her husband's families had known each other since they were children, and that she now felt this part of her life was gone. I present the dialogue in stanza form (McLeod & Balamoutsou, 1996), with lines separated to convey my understanding of importance and emphasis.

DEBBIE: *And . . . you know,*
I've had this, this fam—, this other family.
There's my family—
It's all my family,
Which always included his family as well-his brother, his sister,
And it's as though . . . that's gone, y'know.

THERAPIST: So, *you've lost more than just him.*
You've lost, sort of his brothers and sister—
DEBBIE: *Yeah, that's what I feel*
THERAPIST: *—who were like friends of yours, I mean.*
DEBBIE: *Well, his sis—*
I've never,
I've never really got on well with his mum and his sister
Because—
So that's not so much of a loss as, uh,
she's won.
She's finally got what she wanted,
Which was, she wanted him back.
And she wanted him away from me, basically.
That's how I feel.
Whether that's how she feels,
but that's how I fe—
Y'know.
And this sort of thing's really been getting worse, y'know.
It's getting more mad, I think.
And, um, I still keep in touch with his other brother's wife . . .

The emphasized text near the end ("That's how I feel . . .") was spoken in a distinctive voice, louder, more rapidly, in a lower register, and seemingly much more defiantly and angrily than the rather meek voice of the narrator, who was giving background information to the therapist. The defiant, angry voice seemed to intrude abruptly and unexpectedly, triggered perhaps by the discussion of loss or by the thought that her mother-in-law had won. The defiant voice was interrupted in midword. Was this angry voice related to the problems for which Debbie had sought treatment? Was it related to Debbie's aggressive outburst against her husband on his last visit? I think so, although at this writing we are still working on the analysis of this case and my understanding is tentative.

It emerged that Debbie had a longstanding pattern of angry outbursts, apparently triggered by signs of rejection. The outbursts were mainly verbal; the physical attack on her husband was unusual and extreme. After the outbursts, which she described as uncontrolled, she would feel rejected and horrible about herself. As the therapist formulated it within a CAT framework, Debbie's outbursts seemed to represent her switching into the complementary rejecting role in a repetitive interpersonal procedure. From a signs-and-voices perspective, the abrupt, painful transitions signal the absence of meaning bridges between the defiant voice and the narrator voice. It's a hypothesis that the louder voice in the passage represented a brief intrusion by Debbie's angry self state.

In therapy, Debbie made great progress in reconciling these aspects of herself. She later reported being surprised and pleased that she could have normal conversations with her husband without losing control. She felt less desperately needy and more assertive. How was this achieved?

The following passage was taken from midway in this process, 25 minutes into session eight. Although we hear only Debbie's narrator voice in this passage, it describes a recent internal conversation with her defiant, rejecting voice. In effect, she was constructing a meaning bridge.

Two days before session eight, Debbie's husband had telephoned her just 10 minutes before he was to take their two children to a museum. He said that he couldn't take them because he was going to a boot sale (flea market). Debbie considered this reason utterly inadequate, and a day later she called him back and told him how irresponsible she thought he had been. From her description of this second phone conversation, I imagine that her husband heard the angry, rejecting voice shown as emphasized in the previous passage. But she was less impulsive than in previous episodes, and she did not feel so horrible and rejected afterwards.

DEBBIE: *Yeah, I mean*
Even with that, sort of that rejecting [self-state] *now,*
When I said [to my husband] *yesterday on the phone*
I knew that I would feel rejected after I'd said it [told him he'd been irresponsible]
Because . . .
He'll . . .
He'll reject me
Because I'm not going along with what he says.
And I'm not being nice.
And I'm not being, you know . . .
So I did feel like that a little bit.
But then I thought:
No.
I did the right thing.
I can't start feeling bad
Because I'm saying what I think's right.

This internal conversation—one part of herself telling another part that she shouldn't feel bad, because she's doing the right thing—illustrates a sort of reflexivity that we associate with problem clarification in the assimilation model (APES level 3; Honos-Webb & Stiles, 1998). This was not yet a solution, but it stated the problem in a way that it could be addressed. The exchange of verbal signs was building a meaning bridge that would permit smoother, more modulated, less painful shifts between voices, a step closer to appropriate assertiveness. In other words, the voices were learning to cooperate with each other instead of acting antagonistically.

Summary and Prospects

Assimilation of problematic experiences, I have suggested, is a common therapeutic process that can be understood in terms of signs and voices. This understanding is compatible with the pervasive responsiveness of human interaction, and may be a way to address the frustrations often encountered in research on the process and outcome of psychotherapy.

COMMENTARY

SIGNS AND VOICES 18 YEARS ON

My SPR Presidential Address was delivered at the Snowbird, Utah, SPR meeting in June, 1998 and revised for publication over the next few months (Stiles, 1999a). It reviewed some longstanding intractable problems in psychotherapy research, such as researchers' failure to find expected correlations between treatment processes and outcomes (e.g., Stiles & Shapiro, 1994), and it described a dialogical theory of psychological change that we've called the assimilation model (Stiles et al., 1990). I argued "that the drug metaphor process-outcome correlation problem is a product of responsiveness and that responsiveness can be dealt with in qualitative research" (p. 409).

Sixteen years on, I think the problems remain intractable and the qualitative way forward remains viable. In this commentary, I list some more recent elaborations.

Intractable Problems

The Responsiveness Problem

Human behavior is responsive on timescales ranging from months to milliseconds. Responsiveness refers to behavior that is influenced by emerging context (Stiles, Honos-Webb, & Surko, 1998). Therapists adjust plans and tactics in response to what clients present week by week and moment by moment.

Therapists and clients typically have benign goals, and they respond to emerging context to advance those goals in ways consistent with their principles. This can be called *appropriate responsiveness*: do the right thing. In general, therapists and clients try to be appropriately responsive, although the right thing can vary dramatically across cases, circumstances, and theoretical principles.

Responsiveness is a problem in psychotherapy research because it undermines most hypotheses tested with linear statistics. As I have explained elsewhere (Stiles, 1988, 2009b, 2013; Stiles, Honos-Webb, & Surko, 1998), appropriate responsiveness can account for the failure to find associations of therapy outcomes with (a) theoretically important process components (e.g., Stiles & Shapiro, 1994),

(b) therapists' theoretical approach (e.g., Stiles et al., 2006; Stiles, Barkham, Mellor-Clark, & Connell, 2008), or (c) the duration of treatment in routine practice (e.g., Barkham et al., 2006; Stiles, Barkham, Connell, & Mellor-Clark, 2008).

The Independent Variable is Not Independent

Each client in an experimental condition of an outcome study receives a *different*, responsively tailored treatment. Named treatments, such as CBT, vary not just from study to study (evident from heated controversies about treatment integrity in well-known studies), but from therapist to therapist, from client to client, from session to session, and from minute to minute. The individualization is clinically appropriate, but disastrous for the logic of experiments. The independent variable (the treatment condition) is *causally entangled* with client, therapist, and context variables (Elkin, 1999; Krause & Lutz, 2009). The nature of the independent variable varies systematically with clients and contexts and, even worse, with the dependent variable (outcome), as therapists responsively adjust treatment in light of client progress or lack of progress. Such causal entanglements are more serious than uncontrolled variability in extraneous conditions because they cannot be overcome by randomization (Stiles, 2009b, 2011).

Evaluative Variables Incorporate Appropriate Responsiveness

Evaluative variables, such as alliance, empathy, and competence, reflect whether behavior is appropriate to the circumstances, rather than describing specific behaviors. Unsurprisingly, clients feel and do well, and sessions and relationships are evaluated positively, when therapists and clients do the right thing.

The most popular process and outcome indexes are mainly evaluative. Scales that collect ratings of specific behaviors or symptoms or problems are typically aggregated into global evaluations for statistical comparisons (see, for example, Stiles & Goldsmith, 2010). Measures that nominally assess specific conditions, such as depression, largely reflect global distress and are closely correlated with more global measures (e.g., Leach et al., 2006). Most variables on the list of *evidence-based effective elements of therapeutic relationships* assembled by Norcross (2002, 2011) were evaluative: Alliance, group cohesion, empathy, goal consensus and collaboration, positive regard, congruence/genuineness, repair of ruptures, management of counter-transference, and quality of relational interpretations. These elements represent achievements or desired results rather than specific conditions or volitional behaviors (Stiles & Wolfe, 2006).

Evaluative measures are popular because readers want to know how well a therapy works. They are robust because evaluation is a common denominator in people's diverse understandings. People know what they think is good and what they like. In contrast, substantive descriptors of process and content and theoretical concepts are seldom used consistently across researchers, much less across therapists or clients. Unless respondents all understand and use terms the same way, they do not emerge as common components in rating scales. So most internally consistent self-report measures of process and outcome are evaluative. But a focus on evaluation avoids the theoretically specific descriptions that scientific research is meant to test (Stiles, 2006, 2009a, 2011).

Pre-Theoretical Knowledge

In an underappreciated analysis, Rosenwald (1986) described how social sciences fail to advance because pre-theoretical knowledge trumps research findings. Significant research findings are challenged not for their failure to confirm theoretical expectations but because challengers think some unmeasured variable (i.e., pre-theoretical knowledge) could have accounted for the results. So, rather than building on the original findings, researchers repeat the *same study*, instituting additional controls for the new variable.

Since Rosenzweig (1936) first quoted the Dodo ("*Everybody* has won, and *all* must have prizes"; p. 412), the number of comparative trials has grown enormously, as have methodological sophistication and instrumentation. But the Dodo's verdict remains in force, albeit under continual appeal. Likewise, variations of studies on the statistical association of alliance with outcome run into the hundreds (Horvath, Del Re, Flückiger, & Symonds, 2011).

A Way Forward: Theory-Building Qualitative Research

I have elsewhere argued at length that theory-building qualitative research offers a strategy for advancing scientific understanding, comparing theory with observation and revising theory to fit (Stiles, 1993, 2003, 2005, 2007, 2009a, 2010). I won't repeat my arguments here, but I will reiterate the claims: Theory-building qualitative research is appropriate in the context of justification as well as in the context of discovery. It can use the rich tapestry of clinical observation to a degree unimaginable in statistical hypothesis testing. It does not straightforwardly address which therapy is most effective, but it promises a way forward.

Of course, qualitative research has its own problems. My argument is not that theory-building qualitative research is the only way forward, but rather that, with the traditional gold standard tarnished, it offers a viable alternative with substantial advantages of its own.

Signs, Voices, and Assimilation

The assimilation model (Stiles, 1999a, 2003, 2011; Stiles et al., 1990) has been built primarily by theory-building qualitative case studies. It was conceived partly in response to the Dodo verdict: How could such different operations have such similar results? Assimilation is not a treatment approach, but the theory of psychological change that can inform any treatment. The theory suggests that psychological change is mediated by semiotic tools and that disconnected problematic experiences pass through a predictable developmental sequence as they are integrated into the rest of the personality. Therapists who know what to expect can responsively adjust their interventions to facilitate progress along the path (cf. Powers, 2005).

In my SPR Presidential Address, I explained the assimilation model in terms of signs and voices, and I have increasingly understood psychotherapy as a process of coming to terms interpersonally and intrapersonally (Stiles, 2011), building semiotic meaning bridges between therapists and clients and among clients' internal voices. A meaning bridge is a sign (e.g., word, gesture, image; cf. Leiman, 1992, 2011) or a system of signs that has similar meaning to its author and its addressee. Voice is a metaphor for constellations of traces of people's experiences, which constitute psychological parts of a person. Voices emerge to speak and act when addressed by circumstances that reiterate some aspects of the originating experiences. In the remainder of this commentary, I review some recent directions that assimilation theory and research have taken.

Variations and Elaborations of the Assimilation of Problematic Experiences Sequence

The Assimilation of Problematic Experiences Sequence (APES; Stiles, 1999a, 2003, and many other cited articles), summarizes an eight-stage developmental course of initially problematic experiences, from completely disconnected and alienated from the self to completely integrated and part of the self: (0) warded off/dissociated, (1) unwanted thoughts/active avoidance, (2) vague awareness/emergence, (3) problem statement/clarification, (4) understanding/insight, (5) application/working through, (6) resourcefulness/problem solution, and (7) integration/mastery. Theoretically, in successful psychotherapy, problematic experiences move through some segment of this sequence.

When the APES is used as a quantitative measure, the *S* abbreviates *Scale* (e.g., Caro Gabalda, 2006, 2009; Detert, Llewelyn, Hardy, Barkham, & Stiles, 2006; Honos-Webb, Stiles, & Greenberg, 2003; Osatuke & Stiles, 2011); when used as a qualitative description, it abbreviates *Sequence* (e.g., Brinegar, Salvi, Stiles, & Greenberg, 2006; Gray & Stiles, 2011; Tikkanen, Stiles, & Leiman, 2011, 2013). Though developed with individual adult psychotherapy in mind (Stiles, Meshot, et al., 1992; Stiles et al., 1991), the APES has been extended to couple therapy (Schielke et al., 2011), therapy in cases of mental retardation (Newman & Beail, 2002, 2005), pharmacotherapy (Osatuke, Reid, Stiles, Zisook, & Mohamed, 2011), group therapy for people with dementia (Cheston, 2013; Watkins, Cheston, Jones, & Gilliard, 2006), child neurological evaluations (Tikkanen, Stiles, & Leiman, 2011, 2013), clients' internalization of their therapists (Mosher & Stiles, 2009), supervisory relationships (Osatuke & Stiles, 2012) organizational development (Ostauke, Moore, & Stiles, 2011), and acculturation of immigrants (Henry, Stiles, & Biran, 2005; Henry & Stiles, 2012; Henry, Stiles, Biran, Mosher, Brinegar, & Banerjee, 2009).

As a quantitative scale, the APES can be used for fine-grained, utterance-by-utterance analyses (Caro Gabalda, 2006, 2009; Caro Gabalda & Stiles, 2009, 2013) or for broader descriptions. The fine-grained approach treats each utterance as an expression by some internal voice and suggests inferences about the momentary relation of that voice to the rest of the self as well as to the utterance's addressee.

The APES has changed as new observations have modified investigators' understanding of the developmental sequence. Some versions have been renamed, as the Assimilation of Problematic Voices Scale (Honos-Webb, Stiles, & Greenberg, 2003), the APES-enlarged version (Teusch, Böhme, Finke, Gastpar, & Skerra, 2003), the Assimilation of Problematic and Overwhelming Experiences Scale (Varvin, 2003), the Markers of Assimilation in Dementia Coding Frame (Lishman & Cheston, 2012), the Heidelberg Structural Change Scale (Grande, Rudolf, Oberbracht, & Jakobsen, 2001; Grande, Rudolf, Oberbracht, & Pauli-Magnus, 2003; Rudolf, Grande, & Oberbracht, 2000), and the Resolution of Problematic Experiences Sequence (Schielke et al., 2011). Other investigators have modified the APES and extended its application without changing the name (e.g., see the 2005 special issue of *Counseling Psychology Quarterly*).

Some investigators have elaborated particular segments of the APES. Reid and Osatuke (2006) distinguished substages between unwanted thoughts (APES 1) and the vague awareness/emergence (APES 2) in clients presenting psychosomatic problems. Teusch et al. (2003) divided movement from the vague awareness/emergence to problem statement/clarification (APES 3) into three parts for a study on effects of antidepressant medication. Brinegar et al. (2006) distinguished and named four substages between problem statement/clarification and understanding/insight (APES 4): 3.2 *rapid cross fire*, 3.4 *entitlement*, 3.6 *respect and attention*, and 3.8 *joint search for understanding*. The names describe a systematically changing relationship between a problematic voice and the usual self.

Progress Through the APES and the Therapeutic Zone of Proximal Development

Assessing therapeutic progress or lack of progress requires a continuum along which to progress. By offering such a continuum, the APES permits research on which sorts of therapeutic interventions best facilitate progress within each interval (Meystre, Kramer, De Roten, Despland, & Stiles, 2014).

As an extension of Vygotsky's (1978) developmental concept of the zone of proximal development (ZPD), the *therapeutic ZPD* (Leiman & Stiles, 2001) is the interval on the APES continuum between the client's current ability to accommodate the presenting challenges and a potential ability that can be reached in collaboration with the therapist (Caro Gabalda & Stiles, 2013; Leiman & Stiles, 2001; Ribeiro et al., 2013; Tikkanen et al., 2011). Theoretically, therapeutic work on a problem is most likely to be successful within a zone slightly more advanced along the APES than the problem is currently. Interventions aimed outside the therapeutic ZPD are likely to fail (Ribeiro et al., 2013).

Gonçalves et al. (2011) used the APES in describing failure to progress in therapy attributable to *mutual in-feeding*, a cyclical movement between opposing parts of the Self, which resembles the rapid cross-fire phenomenon described by Brinegar et al. (2006) but which tends to maintain a dysfunctional self-narrative. Even in successful therapy, fine-grained observations show that advances alternate with *setbacks*—speaking turns rated at APES stages below the previous turn. Most setbacks could be attributed to therapists exceeding the client's therapeutic ZPD, or to guided or spontaneous switches from more advanced to less advanced strands of a problem (Caro Gabalda & Stiles, 2009, 2013). That is, most observed setbacks could be reconciled with considering the APES as a series of developmental stages.

A Voices Approach to Psychopathology

Whereas each individual's history is unique, psychological symptoms cluster into patterns, which may be understood within the assimilation model as distinctive configurations of internal voices. Cases of depression have been characterized by conflicts of voices that were internally dominant (overpowering the other voices within the client) but externally submissive with voices that were internally submissive but externally assertive (Osatuke, Mosher, et al., 2007; Osatuke, Stiles, Barkham, Hardy, & Shapiro, 2011). These conflicts may suppress self-affirming voices that represent clients' experiences of continuity, nurturance, and self-worth (Stiles, 1999b). Cases of anxiety, on the other hand, have been characterized by conflicts between a downtrodden main voice and a powerful internal critic that either belittled the client's ability to cope or exaggerated external dangers. Either sort of critic made the clients' usual self excessively vulnerable to—and hence fearful of—external circumstances (Gray & Stiles, 2011). Other cases have suggested still different configurations of voices in cases of trauma (Osatuke & Stiles, 2010; Varvin & Stiles, 1999), psychosomatic conditions (Reid & Osatuke, 2006), borderline personality (Osatuke & Stiles, 2006), and dissociative identity disorder (Humphreys, Rubin, Knudson, & Stiles, 2005).

Conclusion: Cumulative Qualitative Research on Assimilation

Work on signs and voices and the assimilation model illustrates the possibility of cumulative *qualitative* research on psychotherapy theory. The new understanding, like all scientific understanding, is tentative, but it is growing as observations are aggregated in the form of modifications in the theory—changes in confidence, elaborations, and extensions. Note that the theoretical elaborations and extensions (called *abductions* by Peirce, 1931–1958; see Rennie, 2000; Stiles, 2009a) do not have free rein but are strongly constrained by previous research. They must remain consistent with previous observations, or else the previous observations would contradict the theory.

Theory-building qualitative research can incorporate human responsiveness in a way that statistical hypothesis testing cannot. It does not require large numbers of similar instances, only large numbers of theory-relevant observations (Stiles, 2009a). Psychotherapy theories are designed for complex clinical situations in which therapists adjust their thinking and behavior in response to kaleidoscopically changing clinical circumstances. Qualitative observations that show a detailed fit can strengthen confidence in a theory even though those specific circumstances are never repeated within or across cases.

Acknowledgment

I thank Katerine Ostauke for feedback on a draft of this commentary.

Notes

1 At this point, the talk was illustrated by a cartoon (Koren, 1979) in which objects in a park-like setting bore printed signs indicating their metaphoric meaning. For example, a hill was labeled "metaphor for aspiration," a bird was labeled "metaphor for lyricism," a rock was labeled "metaphor for stability," a fence was labeled "metaphor for limits," and a path was labeled "metaphor for the possible."

2 When we coded client speech using the same response modes coding system, however, we found that the clients used similar profiles of modes regardless of what school their therapist adhered to (Stiles & Sultan, 1979; Stiles, Shapiro, & Firth-Cozens, 1988). Mainly the clients used disclosures.

9

CONSENSUS IN PSYCHOTHERAPY RESEARCH AND PRACTICE

Where Have All the Findings Gone? (2000)

Marvin R. Goldfried

I started subscribing to psychology journals when I was in graduate school, and have built up a fairly large professional library. There are times when I sit back and contemplate my collection, looking at the old, faded ones on the left, recalling the many hours I pored over them as a student. At the time, the material in them was new and exciting. Like everyone else, however, my energies are now focused on desperately trying to keep up with those on the right—the current literature. I doubt that many people read the literature of the past, let alone cite it. However, it pains me when I think of those researchers and clinicians who dedicated so much time, energy, and devotion to producing it, especially when I reflect on the negligible impact that much of their work has made on the field.

This concern of mine seems to be a particularly timely one, in that we have made what some feel is a quantum leap, putting the 20th century behind us. The thing about previous centuries is that, by definition, they are thought of as things of the past—the connotation being that they are only of historical interest. As psychotherapy researchers, we have labored long and hard in our attempts to advance the field. A question that we undoubtedly have privately asked ourselves is whether our own contributions will be ignored, or whether they will make an impact. And even if they do make an impact, is it likely that they will be ignored in the future? In our field, the test of time is severe; relatively little survives.

In this article, I would like to explore the question of why it has been so difficult for the field of psychotherapy to build upon the past work of others, a problem that has plagued psychology in general. I would like to do this by taking a clinical approach to this issue; I will begin with a description of the problem, move on to an assessment and formulation of why I believe it exists, and then end with some recommendations for treatment.

The Problem

Whenever psychology or psychotherapy is compared to the natural sciences, we typically fall short of the mark. I once had a conversation about this with a physician, in which I lamented the difficulty we have in agreeing about what we know. He finally looked at me and said: "What do you expect? Psychotherapy is an infant science." One hundred years old and still an infant!

The problem we face is part of a larger one. Thus, Staats (1991) provided an account of the disunity within psychology in general, and pointed to where he believed it needed to head. He described the progression from chaos and disunity to greater unity and consensus as involving a basic shift in scientific goals—moving from preoccupation with finding the novel to the inclusion of efforts to find interrelationships, and to simplify and organize that which has already been found.

While researchers have been busy conducting studies to better understand their particular phenomena, sociologists have been busy studying the researchers. In comparing the advancement of the different sciences, sociologists of science have made a very important distinction—the distinction between the "core" of scientific knowledge and the "research frontier" (Cole, 1992). The core is comprised of those findings that are accepted as being true, that is, findings about which there is a consensus. By contrast, the research frontier consists of cutting-edge contributions that are still being evaluated by the research community. Interestingly enough, a study by Cole (1992) of the grant review process has found that there is just as much disagreement in judging research proposals in the natural sciences as there is in the social sciences. But while we as a field may have just as much disunity at the research frontier as our colleagues in the natural sciences, the place where we differ is that we have difficulty in agreeing on what constitutes our core.

Despite the advances we have made over the past quarter century, psychotherapy research and practice has yet to agree on its core. With some exceptions, psychotherapy researchers and practicing clinicians live in separate worlds. And even within their own worlds, researchers and therapists have their own sub-worlds, based on their theoretical conceptualizations and their regional reference groups. In addition to all of this, there is the all too unfortunate tendency in the field to ignore the past contributions of others.

Assessment and Formulation of Problem

The problem that psychotherapy has in agreeing about its core is complex and multidimensional, involving the following factors: (1) the gap that exists between research and practice, (2) the different theoretical approaches that have been taken in the attempt to understand psychotherapy, (3) the language barriers that characterize the field, (4) the changing nature of our research methodology, (5) the value attached to contributions that are new, and (6) the rules that govern scientific behavior. I will deal with each in turn.

Clinical Research Gap

As I indicated earlier, clinicians and researchers live in different worlds. Research careers are driven by publications, and clinical careers by referrals. Researchers labor over grant applications, while practicing therapists expend considerable energy in their attempt to be granted additional sessions from third party payers.

In addition to being separated by the differing social systems within which psychotherapy researchers and practicing therapists function, there also exists a tension between the two communities. Researchers have long lamented that practitioners typically ignore the research literature and continue to base their practice on what they feel comfortable with, or what seems to work clinically. For their part, clinicians complain that they are not the audience for whom the research literature is written, and that what is studied rarely provides them with useful information on how to proceed clinically. Where therapy research involves the random assignment of patients to different theoretically pure treatment conditions, the practicing therapist needs to select an intervention—often involving a combination of different approaches—based on the needs of the particular case at hand.

The movement toward the specification of empirically supported treatments may certainly be viewed as an attempt to close the clinical-research gap. One of the goals in compiling lists of empirically supported therapies was to aid the practicing clinician in dealing with pressures for accountability coming from managed care, policy makers, and biological psychiatry. However, many practicing therapists have failed to respond with gratitude, and some are indeed distressed, fearing that "the standards and methods of clinical therapy will be set by those who do the least amount of clinical practice" (Fensterheim & Raw, 1996, pp. 169–170). As often happens in distressed relationships, the behavior resulting from one person's positive motivation may have an unintended negative impact on the other.

Theoretical Barriers

Edwin G. Boring, well-known for his contributions to understanding the history of experimental psychology, once commented in an article published in *Science* on the tenacity with which theoreticians hold onto their theories. As he put it: "A theory which has built up its author's image of himself has become part of him. To abandon it would be suicidal, or at least an act of self-mutilation" (1964, p. 682).

I have always felt ambivalent about the role of theory in psychotherapy. Although we certainly need theoretical constructs to organize our findings, I am concerned about the many pitfalls associated with theory. In actuality, my concerns probably have more to do with theorists and the institutional systems that are established to protect their theory. These networks are social, political, and economic in nature, and may continue long after the limitations of the theory have been documented.

In 1950, Skinner wrote an article titled "Are Theories of Learning Necessary?" in which he cautioned the field about the fate of research programs that are designed to test a given theoretical position: "That a theory generates research does not prove its value unless the research is valuable. Much useless experimentation results from theories, and much energy and skill are absorbed by them. Most theories are eventually overthrown, and the greater part of the associated research is discarded" (p. 194). Although Skinner did not mention any names, he was clearly referring to the work by Hull and Tolman, whose extensive research programs were dedicated to proving that each was correct in depicting the mechanisms associated with the learning process. Skinner turned out to be most accurate in his prediction, and all this research was forgotten once their theories fell from popularity.

Kuhn (1962) has suggested that although one can make the case that research findings may be used to construct theories—the kind of bottom-up approach to theory construction advocated by Skinner—it is also likely that theory determines both the questions one asks and what is considered a finding that is worth taking seriously. In this regard, we can think of our theories of therapy as "therapeutic schemas"; they are conceptualizations that can fill in the gaps by allowing us to hypothesize phenomena that might not yet have been observed. When they are accurate, we may be able to do such things as impress our clinical supervisees by making speculations and suggestions that turn out to be clinically accurate. Or we may be able to obtain positive reactions from peer reviewers who evaluate our manuscripts or grant applications. When our theories fall short, however, we have bias.

This bias is illustrated in a study by Mahoney (1976), who sent manuscripts to journal reviewers with identical Introduction and Methods sections, but with different results. He found was that the manuscript was more likely to be accepted for publication when the results were consistent with the reviewers' theoretical orientation, and rejected when they went contrary to theoretical preference. Moreover, the reviewers rated the methodology itself as being less adequate when the findings were inconsistent with their theory.

Language Barriers

Closely associated with the way that theories can prevent us from agreeing on a core body of knowledge is the language barrier they often create. I first noticed this phenomenon some years ago at a case conference that I organized for a meeting of the Association for the Advancement of Behavior Therapy (AABT). So as to provide some diversity of opinion, I invited Hans Strupp to participate, giving us a psychodynamic vantage point. When Strupp began to offer his comments, I noticed an uneasy stirring among members of the audience. In attempting to understand this better, I conducted my own informal process analysis. The result of this observation was the finding that each time Strupp made use of a psychodynamic term (e.g., *ego-dystonic, transference*), there was a noticeable impact on the audience (e.g., people shifted in their seats, whispered to their neighbors, and some even walked out). His language not only served as a barrier to communication, but apparently resulted in what behavior therapists would call a *conditioned emotional reaction* in the audience.

Although different language systems can prevent us from reaching a consensus, a close reading of the literature at times reveals that once we can get beyond an author's theoretical jargon, we may find that what is being said may be quite similar to what others have said, but in different ways. For example, Bandura (1969) has described the reduction of fearful behavior as follows: "Extinction of avoidance behavior is achieved by repeated exposure to subjectively threatening stimuli under conditions designed to ensure that neither avoidance responses nor the anticipated adverse consequences occur" (p. 414). Some years earlier, Fenichel (1941), well-known for his opaque use of psychoanalytic jargon, had described the very same process of fear reduction. In this description, however, he was surprising clear in his use of the vernacular:

> When a person is afraid but experiences a situation in which what was feared occurs without any harm resulting, he will not immediately trust the out-come of his new experience; however, the second time he will have a little less fear, the third time still less (Fenichel, p. 83).

In order to test the way theoretical jargon can be misleading, I once interviewed Howard Rachlin, a colleague known for his radical behavioral orientation, asking about his conceptualization of agoraphobia (Goldfried, Radin, & Rachlin, 1997). We transcribed the interview, translated all the jargon into ordinary language, and asked a group of experienced clinical psychologists to identify his theoretical orientation and indicate the extent to which they agreed with him. We found that relatively few respondents labelled him as behavioral; most thought he was either psychodynamic or eclectic. Further, respondents having a psychodynamic orientation were more likely to agree with his formulation than were those who were behavioral.

The language barrier not only separates therapists on the basis of their theoretical orientation, but it also interferes with communication between researcher and clinician. As researchers, we have developed a unique technical language that succinctly describes the methodological state of the art in therapy research (e.g., end-state functioning). And, while it may serve us well in communicating with other researchers, it serves as a barrier when it is used in the attempt to communicate with clinicians.

Changing Research Methodology

The research methodology associated with psychotherapy outcome research has undergone change over the past several decades (Goldfried & Wolfe, 1998). The first generation of research focused on the very general question of whether psychotherapy worked in bringing about personality change. Relatively little attention was paid to specifying the nature of the clinical problems in question or the methods of intervention. Starting in the 1960s, and receiving most of its impetus from behavior therapy, Generation II methodology defined the target problem more clearly (e.g., public speaking anxiety, unassertiveness) and specified the interventions by means of treatment manuals (e.g., desensitization, role playing). Coming from a tradition of experimental psychology, behaviorally oriented psychotherapy researchers added such aspects to the methodology as random assignment to treatment conditions and other refinements that would ensure internal validity. Generation III outcome research of the 1980s and 1990s, in addition to further refining the methodology of Generation II (e.g., determining the extent to which therapists actually followed the manual), has reflected a marked shift to the medical model. *Outcome research* became clinical trials *and target problems* were replaced by *DSM disorders.*

Just as theory can determine the kinds of research questions that are addressed, so can our research methodology. In fact, sometimes methodological considerations can outweigh theory in determining how we even think about problems. During the APA conference to develop a core assessment battery for psychotherapy outcome research (Strupp, Horowitz, & Lambert, 1997), I found myself in disagreement with two psychodynamically oriented researchers on what needed to be measured in treating anxiety disorders. Although I agreed with them that symptom reduction should be the primary outcome measure, I found myself going to great lengths to try to convince them that other variables were important as well, such as patients' view of themselves and their relationships with other people. The irony was that I had similar arguments with psychodynamic colleagues about the goals of Generation II therapy research in the 1960s and 1970s, dealing with how behavior therapy could reduce target symptoms. However, back then our positions were reversed. Research funding for clinical trials is a powerful reinforcer, capable of changing how we think about clinical problems.

With the requirement that National Institute of Mental Health (NIMH)-funded clinical research make use of DSM diagnoses, there are some research topics and findings that have faded into the background. The extensive Generation II outcome research literature on the treatment of public speaking anxiety is frequently ignored in current studies on social phobia—even though these current studies are, in fact, working with speech-anxious participants. Because unassertiveness is not a diagnosable (and therefore not a fundable) problem, there has been a steady decline (extinction?) in outcome research on that topic—even though virtually every practicing behavior therapist I have ever spoken with maintains that lack of assertiveness seems to play a major role in much of what they encounter clinically. It is also noteworthy that the list of empirically supported therapies generated by the APA Task Force on Promotion and Dissemination of Psychological Procedures (1995) was based mostly on the review of Generation III research, with little recognition given to past outcome studies not using DSM diagnoses.

The Importance of What's New

The amount of clinical, empirical, and theoretical information that has been accumulated over the past 100 years is overwhelming. Even the most conscientious of psychotherapy scholars are unlikely to master the plethora of knowledge that characterizes the field. Moreover, this information overload is compounded with the tendency to equate *new* with *improved.*

In preparing this article, I asked a group of graduate students in clinical psychology to generate as many associations that came to mind during the course of one minute when they thought of the terms *new* and *old.* The results were telling. Virtually every association to *new* had positive connotations, such as *bright, good, better,* and *fresh.* Only about half of the associations to *old* were positive in nature, including such terms as *experienced, wise, solid,* and *established.* The remaining half consisted of terms like *worn out, used, boring,* and *decrepit.*

To confirm that these associations were an accurate reflection of how we tend to react to what is new in comparison to what is old, I checked with *Webster's New Collegiate Dictionary.* Although *new* is defined as "having existed only a short time," it is also said to mean "of dissimilar origin and usually of superior quality" as in "introducing new blood." By contrast, *old* is defined as "from the past—experienced," but also as "showing the effects of time or use" and "no longer in use: DISCARDED," as in "old rags."

To be sure, the focus on what's new is intrinsic to scientific progress in any field; indeed, it is the research frontier. Assuming that the field has an agreed-upon core of knowledge, it is the cutting edge that clearly should receive the most attention. When done in the absence of a core, however, we cannot expect the field to progress in any coherent way.

The Norms of Science

Much has been written about the rules that govern the behavior of scientists. In the early 1940s, it was believed by sociologists studying the behavior of scientists that the norms of science were fairly straightforward and objective. Merton (1942) depicted scientific behavior as having four characteristics:

1. *Universalism:* By this he meant that there existed objective and generally accepted criteria by which knowledge claims may be evaluated. Moreover, there are criteria that are universally applied to anyone who produces the knowledge.

2. *Communality:* Once the knowledge is produced, it belongs to the entire scientific community.
3. *Disinterestedness:* The satisfaction that researchers have in producing knowledge is based solely on the fact that contributions are being made to the field.
4. *Organized skepticism:* Researchers' personal beliefs are set aside, even to the point of doubting one's own views. Instead, judgments are based on logic and data.

A closer examination of the behavior of scientists led Merton (1957) to revise his idealistic, if not somewhat naive views, especially when he began to study the fierce competition that existed among researchers. He observed that science was characterized by fights over priority of discovery—who got there first—and argued that this had more to do with the social system within science itself than with egotism among researchers. For science to advance, original contributions must be made, and professional recognition is given to those who make them. One's career is made by making history, not knowing it.

Merton also suggested that humility was an institutional norm within science—recognizing and acknowledging what one does not know—as in Sir Isaac Newton's statement that he was only able to accomplish what he did by standing on the shoulders of giants. However, Merton weakened his case when he admitted that it is probably easier to accept recognition than to feel humility. He quoted one researcher who presumably confessed: "I possess every good quality, but the one that distinguishes me above all is modesty." What this brings to mind for me is the comment made by Francine Shapiro (1995) in the preface to her book on EMDR, where she likens her contribution to the discovery of flight, landing a man on the moon, and the worldwide popularity of Coca-Cola.

Cole (1992), a student of Merton, similarly laid to rest the positivistic view that the scientific community will agree on findings and theoretical models solely on the basis of objective evidence, namely that nature will win out in revealing the truth. In addition to the quality of the work itself, Cole argued that who the researchers are and the nature of the social processes in the scientific community (e.g., intellectual and political alliances, friendships, institutional loyalties) play crucial roles. Admitting that good guys do not always come in first, Cole suggested that "scientists who are attuned to and adept at manipulating these . . . social processes will experience more career success than those who are not attuned or are less adept" (p. 181).

Based on his study of Apollo moon scientists, Mitroff (1974) has offered an alternative set of norms that govern the behavior of researchers:

1. *Particularism:* Instead of there existing objective criteria that universally apply to all scientists, judgments about knowledge claims are made on the basis of the particular scientist's abilities and experience; it makes a difference whether the researcher is known or unknown.

2. *Solitariness:* Rather than belonging to the entire scientific community, the knowledge that is produced is owned by the particular scientist, and these property rights are not shared prematurely for fear of not getting there first. There is more of an emphasis on *who* is right, than on *what* is right.
3. *Interestedness:* In contrast to producing knowledge for knowledge's sake, researchers do what is likely to be positively received by their own specific reference group and what is likely to further the goals of this group.
4. *Organized dogmatism:* Instead of skepticism about one's own views, skepticism exists about the findings of others; there is firm conviction in one's own beliefs.

This view of how science works is well-known among researchers. Watson (1968) described in his well-known book *The Double Helix* not only how the structure of the DNA molecule was discovered, but also the all-too-human side of scientists. Less well-known is that 30 years earlier, another author—coincidentally named Watson (1938)—published a book titled *Scientists Are Human,* in which he similarly provided an account of the social and personal soft underbelly of research. Researchers are people before they are researchers, and are subject to the same laws of human behavior as are ordinary people.

A particularly "unscientific" aspect of science has to do with the creativity involved in citation practices, which Latour (1987) has referred to as involving "Byzantine political schemes." One such scheme, he argues, is to use the following general strategy: "Do whatever you need to the former literature to render it as helpful as possible for the claims you are going to make" (p. 37). A study by Mahoney (1976) on citation practices found that manuscripts that contained "in press" references to contributions by the author were more likely to be accepted for publication than were identical manuscripts containing "in press" citations to other authors. Being viewed as active and having one's work positively accepted by others apparently helps.

Staats (1983) has written extensively about citation practices in psychology—or, more accurately, the lack thereof. He provides an account of how a well-known but unnamed psychologist presented his own theoretical formulation of human behavior that shockingly overlapped with Staats' own previous work. A documented description of this accusation of plagiarism was originally accepted for publication in the *American Psychologist,* identifying the well-known psychologist by name. Fortunately, the editor subsequently retracted this acceptance, wisely deciding against airing this indiscretion before the entire membership of the APA. Still, we all know that failure to acknowledge the works of others certainly does occur, and therefore contributes to the lack of accumulation of contributions in science.

Scientific facts depend on consensus among scientists. As the comedian Lily Tomlin once put it: "Reality is a collective hunch." However, in order for science to reach a consensus on a contribution, that contribution must be read by others, and "an ignored paper has no more impact than an unpublished one" (Cole, 1992, p. 42). In this context, Latour (1987) has pointed to the distressing observation that most papers are never read at all, leading him to the following conclusion:

> No matter what a paper did to the former literature, if no one does anything with it, then it is as if it never existed at all. You may have written a paper that settles a fierce controversy once and for all, but if readers ignore it, it cannot be turned into a fact . . . You may protest against this injustice; you may treasure the certitude of being right in your inner heart; but it will never go further than your inner heart; you will never go further in certitude without the help of others (Latour, 1987, pp. 40–41).

In short, a fact is not a fact until the community of researchers agrees that it is a fact. Even those psychotherapy contributions that are read, and that are recognized as being important, may fail to have a lasting impact. Once a person leaves the scientific community—through retirement, death, or loss of political influence—his or her influence in the field becomes decidedly less important. An individual's influence in the scientific community becomes less important when other researchers no longer need to rely on him or her for letters of recommendation, peer reviews of their manuscripts, or decisions about grant applications. Once that person is no longer a player and his or her voice becomes less significant, it becomes less essential to cite that person's contribution—a fate we are all likely to share. In short, unless we take steps to establish an agreed-upon core within psychotherapy research and practice, our professional efforts may best be viewed as a process without an outcome.

Treatment: Where Do we Go from Here?

Stating a problem and offering some semblance of an assessment and formulation can certainly help in outlining a treatment plan, but it by no means guarantees one. Complicated problems often require complicated treatments. It also requires active collaboration with, and participation among, those who are experiencing the problem. I view my role in this article more as someone who has identified the issues associated with what we all face as psychotherapy researchers, rather than as the person to suggest how we can set it right. However, my intent has not been to induce a state of depression in either myself or my colleagues, but instead to heighten our awareness of issues that need to be confronted as we begin the next 100 years of psychotherapy research and practice. So, before ending, I will comment briefly on what we need to work toward in helping our field to mature.

In order for psychotherapy to mature, we need to make use of our creative research and clinical energies to build upon, rather than rediscover, what we already know. What has been done in the past is of more than historical interest; it potentially represents the foundation upon which a core consensus may be achieved. Clinical research collaboration is needed; theoretical barriers must be lowered; exclusionary jargon must be translated; findings cannot be limited by currently fashionable methodology; and professional amnesia must be overcome. I have my own opinions on how this might be accomplished (Goldfried, 1995), such as by creating dialogues among therapists of different orientations, making use of a common language, and facilitating a better bond between researcher and clinician. However, these are my own views, and are not necessarily shared by others.

I do believe, however, that the field is closer to arriving at a consensus on certain issues than it has ever been before. The recent movement toward the specification of empirically supported therapies for DSM disorders, however positive its intentions, strikes me as being too oversimplified and, indeed, too dangerously misleading an approach to reaching a consensus. I believe this on the basis of my clinical experience, my research background, and everything I know about the limitations of past efforts at reaching consensus. As a result of the conversations I have had with many respected clinically oriented researchers and research-oriented clinicians, I know that I am not alone in this belief. Indeed, the framers of DSM-IV have made this very point in their introductory chapter:

> Making a DSM-IV diagnosis is only the first step in a comprehensive evaluation. To formulate an adequate treatment plan, the clinician will invariably require considerable information about the person being evaluated beyond that required to make a DSM-IV diagnosis (APA, 1994, p. xxv).

In a report commissioned on behalf of the National Health Service in the United Kingdom, Roth and Fonagy (1996) similarly caution against conclusions drawn solely from DSM-based clinical trials:

> Guidelines should be informed by clinical consensus, to meld training and experience with information gleaned from research findings. Without this, guidelines may be inappropriately narrow and risk so many cases falling outside their range of application that they are seen as clinically unhelpful (p. 50).

Allen Frances and colleagues (Frances, Kahn, Carpenter, Ross, & Docherty, 1996), in part as the result of their experiences in developing DSM-IV, have recognized that attempts at consensus may be heavily influenced by social, political, and economic factors. Moreover, they acknowledge that our research paradigm does not always faithfully generalize to clinical practice. Thus, in developing a methodology to arrive at clinical guidelines for pharmacotherapy, they have used experts involved in both research and practice with a given patient population (e.g., bipolar disorder, schizophrenia) to obtain independent ratings about which drug would be appropriate under differing clinical conditions within that population. The use of this approach to developing research-based and clinically relevant guidelines in determining which psychosocial interventions might be used in various clinical scenarios would seem to hold promise.

Some years ago, Garner, Hake, and Eriksen (1956) wrote about how one might build up a body of knowledge about visual perception that was not confounded by the specific methods used to study the phenomenon. What they addressed was the question of how much of what we learned about perception was a function of the phenomenon, and how much a function of the methods used to study it. Their recommendation was to use more than a single methodology—as they called it, *converging operations*—to investigate the nature of perceptual processes, arguing that firm conclusions could only be drawn from studies that used different methods but arrived at comparable findings. I believe that the same can be said in arriving at a consensus in the field of psychotherapy. Psychotherapy research and clinical practice both focus on the same phenomena, but do so from very different methodological vantage points. To the extent that they arrive at comparable conclusions, the resulting findings are likely to be quite robust. It is *here* that we should look for our core.

COMMENTARY

REACHING CONSENSUS THROUGH EVIDENCE-BASED PRINCIPLES OF CHANGE

My original presidential talk was about the difficulty in obtaining a consensus within the field of psychotherapy. Many of the issues in my presentation continue to remain unresolved. However, here are some of my further thoughts on them.

What Would I Change, Add, or Delete?

If I were able, I would expand my discussion on the clinical-research gap. Much of what has been written about psychotherapy integration over the past several decades has focused on the attempt to reduce the barriers that have existed across the several theoretical orientations. Although we have not yet reached a point where we have a unified paradigm that can help guide our clinical work, the notion of a using contributions from orientations other than our own is no longer taboo. However, the clinical-research gap continues to exist.

Although my original article made a case for the potential complementary contributions of both research and practice, the very longstanding gap between the two continues to exist. This gulf is due, in part, to the fact that most of the research reports in the literature tend to be written for other researchers, and address issues that are more nomothetic nature. There is a tendency for these reports to focus heavily on methodological questions, and relatively few speak directly to the practicing clinician. But it goes beyond this, as there exists an underlying tension between the two communities, where each laments that the other group fails to fully attend to its own contributions.

However, there is nothing like an attack from outside a system to facilitate a united front. The shift from competition and disdain to more fruitful collaboration may now potentially be motivated by the mounting pressure from external forces, such as biological psychiatry and third party payments. As Benjamin Franklin once stated it, "We must all hang together, or assuredly we shall all hang separately." To deal with the attacks from outside the system, the field is very much in need of a consensus, in which there is input from both researcher and clinician as to what constitutes effective psychotherapy.

As indicated above, most of the work on psychotherapy integration has involved the attempt to cross theoretical lines. Because of some of the problems associated with theory that are outlined in my original paper, a fruitful way to arrive at a consensus is with evidence. To the extent that we can demonstrate what works in actual practice, the role of theory becomes secondary. Given the pressures for the field to move toward evidence-based practice, there is very much the need for a two-way bridge between researchers and clinicians.

The distinction between what constitutes empirically supported treatments (ESTs) vs. evidence-based practice is something very much in need of clarification. ESTs consist of those interventions that have been demonstrated to be efficacious through randomized clinical trials (RCTs). Evidence-based practice, on the other hand, includes this and other sources of evidence, such as psychopathology research and findings from basic research on cognition, emotion, behavior, and neuroscience. Moreover, evidence-based practice allows for expert clinical judgment and the fact that the application of interventions to a specific case must take into account characteristics of the patient and relevant moderating variables. As many of these clinically based phenomena may not always appear in the research literature, it is important to recognize the need for building a two-way bridge between practice and research, whereby therapists can have the opportunity to provide feedback to the researcher about their experiences in using ESTs in clinical practice.

Much has been written about the dissemination of research findings to the practicing clinician, and less has been said about the importance of having clinicians disseminate their clinical observations to the researcher. In this sense, clinical practice serves as the context of discovery, highlighting those variables in need of research that can enhance clinical effectiveness. If I were to revise my article, I would spell out in detail the efforts that are being made by Divisions 12 (Clinical) and 29 (Psychotherapy) of the American Psychological Association to build a two-way bridge between research and practice.

Psychotherapy research has made use of the medical model in order to certify interventions that are efficacious. The model is based on the way medications are approved for clinical use by the Food and Drug Administration (FDA) as a result of finding from RCTs. What needs to be recognized, however, is that once a drug has been approved by the FDA, there exists a mechanism whereby practicing physicians can provide feedback with regard to their clinical experiences in using the drug. As noted above, as the result of a collaborative effort between the clinical and psychotherapy divisions of the APA, there now exists a mechanism whereby such clinical feedback can be provided for therapy interventions that have been certified as being empirically supported by RCTs. More information about the two-way bridge project can be found at www.stonybrook.edu/twowaybridge

Another point that could be could be expanded on from the original article has to do with language barriers across therapy orientations that undermine communication and consensus. In 1995, *In Session* was founded as a journal that could not only the link research and practice, but also present conceptual and clinical material without the use of theoretical jargon. The journal continues to exist, is published by Wiley as part of the *Journal of Clinical Psychology*, and appears four times a year.

A point made in the original article that I continue to believe in is the way in which attempts at theoretical development can impede progress in the field. The competitive nature of science drives many to develop theories of therapy, with each theoretical approach being presented as a model for dealing with all problematic human behavior. More often than not, a theorist latches onto a given variable, be it cognition, emotions, or behavior, and attempts to develop a comprehensive model of human behavior and the therapy change process that can apply to all cases. Although there is a certain amount of truth to each of these theoretical models, arguments in the literature that pit one against the other is more likely to obscure, rather than reveal, any of these truths.

What Have I Observed in the Field That is Consistent with My Predictions?

Related to the point made above regarding arguments across theoretical orientations, there has been a new round of competition within an orientation that once presumably had some consensus—cognitive behavior therapy. Although cognitive behavior therapists used to compete with psychodynamic and experiential therapists, they are now arguing among themselves. One such theorist (Steven Hayes) has claimed that his contribution provides a "new wave" of cognitive behavior therapy. He offers evidence for the efficacy of his approach, which has been critiqued by other cognitive behavior therapists that have their own system they wish to advance. This tendency to offer something "new and improved" to the field continues as it has before, and can only serve to undermine efforts to achieve an agreed-upon core of knowledge. Unless the system is changed, so that rewards are given to people who can integrate and find consensus, rather than to provide something new, this tendency is likely to continue to exist. As noted earlier, however, perhaps the attack from outside the system from third party payers and biological psychiatry may finally serve as a source of motivation to engage in fruitful collaboration.

With regard to what changes may have been influenced by my article, I would like to think that current efforts that are directed toward closing the gap between research and practice may have been one of them. However, inasmuch as I am directly involved in these efforts, it is more likely that the influence has been somewhat more subtle, in that I have influenced myself to take action on this issue.

What Are My Thoughts About the Future?

My wishes for the future consist of the attempt to reach a consensus in the field by outlining principles of change that are so robust that they cut across different theoretical orientations. Regardless of orientation, therapy involves: working with patients who have favorable expectations and a certain level of motivation; are functioning within a good therapeutic alliance; become increasingly more aware of those aspects of their functioning and the functioning of others that are creating difficulties; have corrective experiences that allow them to function in a different and more adaptive way; and continue having such experiences over a period of time so as to solidify their therapeutic gains. In order for the field to advance, we need to start with such general principles, and then empirically investigate the parameters that are associated with each, and how they may be used in the context of specific clinical problems. Thus, the principle of increasing awareness may take the form of a reattribution of motive—that is, having patients understand that their anger toward another person is based not on what another person has done, but rather the inaccurate explanation that they have given for this person's behavior. Developing a taxonomy of these parameters of general approaches, and demonstrating how they apply in any given clinical instance, can be a way of reaching consensus within the field.

My actual predictions for the future are much harder to make than are expressing my wishes. Much of where we go as a field depends upon what professional issues and questions are reinforced. The NIMH has always played a key role in moving the direction of the field, and the extent to which they move it in the direction of biological psychiatry will only make progress in psychotherapy research and practice that much more difficult. Skinner was correct in his contention about what influences human behavior, and we as a field need to take steps to counteract the movement away from psychosocial interventions. How this may be done will depend on the creative efforts of those of us that are dedicated to the value of therapeutic intervention.

10

COLLABORATION IN THE NEW MILLENNIUM (2001)

William E. Piper

The year of the millennium has provided us with a special occasion to celebrate the birth, development, and achievements of the Society for Psychotherapy Research (SPR), whose annual meetings began some 31 years ago. Each year, the president starts the conference with an initial address, which has the potential to set a certain tone. Since 1991, each of the Presidential Addresses has been published the following spring in the Society's journal, *Psychotherapy Research*. Thus, there is a complete record of the past 10 Addresses. In chronological order, they include the Addresses of Greenberg (1991), Kächele (1992), Benjamin (1993b), Horowitz (1994), Shapiro (1995), Hill (1996a), Grawe (1997), Crits-Christoph (1998), Stiles (1999a), and Goldfried (2000).

The format of the previous 10 Addresses has been rather consistent from year to year. Typically, the president identifies one or more important issues or questions that characterize the field of psychotherapy research. The issues or questions usually have an unsettled or unanswered quality associated with them. Consequently, a direction for future research is identified. Then, the president indicates how his or her research team has been attempting to advance knowledge regarding the issues or questions that have been identified. In this article, I review some of the major themes addressed by the past presidents, which I believe are relevant not only to the last decade but to the next, consider the implications of the themes for the field, and share some of the related experiences of my own research team.

Just as there is consistency in the format of the past Presidential Addresses, there is consistency in many of the major themes. For example, there is agreement that there are significant weaknesses in some of the basic questions that psychotherapy researchers have addressed, such as "Is psychotherapy effective?" or "Do psychotherapies differ in their effectiveness?" Research questions such as these are currently regarded as being too simplistic or as having already been answered. Similarly, there is agreement that significant weaknesses exist in some of the basic methodologies that psychotherapy researchers have used, particularly in the randomized clinical trial (RCT). The RCT is regarded as flawed in two fundamental ways. First, it is argued that, despite its use of the word *clinical,* much of its methodology differs from what normally occurs in a clinic. For example, therapists usually are not specially selected, usually do not follow strict inclusion and exclusion criteria for patients, do not treat randomly assigned patients, do not use treatment manuals, do not treat patients for fixed lengths of time, and do not assess patients with batteries of process and outcome measures. For all of these reasons, the external validity (or generalizability) of RCTs is regarded as weak. Second, it is argued that despite use of the word *random,* not all of the causal variables in addition to the independent variable are balanced between treatment conditions in RCTs. Imbalance in the treatment conditions is usually due to limited sample sizes and loss of subjects during clinical trials. It is further argued by some (Krause & Howard, 1999) that, even if treatment conditions were perfectly balanced, interactions between undetected variables and the treatment conditions may confound one's conclusions.

Beyond these substantial problems, many of the Presidential Addresses argue that preoccupation with RCTs has led to the neglect of other very important topics regarding change. These include: (1) mechanisms of change, (2) moderators of change, (3) repeated assessments of change, and (4) clinically significant indicators of change. In response to such omissions, the Presidential Addresses suggest many useful ways to carefully study case material to increase our understanding of how therapy works. These include task analysis, narrative analysis, dream analysis, and multifactorial process analysis, among others. Clearly, the weaknesses and limitations of randomized clinical trials have been well documented in the Presidential Addresses of the past decade and some good suggestions have been made. However, having devoted much of my research career to conducting psychotherapy clinical trials, I am conflicted by such strong criticism from people whose work and opinions I respect.

I believe that our research team has been aware of many of the weaknesses and limitations associated with psychotherapy clinical trials. At the same time, we have been aware of some of their strengths, which include (1) careful regulation of independent variables, (2) strong internal validity, and (3) the ability to test theoretically based causal hypotheses. As I will attempt to illustrate, clinical trials also serve to create a structure that permits a variety of objectives and methodologies to be pursued. The lack of recognition of such strengths in most of the previous Addresses was at first puzzling. This led me to suspect that it represented an overreaction to a previous overvaluing of randomized clinical trials in our field and others. Sometimes extreme positions are taken to counter other extreme positions.

The danger, however, is of stereotyping certain questions and methodologies and polarizing researchers who might otherwise communicate with and benefit from each other. As we are aware, polarization has at times not only involved

RCT research vs. process research or RCT research vs. health services research, but other approaches as well, such as quantitative research vs. qualitative research and clinical research vs. analogue research, not to mention polarities created by different theoretical orientations. Rather than succumbing to such polarizations, I believe that the turn of the century is an appropriate time to fully acknowledge the important ways that different methodologies complement each other and advance knowledge in ways that could not occur in the absence of the others.

Next, I would like to examine some of the reasons why collaboration has been difficult to achieve and why it has been easy to fall victim to polarization. To begin, there are: (1) a large number of different objectives for conducting psychotherapy research, (2) a large number of different methodologies for achieving the objectives, and (3) a large number of causal variables for accounting for psychotherapy outcome. I will cite just a few examples of each.

Objectives of research include:

1. discovering powerful treatments that are useful across situations
2. discovering optimal matches among therapies, patients, therapists, and settings
3. discovering causal mechanisms that underlie effective therapies
4. discovering cost-effective treatments
5. protecting patients from ineffectual or harmful treatments, and
6. providing specific guidelines to clinicians.

Methodologies include:

1. randomized clinical trial research, which can be divided into three types:
    A. comparison of different therapies, e.g., traditional comparative studies
    B. aptitude-treatment interaction studies, e.g., matching studies, and
    C. comparison of similar therapies, e.g., dismantling studies
2. statistical modeling research, e.g., multivariate studies based on large samples
3. health services research, e.g., dose-response studies
4. process-outcome research, e.g., aggregated comparison studies, and
5. qualitative research, e.g., nonnumerical task analysis studies.

To this list one might also add the systematic study of catalogued case histories, a traditional approach recently advocated in modern form by Fishman (2000).

In addition to the many different objectives and methodologies, there are many different causal variables. To avoid being inundated and to facilitate communication, psychotherapy researchers usually organize them under a small number of headings. Causal variables include:

1. patient variables
2. therapist variables

3. treatment variables, and
4. setting variables.

If one also includes the interactions among these variables, the total number becomes vast. Just contemplating the number of variables that are capable of affecting psychotherapy outcome is a daunting if not humbling task for any researcher.

To make matters even more challenging, researchers have voiced different opinions as to which objectives are the most important to achieve, which methodologies are the most effective in achieving the objectives, and which causal variables are the most important to study. A special section of the February 1999 issue of the *Journal of Clinical Psychology* was devoted to such a debate.

The large number of objectives, methodologies, and causal variables and the different opinions concerning what is most important to pursue can have two very different effects on the individual psychotherapy researcher. On the one hand, they can be confusing, anxiety arousing, and overwhelming. One can easily find oneself asking such questions as: "Whom should I believe?" "What is the best use of my efforts?" "What if I don't have the resources to pursue the most important objective with the most effective methodology?" "Can I still make a useful contribution to the field?" Because psychotherapy research is time-intensive and methodological requirements have become more and more demanding, it is the rare research team that can pursue several objectives or several methodologies simultaneously. Even well-funded research teams often must pursue objectives in sequence. For example, outcome data is collected, analyzed, and reported, while process data is being transcribed for subsequent ratings or is being rated from recordings. This sequence can result in awkward gaps or considerable delays in understanding the mechanisms that underlie the outcome findings. Because research teams cannot "do it all," they tend to get invested in certain objectives and certain methodologies to the exclusion of others. It becomes easy for one's own objectives and methodologies to become idealized and others to be regarded as less important and less valuable. If we add to this the reality that the processes of obtaining significant funding and publishing one's work in prestigious journals are very competitive, the risk of polarization is clearly high.

On the other hand, I believe that the process of coping with the many different objectives, methodologies, causal variables, and opinions can be stimulating and even reassuring. This can occur if one views the many possibilities as achievable opportunities for making useful contributions.

1. This more positive position is based on several assumptions. For example, in regard to our knowledge base, our field is still at a relatively early stage of development where it is premature to discard objectives and methodologies that have previously proven to be valuable.
2. Each of the objectives addresses a different topic that is important in its own right.

3. Certain methodologies are more effective in achieving certain objectives.
4. Most objectives may be achieved by more than one methodology.
5. Different methodologies can complement one another in advancing knowledge.
6. Progress in advancing knowledge is enhanced by integrating the findings acquired from different methodologies.

Thus, there are many opportunities for individual researchers and individual teams to choose from.

The choice of which objectives and methodologies a researcher pursues is, of course, determined by a number of factors.

1. The researcher's belief in (a) what is important, (b) what is effective, and (c) what is interesting to study.
2. The researcher's wish to present his/her work in high-profile settings and to publish his/her work in the most prestigious scientific journals.
3. The researcher's access to available resources, for example, patients, therapists, research personnel, and funding. As we know, the institutions that we work within and the external granting bodies that we rely on for funding can exert considerable influence on what we study and how we study it.

The problem for a single research team may not only be one of limited time and funds, but also one of limited expertise. For example, a research team that collects outcome data may not be aware of a particularly appropriate process analysis system or, if it is aware, may lack the expertise to apply it well. Conversely, a process analysis team may not have the resources to conduct a well-controlled, large-scale clinical trial, but it does have the expertise and resources to conduct a process analysis of session material. It may welcome an opportunity to apply its system to a new data set. By working together, both teams can benefit. The principle is that of collaboration between researchers and research teams.

SPR is an example of an organization that attempts to promote collaboration. It is an *international, multidisciplinary* scientific organization that emphasizes *inclusiveness.* Its inclusiveness covers: (1) different professions, (2) different levels of training, (3) different theoretical orientations, (4) different treatment modalities, and (5) the different types of objectives and methodologies that I have indicated. Such attributes facilitate both informal and formal communication and collaboration. At an informal level, through presentations and discussions at its annual meetings, attendees become aware of: (1) new variables, (2) new measures, (3) new ways to analyze data, and (4) new ideas that can be applied to data that have been, are being, or will be collected. At a more formal level, attendees arrange to: (1) work on data sets together, (2) write manuscripts together, (3) organize future visits together, and (4) plan future studies together. Processes that originate at annual meetings extend to colleagues at local work sites and to investigators at other settings.

What has become much more possible during the past decade is the opportunity to collaborate across international borders. Advances in ease of communication and travel have accompanied an increasing interest in collaboration. In a recent article on expanding the frontier of treatment research, Norquist, Lebowitz, and Hyman (1999) wrote about the need to form networks of researchers in diverse geographic regions as well as alliances between researchers and clinical providers. SPR is also a good example of an organization that has fully embraced internationalization. Although SPR originated in North America, its annual meetings are now held outside North America every other year. Symposia presented at its annual meetings typically include participants from different countries and continents. At recent annual meetings, there have been attendees from over 25 countries. The Society's Journal, *Psychotherapy Research*, is international in character, with abstracts for its articles printed in four different languages. In addition, SPR's leadership positions are occupied by researchers from throughout the world. Because there are genuine differences in the values attributed to different research objectives and methodologies across international borders, internationalization facilitates the integration of complementary approaches. This has been apparent from the collaborative activities of investigators both within and outside the boundaries of SPR, as evidenced in the research literature.

There is another type of integration that has been emphasized in previous SPR Presidential Addresses, particularly in last year's Address by Marvin Goldfried (2000), that is, the integration between research and practice. Contrary to the process of integration, it has been pointed out that researchers too often have tended to design their studies and write their articles for other researchers, not clinicians. Publications are often replete with statistical and methodological jargon that is not well understood by clinicians. If researchers want their work to have an impact, they will have to convince clinicians that what they have been studying is related to what clinicians do and that their findings are clinically important. These two issues, of course, are related to two of the criticisms of RCTs: that they deal too much with unrepresentative components and they neglect clinical significance. In the following paragraphs, I consider the possibility that it need not be that way, and more specifically that it is possible to put the "clinical" back into randomized clinical trials.

Over a number of years, I believe that the research team I have worked with has moved in that direction. I am aware that other teams in other settings have, as well. I will use the experience of our team to illustrate what I mean. Although our team has involved the collaboration of a large number of people over the years, I would be remiss if I did not mention the names of some of the colleagues that I have worked with most closely. They include: Hassan Azim, Jean-Pierre Bienvenu, Elie Debbane, François de Carufel, Scott Duncan, Anthony Joyce, Mary McCallum, John Ogrodniczuk, John O'Kelly, and John Rosie. Our research team's work is as much theirs as it is mine.

To clearly articulate the weaknesses and limitations associated with RCTs, critics have at times found it convenient to construct a rather thin prototype of RCTs. The prototypical RCT only focuses on pretherapy to post-therapy efficacy in averaged form, only reports results in terms of Statistical significance and effect size, and only studies atypical patients, therapists, and therapies. By today's standards, such a trial would seem to have little value. However, that was not the case in 1973, when I was beginning my career as a psychotherapy researcher in Montreal and beginning to conduct a controlled clinical trial of long-term group psychotherapy (Piper, Debbane, & Garant, 1977). At that time, controlled studies of long-term group psychotherapy were very rare. As a matter of fact, they still are. Although the patients and therapy in our study were typical of those in many outpatient clinics, the rest of the features of our study unfortunately resembled those of the thin RCT prototype. Because of this and other reasons, the scientific value of the findings of our study was probably minimal, although I wouldn't have admitted it then.

However, in contrast to the scientific value of the findings, the study was very valuable to us as a new psychotherapy research team. It provided us with a structure and set of procedures for conducting psychotherapy research that led to more sophisticated and, I believe, more scientifically valuable trials. The procedures had to do with establishing standard ways of: (1) acquiring referrals, (2) assessing patients, (3) allocating patients to different conditions, (4) defining therapy techniques, (5) training therapists, and (6) both recording and rating therapy sessions. Eventually, such procedures became routine in our clinic. The next two group therapy trials that we conducted in Montreal provided findings that were more complex and more valuable. They concerned: (1) ways of preparing patients for group therapy (Piper, Debbane, Garant, & Bienvenu, 1979), (2) ways of coordinating the interventions of cotherapists in groups (Piper, Doan, Edwards, & Jones, 1979), and (3) ways of composing groups to enhance remaining, working, and benefiting (Connelly & Piper, 1989). They also involved fairly detailed process analysis work using a modification of the Hill Interaction Matrix (Hill, 1965).

Our next clinical trial in Montreal was more ambitious (Piper, Debbane, Bienvenu, & Garant, 1984). It compared four forms of time-limited therapy (short-term individual, short-term group, long-term individual, and long-term group). The short-term therapies were of six months' duration and the long-term therapies were of two years' duration. In contrast to the thin RCT prototype that I have described, it was a rather hefty trial that involved detailed process analyses of therapist interventions, outcome assessments during treatment, and focus on patient characteristics as predictor variables. To measure therapist interventions, in particular transference interpretations, we developed a process measure known as the Therapist Intervention Rating System (TIRS; Piper, Debbane, de Carufel, & Bienvenu, 1987). Similarly, our interest in patient personality characteristics led to the development of two interview-based measures of the patient's quality of object relations (Azim, Piper, Segal, Nixon, & Duncan, 1991; Piper & Duncan, 1999) and psychological mindedness (McCallum & Piper, 1997).

Following a geographical relocation to Edmonton, our research team began to use the new measures in a series of RCTs of time-limited psychodynamic therapies. Each trial involved a fairly large group of patients, typically 150–250, who sought services at our psychiatric outpatient clinic. It is worth noting that the therapists in the clinical trials were experienced and the therapies were routinely being provided in the clinic. Data collection usually took between three and four years. The studies included:

1. a controlled trial of short-term individual therapy for a mixed outpatient population (Piper, Azim, McCallum, & Joyce, 1990),
2. a controlled trial of short-term group therapy for patients with complicated grief (Piper, McCallum, & Azim, 1992),
3. a controlled trial of day treatment partial hospitalization for patients with mood and personality disorders (Piper, Rosie, Joyce, & Azim, 1996), and
4. a predictor study of evening treatment partial hospitalization for similar patients (McCallum, Piper, & O'Kelly, 1997).

By this time in our trials, we were routinely including process variables, for example, therapist technique variables in the case of individual therapy and patient work variables in the case of group therapy, using personality measures such as Quality of Object Relations (QOR) and Psychological Mindedness (PM), and analyzing results in terms of clinical significance.

The findings from these trials and the emerging theoretical base led to a new matching study (or aptitude-treatment interaction trial) that involved two forms of short-term individual therapy (interpretive, supportive) and our two patient personality characteristics, QOR and PM. That study was completed about two years ago [1999] and its primary outcome findings concerning patient-treatment matching have been published (Piper, Joyce, McCallum, & Azim, 1998; Piper, McCallum, Joyce, Azim, & Ogrodniczuk, 1999). Currently, we are completing a similarly designed, matching study, but this time with interpretive and supportive forms of group therapy for patients experiencing complicated grief.

In regard to the general findings of our research, I believe that our series of clinical trials has documented the effectiveness of certain time-limited psychodynamic therapies and the importance of certain pretherapy procedures, certain therapist interventions, and certain patient personality characteristics to the process and outcome of those therapies. However, in briefly reviewing the series of RCTs that our research team has conducted over the last 25 years, my intention has not been to emphasize their findings but rather to emphasize their methodology and design. I have been trying to illustrate the evolution of our research team from one that conducted RCTs of the thin prototypical kind that has been the target of extensive criticism to one that has been conducting RCTs that address more complex issues of clinical relevance. It is my impression that this type of evolution has characterized other psychotherapy research teams as well. I believe that it may be time to put the straw-man prototypical RCT to rest and fully embrace the idea that RCTs can be clinically relevant and can complement other research methodologies.

It is clear that, in the case of our own research with time-limited therapies, we could certainly benefit from additional process analysis work of both the quantitative and qualitative types. We have had some experience with task analysis approaches (Joyce, Duncan, & Piper, 1995), but I think not enough. More often than we have liked, we have had to be speculative about patient-therapist interpersonal interactions in therapy and the possible mechanisms underlying our outcome findings. Similarly, our findings would benefit from the methodologies of statistical modeling research and health services research. That would involve large-scale applications of our assessment methods and therapies. Given the time-intensive nature of these methodologies in the current era of health-care reform, this additional endeavor is less feasible. More realistic is the possibility of building in opportunities to replicate our findings in future clinical trials that we will conduct and in the studies that other investigators will conduct in their settings. We have had positive experiences with such collaboration in the past, for example, with our colleagues in Norway (Høglend & Piper, 1995). This brings us back to the theme of collaboration.

The challenge for psychotherapy researchers in the current century is to establish collaboration that integrates different objectives and methodologies of psychotherapy research. For example, Donenberg, Lyons, and Howard (1999) have recently advocated integration and collaboration between clinical trials and mental health services investigations. On the one hand, this involves collaboration among researchers who pursue different objectives and methodologies. As indicated above, individual research teams cannot do it all. On the other hand, it involves collaboration between researchers and clinicians. Last year in his presidential address, Marvin Goldfried referred to the general process as one of dialogue and the general objective as the establishment of a core of knowledge for the field of psychotherapy.

The first step toward the process of collaboration is recognition and acknowledgment of the value of different objectives and methodologies. As Miklowitz and Clarkin (1999) recently suggested, just because findings come from a carefully controlled clinical trial does not mean they are not applicable to community settings, and just because findings come from an uncontrolled, naturalistic community study does not mean that they are scientifically invalid. To avoid dichotomization, or polarization as I have referred to it, respect for alternative approaches such as these is required. In addition, there needs to be dialogue among advocates of alternative approaches. Although organizations such as SPR demonstrate respect for psychotherapy research of diverse objectives and methodologies at its annual meetings and in its journal, in actual numbers, it is easy for some groups to become rather underrepresented. In the case of SPR, this has led to recent efforts to: (1) establish a greater presence of underrepresented researchers, for example, those who focus on cognitive-behavioral techniques, medication, group therapy, family therapy, and marital therapy; (2) establish a greater presence of certain disciplines, such as psychiatry; and (3) establish a greater presence of research-interested clinicians. To the extent to which SPR and other organizations can expand their circles of collaboration, they will increase their chances of achieving a more complete set of objectives and their contribution to knowledge.

As a caveat, however, I must emphasize that collaboration, like most worthwhile activities, does not come without effort and costs. In the international realm of psychotherapy research, it often means dealing with different cultures, different languages, and different styles of working. In addition, the issues of authorship and recognition become more complex and subject to potential conflict when the number of people involved increases. Once again, however, I believe that this is where the experience and nature of SPR and its members emerge as strengths that are up to the task and that can be shared with the wider community of collaborators.

An analogy that to my mind fits the process of collaboration rather well involves the process of assembling a multicolored, multishaped jigsaw puzzle. If you watch people contributing to the puzzle, you notice that their strategies differ. Some people focus on the color, while others focus on the shape of the pieces. Some work on a section outside the boundary of the puzzle and later insert it where they think it belongs; others work solely within the frame. Some insist that the frame must be completed first before further proceeding, others do not. Despite the different strategies and contributions, eventually the puzzle is completed and everyone experiences a sense of accomplishment. There is, however, one notable difference between assembling a puzzle and conducting psychotherapy research. Puzzlers have the advantage of knowing what the finished product looks like; it's on the top of the box. Psychotherapy researchers do not know what the solution looks like until they achieve it. Perhaps that makes achieving it even more enjoyable and satisfying. As we move forward in the 21st century, the opportunities for research collaboration in the field of psychotherapy will only increase. Hopefully, we will recognize their potential and make good use of them.

COMMENTARY

COLLABORATION IN PSYCHOTHERAPY RESEARCH

The Presidential Address that I delivered at the June 2000 annual meeting of the Society for Psychotherapy Research (SPR) focused on the topic of collaboration among psychotherapy research investigators. Collaboration was defined as the combining of resources, both human and nonhuman, to complete a particular therapeutic task. There are both advantages and disadvantages associated with collaboration. On the positive side, collaboration almost always results in an increase in the sample size, which further increases the statistical power of the study. Another potential asset occurs if one or both of the collaborating parties possesses a particular knowledge base, a particular skill set, or both. Ideally, the information from one collaborator complements that of the other. For example, in the field of group therapy, a collaborator may have expertise in regard to a particular process system which captures variables that would not otherwise be included in the study. In addition to using his or her own ratings as study data, the collaborator may also have had previous experience in training others to use the system. This enables the collaborators to accumulate a much larger pool of rated variables. Each collaborator may be quite useful after the completion of the study, when explanations of findings are being sought and interpreted.

Although one usually believes collaboration to be beneficial, it is not without potential problems. On the negative side, there may be competitive strivings associated with the "ownership of the data," the best way to interpret the meaning of the study, and decisions about the best way to proceed in the future. Another possible negative effect of collaboration concerns site effects. These refer to significant variation in the data attributed to aspects of the geographical site of the study. One example is the NIMH Collaborative Study of Depression, which took place at three different sites—University of Oklahoma, University of Pittsburgh, and Washington University (Elkin, Parloff, Hadley, & Autry, 1985). In this study, there were no main effects involving site; however, there were interaction effects. A second example is a recent study that we conducted at two different sites – University of British Columbia and University of Alberta (Piper, Ogrodniczuk, Joyce, Weideman, & Rosie, 2007). In this study, there were no main effects or interaction effects.

Today's clinical trial research in psychotherapy has become a complex endeavor. Typically there are needs for referring agents, therapists, supervisors, research assessors, clinical assessors, research personnel, and principal investigators to carry out related tasks (Bernard et al., 2008). It is not unusual to experience some conflicts between the people who occupy these roles. For example, the criteria for treatment may not be identical to the criteria for the research project. An authoritative leader may be necessary to settle various disputes or differences of opinion.

In preparing my Presidential Address, I discovered that many of the 10 previous Presidential Addresses that I reviewed had similar objectives and were consistent in many of their methodologies. The objectives and methodologies involved identifying significant weaknesses in the methodology regarding basic questions and procedures. Perhaps most predominant were studies that revealed a neglect of topics concerning the understanding of change and over evaluation of the randomized clinical trial. These problems run the risk of polarizing psychotherapy research. The new millennium was a convenient marker to consider the direction and amount of change in collaboration.

Just as there is consistency in the format of the past Presidential Addresses, there is consistency in many of the major themes. For example, there is agreement that there are significant weaknesses in some of the basic questions that psychotherapy researchers have frequently addressed, such as "Is psychotherapy effective?" or "Do psychotherapies differ in their effectiveness?" Research questions such as these are currently regarded as being too simplistic or as having already been answered. Similarly, there is agreement that there are significant weaknesses in some of the basic methodologies that psychotherapy researchers have used, in particular, the randomized clinical trial (RCT). The RCT is regarded as flawed in two fundamental ways. First, it is argued that despite the use of the word "clinical," much of its methodology differs from what normally occurs in a clinic. For example, therapists usually are not specially selected. In addition, therapists usually do not follow strict inclusion and exclusion criteria for patients, do not treat randomly assigned patients, do not use treatment manuals, do not treat patients for fixed lengths of time, and do not assess patients with batteries of process and outcome measures. For all of these reasons, the external validity (or the generalizability) of RCTs is regarded as weak. Second, it is argued that, despite use of the word "random," not all of the causal variables in addition to the independent variable are balanced between treatment conditions in RCTs. Imbalance in the treatment conditions is usually due to limited sample sizes and loss of subjects during clinical trials. It is further argued by some (Krause & Howard, 1999) that, even if treatment conditions were perfectly balanced, interactions between undetected variables and the treatment conditions may confound the conclusions.

Beyond these substantial problems, many of the presidential addresses argue that preoccupation with RCTs has led to the neglect of other very important topics regarding change. These include (1) mechanisms of change, (2) moderators of change, (3) repeated assessments of change, and (4) clinically significant indicators of change. In response to such omissions, the presidential addresses suggest many useful ways to carefully study case material to increase our understanding of how therapy works. These include task analysis, narrative analysis, dream analysis, and multifactorial process analysis, among others. Clearly, the weaknesses and limitations of randomized clinical trials have been well documented in the presidential addresses of the past decade, and some good suggestions have been made. However, being someone who has devoted much of his research career to conducting psychotherapy clinical trials, such strong criticism from people whose work and opinions I respect tends to create dissonance.

I believe that our research team has been aware of many of the weaknesses and limitations associated with psychotherapy clinical trials. At the same time, we have also been aware of some of their strengths. These include: (1) careful regulation of independent variables, (2) strong internal validity, and (3) the ability to test theoretically based causal hypotheses. Cinical trials also serve to create a structure that permits a variety of objectives and methodologies to be pursued.

The lack of recognition of such strengths in most of the previous addresses has been puzzling. This led me to suspect that it represented an overreaction to what previously had been an overvaluing of randomized clinical trials in our field and others. Sometimes extreme positions are taken to counter other extreme positions.

In recent years, it appears that greater attention is being paid to identifying the processes of therapy that serve as effective change agents. To include both measures of effective change agents and outcome is a costly endeavor. As one extends studies to patients with diverse languages, cultures, and traditions of providing psychotherapy, conducting clinical trials becomes quite challenging. It appears that more and more collaborative long-distance studies are being conducted. This is definitely the case for SPR. The use of the computer facilitates collaborative research due to the ease of communication and transfer of data. In spite of this, there appear to be no recent reviews that describe the extent of collaboration either recently or in the past. The same could be said regarding whether collaboration has led to desirable or undesirable effects. It would seem to be worthwhile to conduct a survey that examined the extent of collaboration and its effects, good or bad. In my previous Address, I encouraged practitioners in the field to engage in collaboration with other researchers. Unfortunately, it is not possible to know how much this suggestion has been implemented. Only additional experience will determine whether collaboration as a routine procedure will reward the investigator with valuable information.

11

HERMENEUTIC SINGLE CASE EFFICACY DESIGN (2002)

Robert Elliott

All Gaul, wrote Julius Caesar (BCE 51/1960), is divided into three parts. Similarly, psychotherapy research can be organized into three main areas. Unlike ancient Gaul, these domains are defined not by the rivers that separate them but rather by the scientific questions that motivate them, and by the language, customs, and principles of the researchers who seek to answer these questions.

These three questions and the research territories they define are: (a) Has this client (or group of clients) actually changed? (*outcome research*; e.g., Strupp, Horowitz, & Lambert, 1997); (b) Is psychotherapy generally responsible for change? (*efficacy research*; e.g., Haaga & Stiles, 2000); and (c) What specific factors (within therapy or outside it) are responsible for change? (*change process research*; e.g., Greenberg, 1986).

In this paper I focus on the second question, the causal efficacy of psychotherapy. However, tackling this question requires answering both the first question (whether there is any actual change) and the last question (what processes mediate change). Furthermore, I attempt to meet the challenge of answering these three questions for single therapy clients and nonbehavioral therapies, by proposing the Hermeneutic Single Case Efficacy Design (HSCED).

The Need for a Critical-Interpretive Approach to Causal Research Design

The standard tool for addressing the efficacy of psychotherapy, the randomized clinical trials (RCT) design, is an extremely blunt instrument that suffers from a host of scientific difficulties (Cook & Campbell, 1979; Haaga & Stiles, 2000), especially poor statistical power, differential attrition, and poor generalizability due to restricted samples.

Causal Emptiness

Not the least of these difficulties are two related problems: First, RCTs rely on a stripped-down operational definition of causality (from J. S. Mill; see Cook & Campbell, 1979), in which inferring a causal relationship requires establishing: (a) temporal *precedence* (priorness); and (b) *necessity* & *sufficiency* (that cause and effect covary). Thus, RCTs are "causally empty," offering conditions under which inferences can be reasonably made, but providing no method for truly understanding the specific nature of the causal relationship. For this reason, Haynes and O'Brien (2000) and others have argued that inferring a causal relation requires another condition, the provision of a plausible account ("logical mechanism") for the possible causal relation. Unfortunately, RCTs provide no built-in method for establishing or identifying such plausible causal processes.

Poor Generalizability to Single Cases

Second, RCTs do not warrant causal inferences about single cases. Even when a therapy has been shown to be responsible for change in general, for any specific client, factors other than therapy may actually have been the source of the observed or reported changes, or the client's apparent change may have been illusory. The existence of this inference gap argues for moving the locus of causal inference from the group to the single case, where each client's distinctive change process can be traced and understood.

Rescuing the N = 1 Design

The traditionally sanctioned alternative to group experimental design has been single-participant experimental design. The logic and potential clinical utility of these designs is compelling (Sidman, 1960), and advocates have long argued for the applicability of these designs to non-behavioral treatments (Morgan & Morgan, 2001; Peterson, 1968). Nevertheless, these designs depend on behavioral assumptions about the change process, especially the situational specificity of behavior. As a result, these designs have never caught on outside traditional behavior therapy, not even for cognitive-behavioral therapies.

In order to address the difficulties of applying single case design to non-behavioral therapies, methodologists such as Kazdin (1981) and Hayes, Barlow, and Nelson-Gray (1999) have proposed more flexible alternatives that stretch the guidelines of standard single case design, in particular the clinical replication series. These authors have proposed the following characteristics of single case research as useful for increasing internal validity (Kazdin, 1981):

1. systematic, quantitative data (vs. anecdotal)
2. multiple assessments of change over time
3. multiple cases (a form of multiple baseline design)

4. change in previously chronic or stable problems
5. immediate or marked effects following the intervention.

Sources of HSCED

Kazdin's (1981) general guidelines were one of the sources for HSCED. Another source was Cook and Campbell's (1979) brief description of the *modus operandi* (i.e., one-group post-only design), which they argued can be interpreted when there is rich contextual information and what they called "signed causes" (i.e., influences whose presence is evident in their effects). Mohr (1993) goes even further, arguing that the single case is the *best* situation for inferring and generalizing causal influences, which are obscured in group designs.

The final and most important source for HSCED was Bohart and Boyd's (1997) description of an interpretive approach to examining client qualitative accounts of change over therapy. Starting from a client's assertion that she has changed and her claim that this is the result of therapy, Bohart and Boyd asked, "What would it take to make a convincing case that *therapy* caused a reported change?" In general, the answer to this question takes the form of two types of information: (a) other evidence that the change occurred (corroboration); and (b) plausible ruling out of alternative possible sources of the change.

A *rich case record* of comprehensive information on therapy process and outcome (e.g., using multiple perspectives, sources and types of data) provides a useful starting point. However, *critical reflection* on the claim of therapy-caused change is also required, through maintaining awareness of one's personal expectations and theoretical presuppositions, while systematically searching for evidence that casts doubt on one's preferred account. To do this, Bohart and Boyd (1997) proposed a set of plausibility criteria for evaluating client causal accounts, including evidence for grounding in the client's experience, deviation from expectations, elaboration, discrimination between positive and negative effects and processes, idiosyncraticness, and coherence.

Essentials of Hermeneutic Single Case Design

In our society, experts systematically use practical reasoning systems to make various important judgments, including legal rulings and medical decisions. HSCED is proposed as such a practical reasoning system, with the specific purpose of evaluating the causal role of therapy in bringing about outcome. It builds on Bohart and Boyd's (1997) approach, but examines a larger set of alternative nontherapy explanations, makes greater use of quantitative outcome and weekly change data, and devotes more attention to systematically determining whether change has occurred.

Case Example

To illustrate HSCED, I use a running case example: a depressed, 49-year old male European-American client whom I will refer to as Paul. Paul's main presenting problems were financial worries, general negativity and cynicism, problems communicating with his son, and most importantly, unresolved issues from a rapid succession of the deaths in his family (mother, father, brother), 10 years previously. He was diagnosed with Bipolar II disorder (major depressive episodes plus hypomania) and seen at the Center for the Study of Experiential Therapy for 39 sessions of Emotion-Focused Therapy (EFT, also known as Process-Experiential therapy), primarily focusing on issues of anger and loss. He was seen by a second-year clinical psychology graduate student over the course of 16 months. I did the research interviews.

Rich Case Record

The first prerequisite for a hermeneutic single case efficacy design is a rich, comprehensive collection of information about a client's therapy. This includes background information, as well as data on therapy process and outcome, using multiple sources or measures. I have found the following data to be useful:

a. *Basic facts* about client and therapist, including demographic information, diagnoses, presenting problems, therapeutic approach or orientation (e.g., given above for Paul).
b. *Quantitative outcome measures*. Therapy outcome has both descriptive qualitative (*how* the client changed) and quantitative (how *much* the client changed) aspects. For Paul, quantitative measures included standard self-report questionnaires such as the Symptom Checklist-90 (Derogatis, 1983), the Inventory of Interpersonal Problems (Horowitz, Rosenberg, Baer, Ureño, & Villaseñor, 1988), and the Simplified Personal Questionnaire (PQ; Elliott, Shapiro, & Mack, 1999). At a minimum, these measures should be given at the beginning and end of therapy, but it is also a good idea to give them periodically during therapy, every 8–10 sessions. Paul's quantitative outcome data are given in Table 11.1.
c. *Change Interview*. The Change Interview (Elliott, Slatick, & Urman, 2006) is a semi-structured interview that provides (i) qualitative outcome data, in the form of client descriptions of changes experienced over the course of therapy; and (ii) client descriptions of their attributions for these changes, including helpful aspects of their therapy. (Information on negative aspects of therapy and on medications is also collected.) The Change Interview takes 30–45 minutes and is best carried out by a third party, every 8–10 sessions, at the end of therapy, and at follow-up.

   Paul listed six pre- to post-changes, including "More calm in the face of challenges." "Giving myself more credit for accomplishments." "Doing

TABLE 11.1 Outcome Data for Client PE-04 (Paul)

Measure	*Caseness*	*RC Min (p < .2)*	*Pre*	*Post*	*6-month follow-up*
SCL-90-R GSI	.93	.51	1.17	.80	.47
Inventory of Interpersonal Problems-26	1.50	.57	1.69	1.62	.96
Personal Questionnaire	3.0	1.00[a]	4.44 (4.11)[b]	2.44 (2.78)[b]	2.22

Note: Caseness: cut-off for determining whether client is clinically distressed; RC Min: minimum value required for reliable change at $p < .2$; "+" = reliable improvement from pretherapy. Sources for values given: Barkham, Rees, Stiles, Shapiro, Hardy & Reynolds (1996; Inventory of Interpersonal Problems); Ogles, Lambert & Sawyer (1995; SCL-90-R GSI); Wagner & Elliott (2001).
[a] Corrected from original version.
[b] Using median of three successive weekly scores to smooth instability of scores.

better financially." "Being a happier person." "Being more hopeful about my life." and "(I) don't feel young anymore" (= a negative change). Paul rated these changes as highly unlikely without therapy and described how therapy brought them about: "I don't think I would have looked at those [feelings] on my own . . . I think the therapy actually in some way . . . gave me a process of grieving, maybe not all the stages of grief, but some."

d. *Weekly outcome measure.* A key element in HSCED is the administration of a weekly measure of the client's main therapy-related problems or goals. We used the Simplified Personal Questionnaire (Elliott, Shapiro, & Mack, 1999), an individualized target complaint measure consisting of roughly 10 seven-point distress rating scales.

   Paul's weekly mean PQ scores are given in Figure 11.1, which reveals an erratic pattern of numerous statistically reliable (> 1.0) week-to-week shifts in PQ scores.

e. *Helpful Aspects of Therapy (HAT) form* (Llewelyn, 1988) is a frequently employed qualitative measure of client perceptions of significant therapy events. This open-ended seven-item questionnaire is administered to clients after therapy sessions. In HSCED, HAT data are used to pinpoint significant therapeutic processes which may be associated with change on the weekly outcome measure or to corroborate change processes referred to in the Change Interview.

   In his HAT descriptions, Paul gave 12 significant events ratings of 8 (greatly helpful) or higher. These descriptions provide a summary narrative of what the client considered at the time to be the most helpful events in his therapy.

f. *Records of therapy sessions.* Therapist process notes and videotapes of therapy sessions are collected in case they are needed to pinpoint, corroborate, or clarify issues or contradictions elsewhere in the data.

   For example, in order to make sense out of the largest shifts in Paul's weekly PQ scores, I used his therapist's process notes.

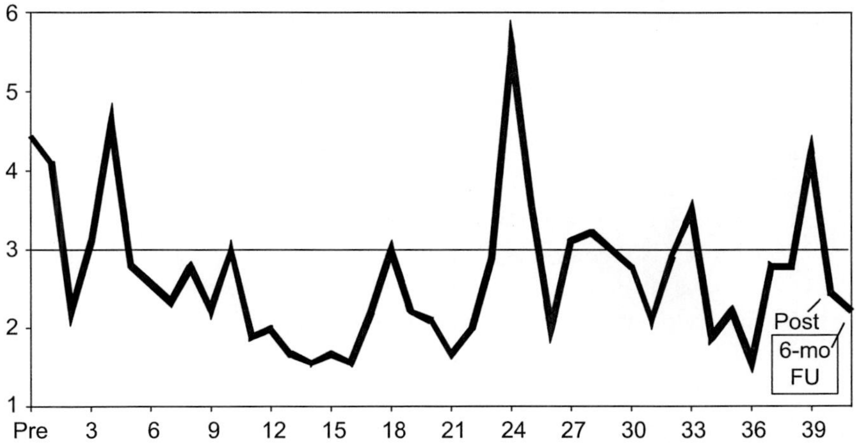

FIGURE 11.1 PQ Means Across Sessions: PE-04 (Paul)

Direct Evidence: Clear Links between Therapy Process and Outcome

In HSCED, the starting point is direct evidence pointing to therapy as a major cause of client change. In order to be confident about proceeding further with the analysis, it is best to have at least two separate pieces of evidence supporting the therapy-change link.

1. *Retrospective attribution.* First, the client may directly attribute a reported change to therapy.

   Clear support for the therapy efficacy hypothesis can be found in Paul's "likelihood-without-therapy" ratings and his description of the role his therapy played in helping him feel more calm in the face of challenges.
2. *Process-outcome mapping.* The content of the client's post-therapy changes corresponds to specific events, aspects, or processes within therapy.

   For example, five of Paul's 12 high-rated significant events (e.g., session 12: "Feeling the hurt, fear, and sadness related to the loss of my family. It enabled me to realize that I can feel what might be under my anger.") refer to work on unresolved loss/grief issues regarding his family of origin, his major post-therapy change.
3. *Within-therapy process-outcome correlation.* In addition, theoretically central in-therapy process variables (e.g., adherence to treatment principles) may be found to covary with week-to-week shifts in client problems.

   To examine this possibility for Paul's therapy, I correlated his therapist's postsession ratings of her use of Process-Experiential treatment principles, tasks, and response modes with difference scores on the Personal

Questionnaire (N = 34 pairs of data points). Only two of the 63 correlations were statistically significant ($p < .05$), less than would be expected by chance. Therefore, at least on this basis, there was no evidence of a therapy-change link.

4. *Early change in stable problems.* Therapeutic influence can be inferred when therapy coincides with change in longstanding or chronic client problems, contrasting with an explicit or implicit baseline.

   Paul's mean PQ scores (Table 11.1) do appear to show a reliable, 2-point drop from pre- to post-treatment. Although we do not know how long Paul's problems had continued at roughly the same level, it is clear that some of them were of many years' standing. Furthermore, his two pretreatment PQ mean scores are consistent with each other (4.44 and 4.11) and in the clinical range (i.e., well above the cut-off of 3). His weekly PQs (Figure 11.1) show some instability, but this appears to be a consequence of three outlier sessions (4, 24, 39). If these are ignored, the largest improvement occurs after Session 1, moving the client into the nonclinical range.

5. *Event-shift sequences.* An important therapy event may immediately precede a stable shift in client problems, particularly if the nature of the therapy process and the change are logically related to one another (e.g., therapeutic exploration of an issue, followed the next week by change on that issue).

   Although Paul's PQ ratings contained many substantial shifts (Figure 11.1), the largest shifts appeared to reflect temporary *blips* associated with the three outlier sessions with no consistent relation to significant therapy events.

Thus, there was supportive evidence linking change to therapy, on three out of five possible indicators.

Indirect Evidence: Competing Explanations for Apparent Client Change

HSCED also requires good-faith efforts to find nontherapy processes that could account for an observed or reported client change. The practical reasoning process involved in evaluating these alternatives is like detective work, with contradictory evidence sought and available evidence weighed carefully. As a result, some nontherapy explanations may be ruled out entirely, while others may be found to partially or even completely explain the observed change. In addition, it is important to weigh both positive and negative evidence. Discrepancies point to complexities or restrictions on the scope of change or the possible role of therapy. A further consideration is the degree of uncertainty considered tolerable. The circumstances under which therapists and their clients operate preclude near certainty ($p < .05$), suggesting "reasonable assurance" or "beyond a reasonable doubt" ($p < .2$) as a more realistic and useful standard of proof. [The rest of this section is significantly abridged from the original version.]

1. *Trivial or Negative Change*

The first four nontherapy explanations assume that apparent client change is illusory or artifactual. First, the apparent changes may be trivial or negative. Trivial changes may be described in such highly qualified or ambivalent terms as to cast doubt on their importance, or may involve changes in other people or life circumstances (one of Paul's changes was "doing better financially"). Similarly, changes on quantitative outcome measures may also fall into the trivial range (e.g., one point on the BDI). Changes might also be negative, casting doubt on the overall effectiveness of the therapy. For example, at an earlier assessment, Paul noted that he and his son were now fighting more than when he began therapy. Changes on quantitative outcome measures may also occur in the negative direction.

In order to assess trivial or negative change, it is useful to define intervals or threshold values that can be used to define change as nontrivial. Jacobson and Truax (1991) proposed two criteria for evaluating change: (a) statistically reliable change and (b) movement past clinical caseness (i.e., clinical significance) cut-offs. Table 11.1 includes these criteria for three key measures (SCL-90-R, IIP, PQ).

Paul's outcome data indicate that from pre- to post-therapy he moved past the caseness threshold on 2 out of the 3 measures (SCL-90 and PQ) but that the amount of change was reliable on only 1 of these measures (PQ).

Next, in order to assess for negative changes, the researcher can ask the client to describe any negative changes that might have occurred over the course of therapy. For example, at posttreatment, when Paul was asked about negative changes, he noted that he did not feel young anymore.

Finally, clients can be asked to evaluate the importance of changes, perhaps using rating scales (cf. Kazdin, 1999). In the Change Interview, the client rates the importance of each change, using a five-point scale. In addition, the manner of the client's description can be examined for qualifiers and other forms of ambivalence.

Thus, in his post-therapy Change Interview, Paul rated all of his positive changes as either very or extremely important; by contrast, he rated his one negative change, feeling old, as slightly important. His descriptions of his changes were directly stated without qualifiers and even included occasional intensifiers ("I am *in fact* more calm than I've been in a *long* time").

2. *Statistical Artifacts*

Related to the possibility of trivial change is statistical error, including measurement error, regression to the mean, and experimentwise error. *Measurement error* involves random inconsistencies in quantitative measures. Jacobson and Truax's (1991) formula provides a confidence interval for defining a minimum *Reliable Change Index* (RCI) value for client change, at either the traditional 95 percent level or the 80 percent level proposed here. Client change which is less than the minimum RCI value is judged to reflect measurement error. Table 11.1 contains RCI minimum values for three common outcome measures: SCL-90, IIP, and PQ.

Paul's pre-to-post change on two of the three outcome measures was less than the prescribed values, although his change on the PQ is statistically reliable. However, the frequent drastic shifts in Paul's weekly PQ scores raised issues about temporal instability (consistent with his atypical bipolar diagnosis) and suggested that it would be a good idea to use the median of his first three and last three PQ scores (Table 11.1 values in parentheses). The difference between these pre- and post-therapy median PQ scores greatly exceeded the minimum RCI value of 1.00.

Regression to the mean occurs when measurements with less than perfect reliability are selected on the basis of their extreme values (Cook & Campbell, 1979). If regression to the mean is operating, then repeating the measurement prior to beginning therapy is likely to reveal a sharp drop; if this occurs, the second measurement can be used as the pretest.

For example, one possible explanation for the numerous sharp spikes in Figure 11.1 is measurement error followed by regression to the mean. However, Paul's two pretreatment PQ scores were fairly stable (both above 4 or moderately distressed), indicating that they were representative of his usual responses; thus, the substantial changes observed in Paul's PQ scores are probably not a function of regression to the mean.

Experimentwise error is a function of carrying out multiple significance tests on change measures. When examining several measures for evidence of change, some apparently reliable differences may occur due to chance alone. For example, when looking at change on three measures at $p < .2$, the probability of one or more measures out of three showing reliable change by chance was .49! The solution here was to require reliable change on two out of three measures, corresponding to a probability of $p < .10$. Requiring replication of reliable change across different outcome measures allows designating a client as demonstrating *Global Reliable Change.*

Using these criteria, Paul showed reliable change at posttreatment on only one out of the three measures, thus failing to demonstrate Global Reliable Change. However, he did satisfy this standard at six-month follow-up (see last two columns in Table 11.1), and his posttherapy PQ change exceeded the $p < .05$ significance level. Thus, it would be most accurate to say that Paul showed reliable but limited change at follow-up but not immediately post-therapy.

3. Relational Artifacts

Apparent client improvement may also reflect interpersonal dynamics between client and therapist or researcher. The classic relational artifact is the legendary (but impossible to attribute) *hello-goodbye effect,* in which the client enters therapy emphasizing distress in order to impress the research staff to accept him/her. Then, at the end of therapy, the client emphasizes positive functioning, either to express gratitude to the therapist and research staff or to justify ending therapy. (I suspect that the use of fixed time limits in most therapy research works to strengthen this effect.)

In order to determine the role of these interpersonal artifacts, client narrative descriptions are invaluable. These accounts are probably most credible when they emerge spontaneously in therapy sessions or research interviews; however, researchers may prefer to obtain these accounts systematically via questionnaire or interview. Because interviews are a highly reactive form of data collection, client qualitative accounts of the effects of therapy need to be read very carefully for nuance and style, using Bohart and Boyd's (1997) plausibility criteria, especially elaboration and discrimination. The validity of client accounts is also enhanced if a researcher (rather than the therapist) interviews the client, and if the researcher conducts an extended, in-depth interview in which he or she encourages thoughtful self-reflection and openness on the part of the client.

Paul's Change Interview data contained substantial detail and at least some negative descriptions. Nevertheless, his manner and choice of language suggested that he may have deferred to me as an apparently successful authority figure, suggesting that he may have held back negative views of his therapy to avoid offending me. This would explain the discrepancy between his mixed quantitative outcome results and his highly positive Change Interview descriptions. Because I was aware of the possibility of his trying to please me, I tried to communicate the attitude that any critical comments would be especially appreciated because they would help improve the therapy.

4. Expectancy Artifacts

Cultural or personal expectations about therapy or wishful thinking may also give rise to apparent client change. That is, clients may convince themselves and others that since they have been through therapy they must therefore have changed. Post-therapy accounts are likely to be particularly vulnerable to this retrospective expectancy bias. Longitudinal measurement of change is no guarantee against clients expecting themselves to do better at the end of therapy and therefore giving themselves the benefit of the doubt when recalling, integrating, and rating subtle or ambiguous phenomena such as mood symptoms, relationships, or self-evaluations.

Examining the language clients use to describe their experience can be useful here, because expectation-driven descriptions are likely to rely on shared cultural *scripts* about the effects of therapy by using standard or clichéd phrases (e.g., someone to talk to). Client accounts of changes that conform entirely to cultural stereotypes are less credible than those that contain idiosyncratic content or word choice (cf. Bohart & Boyd, 1997).

For example, Paul's descriptions generally contained a mixture of stock elements (the idea that releasing blocked feelings is therapeutic), but often qualified in idiosyncratic ways (e.g., typifying this release as a gradual process occurring over the course of a year). Some of Paul's descriptions of his change process did have an intellectualized, self-persuasive quality, for example (italics added): "I *think* I could see the progress, and *that can only help* build self-esteem and self-confidence. So as that goes up, *maybe* proportionately, *maybe* the anxiety goes down." Faced with this self-speculative account, I asked Paul to check the accuracy of his description, which enabled him to elaborate a more experientially-based account of extended, painful grieving for deceased family members. In addition, on four of his six changes, Paul rated himself as "somewhat surprised."

5. Self-Correction Processes

The remaining nontherapy explanations all assume that change has occurred, but that factors other than therapy are responsible. First, client internally generated maturational processes or self-help efforts may be responsible for observed changes. For example, the client may have entered therapy in a temporary state of distress that has reverted to normal functioning via the self-limiting nature of temporary crises or the person's native problem-solving processes. In these instances, client self-healing activities operate prior to or independently of therapy. A general strategy for evaluating the final four nontherapy explanations is to ask the client.

When Paul was asked what brought about his changes, the first thing he said was "Being honest with myself, and being open to change, to trying new things." By itself, this statement would qualify as a report of self-generated change. However, without prompting, Paul then went on to indicate that this self-generated change process was related to therapy: "Since the therapy, I think I've had a lot more courage to really try new things. It's been exciting." In addition, Paul rated three of his six changes as "very unlikely without therapy."

Therapist process notes provide an efficient source of information about client self-help efforts, and can be used in conjunction with shifts in PQ scores. Paul showed a large drop on his PQ after session 1; in her process notes, Paul's therapist noted that Paul had recently made the effort to speak to a friend with similar loss issues, and that this conversion had made him feel less alone.

Self-correction in particular can also be evaluated by comparing client change to a temporal or expectational *baseline*. A temporal baseline requires measuring the duration or stability of the client's main problems or diagnoses. In lieu of repeated pretreatment measurement, clinicians generally measure the baseline of a client's problem retrospectively, by asking the client how long he or she has had the problem.

A review of session tapes and therapist process notes made it clear that two of Paul's main problems—anger/cynicism and unresolved grief—were difficulties of at least 10 years' standing, while his financial problems and anxiety about his son were of relatively recent vintage (i.e., in the order of months). The duration of his central problems make self-correction an unlikely explanation for his change on the PQ. Overall, there is clear support for self-correction as a *partial* influence on Paul's changes, but the evidence indicates that it is unlikely that self-correction was primarily responsible, without themselves reflecting the influence of therapy.

6. Extra-Therapy Events

Extra-therapy life events include changes in relationships, such as crises, deaths, divorces, initiation of new relationships, marriages, births. In addition, clients may change jobs, get fired from jobs, get promoted or take on new work responsibilities, change recreational activities, and so on. Extra-therapy events may be discrete or they may involve chronic situations such as an abusive relationship or the consequences of substance abuse or other problematic behavior. They may also include changes in health status due to physical injuries or illnesses or medical treatments, where these do not directly impinge on psychological functioning. Further, extra-therapy events can contribute both positively and negatively to therapy outcome, and have the potential to obscure the benefits of a successful therapy as well as to make an unsuccessful therapy appear to have been effective. Finally, it is important to consider the bidirectional influence of therapy and life events on one another.

The most obvious method for evaluating the causal influence of extra-therapy events is to ask the client. In the Change Interview, clients are asked what they think brought about changes. If a client does not volunteer extra-therapy events, the interviewer inquires about them. In addition, therapist process notes and session recordings are useful sources of information about extra-therapy events, because clients almost always provide in-session narratives about important positive or negative extra-therapy events. A useful method for locating important extra-therapy events is to look at weeks associated with reliable shifts in weekly change measures such as the PQ.

Extra-therapy events are the major nontherapy counter-explanation in Paul's treatment. When asked, Paul spontaneously described: "Support from my family . . . Reading . . . I have to say my exercise, that's important . . . New activities. Mainly the jobs." His PQ data reveal one large, clinically significant drop at session 2, and three *spikes*, at sessions 4, 24, and 39. Consistent with the drop before session 2, the therapist's process notes describe the client as feeling better, linking this to positive developments in his job and family, as well as a discussion with a friend with similar problems. On the other hand, extra-therapy events had a clear negative influence in the weeks prior to sessions 4 and 25.

7. Psychobiological Causes

The next possibility is that credible improvement is present, but is due primarily to unidirectional psychophysiological or hormonal processes, including psychotropic medications or herbal remedies; the hormonal effects of recovery or stabilization following a major medical illness (e.g., stroke) or after childbirth;

or seasonal and endogenously driven mood cycles. This is a particular problem for psychotherapy research when clients begin or change their medications within a month of beginning psychotherapy, or during therapy. The most obvious approach to evaluating psychobiological factors is to keep track of medications, including changes and dose adjustments. It is also important to ask about herbal remedies. (The Change Interview includes questions about both of these.) Paul had been stable on his anti-anxiety medication since well before the beginning of therapy, and had been taking SSRIs for almost as long, with a minor increase in his latest SSRI one month before the end of therapy.

In addition, client interview data and therapist process notes provide useful sources of information about medication and the effects of other medical and biological processes. For example, at his six-month follow-up interview, Paul disclosed that he had suffered from a major, life-threatening illness during the intervening time, and had experienced a greater sense of focus and appreciation for what was important as a result.

8. Reactive Effects of Research

The final nontherapy explanation involves the reactive effects of taking part in research. These include helpful research activities (e.g., pre-therapy assessment), interactions with the research staff, and enhanced sense of altruism from helping others by taking part in research. On the other hand, research activities can have negative effects on clients, especially if they are particularly evocative or time-consuming. Teasing out the reactive effects of research on client outcome can be difficult, but qualitative interviewing about the effects of research can be useful. Another possibility is to use nonrecruited clients and unobtrusive data collection. Spontaneous comments during sessions, summarized in therapist process notes, are also worth noting.

For example, in session 4, Paul expressed concerns at not being able to be totally open in therapy, because of his concerns about the recording equipment. (Several times during therapy, he referred to "All you assholes watching this.") In addition, he sometimes wrote snide comments on his postsession questionnaire.

Summary and Conclusions of HSCED Analysis of Paul's Therapy

Reviewing the results of applying HSCED to Paul's treatment, there was clear or moderate support for three out of five types of direct evidence: retrospective attribution, immediate perception, and change in stable problems. Since the standard is replication across two or more types of direct evidence, this was more than adequate.

In terms of negative evidence, the standard is that no nontherapy explanation can by itself or in combination with other nontherapy explanations fully explain the client's change, although nontherapy explanations can and usually do play some role in accounting for change. For Paul, there was clear or moderate support against a primary role for all nontherapy explanations, except experimentwise error. The analysis indicates that the change reported on the PQ was unlikely to be due to chance, but identifies Paul's change as narrowly limited to his presenting problems (indicated by lack of change on the SCL-90 and IIP). Self-help, extra-therapy events are also important supporting influences, but not to the exclusion of therapy.

Beyond this, however, what have we learned about psychotherapy from this intensive analysis? First, most simplistically, the analysis supports the claim that Process-Experiential/Emotion-Focused therapy can be effective with clients like Paul, i.e., clients with major depressive disorder plus hypomania (Bipolar II), particularly when they present with issues of anger and unresolved grief. Second, although effective, there was still room for improvement, especially with regard to a broader range of problems and areas of functioning. Third, the analysis makes it clear that therapy exerted its helpful effects within a context of other, supporting change processes, especially extra-therapy events and self-help efforts.

Specific Change Processes

Finally, in the process of sorting out the role of therapy in Paul's change process, I was able to use his descriptions of what he found helpful in his therapy, including post-session descriptions of significant events, but more importantly his descriptions from his post-therapy Change Interview. These accounts provided enough detail to allow me to construct the following model of his change process, providing a plausible account of the chain of events from cause (therapy) to effect (outcome) (Haynes & O'Brien, 2000).

First, in therapy, (a) Paul credited his therapist for "bring[ing] me back to certain areas that she thought I needed to work on, which I might have overlooked"; resulting in (b) "a consistent process of sharing my problems, my frustrations, my heartbreaks"; which (c) "gave me a process of grieving, maybe not all the stages of grief, but some." This grieving process was one of being "able to gradually release it over a year."

As a result of this, he was able to build on in-therapy work through his own efforts: (d) He said, "Then you see a tangible result. And even before [my nephew's] funeral I went out to my family's graves and I was able to cry." (e) After this, Paul said, he "start[ed] maybe for the first time in a long time, to recognize my progress"; and (f) "that can only help build self-esteem and self-confidence." (g) Finally, Paul implied that this extended grieving/release process had begun to undo his earlier problematic functioning ("I kept a lot of things bottled up [before], and I think that just adds pressure, adds to the anger, adds to the anxiety"); leading to (h) reduced anger and anxiety about hurting other people with his anger ("feeling more calm, and not blowing challenges out of proportion").

Issues in Hermeneutic Single Case Efficacy Design

In order to carry out an HSCED study, one needs to: (a) find an interesting and agreeable client; (b) collect appropriate measures; (c) apply them to construct a rich case record; (d) analyze the information to see if change occurred; (e) establish if direct evidence linking therapy to client change is present and replicated; (f) carefully analyze the evidence for each of the eight nontherapy explanations; (g) interpret and weigh the various sets of sometimes conflicting information; and (h) come to an overall conclusion about the likelihood that therapy was a key influence on client change.

HSCED is a new development and clearly needs further testing and elaboration. My team and I have applied HSCED to Paul and other clients (e.g., Elliott, Partyka, et al., 2009). What we have learned so far can be summarized as follows.

First, the "Did the client improve?" question has turned out to be more complex than we first thought. Our clients often present us with a mixed picture, showing improvement on some measures and not others, or telling us that they had made great strides when the quantitative data contradicted this (see Elliott et al., 2009). It is important not to underestimate the complexity of this initial step.

Second, this experience has convinced us that more work is needed on how to integrate contradictory information. We need better strategies for determining where the "weight of the evidence" lies (see Schneider, 1999).

Third, we find ourselves in need of additional creative strategies for evaluating nontherapy explanations, for example, to bolster the self-reflective/critical process of examining nontherapy processes. Bohart (2000) has proposed a form of HSCED that relies on an adjudication process involving separate teams of researchers arguing for and against therapy as a primary influence on client change, with final determination made by a "research jury." However, a less involved process might simply make use of two researchers: one (perhaps the therapist) supporting therapy as an important influence; the other playing "devil's advocate" by trying to support alternative explanations. The researchers might present both sides, leaving the final decision to a scientific review process (cf. Fishman, 1999). We are currently testing a form of adjudicated HSCED (Elliott et al., 2009).

Fourth, in comparing HSCED to traditional RCT design, we have found that HSCED requires fewer resources but is in some ways more difficult and demanding, in that it requires researchers to address complexities, ambiguities, and contradictions ignored in traditional designs. These complexities are present in all therapy research, but RCTs are able to ignore them by simplifying their data collection and analysis. In my experience, every group design is made up of individual clients whose change process is as rich and contradictory as the clients we have studied. The fact that these complexities are invisible in RCTs is yet another reason to distrust them and to continue working toward viable alternatives which do justice to each client's uniqueness, while still allowing us to determine whether: (a) the client has changed, (b) whether these changes have anything to do with our work as therapists, and (c) what specific processes in therapy and in the client's life are responsible for these changes.

Beyond these relatively delimited research applications, HSCED raises broader issues, including the appropriate grounds for causal inference in applied settings, external validity, and the nature of causality in psychotherapy.

Causal Inference in the Absence of RCTs

Skilled practitioners in a variety of settings continually apply useful but implicit practical reasoning strategies to make causal judgments about single events, ranging from medical illnesses to lawsuits to acts of terrorism (see Schön, 1983). For example, forensic and medical practice are both fundamentally systems for developing and testing causal inferences in naturalistic situations. HSCED uses a set of procedures to assess possible alternative explanations for client change. The researcher uses a combination of informant (client and therapist) and observer data collection methods, both qualitative and quantitative. These methods confront the researcher with multiple possible indicators of which they must make sense, typically by looking for points of convergence and interpreting points of contradiction.

External Validity with Single Cases

Logically, what can be demonstrated by a single case such as the one I have presented is the *possibility* that this kind of therapy (EFT, specifically, using primarily empathic exploration and empty chair work over the course of about 40 sessions) can be effective with this kind of client (male, middle-aged, European American, intellectualizing, psychologically reactant) with this kind of problem (e.g., recurrent depression with hypomanic episodes, unresolved multiple losses, current family conflicts). Predicting how effective a similar therapy would be with a similar client would require a program of systematic replication (Sidman, 1960) and, ultimately, a summary of a collection of similar cases, analogous to precedents established by a body of case law (Fishman, 1999).

Nature of Causation in Psychotherapy

Another broad issue concerns the kinds of causal processes that are relevant to understanding change in psychotherapy. The following three propositions seem most consistent with how clients change over the course of therapy:

First, change in psychotherapy involves *opportunity* causes (bringing about change by opening up possibilities to the client), rather than *coercive* causes (forcing or requiring change). Psychotherapy appears to work by offering clients occasions to engage in new or neglected ways of thinking, feeling, and acting and by helping clients remove obstacles to desired behaviors or experiences.

Second, if opportunity causes are the rule in therapy, then, by definition, change in therapy involves multiple *contributing causes* ("weak" or "soft" causation) rather than *sole* causes ("strong" or sufficient causation). After all, opportunities are not commands and can always be rejected or simply ignored. Therapist responses in therapy sessions, and even client-therapist interactions in sessions, can provide at best only a partial explanation of client change. Other factors must be assumed to play important roles as well, including extra-therapy life events, biological processes, and especially client internal self-help processes. A complete interpretation of the change process probably requires weaving together the different therapy and nontherapy strands into a narrative such as the one I presented at the end of the analysis section of this chapter.

Finally, the development of explanations of therapy outcome is a fundamentally interpretive process, involving a *double hermeneutic* (Rennie, 1999) of client (engaged in a process of self-interpretation) and researcher (engaged in a process of interpreting the self-interpreter). The double hermeneutic suggests that the client is a really a co-investigator, who acts always as an active self-interpreter and self-changer. As researchers, we follow along behind, performing a second, belated act of interpretation, carefully sifting through the multitude of sometimes contradictory signs and indicators provided by the client. Although we are sometimes weighed down by methodology, nevertheless, it is our greatest desire to understand how our clients change, in order to become more effective in helping them do so.

COMMENTARY

LOOKING BACK: COMMENTARY ON "HERMENEUTIC SINGLE CASE EFFICACY DESIGN"

When I was a 26-year-old graduate student at UCLA, my advisor invited me to come along to the 1976 annual conference of the Society for Psychotherapy Research, at the Hotel del Coronado in San Diego, California, a couple of hours' drive south from Los Angeles. It was my first scientific conference, and I hadn't been organized enough to arrange for hotel accommodations before I left, so one of the two nights I ended up sleeping in my car. At the conference dinner, I heard Aaron Beck, the founder of cognitive therapy, give his presidential talk. I met Laura Rice, Les Greenberg, Len Horowitz, Bill Pinsof, to name just a few of the people who would later become friends. The conference changed my life; I was electrified by the possibilities of the field of psychotherapy research. At some point during the conference I decided in my youthful enthusiasm that I wanted someday to become president of SPR.

More than two decades later, I got my wish. Now I would have to think of something impressive and interesting to talk about! Fortunately, SPR gives its newly elected General Vice Presidents about two years to come up with something. I had some time to mull over the subject of my talk. But what?

I had spent most of my career as a research methodologist, developing one new method after another. Why not do it again? That sounded like a good idea. I'd been interested in single case design since graduate school, and early in my career had advocated greater use of systematic case studies (Elliott, 1983). More recently, I'd had a long talk with Art Bohart at the 1997 North American SPR meeting in Tucson, Arizona, about some ideas he had for an interpretive alternative to randomized clinical trials (Bohart & Boyd, 1997). What if we could develop a method for using qualitative data from client and therapist in order to help us decide whether therapy had caused the client to change? What would that look like? Art was developing a list of criteria for doing just that. (See Bohart, Berry, & Wicks, 2011, for the latest iteration of his list.)

Together with my team of clinical psychology graduate students at the University of Toledo, I started playing around with some of the data we'd been generating in our research clinic. The method we began to develop, with Art's inspiration, was both interpretive and focused on establishing causality between what happened in therapy (process) and what the client got out of it (outcome). *Hermeneutic* is a fancy word for *interpretive*, while *efficacy* is one of many euphemisms for *causal*. We seemed to have walked into an oxymoron: hermeneutics was supposed to be the opposite of causal research. Instead of beating around the bush, I decided to embrace the apparent contradiction, and called the method "Hermeneutic Single Case Efficacy Design," or HSCED for short. (Pronounced "H-sked," following Rhonda Goldman's helpful suggestion.)

The first HSCED presentations were given in at the Chicago SPR meeting in 2000. After that, the method was further refined, and my SPR presidential talk began to take shape, around an interesting case, a depressed research client for whom I'd acted as researcher. Having heard me in Chicago, Kurt Schneider asked me for a short book chapter (Elliott, 2001), in which I presented the rationale and main procedures of the new method. Eventually, I gave my presidential talk, at the 2001 SPR conference in Montevideo, Uruguay, and after that set about writing up the journal article version (Elliott, 2002).

Looking back, I am very pleased with how the journal article version came out. There is very little I would change about it today. The essentials of the basic HSCED method are clearly laid out in the paper, including guiding principles, design elements, types of linking evidence, a list of eight alternative explanations, plus the research procedures for bringing all this off. Of course, the method has continued to evolve in important ways over the past 10 years.

At this point, the only thing I would want to clarify is the somewhat muddy distinction made between *direct* and *indirect* evidence, which is now more cogently described as the basis for the affirmative and skeptic cases, as part of the legalistic approach used in HSCED today.

HSCED 2.0: The Development of Adjudicated HSCED

In the 10 years since Elliott (2002) was published, the next step in the development of the HSCED method was adding a quasi-judicial component. Because my father was an attorney, I had a longstanding interest in the application of legal principles and practices in research. In this I was once again strongly influenced by Art Bohart, who had also been experimenting with quasi-judicial case study methods (Bohart & Humphreys, 2000).

The result was the case of "George," a client with bridge phobia and panic, who received 23 sessions of emotion-focused therapy (Elliott et al., 2009). We used separate teams of researchers to assemble an agreed-upon set of evidence (the rich case record), along with affirmative and skeptic cases, rebuttals, and closing arguments. The rich case record and the sets of arguments were presented to three judges, well-known psychotherapy researchers representing cognitive-behavioral (Louis Castonguay), psychodynamic (Stan Messer) and humanistic-experiential (Jeanne Watson) approaches. The judges were asked to rule on (a) whether the client had changed, and (b) whether therapy was responsible for the client's changes. In addition, they were asked to describe their understanding of how change had come about. This elaborated HSCED method was cumbersome, but seemed warranted—first, because humanistic therapies are often assumed to be ineffective with anxiety disorders, and, second, because the quantitative and qualitative outcome data contradicted each another. In the end, the three judges unanimously agreed that the client had changed and that therapy was responsible for his changes. In their supporting opinion statements, the judges each explained the change process in terms of their particular theoretical orientation.

As an additional feature (originally introduced because of timing), the 6- and 18-month follow-up data were withheld from the judges. This provided an additional procedure for validating client change, which has since been regularly incorporated in HSCED studies.

In 2006, I moved from the Ohio to Scotland, where it quickly became clear the systematic case studies such HSCED were highly appropriate as master's-level research projects for the counseling and counseling psychology students I was now teaching. Using data from the new research clinic at the University of Strathclyde, students began carrying out adjudicated HSCED studies of clients with social anxiety. Three of these new studies have now been published, looking at the use of person-centered and emotion-focused therapies with this client population (MacLeod & Elliott, 2012; MacLeod, Elliott, & Rodgers, 2012; Stephen, Elliott, & MacLeod, 2011).

This recent wave of HSCED research has led to further refinement and standardization of procedures for constructing rich case record and opposing arguments. In particular, my students and I have experimented with the procedure for judging cases. We have developed a format for judges to use, including more precise questions on which judges are asked to rule, including the use of six-point rating scales. We have also moved toward mixed sets of student and professional-level judges.

Although these developments improve the rigor and appeal of the method, I think that the original version (Elliott, 2002) still has value and provides a useful starting point for understanding the method.

Impact of HSCED (Elliott, 2002) on Psychotherapy Research

According to the Web of Science (accessed June 8, 2013), the journal article version of this talk (Elliott, 2002) has been cited 28 times; the publisher's website lists 61 citations. The most common citing journal is *Psychotherapy Research* (14 citations), but many of the citations are from *Counseling and Psychotherapy Research* (12) or *Person-Centered and Experiential Psychotherapies* (6), journals not indexed in the Web of Science. This locates the focal impact of Elliott (2002) in the readership of these journals—that is, psychotherapy and counseling researchers in the UK and the USA—many of a humanistic-experiential theoretical persuasion.

A recent book on psychotherapy case study research (McLeod, 2010) features a chapter in HSCED as part of "the new case study" movement in psychotherapy research. Systematic case study research, including HSCED, appears to have emerged as an important part of the current zeitgeist in psychotherapy research.

Elliott (2002) and the Future of Psychotherapy Research

What about the future? Human beings are not very good at predicting the future, because their predictions are generally guided either by wishful thinking or simplistic linear extrapolations from the present (Sterling, 2003).

Generalizing from Single Cases

I am going to skip the simple linear extrapolation and go directly to the wishful thinking: What do I hope for the future development of case study research in general, and HSCED in particular? First, dating back at least to Bromley (1986) and Fishman (1999), the goal of contemporary case study research has been to create generalizable, clinically relevant knowledge that practitioners can use, by analogy to the concept of legal precedent in case law. Since conducting large RCTs is out of reach for practitioners, the goal has been to empower them to contribute to the development of scientific knowledge via case research on their own or each other's practice. This is the long-term vision of the new case study movement. However, to do this we will need to develop clear practices and procedures that will provide a basis for generalizing from existing published cases to new cases.

Identifying Specific Causal Processes

Right now, my money is on the specification of key moderator and mediator variables as a basis for generalizing from single case research. As HSCED has developed over the past 10 years, it has become ever clearer that we need to go beyond general causal inference to the specific causal factors responsible for change in therapy. Increasingly, an essential feature of HSCED studies has become an explicit enumeration and justification of: (a) *mediators*, the particular within-therapy processes that helped bring about client change, such as the therapeutic relationship or particular techniques; and (b) *moderators*, the specific contextual or pre-therapy factors that helped the client make use of therapy, such as client social environment and ability to make use of what is offered in therapy. In spite of its ubiquity, standard psychiatric diagnosis seems unlikely to be helpful here.

HSCED as Change Process Research

In the past, the concepts of mediating and moderating variables have been used almost exclusively to group design research. However, as I see it, there is great potential in applying these same ideas to single case research. At the same time, the increasing emphasis on mediating and moderating factors is moving HSCED into the realm of change process research, thus connecting it to the other great traditions in psychotherapy research (Elliott, 2010).

Conclusion

In Elliott (2002), I cited Mohr's (1999) idea that the optimal place to identify causal processes in human behavior is not in randomized group designs. As appealing as they are, group causal designs blur the complex and diverse underlying causal processes, making them harder rather than easier to see. Instead, Mohr argued, the royal road to understanding what causes programs to succeed, or clients to improve, is via in-depth qualitative understanding of the single case. It is only by thoroughly understanding the individual that we can attain essential and generalizable knowledge about how people in general change. Like "hermeneutic" and "efficacy," this is another oxymoron, the seeming contradiction that underlies the emergence of the "new case study" movement in psychotherapy research. I am pleased that my SPR presidential talk, published as Elliott (2002), continues to play an important role in this still-developing approach to psychotherapy research.

12

PSYCHOTHERAPY RESEARCH AND NEUROBIOLOGY (2003)[1]

Challenge, Chance, or Enrichment?

Franz Caspar

It is time for psychotherapy researchers to deal systematically with the challenges and opportunities posed by recent developments in neurobiology. Having done psychophysiological research very early in my development as a psychologist (Strian, Klicpera, & Caspar, 1977), I have continued to look for ways to harmoniously combine cognition, emotions, behavior, and biology. This article is my attempt to formulate some questions and suggest some tentative answers. They do not come from a neurobiology expert and may, therefore, be more intelligible and digestible for readers who are not very familiar with (or fond of) neurobiology while contributing to the discussion for those who are.

What Neurobiology Has to Offer: State and Illustrative Examples

With functional magnetic resonance imaging, procedures in the living brain can be traced with high precision. Can we, as psychotherapists, ignore this? Neurobiological researchers publish actively, and they get attention in public media, strongly driven by a fascination for new ways of making evasive, vague, and subjective psychological phenomena tangible, sound, and objective. The following illustrations introduce readers who are less familiar with neurobiological research and exemplify what progress means in neurobiological research.

With depressed patients anomalies were found in the release of neurotransmitters and sensitivity to neurotransmitters, in sleep patterns measured by physiological indicators (Riemann, Berger, & Voderholzer, 2001), and hyperactivity on the hypothalamus-pituitary-adrenocortical gland axis (Holsboer, 2000). That hypercortisolism and a probably underlying depression represent severe risk factors for cardiovascular disorders (Wulsin, Vaillant, & Wells, 1999) and osteoporosis

(Cizza, Ravin, Chrousos, & Gold, 2001) is an argument in favor of treating depression even if valuing only somatic long-term effects. Several studies have shown changes in the brain of depressed patients, in particular volume reductions in the prefrontal cortex (Cotter, Mackay, Landau, Kerwin, & Everall, 2001; Drevets, 2001; Rajkowska, 2000). It is worth mentioning that considerable changes in the dominant models have already occurred within a relatively short time.

There are some indications for differential treatment selection. Patients with more severely disturbed sleep patterns profited less from psychotherapy (Thase et al., 1997). The same held for patients with more cortisol in the urine (Joffe, Segal, & Singer, 1996). These authors showed also that successful cognitive-behavioral therapy (CBT) leads to a normalization of plasma chemistry. There are, in addition, indications that functional anomalies (Brody et al., 2001; Martin, Martin, Rai, Richardson, Royall, & Eng., 2001) are reversible not only by medication but also by interpersonal psychotherapy.

With obsessive-compulsive disorder patients, it is assumed that a hyperactivation of the frontostriatal system leads to a lack of flexibility and the clinically known stereotypical thought and behavior patterns. For no other disorder have we as clear indications as for obsessive-compulsive disorder that psychotherapy leads to neurobiological changes, which can be demonstrated on brain imaging (Baxter et al., 1992; Schwartz, Stoessel, Baxter, Martin, & Phelps, 1996). With borderline patients, not surprisingly, neurobiological models concentrate on links between neurobiology and affect regulation (Damasio et al., 2000; Hintzen & Pietrowsky, 2001; Soloff, Meltzer, Greer, Constantine, & Kelly, 2000).

Some of the most interesting results are not directly related to psychotherapy but rather to the understanding and treatment of physical disorders and the coping with them. A first example is stroke. A stroke itself is clearly a biological phenomenon, and most of the treatment is biologically based. Research (Liepert, Bauder, Miltner, Taub, & Weiller, 2000; Taub, Crago, & Uswatte, 1998) has shown, however, that there is plasticity. Nonuse of a limb leads to a reduction of this limb's representation in the cortex and thus to a spiral of learned nonuse. Constraint-induced movement therapy (Taub et al., 1998) is, in essence, very simple. The use of the limb that is unaffected by the stroke and is spontaneously used to take over activities from the "paralyzed" limb is restricted. The often not completely paralyzed limb is forced to remain active. This procedure shows amazing effects on motor activities, which are maintained and carried over to everyday life. It also has effects on cortical representations, as Liepert et al. (2000) demonstrated. It is easy to imagine how difficult it is, on a motivational level and on the level of practical details, to conduct such a training with patients of varying motivation. An important point is that the training itself is partly based on biological insights and its effects can be traced biologically, but the main questions related to the treatment are of the kind we know from other active forms of psychotherapy.

A second example is chronic pain. Brain representation changes with different types of chronic pain patients (Flor, 2002). The representation of the back in primary somatosensory cortex of chronic back pain patients enlarges with increasing chronicity, thus making patients more sensitive to pain. Their pain thresholds and tolerance become much lower than normal. Flor, Lutzenberger, Knost, and Birbaumer (2002), in their study of back pain patients, applied electric stimulation at the location where pain in the back was felt versus an unrelated site (a finger). All patients reacted similarly when the finger was stimulated. For the reaction on stimulation of the back, two patient groups need to be distinguished. The so-called solicitous partners group had spouses habitually paying much attention to the pain and behavior related to it. The spouses in the so-called punishing partners group show little interest in the patient's pain. Patients in the latter group have a curve similar to that of nonpatients, whereas those with soliciting spouses show much stronger reactions when the back is stimulated compared with when the finger is stimulated and compared with the other groups. Figure 12.1 shows the differences in brain activity between an assessment situation with the spouse present versus absent. Chronic back pain patients with soliciting partners show a very strong brain reaction but only when the back is stimulated and when the spouse is present! As Flor et al. (2002) reported, Fordyce postulated as early as 1976 that positive reinforcement of observable pain behavior, such as moaning and limping, as well as negative reinforcement of inactivity, the intake of medication, and a lack of positive reinforcement (e.g., being active or working), contribute to the development of pain chronicity. This is seen as a phenomenon parallel to developing generally larger representations of any sensations if behaviorally relevant.

We are now better able to trace what happens in the brain, and we may even be able to intervene more precisely. In principle, the social reinforcement of back pain and its role in the development of chronicity have been known for a long time (Linton, Melin, & Götestam, 1985). Remembering this does not mean to

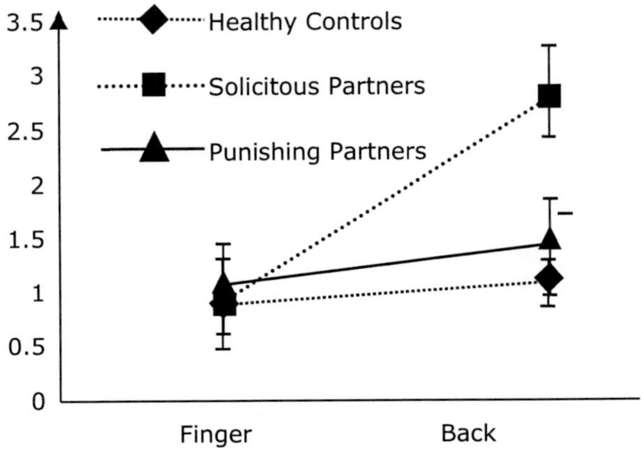

FIGURE 12.1 Back Pain Patients: Electric Stimulation at the Location of Back Pain versus an Unrelated Site, Measured by the Difference in Global Field Power of the EEG (adapted from Flor et al., 2002). Reprinted with permission

undervalue studies as reported here. They are valuable by making mechanisms more understandable, and they can even be used directly in practice. Therapists working with pain patients know that these patients are not always easy. A struggle between the physician/therapist and the patient is common, related to whether the pain is "only subjective" or "real," in the sense of having a reasonably related physical basis.

Such a dispute would be based on a false mind-body separation, as the reported studies suggest. There is probably an objectively different situation not only in the behavior of significant others but also in the brains of chronic pain patients compared with similar patients without or with less chronic pain. Dialogue with pain patients may proceed as follows: "Studies have shown that patients feeling much pain have larger representations of the affected body parts in their brain than those with less pain. Interestingly, this is related to how much attention patients and their significant others pay to the pain. So we have to deal with a vicious circle. What can we do to make you pay as little attention as possible to pain and related matters?"

The utility of such a view in leading out of an often difficult struggle is independent of whether the studies will be replicated. Obviously, the formulations need to be adapted to particular patients, and it is important to know about their goals and motives far beyond diagnosis. All possibilities helping to make a life attractive, which is opposed to concentrating on pain, need to be included, whereas many patients spontaneously concentrate on the pain and, in doing so, change their brain in a maladaptive way. It seems obvious that much can be done against pain by factors psychotherapists use to influence, including the spouse's behavior. Even simple distraction and relaxation are good ways of influencing physical pain via the mind, often neglected by psychotherapists, favoring sophisticated approaches that are more intellectually satisfying and appealing.

The attempt of illustrating the connection between psychology and biology could go on with physiological consequences of traumatization, the role of emotions in psychotherapy in a neurobiological view, and other topics. Given space constraints, the examples reported thus far have to be sufficient to illustrate the current neurobiology-psychotherapy interface and to make plausible that a view of mind and body as essentially separate becomes increasingly obsolete.

Reports in public media often express that research is just one step from explaining schizophrenia, alcoholism, or anxiety from the genes, and just two steps from treating them in a purely biological way. Optimism related to breakthroughs and even neuromysticism seem motivated by other reasons (such as obtaining research money for the allegedly last missing step) rather than being based on a sober evaluation of the situation. This can be annoying for representatives of competing approaches. It is not uncommon that what are seen as conspicuous biological genetic markers (e.g., conspicuous eye movements) are found more often for a group (e.g., schizophrenics), but the phenomena are not specific and also, as it turns out, are found with other groups (e.g., affective patients and their relatives). Effective treatment (e.g., antidopaminergic medication with schizophrenics) may make the existence of a biological deficit plausible, to which the treatment's type of working and effects fit (e.g., dopaminergic hyperactivity with schizophrenics), but such deficits have actually not been found (Clementz & Sweeney, 1990; Harrison, 1999). These are just examples illustrating the fact that much knowledge is still lacking.

When a conspicuous neurobiological phenomenon persists after the remission of psychopathological symptoms, does this neurobiological phenomenon represent a trait that brings about symptoms only in multicausal relation to other factors that are absent after recovery? Is it a "scar" without psychopathogenic importance, or is there no true and relevant relation between the observed phenomenon and psychopathology at all? For every disorder, such questions have to be answered. This will cost not only time but also much money, which will obviously be missing for other types of research.

Even in the absence of a large number of clear, replicable neurobiological findings, which are, in addition, relevant for psychotherapy, neurobiology has an increasing impact in the world of psychotherapy. Grawe's book (2002a), pointing out neurobiological premises of psychotherapy, is a step toward integrating neurobiology and psychotherapy. There is traditionally a particularly strong link between behavioral medicine and neurobiology. Psychoanalysts show a strong interest in neurobiology, as illustrated by the establishment of new journals, meetings, and societies. Even phenomena like attachment are related to neurobiological phenomena: The online "Brain Waves" (spring 2002), by the Society for Neuroscience, familiarizes readers with research (sponsored by DuPont) on parental care and the brain. This research reveals that infants lacking caressing and cuddling show more dying brain cells than normal controls. This has been found with rodents, but it would not be surprising if human binding research as well would heavily include biological parameters very soon. "Brain Waves" covers many interesting topics, and is, as the society declares, a publication for a broad readership; legislators are mentioned in the first place!

Questions and (Tentative) Answers

A number of questions are related to the relation between psychotherapy and neurobiology.

Are Findings and Methods That Are Closer to the Biological Substrate per se More Reliable and Valid?

Even proponents of psychotherapy seem to believe at times that this is the case-neurobiology as the real thing—and such a position seems to have some intuitive appeal. However, for many methodological questions positions are as divergent as in psychotherapy research (Aine, 1995; Filipek, 1999; Fogel, Schiffer, & Rao, 2002). As impressive as colorful pictures are, they still have to be transformed into numbers with which statistics can be calculated. Are human ratings or automated evaluations of such pictures superior; is it better to work with a higher or lower degree of resolution? Such questions are discussed controversially by experts. Some of the methodological questions remind us very much of past and current problems in psychotherapy research.

An essential problem is sample size related to costs. Just as psychotherapy studies tend to be costly and, therefore, sample size much smaller compared with areas of psychological and other research with cheaper data, some neurobiological methods, like brain imaging, are so expensive that sample sizes are also small, thus increasing the number of unreplicable results. Such results will be confusing and waste the time and energy of researchers, but there is no obvious alternative. In addition, if we see conspicuous phenomena (e.g., in brain imaging), we do not know yet whether the clinically and etiologically most important phenomena are actually those that show up most colorfully in the pictures. In addition, because brain imaging has a high level of resolution but is not very sensitive for weak activity, crucial processes may remain hidden for a longer period while we take for most important what is most obvious. Acknowledging such problems and uncertainties does not mean to question the importance of neurobiological research but to avoid burdening it with unrealistic expectations.

Can Psychotherapy Research Already Contribute to Studies That Include Neurobiological Questions and Methods?

Specialized psychotherapy research has much to offer. First, paradoxical as it may seem, neurobiological changes can be better studied with nonbiological interventions than with biological, in particular pharmacological, interventions. When studying the latter, lasting neurobiological changes that are truly related to changes in psychopathology are always confounded with direct pharmacological effects, which may or may not be related to psychopathological phenomena. The most elegant way to eliminate these confounders in neurobiological research is the use of nonbiological interventions. Psychotherapy finds itself in a good starting position as an independent variable in neurobiological research.

Intervention research has reached a high level of sophistication. A good example illustrating the need for sophistication in treatment research is the issue of "researcher allegiance." Luborsky et al. (1999, 2001) found a correlation between rated allegiance and psychotherapy outcomes of .85! [Here the original text explains allegiance as an issue requiring a high level of research expertise.]

Another illustration (shortened here) for the potential usefulness of psychotherapy research is related to a project dealing with neurobiological predictors and consequences of successful psychotherapy. A high success rate is desirable for every treatment study. In such studies, typically more attention is given to the success rates than to the failure rates. When trying to find neurobiological predictors of psychotherapy success, a minimization of the failure rate is absolutely essential, not only because it is complementary to success rates. Once therapy is over, it is not possible to distinguish between neurobiologically caused vs. unnecessary failures. The latter would spoil data gained and analyzed at enormous costs and severely handicap interpretation. Therefore, an effort to reduce the rate of dropouts/failures must be maximal. When planning projects, involved neurobiologists and even psychotherapists among them are, understandably, focused on their new tools and concepts, but good average therapy is no satisfactory answer to the requirements of minimal failure rates.

Funding agencies as well as most reviewers would, in the sense of a risk minimizing strategy, strictly favor manualized procedures. In line with Beutler and others (Beutler, Clarkin, & Bongar, 2000; Beutler & Harwood, 2000), Grawe and I (1996) have maintained that optimal treatment in the sense postulated here requires the consideration of additional aspects beyond those criteria on which patient selection and treatment are normally based in manualized approaches. The process of individualization, of course, adds complexity. We ask therapists to develop individual case conceptualizations based on the approach of Plan Analysis that go far beyond diagnosis. Therapeutic action is seen as an amalgamation of a variety of factors (Caspar, 1995, 2007).

Such an amalgamation is a more demanding procedure than the application of manuals, especially for relatively inexperienced psychotherapists, but unavoidable when trying to increase success and decrease dropout rates. Psychotherapy maximizing treatment effects in line with the approach proposed here and with well-trained, although relatively inexperienced, therapists reaches effect sizes for patients with mixed diagnoses between 1.3 and 1.5 (Grawe, 2002b). The therapeutic relationship, for which we offer the concept of complementary therapeutic relationship (Caspar, 1995; Caspar, Grossmann, & Unmüssig, 2002), is especially important. It is beyond the scope of this article to go into any details of such a procedure. It should be obvious, however, that, although requiring some creativity and intuition, it is highly professional and has to include all available and relevant wisdom accumulated in psychotherapy research.

The second crucial element for optimizing treatment (apart from a general concept guiding individual optimization as postulated previously) is ongoing assessment of the process (Grawe & Braun, 1994) and feedback to the therapist (in the original: pointing out the engagement of several SPR colleagues in this domain). Again, psychotherapy research has much to offer to neurobiologically interested research!

Are There Indications that Biological Treatment is Already More Effective than Psychotherapy?

Effect sizes for psychotherapy are high with several disorders compared to no treatment and alternative treatment (e.g., Grawe, Donati, & Bernauer, 1994). Multiple studies show that there is no general superiority of medication to psychotherapy. In combination, medication seems, as at least some studies suggest (Hautzinger, de Jong-Meyer, Treiber, Rudolf, & Thien, 1996), to add little to psychotherapy, at least for nonpsychotic disorders, or even to reduce long-term effects (Barlow, Gorman, Shear, & Woods, 2000). What are the relative contributions to the cure of disorders? What are realistic models for the interaction of biological and psychological factors? In clinical practice, combined treatment may be based on an implicit or explicit model of some kind of additivity. In research, the uncertainty related to how change actually occurs makes it advisable to use only one type of change agent at a time when trying to shed more light on the interplay of psychological and neurobiological factors, as in the project described previously.

In public, many unrealistic expectations exist related to the amount of help that pharmacological treatment has to offer. The question of relative effectiveness is, of course, complex when going into more details, and this is left to specialized contributions. In sum, empirical findings for depression suggest that, in line with common belief at least among psychotherapists and psychotherapy researchers, psychotherapy has not been outperformed by medication, and, counter to widespread belief, a combination of psychotherapy with medication brings little or no additional effect. Even more surprising for some, empirical findings show that psychotherapy not only saves health-related costs overall (e.g., Baltensperger & Grawe, 2001; Bateman & Fonagy, 1999) but is also less expensive. On the basis of these findings, at the very least biologically based treatments have not yet shown superiority to psychotherapy for depression, and the same applies to most (nonpsychotic) disorders.

Are There Indications that Biologically Informed Psychotherapy is Superior to Psychotherapy Neglecting Biological Factors?

Kandel (1999) assumes that psychotherapy can lead to lasting changes in the brain with a continuing effect on learning. It seems like psychotherapists can bring about neurobiological processes by triggering the release of chemical substances that a patient's body is able to produce. Psychotherapy leading to such effects seems not to require any comprehensive neurobiological training. It is plausible, however, that neurobiologically well-informed therapists can use psychotherapeutic means better and more precisely to stimulate neurobiological processes and empower patients to take control over such processes themselves. Is there empirical support for such expectations? Blatt, Sanislow, Zuroff, and Pilkonis (1996) inspected the personal background characteristics of 24 psychiatrists and psychologists who saw patients in the National Institute of Mental Health study on depression. Although professionals from different backgrounds could not be compared directly, the authors compared those who did versus did not rely on medication in their practices, an indirect index of biological versus nonbiological background. The most effective treatments were offered by those who did not prescribe medication and who maintained a psychological rather than a biological orientation to depression and its treatment, with a modestly strong effect size ($r = .48$). Of course, it could be argued whether or not giving medication in regular practice is a good indicator for being neurobiologically informed. In the absence of studies with better criteria, it may be cautiously concluded that the availability of biological models does not per se have a strong positive effect on the effectiveness of psychotherapists. It would be wrong to see these findings as an argument against the value of acquiring neurobiological knowledge, but this may have to be much more specific to be useful in custom-tailoring psychotherapy, as illustrated next.

Are There Models with a Potential for Contributing to a Reduction of the Mind-Body Gap?

Psychotherapy research in general needs concepts that help overcome the mind-body dualism. For a considerable time, dualism had the advantage of making the world less complex and thus making life easier. This may still contribute to the attractiveness of dualistic concepts while it becomes increasingly obvious that they are too simple.

Should we simply give up our old views and adopt a neurobiological view? Apart from the simple psychological fact that change, also within psychotherapists, does not usually occur by simply replacing old with new concepts, current neurobiological concepts are not a sufficient basis for dealing with the phenomena and processes we are trying to handle in psychotherapy and that we have learned to handle with considerable effects after all. Concepts are needed that are able to mediate between traditional mental and traditional biological models.

Connectionist or neural network models are candidates for such a function; therefore, I have been trying to convey the "the appeal of connectionism for clinical psychology" (Caspar, Rothenfluh, & Segal, 1992) and a "connectionist view of psychotherapy" (Caspar, 1998) since the early 1990s. Much of the remainder of this article is dedicated to a demonstration of how psychological and biological mechanisms can be linked in such models. Because not all readers can be expected to be familiar with connectionist or neural network concepts, a brief explanation of how they work is given. Connectionist models are, in my experience, best understood when contrasted with traditional, nonconnectionist models of human cognitive-emotional-behavioral functioning. [The following explanations have been shortened; more comprehensively see Caspar et al. 1992, Caspar, 1998, Caspar & Berger, 2012.]

In traditional schema models, concepts on a level of resolution at which we normally use them in our everyday or clinical language can be represented in semantic nets with nodes of which each represents meaning. Such localist representation (meaning is located in a particular node) is given up in connectionist models, which are most typically distributed. This means that information on

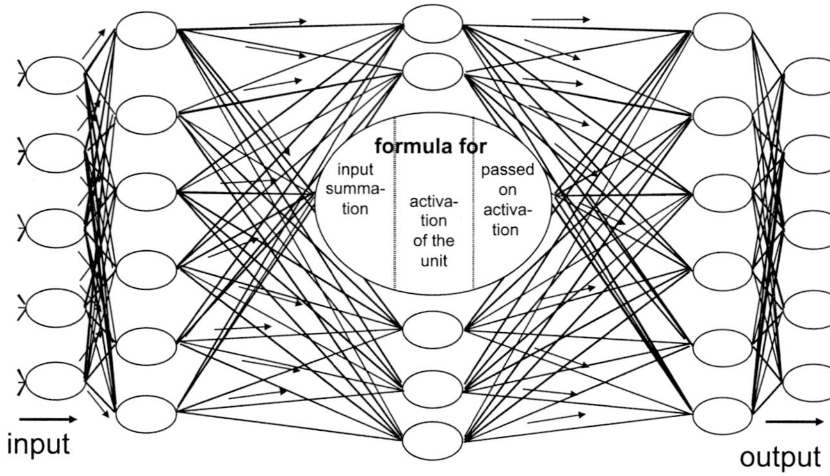

FIGURE 12.2 Schematic Representation of Subsymbolic, Distributed Connectionist Network. (adapted from Caspar (2002b))

an everyday or clinical language level is represented in larger patterns of nodes and their connections rather than in individual nodes. Figure 12.2 shows schematically how information is represented and processed.

One of the myriad units is enlarged in the middle of Figure 12.2, showing that in each node formulas are used for the summation of input activation, calculation of the node's activation, and passing on information. Activation then spreads farther out to an output layer. This is just a simplified schematic figure for how these models work. They have a number of clinically interesting properties (also Stinson & Palmer, 1991). What matters in this context is that information is processed in parallel in the whole system; there is no homunculus required to manipulate stored information. This has clinically relevant implications, such as accounting for implicit, intuitive, holistic processing, and more. Information is represented in a distributed way, which means that when a dog is fed into the system, not a single node becomes activated to represent the presence of a dog but rather a whole pattern. When a cat is fed in, a similar but somewhat different pattern is activated to represent this similar but somewhat different animal. When a table is fed in, a more differing pattern is activated: The remaining similarities represent the existence of four legs.

Many aspects of the functioning of connectionist systems are determined by the principle of spreading activation and changing connections in such a way that the total remaining tension is minimized. The simultaneous activation of incompatible elements always causes tension, the sum of which varies with the different states in which a system can be. This can be represented as tension landscape, which should be understood intuitively here, although it can be modeled mathematically in a precise fashion (Smolensky, 1986). In such a tension landscape (Figure 12.3), there is an ideal global minimum in which tension is

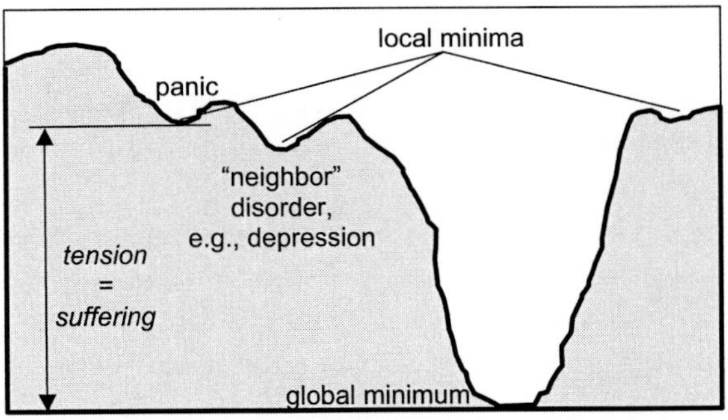

FIGURE 12.3 Global and Local Minima in Tension Landscapes and Disorders

FIGURE 12.4 Local Minima in Everyday Life

at zero, an ideal, never-reached state in which all units fit perfectly together. There are also local minima, corresponding to patterns in which emotions, cognitions, behavior, physiology, and environment fit particularly well together. Every move or change (represented by arrows in Figure 12.3) leads to a tension increase. However, the tension is minimal from only a local, but not a global, point of view. Compared with the global minimum, much tension remains and is experienced as suffering, or "Leidensdruck." Mental disorders can be represented as such patterns. For example, panic goes along with much suffering and tension, but tension in the panic pattern is increased when a therapist tries to interrupt avoidance or if a spouse withholds attention and pampering, which had reinforced panic attacks so far. If seen as a local minimum, a disorder is a solution in the sense of reducing tension to some extent. Unfortunately, problem solving gets stuck on a high level of remaining tension. Grawe (2002a) and others call such minima *attractors,* a term illustrating the effects a local minimum has once it is established.

Charlie Brown may help us comprehend what such local mimima, patterns, or attractors are all about, and why improving one element increases the tension rather than bringing relief, as we know from clinical practice and perhaps from everyday experience (Figure 12.4). The caricature, of course, is in no way meant to be disrespectful of patients with depression.

As stated before, connectionist models can be used metaphorically to help us understand some clinical phenomena that cannot easily be understood by traditional models, such as schema models (Caspar et al., 1992; Stinson & Palmer, 1991). Beyond metaphorical use, connectionist models can be used to actually calculate activations and tensions to simulate relevant dynamic aspects of patients and their disorders. The clinical basis for the illustration given in the original article is the concept of Plan Analysis case conceptualizations (Caspar, 2007). The inclusion of neurobiology happens, among others, via the simulation of neuromodulation: Changes of some parameters mimicking neurobiological states have an impact on the cognitive-emotional-behavioral functioning in the whole network or limited parts of it. Such simulations are used to explore and clarify concepts, but also in the training of psychotherapists' information processing (Caspar, Benninghoven & Berger, 2004). [Here the original text has been cut substantially to comply with the shortening requirements, while leaving as much as possible of the rest of the text complete. The reasons are explained in the Commentary.]

We have used such models for simulating concrete, individual borderline patients in an attempt to increase our insight in the deep structure of their functioning, including biological variables (Berger, 2005). Computer simulations can also be sparring partners for psychotherapists to try out planned interventions before setting them into action with real patients or sometimes retrospectively to understand why interventions were useless.

It is obvious that the effects of psychotherapeutic interventions depend on neuromodulatory states. Psychotherapeutic strategies should be used differentially, depending on the state of a patient. Psychotherapeutic interventions can be used to bring a patient into a particular, more favorable state. Although some psychotherapists are used to including different states caused by pharmacological interventions in their psychotherapy planning, we (including myself) have hardly begun to think about systematic individual treatment planning with an inclusion of psychotherapeutic and neurobiological aspects and their interaction. Our simulations show that such planning is demanding, but they make plausible the notion that psychotherapy leaving out neurobiological parameters remains suboptimal in many cases.

Concentrating on a few simple aspects, models can even be used with patients to further their understanding of themselves. For example, patients often feel the tension increase when they try to come out of a local minimum and take it as an indicator for being on the wrong track. Simple drawings of tension landscapes and, with more sophistication, individual dynamic simulations that can easily be carried into the therapy room on a laptop can make a huge difference when it comes to motivating a patient for tension-increasing therapeutic steps.

All this illustrates what was meant by asking for concepts mediating between "psychological" and "neurobiological" functioning, not only in the abstract, but also for the individual patient. Whatever model is preferred, a pragmatically very important issue involves the manner in which exploding neurobiological knowledge can be incorporated into the existing body of psychotherapy knowledge. It would not make sense to give up old knowledge and replace it with new knowledge. Rather, neurobiology has to be integrated somehow. Models for knowledge acquisition and management and for training psychotherapists will be needed for the acquisition of psychotherapeutic and neurobiological knowledge and for using knowledge when working with our individual patients. What is lost when we give more attention to neurobiology? Close monitoring will be required, a task of minimizing medium or long-term regret.

What Ethical and Political Implications Have to Be Considered?

If future studies show that particular neurobiological markers indicate that a success in the psychotherapy of a particular patient is unlikely, may a patient then be excluded from treatment although he or she continues to seek it? How large does the effect (i.e., the likelihood of failure) need to be to accept it as a reason for excluding a patient from psychotherapy? If a relief from psychopathological symptoms through psychotherapy seems unlikely (e.g., low chances of success for depressed patients with particular sleep anomalies, as reported previously), does psychotherapy make any sense?

Further, the dangers of a reductionist biological view on a political level could be severe. If all mental problems would be taken care of the way a specific medication takes care these days of, for example, attention deficits in children, psychotherapy would be in trouble, and all the good effects it has shown to have would be at risk. The best way to prevent this is to actively integrate psychotherapeutic and neurobiological concepts, preventing a dualistic view (with a biological bias, as the zeitgeist would suggest) in public. These are just a few issues of a bundle of ethical questions we will need to address when including more neurobiology.

Conclusion

It can be assumed that most readers just like myself are lacking sufficient neurobiological training and information. How can we realistically become more familiar with these models? There are wonderful books, such as *Affective Neuroscience: The Foundations of Human and Animal Emotions* by Jaak Panksepp (1998), that can be highly recommended not only for their content but also their readability. There are tremendous websites on the internet, such as "Neuroscience for Kids" (http://faculty.washington.edu/chudler/neurok.html), that are highly recommended for those who would like an introduction with a guarantee of not being overwhelmed. There are even offers on the internet for booking a speaker for the next meeting of one's favored local professional organization. There are many ways for acquiring neurobiological knowledge and a good chance that everyone so desiring will find the way appropriate for them.

No one knows at this point in which direction the development will proceed. However, there is a high potential that we are just in the beginning of a new era of psychotherapy research and practice (Gabbard, 2000). It seems important that all colleagues engaged in psychotherapy and psychotherapy research become involved in dealing with the challenge coming from neurobiology and with discussing the various aspects involved, of which only a selection could be addressed in this article. Psychotherapy researchers should, using their existing strengths, contribute to a cooperation with neurobiology. Although it may be tainted by rivalry, research has the potential of being advantageous for both sides when based on realistic expectations. Dealing with neurobiology is not just another fashion, especially if researchers avoid moving the pendulum to one extreme. It is not recommended that psychotherapy researchers hurry and jump on the bandwagon of neurobiology, throwing treasures of psychotherapy research overboard. It means a combination and cross-fertilization of the two approaches to a field with overlapping and complementary competencies. As yet, psychotherapy has proven effective without being heavily neurobiologically informed, but there is room for higher success rates to which a better understanding of neurobiological factors may contribute. Neurobiology can already contribute to a better understanding of some aspects, while we are still far from being able to ground psychotherapy in neurobiology in any comprehensive way.

We need to keep one issue in mind. Practicing psychotherapists, at least if they treat with open ears, eyes, and minds, are pushed toward a holistic view of their patients and human functioning. Splitting up the world of psychopathology into psychological versus biological disorders cannot be the ultimate solution (Gabbard, 2000). The inclusion of neurobiological concepts and findings as well as neurobiologically grounded interventions should not lead to a new particularism and one-sided concentration on parts of the whole, but rather to a completion in a direction in which gaps are waiting to be filled. Psychotherapy research and neurobiology: Challenge, chance, and mutual enrichment!

COMMENTARY

PSYCHOTHERAPY RESEARCH AND NEUROBIOLOGY: CHALLENGE, CHANGE, OR ENRICHMENT? ARE WE WISER 10 YEARS LATER?[1]

For my Presidential Address I chose to talk about a topic to which I had not dedicated much of my actual research activities. I felt, though, that its importance would rapidly increase, forcing psychotherapy researchers to take position.

The 2002 paper can be summarized as saying that:

1. The attention for neurobiological research is strongly driven by a fascination for new ways of making evasive, vague, and subjective psychological phenomena tangible, sound, and objective.

2. Some neurobiological findings could/can be of great relevance for psychotherapists: information related to differential treatment selection, to traceable psychotherapeutic effects in the brain (comparable to biological interventions), explanations as to why psychotherapy can have a somatic effect, contributions against dualistic view of mind and body.
3. There are limits to neurobiological research:
   - Announcements that (biological) research is just a step from completely explaining/treating a particular mental disorders have usually turned out to be wrong, and such announcements are pretty annoying.
   - It is often unclear whether a neurobiological particularity (when it has no true relation to psychopathology) is a cause (in a multifactorial model) or a "scar" without psychopathogenic importance.
   - Sample sizes in neurobiological research are often small compared to what reviewers demand from psychotherapy researchers.
   - Although stable, replicable findings are still rare, nonprofessional readers and policy-makers are targets of neurobiological publications.
   - To point out and acknowledge the limits of current neurobiological research should free itself from unrealistic expectations
4. There are several ethical dangers, among them the danger of a reductionist biological view among politicians and others who decide about the provision of psychotherapy. An antidote against a dualistic view would be the integration of biological and psychological models.
5. The money invested for costly neurobiological research will be missing for other research, including psychotherapy research.

A number of questions, partly related to the above points, have also been asked in the 2002 paper:

a. *Are findings and methods that are closer to the biological substrate per se more reliable and valid than merely psychological findings and methods?*

   The answer was no: Photo-like pictures have a special suggestive power, but they remain products of "*creative statistics*." The costs which typically have low Ns as a consequence are mentioned as an important factor limiting replicability and therefore reliability and validity. In addition, it is not clear that the most conspicuous phenomena in brain imaging correspond to the clinically most important factors.

b. *Can psychotherapy research also contribute to neurobiological research?*

   The answer was yes, and this was illustrated with examples of tasks in psychotherapy research that require much skill and sophistication, yet are crucial for any neurobiological research related to psychotherapy. It does not make sense to invest into typically expensive neurobiological research without making sure that the involved psychotherapies and psychotherapy research are conducted well. When looking for neurobiological predictors of psychotherapy success vs. failure, it is essential that psychotherapy is as powerful as possible, which requires individualization. The impact of all other than biological factors under study that could contribute to a failure is to be held as low as possible.

c. *Are there indications that biological treatment is already more effective than psychotherapy?*

    The answer given was no.

d. *Are there indications that biologically informed psychotherapy is superior to psychotherapy neglecting biological factors?*

    It has been stated that it is plausible that neurobiologically well-informed therapists can use psychotherapeutic means better and more precisely to stimulate neurobiological processes and empower patients to take control over such processes themselves. There were, however, no proofs for this assumption.

e. *Are there models with a potential for contributing to a reduction of the mind-body gap?* Connectionist network models have been proposed to serve this purpose. In addition, it has been argued that the Plan Analysis (Caspar, 2007) model makes sense also from an evolutionary perspective (what is advantageous for survival is maintained and generalized) and allows one to connect easily psychological, social as well as biological aspects. It has been demonstrated that the functioning of a patient can be simulated in important aspects.

f. *How can the new knowledge be integrated?*

    It is difficult for psychotherapists to add more and more knowledge; the risk of loss of old useful knowledge has been emphasized. It has been postulated that models have to be developed to train therapists in the integration of neurobiological and psychosocial models.

Has the situation changed since 2002, and what would I, as a consequence, write differently? I would reformulate part of the text, but most of the content I see confirmed and unaltered today. In the following, I will concentrate on a number of central issues. Many of the points made were shared by other authors, optimistic (Beutel, 2002; Caspar, Koch, Schneider, Berger, & Wagner, 2011; Fuchs, 2004; Gabbard, 2000; Grawe, 2006; Kandel, 1999; Liggan & Kay, 1999; Schiepek, 2003) as well as skeptical (Fuchs, 2004, 2006; Gauggel, 2006).

Has the situation changed in the sense of showing a superiority of biological over psychotherapeutic treatment? No. Some treatments have been developed, such as deep brain stimulation (Holtzheimer & Mayberg, 2011) or vagus nerve stimulation (Mohr, Rodriguez, Slavíčková, & Hanka, 2011; Rizvi et al., 2011), which seems to be successful with patients who had undergone several unsuccessful previous treatments. Also, transcranial magnetic stimulation might in the future help to attenuate auditory hallucinations (e.g., Freitas, Pearlman, & Pascual-Leone, 2012; Wassermann & Zimmermann, 2012). To date, there is some evidence for effects with some patients, but not enough yet, and luckily much caution has been used to avoid premature acceptance and insufficient consideration of side effects, as in other invasive forms of treatment (Schlaepfer, Lisanby, & Pallanti, 2010). Such promising early results are overall outweighed by reports of other cases for which evidence shows the importance of psychotherapy, such as Cognitive-Behavior Analysis System of Psychotherapy (CBASP; McCullough, 2000) for depressed patients if they were traumatized early (Nemeroff et al., 2003). Skepticism has certainly grown as far as the efficiency of medication is concerned, as illustrated by the meta-analysis by Kirsch et al. (2008) on the treatment of depression and the uproar of those who wish to maintain the belief on the superiority of biological treatment.

New successes with some disorders should not be overvalued as far as superiority is concerned, as also on the side of psychotherapeutic treatments there are new approaches of and new evidence for effective treatment. In a field in which much medication is prescribed, personality disorders and nondiagnostic problems with emotion regulation, the insight is rather increasing that psychotherapy and not pharmacotherapy should be the treatment of choice (Herpertz et al., 2007; Stoffers et al., 2010). The hope of potential investors in the industry in the fast development of new biological treatment approaches seems to be fading (Nutt & Goodwin, 2011), which has so far rather led to increased researcher demands for public resources than to an increased skepticism and reluctance on the side of funding agencies. All involved in the treatment of patients with mental disorders should aim at a balanced approach in which the potential of biological as well as psychotherapeutic is exploited to the advantage of the patient. So far it seems we deal with swings of a pendulum, driven rather by extraneous forces.

Has the number of publications with neurobiological content and potential relevance for how to conduct psychotherapy increased? It certainly has. Since 2002, some fascinating studies combining psychotherapy and neurobiology have been presented (Ritchey, Dolcos, Eddington, Strauman, & Cabeza, 2011). In addition, there were contributions utilizing neurobiological insight for treatment recommendations (DeRubeis, Siegle, & Hollon, 2008). To put things a little more simply than the authors actually do, an underactivation of the prefrontal cortex demands cognitive therapy, while an overactivation of the amygdala demands medication. As depression involves other brain areas as well (e.g., Davidson, Pizzagalli, Nitschke, & Putnam, 2002), somewhat more complex considerations might be more adequate, but DeRubeis et al. (2008) demonstrate an interesting and promising approach. From a practical point of view, recommendations which do not require costly examinations of the individual are—ceteris paribus—more useful than recommendations requiring such examinations, going as far as assessing each individual in an MRI scanner before deciding about therapy.

There have been excellent SPR conference presentations and articles like the one by Strauman and Wilson (2010) or Eddington, Dolcos, Cabeza, Krishnan, and Strauman (2007) on the biological basis of individual differences in the psychotherapeutically important issue of approach vs. avoidance. In the field of addiction, research on subcortical dysfunctions has led to the development of promising treatments specifically targeting automated reactions and functioning. Such developments might be especially promising for patients with high cue-reactivity and low executive control.

In Europe, research with oxytocin (Heinrichs & Gaab, 2007) and its ability to increase empathy have received much attention: Could we use nasal sprays with oxytocin to render patients, in particular male, more empathic during therapy session? Researchers emphasize that much more research will be needed before a use in everyday practice. D-Cycloserine has been discussed as a cognitive enhancer in the treatment of anxiety disorders (Hofmann, Smits, Asnaani, Gutner & Otto, 2011): While cognitive enhancers have—unlike anxiolytic medication—no effect by themselves, they may augment the effect of learning processes in psychotherapy such as extinction processes related to exposure treatments. Obviously, first promising results have yet to be confirmed. It is, however, provoking to think already now about the fact that if these substances should prove to be effective, psychotherapists claiming to treat in line with current empirical evidence would have to argue if they do *not* use such enhancers.

Far from representing a thorough review, these examples illustrate that there is an increase in knowledge. Nevertheless, there are questions such as: "*Is the increase in knowledge in a* reasonable relation to the amounts of money invested for neurobiological research?" and "Are the neurobiologically based insights actually used and do they contribute to better psychotherapy?" For these questions, there is, to my knowledge, still no empirically based answer.

Do we have new proofs that neurobiologically informed psychotherapists deliver better treatment? In 2002 I referred to Blatt, Sanislow, Zuroff, and Pilkonis (1996). They had reported that those who prescribe medication in their regular practice (and can be assumed to be more biologically informed) delivered *inferior* results as psychotherapists (effect size r = .48). We have reports, such as by Misch (2000), on the observation that a neurobiological orientation goes along with a deterioration of the ability to analyze psychosocial factors, but we do not have any more comprehensive empirical insight.

A particular reason why neurobiologically informed therapists could deliver better therapy would be a better insight into the working mechanisms of psychotherapy. Berger and Caspar (2009) have dedicated a (German) paper to the question whether neurobiology helps with understanding and using these mechanisms. Mediators play a particular role, as they explain fully or partly how independent variables (e.g., psychotherapeutic interventions) explain dependent variables (different aspects of psychotherapy success). It is reasonable to assume that part of the mediators are neurobiological, and that the corresponding working mechanisms can hardly be understood in the absence of neurobiological insights. Berger and Caspar emphasize that such insights can inspire approaches to psychotherapy (e.g., Grawe's (2006) *Neuropsychotherapy* and Siegle, Ghinassi and Thase's [2007] *Neurobehavioral Therapy*) even in the absence of concrete

TABLE 12.1 Neurobiological Knowledge about Therapeutic Mechanisms and Potential Gain for Psychotherapy (from Berger and Caspar, 2009)

Neurobiological Knowledge	*Example*	*Potential Gain for Psychotherapy*
Knowledge that psychotherapy works via neuronal processes	High plasticity of the brain; effective psychotherapy brings about lasting changes in neuronal structures and processes (e.g., Kandel, 1999)	• gain in appreciation for psychotherapy in society and politics • concrete use with particular groups of patients (e.g., induction of positive expectations with patients with a medical view of their disorder; new approaches for elderly patients; destigmatization and weakening of taboos related to mental disorders)
Knowledge where and how psychotherapy works on the neuronal level	Behavior therapy with patients with social phobia reduces hyperactivation among others of the amygdala and the hippocampus (Furmark et al., 2002)	• basic knowledge how psychotherapy works; better comprehension of the etiology and the relation between physiological and psychological aspects of mental disorders • neurobiological variables can become the target of psychotherapeutic interventions: o neurofeedback (patients monitor and change their brain activity by themselves) o monitoring of the brain activities of the patient by the therapist during and before the end of a therapy (use: adaptive indication; avoidance of relapses) o in the context of neurobiologically inspired approaches (e.g., neuropsychotherapy: Grawe, 2006; neurobehavioral therapy: Siegle et al., 2007)
Knowledge which intervention works how on the neuronal level	With unipolar depression, antidepressant medication reduces amygdala hyperacticity directly; CBT changes prefrontal hypoactivation (DeRubeis et al., 2008)	• better understanding of the interaction of brain areas → better understanding of where to intervene with whom • development of rules for differential treatment selection on the conceptual level; deduction of psychological markers for rules for differential treatment selection, use of neurobiological markers/ predictors for differential treatment selection

biological assessments with individual patients. Neurobiologically informed therapists could also achieve higher success rates by being selective, if they know based on neurobiological predictors of which patients they might not even try with. Although we are still far from conclusive results, it is fair to state that related to the question of predictors of psychotherapy success vs. failure, a considerable number of studies are under way (McClure et al., 2007; Siegle, Carter, & Thase, 2006; and others).

One idea depicted in the 2002 paper we have not yet developed much further: To use simulation programs in the planning of concrete, individual therapies. The use of such simulations we have demonstrated empirically (Caspar, Benninghoven, & Berger, 2004). It is rather a transition to combined models of self-regulation in the sense of Carver and Scheier (2002), which include more *traditional*, goal-oriented, deliberate regulation as well as the more self-organized kind of regulation as modeled by connectionist models. Berger (2005) has argued that many relevant clinical phenomena can better be understood if one does not move from traditional to connectionist regulation, but focuses on the combination and coordination of these two forms of regulation. It is the very coordination—which may work better or worse—which seems to be responsible for some clinically essential phenomena in diverse areas, such as emotion regulation, drug abuse, repetition compulsion, and suicide, but also therapeutic phenomena, such as corrective experiences (Caspar & Berger, 2012). The combined model includes at least as many neurobiological considerations as the connectionist models that were favored in 2002. New insights led to a search for even better models, but technically and empirically our use of these models is not as advanced as the purely connectionist models were 10 years ago.

What do I and my team do in terms of neurobiological research? Egenolf (2011) and others study implicit information processing in patients with depression with behavioral as well as EEG assessments including localization of activities in the brain. Other members of the team are studying Emotion Focused Therapy (Greenberg) with neurobiological means. Another group is tracing the neurophysiological correlates of motivational incongruence. Several are involved in my old plan of tracing psychotherapist intuition. I am still convinced that the inclusion of neurobiological research questions and methods will contribute to our understanding of the underlying processes of intuition, but although we have a clear view and hypotheses on a macro level, although we followed the advice of collaborating with experts from the outset, and although we have invested already a lot, it has proven difficult to get this research off the ground.

The ongoing efforts in this and our other neurobiologically oriented projects are based on the strong belief that mainly research which *integrates* psychotherapeutic and neurobiological perspectives from the outset will prove useful. The attempts of integrating both perspectives make research more difficult, but it seems to make more sense to invest in the beginning as compared to making vague interpretations and promises at the end of a study.

Four factors keep contributing to the widespread attractiveness of neurobiological research:

1. The belief that the closer we are to the biological hardware, the more solid are methods and findings expected to be. Fuzzy and mostly implicit as this belief is, it is widespread also among outspoken advocates of psychotherapy, and delays in the expected explosive increase in neurobiologically based insights have not changed this deep-rooted belief with many colleagues.
2. Internal validity is easier to achieve in lab studies than in dirty everyday psychotherapy practice. Importantly, internal validity can be assessed more easily by reviewers of submitted manuscripts as well as grant proposals, and reviewers like to be on the safe side. We had an expert meeting and will publish about this issue shortly.

   The European Union spends exciting amounts of money on research on mental heath. €217 million alone in the Seventh Framework Programme (FP7; http://cordis.europa.eu/fp7/projects_en.html), in combination with other topics even more. This money goes almost exclusively into neurobiological research. Patricia Tosetti, scientific officer of the European Commission, in charge of the organization of research related to brain and mental health, reported to me (December 2011, Brussels) an attempt of furthering psychotherapy research—but even psychotherapy researchers in the role of reviewers favored methodological/internal validity criteria, and as a consequence basic neurobiological research. This has killed the initiative. Counter to the declared principle that money should flow where it helps patients most, psychotherapy research remains underfunded.
3. Research with a faster turnover allows a faster accumulation of research skills and experience than research with studies that take much longer to plan, complete, and publish, as is typical for psychotherapy research. A big part of neurobiological research seems faster than most psychotherapy research, which leaves psychotherapy researchers way behind the experience and skill an experimental researcher with less involvement of real patients and therapies can accumulate.

In 2002, I stated that all should contribute: Psychotherapy *researchers* should contribute to a cooperation with neurobiology based on their existing strengths, but based on realistic expectations. I recommended a combination and cross-fertilization of the two approaches in a field with overlapping and complementary competencies. As yet, psychotherapy has proven effective without being heavily neurobiologically informed, but there is room for higher success rates to which a better understanding of neurobiological factors may contribute. Neurobiology can already contribute to a better understanding of some aspects, while we are still far from being able to ground psychotherapy in neurobiology in any comprehensive way.

Practitioners are pushed towards a holistic view by their experiences. Splitting up the world of psychopathology into psychological versus biological factors and disorders cannot be the ultimate solution (Gabbard, 2000). A new particularism has to be avoided: "Psychotherapy research and neurobiology: Challenge, chance, *and* mutual enrichment!" (p. 19).

All this I would repeat without hesitation, although the development seems to take longer than expected 10 years ago, although we understand the frustration of interested practitioners about the long time it takes, and how contradictory the often underpowered findings are, and that a practically useful finding seems to cost much more money than in traditional psychotherapy research.

Note

1 I thank Martina Belz, Thomas Berger, Yvonne Egenolf, Maria Stein, and Tim Strauman for their useful comments.

13

EXTENDING THE SCIENTIFIC FOUNDATION OF PSYCHOTHERAPY RESEARCH (UNPUBLISHED)[1]

Karla Moras

An era of breakthrough progress could be within reach of psychotherapy research on three of our field's most longstanding, difficult, and pivotal questions. The preceding view, which is elucidated in this chapter, is based on two key premises. First, achievements in therapy research over the past 55 years plus related developments have brought three fundamental questions to the fore:

1. What is the nature of the problem to be treated?
2. What are the primary mechanisms of action of efficacious therapies?
3. Can more efficient and efficacious psychotherapeutic methods be developed?

Second, new opportunities exist to answer the questions timely and persuasively from a scientific perspective. The opportunities arise from: (a) methods and findings now referred to as a "scientific revolution" in the neurosciences, and (b) method developments that support causal inference about how and why therapies work, that is, their mechanisms of action.

In sections that follow, prevailing conclusions that provide context for the two key premises are outlined (Section I). Research strategies are highlighted that can yield scientifically strong and relatively rapid progress on the three pivotal questions listed above (Section II). Achievements in psychotherapy research since 1945 are reviewed briefly to help explain why focus on the questions now is crucial to the field's potential to timely yield needed and scientifically valid advances for clinical practice (Section III). Lastly, some examples are given of research strategies that are encouraged to reach the preceding goals (Section IV).

I. The Zeitgeist: Current, Influential Research Conclusions

The view presented here on priorities for psychotherapy research is grounded in six contemporary, research-based conclusions. All contribute to the fund of accepted knowledge within which the field of therapy research now operates.

1. It is established that psychotherapy[2] in general, and some forms of psychotherapy in particular, can "work," that is, are efficacious by accepted standards of scientific evidence (e.g., Chambless & Ollendick, 2001; Smith, Glass, & Miller, 1980).[3]
2. It is widely accepted that some forms of psychotherapy are on par, at least on par, with medications as treatment options for some common problems such as panic disorder and unipolar depression (Barlow, Gorman, Shear, & Woods, 2000; Casacalenda, Perry, & Looper, 2002).
3. The past 20 years of research on the prevailing psychodiagnostic nosology in the US, the *Diagnostic and Statistical Manual of Mental Disorders* (DSM) (e.g., American Psychiatric Association, 1980, 2000), have documented many weaknesses and both the need, and extraordinary opportunities now, to improve its scientific validity (cf. Andreasen, 1997; Houts, 2000; Widiger & Clark, 2000).
4. Genes can induce vulnerability to mental health-related problems but environment (experience) is strongly influential in gene expression.[4]
5. Imaging technologies, like positron emission tomography (PET) and functional magnetic resonance imaging (fMRI), allow changes associated with therapy to be observed from the vantage point of the brain, and also compared with changes associated with medications for the same problems (e.g., Baxter et al., 1992; Goldapple et al., 2004).
6. Neural plasticity is a characteristic of the brain (e.g., LeDoux, 2002).[5]

II. Accelerate Progress on the Pivotal Questions: Increase Use of Strong Science Research Strategies

> "sometimes we need to be reminded of valuable lessons and exhortations from the past."
>
> (Rosen & Davison, 2003, p. 306)

Directions for psychotherapy research advocated in this chapter link to the conviction that needed practice-relevant advances will be speeded by relying more on existing ideas about scientific methods like:

a. Platt (1964) on the value of "strong inference," "[c]ertain systematic methods of scientific thinking may produce much more rapid progress than others" (p. 347);

b. Borkovec (1997) on the value of a "basic science" approach: "the greatest progress in developing more effective psychotherapies will come from a renewed emphasis on designing and conducting therapy research as basic science devoted to the acquisition of cause-and-effect relationships" (p. 145); and
c. Kraemer et al.'s (2002) strategy to identify causal mechanisms of therapeutic action in outcome studies that use a randomized clinical trial (RCT) design.[6]

The title of this chapter implicitly refers to ideas like (a)–(c), and to basic experimental concepts such as internal validity (IV) and external validity (EV) (Campbell & Stanley, 1963).

IV and EV, and other types of experimental validity (see Kazdin, 1994), are critical to the scientific validity and credibility of therapy research findings and, thereby, to their potential persuasiveness both within and beyond the field. IV and EV function scientifically as logic-based rules to guide deductive (IV) and inductive (EV) reasoning. Importantly, for example, IV helps researchers and consumers of research evaluate outcome study results for whether they can be validly interpreted as evidence for hypothesized causal relationships between putatively active treatment(s) and outcomes.

III. Psychotherapy Research: Achievements and Some Continuing Challenges

> "One of the great benefits of looking backward is to be able to see more clearly the present."
>
> (Houts, 2000, p. 957)

Findings and methods development in therapy research since about 1945, plus advances in related fields like psychopathology, and cognitive and affective neuroscience (e.g., Davidson, 1998), support the following conclusion: Achievements have positioned our field to productively focus now on the three questions previously identified here as both pivotal and difficult. Progress since the mid-1940s is considered because forces then spurred recognition of therapy research as a bona fide field, at least in the US (Moras, 2002).

Five basic questions that have driven therapy research for the past 55 or so years are listed in the left-hand column of Figure 13.1. Selected research milestones and contributions to the questions are referenced along timelines, 1945–present, to the right of each one. The contributions shown are illustrative not exhaustive, intended to provide a brief overview of strides and help mark some remaining challenges. Headway on each question is discussed next. Space limitations preclude mention of all contributions cited in the figure.

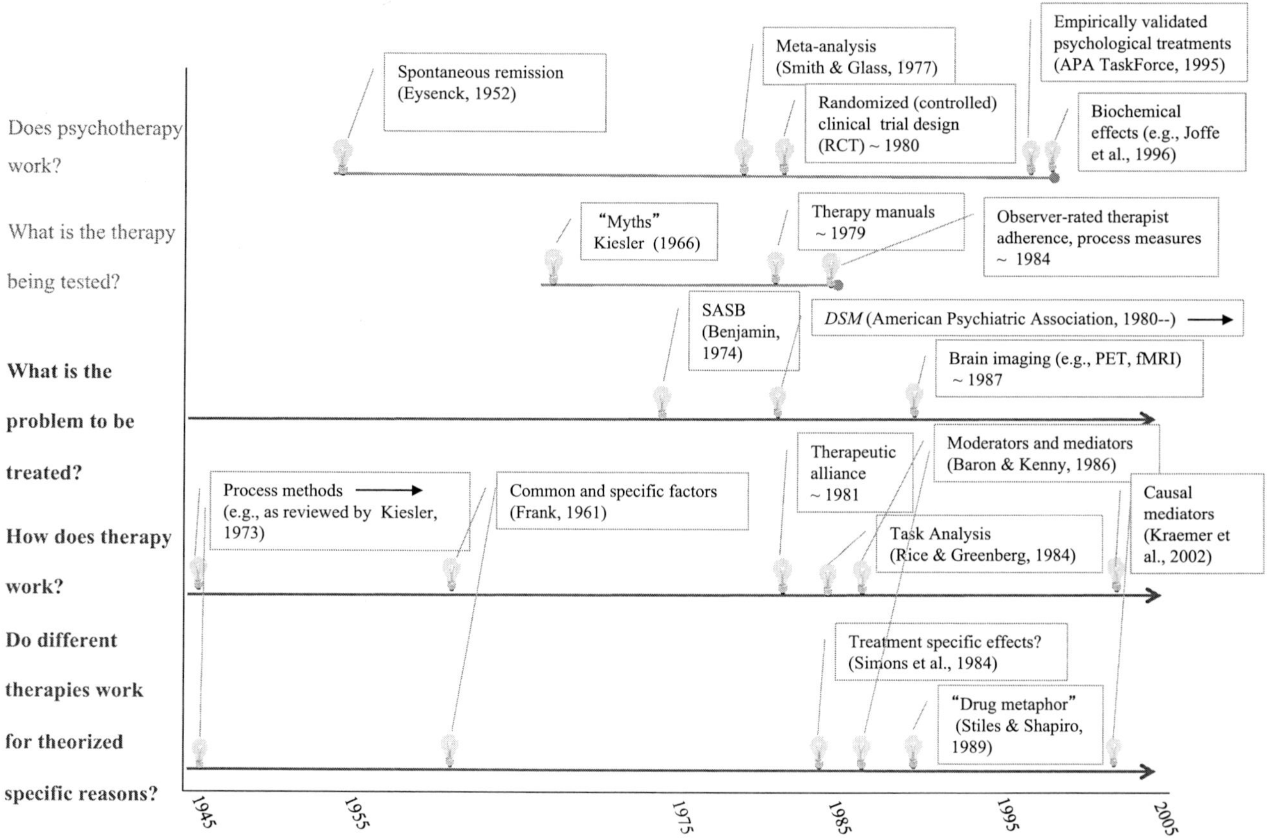

FIGURE 13.1 Psychotherapy Research 1945–2003: Some Achievements and Continuing Challenges

Note: Bold font indicates overarching questions for psychotherapy research not yet satisfactorily answered. SASB = Structural Analysis of Social Behavior; PET = positron emission tomography; fMRI = functional magnetic resonance imaging.

Achievements

Does Psychotherapy Work?

As already noted, our field's *sine qua non* question, "Does psychotherapy work?," has been successfully—and affirmatively—answered. Milestones in the hard won achievement (cf. Parloff, 1984) cited in Figure 13.1 are described next.

Fifty years ago, Eysenck (1952) used data to persuasively argue that existing outcome studies did not show that psychotherapy was associated with higher rates of improvement than "spontaneous remission." The term connotes improvement in problems that can naturally occur over time. It took 25 years for scientifically credible evidence to emerge that successfully challenged Eysenck's conclusion. In 1977, Smith and Glass (1977) reported an application of the statistical technique of meta-analysis to data from nearly 400 therapy outcome studies. A larger meta-analysis soon thereafter, on 475 outcome studies, showed that when findings were pooled from studies in which treated individuals were compared in the same study with either (a) untreated or minimally treated individuals, or (b) people who received placebo treatments or "undifferentiated counseling," the average treated person was better off on outcomes than 80 percent of those who needed therapy but were not treated (Smith et al., 1980). The advantage was larger when the meta-analysis included only studies in which therapy groups were compared to no- or minimal-treatment groups.

Introduction of the multi-site,[7] RCT design to therapy outcome research also helped to defeat doubt that psychotherapy can prompt improvement beyond that which can occur naturally over time or with placebo treatments. The design, when rigorously implemented with necessary research methods, importantly including a treatment control condition, allows scientifically justified causal inference that a tested therapy "works" in the sense of being able to potentiate improvement in a problem that cannot be expected either by chance without treatment or with placebo treatment. (The specific inference allowed depends on the type of control condition.) The RCT design was long used in psychopharmacology research, held as the gold standard for evaluating the efficacy and safety of medications for widespread clinical use for specific problems.

Work of the American Psychological Association's Task Force on the Promotion and Dissemination of Psychological Procedures also was broadly influential. The Task Force developed a set of scientific criteria, grounded in experimental concepts like IV, to guide review of psychotherapy outcome studies. The Task Force's first review in 1995 yielded a list of "empirically validated" forms of therapy for various *DSM* diagnoses such as panic disorder (APA Task Force, 1995).[8] The list was updated as more research accrued.

Additionally, outcome studies began to appear that not only showed associations between response to psychotherapies and biochemical and brain activity changes, but also that the changes could be similar to those associated with medication treatment (e.g., Baxter et al., 1992; Joffe, Segal, & Singer, 1996). Such findings helped strengthen and extend psychotherapy's credibility as a potentially efficacious mental health intervention. Also helpful was successfully answering the second question listed in Figure 13.1, discussed next.

What is the Therapy Being Tested?

The ability to answer the question is another crucial hurdle cleared by our field. For over 20 years (from 1945) outcome studies routinely did not allow the investigators, or anyone else, to be sure of what the therapies tested consisted. Researchers wanted to argue from study results that a therapy worked—or didn't—but could not document to scientific standards the actual content of therapies provided by their study therapists. Kiesler (1966) attended the field to the preceding fatal IV flaw in a classic 1966 paper.

Remedies became widely evident about 15 years later in the form of methods modeled in a landmark study (Elkin, Parloff, Hadley, & Autry, 1985). One was use of therapy instruction manuals that describe in detail how a form of psychotherapy is to be implemented. Scientifically, manuals serve as the required operational definition of the primary independent variable(s) for outcome studies and, importantly, also as a tool to help train study therapists to correctly provide therapies to be tested. Development and use of therapy manuals markedly increased the potential for therapies examined in outcome studies to be done as intended, a necessary condition for a valid test of their efficacy. Manuals also provided a standard, basic reference for another methodological tool that is required to evaluate an outcome study's IV for testing a therapy's efficacy and also specific effects: observer-rated, therapist adherence therapy process measures, such as the Collaborative Study Psychotherapy Rating Scale (Hollon, Waskow, Evans, & Lowery, 1984). Adherence measures and related data collection procedures are needed to reliably assess the extent to which therapies tested were implemented as intended throughout a study (e.g., Hill, O'Grady, & Elkin, 1992).

Continuing, Pivotal Challenges

What is the Nature of the Problem to be Treated?

The third question in Figure 13.1 is fundamental to progress in therapy research but has been intransigent to it and largely also to psychopathology research, the field for which the question is focal. The theory of any form of psychotherapy logically is required to explicitly link the therapy's specific techniques to a theory of "what's wrong?" that they are intended to help remediate. The accuracy, precision, and completeness (identification of causal and maintaining variables) of the theory of what's wrong can be expected to be critical determinants of the potential efficacy, efficiency, and durability of effects of the related form of therapy.

Broad consensus has not emerged on answers to the question despite monumental effort since Kraeplin's pioneering work began in the late 1800s. An instructive example is the aforementioned diagnostic system, the DSM (e.g., American Psychiatric Association, 1980, 2000). Its impact has been vast, shaping much therapy research in the US and also sanctioned and insurance-reimbursed clinical practice since publication of its third revision in 1980. Despite the DSM's pragmatic worth, even its most recent revision (American Psychiatric Association, 2000) remains a mostly pre-scientific classification scheme (cf. Houts, 2000).

The DSM essentially is a descriptive, rationally generated, categorical nosology that represents the consensus efforts, sometimes highly contentious, of "blue ribbon" panels of experts composed at the time each revision is undertaken (cf. Widiger & Clark, 2000). In clinical practice, the presence of DSM diagnoses often is determined mainly from phenomenological self-report (consciously available information) of an identified patient. Basic scientific weaknesses of the DSM as a reliable and valid diagnostic system for research and practice include poor inter-assessor reliability of many diagnoses (e.g., Williams et al., 1992) and extensive co-occurrence (comorbidity) of diagnoses, both within and across DSM's diagnostic categories such as Mood, Anxiety, and Personality Disorders (e.g., Maser & Cloninger, 1990).[9]

How does Therapy Work? Do Different Therapies Work for Theorized Specific Reasons?

> "Therapy is coming of age regarding efficacy for anxiety and depression, but is only a toddler regarding the scientific principles to explain its effects."
>
> (Marks, 2002, p. 200)

The fourth and fifth questions listed in Figure 13.1 are closely related. They also are crucial to extending the scientific foundation of psychotherapy research and making practice-relevant progress. Relevant studies historically have been referred to as *process* and *process-outcome* in the therapy research literature (e.g., Kiesler, 1973; Orlinsky, Grawe, & Parks, 1994). More current terms are *mechanisms of action* and *mechanisms of change* (e.g., Kazdin, 2002).

Editions of the *Handbook of Psychotherapy and Behavior Change* (1971–) include reviews of what has grown to be thousands of discrete process and process-outcome findings. Despite prodigious effort, our field seems to be mostly stalemated with respect to producing important new findings or insights on either question. Nearly 15 years ago, two past presidents of the Society for Psychotherapy Research called progress in process-outcome research "slow" and the yield of about 40 years of such research as of then "disappointing" (Stiles & Shapiro, 1989). Neither the pace nor the yield has picked up detectably. One factor maintaining the impasse is perseverant reliance on simplistic conceptualizations, hypotheses, and study designs, as Stiles and Shapiro suggested. Designs and methods that can support causal inference about how and why therapies work rarely are used.

Answers to both questions are needed to support practice-relevant advances from therapy research such as: (a) refining existing efficacious therapies to make them more efficient by eliminating their non-essential (read: rain dance) elements, and (b) identifying psychological change principles to aid discovery of more efficacious and efficient interventions (cf. Rosen & Davison, 2003). The fifth question in Figure 13.1 points to scientifically critical and progress-essential tasks like (a) testing the theories of therapeutic change of specific forms of therapy, and (b) identifying any mutative processes that are causally prompted by specific therapy techniques that distinguish theoretically different forms of therapy from each other and also from placebo treatments.

Considerations like those above support identifying the question "What are the primary mechanisms of action of efficacious therapies?" as a pivotal one now for therapy research. The question is a condensed restatement of the fourth and fifth questions in Figure 13.1. "Efficacious" emphasizes the importance, given limited research resources, to focus mechanisms research on how and why therapies that can be demonstrated to work do so.

Can More Efficient and Efficacious Psychotherapeutic Methods be Developed?

The question is not listed in Figure 13.1. It is identified here as one of three pivotal questions that merits therapy researchers' attention now due to a troubling byproduct of the field's success in positively answering the question "Does therapy work?"—namely, evidence for unsatisfactory upper limits on the benefits of current empirically supported therapies for many common problems (cf. Borkovec, 1997; Kraemer et al., 2002), such as unipolar depression, obsessive-compulsive disorder, and panic disorder. Even efficacious therapies often, and for many patients, are not adequately helpful or durable. (The same is true of medications, as indicated, for example, by psychopharmacology research on "treatment resistant" depression.) Findings for depression illustrate the point. Notable percentages of those treated with existing psychotherapies, medications, or their combination do not respond, or respond only partially, not meeting recovery criteria. For example, Casacalenda et al. (2002) reviewed randomized, controlled, double-blind outcome studies of unipolar depression (N = 883 outpatients). Remission percentages were 46.4 percent, 46.3 percent, and 24.4. percent for medication, psychotherapy, and control conditions, respectively.

IV. Illustrations: Developments to Mine for Research on the Pivotal Questions

Types of research are illustrated next that could help accelerate scientifically strong, practice-relevant progress on the three pivotal questions discussed in Section III.

1. What is the Nature of the Problem to be Treated?

> "Neuroimaging offers an increasingly powerful method for the development of a scientific psychopathology."
>
> (Teasdale et al., 1999, p. 209)

Toward a Scientifically Valid, Treatment-Relevant Psychopathology

Growing availability and refinement of imaging technologies and methods such as PET, fMRI, and more (cf. Hyman, 2000), and applying them to the brain, make it feasible to advance beyond rudimentary models of psychopathology and related diagnostic systems like the aforementioned DSM (e.g., American Psychiatric Association, 2000). Brain imaging offers critical, additional vantage points to examine the question "What is the nature of the problem to be treated?" For example, the human brain now can be systematically observed in action while a person is: (a) doing experimental tasks that generate emotions, cognitive functions, or mimic hallmark symptoms of some *DSM* disorders; or (b) actually experiencing core, impairing symptoms like auditory hallucinations (Andreasen, 1997). Neuroimaging at last allows observation inside the "black box" while it is at work, and where, it must be assumed: (a) problems of "the mind" are caused and maintained, at least to some extent and in some ways; and (b) psychotherapies have some outcome-relevant effects when they are efficacious.

An experimental fMRI study of brain regions involved in generation of negative and positive affect (Teasdale et al., 1999) illustrates the value of neuroimaging for refining understanding of maladaptive mood and anxiety states. The study also illustrates that neuroimaging already enables detailed examination of neural processes that are posited in theorized of mechanisms of action of some psychotherapies, as per pivotal question number 2. Regarding mechanisms, Teasdale et al. show that the theory that supports the cognitive therapy (CT) (e.g., Beck, Rush, Shaw, & Emery, 1979) technique of cognitive restructuring (to modify negative meanings that a person attributes to experiences) can be examined via neural region activation, while subjects perform experimental tasks that stimulate affect, and manipulate the psychological meaning of emotionally-arousing stimuli. In sum, Teasdale et al. (1999) illustrate breakthrough potential for therapy research due to the ability now to: (a) elucidate neural level processes associated with common problems; (b) experimentally examine theorized mechanisms of action of specific therapies for a problem at the level of neural processes that are more or less explicitly posited (depending on the theory); and (c) refine the theories and related therapy techniques based on findings.

Andreasen's (1997) recent review of developments in psychopathology research elucidates ways that neuroimaging has helped to propel scientifically grounded, treatment-relevant progress in that field. She likens advances to goals that Freud articulated over 100 years ago in his *Project for a Scientific Psychology.* Basic tenets of the 21st-century project for a scientific psychopathology that Andreasen (1997) foresees include:

> the mind is the expression of the activity of the brain and these two are separable for purposes of analysis and discussion but inseparable in actuality. That is, mental phenomena arise from the brain, but mental experience also affects the brain, as is demonstrated by the many examples of environmental influences on brain plasticity. (p. 1586).

Andreasen (1997) credits the current period of progress to "the maturity of the techniques of neuroscience [and to] convergence of efforts from multiple domains: psychiatry, cognitive psychology and neuropsychology, and clinical and basic neuroscience" (p. 1586). Her review signals an era of interdisciplinary rapprochement: "the challenge in developing a scientific psychopathology . . . is to use the power of multiple disciplines" (p. 1586). The time is opportune for therapy researchers to forge collaborations with neuroscientists and (or) develop skill with neuroimaging methods to strengthen the scientific basis of theories of the nature of the problem to be treated that support various psychotherapies (cf. Borkovec, 1997).

One example of direct implications of neuroscience-based psychopathology research for therapy research is Andreasen's (1997) review of findings on unipolar depression. They suggest a causal neural hypothesis for the frequent problem of relapse after treatment (with psychotherapy or medication), and the fact that depressive episodes can occur without being triggered by identifiable troubling events: Neurally encoded memories that are linked to some symptoms of depression (a) might be cued by experiences that bypass conscious brain functions and (b) are not eliminated by existing treatments.

Brain-Imaging Psychopathology Research: Direct Implications for Therapy Research and Practice

Similar to Teasdale et al.'s (1999) experimental use of neuroimaging to investigate affect states, studies of cocaine addiction also illustrate that psychopathology research that uses neuroimaging already can have direct implications for therapy research and practice. Volkow et al. (1992) obtained PET scans from chronic cocaine-abusing males who were recruited from a detoxification unit. A glucose metabolism tracer was used as a marker for regional brain activation. Those who completed a three-month inpatient drug abstinence and rehabilitation program (N = 7) were rescanned. Scans were obtained one to six weeks after last cocaine use and again after three months drug-free. For comparison, scans also were obtained from male control subjects without history of drug or alcohol use, other than caffeine or nicotine. Differences were found in several frontal regions of the controls' compared to the abusers' brains, with the latter group showing lower metabolic activity. Frontal hypometabolism in the abusers' brains persisted after three to four months of drug abstinence.

Such findings have implications for therapy research and practice due to the importance of the brain's frontal areas for judgment, decision making, and willful control over impulses and behavior. The functions are precisely those that cognitively focused therapy techniques (e.g., Beck et al., 1979) are intended to enlist to help a person regulate affects. A figure displaying scans of a cocaine abuser at two times post withdrawal, 10 days and 100 days, and scans of one control subject (Volkow, 2003) helps convey the findings' informative value for therapy research. After 100 days of abstinence, the cocaine abuser's frontal areas remained mostly inactive compared to the same areas of the control's brain, but the scan also showed signs of increased frontal activity compared to 10 days post last use. The findings suggest hypotheses about the use and timing of CT to treat cocaine addiction such as: Therapy techniques that are intended to marshal frontal cortex functions are more likely to be helpful if introduced after some months of abstinence, as part of a sequenced intervention plan.

2. What Are the Primary Mechanisms of Action of Efficacious Therapies?

New Strategy to Identify Causal Moderators and Mediators of Treatment Effects

Kraemer et al. (2002) recently presented a strategy specifically for causal mechanisms research on the effects of treatments. It is "an analytic framework to identify and distinguish between moderators and mediators in RCTs when outcomes are measured dimensionally" (p. 877). The developers describe its intended utility thus: "Rapid progress in identifying the most effective treatments and understanding on whom treatments work and do not work and why treatments work or do not work depends on efforts to identify moderators and mediators of treatment outcome." (p. 877). Moderators are variables that indicate "on whom and under what circumstances treatments have different effects," and "mediators identify why and how treatments have effects" (p. 877).

The strategy draws on but also improves on in crucial ways the Baron and Kenny (1986) method for identifying moderators and mediators. Strengths include conceptual clarity, plus procedural requirements and other elements that sharpen the operational definitions of moderators, mediators, and mechanisms. Importantly, Kraemer et al.'s (2002) approach: (a) allows causal inference which the earlier method does not; (b) adds the concept of "mechanism," defined as a mediator that is demonstrated to have a causal relationship to a treatment effect; and (c) requires temporal precedence for a variable to qualify either as a moderator or a mechanism of a treatment's effects. The latter two elements promise to reduce serious confusion and muddled findings that have been associated with use of the Baron and Kenny (1986) method for therapy research.

Probing Specific and Common Mechanisms of Different Treatments

A preliminary study by Goldapple et al. (2004) illustrates that it already is feasible to use neuroimaging to examine and compare neural correlates of theorized mechanisms of action of theoretically diverse psychotherapies, and also compare the neural correlates to those of medication treatment for the same problem. The study also illustrates that neuroimaging can help investigate common mechanisms of action hypotheses that continue to be posited to account for no difference outcome findings when psychotherapies are compared with each other, or medications (e.g., Wampold, 2001). Neuroimaging methods like Goldapple et al. used, if applied in a stronger study design, could even probe perplexing findings like those from a randomized, partially controlled outcome study in which CT (Beck et al., 1979), medication, and their combination were compared for unipolar depression (Simons, Garfield, & Murphy, 1984). Neither specific nor differential outcomes were obtained as predicted by different theorized mechanisms and the different focal treatment targets of CT and medication. Outpatients treated with CT or medication "demonstrated nearly identical changes on all measures, including cognitive measures, despite the absence of direct focus on cognitive activity [in the medication condition]" (Simons et al., 1984, p. 45).

In brief, Goldapple et al. (2004) collected pre- and post-treatment PET scans of outpatients with unipolar depression who received CT. Pre- to post-changes in activity in some brain regions in CT responders were found and compared with archival PET data from depressed patients who received medication and improved. Some differences and some similarities in brain region activation changes were found to be associated with improvement, suggestive of possible common and also specific neural effects of CT and medication and, thus, of neural mechanisms of action.

Probing Placebo Responses and Mechanisms

The placebo response is one of the most robust and challenging findings in and to medical and mental health treatment research (e.g., Shapiro & Morris, 1978). Clarifying its effects and mechanisms has been an elusive gold key to helping identify common and specific effects of psychotherapies and their respective mechanisms. A recent study by Mayberg et al. (2002) illustrates that brain imaging methods can help reveal mysteries of placebo responses. The development also means that neuroimaging could help identify effects and mechanisms that are common to professionally offered therapies but also distinct from placebo effects and mechanisms. (Mayberg et al.'s findings are not described here. They are preliminary due to study limitations.)

3. *Can More Efficient and Efficacious Psychotherapeutic Methods be Developed?*

Studies and research developments described so far in Section IV point to research directions that are likely to speed discovery of more efficient and efficacious psychotherapeutic interventions. Work by Schwartz and colleagues illustrates use of neuroimaging findings to try to augment the effects of an existing empirically supported therapy, namely exposure and response prevention (ERP), for obsessive compulsive disorder (OCD) (e.g., Schwartz, 1998; APA Task Force, 1995). Imaging findings informed a psychoeducational revision to ERP. Brain scans of OCD sufferers obtained during OCD symptom-provocation tasks are used to teach patients to understand intrusive thoughts and repetitive urges as "false brain messages." One goal of assigning the new meaning to symptoms is to increase patients' confidence that it is safe to ignore compulsive urges like repeated hand-washing. The intent, in turn, is to increase patients' motivation both to resist repetitively performing maladaptive OCD behaviors and replace them with more adaptive behaviors. The latter is another modification of ERP, "behavioral refocusing," also supported by neuroimaging findings on OCD.

V. Summary and General Suggestions

The main aim of this chapter is to encourage efficient and scientifically strong progress on three longstanding, fundamental, and challenging questions for psychotherapy research. It was argued that research on the questions is pivotal to timely, scientifically valid, and practice-relevant progress of the type now needed. To speed advances, mechanisms of action research on psychotherapies and also placebo treatments (to gain requisite comparative knowledge), especially using methods that can identify variables and processes that are causal to desired treatment effects, was emphasized. The utility of brain imaging methods to make progress on all three questions was illustrated and underscored.

Four more suggestions are offered to those stirred to pursue the great task of developing more efficient and efficacious psychotherapeutic principles and techniques. First, take note of Kazdin's (2007) view: "the very best practice will come from the best science" (p. 89).[10] Second, read LeDoux's (2002) *The Synaptic Self: How Our Brains Become Who We Are.* It helped transform at least one therapy researcher's understanding of major determinants of human thoughts, emotional experiences, and behaviors. Third, read Platt (1964) for a broad perspective on research, including his thoughts on why fields advance at different rates and description of Pasteur's methods and pace of accomplishments. Fourth, read Borkovec (1997) for a brief, clear exposition of scientific methods to move therapy research forward.

Notes

1 This chapter is based on a Presidential Address at the 34th annual conference of the Society for Psychotherapy Research, Weimar, Germany, June 26, 2003. The views were the author's not the U.S. National Institute on Drug Abuse. Moras (2006) updates and expands some points, particularly those related to neuroscience.

2 "Psychotherapy" is used broadly to include mental health treatments that rely solely on noninvasive interventions derived from psychologically (including behaviorally) based principles that are delivered by a person, in contrast to medication or other somatic methods such as rapid transcranial magnetic stimulation. For example, psychotherapy includes behavioral treatments like systematic desensitization.

3 "Efficacy" is used with a specific scientific meaning. It refers to experimentally-derived evidence that a putatively active therapeutic intervention is effective in the sense of being causally associated with greater or different benefits than can be expected to be associated with placebo treatment and (or) changes that ordinarily might occur with the passage of time.

4 "Environment" and "experience" are used here as synonyms for non-inherited variables now understood to affect expression of gene-based vulnerabilities.

5 The concept of neural plasticity highlights the brain's flexibility in terms of potential for neuron connections to be changed by experience and not only by experience of which a person is consciously aware. The basic idea is that a routine capacity of the brain is to "rewire" itself at the neural level, that is, to learn via spontaneous modifications as a person interacts with the environment. Described by neuroscientist LeDoux (2002), "Most systems of the brain are plastic, that is, modifiable by experience, which means that the synapses involved are changed by experience" (p. 8).

Neural plasticity replaced the prior dominant conclusion that the adult human brain changes little after development from the neonatal period to early adulthood. The earlier view supported a belief that psychotherapy had negligible value for the middle-aged and older. In contrast, neural plasticity supports psychotherapy's utility both as a treatment modality and across the lifespan. Kandel (1998), psychoanalytically trained psychiatrist, neurobiologist, and Nobel Laureate, described probable causal links between psychotherapy, learning, neural connections, and gene expression: "Insofar as a psychotherapy or counseling is effective and produces long-term changes in behavior, it presumably does so through learning, by producing changes in gene expression that alter the strength of synaptic connections and structural changes that alter the anatomical pattern of interconnections between nerve cells of the brain" (p. 460).

6 See Kraemer et al. (2002) for a synopsis of elements of a well-conducted RCT.

7 In multi-site RCTs, the same research protocol is carried out simultaneously in two or more research settings. The multi-site strategy is scientifically informative and efficient, allowing the generalizability (EV) of outcome findings to be evaluated at the same time that treatment efficacy is tested, e.g., Elkin et al. (1985).

8 In response to controversy, the name of the list was changed to "empirically supported" (Chambless & Ollendick, 2001).

9 Comorbidity is a major threat to the scientific construct validity of the *DSM* because it is categorical classification system. Extensive comorbidity both across and within *DSM's* diagnostic categories indicates that they do not distinguish core underlying pathological processes.

10 The quote is from a chapter by Kazdin published after the Presidential Address summarized in this chapter. It concisely states a central assumption of the Address. For full citation, see Kazdin (2002).

14

THE PERSON OF THE THERAPIST (2005)

Mark Aveline

> "In what is called 'individual psychotherapy,' two people meet and talk to each other with the intention and hope that one will learn to live more fruitfully."
>
> (Lomas, 1981)

This simple statement encompasses the central dimensions in psychotherapy practice: meeting and talking hopefully towards the end of more fruitful living. It is my kind of psychotherapy: a rather ordinary encounter between two people but one of exceptional promise.

This article focuses on the contribution of the person of the therapist to outcome, drawing on my experience as a practitioner and trainer in psychotherapy plus research findings. The view is personal, reflecting my philosophy in life as well as an evolved perspective on what is important in effective psychotherapy. While the conclusions may not apply to all therapies, I am confident that they are important in the kind of psychotherapy that interests me. Their articulation may promote dialogue between clinicians and researchers and initiate research on important issues in clinical practice.

To understand my focus, I need to sketch my formation as a therapist, identify some of the colleagues who have inspired me, and describe the clinical context for which practice methods have had to be evolved. Although this inevitably gives an individual cast to the conclusions, declaring my bias enables readers to compare their position.

My View of Psychotherapy

My training in psychiatry and psychotherapy began at Guy's Hospital, London. I gained experience in Jungian, humanistic, personal construct and behavioral approaches. In Edinburgh, I immersed myself in intense therapeutic milieu work on an inpatient unit with a Freudian emphasis and small group therapy using an object-relations framework. Outside the hospital, I was active in psychodrama and encounter groups. These diverse experiences led me to conclude that there is no royal way in psychotherapy. There are many seemingly different ways for which patients and therapists have different affinities. This is not to say that all therapies are equally good; some may be particularly effective in alleviating specific clinical problems; the essential elements in others may be obscured by redundant relics of tradition. I emerged as a mongrel, proud of my heritage and ready to work as a consultant medical psychotherapist.

I started the Nottingham Psychotherapy Unit in 1974. The primary remit of this specialist National Health Service facility is to provide clinical service and training at specialist and generalist levels. Funded by general taxation, the service is free at point-of-use. Receiving mainly tertiary referrals, the Unit comprises two divisions (psychodynamic and cognitive-behavioral), together providing a one-stop integrated, multidisciplinary service. Prizing diversity within a common framework of assessment, audit, and CPD, the team has a strong emphasis on assessment and matching therapy to patient need through a broad menu of individual and group therapies, both brief and long term.

My ideas have been particularly inspired by four colleagues, most with strong links to SPR, all capable of thinking outside of the box of tradition and willing to be challenged by evidence.

Bob Hobson held a similar post in Manchester. Although not primarily a researcher, his clinical approach was experimental. Entering deep into the space between patient and therapist, he saw psychotherapy as a conversation in which meaning is teased out through paying the closest attention to communications, especially metaphors, and making and testing clinical hypotheses (Hobson, 1985). The idea of co-created intersubjectivity in early studies (Meares, 1976; Meares & Hobson, 1977) foretells later work on the vital importance of recognizing and repairing ruptures in the therapeutic relationship when working with people with complex personality problems (Meares, 2001).

I owe a great deal to Jerome Frank. His seminal book *Persuasion and Healing* (Frank, 1961, 1973) was the first psychotherapy text that made sense to me. The idea that effective psychotherapy is underpinned by the operation of common therapeutic factors helped explain the effectiveness of the diverse therapies that I had come to respect. Looking for ways in my clinical work to instill hope, counter demoralization, and promote mastery through success experiences became a guiding principle.

In 1986, I spent a happy week at Vanderbilt University in Nashville, Tennessee studying Hans Strupp's time-limited dynamic psychotherapy (Strupp & Binder, 1984). On my return, I started teaching my variant: focal therapy (Aveline, 1995, 2002a). Admirably, Hans wanted to address psychotherapy problems at the limits of therapist tolerance, this being a frontier for effectiveness and a marker of major patient disruption.

Group therapy is the poor cousin in the family of psychotherapies, neglected by both practitioners and researchers. This is a great pity because the method has unique potential for therapeutic action (Aveline, 1990, 2006). Irvin Yalom has been a lucid, inspiring advocate for interpersonally focused group therapy. Personal history as told is supplemented by history as shown in the social microcosm of the group, setting the stage for interpersonal learning (Yalom, 1995). His use of the simple Q-sort method highlighted the value that successful group participants place on disclosure, peer acceptance, and honest feedback.

These mentors reinforced my feeling about what is important in effective psychotherapy: conversation, storytelling, the centrality of meaning, making and testing clinical hypotheses, formulation, intersubjectivity, attending to alliance ruptures, the operation of common factors, interpersonal learning, success experiences, and the moral imperative to focus limited resources on patients with major interpersonal problems, the walking wounded rather than the worried well.

In common with other similar specialist psychotherapy departments, the Nottingham Psychotherapy Unit is something of a "last-chance saloon." Patients have severe recurrent problems. Most have had previous therapy in primary or secondary health care and either they or their careers are desperate to find a way forward. I stress these points because sometimes the kind of psychotherapy practiced and investigated elsewhere appears so far removed from what I understand by the term that it might be a different class of activity. One purpose of this article is to assert the character of a more ambitious, classic form of psychotherapy that addresses recurrent maladaptive relationship patterns and aims to modify their more harmful aspects. The argument is not with brevity, of which I am a fan (Aveline, 2001b, 2002b), but with limited ambition and with failure to recognise the benefits of long-term commitment in addressing fundamental problems.

I see psychotherapy being typically for people who have been bruised by life and who, consequently, struggle to form mature relationships. Their disadvantage stems from a combination of inheritance and nurture. Psychotherapy attends to vital feelings of hope, despair, envy, hate, self-doubt, love, and loss that exist between human beings. It works with the meaning of experience and repeated pattern of relationships that people form, in particular those aspects of the patterns for which they responsibility and over which they can come to exercise choice. It encourages personally "significant action,"[1] which, once succeeded in, will begin to rewrite the cramped fiction of a person's life (Aveline, 1979, 2002b).

The stance is interpersonal. It begins with the psychological view that people take of themselves, their situation, and the possibilities that are available. In origin, this is the view that has been taken of them by important others and that they have taken of themselves in the past. Crucially, it will go on being the determining view unless some corrective emotional experience occurs (Alexander & French, 1946). Self-view is illustrated in relationship patterns. My criterion for success is external change rather than inferred intra-psychic change. Recognizing that individuals may need sustained care in order to gather the courage to change tempers this demanding target. Mostly, the process is iterative, revisiting old issues again and again within a therapy and in different episodes of therapy at times of difficulty in a person's life. The intent is not to eradicate neurotic potential but to catalyze sufficient change for the patient's purpose, developing alternative ways of reacting that coexist with old, more limiting patterns and that will become better established if they benefit the patient's life as it unfolds.

The process is interactive. Both in ordinary relationships and the constructed relationship of psychotherapy, the starting points are telling and seeing. In a minor way, this is happening as you read these words. However, to complete the cycle, I have to imagine your reaction. I tell and I see myself. As I tell, you see me, maybe in a new way. I entrust myself to you. If we were to talk, our talking would be shaped by what I said (or did not say). Who I am depends on how you receive me and how you react. Together we create interacting selves. Together we change each other. Furthermore, people show their history in what they feel and do and create their future through a collective authoring of the here-and-now in overlapping systems of interaction. For me, working with these manifestations—wherever they occur—is the way to lever interpersonal change.

Some Concepts That We Could Do Without

In my opinion, what we researchers tend to value complicates the task of evolving effective, relevant psychotherapy. By encouraging unnecessary solutions to false problems, some valued concepts misdirect our energy. Here are four, not wholly true assertions.

1. Diagnosis atomizes what is unitary. For a variety of political and financial reasons, psychotherapy has adopted a form of classification shaped by a medical concept of disease. Categorical diagnosis implies that disorders are discrete entities with different causes and treatments and does not fit the "problems in living" presentations that are the province of psychotherapy and a major part of the work of psychiatry. Stressing difference between conditions underplays the alternative view that the great range of non-psychotic symptomatology is better seen as a single manifestation of disturbance whose origins need to be understood and formulated (Aveline, 1999).
2. Schools overemphasize difference. Furthermore, psychotherapeutic interventions across therapies are much more similar than different and draw heavily on common therapeutic factors.
3. There is no specificity in treatment.
4. The past is unknowable. Each person's history is a work of fiction, reworked as time distances protagonists from events, mellowing or enhancing feelings in line with their residual meaning. Events disappear from the narrative as they are forgotten. When re-remembered, they may appear in transformed form with altered character and meaning, sometimes amalgamated with

> other narratives. The new history is like the history-as-happened but is not the same; often, it has a subtext of justifying the path taken in the person's life. Truly, many favorite memories never really happened. Therapists (and patients) may fall into the trap of accepting narrative at face value and build hypotheses about individual and general causation on shaky ground. Furthermore, a past focus in therapy may encourage the patient to externalize their problems and blame others for their predicament. It is often easier to be the result of the past rather than the cause of the future!

What is left after laying waste to these hallowed concepts? As in Freud's original formulation of anxiety, symptoms are viewed as signals of disequilibrium in a person's homeostasis and indicators of unresolved issues, which may be beneficially understood and addressed rather than simply described. Not all symptoms are meaningless noise in the human machine. Many psychological symptoms are like bubbles, surfacing in a vat of relationship problems as it comes to the boil; they signify that process. The problem is the problem, not the surface disturbance. Effective psychotherapy is a human interactive process, which applies common therapeutic factors. Although some specific techniques add value, most experienced therapists do similar things with most patients. Therapists bring a creative, eclectic professional involvement to sessions, preferentially taking a here-and-now and future-oriented focus. In Adler's (1925) words, "not whence but whither." Therapies do differ in both form and model of the mind, but their effective form is obscured by redundant elements. Therapists differ in aptitude for engaging with particular human problems and therapies. Thus, therapists need to find a form of conversation within which they are comfortable; this is an important function of training. I suspect that therapists educate patients to converse fruitfully within that discourse; those who manage this undeclared task well will have fewer patients terminating prematurely. All therapists have a moral imperative to be aware of the limitations and range of convenience of their preferred approach (Aveline, 2002a).

The Therapist's Contribution to Outcome

Many factors contribute to outcome: intrinsic, extrinsic, generic, and patient specific (Aveline, Strauss, & Stiles, 2005). Patients vary: problems may be more or less entrenched, circumstance sets limits to change, time may not be auspicious, and fortune may smile or frown. Although therapy is effective overall, the Dodo bird finding tells us that psychotherapies are similarly effective and none preeminent, a sobering conclusion for partisans of school or faction (Luborsky et al., 2002; Luborsky, Singer, & Luborsky, 1975). Furthermore, therapist allegiance is a powerful factor in outcome determination. In a review of 29 studies, allegiance was strongly and more highly correlated with outcome than the treatment itself (Luborsky et al., 1999). Between-treatments effects were not large.

As therapists vary in skill, so they vary in outcome. The work of 91 therapists with 1,841 clients over a 2.5-year period in a university counseling center was evaluated using the OQ self-report measure. The best therapists produced better results quicker (average = 2.4 sessions). The worst were slower (average = 7 sessions) and produced deterioration, more than 1 *SD* or 20 OQ points (Okiishi, Lambert, Nielson, & Ogles, 2003). Further evidence of the worth of expertise comes from the performance-tracking system operated by a Californian health-care provider (Lambert, 2003). One therapist specializing in brief therapy had much better outcomes than the average for a training clinic. In a harbinger of the future, the provider is using this type of data to determine referral.

Two analyses by Luborsky et al. (1986, 1997) substantiate the point. Although it is difficult to tease out therapist from therapy effects because of the structure in randomized trials, re-analysis of four major studies of psychotherapy with experienced therapists showed greater variance by therapist than between treatment effects. Some therapists had consistently better outcomes. Even poor therapists had some good outcomes. There were also domain differences, some better at resolving target symptoms and some better at improving interpersonal functioning (Luborsky et al., 1986). Different rates of improvement were shown by 22 therapists across seven samples of substance-abusing and depressed patients. The difference was not related to patient severity or other patient attributes. Some therapists maintained their difference across studies; they were equally good, even when using different techniques (Luborsky, McLellan, Diguer, Woody, & Seligman, 1997).

Two early studies suggest processes whereby therapy can result in negative effects. Seventy replies from 150 prominent clinicians, theoreticians, and researchers identified a range of negative effects that may be engendered by therapy, e.g., decompensation, regression, erosion of relationships, rationalization of hostility, and patients "overreaching" themselves (Strupp, Hadley, & Gomes-Schwartz, 1977). Contributory factors, with considerable face validity, include: poor assessment leading to too deep probing; therapist character factors, e.g., a need to exploit, excessive unconscious hostility and seductiveness; technique factors, e.g., technical rigidity, destructive interpretations conveying abnormality, fostering dependence; and blaming the patient for lack of progress. Similar correlations have been found among encounter group casualties (Yalom & Lieberman, 1971). Of seven types of group leader across a range of groups, aggressive-stimulator leaders (N = 5) produced all but one of the casualties. They were authoritarian, impatient and insisted on immediate self-disclosure, emotional expression, and attitude change—a toxic combination.

Conducting therapy is taxing. Therapy is mostly practiced behind a closed door in a room wherein the therapist has to cope with painful secrets given in confidence and arousing troubling feelings: fear, sadness, helplessness, anger, distaste, fascination, lust, wounded pride, anxiety—the list is long. Maintaining a therapeutic attitude can be difficult. Consider the consequences of two common countertransference reactions from a long list (Bernstein & Bernstein, 1980):

> Do I fear closeness so much that I err by being indifferent, rejecting, and cold?
>
> Do I need to feel important and, therefore, keep patients dependent on me, precluding their independence and assuming responsibility for their own welfare?

Desirable Characteristics

Intriguing data comes from the Development of Psychotherapists Questionnaire (Orlinsky & Ronnestad, 2002): 4,600 psychotherapists from across the world evaluated the character that they show in their friendships; the idea was that this self would be close to that person's core identity. More than 50 percent saw themselves being genial, assured, and engaged, whereas hardly any self-judged as dour or reclusive. Genial means having a pleasant or friendly disposition or manner, which is conducive to life or growth. Genial therapists tend to see their work as a healing involvement and not as stressful. Although therapists with a less welcoming personality can do good work, it seems self-evident that a genial personality fits well with psychotherapy practice and predisposes to doing it well.

What other characteristics are central to effective, ethical psychotherapy? First, the therapist needs to be interested in human stories and good at helping the patient tell them. Understanding another person means beginning with that person's experience, not imposing one's own assumptions. It means tuning into how the other person sees his or her world. Empathic understanding is part inquiry, part deduction, and part intuition.

> A young man came to each assessment session dressed in an immaculate white shirt. As I looked at him, his face appeared to change; it became battered. I said, "Your face is bruised." My intuition scared him; he had not wanted that aspect of him seen so soon. Inwardly, he felt emotionally bruised. Wearing a white shirt was a way of portraying a cleanness in being that he aspired to but did not feel. As a child, he had been sullied by parental abuse and forced to brutalize his siblings. Voicing the intuition precipitated us into exploring dark places, which left us both feeling dirty. Light into dark before emerging in a new light.

Being open to feeling what the patient feels is part of the process of intuition, albeit often an uncomfortable one. Through engaging and feeling, therapists have a partial experience of living the patient's problem; being able to do this requires a certain plasticity of self. Vital information about the clinical issues comes from being with and reflecting on the significance of the interaction and its pattern. Often, much to the therapist's discomfort, that interaction recreates maladaptive parts of the patient's problems.

A school official remarks, "I never know whom I am going to be." Formal and precise, this diligent man is capable both of generous support to his juniors and harsh criticism when he doubts their loyalty. His critical attacks are extreme in their ferocity with no capacity in the heat of the moment to give thought to the consequences. It is only afterward that he senses and regrets the legacy of hurt and understandable caution that his behavior engenders. With his superiors when their loyalty to him is in doubt, he tests them to destruction, taking offense over small slights and attacking them for excluding him when, in truth, he has excluded himself. He appreciates his complexity but "it's like taking two people into the room. Which one will come out?" The switch is dramatic. The trigger, a perceived slight, awakens deep resentment of unfairness and the failure of parental figures in childhood to live up to idealized expectations; friends or neutrals are transformed into hateful figures who must be destroyed. Given these dynamics, I was fully aware of the importance of being meticulous in maintaining therapy boundaries. How did it then happen that one session I forgot to unlock the access door to my consulting room? Realizing my error (so far in its meaning from my self-view as a conscientious, well-intended person), I ran into the street and found him exiting in a rejected rage. My enactment of his hated situation nearly ended the therapy but, fortunately, he was able to hear my apology and we were able to explore what had happened and why.

Therapists need to be able to recognize ruptures in the alliance and be able to repair them (Meares, 2001). Ruptures frequently result from the conjunction of relationship patterns in patient and therapist (Leahy, 2001; Safran & Muran, 2000); therapists have to face not being able to operate with their preferred selves (Aveline, 2005a). Being self-aware is essential in sorting out what aspect of interaction belongs to whom and alerting therapists to their own biases, the stories that they hear too well or do not want to hear at all.

People struggle to get by in their lives. Mostly, they do their best even though their solutions may be maladaptive. Our model therapist will be compassionate and kind in truth telling; being kind does not preclude being tough in confronting issues. Being trustworthy is essential; trust has to be earned through the way that the therapist handles conflict and challenge within the therapy. The therapist will be adaptable in serving the other, not wedded to a personal timetable and preferences. Worthwhile change rarely comes about without taking risks; the therapist will be skilled in encouraging achievable steps at propitious times. Because relationship problems are engrained, their modification requires sustained effort and stamina. Little is to be gained unless the therapist has a basic optimism about the human condition, wanting the best for the other and being sufficiently free of envy to allow it to happen. The therapist has privileged access to patients' lives when they are vulnerable. The therapist may be tempted to exploit or satisfy his or her own needs and has to be abstinent. Being sufficiently content in his or her own life is a great help to the therapist faced with temptation.

Readers may feel that the composite of these descriptors is a saccharine unreal person. Effective therapists do not come in uniform types. Some are attractively eccentric. A supervisee knew that he was unable to feel, neither his own feelings nor those of others, and behaved robotically. However, he was deeply committed to his patients' welfare; they tended to experience his strangeness as part of the magic of therapy and did well. Therapists need to be confident in their method and humble about the limits of their craft. Therapists vary in their aptitude to work well with different problems. Knowing what may be a good match and being able to refer to a better-placed colleague is just as much a part of professional expertise as is being ethical (Aveline, 2001a; Bond, Ashcroft, Casemore, Jamieson, & Lendrum, 2002). In short, the therapist provides tough love.

Research Implications

Although the interpersonal focus is a biasing factor, bringing the therapist once more into the foreground of research attention is surely worthwhile. What the therapist does as a person is more than fostering a good therapeutic alliance, important as that is a background facilitator; it is fundamental to the process as a whole. Of course, personal characteristics are not the only factor in effectiveness, contributing only 10–20 percent to the outcome variance, but what a vital portion (Beutler et al., 2004).

To complement my focus on the person of the therapist, researchers need to take seriously what patients value and reject in therapy. Combining this with evaluations of master therapists and, importantly, ineffective or damaging therapists, identified through the new technology of expected treatment response, could be fruitful. Negative effects are substantially the product of therapist personality; research could substantially improve selection and training. Unrecognized and unrepaired ruptures in the therapy relationship are decisive in many failures of ambitious long-term psychotherapy. Research could identify therapist-specific difficult situations and ways of dealing with patients who complete a "negative fit." Conversely, what are the optimal fits for particular therapists? Finally, much effort during training goes into personal therapy, but could this time be more focused than is customary? Research methods could be developed to identify personally characteristic obstructive countertransferences and provide objective evidence of amelioration through training.

If psychotherapy as we know it is but one systematization of age-old human capacity to be helpful to one another, we need to broaden our focus. Our concept of how people change is profoundly structured by the circularity of clinical work with case populations. What happens in that special situation is well documented but relatively little is known about what happens in everyday relationships and how issues get resolved naturally. Therefore, study natural social systems and compare change interactions with those already identified in therapy.

Final Word

By concentrating on the person of the therapist, elements in the change process that are often taken for granted and consigned to the background are brought forwards, reversing the usual primacy of technique and theoretical school. The described characteristics embody a set of values for living and facilitate a particular kind of ambitious psychotherapy. They model a passionate, committed, non-exploitative relationship, in which the therapist seeks the best for the other; the therapist acts in good faith, minimizing selfishness. The person of the therapist is not all-important in therapeutic action, but without the therapist's contribution there would be no therapy.

COMMENTARY

"THE PERSON OF THE THERAPIST" REVISITED

I revisit my address with an older sensibility and a dwindling involvement in academic work. The task of getting the resource to provide publicly funded specialist psychotherapy and training has passed to others. But the person I was continues. I feel just as passionate about justice, fairness, ethics, evidence-based practice and pluralism as ever (Aveline, 2011).

If it is not too conceited, I am pleasantly surprised by what I wrote in 2004. My grading: experience rich, somewhat research-lite, written from the heart. I take this opportunity to say more about language and raise new concerns.

I advocated an ambitious psychotherapy, interpersonally focused and prioritizing the walking wounded rather than the worried well (Aveline, 2005: 157). Building on findings of difference in outcome between therapists, I described personal qualities linked to effectiveness. Within an approach that one might call "tough love," I called for compassion and kindness in truth-telling, earned trustworthiness, adaptability in serving the other, skill in encouraging risk taking at propitious moments, stamina, optimism and abstinence in the face of temptation. I should have added respect for other people's solutions. These easily understood elements cut across artificial distinctions between therapies and diagnosis-focused interventions.

The Language of Therapy

In training psychiatrists, two complementary strands are present: external description of symptoms and signs to serve diagnosis and communication and internal understanding of meaning. Psychotherapists are mainly interested in the latter. *Dasein*, meaning the person's being-in-the-world (Binswanger, 1963), is not only, I believe, the right focus but has implications for how we learn to be therapists and depict our field. Let us look beyond science for some of our understanding and pay attention to the words used when we write and talk about our work.

Who could not be moved—and informed—by Chekov's insights into the human condition. *The Death of a Clerk* begins with the Clerk sneezing at the opera (Chekhov, 2001). The Clerk fears that he has sneezed on a senior official. Over a few short pages, Chekhov shows how anxiety for the imagined offence against General Brizzhalov becomes overwhelming and the protagonist's attempts to make amends become offensive to the General and, in turn, fatally self-damaging to the Clerk. Or the desperate tale of toxic interaction between an unwilling mother and her malign child and the tragic, unrelenting consequences for the family, marriage and community in *We Need to Talk About Kevin* (Shriver, 2005). Or in *Of Mice and Men*, how George tries to protect Lennie, his friend, a giant of a man but limited in intellect and knowledge of the adult world, from accidental disaster, fails and, through love, has to end Lennie's life to save him from the horrors of the lynch mob (Steinbeck, 1958). In these fictions, I am not asserting that life is necessarily tragic and predetermined, but am making the case for the way that literature can illuminate consequences when sustainable fragile lives spiral into disaster. Therapy offers hope that lives can be brought back from the brink and, sufficiently, redirected to more successful continuations.

Words are important. They shape the way we see things. From perception comes the meaning we take from experience. Used words express and delineate our understanding of the world. Some fail the test of verisimilitude. Top-executives' "compensation" rather than "pay," "passed away" instead of "died," and "discomfort" instead of "pain." These are mealy-mouthed words whose purpose is to divert attention from reality and justify injustices and platitudes. In our field, we need raw language to remind practitioners and researchers of what they are dealing with—pain, despair, loneliness, guilt, shame, hate, envy, courage, self-sacrifice, devotion and love. Of course, good science should be neutral about findings and outcome, but journal articles are often too neutral, obscuring the personal behind opaque jargon. This is not an argument for being simply swayed by emotion and the allure of moving, plausible stories but for combining the two in the way that we conceptualize and communicate.

A Faustian Pact

In England and Wales since 2005, there has been a very substantial increase in provision of short-term, state-funded CBT through the IAPT program (www.iapt.nhs.uk). Two forces drive the increase: a political imperative to facilitate return to work by relieving depression among the unemployed, and the research evidence. While increasing access to psychological therapies in the plural as the acronym states is self-evidently a good thing, the resultant monoculture is not (Cooper & McLeod, 2010). CBT is being favored over other approaches, often to the detriment of alternative, valued services. Favorable research evidence for CBT is being interpreted as evidence of ineffectiveness for less tested therapies.

NICE (National Institute for Health and Care Excellence) is the prime mover, prioritizing RCTs over other forms of evidence despite its chairman saying that the notion that evidence can be reliably or usefully placed in "hierarchies" is illusory (Rawlins, 2008).

One can hardly object to colleagues making a living through using hard-won skills and, doubtless, benefiting many patients, but there are two problems: a misreading of the evidence, and a development ending in tears if effectiveness in routine practice does not live up to service-justifying predictions based on controlled experimental studies. A similar concern is about tying clinical services to particular diagnoses. While a good case can be made for separate integrated provision for eating disorders and addiction, singling out one form of personality disorder—for example, borderline—because it has some treatment research evidence, does not. There is a Faustian pact whereby resources are only or plentifully available when diagnostic groups are treated as discrete entities rather than as persons manifesting particular concentrations of personality characteristics whose difficulties could be and were addressed in more generic psychotherapy. Resource and fame is always tempting. Psychotherapy risks fragmentation and underplaying the importance of common therapeutic and therapist factors, a high price for short-term gain. Will SPR hold to its non-denominational stance?

It is never going to be possible for all the psychotherapies to be tested in RCTs. Or for the weight of efficacy evidence to equal that accumulated by CBT through its special position in the clinical psychology practitioner-researcher model of training. Please note that I am not criticizing CBT but am mounting a case for equivalence. An outcome comparison of 5,613 therapies (CBT, person-centered and psychodynamic) from 32 NHS primary care services over a three-year period showed overall marked improvement on CORE-OM (Stiles, Barkham, Mellor-Clark, & Connell, 2008). Groups started with equivalent scores. No treatment yielded significantly better results. As a naturalistic study of routine practice, the limitations are several—poor treatment definition, unequal groups, no randomization, and failures to complete—but, as a pointer to a way ahead, it is very interesting.

If results are replicated, an alternative way of validating therapies opens up. The criterion would be: can an alternative therapy equal the effectiveness of the recommended RCT-validated therapy in routine practice? If it does, the result should be accepted as substantial evidence of effectiveness. In short, equivalence of outcome equals equivalence of effectiveness. Matching efficacy would be even stronger evidence. SPR is well placed to facilitate such testing. Members have access to diverse clinical populations, which, in combination through a central database, would form a significant dataset. For the shared element, researchers would use a common set of profiling and outcome measures, scoring and outcome analysis being done online. SPR could provide the paraphernalia needed to gather practice-based evidence, the foundation of evidence-based practice (Barkham, Hardy, & Mellor-Clark, 2010).

Generalization

Recently, Sue Wheeler, Michael Barkham, and I tried to improve research into clinical supervision (Wheeler, Aveline, & Barkham, 2011). By proposing a small toolkit of measures to be selected from in all studies (plus extras of choice), we hope to facilitate communication, comparability, and collaboration. Surveying supervision studies since 1980 identified 150 measures. Many were used once or with comparison-reducing modifications of the original; hard copy could be retrieved for only 67. This use pattern makes comparison between studies difficult and limits opportunities for aggregation. The golden goal of synergy of research effort is being lost.

The paucity of use points up a weakness of much research. Not enough of it revisits earlier work. When an area has few studies, these tend to be disproportionately influential. It is only by replicating the index work that partialities in selection, practice, and researcher bias may be revealed. Researchers, grant-giving bodies, and publishers can be drawn to the new instead of the less exciting but vital work of testing the role of chance or particularity in the original findings. Longer follow-ups would be good too.

Stories are our life-blood. They tell us—and others—who we are and who we would like to be. In psychotherapy and other storytelling processes, our stories may be reshaped. Qualitative research, thus, has an immediate appeal and may appear deceptively easy to do and overly persuasive to investigators (Aveline, 2005). Implementing good practice guidance is an essential step towards more robust appraisal of narratives and optimizes their generalization (Eliott, 2002; Elliott, Fischer, & Rennie, 1999); see guidance on how to read a research paper (Aveline, Strauss, & Stiles, 2005, pp. 561–462).

It would be good if quantitative and qualitative research gave priority to investigating the management of practice-critical problems, as these are so important in outcome and span the therapies. Examples are repairing alliance ruptures, risk to self and others, boundary violations, and containment of toxic mental states.

Large-Scale Concerns

In the scientific community, concern is growing about trial integrity. Fraud and biased results through withholding data and selective publication undermine confidence in trial validity (Moynihan, 2011). A review of 200 trials of cholesterol-lowering drugs showed that studies with positive findings were 20 times more likely to have been funded by the drug manufacturer. Not publishing antidepressant studies with unfavorable results created an overly positive impression of the published favorable ones (Turner, Matthews, Linardatos, Tell, & Rosenthal, 2008). These examples of bias are associated with commercial funding, but therapist and researcher allegiance is another confound.

It is a tribute to the rise in respect of science that evidence is now so influential in health-care decisions but evidence has to have integrity; anything less debases the currency of research. Many countries have legislated that trials be registered. From 1997, the US ClinicalTrials.gov information resource has registered clinical trials of experimental treatments for serious or life-threatening diseases or conditions (www.clinicaltrials.gov). Post-2007, summary results can be posted, including information on participant flow, baseline characteristics, outcome measures, statistics, and adverse events. The intention is to reduce duplication of research effort, publicize outcomes and make it harder for authors to report selectively when the demographics of the intake population is publicly known. In 2005, the International Committee of Medical Journal Editors declared that they would consider a trial for publication only if it has been registered before the enrollment of the first patient (www.icmje.org/update_may05.html). Integrity is a personal moral matter, where the practitioner has to balance complex responsibilities to patient and science (Miller, Rosenstein, & DeRenzo, 1998). The message is reinforced by the development in many countries of institutions to promote integrity and investigate suspected unscrupulous behaviour (Tavare, 2012).

What can be done in our area? Declaration of conflicts of interest and funding sources is standard practice in many journals. Researcher allegiance should be declared and consideration given to publishing allegiance-corrected results as well the usual analyses. Earlier, I suggested a role for SPR as tester of naturalistic equivalence, but more could be done if SPR was a repository for raw trial data, open to members who have opted in. With shared core measures, ethical protection, and stratification, aggregated data would extend the range of small studies and, more radically, be available for re-analysis. Re-analysis would be a form of SPR-sponsored quality control, not as the norm but as a useful option when the original statistics or design are controversial or when the consequences for public policy and funding are major.

Last Word

Research can help answer the perennial question of responsible practice: what in the therapy and this person's life helped, could the end have been achieved more expeditiously and was anything done that was detrimental (Aveline, 2007)? I look forward to SPR continuing its four decades of work in providing answers and raising new questions.

Note

1 What is significant action is revealed through understanding the patient's assumptive world (Frank, 1961, 1973). These acts may be very simple and appear to be insignificant to an uninformed onlooker, but both the patient and I know that they have dynamic significance. Once succeeded in, they indicate a yielding of these dynamics. Action may take place within the session or in the patient's ordinary life, e.g. a timorous person may assert their view or someone who is insecure in their attachments may, on taking leave of a friend, delay making plans to meet again (Aveline, 1988).

15

CONCEPTUALIZATION AND TREATMENT OF PERSONALITY DISORDERS (2006)

John F. Clarkin

The focus of this Presidential Address is on the often-neglected understanding and treatment of individuals with personality disorders. The advent of Diagnostic and Statistical Manual of Mental Disorders (DSM-III; American Psychiatric Association) in 1980, with its separate axis for personality disorders, was a boon to this area of inquiry but hardly the originator of such an enterprise. With the combination of phenomenology and longitudinal research, we can now discern the difference between acute, episodic symptoms and difficulties; and structural characteristics that form the backbone of the individual's trajectory across time. With the tools of modern affective neurocognitive science, we can begin to understand how the individual perceives incoming stimuli in the light of stored memories and expectations from interactions in the past. Furthermore, psychotherapy researchers can construct treatment structures that provide a safe interpersonal context in which the personality-disordered patient's perceptions and expectations from self and others can be re-evaluated. This Address draws on 30 years of experience in research on the phenomenology and treatment of patients with severe personality disorder, more commonly called borderline personality disorder (BPD). This effort has culminated in our recent attempts to involve neurocognitive scientists, psychoanalysts, attachment researchers, and psychotherapy researchers in a broad-based interdisciplinary project to understand and treat these individuals. The central points I wish to emphasize are: (a) an approach to personality pathology that identifies and measures certain key processes or functions that are characteristic of the individual across time, and (b) the attempt to modify these cognitive and affective functions in psychotherapy.

Personality

There are two central approaches to the question of how to conceptualize personality. Trait theorists have attempted to survey human traits or behavioural dispositions that are posited as relatively stable over time. A second approach championed by Mischel and Shoda (1999) is a dynamic processing approach that conceptualizes personality as a system of mediating units such as encodings, expectancies, motives, and goals at various levels of consciousness that enable the individual to interact with the environment. This cognitive-affective personality system (CAPS) posits that individuals differ in their proclivity to activate particular cognitive–affective mental representations in their interactions with the environment, especially in social interactions. It is the organization of the relationships among the cognitive-affective representations that form the essential aspect of the personality.

Compared with the trait approach to personality, the process approach has the advantages of capturing the individual in the dynamic moment and lends itself to neurocognitive investigation. From a clinical point of view, most clinicians in their everyday work do not systematically use trait instruments to plan psychotherapeutic intervention. The process approach can be used to guide the clinical assessment interview and focus the moment-to-moment interventions in psychotherapy.

Theories of Personality Disorder

The development of theories about personality disorder (Lenzenweger & Clarkin, 2005) is less advanced than theories of personality. However, even at this stage of development, one can discern constructs across theories that point to basic psychological and related biological processes, cognitive and emotional processes. There is an emerging consensus that the heart of personality pathology is composed of problems with self or identity and chronic interpersonal dysfunction (Livesley, 2001; Pincus, 2005). Clinicians from the cognitive, interpersonal, attachment, and psychodynamic object-relations points of view are emphasizing concepts, articulated somewhat differently, around these two key areas.

Developmental Perspectives

The human being develops from a condition of total dependency on a caregiver. Given the importance of the child's dependence on others, it is not surprising that the child's affect expression and regulation is related to the caregiving context (Kochanska, 2001). Mother-child attachment patterns as early as 14 months are related to the children's affect display in laboratory settings. As they develop, secure children became less angry, and insecure children demonstrate more negative affect. Through an integration of temperamental disposition and learning from modeling of the caregivers, capacities for attention regulation and effortful control are developed. Effortful control is a self-regulation dimension of temperament, described as the ability to inhibit a dominant response to perform a subdominant response (Posner & Rothbart, 2000). The individual with effortful control is able to voluntarily inhibit, activate, or change attention and thus potentially modify affective responses. In fact, the development of effortful control in infants and toddlers is central in the regulation of affect and social relations and in the development of conscience (Eisenberg, Smith, Sadovsky, & Spinrad, 2004).

Conceptions about oneself and others develop from an early age and depend on the emergence of language and the encoding of semantic and episodic memories. Disruptions in the relationship between the child and caregivers have a profound effect on children's developing conception of self and others (Harter, 1999). Whereas early sexual abuse occurs in the history of some borderline patients, there are additional factors of caregiver neglect, indifference, and empathic failures that have profound deleterious effects (Westen, 1993). Children reared in these disturbed environments form insecure attachments with their primary caregivers (Cicchetti, Beeghly, Carlson, & Toth, 1990). In this insecure relationship pattern, the development of capacities for effortful control and self-regulation and the internalization of conceptions of self and other are compromised by intense negative affect and defensive operations that distort the information system in order to avoid pain. There appears to be a natural sequence in the development of self-representations, one in which there is a progression from unrealistically positive evaluations in childhood to the presence of positive and negative evaluations with the ability to integrate opposing attributes in middle to late childhood.

A picture emerges of a developmental trajectory characterized by the gradual use of effortful control and other self-regulatory skills that emerge in the context of a nurturing and securely rhythmic and predictable relationship between child and caregiver. The interaction between the benevolent, empathic, attentive caregiver and the child leads to growing self-regulation, the predominance of positive over negative affect, the beginnings of conscience, and increasingly smooth and satisfying interactions with peers. This path of normal development can be disrupted by a vulnerable temperament or an environment marred by physical or emotional neglect and abuse. In this context, the child demonstrates negative affect, poor self-regulation, disruptions in conceptions of self and others, and disturbed relations with peers. There are no existing developmental studies of borderline patients as yet, but this emerging picture resembles the adult presentation of borderline personality organization with its identity diffusion, preponderance of negative affect, poor self-regulation, and compromised relations with others.

Empirical Heterogeneity of BPD Patients

One of the most vexing problems that impedes advance in the understanding and treatment of borderline patients is the heterogeneity of the group that meets the polythetic definition of BPD both in terms of the number and specific criteria that lead to the diagnosis. We have used various methods (e.g., factor analysis, conditional probabilities, cluster analysis, Q factoring) to attempt to understand possible meaningful relationships between the criteria that reveal subgroups of patients.

By factor analysis, we found three factors formed by the criteria: an affective factor, an identity factor, and an impulse factor (Clarkin, Hull, & Hurt, 1993). Because the diagnosis of BPD only requires five of the set of nine criteria, it means that a particular patient may suffer from one or two of these factors and not from the third. In examining the conditional probability of the co-occurrence of the BPD criteria, we found that the combination of identity disturbance with unstable/intense relations predicted the diagnosis of BPD with certainty (Clarkin, Widiger, Frances, Hurt, & Gilmore, 1983). This is reminiscent of the centrality of identity diffusion and disturbed interpersonal behavior at the core of personality disorders.

Most recently, we used Q factoring as a technique for generating prototypic Axis II profile patterns of comorbidity using all of the International Personality Disorder Examination (IPDE) dimensional ratings (Clarkin, Critchfield, & Levy, 2005). A three-factor solution was judged to be the most appropriate and accounted for 75 percent of the variance in cases. Assignment of cases to groups yielded three prototype profiles differentiable mainly because of the marked presence of paranoid, histrionic/narcissistic, and avoidant features, respectively. The different subgroups of BPD patients identified in this study may have prognostic value in psychotherapy. It remains clear that we must go beyond the criteria to understand the disorder.

In one step removed from the diagnostic criteria, there are two areas of functioning central to personality disorders: identity formation and self-control. Even at these levels, as we see later, the patients show heterogeneity that must inform theory and psychotherapeutic intervention.

Identity: Conception of Self and Others

The developing child evolves a working conceptualization of self and others, especially under the influence of affectively charged interactions with others that are comforting and pleasurable or aversive and dangerous (Bowlby, 1979; Kernberg & Caligor, 2005). It is from these early interactions that the developing individual builds up an internal model of self and others that lead to expectations in later interactions with others.

This process can go awry. Influenced by vulnerable temperamental disposition, environmental (traumatic) events, or a combination of both, a secondary level of intrapsychic organization may take place that determines the clinical syndrome of identity diffusion (Kernberg & Caligor, 2005). Identity diffusion is a relatively chronic condition characterized by a lack of integration of the concept of self and the related concept of significant others. These unintegrated conceptions of self and others are derived from an excessive dissociation (sometimes referred to as dichotomous thinking) between positive and negative affective investment of self and other representations, leading to the chronic deficiency in the assessment of others' motivations. The clinical characteristics of identity diffusion are chronic immaturity in judgments of emotional relationships, difficulties in the commitment to intimate relations, disturbances in sexual and love life, and problems with commitment to work or a profession.

Attachment Style

Some clinical researchers are conceptualizing fundamental aspects of BPD (e.g., unstable, intense interpersonal relationships, feelings of emptiness, bursts of rage, chronic fears of abandonment, and intolerance for aloneness) as stemming from impairments in the underlying attachment organization (Fonagy, Target, & Gergely, 2000; Gunderson, 1996). The research stimulated by John Bowlby has influenced both clinical thinking and research on normal individuals and, subsequently, on patient populations such as borderline patients. There is a growing empirical literature on the attachment status of borderline patients. Compared with dysthymic patients, borderline patients are significantly more likely to be fearfully preoccupied and unresolved for trauma even though both groups had experienced similar trauma histories (Patrick, Hobson, Castle, Howard, & Maugham, 1994). In a sample of women with a history of childhood sexual abuse, those with a borderline diagnosis had the attachment status of preoccupied or dismissive, and the majority were unresolved for trauma (Stalker & Davies, 1995). In a sample of hospitalized adolescents, the majority of BPD patients were preoccupied, with a significant subgroup (28 percent) dismissing (Rosenstein & Horowitz, 1996). In a large sample of nonpsychotic inpatients and matched controls, Fonagy et al. (1996) found that 75 percent of the borderlines were preoccupied and 47 percent were E3. In our own work with carefully diagnosed BPD patients (Levy, Meehan, Weber, Reynoso, & Clarkin, 2005) we have found 44 percent preoccupied, 32 percent dismissing, 8 percent secure, and 4 percent unclassifiable. In summary, BPD patients are likely to be either preoccupied or dismissing in attachment status and often unresolved for trauma. There is a growing but still small research literature on the impact of attachment state of mind and its influence on the capacity to make use of therapy, the quality of the therapeutic alliance and relationship, and treatment outcome (Diamond et al., 2003).

Self-Control Mechanisms

The interaction of temperament and environment is central to the development of self-control, emotional control, empathy, and social behavior (Posner & Rothbart, 2000). Temperament refers to individual differences in motor and emotional reactivity and self-regulation. Temperament is grounded in genetic endowment

(Rothbart, Ahadi, & Evans, 2000), but temperamental systems are influenced by the environment and follow a developmental course (Rothbart & Bates, 1998). Both empathy and the development of conscience are related to the development of effortful control mechanisms (Kochanska, 2001; Rothbart, Ahadi, & Hershey, 1994).

A central feature of borderline pathology is unstable and variable inhibitory control over emotion, cognition, and behavior (Siever & Davis, 1991; Zanarini, 1993). This deficit in self-regulation is manifested in impulsive behaviors, including impulsive self-destructive behaviors, and difficulties in modulating affective experience. An impulse action score is the best predictor of borderline psychopathology at follow-up (Links, Heslegrave, & van Reekum, 1999).

There is a link between impulsivity and underlying biological systems. Both impulsive aggression and affective instability show a stronger familial relationship than the diagnosis of BPD itself (Silverman et al., 1991). In twins, impulsivity and affective instability are heritable (Torgersen et al., 2000). Biological, neuroendocrine, and imaging studies provide evidence for the involvement of serotonergic activity in impulsive aggression (Coccaro et al., 1989; Gurvits, Koenigsberg, & Siever, 2000). In our own work, we have found that impulsivity and aggression are two separate factors, both of which are prominent in borderline patients (Critchfield, Levy, & Clarkin, 2004).

The evolution of self-regulation in the developing child is of central importance in understanding both the development of normal personality and personality pathology (Posner & Rothbart, 2000). Effortful control has a developmental course in which some children by age 3 are capable of efficiently making choices in conflict situations, especially those involving the suppression of dominant response modes. We examined the clusters of borderline patients formed by a consideration of varying degrees of effortful control (Hoermann, Clarkin, Hull, & Levy, 2005). Once the patients were empirically grouped by the effortful control construct, we examined hypothesized differences between the groups in terms of symptoms, interpersonal behavior, and self-conception or identity diffusion. In general, borderline patients with the highest effortful control scores were the least symptomatic and the least identity diffused compared with two other groups of patients with lesser effortful control.

Borderline patients have deficits in executive neurocognition (i.e., difficulty in the delay or termination of a cognitive or motor response in order to achieve a less immediate goal; Fertuck, Lenzenweger, Clarkin, Hoermann, & Stanley, 2006). Various laboratory tasks have been used to assess these control functions in borderline patients. For example, compared with controls, borderline patients showed deficits on tasks that required controlled information processing such as executive functioning (Lenzenweger, Clarkin, Fertuck, & Kernberg, 2004). Not only are borderlines and controls significantly different in impaired executive neurocognition, but the extent of BPD pathology is associated with greater impairment on these neurocognitive tasks (Fertuck, Lenzenweger, & Clarkin, 2005).

With regard to the processing of affective stimuli, we (Silbersweig et al., 2007) and others (Donegan et al., 2003) have used functional magnetic resonance imaging (fMRI) to examine borderline patients. We used a specifically designed fMRI activation probe, an emotional linguistic go/no-go task, to test hypotheses concerning decreased prefrontal inhibitory function in the processing of negative emotion in these patients. We found decreased ventromedial activation under conditions associated with the interaction of behavioral inhibition and negative emotion in BPD patients compared with normals. These findings are suggestive of plausible neural substrates associated with the core clinical features of emotional and behavioral dyscontrol in BPD. In the near future, these neural substrates will provide the focus for pre- and post-psychotherapy evaluation.

Treatment

Both psychodynamic and cognitive-behavioral therapies are effective treatments of personality disorders (Leichsenring & Leibing, 2003). Given the complexity and heterogeneity of patients who meet the diagnosis of BPD, however, one can see why there is currently no one treatment of choice for BPD individuals. Linehan (1993) has developed a complex package of cognitive-behavioral strategies and techniques for the subset of borderline patients who exhibit current self-destructive and suicidal behavior. This treatment is better than treatment as usual in reducing self-destructive and suicidal behavior (Linehan, Armstrong, Suarez, Allmon, & Heard, 1991). The overall results of studies on DBT are suggestive of the value of this cognitive-behavioral treatment, but results from the naturalistic follow-up of patients in DBT showed variable maintenance of treatment effects and ongoing impairment in functioning in patients who initially experienced symptom relief. More information is needed on the mechanisms and durability of change effected by DBT (Scheel, 2000; Westen, 2000) and other treatments for BPD.

Bateman and Fonagy (2004) have developed a psychodynamic day-hospital treatment for borderline patients. The effectiveness of this mentalization-based day-hospitalization program over 18 months has been compared with routine general psychiatric care for patients with BPD. Patients randomly assigned to the day-hospital program showed a statistically significant improvement in depressive symptoms and better social and interpersonal functioning, as well as a significant decrease in suicidal and self-mutilatory acts and number of inpatient days (Bateman & Fonagy, 1999).

Our own research group has developed an object relations approach to BPD (Clarkin, Yeomans, & Kernberg, 2006). In a randomized controlled trial comparing our treatment (transference-focused psychotherapy; TFP), a psychoanalytic supportive treatment, and DBT, all three treatments resulted in significant patient change in symptoms and global functioning, with few differences between the three treatments (Clarkin, Levy, Lenzenweger, & Kernberg, 2007). However, in all three treatments, properly delivered to different subsets of BPD patients, there are patients who do not respond to the treatment. The extent of the response varies, from symptom change to improvements in intimate relations and work. Clearly, further development is needed.

Limitations of Existing Treatment Studies

Treatment studies of BPD are growing in number, but the total number of patients investigated is small, power is low in many of these studies, and the outcome domains have been limited and focused almost entirely on symptoms. The mechanisms of change have rarely been examined, so that the evidence for the specific factors hypothesized in the treatment manuals is lacking. There has been very little systematic attention to therapist adherence and competence in the delivery of these lengthy treatments. Finally, as has been emphasized in this address, because the DSM-IV Axis II criteria for BPD select such a heterogeneous group of patients, it is difficult to compare the treatments at different sites with one another. The most parsimonious conclusion is that structured treatments are better than nonstructured treatments, but it is difficult to empirically disentangle the hypothesized mechanisms of change in these treatments from the structure provided (Roth & Fonagy, 2005).

Mechanisms of Change

With the emergence of some consensus about the need for treatment to address the characteristic conceptions of self and other in patients with personality disorder, the research question turns to the issue of examining the mechanisms of change; that is, how do the various treatments focus the therapeutic interaction on the patient's conception of self and other, and how do they measure the changes in this process? This is a somewhat new focus from simply measuring symptom and behavioral change and addresses the hypothesized ways in which the treatments operate. With a growing consensus on the need to change the personality disorder patients' conception of self and others, we can examine how cognitive, cognitive-behavioral, interpersonal, and psychodynamic treatments accomplish this task.

In our own work, we have used the construct of reflective functioning to approach the question of how TFP operates for change. Reflective functioning is the functional capacity to articulate a conceptualization of the mental processes that occur in both self and others such as feelings, beliefs, intentions, conflicts, and motivations. There is some empirical evidence that reflective capacity may serve as a mediating variable between current adjustment and the impact of an early abusive environment (Fonagy et al., 1996, 2000).

In our view, identity diffusion is the central pathology in borderline patients; thus, successful treatment would enhance the patient's ability to conceptualize self and others. TFP allows the full activation of the patient's distorted internal representations of self and other in the present and ongoing and unfolding relationship between therapist and patient. The patient's object relations are activated in the treatment setting, because they are active constantly in the patient's life and are the dominant motivational systems in the patient's life. The therapist attempts to clarify cognitively what the patient perceives at the most profound level. TFP creates a treatment frame, which makes it safe to reactivate those past pathogenic experiences. The safety and stability of the therapeutic environment permit the patient to begin to reflect about what is going on and what went on in the past, because his or her perceptions are based more on internal representations than on what is realistically going on in the present.

We have examined changes in reflective functioning (RF) from ratings on the Adult Attachment Interview in patients completing one year of outpatient treatment in three types of treatment: supportive, TFP, and DBT (Levy & Clarkin, 2006). In a comparison of data collected before treatment and after one year of treatment, we found that changes in RF were specific to TFP. Patients in TFP as a group significantly improved in level of RF, whereas those in the other two treatments did not improve. These data provide preliminary confirmation that TFP, which constantly seeks patient articulation of the relationship between patient and therapist, contributes to an improvement in identity formation (i.e., a richer and more nuanced capacity to reflect on self and other).

Conclusions

Psychotherapy research concerning the personality disorders is in its infancy. For psychotherapy research in this area to stay in the mainstream, it must be infused with information from the fields of personality, developmental psychology, and psychopathology and neurocognitive science. The DSM diagnostic system is insufficient to guide the treatment of personality disorders, because personality dysfunction is not synonymous with the lists of criteria. Treatments must be differentiated and multifaceted, respecting subgroups of patients with severe personality disorders. Advances in neurobiology, laboratory tasks, and interview techniques will assist in the measurement of personality organization and identification of subgroups of patients for more refined treatments. A focus on the human functions that need modification and change will bring attention to the mechanisms of change in psychotherapy, which, in turn, will inform the essential features of psychotherapeutic intervention. To be truly humane, treatments must go beyond symptom relief, introducing the patient to fruitful relations and productive work. The era of schools of psychotherapy will be superseded by focus on the ways in which treatments provide not only alleviation of symptoms but also the resumption of individual development.

COMMENTARY

CONCEPTUALIZATION AND TREATMENT OF PERSONALITY DISORDERS: 2005 TO THE PRESENT

My 2005 SPR Presidential Address was focused on various aspects of personality disorder (especially, borderline personality disorder) theory and research at that time. This update explores subsequent developments in our understanding of personality disorders and treatment with special emphasis on borderline personality disorder (BPD).

Personality and Personality Disorders

The theoretical description of the personality disorders remains relatively isolated from the understanding of personality in academic psychology. This disjunction in traditions has left the field of personality disorders with partial theories of the personality pathology that need advancement and amplification, both on the theoretical and empirical levels (Lenzenweger & Clarkin, 2005).

One marker of the developing understanding of the personality disorders is the evolution of the DSM approach to the personality disorders. The re-evaluation of the DSM-IV diagnostic system in preparation for the DSM-5 has emphasized the limitations of a categorical system and an appreciation of the underlying biological systems that form important domains of pathology that are best captured in dimensions (Hyman, 2011). One aspect of academic psychology that was proposed for the description of the personality disorders in DSM-5 was the utilization of trait theory. Proponents of trait theory emphasize the continuity between normal personality and personality disorder, and the dimensional nature of traits (Clark, 2007). In contrast to a trait approach to the personality disorders, others focus on the clinical usefulness of functioning (Westen, 2006), the organizational structure of the personality which a list of traits does not capture (Kernberg & Caligor, 2005), the clinical utility of identifiable prototypic personality disorder types (Shedler & Westen, 2010), and the research these types have accumulated, such as that on BPD.

Heterogeneity of BPD Patients

A major difficulty in furthering the understanding and treatment of patients with borderline personality disorder is the heterogeneity of those selected by the diagnostic criteria (Lenzenweger, 2010). This heterogeneity at the phenotypic level impedes a search for the genetic background of the pathology and confounds the empirical investigation of treatment of borderline patients. All existing randomized clinical trials at this point do not identify subgroups of borderline patients in their examination of treatment effects, nor do they select for a specific type of borderline patient.

One approach to understanding the heterogeneity of BPD patients has been to utilize factor analysis of the DSM criteria. We (Clarkin, Hull, & Hurt, 1993) and others (e.g., Sanislow, Grilo, & McGlashan, 2000) have utilized this approach, and the current understanding is that there are two to four dimensions in the disorder, including identity diffusion, preponderance of negative affect, and problems in self-regulation, including emotion dysregulation.

Since the factor analysis of the BPD criteria is not the most effective way to identifying clinically relevant subgroups of individuals (in contrast to dimensions across individuals) with BPD, we have utilized finite mixture modeling to approach this problem. Three subgroups of BPD patients were identified (Lenzenweger, Clarkin, Yeomans, Kernberg, & Levy, 2008) characterized by different combinations of paranoid and suspicious orientation to others, aggressive attitudes and behavior, and antisocial behaviors and traits. These results suggest that treatment foci and related techniques must adapt to the three different constellations to be optimally effective.

Stimulated by the problems with categorical diagnoses, a recent initiative of the NIMH to abandon the DSM diagnostic system to guide research has been proposed (Sanislow et al., 2010). This research domain criteria (RDoC) approach will focus research on neurobiological systems (i.e., positive affect, negative affect, cognition, regulatory processes, social processes) that extend across the various categorical diagnoses. This research orientation will capitalize on attention to the moment-to-moment functioning of patients at various levels of the organism (e.g., neurotransmitters, neurocognitive functioning, psychological functioning).

Real-Time Functioning in BPD Patients

The most salient development since my presidential address which is consistent with the RDoC initiative has been the growing recognition of emotional and cognitive systems of functioning of the borderline patient in real time (see Clarkin & De Panfilis, 2013 for details). The use of real-time sampling of patient behavior has allowed us to see the borderline patient in action, especially in the daily control/dyscontrol of affect in social interactions. In addition, the emergence of social neurocognitive science, with its emphasis on behavioral tasks with concomitant readings at various brain systems, has focused our attention on the psychological functions that the human being must execute in the immediate present to function on cognitive and interpersonal tasks. Social neurocognitive science enables the field to progress beyond a trait description of the personality disorders, and enter into the realm of how these troubled individuals function psychologically and neurobiologically in social interactions.

The intense negative states that borderline patients experience are often stimulated by perceived interpersonal events (Jovev & Jackson, 2006), especially rejection (Herpertz, 1995; Stiglmayr, Shapiro, et al., 2001). In an event-contingent recording procedure study (Russell et al., 2007), borderline patients experienced more unpleasant affect, were less dominant and more submissive, and more quarrelsome in their interpersonal behavior than were controls. They also showed greater variability in the use of these behaviors. These finding are consistent with the clinical hypothesis that borderline patients lack a stable and positive sense of self to guide them efficiently and adaptively through various interpersonal situations (Kernberg & Caligor, 2005).

Beliefs about the social world, such that one is powerless and vulnerable in the face of a malevolent social environment, may bias appraisal of the environment. A clear example of such bias is rejection sensitivity. Individuals prone to rejection sensitivity, including those with BPD, are hyper-alert to any stimuli suggesting rejection, and tend to react with emotional dysregulation and anger outbursts (Berenson, Downey, Rafaeli, Coifman, & Paquin, 2011). However, those rejection sensitive individuals with effortful control can modulate their response to perceived rejection, and emit interpersonal behavior that is more socially appropriate and therefore more interpersonally adaptive.

The functional domain of self-regulation including affect regulation is most illustrative and central to understanding BPD. Self-regulation dysfunction is reflected in the cognitive functioning of BPD patients on tasks that require considerable executive processing resources reflective of control for successful performance (Lenzenweger, Clarkin, Fertuck, & Kernberg, 2004; Fertuck, Lenzenweger, Clarkin, Hoermann, & Stanley, 2006; Posner et al., 2002, 2003).

Functional imaging studies of borderline patients suggest some specific areas of difficulty these patients experience in the processing of emotional stimuli. Borderline patients rely on reflexive, automatically responding networks, whereas healthy controls use networks with access to higher level conscious cortical processing (Koenigsberg et al., 2009). It is especially negative stimuli that borderline patients have difficulty processing efficiently and effectively (Silbersweig et al., 2007). Furthermore, borderline patients are deficient in the ability to reduce negative affect by reappraisal (Koenigsberg et al., 2009). This finding is quite important to borderline pathology and potential treatment implications, as in normal individuals affect regulation by reappraisal in contrast to suppression is associated with greater positive emotion and reduced negative emotion and better interpersonal functioning (Gross & John, 2003).

Treatment Development for BPD Patients

There have been major advances in the empirical investigation of treatment for borderline patients. Our group at Weill Cornell Medical College has been guided by sequential steps in treatment development as articulated by Kazdin (2004). Our treatment manual (Clarkin, Yeomans, & Kernberg, 2006) is a principle-driven description of how to structure the treatment in a way to enable the patient to relive and reappraise symbolic representations of self and others, and gradually improve affect dysregulation. In a treatment development study funded by NIMH

(PI: John Clarkin), we generated initial effect sizes that suggested further empirical investigation of what became known as transference-focused psychotherapy (TFP). In a subsequent randomized clinical trial, we compared TFP to DBT and a structured supportive treatment. All three treatments resulted in significant symptom reduction, with some superiority of TFP in several areas (Clarkin et al., 2007). Only TFP made significant changes in the patients' ability to think of self and others in reflective ways (Levy et al., 2006).

The measurement of neurocognitive functioning offers a new level of development in the assessment of treatment effects for psychiatric patients including borderline patients. Our group has recently completed a demonstration study using fMRI technology to measure borderline patient change in one year of TFP. We prepared for this treatment study by investigating an emotional go/no-go task in a cross-sectional study that revealed differences between borderline patients and normal controls in efficient regulation of negative affect (Silbersweig et al., 2007). The results of this study are consistent with others indicating that borderline patients are inefficient in the modulation of negative affect, and this functional impairment is manifested by amygdala overresponse and underregulation in the prefrontal cortex. This knowledge sets the stage for psychotherapy intervention with borderline patients who are affectively labile with the use of psychological and fMRI measures of affect regulation as outcome markers.

There are now a number of empirically supported treatments for BPD (Bateman & Fonagy, 2008; Clarkin, Levy, Lenzenweger, & Kernberg, 2007; Linehan, 1993). These treatments come from a variety of theoretical approaches, and yet each includes a number of common elements. Any enthusiasm over the multiplicity of available treatments for those with BPD must be tempered by the fact that in every empirical investigation of borderline treatment, there is a substantial minority of patients who do not respond to treatment, and improvements in symptoms far outweighs improvement in social functioning. Most important to the future development of the field is the need for a more refined research attempt to identify the mechanisms of change, that is, what are the ways in which each of these treatments accomplishes the outcome, i.e., reduction in symptoms.

16

WHAT WE HAVE LEARNED FROM A DECADE OF RESEARCH AIMED AT IMPROVING PSYCHOTHERAPY OUTCOME IN ROUTINE CARE (2007)

Michael J. Lambert

The effects of psychotherapy have been found to be generally positive across a variety of studies and over a substantial period of time dating back to the 1930s (Lambert & Ogles, 2004). In randomized clinical trials (RCTs), in which treatments are offered by carefully selected and closely supervised therapists to carefully screened patients with a specific disorder, about 35–40 percent of patients experience no benefit and a small group of patients, perhaps between 5 and 10 percent, deteriorate (Hansen, Lambert, & Forman, 2002). In our program of research, we have endeavored to improve psychotherapy outcome in routine care through monitoring patient progress and providing this information to clinicians in order to guide ongoing treatment, especially for the patient who is not having a favorable response to treatment (not-on-track [NOT] cases). This research is an extension of quality-assurance action research and represents one effort to bridge the gap between research and practice while enhancing patient outcome before treatment termination. It is also well suited to models of care in which clinicians attempt to step up or step down the intensity of treatments after assessing a patient's treatment response (Otto, Pollack, & Maki, 2000). I have documented here our progress in enhancing patient outcome by describing how we have operationally defined outcome, treatment success and failure, and our experience with monitoring treatment response and feeding back this information to therapists and patients before treatment termination.

Defining Outcome

Our program of research began with the development of a suitable but brief (five-minute) outcome measure, the Outcome Questionnaire-45 (OQ-45; Lambert, Morton, et al., 2004), which provides both a measure of weekly change as well as the criterion measure for classification of a patient into outcome categories (recovered, improved, no change, and deteriorated) after treatment. It was designed to assess four domains of functioning: symptoms of psychological disturbance (mainly depression and anxiety); interpersonal problems; social role functioning (e.g., problems at work or school); and quality of life (positive aspects of life satisfaction). Factor analysis of the OQ-45 has confirmed the presence of symptom (depression, anxiety, and somatic), interpersonal, and social role subscales but also that a general mental health factor is described by the total score (de Jong et al., 2007; Mueller, Lambert, & Burlingame, 1998). Even though the diverse elements of outcome measured by the scale have been validated, we have focused our outcome studies on the total score because of the small number of items that have been used to measure some factors. Two large-scale studies have shown that the OQ-45 items, subscales, and total score are sensitive to change in patients over short time periods (nine weeks) but remain stable in untreated individuals (Vermeersch, Lambert, & Burlingame, 2002; Vermeersch, Whipple, Lambert, Hawkins, Burchfield, & Okiishi, 2004). We consider these sensitivity studies as good examples of one of our unique contributions to methodological advancements in scale development. Through the collection of weekly measurement of patient progress, we were able to assess the speed of change on each item of the OQ-45 and its value as a scale for change measurement (in contrast to usual procedures that emphasize diagnostic value or usefulness in treatment planning). Based on these studies, the OQ-45 appears to be well suited for tracking patient treatment response and can be used on a weekly basis with limited test-retest artifacts (Durham et al., 2002).

A series of studies have provided information about the psychometric properties of the OQ-45 (Lambert et al., 2004). Using formulas developed by Jacobson and Truax (1991), clinical and normative data for the OQ-45 were analyzed by Lambert et al. (1996) to provide cutoff scores for the reliable change index (14 points) and clinically significant (CS) change (dysfunctional/functional cut-off: 64/63). This latter cut-off score requires that the patient score within 1 SD of the mean of normal functioning ($M = 45$). Individuals are defined as recovered when they leave therapy with an OQ-45 score that has improved by at least 14 points and is below 64. Patients who improve by 14 points are considered improved and those who worsen by at least 14 points are regarded as deteriorated if they leave treatment in the dysfunctional range. These cut-off scores provide a means for individualizing change at the end of treatment and follow-up and can also be used to raise questions about the necessity of further treatment. They have the advantage of providing absolute standards for classification that apply across all studies we conduct rather than having standards of improvement and deterioration that are sample-specific and vary from study to study.

Support for the validity of the OQ-45's reliable change and clinical significance cut-off scores have been reported by Lunnen and Ogles (1998), Beckstead et al. (2003), and Bauer, Lambert, and Nielsen (2004). This research suggests that the

Jacobson-Truax formulas provide a sound basis for estimating cut-off scores and that classification of change based on other measures results in considerable consensus with OQ-45 classifications. Despite this encouraging evidence, much additional work is necessary to understand the relationship between these cut-off scores and their practical meaning for overall patient health and well-being.

In the course of collecting weekly outcome ratings from patients undergoing treatment in routine clinical practice, a number of findings have emerged that have clear implications for social policy and theoretical concerns. Before highlighting the research aimed at improving outcomes for specific clients, I address several important findings.

Treatment Length

The amount of psychotherapy necessary to bring about positive outcomes has been a concern for decades and remains a topic of serious debate (Lambert, Bergin, & Garfield, 2004). Early concerns about excessively long, mainly psychodynamic therapy resulted in rejections of this form of care in the community mental health movement that emerged in the 1950s and 1960s because long treatment lengths were associated with unacceptably long waiting lists. Traditional long-term psychodynamic treatments were shortened, with numerous planned short-term therapies (25 or fewer sessions) being developed and advocated in the 1960s. More recent concern about treatment length has been associated with the management of skyrocketing medical costs and based on the assumption that positive outcomes can be achieved with few sessions. The usual method of cutting costs in the United States has been to limit treatment to four to eight sessions, providing standard limits for all patients.

It should be noted that many organizations claim to be delivering evidence-based services while ignoring the fact that the clinical trial treatments that they are attempting to duplicate were based on 12 to 14 sessions, not four to eight sessions. Even a casual observer of the worldwide diversity of policy and practices concerning treatment length might be quite puzzled at the absence of the use of empirical data to shape important policy decisions concerning treatment length. In our mind, treatment length is most appropriately driven by patient treatment response rather than theoretical or cost-based decisions. How much therapy is enough?

Howard, Kopta, Krause, and Orlinsky (1986) made an early attempt to address the question "How many sessions are required to produce meaningful change?" and suggested that 50 percent of patients derive such a benefit by the ninth session and that the dose-effect relationship in psychotherapy could best be characterized as negatively accelerating, a finding that is usually interpreted as indicating that each successive session of therapy has less impact on a patient's well-being. Following the lead of these researchers, we addressed the issue of dosage in an attempt to shed further light on the relationship between number of sessions received and patient benefit, with the advantage that we used a standard definition of good outcome and session-by-session data rather than statistical modeling based on pre-post data.

Survival Analysis

Using data (N > 6,000 patients) from a variety of U.S. clinical samples that received routine clinical care (ranging from employee assistance programs to community mental health centers), we have published five studies that estimated the dose-effect relationship (Anderson & Lambert, 2001; Hansen & Lambert, 2003; Kadera, Lambert, & Andrews, 1996; Snell, Mallinckrodt, Hill, & Lambert, 2001; Wolgast, Lambert, & Puschner, 2003). In each of these studies, patients rated their functioning at each session of treatment on the OQ-45. Our standard definitions of reliable and CS change were used as dependent variables (the binomial event of interest), and the Kaplan-Meier survival analysis statistic (or related technique) was used to provide a population estimate of the distribution model of sessions needed to reach the event of interest (normal functioning and reliable improvement). Across these studies, the session at which 50 percent and 75 percent of patients reached criteria for recovery ranged from Sessions 11 to 21 and Sessions 25 to 45, respectively.

These data provide an important source of information for policy decisions aimed at limiting the amount of psychotherapy a patient may receive. These data also allow government agencies, insurance companies, employers, clinics, and consumers to understand the consequences of such policies. The findings suggest that limiting treatment to four sessions, a common practice, will result in insufficient treatment for the vast majority of patients. Even policy decisions that permit more than twice this amount of treatment cannot be justified on the basis of empirical findings. For example, data from the directors of counseling centers at 73 U.S. colleges and universities show that more than half of such centers have a self-imposed session limit of 10 sessions (Stone & McMichael, 1996). Our findings suggest that limiting psychotherapy to this amount is likely to be appropriate for fewer than half of the clients who seek treatment, even when the least rigorous criterion, reliable change, is used to define a positive treatment response. It is also clear that such a policy is particularly disadvantageous to the most disturbed clients, whose time to recovery is slower and who are most at risk for personal failures, self-harm, and hospitalization. The most important determinant of treatment outcome is initial patient functioning; variables such as severity, complexity of disorder, somatization, dual diagnosis, personality pathology, and the like are very important (Clarkin & Levy, 2004; Lambert & Anderson, 1996).

It is also worth noting that the estimated time to recovery for patients in routine care produces recovery estimates that are similar to actual CS outcomes of patients treated in RCTs (50 percent in 14 sessions; Hansen & Lambert, 2003).

Actual CS outcome (rather than modeled outcome) of patients in routine care is closer to 30 percent, with an average dosage of about four sessions. These data suggest the need for providers and service managers to give high priority to keeping patients in treatment longer rather than setting session limits. In college counseling centers, about 90 percent of patients have terminated treatment by Session 15 (Nielsen & Lambert, 2006; Wolgast et al., 2003); the remaining 10 percent of clients use 30 percent to 40 percent of the total sessions delivered. Survival curves also show the same tendency to flatten as the number of sessions increases, with few patients meeting criteria for reliable change and CS change at subsequent sessions after Session 25, which is equivalent to six months of weekly treatment. We interpret such data as indicating that if a general session limit is set, it would be more reasonable to think in terms of 20 to 25 sessions for most patients, depending on initial severity and treatment setting.

Although setting general session limits has great advantages for managing costs and making the life of administrators easier, it is not to the advantage of most patients and diminishes the overall value of services, especially for the most disturbed patients. Our data suggest that the highest quality of care will be provided by monitoring each client's treatment response and making treatment length a function of treatment response and mental health status rather than arbitrary or theory-driven limits. Limiting treatment in such a circumstance requires frequent assessment of patient well-being and would be instigated only when it becomes clear that no further progress can be expected if a patient continues to receive the same treatment.

Managing Treatment by Measuring Treatment Response and Outcome

An alternative to setting general session limits is to make the length of treatment responsive to each individual patient. A primary focus of our research has been to understand and apply information about usual treatment response in routine care through the use of longitudinal data analysis.

Expected Treatment Response

Survival statistics are ideal for providing estimates of an event of interest (e.g., recovery) that can be used to guide policy decisions. Different statistical procedures are necessary to model the shape and speed of change over time for the purpose of understanding expected treatment response for the individual patient. For this purpose, we have used hierarchical linear modeling (HLM) of session-by-session ratings of functioning produced by patients. HLM is especially useful in analyzing longitudinal data from routine care, a situation in which patients begin treatment at diverse levels of initial disturbance and have treatment lengths that are highly varied. The results of such modeling can be examined for subsets of patients who meet criteria for an event such as clinically significant or reliable change (or deterioration) but are most valuable as a means of establishing session-by-session expectations for a course of psychotherapy in relation to unique levels of initial disturbance.

Finch, Lambert, and Schaalje (2001) applied HLM to a large database consisting of 11,492 patients treated in a variety of settings, including employee assistance programs, university counseling centers, outpatient clinics, private practice, and a clinical psychology training clinic. An initial graphic analysis of the data revealed decelerating growth curves similar to those identified in dose-response studies, a lawful linear relationship between the log of the number of sessions and the normalized probability of patient improvement, again illuminating the tendency for larger and larger doses (number of sessions) in order to find a higher percentage of recovered patients.

Tolerance intervals calculated in this model allowed for the identification of the 10 percent and 15 percent of patients in a given sample whose rate and trajectory of progress, respectively, deviated significantly from what might be the predicted course of recovery for others entering therapy with a similar intake score. The tolerance intervals created were primarily aimed at identifying this 10 percent of the patient population who deviate from the recovery track and formed the core of an empirical warning system by providing table values and charts of predicted therapeutic gains against which the data of any given patient can be compared. If at any session after intake the OQ-45 total score for a patient does not exceed the tolerance interval, then therapy is judged as proceeding as anticipated for this particular patient, and a green light message can be given as feedback for therapists to proceed as they have been. If the same OQ-45 score falls outside of the upper 15 percent and does not surpass the upper bound of the 10 percent tolerance interval, the patient is considered to be deviating by more than 1 SD from what is expected of a typical person at this point in therapy, and the therapist would receive a yellow message as a warning to attend to this patient's progress. This 1 SD unit approximates a 14-point increase in the OQ score (the marker for reliable change) but varies depending on the patient's initial level of disturbance. If this same OQ-45 score falls above the upper limits of the 10 percent interval, then the patient is deviating significantly in a negative direction from what is predicted at this point in therapy. The 10 percent boundary is consistent with the estimate that about 10 percent of patients deteriorate after psychotherapy (Lambert & Ogles, 2004). At this point, the therapist would receive a red warning message that therapy may be heading toward an unsuccessful conclusion and that the therapist needs to consider an alternative course of action. In our program of research, we consider patients whose treatment response crosses either the yellow or red boundary to be alarm-signal or NOT cases.

An opposite pattern can be described for scores falling on the lower side of the low tolerance bands, indicating that the individual is deviating significantly in a positive direction from what is normally expected at this point in therapy, and the therapist would receive a blue message indicating confidence that the patient will leave treatment with a positive outcome and maintain gains for at least one year (Haas, Hill, Lambert, & Morrell, 2002).

Early, Dramatic Treatment Response

Before turning to the effects of providing therapists with alarm signals for patients who are deviating from expected recovery, presentation of findings concerning extraordinary positive courses of treatment is in order. Few studies have investigated the timing of response in psychotherapy. Among those studies that have addressed this issue, the apparent finding is that early dramatic (as opposed to delayed or worsening) response to psychotherapy is positively related to better intermediate and long-term outcomes.

Haas et al. (2002) used a unique method of quantifying early dramatic treatment response by using session-by-session ratings of client symptomatology in relation to expected recovery curves, as just described (blue signals). This strategy allowed for the creation of a standardized method for determining the timing of treatment response and its size in relation to a typical response, thereby providing a data-based standard rather than a sample-relative standard of early response. Data analytic techniques allowed for examination of early dramatic response as both a continuous and a discrete variable aimed at evaluating the clinical significance of change.

Clients with faster rates of response to psychotherapy reported lower end-of-treatment OQ-45 scores. In the second hierarchical regression, which used the same format but utilized OQ-45 scores at follow-up as the dependent variable, an effect for early response and follow-up scores was also found. Clients with faster rates of response reported lower OQ-45 scores at follow-up an average of one year post-therapy. An examination of response rate and the clinical outcome categories showed that early responders were more likely to benefit to a clinically significant degree at both termination and follow-up.

At present, the active mechanisms linking early dramatic response to long-term outcomes are unknown. They might include a "flight into health" or other unrealistic reflections of resistance, medications beginning to work, significant reductions in psychosocial stressors, or simply a very rapid response to psychotherapeutic interventions coming from insight or important realizations. Whatever the active ingredients are, they appear to work quickly in many cases. The timing of improvements during psychotherapy has theoretical implications beyond placebo explanations for change. If response to therapy precedes introduction of theoretically important techniques, then it is difficult to attribute central importance to these techniques in the healing process. Early dramatic responders to psychotherapy may be more resilient, better prepared, more motivated, and thus more receptive to therapeutic influences of any kind. Early responders may be more likely to proceed from one problem to the next in therapy (a sequential pattern), whereas delayed responders continue to revisit the same therapy topic across sessions (Fennel & Teasdale, 1987). Early response may also indicate a better fit between client and therapist and reflect the positive effects of the working alliance, which often can be detected by Session 3 of treatment (Krupnick et al., 1996).

Whatever the mechanism of change, the emerging findings suggest that early dramatic treatment response is relatively common (perhaps 25 percent of patients) and foretells recovery and maintenance of gains. It suggests that these patients, were their progress monitored, could be discharged from treatment after just a few treatment sessions. We could then focus on maximizing the outcome of patients whose early positive response cannot be detected and, even more important, those patients who outright worsen during treatment.

Accuracy of Predicting Treatment Failure

If treatment failure is to be minimized, it is necessary to predict poor outcomes before they occur. We have conducted six studies aimed at examining the accuracy of our predictive methods (Ellsworth, Lambert, & Johnson, 2006; Hannan et al., 2005; Lambert, Whipple, Bishop, et al., 2002; Lutz et al., 2006; Percevic, Lambert, & Kordy, 2006; Spielmans, Masters, & Lambert, 2006). These studies vary with regard to patient populations, methods, and findings. The general finding is that deterioration can be predicted before it occurs through the use of information about patients' initial level of disturbance and their treatment response after one or more sessions of psychotherapy (empirical algorithms). Once these variables are taken into account, little improvement in predictive accuracy is achieved by adding such variables as diagnosis (i.e., what matters most is how disturbed a patient is, not which disorder they have or if they have comorbid conditions, because both these variables correlate with degree of disturbance), sex, age, ethnicity, type of treatment, and experience of therapist.

The hit rate (overall correct classification rate) for OQ-45 feedback appears to be about .80. The sensitivity of the predictive system is defined as the proportion of people who ultimately deteriorate in treatment who were predicted to deteriorate by the feedback system. Sensitivity in our studies typically is about .88. In this context, the algorithms we have developed show that if a patient never receives red or yellow signals, it is almost certain that he or she will not deteriorate.

The accuracy of empirical systems for predicting whether a patient will deteriorate has been contrasted with the accuracy of therapist judgment. Hannan et al. (2005) examined therapist accuracy by asking 40 therapists (20 trainees and 20 experienced professionals), at the end of each session, whether they believed a patient would leave treatment in a deteriorated state and whether a patient was worse off at this particular session compared with functioning at therapy entry. Therapists were aware of the purpose of the study, the dependent measure

(OQ-45), and cut-offs for judging deterioration and that the base rate for deterioration was likely to be 8 percent. During the three-week period, predictions were made for 550 clients and compared with our empirical prediction method. Only three of 550 clients were predicted to deteriorate, one of whom actually deteriorated. The therapists did not identify 39 additional clients who deteriorated during treatment. Despite being armed with base-rate information and having familiarity with the outcome measure used in the study, therapists showed an inability to accurately forecast negative outcome. Their predictions of deterioration would have improved markedly if they had simply used their judgment that a patient was worse off at any particular session. Although correctly identifying 16 clients who had worsened during treatment, they did not interpret this information as a predictor of final patient outcome. In contrast, the statistically based alarm system, applied to patient scores during the same three-week time period, identified 77 percent of the deteriorators but generated numerous false-positive results.

Methods of Preventing Treatment Failure

We have applied the foregoing statistically based alarm system as an intervention for preventing deterioration and enhancing positive outcomes in patients. In addition, we have created, and provided therapists with, problem-solving guidelines (clinical support tools [CSTs]; Lambert, Whipple, Harmon, et al., 2004) for helping such patients and provided direct feedback about progress to patients themselves. In our current research, we have incorporated administration of the OQ-45 (by means of hand-held computers), scoring, and application of algorithms into software called OQ-Analyst. A screen shot of the software output is presented in Figure 16.1, which illustrates the progress of a fictional patient, Brad News. The OQ-45 is typically administered before each session, making the Session 1 score a reflection of the patient's status before Session 1 and the Session 8 score reflecting his status before Session 8. Brad was predicted to have a negative treatment outcome after undergoing a single session of treatment (at Session 2). He again passed the cut-off score for a red warning after seven sessions of treatment. Messages consistent with his progress at any session of interest are provided by OQ-Analyst. At Session 8, another red alarm was sent. The therapist could look below the graph and read the message that is provided. Messages vary depending on the size of the deviation from expected treatment response (the dark sloping line) and amount of therapy. Patient scores are displayed in the graph in relation to the horizontal line at a score of 63, which demarcates normal functioning. As can be seen, the feedback report provides information about Brad's answer to five critical items, as they were answered just before Session 8.

Five controlled studies have been published that examine the effects of providing progress feedback to patients (Harmon et al., 2007; Hawkins, Lambert, Vermeersch, Slade, & Tuttle, 2004; Lambert et al., 2001; Lambert, Whipple,

Name:	news, brad	**ID:**	
Session Date:	10/25/2005	**Session:**	8
Clinician:	FP	**Clinic:**	Clinic A
Diagnosis:	Unknown Diagnosis		
Algorithm:	Empirical		

Alert Status:	**Red**
Most Recent Score:	106
Initial Score:	85
Change from Initial:	Reliably Worse
Current Distress Level:	High

Most Recent Critical Item Status:

8. **Suicide -** I have thoughts of ending my life.	**Frequently**
11. **Substance Abuse -** After heavy drinking, I need a drink the next morning to get going.	**Frequently**
26. **Substance Abuse -** I feel annoyed by people who criticize my drinking.	**Frequently**
32. **Substance Abuse -** I have trouble at work/school because of drinking or drug use.	**Sometimes**
44. **Work Violence -** I feel angry enough at work/school to do something I might regret.	**Sometimes**

Subscales	**Current**	**Outpat. Norm**	**Comm. Norm**
Symptom Distress:	61	49	25
Interpersonal Relations:	26	20	10
Social Role:	19	14	10
OQ-45 Total:	**106**	**83**	**45**

Graph Label Legend:

(R) = Red: High chance of negative outcome
(Y) = Yellow: Some chance of negative outcome
(G) = Green: Making expected progress
(W) = **White**: Functioning in normal range

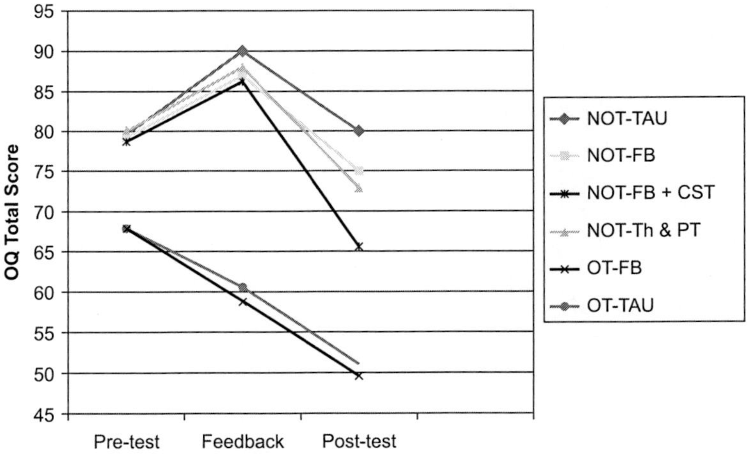

Feedback Message:

The patient is deviating from the expected response to treatment. They are not on track to realize substantial benefit from treatment. Chances are they may drop out of treatment prematurely or have a negative treatment outcome. Steps should be taken to carefully review this case and identify reasons for poor progress. It is recommended that you be alert to the possible need to improve the therapeutic alliance, reconsider the client's readiness for change and the need to renegotiate the therapeutic contract, intervene to strengthen social supports, or possibly alter your treatment plan by intensifying treatment, shifting intervention strategies, or decide upon a new course of action, such as referral for medication. Continuous monitoring of future progress is highly recommended.

FIGURE 16.1 OQ-Analyst Screen Shot Illustrating Feedback Graph and Report of Patient Progress

Vermeersch, et al., 2002; Whipple et al., 2003). Each study required about one year of daily data collection and evaluated the effects of providing feedback about a patient's improvement through the use of progress graphs and warnings about patients who were not demonstrating expected treatment responses (alarm-signal cases).

Our primary question was: Does formal feedback to therapists (or patients) on patient progress improve psychotherapy outcomes? We hypothesized that patients identified as alarm-signal cases (those predicted to have a poor final treatment response) whose therapist received feedback will show better outcomes than similar patients whose therapist did not receive feedback (see also Lambert, Whipple, et al., 2003).

The studies shared many things in common: (a) Each included consecutive cases seen in routine care regardless of patient diagnosis or comorbid conditions (rather than being disorder specific); (b) random assignment of patient to experimental (feedback) and treatment-as-usual (TAU) conditions (no feedback) was made in all but one of the studies; (c) psychotherapists provided a variety of theoretically guided treatments, with more clinicians adhering to cognitive-behavioral and eclectic orientations followed by psychodynamic and experiential orientations; (d) a variety of clinicians were involved (postgraduate psychotherapists and graduate students each represented about 50 percent of the therapists); (e) therapists saw both experimental (feedback) and TAU (no feedback) cases, thus limiting the likelihood that outcome differences between conditions could be due to therapist effects; (f) the outcome measure as well as the methodology rules or standards for identifying alarm-signal patients (failing cases) remained constant; (g) the length of therapy (dosage) was determined by patient and therapist rather than by research design or arbitrary insurance limits; and (h) patient characteristics such as gender, age, and ethnicity were generally similar across four of the studies and came from the same clinic, whereas the fifth sample (Hawkins et al., 2004) was older, more disturbed, and treated in a hospitalbased outpatient clinic.

Another notable difference in the studies was that two of the studies (Harmon et al., 2007; Whipple et al., 2003) extended the design of the first two studies by including a second experimental condition. This was intended to strengthen the feedback intervention by encouraging therapists to use Clinical Support Tools (CSTs) (a problem-solving decision tree and additional measures) with alarm-signal cases. The Harmon et al. (2007) and Hawkins et al. (2004) studies also included two experimental conditions aimed at comparing TAU with feedback to therapists and feedback to therapists and patients.

Results from the combined studies are presented graphically in Figure 16.2. As can be seen, the patients identified as NOT (alarm-signal patients) had a different outcome course depending on assignment to the no-feedback or feedback treatment conditions. Up to the point at which these alarm-signal cases were first signaled or, in the case of the no-feedback treatment-as-usual condition,

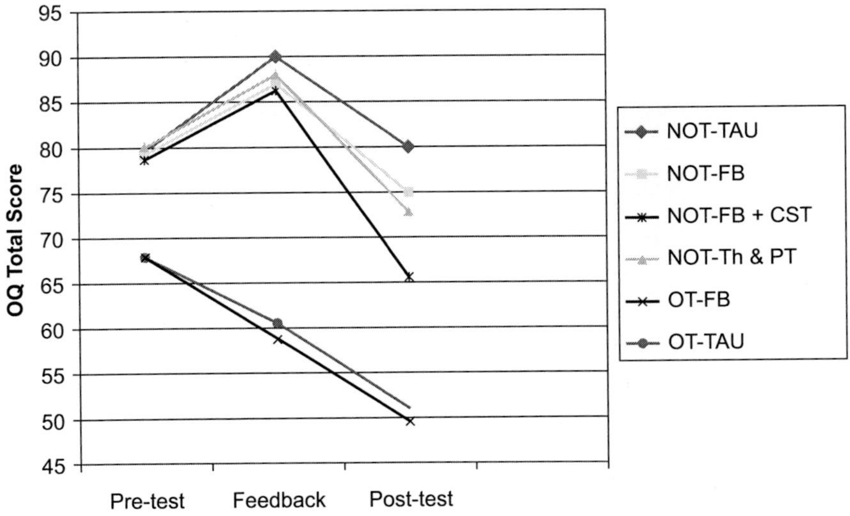

FIGURE 16.2 Change from Pre- to Post-Testing of Not-on-Track (Alarm-Signal) and On-Track Patients

could have been signaled, the graph illustrates an average worsening of about 10 points (about 0.5 SD on the OQ-45). From the point of the alarm signal, all the experimental (feedback [FB]) groups (NOT-FB, NOT-FB + CST, and NOT-Th & PT) improved, whereas the no-feedback control (NOT-TAU) cases improved to an average score near 80 and were, as a group, slightly worse off than when they entered treatment.

Also displayed is the outcome for on-track (OT) cases that did (OT-FB) and did not (OT-TAU) receive feedback. As can be seen, these patients made steady progress and left treatment, as a group, well within the ranks of normal functioning. It appeared to make little difference in outcome for feedback (green or white messages) to have been given.

In the individual studies themselves, the effect sizes (standardized mean differences) for the difference between various feedback conditions for the NOT patients and NOT-TAU controls ranged from .34 to .92. Such effect sizes are surprisingly large when one considers that an average effect for comparative studies (active treatments) typically falls between .00 and .20 (Lambert & Ogles, 2004) and is widely considered important enough to lead to a recommendation of a best practice. Across the five studies, some inconsistent results have been found. Usually the provision of NOT feedback increases the number of sessions that patients attend by about two to three sessions and decreases sessions for OT cases by 0.66 session, but not in Hawkins et al. (2004). In about half the studies, feedback to OT cases improved outcomes despite reducing treatment length. Direct feedback to patients in the form of a written message improved outcomes dramatically in Hawkins et al. (2004) but had no impact in the Harmon et al.

TABLE 16.1 Percent of Not-On-Track (Signal-Alarm) Cases Meeting Criteria for Clinically Significant Change at Termination Summed Across Five Studies

Outcome Classification	*NOT-TAU*[a]	*NOT-FB*[b]	*NOT-T FB + CST*[c]	*T/P-FB*[d]
	N (%)	*N (%)*	*N (%)*	*N (%)*
Deteriorated[e]	64 (20%)	90 (15%)	12 (8%)	19 (13%)
No Change	184 (58%)	316 (53%)	73 (47%)	71 (48%)
Reliable/or Clinically Significant Change[f]	70 (22%)	196 (33%)	169 (45%)	57 (39%)

Notes:
[a] NOT-TAU = patients who were not on track and whose therapist was not given feedback.
[b] NOT-FB = patients who were not on track and whose therapist received feedback.
[c] NOT-T-FB+CST = patients who were not on track and whose therapist received feedback and used clinical support tools.
[d] T/P-FB = therapist feedback plus written direct feedback to patients.
[e] Worsened by at least 14 points on the OQ from pre-treatment to post-treatment.
[f] Improved by at least 14 points on the OQ or improved and passed the cut-off between dysfunctional and functional populations.

(2007) replication. A second replication study is in the final stage of data analysis.

Table 16.1 presents a classification of alarm-signal patients based on their final treatment status at termination. As shown, 20 percent of the alarm-signal cases seen by therapists who received no feedback (NOT-TAU) showed a negative treatment outcome at termination. In contrast, when therapists received feedback that identified their patient as NOT, only 15 percent, 13 percent, and 8 percent of T-FB, T/P-FB patients and TFB+ CS, respectively, deteriorated. The rates for alarm-signal cases showing clinically significant or reliable change were also markedly different; the highest rates of improvement were in the T-FB + CST condition (45 percent) compared with 22 percent in the NOT-TAU condition. These data suggest that the improved outcomes for patients in the experimental conditions are not only statistically significant but also of considerable clinical meaning for the individual client.

Improving Outcomes Through Examination of Therapists' Effects

Because of the rather large database that has accumulated over the years, and with the permission of therapists, we have been able to evaluate the outcome of patients as it relates to specific therapists in two overlapping studies (Okiishi et al., 2003, 2006). After testing for the effects of therapeutic orientation, therapist experience, gender, and age, and finding that these variables were unrelated to patient outcome, we sought to compare outcome across 71 therapists who treated clients with equivalent levels of initial severity. Each therapist saw a minimum of 30 patients (range = 30–350+). As might be expected, there was considerable variability in patient outcome as a function of which therapist treated a patient. Patient outcome was normally distributed across therapists. In general, therapists in the second and third quartiles could not be distinguished from one another based on their patients' outcome, but comparisons between the top and bottom quartiles revealed statistically significant differences.

Because therapists were given anonymity in return for participation in the data analysis, this information could not be directly and immediately used to enhance patient outcome, but further understanding and use of this information for scientific and humanitarian purposes are highly desirable. One is reminded of the progress made in treating cystic fibrosis as described by Gawande (2004) in an article for the *New Yorker*: "The Bell Curve: What Happens When Patients Find Out How Good Their Doctors Really Are?" In the case of cystic fibrosis, life expectancy was dramatically increased, presumably as a function of examining and sharing (making public) outcome data showing the variability in time to death across specialty clinics and subsequent examination of practices engaged in by the most successful clinics. Certainly examining psychotherapy outcome as a function of provider holds considerable promise for patients, but little has been done to facilitate such research or use the research to enhance patient outcome. Several limitations to our research can be noted (Lambert, 2007).

A few comments on the practicality of implementing a feedback system in routine care are in order. Generally, clinicians do not see the value of frequent assessments based on standardized scales (Hatfield & Ogles, 2004), possibly because they are confident in their ability to accurately observe patient worsening and provide an appropriate response. Despite evidence suggesting that psychotherapists are not alert to treatment failure (Hannan et al., 2005; Yalom & Lieberman, 1971) and strong evidence that clinical judgments are usually found to be inferior to actuarial methods across a wide variety of predictive tasks (Meehl, 1954), therapist confidence in their own clinical judgment stands as a barrier to implementation of monitoring and feedback systems. In addition, clinicians are used to practicing in private and with considerable autonomy. Monitoring patient treatment response makes the effects of practice somewhat public and transparent. Such transparency inevitably raises evaluation anxiety and fears of losing control. Implementation requires the cooperation of therapists and takes time before it is apparent to clinicians that the feedback is helpful.

The practical difficulties of adding monitoring activities to busy practices can be an important barrier to implementation. Fortunately, recent developments in software programs make the possibility of instantaneous feedback to clinicians easy to implement. If the patient takes the OQ-45 immediately before the scheduled psychotherapy session, feedback through the OQ-Analyst is available to the therapist before beginning that session.

We continue to work on implementation issues in combination with further research studies. With regard to implementation, we are incorporating our problem-solving decision tree and CSTs into the OQ-Analyst software. This will enable alarm-signal patients to readily take assessments that facilitate clinician problem solving and will provide interventions strategies for therapist consideration more rapidly. In addition to making implementation automatic, we continue to modify our CSTs and test their effects to facilitate problem solving with the failing case.

We hope that the results of our feedback studies convinces practitioners that systematically monitoring their patients with the methods described here is in the best interest of patients and that researchers will consider replication, improvement, and expansion of our methods and findings.

Acknowledgements

The following list of individuals made significant contributions to various aspects of the research reported in this summary. Without their help the findings reported here would never have emerged. In addition to their intellectual contributions and tireless efforts I have been lucky enough to have enjoyed their company and emotional support. They are listed in alphabetic order: Ed Anderson, Steffi Bauer, Matthew Bishop, Jeb Brown, Gary Burlingame, Taige Bybee, Kara Cattani-Thompson, Arthur Finch, Eric Haas, Corinne Hannan, Wolfgang Hannover, Nathan Hansen, Cory Harmon, Derek Hatfield, Eric Hawkins, Scott Kadera, Hans Kordy, Wolfgang Lutz, Kevin Masters, Stevan Nielsen, Ben Ogles, John Okiishi, Robert Percevic, Bernd Puschner, Matthias Richard, Karstin Slade, David Smart, Glen Spielmans, Richard Tingey, Val Umphress, David Vermeersch, Jason Whipple, and Bob Wong.

I would also like to thank Brigham Young University, the College of Social Home and Family Life, and the Counseling and Career Center for their generous financial contributions in support of this program of research. An atmosphere has been created in which success is encouraged. I would also like to thank the therapists and clients at the counseling center, and in many other settings, who joined with us in exploring new methods for enhancing patient outcome.

COMMENTARY

FORMALLY TRACKING PATIENT TREATMENT RESPONSE REDUCES TREATMENT FAILURE AND ENHANCES PSYCHOTHERAPY OUTCOMES: COMMENTARY ON MY PRESIDENTIAL ADDRESS

The Editors of Visions provided the opportunity to reflect on my Presidential Address to the Society in 2005, taking stock of the present, and looking toward the future. The talk I gave focused on a decade of work undertaken at Brigham

Young University directed at improving psychotherapy outcomes and more broadly at examining patterns of change over time and their implications for theory and practice. The research began with the development of brief scales intended to operationally define mental health and dysfunction that would be suitable for repeated administration over the course of psychotherapy in order to track patient progress. For adults we defined mental health as internal subjective distress and well-being, interpersonal problems and satisfaction, and functioning in societal roles. These constructs and the items used to define them provide the basis for quantifying mental health and tracking it over time. I am pleased to say that the measures have become widely used in English and translated into over 20 different languages for use across the world.

Having an index or mental health vital sign then allowed exploration of patterns of change in treated and untreated individuals, estimating the number of sessions needed for return to normal functioning, examining discontinuities in change such as sudden gains, sudden declines, modeling treatment success and failure, and most importantly predicting treatment failure. This latter task was especially important since the major goal of the research was to identify patients who had a high probability of leaving treatment worse off than when they started, and notifying therapists before patients left treatment so that they could make timely interventions. Before discussing this topic in more detail it is worth noting that there is more information coming from the field on the other topics alluded to in my Presidential Address.

The Dose-Response Relationship

The number of sessions needed to bring about positive change remains controversial. Estimates from our research suggested that the session at which 50 percent and 75 percent of patients returned to normal functioning ranged from 11 to 21 and 25 to 45, respectively. The more disturbed a patient, the more sessions that are needed, so that estimates vary from setting to setting. In answer to our original question—How much therapy is enough?—research now suggests some modification to the idea that more therapy will lead to better outcomes. It appears that there is a dose-response relationship as we suggested, but possibly that this relationship is most clear in just the first eight sessions, as the dosage increases beyond that limit the dose-response relationship becomes less detectable (Baldwin et al., 2009).

In the future this kind of information will continue to be important for theories of change, social policy, and treatment planning. On the other hand it would be nice to live in a world where the amount of treatment one received was more a function of clients' health needs rather than economic policy or even theoretical considerations. In the future I expect to see refinements in predictions that become more specific (type of problem, type of therapy), but no radical changes in the current estimates. But there is a growing trend in the

United States to ration treatment by diluting dose over time (providing less than weekly psychotherapy. Most predictions of dose and outcome have been based on weekly psychotherapy. It may well be that the practice of spreading sessions out to every two or three weeks will not only slow the effects of treatments but diminish the effect of each session in addition. If this is the case such practices should be stopped for the patient's sake and for the reputation of the profession or the kind of treatment offered may need to be modified for slow delivery (e.g., every third week). Of course, it may be that spreading treatment out only prolongs patient suffering but does not diminish its effects and that low dose therapy in the face of no or shortened waiting lists is a reasonable trade-off.

Expected Treatment Response

In a related line of research we modeled expected treatment response for the purpose of predicting final outcome. As it turned out we could predict treatment failure before it occurred and with much greater accuracy than a specific client's therapist could. Since our original work other individuals have taken on this task using a variety of sophisticated and creative statistical methods (e.g., Lutz et al., 2007). With advances in longitudinal data analysis and greater specificity in predicting for specific disorders and treatments, we can expect to improve predictive accuracy, but if such work is not incorporated into routine care such advances will be largely academic exercises. Who needs an excellent predictive method that is not used to help a single individual? So far predicting treatment failure and delivering this information to therapists and clients to improve outcomes has not moved as far as I had hoped in the field in general—with regards to improving patient outcome. To be optimistic, it is just a matter of time (and concentrated effort) before advances in this area pay dividends with regards to patient benefit.

Early, Dramatic Treatment Response

In the course of examining patient change it became obvious that rather than incremental session-by-session improvement many patients, and particularly patients whose outcome is most positive, responded to therapy very early on and very dramatically. This phenomenon was first reported in the 1990s within drug trials and was thought to represent a placebo response (since it occurred before the active medication effects should be observable). Tang and DeRubies (1999) noted this phenomenon while studying CBT for depression and titled it "sudden gains." Our own explorations of this phenomenon suggested that it was not just a characteristic of CBT for depression as demonstrated originally by the authors, but that it was found across patient diagnosis (e.g., bulimia nervosa, panic) and therapist treatment orientations (even occurring in supportive psychotherapy). More recently sudden gains have been found even in couple therapy

(Doss et al., 2011). Over the years more researchers have explored various aspects of sudden gains. Among the many implications of this pattern of change is that it can occur very early in treatment (in the first three sessions), that the gains usually persist over the course of treatment, and well after, and it preceeds much of what are considered to be the necessary ingredients of psychotherapy (e.g., homework assignments, exposure, practice).

In our own research we define a sudden gain as improvement so large that it only occurs in 10 percent or less of the patients at a particular session of treatment (in comparison to expected change at that session). I think we were correct in perceiving this phenomenon to be very interesting and important and that future research will tell us more about its frequency, and causes. Anecdotally, it can be observed to occur following sessions in which a patient exposes to the therapist a long-held, shameful secret, subsequently received without judgment or condemnation. The impact of such disclosures appears to come from a kind of confessional process—hardly emphasized in most theoretical systems and even incidental to the intent of the therapist. It also appears to have the qualities of patient insight, or realization; instances of which lead to self-reorganization. Whatever the causes, further study of such changes is likely to help us better understand change and promote change. Continuing study of this phenomenon will pay large dividends. Use of the information (that there has been a sudden gain) clinically may also be of value in understanding the effects of psychotherapy.

Improving the Effects of Treatment

My Presidential Address emphasized the degree of progress we had made in preventing treatment failure. I summarized four published studies done by myself, my graduate students, and treatment center staff. Since publication of these four articles we have published five more randomized clinical trials (Crits-Christoph, et al., 2011; Harmon et al., 2007; Simon et al., 2012, 2013; Slade et al., 2008), a meta/mega-analytic review of our first six studies (Shimokawa, Lambert, & Smart, 2010). I am happy to report that the beneficial effects reported in my Presidential Address based on our first four studies have, by and large, been replicated by those that followed. This later research essentially showed that combining patient progress feedback (with alarm-signals) and Clinical Support Tools for predicted treatment failures produced strong effects, more than doubling positive outcomes while reducing deterioration rates by 75 percent. In initial attempts to see if these feedback methods could help clients being treated for substance abuse, Crits-Christoph et al. (2011) found that they did, but that the effects were much smaller. Simon et al. (2013) extended the feedback methods to inpatient care with females suffering with eating disorders. In this setting, where 90 percent of patients were on medication, and a host of treatments were provided on a daily basis, the consequences of feedback were again found to be positive, though not as large as in our original studies. Thus it is fair to conclude that our initial work on feedback was replicated and extended in the years following the Presidential Address. Other research groups are replicating and extending this research in new settings and cultures, but it is too soon to know the degree to which the same strong findings are replicated.

There are a variety of other feedback systems that overlap with the OQ-Analyst System, but also take different directions. I have reviewed elsewhere several of the most well developed systems (Lambert, Hansen, & Harmon, 2010). As with psychotherapy itself, where large differences in procedures appear to be overshadowed by factors common to all, the various assessment-based feedback systems may end up having rather similar effects on patients. Certain aspects of the OQ-Analyst approach that seem necessary to us may not be found to matter. For example, we believe feedback is effective for clients who are predicted to be treatment failures, not all clients. The evidence we have collected to date shows small impacts on cases who are on track and large effects on those who are not. Others see the feedback as generally helpful. We see what we do as a method for preventing treatment failure, and emphasize, through our Clinical Support Tools, problem solving for the off-track case. The Clinical Support Tools provide a decision tree to organize problem solving, assessment of the therapeutic alliance, motivation/expectations, social supports, and untoward life events. The Clinical Support Tools are unnecessary and inappropriate if patients are improving.

We feel that CST feedback is best when delivered at the item-level, not just the subscale-level, and we believe this type of information (item-level feedback) leads to the most effective therapist problem solving. In contrast to Miller and some others, we believe that factors, other than the alliance, are important for turning the course of therapy around. We also ask therapists to reconsider patient diagnosis and the need for a medication consultation or to consider changing the nature of treatment. We do not believe it is important or necessary to measure the alliance and the other factors and provide feedback to therapists when the patient is improving as expected. It may be that the major reason that feedback systems work is that they prompt a discussion between client and therapist about progress in treatment and aspects of treatment that are unhelpful. This discussion can be prompted in many ways and the specifics of the systems may be unimportant as long as they facilitate such a discussion.

With regards to the applied science of including progress feedback and problem-solving tools in routine care, we are at the stage of discovering the effect sizes for these interventions and estimating the extent to which they emerge in different settings and patient populations. The next steps might well include comparisons of the major systems and exploration of the active mechanisms across systems. It remains an important task of future research to discover the most impactful kind of feedback and effective ways of delivering feedback. For individual researchers and research groups who make modifications to the methods that we have used, it is important to reflect on the nature of the changes that are being made—Are they trivial or crucial to what is necessary to having a positive impact on patients?

Summary

Looking back at my Presidential Address I remain proud of its focus and findings. The field has produced research that refines and strengthens the findings that were summarized. It has been only a short period since its publication but the amount of research that we and others have contributed is rather large. We can expect to learn much in the coming decade about patterns of change that emerge as we practice psychotherapy, and that this information will benefit those who enter treatments. Most important will be the fundamental changes in the way we routinely practice that will include methods of formally measuring, monitoring, and feeding back information to therapists, clients, systems of care, as well as policy makers. This work provides a good example of bridging the gap between science and practice for the benefit of the client.

17

RESONATING MINDS

A School-Independent Theoretical Conception and its Empirical Application to Psychotherapeutic Processes (2008)

Erhard Mergenthaler

Psychotherapy works. This has been demonstrated by a number of authors focusing on outcome research (most recently, Joyce, Wolfaardt, Sribney, & Aylwin, 2006; Ogrodniczuk, 2006). Psychotherapy is superior to the absence of treatment, with recovery and improvement rates of about 60 percent and 65 percent, respectively, if no distinction is made between therapeutic orientation and diagnostic groups and with a 5 percent to 10 percent patient deterioration rate (Lambert, 2007). Nevertheless, the exact mechanisms of change are still not known. To learn more about this psychotherapy process, research is needed. This article introduces a theory and the corresponding model for its empirical assessment with computer-assisted text analysis, developed over the last 20 years, that maps the therapeutic process and enables the process researcher to identify clinical processes and significant clinical events, to analyze them in detail, and to relate them to concepts stemming from neuroscience, experimental, and cognitive psychology. A critical overview of studies that provide first evidence and steps of validation for both theory and model concludes the article.

The Resonating Minds Theory

A target of process research is the investigation of the mind, both the patient's and the therapist's. To observe what they are doing with words, the single steps of meaning making in the therapeutic talk have to be understood in order to learn about the conditions that lead to therapeutic change. They communicate and interact in specific ways, a process I call the "resonating mind," and I differentiate two aspects. First, the interpersonal view that is found in concepts like therapeutic alliance, emotional communication, or, on a more biological level, the mirror neurons as neurophysiological mechanisms underlying the understanding and imitation of action as well as experiences. Second, the intrapersonal view is found in concepts regarding the flow of information within a person's mind or, seen from a neurobiological view, activities between specific brain areas and between the hemispheres, marked by the asymmetry of the brain. The resonating minds theory (RMT) takes up these perspectives and extends them to the interactive system between therapist interventions and the modalities of patients' behavior. The key concepts in RMT are therapeutic process and change, brain asymmetry, cognition and emotion, and therapeutic interventions.

Therapeutic Process and Change

The RMT distinguishes three factors: affective experiencing, cognitive mastery, and behavior. All these factors are at work all the time. They are brought into the therapeutic situation by means of talking about experiences, by reflecting on them, and by telling stories that reflect real behavior. Therapeutic change thus can be understood as a change from a pathological toward a normal regulation of emotional, cognitive, and behavioral processes. The psychotherapeutic process can be seen as a set of verbal, psychotropic, or other therapeutic interventions that directly influence a patient's emotional, cognitive, and behavioral regulation. Therapeutic interventions are sought by therapists in such a way that gradually a pathological system of regulation will turn into a more adaptive one.

Psychotherapy research has followed this understanding for a long time. However, from a more current point of view, an important link was missing: the neurobiological level or, more precisely, the brain. Whatever is done on the level of interventions, it will first reach the brain, alter the state of the brain or specific areas of it, and only then, as a consequence of the changes in the brain, will the emotional, cognitive, and behavioral regulation change. In the case of medication as a major therapeutic intervention, this always seemed to be quite apparent, because it is obvious that the drug will alter the chemistry of the brain and, consequently, a patient's experiences. With regard to verbal interactions, change in the brain did not seem to be that evident.

That psychotherapy changes the brain no longer may be seen as an unsupported claim. One of the earlier studies that provided evidence for this was by Brody et al. (2001), who reported on regional brain metabolic changes in patients with major depression treated with either Paroxetine or interpersonal therapy. Both groups showed decreased activity in the prefrontal cortex. Patients on medication showed the decrease in both hemispheres, whereas those who received verbal treatment only changed in the right hemisphere. Roffman, Marci, Glick, Dougherty, and Rauch (2005) gave an informative overview on neuroimaging findings and concluded that psychotherapy and pharmacotherapy yield similar but not identical changes in the regional cerebral bloodflow. The fact that these changes are not identical is not surprising. Psychotropic drugs essentially either inhibit or activate major brain areas in a mostly unspecific way. Words can activate or inhibit many and even small brain areas, and groups of words like sentences or thought streams can do this in even more specific ways. The RMT is supposed to provide a theoretical conception that allows the development of methodological approaches to empirically assess and validate these assumptions.

Psychotherapy process research needs to integrate mind, brain, and therapeutic interactions, to link aspects of emotional, cognitive, and behavioral regulation with neurobiology and with various types of interventions. The question remains: What are the specifics of "psycho"-therapy? It is effective, causes changes in the brain, and can be done with a variety of therapeutic interventions that obviously dispose of the capacity to specifically contribute to change. Can these characteristics be identified?

Evidence from Neuroscience

During the past few years, an increasing number of findings in neuroscience have emerged that might be related to one or more characteristics of psychotherapeutic interventions. I refer to two examples to give an idea of how the process of linking findings from brain imaging with types of therapeutic activity such as patient narrative and therapist interventions could work.

The first example is a functional magnetic resonance imaging study by Yomogida et al. (2004) that shows the effect of watching concrete stationary objects and imagining that they move, like an internal movie. The participants were asked to look at drawings of a ladder and a cat. They then were instructed to imagine how these two objects might interact (e.g., the cat climbs up the ladder). This task caused a strong activation, specifically in the left hemisphere. I conclude that similar activations take place when a patient reports a dream. This assumption is supported by other findings regarding concrete versus abstract words, with concrete words being processed in the left brain (e.g., Perani et al., 1999). To put it concisely, I am suggesting that all kinds of interventions that evoke an internal imagery or cause a narrative report are likely to activate the left hemisphere.

The second example is a study that focused on participants' attention to visual speech gestures while observing a female face silently articulating vowels (Pekkola et al., 2006). The instructions required the participants to direct their attention either to the articulation of sounds or to the direction of movement of elliptic circles that were projected over the mouth area, as a nonverbal visual stimulus. This task enhanced activity in the left planum temporale for the articulation discrimination compared with the non-speech motion discrimination task. This could mean that, in face-to-face settings, it may be interesting to pay attention to moments in which patients avoid gazing or eye-to-eye contact and thus avoid possible left hemispheric activation.

However, therapeutic interventions focus not only on the left hemisphere. Rhythmic movements of the legs, for example, cause activity in the right brain, whereas listening to music activates both hemispheres (Brown, Martinez, & Parsons, 2006).

These and the many other studies suggest that there is ample evidence for a lateralization of cognitive skills (Hugdahl & Davidson, 2003). This certainly will be of relevance for clinical practice. It even seems to be a natural consequence that therapeutic interventions and certain types of verbal activities have the potential to contribute to the asymmetric activation of the brain.

Along with this, two additional principles, activation spreading and neural plasticity, (McClelland, Rummelhardt, & the PDP Research Group, 1986) are useful.

Activation Spreading

This means that areas in the brain that are neighboring or reside in the same hemisphere of an active area are more likely to become active themselves. It is important to use the phrase "more likely" because it is not a law that it has to be; it is just an increased likelihood, and it may need some additional input to really make such an area active. Thus, activating an internal imagery, like when telling a dream, may be the cause for a subsequent increase of positive emotion, because both phenomena are assumed to be predominantly processed in the left hemisphere. This may even be true in the case of a nightmare, because it is possible to activate areas in both hemispheres and, later, to experience both positive and negative affect at a time (Russell & Carroll, 1999). However, because of either some pathological information processing or a possibly counterproductive intervention or other reasons, an activation of positive emotions also may become blocked despite the processing of the imagery in the left brain when reporting the dream.

Neural Plasticity

This concept basically explains why a brain undergoes functional and structural alterations in response to external and internal environmental changes (May et al., 2007) and why it persists (Wang, 2003).

Evidence from Experimental Psychology

Broadening

Isen, in the late 1980s, did some pioneering work relating specific cognitive skills with the valence of emotion. She convincingly demonstrated that positive emotions widen the array of the thoughts and actions that come to mind and in this way support or even enable creative or problem-solving processes (Isen, Daubman, &

Nowicki, 1987). Fredrickson (1998) further developed the notion that positive emotions "broaden-and-build," a process she labels *broadening*. I conclude from this that broadening is an important aspect of the psychotherapeutic process: Patients need to focus on emotion-relevant domains but have to be generative of, or receptive to, a wide range of ideas and actions that may come into mind and may help to undergo change as, for example, through some new insight.

Deepening

Again from the work of Isen (1990) stems the concept that negative emotions focus our cognitive organization. They are more focused on the seeking and use of information (Spering, Wagener, & Funke, 2005). I conclude from this that negative emotions provide or prepare pathways to relationship episodes, autobiographical material, and closely related topics. Analogous to Fredrickson's "broaden-and-build," I labeled this state "deepen-and-provide." Patients in a state of *deepening* typically retrieve conflict-related material to be worked through in the psychotherapeutic process. This fits well with the clinical observation that patients typically present their problems with negative emotions and report a higher preponderance of negative relationship episodes during therapy. How does this relate to the brain, to neural networks that may be involved? Taking up the thread of brain asymmetry and concentrating on the three change factors mentioned previously, emotion might be a good candidate for investigating this.

Lateralization of Emotion

Davidson (1993) presented three alternatives: (a) that emotions are located in the right hemisphere; (b) that emotions associated with approach are located in the left hemisphere, whereas emotions associated with withdrawal are located in the right hemisphere; and (c) that positive emotions are located in the left hemisphere and negative emotions in the right hemisphere (valence hypothesis). More recently, additional perspectives about the lateralization of emotions have emerged (e.g. Olko, 2002). There is good support for the valence hypothesis, with negative emotions on the right and positive emotions more likely on the left, and with males showing more lateralization to emotional activity (Wagner, Phan, Liberzon, & Taylor, 2003). To conduct empirical research, it is important to make assumptions. The RMT follows the valence hypothesis, and I base my further reasoning on these assumptions.

Returning to the concepts of broadening and deepening from experimental psychology, as well as from neuroscience, there is sufficient evidence that the deepen-and-provide notion is supported by studies that located negative autobiographical memories in the right hemisphere (Fink et al., 1996; Piefke, Weiss, Zilles, Markowitsch, & Fink, 2003) and found right brain activity during recall of traumatic memories (Schiffer, Teicher, & Papanicolaou, 1995).

Another concept central to cognition is deductive and probabilistic reasoning. There is also evidence for distinct right and left brain systems for deductive versus probabilistic "Aha!" types of reasoning (Kounios et al., 2006; Parsons & Osherson, 2001). Thus, negative emotions, deepen-and-provide states, as well as deductive reasoning, tend to be processed in the right brain, whereas positive emotions, broaden-and-build states, and probabilistic reasoning tend to be processed in the left brain.

Shift Events

In my view, both deepening and broadening are essential in therapy. Ideally, deepening should be followed by broadening as a sign of working through conflictive material that has been provided. *Shift events* are supposed to achieve such a transition from a state of deepen-and-provide to one of broaden-and-build. They can be triggered by either the therapist or the patient. Typical shift events occur during narratives, dream reports, chair work, empathic responses, systemic evocative unfolding, and more. Shift events may be shared or specific for different therapeutic orientations.

Summary

The therapist-patient interaction is marked by resonating processes that include affective experiencing, cognitive mastery, and behavioral regulation. Therapeutic interventions are key to RMT. They explicitly trigger brain areas by asking for activities that, as an immediate consequence, activate specific areas. They also may trigger brain areas implicitly by providing cues that will be processed in specific areas and, based on the mechanism of activation spreading, tend to activate the same and neighboring areas. In the therapeutic process, deepen-and-provide has the function of problem activation, whereas broaden-and-build accounts for problem solving. It is assumed that in existing psychotherapies therapists and patients "resonate" in such a way that a problem will be activated and then problem solving will follow. Given the asymmetry of the brain and the assumed lateralization of emotions, interventions will be chosen in such a way that right hemisphere activation will be followed by left hemisphere activation, both steps either explicitly or implicitly. In the following section, this theoretical conception is applied to a viable method for the empirical assessment of the RMT principles.

The Therapeutic Cycles Model

The therapeutic cycles model (TCM) may be seen as an instantiation of the RMT as a means for empirical research. It views the therapeutic process from a linguistic perspective because it can be observed within psychotherapy transcripts and other related textual data, making the assumption that the three factors distinguished by the RMT—affective experiencing, cognitive mastery, and behavior—will be represented at the level of the discourse. The corresponding linguistic measures used by the TCM are emotional tone, abstraction, and narrative style. It relies on computer-assisted content analysis that is based on dictionaries of words identified as markers for affective language (emotional tone; Mergenthaler, 1996), for conceptual language (abstraction; Mergenthaler, 1996), and for storytelling and narration (narrative style, see also Mergenthaler & Bucci, 1999).

In its earlier version (Mergenthaler, 1996), the TCM was composed of its main elements, emotional tone and abstraction, and their temporal variation was assumed to follow a curve ideally resonating like the sine (Figure 17.1, upper graph). There was no rationale available for predicting which of the two variables might increase first and why these variables might behave in a cyclical manner at all, except for anecdotal evidence and support from everyday experience that no healthy person likes to or even can remain in a high (or low) level of arousal or abstract thought for an extended period of time. It also was assumed that there is a time lag between emotion tone and abstraction. The current version is an extension of the previous one and additionally differentiates the valence of emotional tone. It is now grounded on the RMT by reflecting that negative emotion and deepening will occur first, followed by an increase of positive emotion and broadening, which then leads to change. In Figure 17.1, this is represented in the lower graph showing an idealized flow of positive and negative emotional tone across the time. Both upper and lower graphs together represent the TCM.

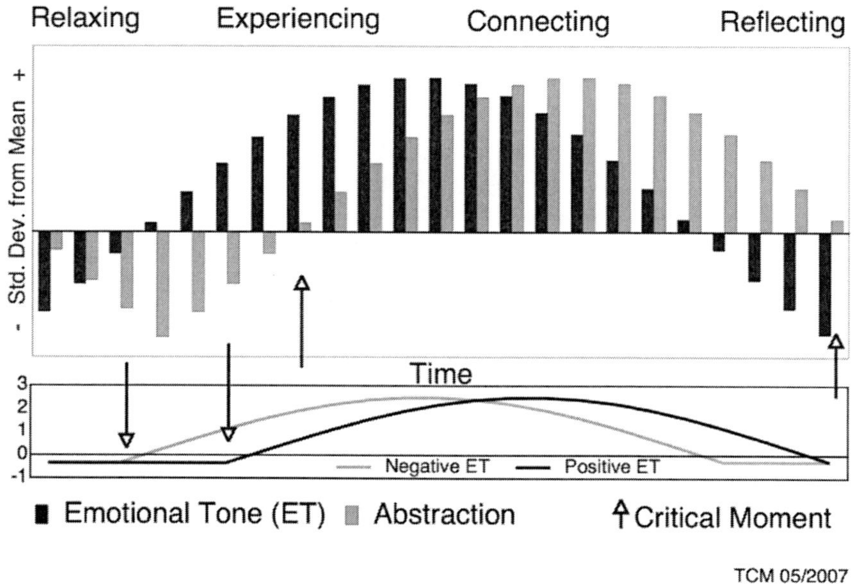

FIGURE 17.1 The Therapeutic Cycles Model

The flow of variables as shown in Figure 17.1 represents one prototypical cycle. It is theoretically derived and represents an idealized flow. The left and right ends of the graphs mark the beginning and end of the prototypical cycle. The observation unit can be a therapy session, referred to as microanalysis later, with segments like word blocks (other segmentation criteria, like turn of speech or time segments, are also possible). On a macro-analytical level (for more details, see Mergenthaler, 1996), the model may be applied across sessions describing complete treatments. For the sake of clarity, all further descriptions and examples within this section of the article relate to microanalyses on a within-session level. The cycle is not expected to occur frequently or repeatedly within a session or even in every session. A good therapy, however, following the RMT will be marked by an increasing number of successfully passed cycles. Patients who do not succeed in connecting emotion tone with abstraction during their therapy are likely not to improve.

Emotion-Abstraction Patterns

The quantitative dimension of emotion tone and abstraction allows the differentiation of at least four classes that are henceforth referred to as emotion-abstraction patterns. Graphically they are represented as a combination of the z-scored relative frequencies for emotional tone and abstraction words (see Figure 17.1). The four patterns are labeled and interpreted as follows.

1. *Relaxing*: little emotional tone (equal to or below the mean) and little abstraction (first three bars in Figure 17.1). Patients talk about material that is not manifestly connected to their central symptoms or issues. They describe rather than reflect. Further, it is a state to which patients return as often as they feel the need, thus regenerating both physically and mentally to prepare themselves for the next step of their "talking cure."
2. *Experiencing*: much emotional tone and little abstraction (bars 4–7 in Figure 17.1). Patients find themselves in a state of emotional experiencing. Patients may be raising conflictual themes and experience them emotionally. With regard to the valence of emotion, positive and negative experiencing additionally will be differentiated depending on whether positive or negative emotional tone is dominating and above the mean.
3. *Connecting*: much emotional tone and much abstraction (the middle bars in Figure 17.1). Patients have found emotional access to conflictive themes and they can reflect on them. This state marks a clinically important moment that often coincides with a moment of insight or possibly a moment of change.
4. *Reflecting*: little emotional tone and much (above the mean) abstraction (the last four bars in Figure 17.1). Patients discuss topics with a high amount of abstraction and without intervening emotions. This may be an expression of the defense known as intellectualization.

Critical Moments

Returning to the graphic representation of the TCM (see Figure 17.1), four arrows have been inserted to mark what I call critical moments, where pathological behavior may differ from more normal ways of emotional, cognitive, and behavioral regulation. In the case of a problematic event, a healthy person might be expected to pass through the cycle, as shown in Figure 17.1, easily and perhaps quickly. However, this might depend on the nature of the event that causes the cycle to start. In the case of being confronted with bad news like the illness of a good friend, it may take longer, maybe an hour or even days, to go through the cycle. In the case of a small misfortune or daily hassle, like a slip of tongue, this is likely to be a very fast process, realizing the negative experience coming along with it, searching for an explanation, smiling or laughing, and resolving the problem. Patients, however, may experience considerable difficulties in proceeding past one, some, or all of these critical moments and need a therapist to support them with appropriate interventions to successfully pass through a cycle. I describe these critical moments briefly and propose some interventions a therapist might use to assist the patient in proceeding to the next phase of the cycle. These critical moments are generalizations from typical patterns that have been found across lots of patients. The examples for interventions are drawn from real cases.

The first critical moment is when a patient has difficulties accessing conflictual material. Therapists typically initiate deepening. Examples might be to trigger negative feelings ("You seem sad today" or "What bothers you?"), to emphasize negative feelings ("Say that again, 'I hate my mother'" or "You are alone, abandoned, lost"), or to ask for a detailed symptom description, just to mention a few.

After a successful deepen-and-provide experience, the patient may be stuck in negative experiencing, the second critical moment, and the therapist may want to start broadening, a broaden-and-build phase, by initiating a shift event. Here the disparate therapeutic orientations may differ most. Some try to elicit a narrative: "Do you have a memory of this?" Others, for example, initiate empty- or two-chair work or propose homework. If a patient, despite the successful initiation of a shift event, cannot start to broaden-and-build, the therapist may try to foster a positive experiencing by taking up positive aspects that have been presented by the patient in his or her most recent statements. An example of this is the dream presented in the next section, in which a sexual topic was taken up. Very often in transcript analyses we found a specific "language tool," with the therapist expressing negative thoughts of the patient in positive terms:

PATIENT: I hate her.
THERAPIST: You don't love her any longer?

Using a negation along with a positive term holds up the semantic meaning but causes the processing (resonating) of a positive aspect for the patient and, as a likely consequence, an activation shift toward the left brain. Also, use of humor may cause a shift toward broaden-and-build.

The third critical moment is marked by a lack of reflecting about feelings. Again, here we found a typical set of therapist interventions that may trigger and encourage the connecting process: "What does this mean to you?" or "What other ways could you think about this?"

Finally, if all these barriers are overcome, a new cycle may begin. This might happen, for example, by the therapist asking for more symptom-related information or by resuming reflection on feelings. Patients who in the course of a therapy do not learn to pass the critical moments—and, therefore, to pass a cycle completely—are less likely to improve.

A Sample Clinical Illustration of the TCM

The following description is inspired by a real case (Amalia X., Session 152; Kächele et al., 2006) and presents in a condensed way the essentials of a psychoanalytic session to illustrate the temporal sequence of the phases of the model (see Figure 17.1) in a way clinicians might be more familiar with. An example with real data is shown later. The patient begins the session without really knowing what to start with, which in the model corresponds to relaxing (first three bars, emotional tone and abstraction below the mean). Then, at the first critical moment, she turns to negative feelings, a negative experiencing (emotional tone above the mean, abstraction below the mean, and negative emotional tone above the mean), with the remark that she has not slept well, that she thought she might have a heart attack. Then she recalls a dream: She is lying on the floor, dead, with a knife in the back, and her skirt far up, which was embarrassing because a former colleague passed by; a couple then came up to her and cut off her hair; finally she stands up and goes to see a hairdresser. The therapist responds to her being dead in a mode of "deepen-and-provide" by reflecting: "So you were dead; you had that knife in your back." The patient reminds the therapist that, despite the knife in her back, she obviously was alive because she went to the hairdresser. This happens around the second critical moment and can be seen as a step toward positive experiencing (emotional tone above the mean, abstraction below the mean, and both negative and positive emotional tones above the mean). A "broaden-and-build" shift occurs near the third critical moment, when both the patient and the therapist refer to the sexual image regarding the patient's skirt in the dream. This association then leads to a connecting event, an insight with regard to her shame (anxiety) and her relationship with the former colleague she saw in the dream. This is considered to be a moment of change, yielding a mini-outcome that was followed in the last phase of the model by some abstract thoughts without emotional ground, reflecting (emotional tone below the mean, abstraction above the mean). Another cycle may now begin.

Using the TCM on Case Material

The Software

Session transcripts are analyzed by the CM software. CM takes as an input the text file of a transcript and produces as an output a graphic representation of the session (Figure 17.2). The session is automatically segmented into word blocks of 150 words each, and additionally the window moves in steps of 75 words, providing a finer-grained representation of the flow. The black bars in the top and bottom graphs represent emotional tone, the gray bars abstraction. The second graph from the top shows the speech proportion: black and above the axis for the activity of the patient, gray and below the axis for the therapist. Both together represent 100 percent. The bottom graph displays the valence of emotion, with black representing positive emotion and gray representing negative emotion.

Patients as well as healthy people do not behave like the textbook says or a model prescribes; similarly, they do not perfectly follow the TCM. Thus, to apply the model and to work with empirical material, definitions are needed to translate the prototypical cycle into a real situation. A cycle for this purpose is defined as any sequence of emotion-abstraction patterns that includes at least one connecting block and is delimited by a relaxing block before and after. Where there is no relaxing word block before a connecting word block, the beginning of the session will count as the beginning of the cycle. The same applies to that case at the end of a session. For a connecting word block to form the basis for a cycle, at least one of the two variables must be above 1 SD, and the other must reach at least 0.25 SD above the mean.

Optionally, as shown in Figure 17.2, the software generates a circle around the cycles present in the session based on the prior definition. The vertical lines and arrows in Figure 17.2 (not provided by CM but inserted manually in the graph) indicate shift events, moments in which positive emotion changes above the mean after a dominating negative period. These are expected to be moments when the necessary preconditions are given for connecting and thus insight or change to follow.

In addition to the graphic representation, CM also provides a data file for statistical analyses, a postscript file to reproduce the graph, a statistics summary, left-over lists with words in the text but not in the dictionaries, and more.

The Interpretation of a CM Graph

The CM graph may be used as a guide to the session. Typically, with the prototypical cycle in mind, the therapist would locate one or a sequence of outstanding word blocks in the graph and then return to the transcript—the software also provides a version of the text file with word block markers—in order to

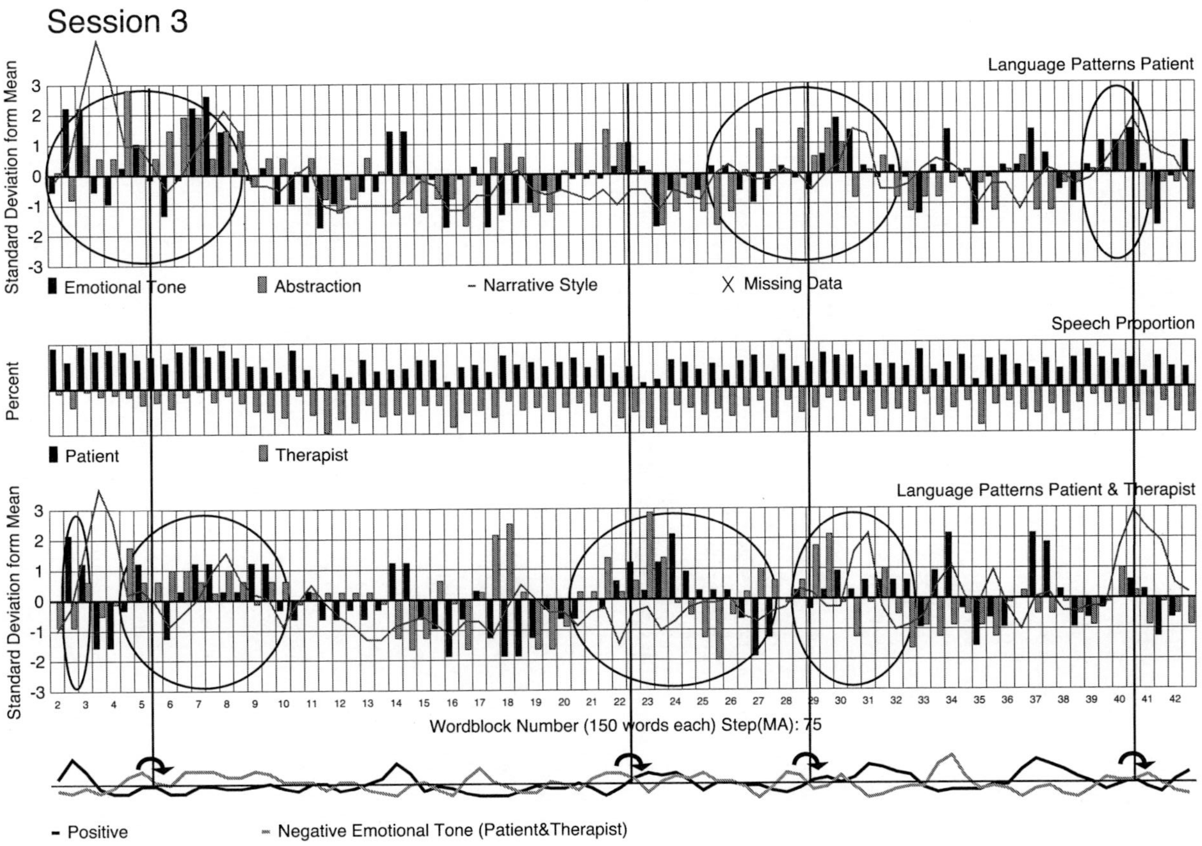

FIGURE 17.2 Sample Graphic Output from CM

have a closer look at the turn-by-turn discourse. Such moments could be instances of critical moments (e.g., positive experiencing has been reached but no connecting follows, as in Word Block 14 in Figure 17.2) or complete cycles, or differences between the patient's graph and the one for patient and therapist together (e.g., Word Blocks 23–25 in Figure 17.2, where obviously the therapist only contributed to connecting). The following example again refers to Figure 17.2, starting with Word Block 29, where a shift event can be observed that leads to a connecting in patient's language patterns in Word Block 30. The whole sequence is part of a cycle.

Start Word Block 29:

THERAPIST: How do you feel about him when you remember that absence?
CLIENT: Um, maybe not wanting to be there.
T: It kind of hurts?
C: Yeah, um, I realize that . . . it's, um, a disease thing, that can't be controlled.
T: Mm-hm.
C: Or emotions could have been part of why he couldn't express himself, or had such strong emotions that he escaped to that.

Therapist initiates two-chair work:

T: Uh-huh. /// talking, can you switch over here?
C: Okay.
T: What are you saying to C.? You're saying that I couldn't control it, I had strong emotions?
C: Yes, you're right C., that was more of an escape for me, because to get out of reality . . .
T: I needed to escape.
C: Yeah, it's like a high, it's almost like feeling high when, um, I got into the gambling and was away from the family and didn't have to face my problems [laugh].

Start Word Block 30:

T: I could, I could shut the world out this way.
C: Yeah.
T: Shut out the pain.
C: When really I should have been at home helping your mother out and, just being there with you kids.
T: Mm-hm, so that's like, I should have been there.
C: Yeah, I should have been there, helping mom out.
T: Mm-hm.

C: So she wouldn't be so, um, tired—or depressed, given her a break, if she wanted a little time away from you kids if she needed it.

T: And how did you feel? Why did you say that?

C: Um, angry, um, I'm sorry, sorry that I wasn't there and sorry that I didn't do anything about it.

T: Mm-hm.

C: I just thought I'd make money and come home and be able to pay the bills with it and everything else would be alright.

T: I thought that, my contribution was enough.

Start Word Block 31:

C: I thought I was—trying to support a family, and, and to me that was—what I had to do.

T: Uh-huh, and so I thought that that was good enough, is that what you're saying.

C: Yeah, under my, power and faith and belief, I thought that was what I should be doing.

End of chair work:

T: Uh-huh change.—How do you respond to that? He says that he thought that was good enough. What happens . . .

C: Um, I'll feel relieved.

T: You feel relieved like a weight has lifted.

C: Just talking about it.

T: Uh-huh, can you tell him, "I feel relieved to be able to tell you about this, these feelings"?

C: Yeah, I do. It feels really good to be able to say this to you, to let it out of me, I shouldn't have to [crying] carry these feelings.

T: Mm-hm.

C: It's really overwhelming.

T: Do you feel overwhelmed right now?

Start of Word Block 32:

C: Um, like uh . . .

T: Kind of like a rush of all these feelings, is that it?

C: Yeah, yes [sniff].

In the prior example, we see that the therapist changes the setting to start two-chair work. The patient accepts, and in the graph for patient's language patterns we observe an increase of emotional tone while maintaining a high level of abstraction in the second half of Word Block 29 followed by connecting in Word Block 30. Then the language measures "relax" approaching their session mean and finally, starting with Word Block 32, falls below the mean, and relaxing can be observed.

Empirical Evidence for the TCM

To provide empirical evidence for the underlying assumptions of the RMT and the findings with TCM, it will be necessary to conduct studies that focus on its specific aspects finally yielding a convergent validity. I briefly refer to a number of studies that may provide contributing evidence following Kazdin's (2007) seven criteria or requirements that a theory with its proposed mediators and mechanisms of change needs to meet.

Strong Association

We have accumulated evidence suggesting significant correlations between the psychotherapeutic intervention and connecting and between connecting and therapeutic change (Fabi & Mergenthaler, 2004; Mergenthaler, 2003, 2004; Nicolò, Mergenthaler, Pontalti, Semerari, & Catania, 2000). The weakest aspect in our findings is that we have had access to outcome data after every session in only two cases (Kraemer, Lihl, & Mergenthaler, 2007). In the other studies, outcome was measured pre- and post-therapy, and hence we cannot definitely conclude that connecting caused change.

Specificity

The specificity of the association among the intervention, the mediator connecting, and outcome should ensure that only the connecting events account for change. In none of the studies done so far have patterns other than connecting been associated with outcome. With regard to therapist interventions, Walter (2008) has investigated the role of four types of therapeutic interventions on patient responses in terms of emotion-abstraction patterns, and found that challenge to facts resulted in a relaxing pattern, challenge to cognition resulted in a reflecting pattern, challenge to emotion resulted in an experiencing pattern, and challenge to integration of cognition and emotion resulted in a connecting pattern. This supports the specific function of each of the four patterns. Limberg (2008) took a closer look at therapist interventions before and after connecting events. He found that "encouraging patient to reflect" occurred significantly more often before connecting and "asking patient for facts" was significantly more frequent after connecting blocks.

Mergenthaler and Horowitz (1994) found that "therapeutic processing of conflictual topics is often accompanied by Shimmering States of Mind, which are associated with Connecting and Experiencing in the text analyses" (p. 392). Di Marino and Mergenthaler (2003) compared States of Mind that were rated from videotape without use of the soundtrack with emotion-abstraction patterns as derived from the transcript. They found that Well-modulated states correspond with Relaxing, Over-modulated with Reflecting, Under-modulated with Experiencing, and rapid shifts between the latter two states, that Horowitz calls Shimmering, with Connecting. This finding suggests a strong relationship between different levels of communication. What is said is also expressed with gesture and mimicry. It also supports the notion that Connecting is a moment of therapeutic change, as has been shown for the corresponding state of Shimmering independently in Horowitz' work (Horowitz, Ewert, & Milbrath, 1996).

Consistency

This is a requirement that concerns the replication of an observed result across studies, samples, and conditions. We have had the opportunity to apply the TCM to many different therapeutic orientations in individual therapy—client centered (Mergenthaler, 2003), cognitive (Nicolò et al., 2000), cognitive-behavioral (Kraemer et al., 2007), emotion focused (Lepper & Mergenthaler, 2008; Mergenthaler, 2004), psychoanalysis (Bucci, 1997, pp. 280–304), psychodynamic (Mergenthaler, 1996; Pfäfflin & Mergenthaler, 1998; Roussos, Acosta, Juárez, & Mergenthaler, 2001), and systemic (di Marino & Mergenthaler, 2003)—as well as in group therapy (Fontao & Mergenthaler, 2002; Lepper & Mergenthaler, 2005; Sabel, 2007). We found connecting events across all those therapies to be associated with outcome and treatment success. We have also examined a number of different diagnostic groups, including borderline personality disorder (Nicolò et al., 2000), schizophrenia (Kraemer et al., 2007), eating disorders (Fontao & Mergenthaler, 2005b; Michal, Overbeck, Grabhorn, Stirn, Mergenthaler, & Jordan, 2001), depression (Lepper & Mergenthaler, 2007; Mergenthaler, 2003, 2004), trauma (Mergenthaler, 1999), and more. Again here, we found connecting events across all those diagnostic groups to be associated with outcome and treatment success.

Experimental Manipulation

We have conducted two experimental studies that manipulate single aspects of the model to provide evidence for their effect within the model. One of these studies explored the effects of negation on cognitive skills (Maier, 2008). This aspect is important when broadening needs to be activated. A possible intervention is to use negated positive terms instead of negative formulations. The study supported the hypothesis that negated positive formulations such as "no good" result in a better performance on a problem-solving task than the linguistically corresponding negative term "bad," although semantically these two statements are similar.

In a speaking/writing task, Pfeiffer (2006) found evidence that the stimulation of the left hemisphere will result in more positive emotion and therefore in an increased capacity to solve problems.

Time Line

Causes and mediators must temporally precede change. We have some evidence from qualitative and clinical evaluations of cycles that they precede or coincide with change. Statistical support needs to be provided.

Gradient

The question of whether a gradient can be shown in which stronger doses or greater activation of connecting or more frequent cycles will be associated with greater change in the outcome has not yet been addressed. Clearly, it needs more than just a few cycles and connecting to achieve several mini-outcomes that lead to a general outcome. Possible answers and study plans may come from neurobiology, because it appears to be rather a question of at what rate neuro-plasticity occurs, of how much firing neural nets need to change their behavior and constitute persistent change. Phenomena like sudden gain and their neural correlates should be considered here.

Plausibility or Coherence

One of the major goals was to demonstrate plausibility or coherence of the explanation given with the resonating minds theoretical conception of how the TCM operates and how it is integrated in findings with other and broader scientific knowledge. Above all was the question, How plausible, or How feasible, is this approach to clinical practice? The TCM was first presented at the 1992 Society of Psychotherapy Research annual meeting at Berkeley, and initial feedback indicated that the model made sense to clinicians and that they could think of moments in their practice where they made an observation that fit the model. I give a very brief overview of ongoing and completed studies in which other scientific domains become integrated with the cycles model: attachment, conversation analysis, group therapy, metaphor, silences, rate of speech, meta-cognition.

Attachment

Several studies have shown that attachment style and connecting seem to be related. Dismissing participants had least connecting, preoccupied participants had most connecting, and securely attached participants showed a medium amount of connecting in the Adult Attachment Interview (Buchheim & Mergenthaler,

2000, 2002). Using the Adult Attachment Projective, securely attached participants were found to prefer preconstructed stories that represented a connecting pattern, in contrast with insecurely attached participants, whose preference was for experiencing or reflecting stories (Hölzer, 2007). Gril, Altmann, and Mergenthaler (2000) showed that connecting events were associated with signs of secure attachment of the mother with her baby.

Conversation Analysis

Conversation analytic theory is predicated on the assumption that speakers create interpersonal meaning by building each turn on the previous turn and creating the conditions for the following turn. It is a way of observing how minds resonate at the level of observable interaction. In a set of three studies—a single group therapy session (Lepper & Mergenthaler, 2005), a short-term psychodynamic individual therapy of eight sessions (Lepper & Mergenthaler, 2007), and a 15-session emotion-focused therapy (Lepper & Mergenthaler, 2008)—it has been shown that topic coherence and topic sequence length, key concepts in conversation analysis, are significantly higher within cycles and connecting word blocks. Further, the CM graphs identified moments in therapy sessions of heightened activity and therapeutic change, but also identified ruptures in the turn-by-turn interaction that could then be analyzed in more detail.

Group Therapy

CM analysis of the talk of patients in group therapy, taken as a whole, shows that cycles occur in the same way as in individual therapy (Fontao & Mergenthaler, 2002). This is striking evidence for resonating minds, connecting correlates with insight (Fontao & Mergenthaler, 2005a, 2005b, 2008).

Metaphor

Unconventional metaphors are more frequent in and before moments of connecting (Gelo, 2008; Gelo & Mergenthaler, 2003). This is seen as evidence for therapeutic change, because patients in such moments often miss words and use unconventional metaphoric language to express their new thoughts and feelings.

Silences

Following the Pausing Inventory categorizing system (Frankel, Levitt, Murray, Greenberg, & Angus, 2006), it has been shown that high reflective pauses—one of the productive silences—occur more often within a cycle and before connecting events. After high reflective pauses, we found more often experiencing (Mergenthaler & Levitt, 2005).

Rate of Speech

Tonti (2006) developed a computer-assisted system to measure rate of speech from audiotapes. Comparing these data with the CM language measures showed that high levels of emotion and abstraction tend to slow down speed. This may be due to elaboration or retrieval processes.

Meta-cognition

Semerari, Carcione, Dimaggio, Nicolò, and Procacci (2007) reported that difficulties with self-reflection as obtained with their Meta-Cognition Assessment Scale coincides with low frequency of connecting.

Other Applications

Kraemer et al. (2007) compared two cases of a cognitive-behavioral therapy (one good outcome, one poor outcome) and found key sessions marked by connecting in the good-outcome case and experiencing, which leads to a psychotic episode, in the poor-outcome case. A single case study with a sexual offender has provided a clear example of how this patient learned from the therapist how to connect feelings and thoughts (Böhmer, Mergenthaler, & Pfäfflin, 2003; Pfäfflin, Böhmer, Cornehl, & Mergenthaler, 2005). Ways of how the therapeutic cycles model and CM could be applied to supervision and training were shown by Mergenthaler (2002).

Most of these findings provide support for the concept of resonating minds and its empirical assessment with the TCM. It might be worth mentioning that no studies revealing inconsistencies or contradicting results have been found so far.

Future Directions

The RMT is a neurobiologically informed approach to the description and explanation of psychotherapeutic change. The TCM may provide a window for observation of the relationship among the neurobiological, psychological, and interpersonal levels of resonating minds. It associates psychological shifts with underlying shifts of regional cerebral blood flow or cerebral activity from the right hemisphere toward the left. In TCM, such shifts are observable on the psycholinguistic level.

Not represented in the resonating minds theoretical conception or in RMT are moderators like gender, setting, frequency, and therapist effect. Especially for language processing, an increasing number of studies (e.g., Kansaku, Yamaura, & Kitazawa, 2000) suggest that women use some brain areas more bilaterally during linguistic processing of global structures in a narrative than men do. However, hormonal dispositions, along with the menstrual cycle, have also been shown to influence emotion processing and interpersonal relations (e.g., Turner, Altemus, Enos, Cooper, & McGuinness, 1999). With regard to frequency, the effect of therapeutic interventions seems to be completely understudied. This and other criteria will have to inform our future research plans. The timing of interventions has had some attention (Gilboa-Schechtman & Shahar, 2006). It also might be of interest to see how the method presented here, and operating on a rather formal level, might converge with other more clinically oriented approaches to process research like the task analysis and especially the "events" that seem to show a similar structure as the therapeutic cycle (Greenberg, 2007).

Conclusions

We have been able to observe therapeutic cycles in at least nine distinct and common approaches to psychotherapy. Given Kazdin's notion that "it is not very likely that the different treatments produce change for different reasons" (2007, p. 4), shift events can be understood as interventions that lead to and are responsible for change regardless of the diverse therapeutic orientations. Connecting may be what many of these orientations share as a common mediator.

Advances in neuroscience research have led to a better understanding of how psychotherapy may affect the brain. The resonating minds theoretical conception takes this up, linking mind, brain, and psychotherapeutic activity with each other. All three are inseparable. This is not always reflected in the literature, although we find plenty of writing bringing together two corners of this triangle: mind with brain, brain with psychotherapy, and psychotherapy with mind. With this article, I hope to have started a reconstruction of the triad.

COMMENTARY

RESONATING MINDS THEORY—ANY RESONANCE?

The Resonating Minds Theory (RMT) and the Therapeutic Cycles Model (TCM) mainly were thought for psychotherapy process researcher in order to provide them with a theoretical framework and a tool for the empirical assessment of therapeutic discourse, but also for psychotherapists in clinical practice. The latter group resonated astonishingly well. It appears that the model that follows from the RMT fits clinical thinking and helps to better understand what is going on in a session. This seems to be independent from the therapeutic orientation. One therapist recently said that in a session with a patient, he found himself asking if his patient would have had already a "Connecting" today. Another one commented that he very often would realize the cycles that the model provides and thus he would have a better idea of the structure a session has.

On the research side, too, there was encouraging feedback and activity. Naturally, this was limited to some extent, as the empirical realization into a research endeavor needs transcripts from therapy sessions or other discourse. These are still costly resources and limit the potential circle of researchers.

Finally, and interestingly, the RMT found interest in fields other than psychotherapy. Currently there is a study under way where witnesses of the so called "Hamburg Fire Storm"—a massive fire in 1943 after the bombing of major parts of the city of Hamburg, Germany, in World War II—reported their memories 65 years later.

Since the publication of my Presidential Address a number of studies have been published that directly are based on the RMT. Gelo and Mergenthaler (2012) investigated the relationship between unconventional (i.e., creative) metaphors and emotional-cognitive regulation in a metacognitive interpersonal therapy (MIT). The occurrence of unconventional metaphor was identified using the Metaphor Analysis in Psychotherapy (MAP) model, and emotional-cognitive regulation was assessed by the TCM. The results showed that the dyad's frequency of unconventional metaphors is significantly related to emotional-cognitive integration, reflective processes and moments of therapeutic engagement based on the quality of such regulation. More specifically, client metaphors were associated with emotional-cognitive integration and moments of therapeutic engagement, while therapist metaphors were associated with reflective processes. The results suggest that unconventional metaphors may be considered markers for different cognitive-emotional regulatory processes and moments of heightened therapeutic work and change in MIT.

McCarthy et al. (2011) focused on psychodynamic change that is understood to occur in part through the unique therapeutic relationship developed between therapist and patient, and the subtle cycles of their conversation from relaxed connection to intense experiencing. The TCM and the Heidelberg Structural Change Scale (OPD Task Force, 2008) were used to investigate therapist-patient dynamic processes across 16 sessions of psychotherapy. The TCM identified interventions of the therapist instigating change in emotion-abstraction patterns. Structural personality change was higher in TCM cycles, and differed according to emotion-abstraction patterns. The interventions of the therapist promoted dynamic structural change in the patient. The findings demonstrate for the first time the interconnection between specific types of therapist and patient dialogue that promote deep changes.

Fontao et al. (2011) explored the therapeutic processes of a parents' group. The theoretical framework was the RMT, which describes therapeutic change by means of processes termed as "deepen-and-provide" and "broaden-and-build." In verbatim protocols, adherence to the therapy focus and group interaction were assessed. Furthermore, verbatim protocols were examined with a computerized text analytic tool to identify emotion-abstraction patterns. Evidence of the presence of "deepen-and-provide" processes was found in the initial phase.

Emotional tone was higher in later sessions. In patient protocols, evidence was found for "deepen-and-provide" and "broaden-and-build." The results are discussed taking into account the limits of a single case study.

Walter et al. (2010) examined the question of whether the dynamics of interpersonal plans in the psychotherapeutic process are reflected in the RMT, especially in the emotion-abstraction patterns (EAP; Relaxing, Experiencing, Connecting, Reflecting) in a single-case study. The activation of interpersonal plans was encoded in 10-second intervals by means of sequential plan analysis on the basis of video recordings. The EAP were identified in two-minute intervals on the basis of a transcript of the nine-session short-term therapy. The hypothesis that the dynamic complexity of plan activation time series of the patient increases during intensified phases of the EAP connecting was examined and supported. This can be considered an indicator for the occurrence of critical instabilities in the environment of order transitions in the direction of more strongly integrated states of processing.

In a single-case-design study, Fontao and Mergenthaler (2008) examined the relationships between therapeutic factors in group therapy and the language features of the group dialogue. Forty-two transcripts from a group treatment were investigated. EAP were identified for the group as a whole using computer-assisted text analysis, and therapeutic factors were rated by external judges using the Kiel Group Psychotherapy Process Scale. Significant positive relationships were found between insight and the EAP connecting and between catharsis and the EAP experiencing. Interpersonal learning output, catharsis, and self-disclosure showed higher scores in connection with the therapeutic cycle, which, according to the therapeutic cycle model, represents a sequence of EAP related to a successful therapeutic process. The current findings show that the use of EAP allows the identification of key moments in a group therapy process.

Lepper and Mergenthaler (2008) presented a pilot study that seeks to validate a method for the identification and analysis of clinically significant interactions in the psychotherapy process. Using a combined method, the authors demonstrate that the TCM can be used reliably to identify clinically significant events across sessions, which can then be analyzed at the level of the therapist-client interaction using conversation analysis, a discipline that has generated a substantial body of knowledge of how meaningful interaction is achieved by speakers on a turn-by-turn basis. The authors demonstrate that significant events can be compared within and across cases in order to understand how therapist interventions contribute to within-session micro-outcomes and, ultimately, to outcomes across populations of cases.

A few more studies and books that have been published in the mean time and related to the RMT were Walter et al. (2009), Mergenthaler & Gelo (2009), Mergenthaler and Casonato (2009), Casonato and Mergenthaler (2008), Gelo (2008), Toranzo, Taborda, Ross, Mergnethaler, and Fontao (2008), Angus, Goldman, and Mergenthaler (2008), and Walter (2008).

What I have not outlined in my Address, and only recently came to my attention and mind, is the fact that the RMT and the TCM may be used and understood beyond the limits of transcripts. It might well be that the basic variables like emotional tone, abstract thoughts and narrative style may be determined by other means than transcript analysis. A rating procedure of audio or video recordings may be one, but also a rating of a speaker's gesture and mimic may be subject to such an application.

Psychotherapy Research in the Near Future—What to Pay Attention to

Psychotherapy Process research will have to overcome boundaries that still seem to be given by the frame of a single session. The next step is to break up sessions into the next-smaller units given by the interaction of therapist and patient. The next goal of practice-oriented process research is to learn more about the impact of therapist interventions, about the meaning of patient statements, and the consequences of both in the interaction with regard to change. Such a new research paradigm nowadays can build on a solid amount of measures for session outcome, treatment outcome, change in all kinds, but also on typologies for therapist interventions and patient statements, and finally on methods and findings from qualitative research approaches. Additionally there is now an increasing number of studies and findings from neuroscience that can help to learn more about the brain and how it works in relation to verbal and other therapeutic interventions. What is missing are models of the psychotherapeutic process at the level of within-session interaction that allows to predict change and formulate hypotheses that can be assessed statistically. The RMT has made one first step toward such a new paradigm and, with the TCM, also has provided a tool to assess empirically therapeutic discourse guided by a theory.

18

TOWARD A WORKING THROUGH OF SOME CORE CONFLICTS IN PSYCHOTHERAPY RESEARCH (2009)[1]

Jacques P. Barber

The goal of this article is to review some core conflicts in the field of psychotherapy research by exploring the core beliefs that may be responsible for these disagreements. Specifically, I address six key statements, viewed as true by some and false by others, with a number of researchers' and clinicians' opinions falling somewhere between these two extremes.

The first of these statements is that the therapeutic alliance has a causal role in outcome. Second, therapeutic techniques are important in explaining patients' outcome. Third, the therapist determines psychotherapy outcome. Fourth, the patient determines therapy outcome. Fifth, randomized controlled trials (RCTs) provide valuable data and should be considered the gold standard of research methodology. Sixth, data from RCTs are almost worthless. Clearly, some of these statements appear to conflict with one another and, at least on the surface, could be considered mutually exclusive. These "truths," which some researchers take to be self-evident, can be compiled into three core conflicts as follows: (1) Is good therapeutic outcome a result of the alliance or of techniques? (2) Does the patient or therapist determine the outcome? (3) Are RCTs a blessing or a curse? In other words, are RCTs the main gateway to knowledge about the efficacy of psychotherapy or is the information they provide misleading?

Although one could also charge that these are "straw man" positions, I have seen exemplars of all of these statements made in various forms at different presentations or conferences, and it is perhaps not surprising that Society of Psychotherapy Research conventions generate such lively discussions. Further, it is not rare to see articles addressing only one side of the conflict. For example, we see numerous studies examining the relation between alliance and outcome, but few examining the impact of the Alliance x Technique interaction on outcome (e.g., Crits-Christoph & Connolly, 1999), as is shown later. I will not attempt to cover the large, often relevant, body of existing literature addressing these three core conflicts but will rather aim (1) to present some of the research that I have conducted that is relevant to these issues and (2) to convey some of my thoughts on how compromises can be created among these conflicting viewpoints and to delineate future research paths.

This article does not address other "big issues" or conflicts (e.g., the increasing use of drugs for psychological ailments and the fact that many psychotherapy patients are presecribed pharmacotherapy, the lack of funding for psychotherapy research despite its importance when disaster occurs).

First Core Conflict: Is Psychotherapy about the Alliance or about Techniques?

The Role of the Therapeutic Alliance

One of the most commonly studied psychotherapy constructs is the therapeutic alliance and its small but robust association with outcome (e.g, Martin, Garske, & Davis, 2000). Although alliance has a reliable effect, it unfortunately does not explain much outcome variance. An important question to ask is whether the therapeutic alliance has a causal role in outcome. The problem with some of the existing research, as pointed out by DeRubeis and Feeley (1990), is that many researchers have examined the correlation between the alliance measured at session X and change in some outcome measure from intake to termination. Therefore, as discussed in Barber, Connolly, Crits-Christoph, Gladis, and Siqueland (2000), many of these correlations may reflect the fact that the alliance itself is the product of earlier symptomatic change. For example, Barber et al. (2000) reported that that early change in symptoms predicted alliance level at session 5, and that alliance at session 5 predicted change in depressive symptoms from session 5 to the end of treatment. Furthermore, alliance predicted subsequent change in symptoms even after partialing out the impact of early change of symptoms on the alliance. Thus, this study showed that, although initial change in symptoms predicted alliance, alliance itself still predicted or induced subsequent change in symptoms (see also Klein et al., 2003), Table 18.1 summarizes all the studies that have examined this question suggesting no strong support for the hypothesis that the therapeutic alliance causes further improvement in symptoms. Because the studies from our group and from Klein et al. were based on therapies possessing a strong interpersonal emphasis, one could speculate that the alliance may have more of a causal role in those therapies. If alliance is not causally related to outcome, perhaps it could be associated with good outcome in the sense that if the alliance is high, then the therapy is going well.

TABLE 18.1 Predicting Subsequent Outcome from Alliance, Taking into Consideration the Temporal Sequence

Study	*N*	*r*	*Significance*
DeRubeis & Feeley (1990)	25	.10	No
Feeley, DeRubeis, and Gelfand (1999)	25	−.27	No
Barber et al. (1999)	252	.01[a]	No
Barber et al. (2000)	88	.30[a]	Yes
Barber et al. (2001)	291	.01[a]	No
Klein et al. (2003)	367	.14	Yes
Strunk, Brotman, and DeRubeis (2008)	60	.15	No

Source: Adapted from Strunk, Brotman, and DeRubeis (2008).

Note. [a]The average of more than one correlation.

Future Challenges for Research on the Alliance

I now focus on what may be five fruitful lines for additional research on the alliance:

1. Is the alliance a cause for change in different forms of psychotherapy (cognitive-behavioral therapy [CBT] vs. dynamic), or is it more akin to a thermometer?
2. Does the patient's main problem make a difference? The Barber et al. (1999, 2001) studies did not find support for the causal role of the alliance in the treatment of cocaine dependent patients. However, Barber et al. (2000) showed that alliance was causally related to outcome in depressed, anxious, and personality disorder patients in dynamic therapy. Thus, more systematic data are needed on the role of the alliance not only in different therapies but also with different kinds of patients (see DeRubeis, Brotman, & Gibbons, 2005).
3. Is there a ceiling effect with current measures of the alliance? Patients completing alliance measures usually rate their therapists very highly. This is not likely due to the patients' concern about hurting the therapists' feelings, because most studies keep therapists blind to results. It is also possible that most patients who have low alliance ratings drop out of therapy, leaving the rest in treatment. However, more data addressing this issue are needed.
4. What participant qualities are associated with good alliance? We know that good alliance is created very early in treatment. In fact, we have found that it is high before some patients even meet their therapists (Iacoviello, McCarthy, Barrett, Rynn, Gallop, & Barber, 2007). However, more research is required to demonstrate which specific participant qualities help create a good therapeutic alliance (see, for example, Connolly Gibbons, Crits-Christoph, de la Cruz, Barber, Siqueland, & Gladis, 2003).

5. How much does the patient or the therapist contribute to the strength of the therapeutic alliance? There are very few data on this issue, with the exception of the findings of Baldwin, Wampold, and Imel (2007), who showed that therapists are mainly responsible for the relation between alliance and outcome (this issue iscovered in more detail later).

The Role of Technique in Psychotherapy Research

A cursory review of the literature may convey the impression that many therapists feel that the alliance is the most important aspect of psychotherapy. However, when training young therapists, most instructors do not ask the trainees to focus only on the alliance and most also train their students in the skillful implementation of therapeutic techniques. I have been studying the role of techniques and alliance and their impact on outcome using measures of adherence and competence. Adherence is typically defined as the extent to which the therapist used prescribed techniques and avoided proscribed techniques as dictated by treatment manuals. Competence is the degree of skillfulness, nuance, and responsiveness with which the therapist delivers these interventions (Sharpless & Barber, 2009). Although my focus has been on the use of adherence-competence scales, it is important to acknowledge that a range of other methods exist for examining therapist techniques in psychotherapy, and these other methods have been useful in understanding the process of both naturalistic and manual-based psychotherapies (e.g., Stiles, Honos-Webb, & Surko, 1998).

How are techniques related to outcome? There is an implicit belief that the more therapists do something prescribed by the treatment protocol, the better the outcome will be. Thus, more interpretation of underlying conflicts and defenses will lead to more change. But what is the evidence that greater adherence to a particular manual leads to a better treatment outcome? Several authors did not did not find a relation between adherence and outcome (Elkin, 1988, for interpersonal therapy or CBT; Barber, Crits-Christoph, & Luborsky, 1996 in supportive expressive therapy [SET]). DeRubeis and Feeley (1990), however, found a relation between the use of concrete cognitive therapy (CT) techniques and outcome in CT for depression. Perhaps surprisingly, there appears to be no consistent evidence for a strong relation between adherence and outcome (e.g., Barber, Triffleman, & Marmar, 2007b). If adherence is not directly related to outcome, then how are the two related? Like many clinicians, Barber et al. (2006) suggested that the relation between adherence and outcome may be curvilinear and tested that hypothesis using data from the National Institute on Drug Abuse Collaborative Cocaine Treatment Study (CCTS; Crits-Christoph et al., 1999, N = 487). Those patients received individual drug counseling (IDC), CT, SET, or group drug counseling. The individual treatments were supplemented with group drug counselling. All providers were extensively trained. Contrary to expectations, this study demonstrated that IDC was more effective than the other treatments.

To understand what was helpful about IDC, Barber et al. (2006) found that linear adherence was not associated with drug use. Because the authors had access to a large sample (N = 95), they were able to examine several process research questions, including testing the clinically relevant hypothesis that a moderate amount of adherence was more effective than a high or low amount. As expected, they found a moderate effect size (*d* = 0.44) curvilinear relation between adherence and outcome.

An important question raised by these findings is whether they are specific to IDC. Barber et al. (2008) tested those questions in the 108 of the patients randomized to SET who had been treated by 13 therapists (nine women, four men) and who had the needed outcome data and adherence ratings The scale assessed therapist use of both supportive and expressive (interpretative) techniques with an additional emphasis on the SET techniques related to cocaine dependence (Barber, Krakauer, Calvo, Badgio, & Faude, 1997). An example of a cocaine-related technique is whether the therapist relates the appearance of urges during the session to components of the core conflictual relationship theme.

Barber et al. (2008) also reported that, contrary to predictions, the relation was that the more a therapist was adherent to SET principles, the worse the patient's outcome was. Similarly, the less competently delivered the dynamic therapy, the lower the patient's drug use. These findings were certainly puzzling, because SET patients improved quite a lot, even if they did not improve as much as patients who received IDC. In light of the fact that the greater use of SET techniques was associated with worse outcome, the authors examined whether the dynamic psychotherapists were doing something else in addition to the techniques prescribed by the manual. Barber, Foltz, Crits-Christoph, and Chittams (2004) used each individual treatment adherence-competence scale to rate each of the three individual therapies (SET, IDC, and CBT). Using the IDC adherence and competence ratings from a subgroup of patients (N = 34) who had received SET, they reported a large effect size (*d* = 0.81) curvilinear relation between the use of IDC techniques and outcome in SET patients. More specifically, those SET patients who received a moderate amount of (presumably unintentional) IDC interventions during their treatment improved the most. The number of IDC interventions found in SET was somewhat lower than in IDC. Again, however, the pattern of results reported by Barber et al. (2006) in regard to the IDC group using the IDC scale was replicated among the SET patients using the IDC scale. Barber et al. (2008) then tested how the combination of dynamic psychotherapy techniques and direct counseling techniques helped patients' outcome. They found that both sets of adherence scales (IDC *d* = 1.33; SET *d* = 0.88) predicted patients' outcome. As shown in Figure 18.1, it is clear that, as adherence to IDC increases and adherence to SET decreases, patients'

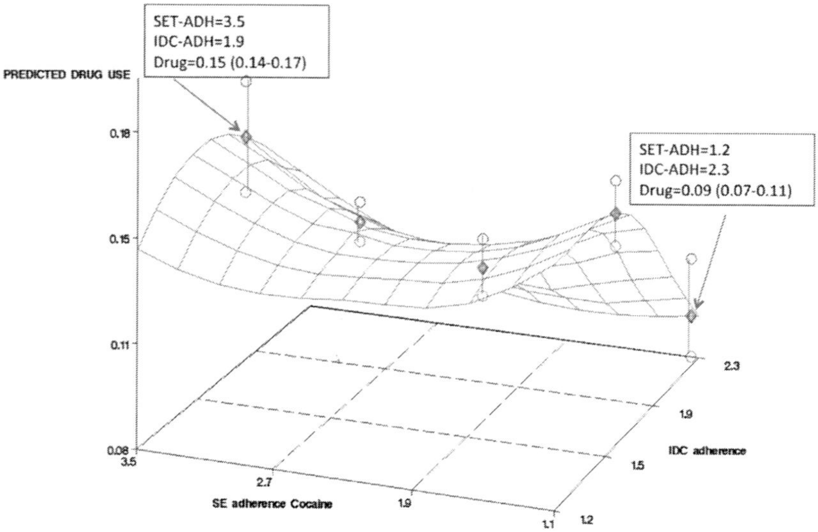

FIGURE 18.1 Patients' Drug Use as a Function of Adherence (Adh) to Dynamic Therapy and to Individual Drug Counseling (IDC)

Note: SET = supportive-expressive therapy.

outcomes improve. Focusing on two actual patients depicted in Figure 18.1, one can see that the patient on the left was still using a moderate amount of drugs (predicted Addiction Severity Index Composite Drug Use [ASI] = 0.14–0.17), and his therapy was characterized by relatively high adherence to SET and moderate adherence to IDC. In contrast, the patient on the right of the "saddle" had low adherence to SET but high adherence to IDC, and his predicted ASI Composite Drug indicated decreased drug use.

Another means of explaining the lack of a direct, linear relation between adherence and outcome is whether or not the competent delivery of treatment may be responsible for patients' outcome rather than adherence. A few studies have found evidence for the role of competence (e.g., Barber et al., 1996; Shaw et al., 1999). However, others have shown that competent delivery of dynamic techniques ended up being associated with poorer outcome (Barber et al., 2008; Svartberg & Stiles, 1994).

Finally, another reason why linear adherence may not be associated with outcome is perhaps explainable by the more global nature of these measures and the obvious fact that they do not focus on the occurrence of a specific technique at a specific point in treatment. Similarly, it could be that examining adherence alone does not allow for the evaluation of the interactive nature of the therapeutic encounter, where therapists are responsive to patients' expressions (e.g., Stiles et al., 1998).

Summary of the Role of Techniques

The research presented here regarding the role of techniques in relation to outcome leads to the following conclusions. First, delivery of therapeutic techniques is related to outcome in a way that is not necessarily linear. Second, the competent delivery of techniques is associated with outcome. Third, the use of intended interventions may have unintended consequences. Fourth, outcome is associated at times with the use of unintended interventions or even a combination of both intended and unintended interventions (e.g., Jones & Pulos, 1993). Some of these findings are associated with RCT research, and it is undoubtedly the case that working with RCTs enables one to explore these types of questions. At the same time, the research presented here does not address the all-important question relating to how the delivery of one specific intervention (rather than a treatment or a package of interventions) impacts a theoretically relevant construct, which then results in a more distal outcome. Undoubtedly, more theoretically derived research of the impact of specific interventions on targeted theoretically relevant constructs is needed.

Future Questions Regarding the Study of Techniques

Many questions remain in the domain of studying techniques including the need for greater theoretical knowledge and specificity about which techniques really matter and which may better be classified as clinical lore. A second issue is how supportive techniques (including acceptance) complement and possibly interact with more active techniques (such as interpretation) in explaining good outcome. A third question to address is how the use of different therapeutic techniques changes during the course of therapy. A fourth question is to what extent evaluating therapists' competence involves the assessment of therapists' responsiveness (Stiles et al., 1998). Finally, to what extent is outcome due to unintended or even nontheoretically relevant interventions?

Possible Steps Toward a Resolution of the Core Conflict Between Relationship Variables and Therapeutic Interventions

The way I have described my research on alliance and techniques thus far seems to indicate that when I conduct research on technique, I ignore the therapeutic relationship. However, it is quite obvious that the therapeutic relationship and techniques are intertwined and indeed work together. Surprisingly, there is relatively little empirical work in this area (e.g., Crits-Christoph & Connolly, 1999; Gaston, Thompson, Gallagher, Cournoyer, & Gagnon, 1998). Barber et al. (1996) examined whether the competent delivery of expressive techniques predicted outcome over and above the effect of alliance. In this sample of depressed patients treated with SET, the competent delivery of interpretive (expressive) technique

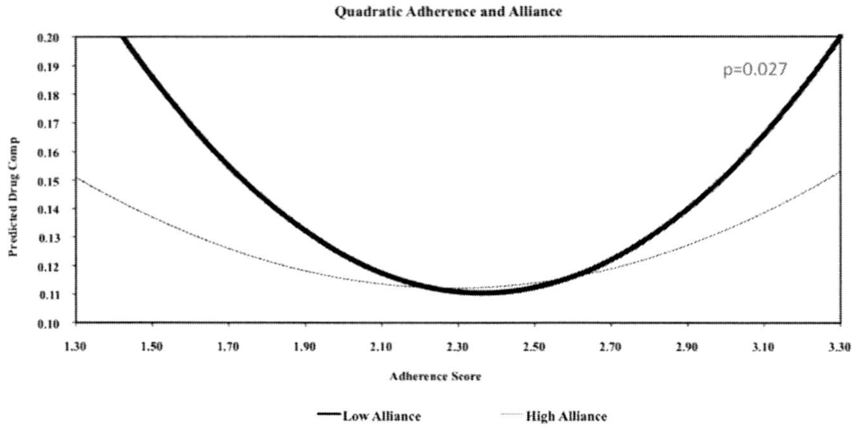

FIGURE 18.2 Do Alliance and Techniques Predict Outcome in Individual Drug Counseling?

Source: Barber et al. (2006).

was the main predictor of outcome, and not the alliance (Barber et al., 1996). In fact, competent delivery of expressive techniques predicted subsequent change in depressive symptoms over and above both the level of the therapeutic alliance and the earlier change in symptoms.

In the aforementioned study of IDC for cocaine dependence, Barber et al. (2006) explored more complex relations between adherence and alliance and found that alliance interacted with curvilinear adherence in predicting outcome (Figure 18.2). A significant interaction between alliance and curvilinear adherence was found. The magnitude of the effect size of this interaction suggested that it was moderate in scope (d = 0.44). For patients who had a low alliance with their therapists, the curvilinear relation between adherence and outcome was more pronounced. In other words, for those patients a moderate amount of adherence generated a good outcome. For patients with a high alliance, the relation between adherence and outcome was less pronounced. In summary, one could say that a strong therapeutic alliance negated the impact of the counselor's adherence to IDC model, but that adherence was critical to the improvement of patients with low alliance.

Thus, it seems quite clear that patient outcome is associated with both alliance and technique. A difficulty is how to be simultaneously mindful of both of these aspects of therapeutic process. The relation among the therapeutic relationship, techniques, and outcome is a complex phenomenon that is constantly changing over time. This complexity is further compounded by the fact that these relations may vary as a function of patients' presenting problem and perhaps as a function of the type of therapy they receive as well. Working through what is perhaps an exaggerated dichotomy between the therapeutic relationship and techniques requires the ongoing confrontation of incorporating these two aspects of the therapeutic encounter in their research.

Future Research on the Alliance and Techniques

An issue that should be addressed in the future is how to pinpoint what the essential techniques are and how these interact with alliance to bring about patient improvement. As techniques and alliance impact on outcome, are they dependent on patients' problems, the specific therapies, or both? Many clinical researchers and clinicians conduct treatment using interventions that they believe are effective, and in many cases patients change. At times, one may conclude that these changes are due to interventions that are believed to have been delivered (whether that intervention is interpretation, exposure, or acceptance). However, there are other possibilities, because it is conceivable that patients change because of: (1) something that was done but the therapist did not think much of it, (2) therapists not thoroughly doing something they thought they did, or (3) the fact that techniques outside of their chosen modality were included. In addition, sometimes it might be a combination of both the intended and unintended interventions that induces change which may require researchers to keep an open mind about which interventions they should assess when studying the therapeutic process. Further, do these processes change with different patients and withn different forms of therapy? Creating and using multitheoretical scales to examine therapists' interventions is of great theoretical and practical utility (e.g., McCarthy & Barber, 2009). Finally, it is important to gather knowledge about what the therapist and patient respectively contribute to these diverse processes.

Second Core Conflict: Is it All About the Patient or All About the Therapist?

In thinking about the kinds of findings reported previously, one may have the tendency to assume that therapists are responsible for the outcome, and that they have a major role in developing the interaction between adherence and alliance (i.e., that this is what really predicts patient outcome). Barber and Gallop (2008) have shown that in the IDC condition there was a range of outcomes for each therapist and that some therapists, on average, were better than others. Barber and Gallop also demonstrated that therapists differed in their overall level of adherence, with some therapists having overall higher adherence. However, there was a range of adherence scores for each patient that the therapist saw. Furthermore, significant differences between therapists (in terms of the levels of their scores) were found, and this likely reflects the interaction of the alliance with curvilinear adherence. One may infer that therapists were responsible for those differences.

So how can one determine whether these differences are due to the patient or the therapist? Using multilevel modeling, Baldwin et al. (2007) showed that the variance among therapists was responsible for the impact of alliance on outcome. Using the same methods, Barber and Gallop (2008) found that patient variance was responsible for the impact of the interaction of alliance and curvilinear adherence on outcome, and almost no variance was due to differences between therapists. More specifically, they found that patients explained about 24 percent of the outcome variance, whereas the therapist only explained 4 percent, and that finding of 4 percent was not even significant.

Conclusions Regarding Patient and Therapist Contributions to Outcome

Like prior researchers, Barber and Gallop (2008) have shown that therapists differ in their efficacy. However, they have also shown that patient factors seem to impact on important process variables such as adherence, the therapeutic alliance, and their interactions, which all have a bearing on outcome. Steps toward working through the conflict of emphasizing patients' variance on one hand or, instead, emphasizing therapists' variance on the other hand, require researchers to keep in mind that both patients and therapist variables seem to make a difference. Most importantly, the field now has the tools to study these kinds of questions.

Future Research on Patient and Therapist Contributions to Process and Outcome

Research on patient and therapist contributions to the process and outcome of therapy is going to blossom. Until now, the methodological tools (or maybe the interest) to dissect the contributions of the patient and therapist were not available. Using these tools, researchers will be able to investigate the relative contributions of using a variety of both outcome and process variables across a wide range of disorders and interventions. Finally, one will need to investigate the source of these contributions: What is it about the patient and about the therapist that can really make a difference? Hill (2005) suggested patients' involvement, and others have considered motivation for change.

Third Core Conflict: Do Randomized Controlled Trials Provide Valuable Data or Not?

Let me begin by suggesting that if the readers require treatment for a loved one who is ill, they would appreciate having data available from an RCT to help determine the best course of treatment, and they would prefer data coming from an RCT to data from a naturalistic trial or clinical lore. RCTs have many advantages—they reduce biases, minimize uncontrolled differences between groups, increase confidence that results from the experimental group differ from those of the control group, provide opportunities to define clearly both the treatment and the population to adequately generalize results, enable researchers to use powerful statistical analyses.

Despite these advantages, RCTs also have many shortcomings (e.g., Kazdin, 2008). Before focusing on criticisms of RCTs that, to the best of my knowledge, have not been often made (yet may be valid), it is important to discuss a common criticism of RCTs that, in my experience, is not valid. One assumption of RCTs is that the patients involved are representative of the patient population at large. Critics of RCTs claim that these trials include easy and simple cases only, and that these patients are dissimilar to patients seen in private or community practices. In my experience, this may have been the case in the past; however, in recent studies, this has clearly changed, and most clinicians who participate in RCTs would readily agree. Many practitioners treat clients who pay large sums of money (out of pocket) for psychotherapy. Such fortunate patients, generally, do not often come to psychotherapy RCTs. In the United States today, most of the patients seen in psychotherapy trials are those who cannot afford to pay even $20 per session to see a therapist. With such financial limits, the patients seen in RCTs may not be representative of the patients other clinicians see, but they are certainly not easy, straightforward cases. Stirman, DeRubeis, Crits-Christoph, and Brody (2003) presented data suggesting that samples in RCTs of psychotherapy are representative of community outpatients, except for the fact that patients with adjustment disorders who are often seen in clinical work are not often studied in RCTs.

I now raise criticisms of RCTs that are rarely made but that appear to be valid. One concerns the belief that there should be only one difference between the treatment group and the control group. In reality, it is rarely the case that there is only one difference between the two groups when one conducts psychotherapy research. For example, most RCTs involve different therapists. By using different therapists (who cannot be randomly assigned) and different patients, there is already more than one difference between the two groups (Borkovec & Castonguay, 1998). One obvious solution is to use the same therapists in both treatment groups. However, using the same therapist creates new problems, because there is now the possibility of allegiance effects for one treatment over another. Even if the therapists in these studies have no allegiance to a specific modality, it may not be representative of clinical practice (where therapists tend to be committed to a certain way of conducting therapy).

RCTs also have the implicit assumption that patients with the same diagnoses are similar and that they will respond to the same treatment. However, in light of the high comorbidity of psychological problems and heterogeneity of symptom presentations, it is quite likely that two patients with the same Axis I diagnosis will have different responses. In their reanalysis of Elkin et al.'s (1989) study, Barber and Muenz (1996) showed that depressed patients with avoidant personality disorder benefited more from CT, whereas those with obsessive-compulsive personality disorders benefited more from interpersonal therapy.

Connected to the earlier discussions of adherence and competence, another problem with RCTs is that different experts might not consistently agree that a specific therapy session was delivered accurately and with finesse, raising questions about the treatment integrity of the way the therapies are conducted, even in RCTs. This is especially a problem for the cognitive, humanistic, and dynamic therapies, although possibly less of a challenge in the case of structured behavioral therapies such as prolonged exposure (e.g., for PTSD). More work, both theoretical and empirical (as discussed in Barber, Sharpless, Klostermann, & McCarthy, 2007a, and Sharpless & Barber, 2009), could help to remedy this difficult situation.

The final problem I raise in regard to RCTs is more pragmatic. RCTs are enormously expensive and time-consuming. There is obviously a real and very finite limit to the number of RCTs that even very productive leaders in the psychotherapy research field can conduct during their lifetimes. Very few researchers will conduct more than five trials in their career. So how many RCTs can all psychotherapy researchers as a group conduct? And at what financial and temporal cost? Keep in mind that there is a large number of possible diagnoses and a very large number of possible comorbidity combinations, and that there are many forms of therapy to remedy these diagnoses and diagnostic combinations, so there is no feasible way to conduct enough RCTs to cover all disorders and treatments.

In summary, RCTs are crucial and provide important, high-quality data, but they have real limitations when applied to the study of psychotherapy. Even if there were no epistemological or methodological problems with RCTs, it is impossible to conduct enough of them to meet our needs for evidence and accountability. So it is apparent that RCTs must be somehow supplemented with other types of evidence. A question remains, of course, as to how to best accomplish this task.

Toward a Multifaceted Approach to Study Psychotherapy Research

One way of addressing these issues is to conduct naturalistic studies with large samples. Stiles, Barkham, Mellor-Clark, and Connell (2008) collected data from 33,587 patients seen by 637 therapists at 34 primary care services. They focused on therapists who delivered CBT, client-centered psychotherapy, and psychodynamic psychotherapy. Using patients' self-report, they found no significant difference in outcome between the three groups. However, see the criticisms from Clark, Fairburn, and Wessely (2008). Although there are perhaps methodological problems with Stiles et al.'s particular study, future studies could clearly learn from this discussion and be improved in ways that they can better answer Clark et al.'s criticisms, remain fairly naturalistic, and not utilize randomization. A relatively simple way to improve such naturalistic studies would be to assess patients more thoroughly so as to engender confidence in the patients' diagnoses. One would also need to know more about why specific therapists included specific patients in the study and, further, why particular patients approached a particular therapist as opposed to another. Finally, it would be advisable to have a better operationalization of the treatment while maintaining fidelity to practice in order to ensure that the CBT or dynamic therapies that were implemented were indeed acceptable versions.

As stated, psychotherapy RCTs are important and beneficial but very expensive. For the most part, only governmental agencies are funding them, in contrast to pharmacotherapy trials funded by pharmaceutical companies. Therefore, they are difficult to implement in high numbers. These issues related to RCTs are not often mentioned as problems in the field, and it may be that the manifest difficulty of the conflict makes researchers not want to keep them in the foreground. Even if readers do not agree with these points, they are still likely to agree with the appraisal that there are clearly major strengths and weaknesses to both RCTs and the more naturalistic studies of psychotherapy outcome. It seems clear that methodological pluralism could be a fruitful approach for the study of both the efficacy and the mechanisms of psychotherapy.

As a corollary of this, one often considers data from these divergent methods when thinking practically about which types of treatment would benefit our patients. Flexibility is an important quality that most psychotherapists and researchers value in their own lives and the lives of their patients. This is important, because there might not be clear and simple answers that work for all patients, treatments, therapists, and disorders. In closing, I foresee an interesting future for our field of psychotherapy research, and there appears to be a sufficient number of questions and problems to keep at least several generations of researchers quite busy. More work needs to examine why some patients change in some treatments and whether there are ways to help more treatment-refractory patients. In light of our subject matter's inherent high level of complexity, it seems reasonable for us to proceed with a measured respect for what has worked, an openness to new approaches, and a healthy skepticism toward methods that promise more than seems reasonable. Looking at the larger picture, it is my hope that what we have learned in the clinics regarding what helps and what impedes change can be used by the next generation of researchers to solve some of the problems facing humanity such as war and intolerance.

Note

1 This article was written with support from National Institute of Mental Health Grants DA MH 061410 and MH 070664. I thank Louis Castonguay, Dianne Chambless, Paul Crits-Christoph, Robert J DeRubeis, Edna Foa, Shabad-Ratan Khalsa, J. Christopher

Muran, Michelle Newman, and Brian Sharpless for their comments on earlier versions of this Presidential Address and for their overall support. I also thank my research colleagues around the world who have contributed to my research in general, including some of the work included in this Address. At the University of Pennsylvania, I especially would like to mention Marna Barrett, Dianne Chambless, Paul Crits-Christoph, Robert J DeRubeis, Guy Diamond, Robert Gallop, Mary Beth Connolly Gibbons, Lester Luborsky, Brian Sharpless, and Michael Thase; at Cornell University (New York), Barbara Milrod; at the Karolinska Institute (Stockholm), Marie Asberg, Alexander Wilczek, Bo Vinnars, and my late friend Robert Weinryb; and in Israel, Hadas Wiseman, Orya Tishby, Gary Diamond, and Gaby Schefler. Finally, I thank my wife, Smadar Auerbach-Barber, and my children, Natalie and Adam, whose father was always disappearing around Father's Day to go to the Society for Psychotherapy Research meeting.

19

LEAVING "SPLENDID ISOLATION"

Why Psychotherapy Trainees and Researchers Should Communicate with Each Other (Unpublished)[1]

Bernhard M. Strauss

Many former SPR presidents have emphasized the problematic relationship between research and practice (e.g., Greenberg, 1991), yet the relationship between *psychotherapy training* and research has remained a back seat topic over the past 20 years (with some marginal exceptions, e.g., Aveline, 2005b). Empirical evidence about psychotherapy training has been summarized in a handful of review articles during the last decades. These reviews have uniformly stressed the urgent need to promote training research and to organize psychotherapy training according to evidence based principles (e.g., Binder, 1993; Boswell & Castonguay, 2007; Laireiter & Botermans, 2005; Matarazzo & Petterson, 1986).

This Presidential Address is focused on training and is formulated from a European perspective. The selection of the training focus was motivated by many personal experiences from training programs which, in a "*splendid isolation,*"[2] often seem to be satisfied if "established answers" remain unquestioned by researchers (cf. Greenberg, 1991). Another motive to accentuate training aspects in this manuscript arose from the intensive work on a research expertise under the aegis of the author which was initiated by the German Ministry of Health with the aim to evaluate the training of "psychological psychotherapists and child and adolescent psychotherapists" in Germany. This expertise (Strauss et al., 2009) is based on several training related studies and was sent to the Ministry in May 2009 in order to stipulate a reform of the current training system in this country.

This article will focus on three different issues:

1. Some central questions of psychotherapy training research will be stressed and related to a tentative schema for organizing psychotherapy training research

based on selected results from the German expertise which aimed to evaluate an entire national training system.

2. Since psychotherapy training curricula in European countries are clearly connected to specific theoretical models (e.g., CBT, psychodynamic, humanistic therapy, etc.), it is suggested that trainees should be systematically taught about integrative and overarching, but also about research-based concepts to expand their theoretical perspectives. This will be exemplary discussed in relation to interpersonal theories and the author's studies focusing on attachment issues. In addition, the group setting is advocated as an excellent field to study these theories and as an important area for trainees to experience the interpersonal process and the group's potential for psychotherapeutic change.
3. Finally, based on the observations that there is an increasing isolation of training curricula from societal and political discussions and perspectives, the article concludes with some subjective reflections on the question of what psychotherapy trainees *and* researchers should do to maintain a critical view of the current cultural, economic, and social developments that will necessarily affect psychotherapy in the future.

Psychotherapy Research Related to Psychotherapy Training: Selected Results from the German Research Expertise

In the following, psychotherapy training (usually conceptualized as a postgraduate training) is defined as a process lasting several years and ranging from stages where the training is focused on skills and basic theory to more advanced stages where clinical practice and supervision becomes more important. The training aims to enable trainees to practice as a psychotherapist. Many of the following results are related to the German health system, but may also apply to other training systems. A recent discussion about changes of the training systems in Europe was initiated because of changes related to the entry requirements for training candidates. These changes were due to the introduction of Bachelor and Masters programs in the entire European university system (which was called the "Bologna process," because the European countries decided to reform the system during a meeting in Bologna, Italy). The decision to introduce the Bachelor and Masters curricula has led to a radical change of the entire educational system in German colleges and universities. This was the main reason why the German Ministry of Health ordered a research expertise to evaluate the current psychotherapy training system in Germany. An additional reason was the fact that the German system still continues to differentiate between the entry requirements for psychotherapists treating adults and for those who treat children and adolescents. Accordingly, the experts were expected to address the future organization of these two different training models. The current psychotherapy training—at least for non-medical professionals—is organized according to a German "Psychotherapy Law" that was incepted in 1999 (cf. Strauss, 2009).

After 10 years of experience with this training system, some problems were obvious. Financial difficulties are one of the most prominent problems trainees have to face, especially during their time as interns in psychiatric hospitals, and these are usually not recompensated. In addition, there are still discrepancies between the medical and the non-medical psychotherapy training systems leading to the question whether the two systems should be revised in the future.

Hence, the research highlighted the following major goals:

a. an evaluation of the current situation of psychotherapy training in Germany, i.e. the entire training system
b. a description of current training developments in Germany in comparison to other (European) countries
c. recommendations for the content and organization of the Bachelor and Master's programs for psychology, education and social sciences as a basis for psychotherapy training
d. recommendations for the future entry requirements for the training in psychotherapy, adult psychotherapy and child and adolescent psychotherapy.

Many of these questions are clearly connected to the German health and educational system, which has some unique features when compared to other European countries (for a detailed description of the pattern of psychotherapeutic professionalization and practice in Germany, cf. Strauss, 2009).

The data sources for the evaluation primarily consisted of a number of surveys from training institutions (i.e., organizations that provide almost all components of training, most of them are privately organized, some are associated with university programs; we first surveyed in two waves: 161 and then again 129 training institutions out of a total 173 at the time of the study), graduate students in psychology (N = 480), trainees (N = 3,223), trainers and supervisors (N = 2,196) as well as alumni (N = 666). In addition, data were collected from hospitals providing internships and from all 16 governmental institutions regulating the training in the different (16) states of the Federal Republic of Germany. An international survey was conducted to gain perspective on the situation in different European countries. Finally, a Delphi-survey was performed, including a large number of experts in the field, as well as scientific and professional organizations. The surveys were combined with qualitative analyses of training programs and curricula. The data collection was concluded with an expert panel held in Berlin in January 2009. The samples were large enough to draw generalizable conclusions especially among the alumni (N = 666), the current trainees (N = 3,223), as well as the current trainers and supervisors (N = 2,196).

Detailed results from the entire research (Strauss et al., 2009) and the single surveys have been published in several articles (e.g., Glaesmer et al., 2010; Kohl et al., 2009; Michels-Lucht et al., 2009; Sonntag et al., 2009; Strauss & Kohl, 2009).

In general, the surveys revealed that different subgroups indicated a high level of satisfaction with the current training system and its components. The most important component for most of the current trainees and the alumni was the *therapeutic practice under supervision.* Learning specific skills and techniques, theoretical knowledge related to different therapeutic orientations as well as case-related learning, were mentioned as the most important tasks. In general, the surveys indicated a preference for a postgraduate training following a degree in Psychology with a focus on one specific psychotherapy theory (in Germany, this means predominantly either CBT or Psychodynamic Psychotherapy).

The following paragraphs summarize a small selection of results that might be of interest for an international readership and that relate to other issues discussed in this article.

The trend towards CBT in training: According to our surveys, the German training system comprises a total of 173 training institutions (with only a minority related directly to university programs). Of these, 99 institutes provide psychodynamic training; and 81, CBT training. There were only two institutes which provide training in client-centered therapy (CCT). Although CCT has been accepted for training from a scientific point of view, it has not been certified from the perspective of social legislation (cf. Strauss, 2009). In contrast to the distribution of the treatment modalities in the institutes, the current percentage of candidates undergoing CBT training was 71 percent, whereas only 28 percent of the trainees had chosen a psychodynamic training (1 percent, a client centered training). In our sample of the alumni, the relationship was 78 percent CBT versus 22 percent other. The distribution appeared to be slightly different in the field of child and adolescent psychotherapy, with 62 percent in CBT, and 38 percent in psychodynamic training. This might be due to the fact that trainees within the child and adolescent field cover a broader spectrum of university education (including education and social sciences), whereas trainees in adult psychotherapy are exclusively psychologists.

As expected, we found a wide range of *reasons for the selection of a specific treatment* approach. One result of our studies was, that psychology students from universities with a clear focus on CBT also indicated a clear preference for a CBT training, whereas students from those universities (a dramatically shrinking minority) with a psychodynamic focus showed a higher preference for a psychodynamic training (cf. Figure 19.1). Table 19.1 summarizes the reasons for the selection of CBT versus psychodynamic training, clearly indicating that those with a preference for CBT value more pragmatic reasons (e.g., costs, scientific background) compared to those preferring psychodynamic psychotherapy (e.g., specific personal interest, the specific idea of man, etc.).

The research expertise thoroughly evaluated the individual *components of the psychotherapy training*, such as the training in theory, personal therapy, internships, supervision, or practical training. Interestingly, the surveys of the trainees and the alumni suggested that trainees undergoing psychodynamic training were

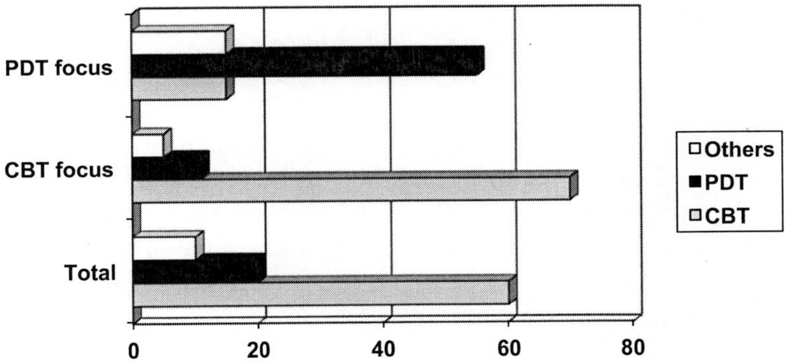

FIGURE 19.1 Percentage of Students (Total Sample N = 480) Who Prefer PDT, CBT, or Other Training Depending on the Theoretical Focus of Their Psychology School (from Strauss et al., 2009)

TABLE 19.1 Reasons for Selecting a Specific Psychotherapy Training (CBT vs. PDT)

Reasons	*CBT (%)*	*PDT (%)*
Costs	28	10
Most knowledge	18	6
Requested by institutions	11	2
Expected scientific background	33	9
Evidence based	56	10
Most agreement	44	49
Specific personal interest	39	63
Allows access to health system	61	55
Convincing theory	57	57
Idea of man	45	73

significantly more satisfied with theoretical training, personal therapy, and supervision, whereas CBT trainees judged the value of personal therapy as the least important component in their training program. On the other hand, psychodynamic training was seen as more profound, but also of longer duration and consequently more expensive. Taken together, this may explain the differences in the trainees' satisfaction.

Some further detailed results of the survey are mentioned below in relation to the international literature on training research. One specific result that appears precarious to mention at this point relates to the marked differences of the psychotherapy (training) systems in the European countries despite the political movement towards a unified Europe. Our data are based on an *international expert survey* from 21 countries, all members of the European Union (EU, for details see Strauss & Kohl, 2009). While all countries allow medical doctors and psychologists to have access to psychotherapeutic training, there are tremendous differences in the training from country to country for the professions such as social workers, pedagogues, nurses, theologists, or teachers. In addition, the most marked differences in the training and health service systems were found with respect to the existing legal regulations (only 47 percent of the countries possess a legal regulation of psychotherapy at all). Differences were also found regarding the protection of the title of a psychotherapist, the compensation of psychotherapy within the health system, the differentiation between adult and child/adolescent psychotherapy, the number of accepted treatment modalities (ranging from 2–4, i.e., CBT, psychodynamic, humanistic, systemic, to even 22 in some countries), the institutionalization of the training (university versus private institutes), rules for examinations and licensing, as well as the duration of the training and its costs. Apart from quality standards, the differences between EU countries raise questions about the future European legal regulations that inescapably must be expected within the next decade. One observation from our international survey was that those countries with a high quality standard for psychotherapy training appear to have the highest probability that psychotherapy will be included in and compensated by the national health system.[3]

Many of the questions and results from the German research expertise may be connected to some central questions of psychotherapy training research. These will be discussed in the following section.

Some Central Questions of Psychotherapy Training Research

Questions regarding the training situation have stimulated the development of a tentative schema to organize psychotherapy training research which is shown in Table 19.2.

This schema mainly differentiates between three levels of variables which have been proven to be useful in another model that is very common in psychotherapy research, i.e., the generic model of psychotherapy (Orlinsky & Howard, 1987). The generic model also discriminates between input, process and output variables, and implicitly—as seen in Table 19.2—includes the background perspective of cultural, legal, social, ethical, and financial regulations of psychotherapy, which normally constitute the basic conditions for the provision of psychotherapeutic help within a country or a sociological entity (Orlinsky, 2008).

From the *input variables*, the entire personal background of the trainees, their personality, pre-training, and clinical experience could be summarized as well as variables determining the choice of specific training, their individual motivation and interest, but also psychological variables that might be subject of change during the entire training period. Additionally, from the input variables basic

TABLE 19.2 A Schema for the Arrangement of Research Results Related to Psychotherapy Training

Background	**Culture** legal, ethical, social and financial regulations/foundations of psychotherapy-entry requirements, general status of psychotherapy within the health system
Input	Personal background of the **trainees**, motives for professional decisions, personality (self-efficacy, vulnerability, etc.)(clinical) experience, selection/preference of a psychotherapeutic orientation, general motivation, specific interest **Training institute, teachers, therapists, supervisors** curriculum, admission requirement, examinations, teaching concept, psychotherapeutic theory, qualification and personal background of the staff, standards of quality assurance
Process	Goals, content, and concept of training (e.g. disorder-, general factor-orientation), quality characteristics, operationalizations (e.g., helping skills), training methods, psychotherapeutic skills and their mastery **Group process** within the training groups, the institution, etc.negative effects, general development (individualization, autonomy, dependency, [over-] identifications) **Training components:** personal therapy, practical training, theoretical training, supervision, internships, additional choices, satisfaction and evaluation
Output	Micro- and macro-outcomes (examinations, goal attainment, etc.) expertise/competence, negative effects, professional integration, lifelong learning, change of interests, post-training socialization, personal growth, distress, self-care

conditions and characteristics of the training institution and its staff such as program features, curricula, program structure and the qualification of supervisors, trainers, and teachers can be considered.

One example of research questions related to input, has already been mentioned as a result of the research expertise, i.e., the *question of the determinants for choosing a therapeutic orientation.* In a recent study, Heffler and Sandell (2009) differentiated several "learning styles" (Kolb, 1984; classified as a preference for either doing, thinking, watching, or feeling) in a sample of trainees by examining the relationship between the individuals´ learning styles and their preference for a specific theoretical orientation: One of the major results of the study was that students who selected a psychodynamic treatment for their training continuously preferred a "feel and watch" style of learning, whereas the CBT candidates increasingly favored a "think and do" style. This result highlights the seemingly more pragmatic background of the CBT trainees' decisions, which has already been mentioned above (cf. Table 19.1).

Process variables within psychotherapy training combine all components of the training such as personal therapy, supervision, intensive practice, etc., as well as the development of the trainees´ skills and their mastery, microscopic processes of interaction between training staff and the trainees with respect to professional and psychological issues, the development of a basic psychotherapeutic attitude related to the profession, the psychotherapeutic theories, and the role as a helping professional. Castonguay (2000), for example, proposed a model to structure psychotherapeutic training related to the individual development of a trainee that differentiates the phases of preparation, exploration, identification, consolidation, and integration, which might provide a process model for empirical examination.

Here are some examples of a process-related research question: An extensive body of literature already covers the *evaluation of single training components*, such as personal therapy, supervision, etc., and aspects of quality assurance (cf. Laireiter & Botermans, 2005). Methodologically, only a very small number of studies examined mixed perspectives such as clients, therapists in training, as well as their supervisors (see, for example, the study of Ladany, Walker, et al. [2008], where therapy and supervision-related variables were closely combined leading to a variety of recommendations for the practice of counseling).

Compared to other sciences, the *development of didactic concepts* for psychotherapy training still seems to be limited (e.g., the use of e-learning models). Psychotherapy training institutions could learn from recent developments in the medical education, where—during the last two decades—dramatic progress has been made due to new approaches in training and examining specific skills. Among these different approaches, the method of using standardized patients seems to be promising for psychotherapy, with some studies already indicating benefits of this method (e.g., Wündrich et al., 2008). Also "practical" examinations following the model of the objective standardized clinical examination (OSCE) in medicine seem to be promising.

A challenge within psychotherapy training which has caused discussions—still unresolved—during the last decades is the question of *how research can be better integrated into training and what methods should be used to integrate research*. In our German studies (Strauss et al., 2009), we asked a total of 1,704 individuals who were active in training, teaching, and supervision, etc. how important they felt psychotherapy research would be for the entire psychotherapeutic training. On a seven-point Likert scale, the overall mean of the ratings of this question was 4.1 (SD = 1.0), indicating that trainers and teachers were only moderately convinced that research is an important issue within the training of psychotherapists.

The model in Table 19.2 discriminates *outcome variables as either* micro- or macro outcomes. Micro-outcomes may be best defined by the increase of knowledge and expertise during training and may be tested during (final) examinations. Macro-outcomes, on the other hand, probably combine the psychotherapeutic knowledge with the professional practice of a psychotherapist and are influenced by many other factors, such as the therapists' psychological status, satisfaction, his or her professional integration, continuing education, post-training professional growth, self-care, and other determinants of expertise and competence.

With respect to the outcome, one of the most crucial questions in psychotherapy training is "*What [finally] makes a good therapist good?*" (Luborsky & Spence, 1971). Interestingly, the literature provides some conceptual consensus regarding psychotherapeutic competence, although there is a lack of an empirical basis. During a discussion held at SPR, Robert Elliott, for example, summarized the following features of a good therapist (in a panel at the Annual SPR Meeting, 2000): "Specific skills (e.g., facilitate the development of a positive relational environment), General interpersonal ability (caring, interest, tolerance, listening, empathy, setting aside own interests, flexibility, creativity, responsiveness . . .), Interpersonal functioning (self awareness/self acceptance, including internal complexity and contradictions, blind spots, limits; a *balanced attachment pattern, e.g., attached but not too secure, slightly distant but not detached*)."

Accordingly, trainees should be monitored according to their helping skills (and experience), their interpersonal skills and abilities, and to their intrapersonal functioning. Only recently has the German Chamber of Psychotherapy formulated very similar concepts as the pillars of psychotherapeutic competence, i.e., professional-conceptual, personal, and interpersonal competence (BPtK, 2009).

A crucial question related to the issue of competence is *how competence and expertise of psychotherapists can be assessed.* There is a vast amount of literature related to expertise and competence within the field of educational psychology, or about helpful skills for psychotherapeutic professionals (Hill, 2009). In a recent German study, Eversmann (cf. Caspar & Eversmann, 2009) investigated a cohort of 40 trainees during a five-year-period to test which variables were the best predictors of competence (i.e., empathy, talent, acceptance, openness, flexibility and understanding in a real situation). Among the variety of predictors, such as intelligence, academic achievement, interpersonal intelligence and competence, demographic variables and personality, interpersonal competence clearly outperformed all other variables and predicted both, objective as well as subjective training outcome criteria.

Another central question of psychotherapy training research accentuates the *differentiation of successful and unsuccessful,* or "happy and unhappy" therapists. Within the past few years, a variety of studies have been published demonstrating systematic differences between psychotherapists with respect to the quality and outcome of their treatments, indicating huge individual differences between therapists (e.g., Okiishi et al., 2003, Sandell, 2007). It would be interesting to see if therapists showing systematically different outcomes could also be differentiated according to their training experiences. In Orlinsky and Ronnestad's legendary study on the personal development of psychotherapists (Orlinsky & Ronnestad, 2005), a significant subgroup (about 10 percent of the total sample) indicated a high amount of stressful work combined with a low amount of healing leading to a "distressing practice."

An organized "generic" model of psychotherapy training could facilitate the combination of research results which are implicitly and explicitly related to training aspects and questions of psychotherapeutic competence. The model could also serve as a basis for the development of more measures and instruments specifically related to training issues (e.g., Ladany, 2004; Zarbock, Drews, Bodansky, & Dahme, 2009).

Integrative Research-Based Concepts for Psychotherapy Training

One of the most difficult challenges in psychotherapy training is to find a concerted balance between "eminence-based" and "evidence-based" training. With respect to research, trainees usually learn that the results of psychotherapy research are relatively clear and straight forward in relation to outcome, process- and patient-by-treatment-aptitude questions. Recently, an additional extensive amount of results related to the health service system and basic psychobiological research has been added, including studies from neuroscience that propose biological markers of psychotherapeutic change (cf. Caspar, 2003).

On the other hand, if trainees take a closer look at the situation in psychotherapy research, they will learn that there are still many open questions in the field, such as "What really works for whom?" (Roth & Fonagy, 1996) or "How and why psychotherapy really leads to change?" (Kazdin, 2008). They also learn, that "in essence, the dodo bird verdict has been fortified" (Lambert & Ogles, 2004), although many psychotherapeutic orientations appear to be clearly superior to others. With respect to the psychotherapy process, trainees can discover that there are "some core conflicts" (Barber, 2009) and that technical variables seem to explain only a very small amount of variance in comparison to therapist variables, common factors, client variables, and extra-therapeutic changes (Lambert & Barley, 2002; Wampold, 2001).

Our German studies mentioned above (Strauss et al., 2009) came to the manifest conclusion that the large majority of the trainees, alumni, and teachers clearly prefer a continuation of the training system which is based on specific psychotherapeutic "schools" or theories, such as CBT or psychodynamic therapy (PDT). In addition, a significant amount answered positively to the question of whether theoretical issues beyond specific therapeutic orientations should be increasingly included in training. Not surprisingly, more than 50 percent of the *alumni* answered positively to this question, whereas only 35 percent of the candidate teachers did, indicating that progress in the training process might open the trainees' minds.

Beyond any specific psychotherapeutic orientation, there are a couple of theoretical approaches overarching all psychotherapeutic methods. Consequently, these theoretical approaches should receive much more focus in training activities to provide trainees a more general model of psychological interventions more or less independent from the specific assumptions of their schools (Grawe, 1997).

Of course, we overlook a variety of such overarching principles and concepts. Interpersonal theory (e.g., Horowitz, 2004) and attachment theory (Strauss, 2008) are examples of prominent theoretical approaches that could be increasingly integrated into all psychotherapeutic orientations. Both theoretical models are rooted in basic psychological (and psychodynamic) research (either developmental or personality-related), and may serve as good examples of how evidence-based theoretical models have generated a vast amount of knowledge resulting in the development of specific treatment approaches (e.g., interpersonal reconstructive therapy in the case of the interpersonal model, Benjamin, 2003a; or mentalization-based treatment in the case of attachment theory, Bateman & Fonagy, 2003).

The Attachment System as a Basis for Psychotherapeutic Change

There has been a huge amount of research revealing basic results on the attachment system. The system reflects universal needs and invites reciprocal behaviors (Fonagy, 2009). It is undoubtedly biologically significant. Recent studies from the field of neuroscience indicate that social attachment seems to be like "an addictive disorder" (Insel & Young, 2001). This implies that drug abuse and addiction may be considered as an attempt to replace opiates and endogen factors that are normally provided by social attachments. fMRI studies by Bartels and Zeki (2004) and others have shown that attachment stimuli provoke common activation and deactivation if the stimuli represent maternal or romantic love. One of the major results of these studies is that reinforcement systems are activated if provoked by attachment stimuli, and that the frontal regions normally representing critical thinking and evaluation seem to be deactivated (Strauss, 2007).

The theory behind the attachment system, going back to John Bowlby's trilogy on attachment and loss, has been integrative and empirically supported during recent years. It parallels many other (clinical) theories and it particularly incorporates modern models of developmental psychobiology (Schore, 2000).

Developmental findings highlight the importance of the attachment system. It has been shown that infant attachment is clearly measurable (e.g., using the strange situation paradigm), and that infant attachment even allows predictions of adult personality and mental disorders. Adult attachment can also be measured using different approaches such as interviews, questionnaires, or projective measures (Buchheim & Strauss, 2002; Strauss, Lobo-Drost, & Pilkonis, 1999). Although these measures still need clarification and construct validation, the current evidence shows that adult attachment, specifically maternal attachment, predicts infant attachment to a large degree and influences social cognition and mentalization (Fonagy, 2009).

Clinical findings claim that attachment security predicts treatment outcome (e.g., Strauss et al., 2006) and seems to be susceptible to change, at least in specific treatment approaches (e.g., Fonagy et al., 1996; Levy et al., 2006; Strauss et al., 2011; Kirchmann et al., 2011). Attachment also predicts therapeutic alliance in individual (Mallinckrodt, 2000; Romano et al., 2008) and group psychotherapy (e.g., Kirchmann et al., 2009), and it works as a determinant of treatment expectations, service use, as well as group process and the perception of others (Chen & Mallinckrodt, 2002; Strauss & Schwark, 2007). In a recent study (Kirchmann, 2009) from our group, it could be shown that patients with a more secure attachment style at the beginning of an inpatient treatment for depressive symptoms showed the best prognosis related to post-treatment and one-year follow-up scores. The study also indicated that patients with ambivalent and avoidant attachment needed more time to reach the secure patients' post-treatment depression scores. On the other hand, it could be shown that the percentage of patients needing outpatient psychiatric or psychotherapeutic help during the one-year follow-up period differed markedly from 30 percent in the secure subgroup to 55 percent in the ambivalent subgroup.

How the attachment system affects the therapeutic relationship remains unexplained to some degree. But there is an increasing number of studies indicating that attachment might affect interactive and countertransference processes. For example, Martin et al. (2006) studied the impact of narratives as part of the adult attachment interview from an autonomous, dismissive, and enmeshed person on the perception of this person by a group of listeners (students as well as psychotherapy trainees). The study demonstrated that students as well as therapists(!) listening to the narratives of a secure person showed much more positive countertransference reactions, better well-being, and more friendly interpersonal interactions compared to the responses to the narratives of insecure patients that caused much more negative interpersonal countertransference reactions. The study is described in detail by Martin et al. (2006) and is currently being replicated, with a focus on the question of whether the attachment status of the listener might affect the response to the attachment stimulus (cf. Kirchmann et al., 2011).

The attachment system as a basis for psychotherapeutic change is increasingly related to specific mechanisms: Fonagy (2009) pointed out that successful psychotherapy shows parallels to developmental processes of affect and self-regulation through mirroring, and that psychotherapy preferably co-activates the attachment system and mentalization. Mentalizing, according to Fonagy (2009), is a form of imaginative mental activity, namely, perceiving and interpreting human behavior in terms of intentional mental states (e.g., needs, desires, feeling, beliefs, goals, purposes, and reasons): "Simultaneously with the activation of attachment, the therapist attempts to enhance mentalization" (Fonagy, 2009). The development of mentalization-based treatment approaches, which are increasingly elaborated and developed, seems to be a promising development that contrasts "school specific psychotherapy."

Extending the Repertoire: Group Therapy as Part of Psychotherapy Training

The research expertise (Strauss et al., 2009) asked the experts in the field of psychotherapy which additional qualifications would be worth requiring for psychotherapists in the future. Some answers were related to the work with minorities, or qualifications related to relaxation techniques, but the huge majority of the experts (64 percent) voted for *group psychotherapy*. In fact, during regular psychotherapy training, groups are only marginally featured, although, as research shows, group treatment has been proven to be a very effective form of treatment for a large number of specific disorders (Burlingame, MacKenzie & Strauss, 2004).

If work with groups was included in training concepts, the repertoire of measures and concepts would be largely extended: Recent research on groups has brought forth promising methods to select patients for group psychotherapy, such as the group selection questionnaire (GSQ; Löffler et al., 2007). The GSQ is a quick screen for client expectations prior to assignment to group and might serve to identify clients that could be at risk for premature dropout or negative effects. The GSQ comprises the subscales expectancy, participation, and domineering and has proven to predict group climate and outcome.

Working with groups could also extend the common models of the helping alliance and the therapeutic relationships that are seemingly more complex within groups. Studies initiated by Johnson (2003) have validated a model which discriminates three basic factors of a helping alliance in group psychotherapy, e.g., positive bonding, positive working, as well as negative relationship. This model has been replicated several times in German samples (Bormann & Strauss, 2007), and has led to the development of an economic questionnaire, the Group Questionnaire (GQ; Krogel, 2008), comprising these dimensions of group-related alliances.

Group researchers can also use precise general practice guidelines (Leszcz & Kobos, 2008) and a core instrument developed by a task force of the American Group Psychotherapy Association (Strauss et al., 2008). The core instrument consists of a number of handouts and selection tools for pre-group preparation and member selection, as well as a number of specific outcome and process measures. The core instrument may provide an economic basis for patient-oriented research in group psychotherapy and has been increasingly accepted among practitioners.

Extending the psychotherapeutic repertoire by focusing on group psychotherapy may contribute to a more complex view of the forces that govern therapeutic effectiveness in psychotherapy by considering the factors that were included into a model by Burlingame et al. (2004; e.g., patient factors, leader factors, structural factors, the formal change theory, and specific small group processes). The complexity of the group has the potential to shape trainees' experiences and there is a common subjective belief that competence in leading groups also increases the competence to cooperate in future scientific or clinical networks.

Societal and Political Aspects of Psychotherapy: An Issue for Trainees and Researchers

I will conclude my reflections about the interaction between research and training with some more general thoughts on the position of psychotherapy and psychotherapy research related to social and cultural processes in the time of globalization. Many authors from other fields, especially sociology, have criticized psychotherapy research and psychotherapists and sometimes blamed them "to systematically neglect social and cultural issues" (e.g., Keupp, 2009)—creating another "splendid isolation."

I will formulate some theses related to sociocultural aspects of psychotherapy and how psychotherapy training should be considered in future discussions.

1. *Psychotherapy training (and research!) is increasingly driven by economic aspects.* There are several indicators supporting the first thesis that a psychotherapy is driven by economic aspects. In the United Kingdom, for example, the so-called Layard Depression Report has clearly shown that psychotherapy may have positive economic effects. Instead of thoroughly discussing the clinical consequences of these economic findings, economic arguments appear to have been used as an argument against individualized psychotherapy through the implementation of the program "improving access to psychological therapies" (IAPT), which is so far clearly dominated by brief CBT techniques.

The EST movement (Elliott, 1998) and the promotion of guidelines are obviously (besides the intention of summarizing evidence) also a result of the economic pressure in the health system. Only a few researchers ask the critical question of whether guidelines really are effective. Within general medical practice, there have recently been some studies critically analyzing the effectiveness of guideline driven therapy, such as the study by Bebb et al. (2007) which showed that—in a randomized controlled trial—a guideline-based treatment algorithm for patients suffering from hypertension and type-2 diabetes was not more effective than treatment as usual.

2. *Psychotherapy training is (still) mostly determined by psychotherapeutic orientations (e.g., schools, "confessions", "churches") and is less research-driven.* One of the former presidents of the SPR, Klaus Grawe (1997), had the vision that psychotherapy researchers would once participate in a "funeral of therapy schools replacing them with a new research informed psychotherapy" (p. 17). The funeral of therapeutic schools has in fact often been discussed, but has never happened. Although training models may have become a bit more integrative (e.g., Castonguay, 2000, 2005), they are still mostly based upon one method or orientation (usually CBT or psychodynamic psychotherapy). This is surprising in view of the findings of psychotherapy research that—to a large extent—has supported arguments for a

contextual instead of a medical model of psychotherapy (Wampold, 2001). A contextual model of psychotherapy, per definition, cannot be a school-based model.

In the above mentioned German research expertise (Strauss et al., 2009), a Delphi survey of experts showed a strong preference for a specific orientation, at the most combined with the knowledge of other orientations (85 percent). A minority of the experts voted for a disorder-oriented training structure (9 percent), and an even smaller minority (4 percent) favored a common factors or principle of change-oriented training as it has been described by Castonguay (2000).

3. *Unfortunately, there is no real dialogue between psychotherapeutic methods, instead fighting and dishonesty, and an incorporation of prevailing theories and techniques, disregarding historical facts.* The predominance of the specific orientations combined with economic pressure has plainly had a negative influence on the "emotional climate" and on the dialogue between psychotherapeutic orientations. How the economy increases undue hardship in the debate between the schools may be best shown by the reactions to a recent meta-analysis of the effects of psychodynamic long-term psychotherapy (Leichsenring & Rabung, 2008). Although this meta-analysis may have a number of obvious shortcomings, the arguments against it were particularly harsh, including the accusation that publishing such results would be unethical and cause damage to potential patients (Rief & Hofmann, 2009). These accusations go far beyond the style of scientific discourse and reflect a recent trend of some psychotherapists and psychotherapy researchers to neglect historical facts and findings by rejecting established knowledge on the one hand, and integrating interventions, theoretical assumptions, and thoughts into their existing psychotherapeutic theories on the other hand (according to the motto "If it works, it belongs to us").

To understand why "the funeral of therapeutic schools" fails to occur, a group theory dealing with power, identity, and conflict might be helpful. In his monograph *Taking the Group Seriously,* Farhad Dalal (1998) formulated the interesting thesis that identity (including psychotherapeutic identity) results from a "labeling of relationships between people" (e.g., members of a therapeutic orientation/theory, or a tribe). Although, according to Dalal, natural groups do not really exist, people tend to create groups (at least in their minds) to construct an illusion of stability (Who am I? What am I? = Where do I belong?). Identities formed in this way are, of course, continuously threatened (for example, by outsiders from other groups defining themselves according to different labels). According to Dalal's opinion, people fight against threats to their identity by sticking to "names" and declaring these to be essential. He concludes: "If this tendency gets too strong, we speak of fundamentalism" (Dalal, 1998, p. 145).

There are some ways to treat informed trainees in order to avoid such forms of fundamentalism. Trainees, for example, should know that many experienced

FIGURE 19.2 Learning from Many Masters

(www.cartoonstock.com)

psychotherapists usually classify themselves mostly as eclectic and independent of psychotherapeutic schools as a cartoonist has shown it in Figure 19.2, and that they should try to learn from "many masters" (Orlinsky, 1995). Research results should be a more crucial part of the psychotherapy training in the future, although these results may sometimes threaten the professional identity. In our training programs, we should begin to focus much more on the training of people instead of programs or even manuals. We should also focus on contextual and conceptual aspects of psychotherapy. Training should not be polarized by supporting idealization of insiders and stigmatization of outsiders, instead, similarities between different modalities and the differences within these modalities should be highlighted. Dialogues between different "tribes" within practice and research could finally lead to more integrative role models.

We can learn from attachment theory that over-attachment is usually a disadvantage. Instead, those who organize the training may take the advice of the famous German classical writer Johann Wolfgang von Goethe (1749–1832), who may be considered a harbinger of modern attachment theory, when he said, "*It is two things that children should get from their parents: roots and wings.*" That is exactly the message teachers should provide to their trainees.

COMMENTARY

SOME REMARKS IN RETROSPECT

The Presidential Address summarized in this chapter's paragraphs was delivered in 2009. One of the motivations for the presentation was to increase the sensitivity of SPR researchers to training issues. Fortunately, SPR has meanwhile established a Special Interest Section dealing with training issues (SPRISTAD) that plans to initiate and coordinate research activities around the training of psychotherapists. Discussions about integrative concepts within psychotherapy research and practice have progressed. The idea to use attachment theory and related research as a conceptual framework for psychotherapy integration has recently been propagated in a series of articles in the *Journal of Psychotherapy Integration* (2011). The idea to include the group setting in the training of psychotherapists as a learning field and as an application of an economic and efficacious form of psychotherapy has received support by recent systematic reviews confirming the value of group therapy for a wide range of psychological disorders (Burlingame, Strauss, & Joyce, 2013). In a study based on a representative survey in the German population, we found that the public attitudes towards groups in general, and group psychotherapy specifically, were surprisingly positive, which instills the hope that groups will have a future in our field, not only because of the cost-effectiveness (Strauss, Spangenberg, Brähler, & Bormann, 2014).

The research expertise mentioned several times in this article was ordered to revise the current legal conditions in Germany, but has not yet had any consequences, due to other political priorities in the health sector, although the discussion about the future of psychotherapy training is in full swing. Unfortunately, we cannot really observe an increased commitment for societal issues within the psychotherapeutic profession. Instead, the tendency to fight against each other under the flags of a specific psychotherapeutic orientation seems to be even more pronounced now (at least in some subgroups) than several years ago, with a clear tendency for anti-psychodynamic arguments.

Notes

1 Written and revised version of the author's SPR Presidential Address held at the 40th Annual Meeting of the Society for Psychotherapy Research, Santiago de Chile, June 24, 2009.

2 The term "splendid isolation" was used to describe the foreign policy pursued by Great Britain during the late 19th century under the Conservative premierships of Benjamin Disraeli and the Marquess of Salisbury. The term was coined by a Canadian Member of Parliament to praise Britain's lack of involvement in European affairs. Today, the metaphoric meaning is the voluntary avoidance of an alliance that seems to be

appropriate to describe the relationship between research and training in the field of psychotherapy research.

3 Based on an initiative by David Orlinsky within the special interest group on culture, SPR has collected systematic descriptions of psychotherapy (training) systems in different countries. A survey of almost 20 different countries is available under the URL www.psychotherapyresearch.org/displaycommon.cfm?an=1&subarticlenbr=89 on the SPR website.

20

PSYCHOTHERAPY, PSYCHOPATHOLOGY, RESEARCH, AND PRACTICE

Pathways of Connections and Integration (2011)

Louis G. Castonguay

Scholars typically work within conceptual, pragmatic, and/or epistemological frameworks or paradigms (Kuhn, 1962). Figuratively speaking, most researchers and practitioners live within fairly distinct or delimited communities of knowledge seekers. As in other scientific and professional fields, distinctive frameworks or paradigms of knowledge have shaped psychotherapy and psychotherapy research (Goldfried, 2000). Theoretical orientations (e.g., cognitive behavioral, humanistic, psychodynamic, systemic), methodological preferences (e.g., quantitative, qualitative), and primary "residence" (e.g., academia, clinical milieu) have an undeniable influence on what one sees as the most relevant source or object of knowledge, as well as the most valid strategy to acquire such knowledge. At various times, the boundaries that separate different knowledge communities have been described as impassable, and the views about psychopathology and therapy prevailing within each of them have been perceived as irreconcilable. Historically, such professional and conceptual divisions have fueled hostile statements and exchanges among respected figures of our field (see Castonguay & Goldfried, 1994). One could also argue that some of these divisions have played a role in (and are being reinforced by) dichotomous and divisive positions that are parts of current discussions about the process of change, as well as the practice and training of psychotherapy (e.g., techniques vs. relationship, empirical evidence vs. clinical experience).

However, considering the complexity of psychotherapy, it is unlikely that one theoretical orientation, method of investigation, or one type of knowledge seeker will ever be able to provide the field with a comprehensive view of therapeutic change and a complete set of interventions to alleviate psychological problems. Accordingly, a fruitful way to enrich our understanding and increase the impact of therapy may be to foster connections between communities of knowledge—or to build bridges across different empirical, theoretical, pragmatic, and philosophical quests about understanding suffering and ways to reduce it.

The goal of this paper is to describe three pathways of knowledge connections: Integration of psychotherapeutic approaches, integration of psychotherapy and psychopathology, and integration of research and practice. For the most part, these are distinct pathways, except for the fact that each reflects efforts of rapprochement built on convergence and complementarity across communities of knowledge seekers—as well as the fact that they represent meaningful contexts within which I have conducted most of my empirical, conceptual, and clinical work. By pointing out intrinsic and synergic connections between research and clinical practice that are emerging from these pathways, I hope to demonstrate that these connections may facilitate the actualization of the scientist-practitioner model.

Integration of Therapeutic Approaches

Psychotherapy integration has become a leitmotif in our field. There are, of course, numerous factors that can explain such a zeitgeist (see Castonguay, Reid, Halperin, & Goldfried, 2003), but one could argue that fundamentally it is a reaction against the orthodox rigidity within and acrimony between traditional schools of therapy that predominated our field up until the 1970s. It can be seen as a response to the theoretical, clinical, and epistemological limitations of modern approaches to psychotherapy: a humble and open response to the unsatisfactory status of our field and one that is based on the assumption that the richness of plurality may be a promising strategy to approach the complexity of human functioning and difficulty of facilitating change.

The efforts of rapprochement and connection that have emerged from this attitude have taken several forms (see Castonguay et al., 2003), such as the construction of new theories of human functioning and/or change, the prescription and combination of particular interventions for different clients, the delineation of common factors or convergences across different orientations, and the improvement of major systems of psychotherapy based on the assimilation of complementary perspectives from other orientations. Focusing only on the last two of these four themes, I will describe initiatives and a few examples of research that are relevant to the integration movement. I will also present some directions for future research related to these efforts and that may be relevant to practicing clinicians.

Common Factors

Although current forms of psychotherapy are based on divergent theories and are associated with various types of interventions that are assumed to be unique to each of them, a large number of common factors (see Castonguay, 2006;

Grencavage & Norcross, 1990) have been identified by scholars of different theoretical orientations. In my view, two general types of common factors are of particular conceptual and clinical importance, as they can shed light on the complexity of psychotherapy by challenging simplistic views about therapeutic change (such as technique vs. relationship, common vs. unique variables). These two sets of common factors, principles of change and "faux-unique" variables, are discussed in the next sections.

Principles of Change

Consistent with the seminal contribution of Marvin Goldfried (1980), I define such principles as general guidelines and/or foci of interventions that cut across different approaches, with a number of them underlying many of the specific techniques that are frequently considered to be unique to a particular orientation. In addition to the research that I have conducted with my colleagues and students over many years (for selective reviews, see Castonguay, 2006; Castonguay et al., 2003), I have been involved in two distinct but complementary strategies that led to the delineation of principles of change, in depth examination of some of them, as well as suggestions for future studies.

One of these initiatives was the Task Force sponsored by the North American Society for Psychotherapy Research (NASPR) and the Division of Clinical Psychology of the American Psychological Association (APA, Division 12) that Larry Beutler and I chaired (Castonguay & Beutler, 2005a). The first goal of this task force was to delineate and integrate what we know about numerous variables that contribute to change in psychotherapy, by reviewing the contributions of three sets of variables (i.e., participant characteristics, relationship variables, and technical factors) that have not only been shown to be related to outcome but that more than likely operate in constant interaction in clinical practice. The members of the Task Force were respected psychotherapy researchers who worked in pairs, most of which comprised researchers of different theoretical orientations for the sake of fostering connections between different communities of knowledge. These scholars were asked to review the role of therapeutic variables for four clusters of clinical problems frequently encountered by clinicians: dysphoric, anxiety, personality, and substance use disorders. In addition, they were asked to translate the research-based evidence into principles of change that could serve as helpful guidelines to clinicians without being tied to particular jargon or theoretical model.

One of the end results of this effort was the identification of 61 "Research Informed Principles" that can be used to help clinicians of different theoretical orientations to plan and deliver treatments that are consistent with contemporary research findings. For example, based on a review of psychotherapies that have received empirical support, Follette and Greenberg (2005) have derived six principles related to techniques for the treatment of depression, including the challenging of cognitive appraisals, increasing positive reinforcements in the client's life, improving client's interpersonal functioning and social environment, as well as fostering emotional awareness, acceptance, and regulation. As a source of clinically relevant information, these heuristics are precise enough to guide the focus of clinicians' interventions without being restricted to a narrow and orientation-specific set of prescribed procedures (there are, for instance, many techniques, e.g., interpretation, cognitive restructuring, that therapists can use to challenge clients, all of them aimed at providing an alternative view of self and others; Goldfried, 1980). In addition, this list of principles can help therapists to increase their repertoire of interventions if the treatments they typically conduct with their depressed clients do not systematically target dimensions of functioning that may be involved in the cause or maintenance of depression (e.g., interpersonal skills, dysfunctional marital or familial relationships). Furthermore, as described elsewhere, such empirically anchored principles (along with principles of change related to relationship and participant variables) have provided the foundation for training guidelines to prevent or reduce harmful effects in therapy (Castonguay, Boswell, Constantino, Goldfried, & Hill, 2010).

Another result of this task force was the identification of recommendations for future research on principles of change (Castonguay & Beutler, 2005b). Perhaps the two most important of them related to: (a) personality disorders, which evidence a limited amount of research regarding all three domains of therapy examined; and (b) the interaction between participants, relationship, and technique variables for all disorders investigated. Considering the prevalence of the former and the omnipresence of the latter (let alone the complexity of both of them), these research priorities would no doubt be viewed as highly relevant by many clinicians.

A second initiative that has led to further exploration of principles of change is a continued series of conferences that Clara Hill and I have organized at Penn State University since 2001. Also aimed at fostering connections between different communities of knowledge seekers, these series of conferences are primarily based on open discussions among influential psychotherapy researchers from different orientations and with diverse methodological expertise. These conferences also serve as a steppingstone to stimulate new and creative theoretical, clinical, and empirical projects toward specific processes of change. Finally, after the completion of these projects (each of them leading to a book chapter), the last meeting of each series of conferences is set to foster a consensus about four specific questions: What is the nature or definition of the process investigated? What facilitates it? What follows it? and What are the most important questions that future research should address in order to better understand this process?

The first series of conferences was on insight (Castonguay & Hill, 2006) or, using Goldfried's conceptualization of principles of change, the acquisition of a new understanding of self. As an example of the type of innovative and creative ideas that can emerge from active and long-term collaboration of researchers typically working within different communities of knowledge, a consensus was achieved on 19 specific (and clinically relevant) directions of future research (e.g., Does insight need to be true or historically accurate? Are insights better if they are client-generated, therapist-generated, or co-constructed? Do more complex, emotionally intense, central insights lead to stronger, and longer lasting changes? Hill et al., 2005). Further reflecting Goldfried's influence, the second series of Penn State Conferences is on another principle of change: corrective experiences.

"Faux-Unique" Variables

Raising doubts about the theoretical boundaries between some of our communities of knowledge, research has suggested that a number of components of therapy that are typically associated with a particular orientation may play a role in the effectiveness of other approaches. I call these "faux-unique" variables.

Consistent with their underlying models of change, for example, research suggests that cognitive-behavioral therapists focus less on client's interpersonal experience than psychodynamic-interpersonal (PI) therapists (Blagys & Hilsenroth, 2000). Despite this, some process studies have suggested that clients improve more when cognitive behavior therapists focus on interpersonal issues that are associated with psychodynamic treatment. For instance, Hayes, Castonguay, and Goldfried (1996) found that the therapist's focus on early attachment patterns predicted positive outcome CBT. Therapists' connections between the therapeutic relationship and other relationships were also part of a set of psychodynamic techniques correlated with change in CBT (Jones & Pulos, 1993).

In their review of the empirical literature, Blagys and Hilsenroth (2000) also demonstrated that CBT therapists focus less on clients' expression of emotion than do PI therapists. In line with a seminal paper written by Stan Messer (1986), a study conducted by Wiser and Goldfried (1993) suggests that, while PI therapists see the exploration and experience of affect as significant in therapeutic episodes, cognitive behavior therapists see the decrease of emotional experiencing as a significant therapeutic event. In a number of studies, however, the client's emotional experience in CBT has been found to relate positively with treatment outcome (e.g., Castonguay, Goldfried, Wiser, Raue, & Hayes, 1996; Jones & Pulos, 1993). These findings (along with the studies on interpersonal issues mentioned above) suggest that what leads to change may not be restricted to those variables assumed to be mutative in a particular treatment and may involve factors typically associated with other orientations (Barber, 2009; Castonguay et al., 2003). In other words, while our current theories of change are not "wrong" (CBT therapists do focus more on cognition and less on emotion), they may not entirely capture the complexity of the process of change. As described below, these studies on "faux-unique" variables also suggest directions for how to potentially improve the effectiveness of traditional approaches by considering and incorporating processes of change emphasized by other orientations.

In addition to questioning the solidity of conceptual boundaries that separate orientations, as well as the validity or usefulness of dichotomies that prevail in current dialogues about process of change, empirical evidence on common factors also addresses core conceptual and clinical needs of practitioners. Clinicians are likely to be interested in knowing what variables are predictive of or facilitate change, irrespective of the treatment used. Trainers and supervisors will find it helpful to learn more about the relationship and technical interventions that should be considered as foundational pillars of psychotherapy training, even if such factors may take different forms when implemented in different types of therapy (see Castonguay, 2000). In addition, clinicians are likely to be interested in knowing that some variables not typically associated with their preferred approach may nevertheless explain parts of its effectiveness, thereby inviting them to pay more attention to these variables.

Improvement of Major Systems of Psychotherapy

A number of scholars associated with particular schools of therapy have attempted to improve their preferred orientation by integrating constructs and clinical venues developed in other traditions. Aptly defined by Messer (2001) as "assimilative integration," such efforts refer to "the incorporation of attitudes, perspectives, or techniques from an auxiliary therapy into a therapist's primary, grounding approach" (p. 1).

Examples of assimilative integration have been anchored within different theoretical bases. A well-known attempt to do so is Jeremy Safran's expansion of cognitive therapy. Relying on contributions from humanistic, interpersonal, and psychodynamic approaches, Safran (e.g., Safran & Segal, 1990) has offered a revision of the concept of schema that allows for a recognition of dimensions of human functioning (i.e., emotional, developmental, and interpersonal) that have not always received full attention in more traditional CBT models. A complementary (and, as will be noted, not at all mutually exclusive) way to improve the outcome of psychotherapies may be to modify existing treatments based on research, including process research. One example of such an effort is the work that my colleagues and I have been involved in exploring the possibility of improving the efficacy of cognitive therapy (CT) based on findings related to common and unique variables in CT.

Integrative Therapy for Depression

In a process study on CT for depression, Castonguay et al. (1996) found that, while the alliance was positively related to outcome, therapists' focus on issues at the core of CT (such as the causal relationship between cognition and emotion) was negatively related to outcome. Content analyses conducted to shed light on this negative finding revealed that when attempting to repair alliance ruptures (e.g., client's reluctance to accept or engage in prescribed procedures), therapists frequently increased their adherence to cognitive interventions – either by further emphasizing the validity of the CT rationale or by identifying the client's negative therapeutic reactions as a manifestation of distorted thoughts about the therapist or therapy. These interventions, however, did not appear to repair the alliance problems and may have perpetuated and/or worsened them (interestingly, similar patterns of adherence to prescribed techniques in the context of alliance ruptures have also been observed in psychodynamic therapy, e.g., Piper et al., 1999; Schut et al., 2005).

These findings suggest that one way to increase the effectiveness of CT is to add to its protocol new interventions to address ruptures in the therapeutic alliance. Based on the work of David Burns (1990) and Jeremy Safran, I have developed a treatment protocol, called integrative cognitive therapy (ICT), that involves procedures of meta-communication typically associated with or derived from non-CT approaches (i.e., humanistic, interpersonal, and psychodynamic). Specifically, therapists conducting ICT are asked to follow the traditional cognitive therapy protocol (cf., Beck, Rush, Shaw, & Emery, 1979), except when confronted with signs of alliance ruptures. Rather than increasing their adherence to the treatment rationale and/or methods in response to such ruptures (as was observed in cognitive therapy by Castonguay et al., 1996), therapists are instead instructed to use the strategies developed by Burns and Safran: inquiring about the relationship problems, empathizing with the client's experience related to the alliance ruptures, and recognizing the therapist's contribution to these ruptures. Once the relationship problems have been explored and resolved, therapists then resume cognitive therapy, either by continuing to use the procedures they were using prior to the emergence of the alliance rupture or by shifting to other techniques prescribed by traditional CT.

ICT has currently been investigated in two preliminary studies (Castonguay et al., 2004; Constantino et al., 2008). Although systematic assessment of the therapeutic process has yet to be conducted, observations of a large number of therapy sessions revealed that alliance problems emerged relatively frequently during the application of cognitive techniques and that these problems seemed to be adequately addressed by the use of meta-communication strategies. With regard to outcome, the first study found that ICT led to significantly greater improvement than a wait-list condition, achieving a pre-/post-effect size of $d = 1.91$ on the BDI (Castonguay et al., 2004), which is more than twice the size of comparable studies of traditional CT. In a second study, Constantino et al. (2008) found ICT to be superior to standard CT with a medium effect size, $d = 0.50$ (also on the BDI). The second study also found higher alliance and therapist empathy ratings were reported in ICT.

Although preliminary, these studies are consistent with other recent investigations that have provided support for the positive effect of alliance-repair strategies (Muran, Safran, Samstag, & Winston, 2005), as well as the positive impact of training in alliance-fostering interventions (e.g., Crits-Christoph et al., 2006). Considering the relatively high frequency with which alliance ruptures may occur, as well as how challenging such events can be for therapists (see Eubanks-Carter, Muran, Safran, & Hayes, 2010 for a review), more research on alliance rupture and repair is likely to help researchers, clinicians, and supervisors to prevent or reduce harmful effects in therapy (Castonguay, Boswell, Constantino et al., 2010).

Integrative Therapy for Generalized Anxiety Disorder (GAD)

With other colleagues, I have also been involved in an assimilative effort aimed at improving CBT for GAD by adding a range of interventions used in humanistic, interpersonal, and psychodynamic therapies (Newman, Castonguay, Borkovec, & Molnar, 2004). As in the case of ICT, the choice of the specific techniques added to CBT was based on research findings. For instance, procedures to deepen emotions (e.g., two chair) have been added to CBT not only because (as mentioned above) emotional experience has been linked to outcome in this treatment but also because several studies have suggested that worry, the central feature of GAD, serves as a cognitive avoidance of painful emotion (Borkovec & Newman, 1998). Therefore, helping the client to become aware of, stay with, and fully experience their emotions may provide them with an exposure to affect that they may be trying to avoid by worrying and ruminating. A large number of applied and basic findings have also led us to add therapeutic interventions addressing several interpersonal issues. As demonstrated by Newman & Erickson (2010), individuals with GAD present with significant past (attachment) and current interpersonal problems. As mentioned above, however, traditional CBT protocols tend to focus more on intrapersonal issues than on interpersonal issues (or at least focus significantly less on interpersonal issues than do psychodynamic treatments). Findings obtained by Borkovec and colleagues indicate that failure to solve interpersonal problems at the end of CBT predicts worse response at follow-up (Borkovec, Newman, Pincus, & Lytle, 2002). Paradoxically, and also mentioned above, evidence suggests that a focus on past and in-session interpersonal issues is related to outcome in CBT.

Taken together, these findings led my colleagues and me to predict that if we were able to construct a treatment protocol that maintains the coping skills components of effective CBT while also including interventions aimed at directly and systematically processing emotional and interpersonal issues, we would be able to increase the efficacy of the only treatment currently judged to be empirically supported for GAD. As described elsewhere (Castonguay et al., 2005; Newman et al., 2004), the cohesive combination of CBT and non-CBT interventions were anchored in integrative model of human functioning, specifically, Safran and Segal's (1990) expansion of the cognitive model. At a clinical (or procedural) level, our attempt to combine these interventions was structured around Goldfried's principles of change (reflecting what Boswell, Nelson, Nordberg, McAleavey, & Castonguay [2010] refer to as "principle based assimilation"). A first and preliminary (open trial) study revealed that the average within-participant effect sizes obtained for our integrative treatment were superior to those obtained in previous CBT studies (Newman et al., 2008). Clearly suggesting that improvement of an existing approach may be even more complex than what we anticipated, however, a follow-up randomized clinical trial failed to show many significant differences between our integrative treatment (CBT+Interpersonal and Emotional Processing Therapy [I/EP]), and a control condition that added a supportive listening segment (to control for common factors, such as time and therapist attention) to CBT (i.e., CBT+Supportive Listening Therapy [SL]) (Newman et al., 2011).

These results warn us of a possible "all-or-none" (and even perhaps a rigid and complacent) attitude that one can sometimes hear expressed, implicitly or explicitly, in the discourse of proponents of psychotherapy integration (the specific type of attitude against which this movement was a reaction); that is, that a combination of techniques (even the best of them) from several approaches will always be superior to a pure form of therapy. The fact of the matter is that we know that there is a substantial percentage of clients who evidence clinically significant change from empirically supported therapies, including CBT for GAD (see Borkovec et al., 2002). For these clients, the addition of non-CBT interventions may be unlikely to lead to further improvement to, and may even interfere with, the therapeutic impact of CBT interventions. Although comparing integrative treatments with empirically supported therapies is an important scientific step, a more conceptually sophisticated and clinically relevant avenue of research is to investigate which clients are the most likely to benefit from the addition of interventions not already included in treatments that have been shown to be effective.

It should be mentioned that the integrative treatments described above are not the only ones that have been built with the aim of improving effective therapy while relying on process and basic findings. For example, the treatment for depression developed by Hayes and Harris (2000; integrating emotional deepening strategies to "destabilize" core schema), the assimilation (based on the work of Klaus Grawe and Franz Caspar) of clients' motivational goals within different therapies (see Grosse Holtfort and Castonguay, 2005 for a review), as well as Constantino's integration of strategies to enhance expectations in cognitive therapy (Constantino, Klein, Smith-Hansen, & Greenberg, 2009), are worth highlighting. More efforts of this type will likely be viewed as relevant by many clinicians—those who base their practice on a preferred approach but who are also open to using interventions associated with other orientations (in theoretically cohesive and/or empirically informed ways), with the goal of developing broader case formulations and treatment plans, and thus better addressing the complexity of therapeutic change.

Integration of Different Knowledge Domains

Another possible way of increasing our understanding of the complexity of change and improving the effectiveness of different forms of psychotherapy is to establish or solidify connections with groups of researchers who seek knowledge outside our field. As argued by a number of authors, research from different domains of basic psychology is likely to be beneficial for psychotherapy researchers, scholars, and clinicians (Constantino & Castonguay, 2003; Goldfried & Wolfe, 1996). For example, the Penn State University conferences mentioned above illustrated how research and theory from social, cognitive, and developmental psychology can provide new ways of understanding and investigating insight in psychotherapy (see Castonguay & Hill, 2006). Connections between psychopathology and psychotherapy might be particularly fruitful. As noted by Arkowitz (1989), while psychopathology research can tell us what to change, psychotherapy research can tell us how to change it.

Research in psychopathology has led to a wealth of information related to symptomatology, clinical features, epidemiology, course, co-morbidity, and etiology of disorders frequently seen in outpatient or training clinics. A careful attention to findings from most if not all of these aspects of basic research may help us delineate clinical guidelines in terms of assessment foci, case formulations, and treatment planning. And, since these guidelines are drawn from research that is not tied to a particular school of therapy, most if not all of them could potentially be included in the clinical repertoire of therapists from different theoretical orientations.

Using depression as a case in point, psychopathology research suggests, for example, that vegetative symptoms may be crucial to assess (at the beginning and end of therapy). In a study based on the DSM-III criteria, Buchwald and Rudick-Davis (1993) found that the best single predictive symptom of a major depressive episode was psychomotor change, while the worst was "thoughts of death." Numerous empirical studies have shown that interactions between individuals who suffer from depression and other people are frequently characterized by anger, frustration, and lack of cooperation (Joiner, 2002). Such research, addressing issues as basic as symptomatology and clinical features, has helpful clinical implications. Specifically, in assessing the client's needs and the progress of therapy, the therapist should look beyond the psychological symptoms (such as feelings of worthlessness or guilt) that many psychotherapy books or manuals emphasize when referring to the symptoms of depression. Therapists, irrespective of their orientation and level of experience, should also be reminded that negative interpersonal processes are likely to emerge in the therapeutic relationship. Clinical skills are required to discern the extent to which such processes are manifestations of a client's depressive (emotional and interpersonal) reaction patterns, and how much of these are responses to an alliance rupture specifically due to therapy. Irrespective of their sources (and it is not likely to be an all-or-none phenomenon), focusing on such negative processes and their impact on a client's life may lead to important change, perhaps providing unique opportunities for corrective experiences in the safety of the therapeutic relationship.

Clinical guidelines can also be derived from epidemiological research. Such research has demonstrated that the prevalence of depression has been climbing sharply over recent decades (Seligman, 1989). According to Seligman (1989), this increase points to environmental determinants of depression. Contrasting a tenfold increase in prevalence observed in the general population with the rate of depression in some "non-modern" cultures (e.g., Amish), he argued that there is something in contemporary society that causes depression: a focus on individualism rather than the common good. The lack of commitment to common projects, one could suggest, has robbed individuals of buffers against depression when they are confronted with personal difficulties or failures. Our overinvolvement in activities aimed at increasing our individualistic accomplishments, wealth, and comfort might well make it more difficult to reach out for and obtain help and support from others when we experience serious difficulties in our lives. What this implies with regard to clinical practice is that irrespective of their orientation, clinicians should help clients renew or create meaningful relationships. They should encourage clients and/or teach them skills to appropriately and safely open themselves to others, as well as to get involved in purposeful and/or pleasurable activities with others.

These clinical implications, emerging from purely basic research, are consistent with some of the principles of change that were mentioned above and that were derived from another domain of research: empirically supported treatments. Such convergence of findings across different communities of knowledge may not be surprising considering the core aspects of human functioning to which they appear to be linked. As argued by MacLean (1985), communication and play are two of the evolutionary developments that differentiate not only humans but all mammals from reptiles. Denying or not attending to such ways of being forces our clients and us to fight a losing evolutionary battle!

Research on the etiology and maintenance of depression can also provide helpful heuristics for treatment planning. Investigations based on cognitive psychology have demonstrated that depressed individuals show information-processing (e.g., memory) biases. In a series of studies, Joorman and her colleagues have showed that such biases can be attributed to deficits in cognitive inhibition (see Joormann, 2009). It is not that depressed people automatically pay more attention to all instances of negative information; rather, they have difficulty disengaging from (and they further elaborate on) such information. Among other things, such a problem of disengagement suggests that, while benefits can be derived from focusing on a client's internal experience (e.g., examining distorted thoughts, exploring the meaning of such thoughts, or evoking and staying with feelings), therapists may also want to help clients develop strategies to shift their attention, at appropriate times, away from negative emotions and cognitions. Blasting Beethoven's 9th Symphony on one's iPod in response to pervasive and recurrent ruminations late at night, for instance, may well be a powerful adjunct to a verbal/insight-oriented form of therapy!

These are just a few examples of basic findings that can help clinicians more comprehensively assess and treat depressive symptoms. This does not mean that we have to reinvent the wheel and create new treatment approaches for different disorders exclusively or primarily based on basic research. What it does mean is that most, if not all, effective psychotherapy treatments are likely to be enriched by integrating, in a theoretically cohesive way, clinical guidelines that can be derived from the findings emerging from complementary communities of knowledge seekers (as noted by Joiner [2002], even interpersonal psychotherapy has not relied heavily and specifically on basic findings on interpersonal aspects of depression that are complementary to its therapeutic focus).

With the hope of creating new bridges between science and practice, Thomas Oltmanns and I are editing a textbook (for graduate students and experienced clinicians) aimed at weaving together information about basic research on psychopathology and the treatment of mental disorders (Castonguay & Oltmanns, 2013). Covering psychological disorders most frequently seen in clinical practice, each chapter is written by a pair of experts, most of which include a visible scholar from psychopathology research and an influential treatment researcher (or, for some chapters, researchers who have significantly contributed to both psychopathology and psychotherapy research). Each chapter covers major issues of psychopathology, such as the ones mentioned above. Adding a new dimension to the movement toward evidence-based practice, each chapter also provides readers with relevant clinical guidelines, in terms of assessment and treatment planning, derived from basic research in psychopathology.

By fostering connections between people from different research and/or theoretical backgrounds, this project, like the Task Force on Principles of Change (co-chaired with Larry Beutler) and the Penn State University Conferences (co-chaired with Clara Hill), has been leading to new, fresh, and collaborative ways of thinking about clinical practice. In the case of this book, specifically, the two-way street it aims to build is also likely to be valuable to investigators doing basic research on psychopathology, as it highlights issues from clinical practice that have an important bearing on phenomena and problems that they ought to address. To borrow Arkowitz's (1989) eloquent words, considerable learning about how to treat psychopathology can be derived from the knowledge community of basic researchers, and much can be learned from psychotherapy scholars in terms of how psychopathology manifests itself and is caused or maintained by issues that have been observed or investigated in assessing and treating clinical problems.

What About the Therapist?

Basic research on therapists' individual differences (including variables related to psychopathology) is also likely to provide helpful guidelines to improve the effectiveness of therapy. Moreover, such research could directly address one of the paradoxes that we are currently facing in our field today.

Based on the seminal contribution of Bruce Wampold (2001) and his colleagues, we know that a significant proportion of the outcome variance is explained by a therapist effect. Not only do we know that some therapists are more effective than others, data are beginning to show that this effect is specific. Based on an assessment tool measuring a wide range of symptoms and dimensions of functioning, a recent study suggests that, while a few therapists have superior results with most clinical problems (and a few others demonstrate ineffectiveness at treating most clinical problems), most therapists appear to have superior outcomes with respect to particular problems (e.g., depression, anxiety, suicide, substance abuse) but not with others (Kraus, Castonguay, Boswell, Nordberg, & Hayes, 2011). However, our understanding of the variables responsible for these general and specific effects of the therapist appears to be lacking (Wampold, personal communication, 2009).

One way to elucidate therapist effects might be to investigate interactions between individual differences and various components (affective, cognitive, and behavioral) of therapists' engagement that have been identified as common factors (Castonguay, 1993, 2006). To build on our current state of knowledge, it may be particularly indicated to study the possible interaction between personal characteristics and advanced therapeutic skills that have shown promising links with outcome, such as meta-communication (Eubanks-Carter et al., 2010), self-disclosure (Hill & Knox, 2002), and management of countertransference (Gelso & Hayes, 2002). From a practical point of view, focusing on who the therapist is and what he/she should do in therapy to facilitate change is likely to be of great interest to clinicians. Furthermore, considering our duty to "First, do no harm," perhaps it is even more urgent that we focus on how these factors may interfere with change (Castonguay, Boswell, Constantino et al., 2010).

Integration of Research and Practice

It seems fair to say that in the current state of our field the connection between psychotherapy research and clinical practice is not a strong one. It has been argued that few full-time practitioners are substantially guided by empirical findings, in part because many studies fails to address the concerns and questions that clinicians faced in their day-to-day practice (Goldfried & Wolfe, 1996). To a certain extent, this might reflect what I have described elsewhere as "empirical imperialism" (see Castonguay in Lampropoulos, Goldfried, Castonguay, Lambert, Stiles, & Nestoros, 2002), when scientists who often treat very few patients decide what should be studied (and how it should be studied) in order to understand and improve psychotherapy.

As also argued elsewhere (Castonguay in Lampropoulos et al., 2002) a likely antidote to such empirical imperialism is to foster clinicians' full participation in all aspects of empirical studies, from the selection of issues to be investigated, delineation of hypotheses to be tested, construction and implementation of research design, as well as dissemination of the findings. The formation of Practice Research Networks (PRNs), which rests on an active collaboration between researchers and clinicians in the development of clinically relevant and scientifically rigorous studies, has been viewed as a promising vehicle or infrastructure to foster such engagement. Established under the leadership of a full-time academician (Tom Borkovec) and a full-time clinician (Steve Ragusea), the Pennsylvania Psychological Association Practice Research Network (PPA-PRN) is, to my knowledge, the first PRN to be specifically devoted to this type of collaborative research on psychotherapy. The PPA-PRN has now completed two studies. Launched in the mid-1990s, the first was aimed at testing the feasibility of conducting scientifically sound research within the practice setting using a core assessment battery for obtaining pre- and post-outcome data within a state-wide infrastructure (Borkovec, Echemendia, Ragusea, & Ruiz, 2001).

The second completed study is the focus of two recently published papers (Castonguay, Boswell, et al., 2010; Castonguay, Nelson, et al., 2010); the first presents the findings obtained in this second study (discussed further below), and the second describes the experiences of clinicians who collaborated with full-time researchers not only in the implementation, but also in the design (which alone required regular meetings for one full year) of this investigation. I want to briefly discuss this study, not by emphasizing its results but by highlighting the level of involvement that clinicians can commit toward research within their own private practices, as well as some of the lessons that can be derived from the active collaboration of knowledge seekers living in different worlds.

The primary goal of the PRN study upon which these papers are based was to assess what clients find helpful and/or hindering during treatment in order to help therapists better address their clients' needs. As described in detail in Castonguay, Boswell, et al. (2010), the research protocol required clients and psychotherapists (or only the psychotherapist, depending on the experimental condition to which a client was assigned) to fill out parts of the Helpful Aspects of Therapy questionnaire (HAT; Elliott, Slatick, & Urman, 2006) at the end of every session. Specifically, participants were asked to: (1) answer two questions on small index cards (Did anything particularly helpful happen during this session? and Did anything happen during this session which might have been hindering?); (2) briefly describe the event(s) if applicable; and (3) rate these events in terms of the degree to which they were helpful or hindering, respectively.

Thirteen therapists of varying theoretical orientations participated in the design and implementation of this study. For a period of 18 months, psychotherapists invited all of their new clients (adults, adolescents, and children) to participate in the study (except when psychotherapists judged such participation to be clinically contraindicated). Combining the child, adolescent, and adult groups, 146 clients participated, and more than 1,600 helpful or hindering events were collected. These events were coded by three independent observers, using a therapy content analysis system. Among the findings obtained with the adult and adolescent groups, both clients and therapists perceived the fostering of self-awareness as being particularly helpful. The results also point to the importance of paying careful attention to the therapeutic alliance and other significant interpersonal relationships.

A qualitative analysis of interviews conducted with the participating psychotherapists led to the delineation of several benefits to therapists (e.g., learning information that improved their work with clients and feeling that they were contributing to research that would be useful for psychotherapists), difficulties for them and their clients (e.g., time and effort required to integrate research protocol into routine clinical practice), as well as general recommendations for future PRN studies (Castonguay, Nelson, et al., 2010). As we noted,

> Perhaps the most important recommendation for future PRNs is to conduct studies that intrinsically confound research with practice—studies for which it is impossible to fully distinguish whether the nature of the questions investigated, tasks implemented, or the data collected are empirical or clinical. We would venture to guess that psychotherapists and researchers will be most successful in designing and implementing PRN studies when their empirical goals are intertwined with day-to-day clinical tasks and/or concerns (as when clinicians are able to learn about what could facilitate and/or interfere with change as they are involved in the process of collecting data with each individual client). To paraphrase a commonly used term ("ego-syntonic"), research has to be "clinically-syntonic." It could be argued that clinicians truly integrate science and practice every time they perform a task in their clinical practices and are not able to provide an unambiguous answer to questions such as: "Right now, am I gathering clinical information or am I collecting data?" or, "At this moment, am I trying to apply a helpful intervention with my client or am I implementing a research task?" Frequently setting up rigorous empirical investigations that will lead them to answer these questions by saying, "Perhaps both," may be the most fruitful and exciting pathway to bridge research and practice (pp. 352–353).

Private practice, of course, should not be viewed as the only anchor for PRNs. Clinic training programs in psychology departments can also be optimal sites for such networks, as they can foster another level of healthy confusion between three goals or tasks that are frequently viewed as mutually exclusive: clinical, research, and training. One might argue that simultaneous, seamless, and repeated integration of science and practice activities as early as possible in a psychotherapist's career might create an intellectual and emotional (hopefully secure) attachment to principles and merits of the Boulder model.

My colleagues and I at Penn State have transformed our psychology clinic into such a PRN by creating and/or incorporating four major components into our training program: a core outcome battery, standardized diagnostic assessment procedures, a selection committee for the evaluation of research proposals (including representatives from the faculty, clinical staff, students, and practitioners from the community), and an innovative agreement with the office of research protection to efficiently streamline the Institutional Review Board (IRB) assessment process. This infrastructure has allowed several of our students to find themselves in a situation in which they are seeing clients, meeting their clinical hour requirements, and collecting their masters and/or dissertation data, while at the same time discovering, for example, that the trajectory of change of their clients can be predicted by their initial severity level on assessment (Nordberg, Boswell, Castonguay, & Kraus, 2008) or that cognitive-behavioral interventions can have a negative impact on particular clients, especially when used by particular therapists (Boswell, Castonguay, & Wasserman, 2010).

However, while such PRN initiatives can lead to fruitful investigations, individually each particular site or network will be restricted in terms of the sample it can provide, the expertise it can represent, and thus the connections of knowledge it can foster. Hence, I believe that an important next step for the future growth of the integration of science and practice is the creation of large infrastructures where clinicians (of different level of training) and researchers (in applied and basic sciences) will design and conduct descriptive (including single-cases), correlational, and experimental studies based on the same assessment tools. Examples of such infrastructures include the Network of Practice-Research Networks that my colleague David Kraus and I are in the process of building with groups of researchers and clinicians working together in different regions of North America, a similar type of infrastructure (proposed by Borkovec, 2002) that would connect a large number of training clinics across clinical and counseling masters and doctoral degree programs, and the major infrastructure developed by Ben Locke (Locke, Crane, Chun-Kennedy, & Edens, 2010) that now includes more than 120 counseling centers providing clinical services to college students in the USA (and which has recently led to a number of "preliminary" studies involving 28,000 clients (see Castonguay, Locke, & Hayes, 2011).

Concluding Words and Wishes

Psychotherapy research is at least 60 years old. These decades of empirical efforts have led to important and exciting findings, which in turn have firmly established the scientific credibility of psychosocial interventions, as well as confirmed, advanced and sometimes challenged some of our views of therapeutic change. To a large extent, these contributions, including those by many leaders of the SPR (see Castonguay, Muran, et al., 2010), have been facilitated by (and have fostered the growth of) diverse theoretical, methodological, and professional communities. At various times, however, myopic or rigid adherence to a preferred tradition has led to dismissing views about the potential contributions of others, and/or to restrictive and divisive perspectives about what treatments work, how they work, and how we should train future therapists. The aim of this paper is to suggest that one way, and by no means the only one, to challenge such perspectives (and potentially improve our understanding of and the impact of psychotherapy) is by fostering and deepening connections within and between communities of knowledge seekers.

As mentioned above, we have so many difficult and important responsibilities (preventing harmful effects being one of them), that it behooves us to explore and hopefully establish synergetic connections between different research methods, theoretical approaches, research domains, and world-views/experiences. Although they will no doubt continue to evolve on their own distinct paths, the crossings of communities of knowledge seekers will likely provide scholars and/or clinicians with unique opportunities to enrich their view of complex realities, such as psychotherapy and psychopathology.

21

WHAT THE FUTURE HOLDS FOR PSYCHOTHERAPY RESEARCH

Bernhard M. Strauss, Louis G. Castonguay, and Jacques P. Barber

The main chapters of this book provide the messages of 20 former presidents of the Society for Psychotherapy Research (SPR), all of whom represent very heterogeneous research traditions, theoretical perspectives, as well as biographical and cultural backgrounds. In their retrospective remarks, some presidents reached the conclusion that their recommendations for the future did not have the impact they had hoped for, but the majority believed that their work had some influence on subsequent studies in their own as well as other research labs. The goal of this concluding chapter is to offer a brief synopsis of these contributions, as well as to present some of our own predictions and/or recommendations for future research in psychotherapy.

Messages of 20 SPR Past Presidents: A Synopsis

Covering the Bases: Research, Theory, and Practice

From a *general perspective*, the messages of the Presidential Addresses and the commentaries emphasize the importance of anchoring the advancement of the field to strong research programs, the need to build psychotherapeutic work upon solid theories, as well as the critical value of pursuing empirical knowledge that could lead to a consensus about what effective therapy really is. In order to foster the impact of research on practice, several chapters' authors also underline the need to present research findings without relying too heavily on methodological questions and scientific jargon. Furthermore, some authors argued that researchers should distance themselves from major theoretical traditions and, instead, recommended efforts to build a research-informed psychotherapy (Grawe) based on interventions that cut across different approaches (Goldfried).

Combining these recommendations, Clarkin predicted, "That it is quite possible that future treatment development will be guided less by theory (i.e., cognitive behavioral, schema, psychodynamic), but more by the empirical understanding of the sequence of cognitive-affective reactions that disturb interpersonal functioning" (p. 268).

Interestingly, while some questioned the merit of having research being guided by (or aimed at supporting) major models of psychotherapy, there appears to be a consensus among past presidents that future treatments should take into consideration multiple concepts and theories related to scientific fields such as cognitive and social psychology, as well as neurosciences (e.g., Caspar, Clarkin, Horowitz, Mergenthaler, Moras). Clarkin, for example, mentions initiatives to promote a research domain criteria (RDoC) approach focusing on neurobiological systems and to "the moment-to-moment functioning of patients at various levels of the organism (e.g., neurotransmitters, neurocognitive functioning, psychological functioning)" (p. 269). Research on common factors are seen by some of the past presidents as an important link between psychotherapy and psychopathology research and as a fruitful avenue for the integration of different types of knowledge (e.g., Castonguay, Goldfried, Horowitz, Moras).

Exploring the possibility of further expansions of scientific boundaries, different opinions were expressed with regard to whether and/or how natural sciences might function as a model for research and as a source of constructs relevant to psychotherapy. Whereas some authors argued for a paradigm shift guided by important discoveries and advances in natural sciences, others note the "uniqueness of our subject material" (Benjamin) needing specific scientific approaches. For others, biological sciences may actually be a major threat to psychotherapy research because of the fact that, at least in some countries, political and economic issues have led to funding priorities for biological research. Shapiro even states that "science is for sale" (p. 103) and that universities increasingly have become commercial enterprises that are also under the influence of external forces causing conflicts of interest.

In contrast with some disagreements noted about the types and level of connections between psychotherapy and basic sciences, many authors voiced the same need to develop a partnership between scientists and practitioners; as well as to closely link empirical data with clinical reality (e.g., Aveline, Barber, Castonguay, Goldfried, Kächele, Piper, Shapiro). As noted by Kächele, "It is the interaction between clinical work and scientific study that should become standard in our field" (p. 38). This interactive pathway should be viewed as a two-way process. On the one hand, rather than limiting ourselves to controlled studies, it is important to conduct research in naturalistic settings (in the "real world") in order to maximize the ecological value of studies for clinicians (Barber). On the other hand, researchers should also listen to practitioners' concerns (what they need to know in order to better address difficult clinical situations), as well as their evaluations of research (e.g., EST) as it is applied in clinical settings

(Goldfried). In addition, several authors pointed to the need of more research on training, not only to help trainers and supervisors to select and train therapists, but also to make research an educational experience for trainees (e.g., Aveline, Castonguay, Crits-Christoph, Hill, Shapiro, Strauss).

Research Foci in Psychotherapy: Does it Work, How, for Whom, and with Whom?

The authors of the chapters have investigated many questions, which reflect central themes in psychotherapy research. Although the efficacy of psychotherapy has been established for at least three decades (Smith, Glass, & Miller, 1980), the *outcome* question is still at the heart of the research program of many past SPR presidents. Undoubtedly, outcome research has become more elaborated using, for example, sophisticated statistical methods that better model changes or by investigating more specific issues such as sudden gains. Refinements have also included the focus on predictions of treatment failure and the use of strategies to reduce deteriorations, such as providing feedback to therapists (Lambert).

Process research represents a specific (if not unifying) tradition within SPR, a tradition that has been highlighted and pursued by several past presidents (e.g., Barber, Benjamin, Clarkin, Crits-Christoph, Goldfried, Greenberg, Elliott, Hill, Kächele, Mergenthaler, Moras, Shapiro, Stiles). This is reflected in this book by many statements about the primary goal of psychotherapy research, such as explaining the "process of change" (Stiles) (p. 149), pursuing "a basic science of psychotherapy, with the emphasis on understanding mechanisms of change" (Shapiro) (p. 100), or that "for a true science, we need to specify client and therapist processes as well as their interaction" (Greenberg) (p. 23).

Most studies examining what happens during psychotherapy sessions are located in the *"interpersonal environment of psychotherapy"* with a focus on constructs such as alliance and alliance ruptures, transference, or attachment and interpersonal models of therapeutic interaction (e.g., Aveline, Barber, Benjamin, Castonguay, Clarkin, Crits-Cristoph, Goldfried, Hill, Horowitz, Lambert). Although they have received less attention at SPR (and in the field of psychotherapy research in general), "non-relational" process constructs have been investigated by some past presidents, including therapists' interpretations (Crits-Christoph, Barber), as well as client insight and corrective experiences (Castonguay). Also emphasized in some of the previous chapters are methodological strategies in process research (including qualitative and/or single-case approaches [e.g., Aveline, Elliott, Greenberg, Hill, Kächele, Mergenthaler, Stiles], as well as theories about specific aspects of the change process (e.g., therapeutic cycle model, Mergenthaler).

In addition to examining the impact and process of psychotherapy, a number of past presidents have investigated variables related to its participants. This involves, for example, clients' characteristics such as interpersonal problems, personality disorder, defenses, and attachment (Barber, Benjamin, Crits-Christoph,

Clarkin, Horowitz, Strauss). The therapist effect (as it relates to harmful impact of psychotherapy, for example) has recently received considerable attention by many SPR presidents of the recent years (e.g, Aveline, Barber, Benjamin, Castonguay, Crits-Christoph, Lambert). As mentioned above and described in more detail below, the training of therapists (including supervision) has also become an important theme of research (Aveline, Crits-Christoph, Hill, Strauss).

Research Strategies and Methodology

Readers of the presidents' chapters will have certainly noticed the extensive discussions about research strategies and methodology in our field (e.g., Aveline, Barber, Benjamin, Crits-Christoph, Elliott, Greenberg, Hill, Stiles). Frequently expressed in these discussions are critical positions about the increased focus on specific disorders and the fact that too much weight might be put on randomized clinical trials (RCT) studies as the ultimate type of evidence (as it is understood by several guideline committees, such as National Institute for Health and Care Excellence NICE in the UK). Accordingly, several past presidents have urged the field to go beyond RCTs (and the related concept of Empirically Supported Treatments, EST) and recognize a wider range of methods and approaches in building a valid empirical foundation to psychotherapy (Barber, Castonguay). It has also been suggested that future research focus less on specific disorders and more on areas of dysfunction (Clarkin). It should be mentioned, however, that some presidents have argued that unfair and excessive critiques of specific methodologies (especially RCT) have been voiced in the SPR community, which may in turn have contributed to the polarization of the field on the issue of evidence based practice (Piper).

However, there appears to be a broad consensus that a wide range of quantitative and qualitative studies can be helpful for the progress of psychotherapy research (e.g., Hill). One of the leitmotifs that emerged from the presidential statements is the view "that psychotherapy research should comprise a variety of approaches including a discovery oriented mixture of rational and empirical approach that heavily relies on a qualitative approach" (Greenberg). Although serious problems have been associated with quantitative approaches (Stiles), many past presidents have acknowledged them as important tools for outcome, process-outcome and dose-effect research (Piper, Lambert). Considering the strengths and limitations of all research strategies, it has been suggested that different methodologies be used to understand same cases and phenomena (Barber, Castonguay, Goldfried, Stiles).

A plea for Pluralism: SPR's Position in the Scientific Field

During times of a continuing medicalization of mental health and an economization of the mental health systems in most industrialized countries, it is helpful for psychotherapists to have the "secure base" of a scientific organization that is active in the dissemination of recent developments in the field. The SPR has provided such a basis for more than 40 years (see the Introduction). The presidential presentations included in this book provide a picture of the wide theoretical and epistemological spectrum that is represented in this organization. While SPR is frequently described in the scientific field as prominently psychodynamically oriented, as well as predominantly focused on process and on qualitative research, we believe this book's chapters demonstrate that such stereotypes are inaccurate.

SPR is an organization that attempts to integrate a diversity of cultures, psychotherapeutic traditions, professional backgrounds, clinical settings and populations, theories and findings, as well as research models. It is proudly viewed by its members as a truly international society, a status that is reflected by its former presidents, the profile of its journal and the locations of its meeting (see the Introduction).

We believe that the stereotypical views regarding SPR are in part the result of false dichotomies or "core conflicts" in the field, such as between process and outcome research, technique and relationship (Barber), psychological and biological factors (Casper), RCTs and other approaches supporting the effectiveness of interventions, or between efficacy research and the search for significant principles of change. We have experienced SPR as an environment in which different approaches and views are not only permitted but frequently integrated in the quest of developing a better understanding of psychotherapy. By being constantly confronted with those differing points of view, some research of course withdraws, but others are galvanized to attempt to resolve those conflicts or tensions within our field. As Mark Aveline has formulated in his commentary, "SPR could provide all the paraphernalia that is needed to gather and marshal practice-based evidence so as to inform evidence-based practice."

Future issues of psychotherapy research

Reaching the end of this book, it is hard to add something significant to all the "visions" that have been formulated. Based upon our discussion of major themes represented in the last 20 years of psychotherapy research, we nevertheless would like to conclude this book with a brief list of recommendations that, in our opinion, might be candidates to guide psychotherapy research in the years to come:

- As mentioned above, criticisms have been voiced about the current emphasis on specific disorders in psychotherapy research. It may well be that the current attention given to *transdiagnostic* interventions or principles (e.g. McHugh, Murray, & Barlow, 2009) will become a predominant theme in future research. At least in the field of group psychotherapy, there is a clear tendency for studies examining the effects of *mixed diagnosis* groups for mood and anxiety, anxiety and post-traumatic stress, mixed anxiety (social phobia, generalized, obsessive compulsive disorder and panic) and co-occurring disorders (Burlingame, Strauss, & Joyce, 2013) reflecting the reality for many clinicians that it is very difficult composing diagnostically homogeneous groups. A greater attention to transdiagnostic interventions would also be consistent with the fact that co-morbidity is the norm rather than the exception in psychopathology (Castonguay & Oltmanns, 2013).

- Similarly, there is a great need to examine which subgroups of patients derive more benefits from successful interventions (e.g., Barber & Muenz, 1996; Barber et al., 2012). As we know, not one intervention works for all patients with a certain problem or diagnosis. There is a need to continue developing more sophisticated theories of what works for whom, and to test those theories on existing database and in new studies. In other words, there is a need to recognize the role of the patient complex presentation in making the best treatment decision.
- Together with a greater emphasis on, and an acknowledgement of the importance of therapist factors (e.g., Baldwin & Imel, 2013), there has also been an increasing interest in the questions of how to describe the *professionalization* of therapists, what training tools are effective, and what facilitate and interfere with the development of effective therapists. SPR's recent special interest group on training and therapists' development has taken the lead in coordinating studies and initiating research cooperation on these important issues. In view of huge differences in the training and health service systems across different countries and continents, an international perspective on training standards is of utmost importance.
- As a part of initiatives to foster training research in psychotherapy, it is important to systematically develop and study empirically based approaches that would provide alternatives to standard "school-oriented" psychotherapy training, such as integrative training models, training based upon principles of change, or common factors.
- The *development and evaluation of instruments* for psychotherapy research has been a long tradition in SPR, including early attempts to create core batteries of measures aimed at enabling better comparisons of single studies (Strupp, Horowitz, & Lambert, 1997; Waskow & Parloff, 1975). Unfortunately, the situation has not changed very much, with many different measures still being used, and researchers often developing new instruments instead of resorting to previously developed and validated ones. The time may well be ripe for other efforts to achieve minimal level of consensus in the field (and consistency across future research) with regard to core issues of measurement.
- Over the last few years, an increasing number of studies have emerged using neurobiological approaches in psychotherapy, such as investigations of changes in the brain function following psychotherapeutic intervention, and attempts to refine clinical diagnoses and predicting treatment outcome based

upon neuroimaging. While we recognize the potential benefits of biological research of this kind, we also hope that the funding priority that this type of research is currently enjoying will not overshadow the investigation of other dimensions of functioning (intra-personal, interpersonal, social, and cultural), and that the studies conducted within this zeitgeist will be less guided by purely academic pursuits (i.e., "l'art pour l'art") than by questions of high relevance for the practice of psychotherapy.

- We see an urgent need to expand upon psychotherapy researchers' knowledge of, and collaboration with, a wide range of other disciplines such as behavioral medicine, psychosomatics, psychopathology, basic sciences (including cognitive, developmental, and social psychology), sociology, anthropology, etc.
- We also see the need to develop new statistical methods and to critically discuss the standards of statistical analyses in our field with statisticians, especially to evaluate the fit between the methods and the quality of the data that is typically collected in psychotherapy research.
- We would also argue that more attention should be given to a diversity of epistemologies (e.g., hermeneutic, phenomenology). Convergences and complementarities that are likely to emerge from different methods of knowledge acquisition could indeed deepen and expand our understanding of psychotherapy.
- We also believe that a fruitful strategy to conduct more clinically relevant research, as well as to facilitate the use of research in naturalistic settings, is to establish better collaborations with practitioners (in diverse form of practice-oriented research, including the development of research-practice networks, see Castonguay, Barkham, Lutz, & McAleavey, 2013), stakeholders (such as insurance companies as, e.g., in some recent practice-based research programs in Germany), and clients or client organizations (such as the National Alliance on Mental Illness). These collaborations could enhance the role and influence of psychotherapy as a central element in the mental health systems.
- There is no doubt in our minds that ethical issues psychotherapy will be an important focus of future research. These include the question as to how negative or even harmful effects of psychotherapy can be documented, explained, reduced, and prevented.
- We also predict that more attention will be given in the future to specific questions such as the impact of intense and long-term psychotherapy as an alternative to brief and manualized interventions. We also think that it would be important to learn more about individuals who may not frequently seek or receive psychotherapy, including members of lower social classes, minorities, complex disorders, or severe and persistent mental illness such as bipolar disorders and schizophrenia.
- In the context of globalization, we believe that research should be guided by a sociocultural view of psychotherapy that allows reflections about, and

investigations of, specific needs of patients and the social and cultural manifestations of psychotherapeutic interventions in different parts of the world.

- Finally, we realize that psychotherapy research and training is increasingly endangered to become "ahistoric." Many interventions that are supposed to be "innovative" are nothing more than reinventions of earlier treatment approaches. Researchers, supervisors, trainees, and practitioners should be aware of the historical roots of their current knowledge and practices. As for the recent book on SPR leaders it was aimed to complement (Castonguay, Muran, Angus, Hayes, Ladany, & Anderson, 2010), the preservation of the knowledge of decades of psychotherapy research has been one of the major motivations to create this book.

REFERENCES

Abramson, L. Y., & Sackeim, H. A. (1977). A paradox in depression: Uncontrollability and self blame among abused women. *Canadian Journal of Psychiatry, 40,* 234–240.

Adler, A. (1925). *The practice and theory of individual psychology* (pp. 1–15). London: Routledge.

Agnew, R. M., Harper, H., Shapiro, D. A., & Barkham, M. (1994). Resolving a challenge to the therapeutic relationship: A single-case study. *British Journal of Medical Psychology, 67,* 155–170.

Aine, C. J. (1995). A conceptual overview and critique of functional neuro-imaging techniques in humans: I. MRI/fMRI and PET. *Critical Reviews in Neurobiology, 9,* 229–309.

Ainsworth, M. D. S., Blehar, M. C., Waters, E., & Wall, S. (1978). *Patterns of attachment. A psychological study of the strange situation.* Hillsdale, NJ: Erlbaum.

Alden, L. E., Wiggins, J. S., & Pincus, A. L. (1990). Construction of circumplex scales for the Inventory of Interpersonal Problems. *Journal of Personality Assessment, 55,* 521–536.

Alexander, F., & French, T. (1946). *Psychoanalytic therapy: Principles and applications.* New York: Ronald Press.

American Psychiatric Association (1980). *Diagnostic and statistical manual of mental disorders* (3rd ed.). Washington, DC: American Psychiatric Association.

American Psychiatric Association (1987). *Diagnostic and statistical manual of mental disorders* (3rd ed., revised). Washington, DC: American Psychiatric Association.

American Psychiatric Association (1994). *Diagnostic and statistical manual of mental disorders* (4th ed.). Washington, DC: American Psychiatric Association.

American Psychiatric Association (2000). *Diagnostic and statistical manual of mental disorders* (4th ed., revised). Washington, DC: American Psychiatric Association.

American Psychological Association (2013). Recognition of psychotherapy effectiveness. *Psychotherapy, 50,* 102–109.

American Psychological Association Task Force on Promotion and Dissemination of Psychological Procedures (1995). Training in and dissemination of empirically validated treatments: Report and recommendations. *Clinical Psychologist, 48*(1), 3–24.

Anderson, E. M., & Lambert, M. J. (2001). A survival analysis of clinically significant change in outpatient psychotherapy. *Journal of Clinical Psychology, 57,* 875–888.

Andreasen, N. (1997). Linking mind and brain in the study of mental illnesses: A project for a scientific psychopathology. *Science, 275*(5306), 1586–1593.

Angus, L., Goldman, R., & Mergenthaler, E. (2008). Introduction. One case, multiple measures: An intensive case-analytic approach to understanding client change processes in evidence-based, emotion-focused therapy of depression. *Psychotherapy Research, 18,* 629–633.

Angus, L. E., & McLeod, J. (Eds.). (2004). *The handbook of narrative psychotherapy: Practice, theory and research.* London: Sage.

Arkowitz, A. (1989). The role of theory in psychotherapy integration. *Journal of Integrative and Eclectic Psychotherapy, 8,* 8–16.

Aveline, M. (1979). Towards a conceptual framework of psychotherapy—A personal view. *British Journal of Medical Psychology, 52,* 271–275.

Aveline, M. (1988). The process of being known and the initiation of change. In W. Dryden (Ed.), *Key cases in psychotherapy* (pp. 21–47). London: Croom-Helm.

Aveline, M. (1990). The group therapies in perspective. *Free Associations, 19,* 77–101.

Aveline, M. (1995). How I assess for focal therapy. In C. J. Mace (Ed.), *The art and science of assessment in psychotherapy* (pp. 137–154). London: Routledge.

Aveline, M. (1999). The advantages of formulation over categorical diagnosis in explorative psychotherapy and psychodynamic management. *European Journal of Psychotherapy, Counselling and Health, 2,* 199–216.

Aveline, M. (2001a). Complexities of practice: Psychotherapy in the real world. In F. Palmer-Barnes & L. Murdin (Eds.), *Values and ethics in the practice of psychotherapy and counselling* (pp. 128–143). Buckingham, UK: Open University Press.

Aveline, M. (2001b). Very brief dynamic psychotherapy. *Advances in Psychiatric Treatment, 7,* 373–380.

Aveline, M. (2002a). Focal therapy, a brief interpersonally focussed psychotherapy. *Psychiatry, 1,* 2–9.

Aveline, M. (2005a). Clinical case studies: their place in evidence-based practice. *Psychodynamic Practice, 11*(2), 133–152.

Aveline, M. (2005b). The person of the therapist. *Psychotherapy Research, 15*(3), 155–164.

Aveline, M. (2006). Group psychotherapy. In S. Bloch (Ed.), *An introduction to the psychotherapies* (4th ed., pp. 237–263). Oxford, UK: Oxford University Press.

Aveline, M. (2007). The training and supervision of individual therapists. In W. Dryden (Ed.), *Dryden's Handbook of Individual Therapy* (5th ed., pp. 515–548). London: Sage.

Aveline, M. (2011). Questionnaire. *Therapy Today, 22,* 21.

Aveline, M., Shapiro, D. A., Parry, G., & Freeman, C. (1995). Building research foundations for psychotherapy practice. In M. Aveline & D. A. Shapiro (Eds.), *Research foundations for psychotherapy practice* (pp. 299–320). Chichester: John Wiley.

Aveline, M., Strauss, B. M., & Stiles, W. B. (2005). Psychotherapy research. In G. Gabbard, J. Beck, & J. Holmes (Eds.), *Concise Oxford textbook of psychotherapy* (1st ed., pp. 449–620) Oxford, UK: Oxford University Press.

Azim, H. F. A., Piper, W. E., Segal, P. M., Nixon, G. W. H., & Duncan, S. (1991). The quality of object relations scale. *Bulletin of the Menninger Clinic, 55,* 323–343.

Bagot, R., & Meaney, M. J. (2010). Epigenetics and the biological basis of gene x environment interactions. *Journal of the American Academy of Child & Adolescent Psychiatry, 49,* 752–771.

Bakhtin, M. M. (1981). Discourse in the novel. In M. Holquist (Ed.), *The dialogic imagination*. Austin: University of Texas Press.

Baldwin, S. A., Berkeljon, A., Atkins, D. C., Olsen, J., & Neilsen, S. (2009). Rates of change in naturalistic psychotherapy: Contrasting dose-effect and good-enough level models of change. *Journal of Consulting and Clinical Psychology, 77*(2), 203–211.

Baldwin, S. A., & Imel, Z. E. (2013). Therapist variables. In M. Lambert (Ed.), *Bergin and Garfields' handbook of psychotherapy and behaviour change*. New York: Wiley.

Baldwin, S. A., Wampold, B. E., & Imel, Z. E. (2007). Untangling the alliance outcome correlation: Exploring the relative importance of therapist and patient variability in the alliance. *Journal of Consulting and Clinical Psychology, 75*, 842–852.

Baltensperger, C., & Grawe, K. (2001). Psychotherapy from a health-economics point of view. *Zeitschrift für klinische Psychologie und Psychotherapie, 30*, 10–21.

Bandura, A. (1969). *Principles of behavior modification*. New York: Holt, Rinehart and Winston.

Barber, J. P. (2009). Toward a working through of some core conflicts in psychotherapy research. *Psychotherapy Research, 19*, 1–12.

Barber, J. P., Barrett, M. S., Gallop, R., Rynn, M., & Rickels, K. (2012). Short-term dynamic therapy vs. pharmacotherapy for major depressive disorder. *Journal of Clinical Psychiatry, 73*(1), 66–73.

Barber, J. P., Connolly, M. B., Crits-Christoph, P., Gladis, M., & Siqueland, L. (2000). Alliance predicts patients' outcome beyond in-treatment change in symptoms. *Journal of Consulting and Clinical Psychology, 68*, 1027–1032.

Barber, J. P., Crits-Christoph, P., & Luborsky, L. (1996). Effects of therapist adherence and competence on patient outcome in brief dynamic therapy. *Journal of Consulting and Clinical Psychology, 64*, 619–622.

Barber, J. P., Foltz, C., Crits-Christoph, P., & Chittams, J. (2004). Therapist's adherence and competence and treatment discrimination in the NIDA Collaborative Cocaine Treatment Study. *Journal of Clinical Psychology, 60*, 29–41.

Barber, J. P., & Gallop, R. (2008). *Disentangling the contribution of the therapists and the patients in complex therapeutic processes predictive of outcome*. Submitted for publication.

Barber, J. P., Gallop, R., Crits-Christoph, P., Barrett, M. S., Klostermann, S., McCarthy, K. S., et al. (2008). The role of the alliance and techniques in predicting outcome of supportive-expressive dynamic therapy for cocaine dependence. *Psychoanalytic Psychology, 25*, 461–482.

Barber, J. P., Gallop, R., Crits-Christoph, P., Frank, A., Thase, M. E., Weiss, R. D., et al. (2006). The role of therapist adherence, therapist competence, and the alliance in predicting outcome of individual drug counseling: Results from the NIDA Collaborative Cocaine Treatment Study. *Psychotherapy Research, 16*, 229–240.

Barber, J. P., Krakauer, I., Calvo, N., Badgio, P. C., & Faude, J. (1997). Measuring adherence and competence of dynamic therapists in the treatment of cocaine dependence. *Journal of Psychotherapy Practice and Research, 6*, 12–14.

Barber, J. P., Luborsky, L., Crits-Christoph, P., Thase, M. E., Wiess, R., Frank, A., et al. (1999). Therapeutic alliance as a predictor of outcome in treatment of cocaine dependence. *Psychotherapy Research, 9*, 54–73.

Barber, J. P., Luborsky, L., Gallop, R., Crits-Christoph, P., Weiss, R. D., Thase, M. E., et al. (2001). Therapeutic alliance as a predictor of outcome and retention in the National Institute on Drug Abuse Collaborative Cocaine Treatment Study. *Journal of Consulting and Clinical Psychology, 69*, 119–124.

Barber, J. P., & Muenz, L. R. (1996). The role of avoidance and obsessiveness in matching patients to cognitive and interpersonal psychotherapy: Empirical findings from the Treatment for Depression Collaborative Research Program. *Journal of Consulting and Clinical Psychology, 64,* 951–958.

Barber, J. P., Sharpless, B. A., Klostermann, S., & McCarthy, K. S. (2007a). Assessing intervention competence and its relation to therapy outcome: A selected review derived from the outcome literature. *Professional Psychology: Research and Practice, 38,* 493–500.

Barber, J. P., Triffleman, E., & Marmar, C. (2007b). Considerations in treatment integrity: Implications and recommendations for PTSD research. *Journal of Traumatic Stress, 20,* 793–805.

Barkham, M., Hardy, G. E., & Mellor-Clark, J. (Eds.) (2010). *Developing and delivering practice-based evidence: A guide for the psychological therapies.* Chichester: Wiley.

Barkham, M., Rees, A., Stiles, W.B., Shapiro, D. A., Hardy, G. E., & Reynolds, S. (1996). Dose-effect relations in time-limited psychotherapy for depression. *Journal of Consulting and Clinical Psychology, 64,* 927–935.

Barkham, M., Stiles, W. B., Lambert, M. J., & Mellor-Clark, J. (2010). Building a rigorous and relevant knowledge-base for the psychological therapies. In M. Barkham, G. Hardy, & J. Mellor-Clark (Eds.), *Developing and delivering practice-based evidence: A guide for the psychological therapies* (pp. 21–62). New York: Wiley Blackwell.

Barkham, M., Stiles, W. B., & Shapiro, D. A. (1993). The shape of change: Longitudinal assessment of personal problems. *Journal of Consulting and Clinical Psychology, 61,* 667–677.

Barlow, D. H., Gorman, J. M., Shear, M. K., & Woods, S. W. (2000). Cognitive-behavioral therapy, imipramine, or their combination for panic disorder: A randomized controlled trial. *Journal of the American Medical Association, 283,* 2529–2536.

Baron, R. M., & Kenny, D. A. (1986). The moderator-mediator variable distinction in social psychological research: Conceptual, strategic, and statistical considerations. *Journal of Personality and Social Psychology, 51*(6), 1173–1182.

Bartels, A., Zeki, S. (2004). The neural correlates of maternal and romantic love. *Neuroimage, 21,* 1155–1166.

Barton, S. (1994). Chaos, self-organization, and psychology. *American Psychologist, 49,* 5–14.

Bateman, A., & Fonagy, P. (1999). Effectiveness of partial hospitalization in the treatment of borderline personality disorder: A randomized controlled trial. *American Journal of Psychiatry, 156,* 1563–1569.

Bateman, A. W., & Fonagy, P. (2003). The development of an attachment-based treatment program for borderline personality disorder. *Bulletin of the Menninger Clinic, 67,* 234–267.

Bateman, A., & Fonagy, P. (2004). *Psychotherapy for borderline personality disorder.* Oxford, UK: Oxford University Press.

Bateman, A., & Fonagy, P. (2008). 8-year follow-up of patients treated for borderline personality disorder: Mentalization-based treatment versus treatment as usual. *American Journal of Psychiatry, 165,* 631–638.

Bauer, S., Lambert, M. J., & Nielsen, S. L. (2004). Clinical significance methods: A comparison of statistical techniques. *Journal of Personality Assessment, 82,* 60–70.

Baxter, L. R., Schwartz, J. M., Bergman, K. S., Szuba, M. P., Guze, B. H., Mazziotta, J. C., et al. (1992). Caudate glucose metabolic rate changes with both drug and behavior therapy for obsessive-compulsive disorder. *Archives of General Psychiatry, 49*(9), 681–689.

Bebb, C., Kendrick, D., Coupland, C., Madeley, R., Stewart, J., Brown, K., et al. (2007). A cluster randomised controlled trial of the effect of a treatment algorithm for hypertension in patients with type 2 diabetes. *British Journal of General Practice, 57,* 136–143.

Beck, A. T. (1983). Cognitive therapy of depression: New perspectives. In P. J. Clayton & J. E. Barrett (Eds.), *Treatment of depression: Old controversies and new approaches* (pp. 265–290). New York: Raven Press.

Beck, A. T., Rush, A. J., Shaw, B. F., & Emery, G. (1979). *Cognitive therapy of depression.* New York: Guilford Press.

Beck, A. T., Ward, C. H., Mendelson, M., Mock, J., & Erbaugh, J. (1961). An inventory for measuring depression. *Archives of General Psychiatry, 4,* 561–571.

Beckstead, D. J., Hatch, A. L., Lambert, M. J., Eggett, D. L., Goates, M. K., & Vermeersch, D. A. (2003). Clinical significance of the Outcome Questionnaire (OQ-45.2). *Behavior Analyst Today, 4,* 79–90.

Beermann, S. (1983). *Linguistische Analyse psychoanalytischer Therapiedialoge unter besonderer Berücksichtigung passivischer Sprechmuster.* Hamburg: Diplomarbeit.

Benjamin, L. S. (1974). Structural analysis of social behavior. *Psychological Review, 81,* 392–425.

Benjamin, L. S. (1979). Structural analysis of differentiation failure. *Psychiatry: Journal for the Study of Interpersonal Processes, 42,* 1–23.

Benjamin, L. (1981). *Manual for coding social interacts in terms of Structural Analysis of Social Behavior (SASB).* Madison: University of Wisconsin Press.

Benjamin, L. S. (1984). Principles of prediction using structural analysis of social behavior. In R. A. Zucker, J. Aronoff, & A. J. Rabin (Eds.), *Personality and the prediction of behavior* (pp. 121–173). New York: Academic Press.

Benjamin, L. S. (1986). Adding social and intrapsychic descriptors to Axis I of the DSM-III. In T. Millon & G. Merman (Eds.), *Contemporary directions in psychopathology* (pp. 599–638). New York: Guilford Press.

Benjamin, L. S. (1991). Brief SASB-directed reconstructive learning therapy. In P. Crits-Christoph & J. P. Barber (Eds.), *Handbook of short-term dynamic psychotherapy* (pp. 248–286). New York: Basic Books.

Benjamin, L. S. (1993a). *Interpersonal diagnosis and treatment of personality disorders.* New York: Guilford Press.

Benjamin, L. S. (1993b). Every psychopathology is a gift of love. *Psychotherapy Research, 3,* 1–24.

Benjamin, L. S. (1996). Introduction to the special section on Structural Analysis of Social Behavior (SASB). *Journal of Consulting and Clinical Psychology, 64,* 1203–1212.

Benjamin, L. S. (2003a). *Interpersonal diagnosis and treatment of personality disorders* (2nd ed.). New York: The Guilford Press.

Benjamin, L. S. (2003b). *Interpersonal reconstructive therapy.* New York: Guilford Press.

Benjamin, L. S. (draft). *Interpersonal Reconstructive Therapy for anger, anxiety and depression: it's about broken hearts, not broken brains.* Washington, DC: American Psychological Association.

Berenson, K., Downey, G., Rafaeli, E., Coifman, K., & Paquin, N. (2011). The rejection-rage contingency in borderline personality disorder. *Journal of Abnormal Psychology, 120,* 681–690.

Beretta, V., Despland, J. N., Drapeau, M., Michel, L., Kramer, U., Stigler, M., & de Roten, Y. (2007). Are relationship patterns with significant others reenacted with the therapist? A study of early transference reactions. *Journal of Nervous and Mental Disease, 195*(5), 443–450.

Berger, T. (2005). Die Dynamik psychischer Störungen. Strukturen und Prozesse aus der Perspektive konnektionistischer Netzwerke [Dynamics of mental disorders. Structures and processes from a perspective of connectionist models]. Doctoral dissertation, University of Freiburg. Available at: www.freidok.uni-freiburg.de/volltexte/1968/

Berger, T., & Caspar, F. (2009). Gewinnt die Psychotherapie durch die neurobiologische Erforschung ihrer Wirkmechanismen? *Zeitschrift für Psychiatrie, Psychologie und Psychotherapie, 57*(2), 77–85.

Bergin, A. E., & Garfield, S. L. (1994). Overview, trends, and future issues. In A. E. Bergin & S. L. Garfield (Eds.), *Handbook of psychotherapy and behavior change.* (4th ed., pp. 821–830). New York: John Wiley.

Berlin, S., & Johnson, C. (1989). Woman and autonomy: Using structural analysis of social Behaviour to find autonomy within connections. *Psychiatry, 52,* 79–95.

Bernard, H., Burlingame, G., Flores, P., Greene, L., Joyce, A., Kobos, J. C., et al. (2008). Clinical practice guidelines for group psychotherapy. *International Journal of Group Psychotherapy, 58,* 455–542.

Bernstein, L., & Bernstein, R. S. (1980) *Interviewing: A guide for health professionals.* New York: Appleton-Century-Crofts.

Beutel, M. E. (2002). Neurowissenschaften und Psychotherapie. Neuere Entwicklungen, Methoden und Ergebnisse. *Psychotherapeut, 47,* 1–10.

Beutler, L. E. (1991). Have all won and must all have prizes? Revisiting Luborsky et al.'s verdict. *Journal of Consulting and Clinical Psychology, 59,* 226–232.

Beutler, L. E., Clarkin, J. F., & Bongar, B. (2000). *Guidelines for the systematic treatment of the depressed patient.* New York: Oxford University Press.

Beutler, L. E., & Harwood, T. M. (2000). *Prescriptive psychotherapy: A practical guide to systematic treatment selection.* New York: Oxford University Press.

Beutler, L. E., Malik, M., Alimohamed, S., Harwood, T. M., Talebi, H., Noble, S., et al. (2004). Therapist variables. In M. Lambert (Ed.), *Handbook of psychotherapy and behavior change* (5th ed., pp. 227–306). New York: Wiley.

Binder, J. (1993). Is it time to improve psychotherapy training? *Clinical Psychology Review, 13*(4), 301–318.

Binswanger, L. (1963). *Being-in-the-World.* New York: Basic Books.

Blagys, M. D., & Hilsenroth, M. J. (2000). Distinctive features of short-term psychodynamic-interpersonal psychotherapy: A review of the comparative psychotherapy process literature. *Clinical Psychology, 7,* 167–188.

Blatt, S. J. (1974). Levels of object representation in anaclitic and introjective depression. *Psychoanalytic Study of the Child, 29,* 107–157.

Blatt, S. J., Sanislow, Ch. A., Zuroff, D. C., & Pilkonis, P. A. (1996). Characteristics of effective therapists: Further analyses of data from the national institute of mental health treatment of depression collaborative research program. *Journal of Consulting and Clinical Psychology, 64*(6), 1276–1284.

Blatt, S. J., & Schichman, S. (1983). Two primary configurations of psychopathology. *Psychoanalysis and Contemporary Thought, 6,* 187–254.

Blatt, S. J., Zuroff, D. C., Quinlan, D. M., & Pilkonis, P. (1996). Interpersonal factors in brief treatment of depression: Further analyses of the NIMH Treatment of Depression

Collaborative Research Program. *Journal of Consulting and Clinical Psychology, 64,* 1276–1284.

Bohart, A. C. (2000). A qualitative "adjudicational" model for assessing psychotherapy outcome. Paper presented at meeting of Society for Psychotherapy Research, Chicago, IL.

Bohart, A. C., Berry, M., & Wicks, C. (2011). Developing a systematic framework for utilizing discrete types of qualitative data as therapy research evidence. *Pragmatic Case Studies In Psychotherapy,* 7(1).

Bohart, A. C., & Boyd, G. (1997). Clients' construction of the therapy process: A qualitative analysis. Poster presented at meeting of North American Chapter of the Society for Psychotherapy Research, December.

Bohart, A. C., & Humphreys, C. (2000). A qualitative "adjudicational" model for assessing psychotherapy outcome. Paper presented at the meeting of the International Society for Psychotherapy Research, Chicago, IL, June.

Böhmer, M., Mergenthaler, E., & Pfäfflin, F. (2003). Change events during the psychotherapy process of a patient detained by court order due to sexual offence in a high security forensic clinic. *Psychiatrische Praxis, 30,* 145–151.

Bond, T., Ashcroft, R., Casemore, R., Jamieson, A., & Lendrum, S. (2002). *Ethical framework for good practice in counselling and psychotherapy.* Rugby, UK: British Association for Counselling and Psychotherapy.

Boring, E. G. (1964). Cognitive dissonance: Its use in science. *Science, 145,* 680–685.

Borkovec, T. D. (1997). On the need for a basic science approach to psychotherapy research. *Psychological Science, 8*(3), 145–147.

Borkovec, T. D. (2002). Training clinic research and the possibility of a national training clinics practice network. *Behavior Therapist, 25,* 98–103.

Borkovec, T. D., & Castonguay, L. G. (1998). What is the scientific meaning of "empirically supported therapy"? *Journal of Consulting and Clinical Psychology, 66,* 136–142.

Borkovec, T. D., Echemendia, R. J., Ragusea, S. A., & Ruiz, M. (2001). The Pennsylvania Practice Research Network and future possibilities for clinically meaningful and scientifically rigorous psychotherapy effectiveness research. *Clinical Psychology: Science and Practice, 8,* 155–167.

Borkovec, T. D., & Newman, M. G. (1998). Worry and generalized anxiety disorder. In A. S. Bellack, M. Hersen, & P. Salkovskis (Eds.), *Comprehensive clinical psychology,* Vol. 6., *Adults: Clinical formulation and treatment* (pp. 439–459). Oxford: Pergamon Press.

Borkovec, T. D., Newman, M. G., Pincus, A. L., & Lytle, R. (2002). A component analysis of cognitive-behavioral therapy for generalized anxiety disorder and the role of interpersonal problems. *Journal of Consulting and Clinical Psychology, 70,* 288–298.

Bormann, B., Strauss, B. (2007). Group climate, cohesion, alliance and empathy as components of the therapeutic relationship in group treatments. *Gruppenpsychotherapie und Gruppendynamik, 43,* 1–20.

Boswell, J. F., & Castonguay, L. G. (2007). Psychotherapy training: Suggestions for core ingredients and future research. *Psychotherapy: Theory, Research, Practice, Training, 44*(4), 378–383.

Boswell, J. F., Castonguay, L. G., & Wasserman, R. H. (2010). Effects of psychotherapy training and intervention use on session outcome. *Journal of Consulting and Clinical Psychology, 78,* 717–723.

Boswell, J. F., Nelson, D. L., Nordberg, S. S, McAleavey, A. A., & Castonguay, L. G. (2010). Competency in integrative psychotherapy: Perspectives on training and supervision. *Psychotherapy: Theory, Research, Practice and Training, 47,* 3–11.

Bowlby, J. (1979). *The making and breaking of affectional bonds.* London: Tavistock.
BPtK (Bundespsychotherapeutenkammer) (2009). Core competencies of psychotherapists. Positionspapier. Available at: www.bptk.de
Bressi, C., Amadei, G., Caparrelli, S., Cattaneo, C., Cova, F., Crespi, S., et al. (2000). A clinical and psychodynamic follow-up study of crisis intervention and brief psychotherapy in psychiatric emergency. *New Trends in Experimental and Clinical Psychiatry, 26,* 31–37.
Brinegar, M. G., Salvi, L. M., Stiles, W. B., & Greenberg, L. S. (2006). Building a meaning bridge: Therapeutic progress from problem formulation to understanding. *Journal of Counseling Psychology, 53,* 165–180.
Brody, A. L., Saxena, S., Stoessel, P., Gillies, L. A., Fairbanks, L. A., Alborzian, S., et al. (2001). Regional brain metabolic changes in patients with major depression treated with either paroxetine or interpersonal therapy. *Archives of General Psychiatry, 58,* 631–640.
Bromley, D. B. (1986). *The case-study method in psychology and related disciplines.* New York: Wiley.
Brown, S., Martinez, M. J., & Parsons, L. M. (2006). The neural basis of human dance. *Cerebral Cortex, 16,* 1157–1167.
Bruner, J. S. (1957). On perceptual readiness. *Psychological Review, 64,* 123–152.
Brunink, S. A., & Schroeder, H. E. (1979). Verbal therapeutic behavior of expert psychoanalytically oriented, gestalt, and behavior therapists. *Journal of Consulting and Clinical Psychology, 47,* 567–574.
Bucci, W. (1997). *Psychoanalysis & cognitive science. A multiple code theory.* New York: Guilford Press.
Buchheim, A., & Mergenthaler, E. (2000). The relationship among attachment representation, emotion-abstraction patterns, and narrative style: A computer-based text analysis of the Adult Attachment Interview. *Psychotherapy Research, 10,* 390–407.
Buchheim, A., & Mergenthaler, E. (2002). Adult attachment representation and computer-assisted language measures: What can we learn from the therapeutic cycle model for the Adult Attachment Interview and vice versa? *International Congress Series, 1241,* 353–360.
Buchheim, A., & Strauss, B. (2002). Interview methods in clinical attachment research. In B. Strauss, A. Buchheim, & H. Kächele (Eds.). *Klinische Bindungsforschung [Clinical attachment esearch]* (pp. 27–53). Stuttgart: Schattauer.
Buchwald, A. M., & Rudick-Davis, D. (1993). The symptoms of major depression. *Journal of Abnormal Psychology, 102,* 197–205.
Burlingame, G.M., MacKenzie, K.R., & Strauss, B. (2004). Small group treatment: Evidence for effectiveness and mechanisms of change. In M. J. Lambert (Ed.), *Begin and Garfield's handbook of psychotherapy and behavior change* (4th ed., pp. 647–696). New York: Wiley.
Burlingame, G. M., Strauss, B., & Joyce, A. (2013). Change mechanisms and effectiveness of small group treatments. In M. J. Lambert (Ed.), *Begin and Garfield's handbook of psychotherapy and behavior change* (5th Ed.). New York: Wiley.
Burns, D. D. (1990). *The feeling good handbook.* New York: Plume.
Campbell, D. T., & Stanley, J. C. (1963). Experimental and quasi-experimental designs for research on teaching. In N. L. Gage (Ed.), *Handbook of research on teaching* (pp. 171–246). Chicago, IL: Rand McNally.
Caro Gabalda, I. (2006). The assimilation of problematic experiences in linguistic therapy of evaluation: How did María assimilate the experience of dizziness? *Psychotherapy Research, 16,* 422–435.
Caro Gabalda, I. (2009). Convergence of voices in linguistic therapy of evaluation. *Clinical Psychology and Psychotherapy, 16,* 182–198.

Caro Gabalda, I., & Stiles, W. B. (2009). Setbacks in the context of linguistic therapy of evaluation. *Análise Psicológica, 27,* 199–212.

Caro Gabalda, I., & Stiles, W. B. (2013). Irregular assimilation progress: Setbacks in the context of linguistic therapy of evaluation. *Psychotherapy Research, 23,* 35–53.

Carroll, L. (1865). *Alice's adventures in wonderland* (de luxe Ed., undated, 1946). New York: J. J. Little Ives Co.

Carson, R. (1991). Dilemmas in the pathway of the DSM-IV. *Journal of Abnormal Psychology, 100,* 302–309.

Carson, R. C., & Butcher, J. N. (1992). *Abnormal psychology and modern life* (9th ed.). New York: HarperCollins.

Cartwright, R. D. (1993). Who needs their dreams? The usefulness of dreams in psychotherapy. *Journal of the American Academy of Psychoanalysis, 21,* 539–547.

Cartwright, R. D., Tipton, L. W., & Wicklund, J. (1980). Focusing on dreams: A preparation program for psychotherapy. *Archives of General Psychiatry, 37,* 275–277.

Carver, C. S., & Scheier, M. F. (2002). Control processes and self-organization as complementary principles underlying behavior. *Personality and Social Psychology Review, 6,* 304–315.

Casacalenda, N., Perry, J. C., & Looper, L. (2002). Remission in major depressive disorder: A comparison of pharmacotherapy, psychotherapy, and control conditions. *American Journal of Psychiatry, 159*(8), 1354–1360.

Casonato, M., & Mergenthaler, E. (2008). *Freud e l'uomo dei topi.* Urbino: Quattro Venti.

Caspar, F. (1995). *Plan analysis: Towards optimizing psychotherapy.* Seattle, WA: Hogrefe.

Caspar, F. (1998). A connectionist view of psychotherapy. In D. J. Stein & J. Ludik (Eds.), *Neural networks and psychopathology* (pp. 88–131). Cambridge, UK: Cambridge University Press.

Caspar, F. (2003). Psychotherapy research and neurobiology: Challenge, chance, or enrichment? *Psychotherapy Research, 13,* 1–23.

Caspar, F. (2007). Plan analysis. In T. Eells (Ed.), *Handbook of psychotherapeutic case formulations* (2nd ed., pp. 251–289). New York: Guilford Press.

Caspar, F., Benninghoven, D., & Berger, T. (2004). Kohärenz in psychotherapeutischen Fallkonzeptionen. *Zeitschrift für Psychiatrie, Psychotherapie und medizinische Psychologie, 54,* 320–329.

Caspar, F., & Berger, T. (2012). What can we learn from different models and research in basic psychology? In L. G. Castonguay & C. E. Hill (Eds.), *Transformation in psychotherapy: Corrective experiences across cognitive behavioral, humanistic, and psychodynamic approaches* (pp. 141–157). Washington, DC: American Psychological Association-

Caspar, F., & Eversmann, J. (2009). What do candidates have to have to become a good therapist? *Psychotherapie, Psychosomatik, Medizinische Psychologie, 59,* 213–215.

Caspar, F., & Grawe, K. (1996). What speaks for, what against individual case conceptualizations? In F. Caspar (Ed.), *Psychotherapeutische Problemanalyse* (pp. 65–86). Tübingen, Germany: DGVT.

Caspar, F., Grossmann, C., & Unmüssig, C. (2002). *Complementary therapeutic relationship Therapist behavior, interpersonal patterns, and therapeutic effects.* Manuscript submitted for publication.

Caspar, F., Koch, K., Schneider, F., Berger, T., & Wagner, G. (2011). Psychotherapie und ihre neurobiologischen Voraussetzungen. In W. Senf & M. Broda (Eds.), *Praxis der Psychotherapie* (pp. 48–69). Stuttgart: Thieme.

Caspar, F., Rothenfluh, T., & Segal, Z. V. (1992). The appeal of connectionism for clinicalpsychology. *Clinical Psychology Review, 12,* 719–762.

Castonguay, L. G. (1993). "Common factors" and "nonspecific variables": Clarification of the two concepts and recommendations for research. *Journal of Psychotherapy Integration, 3,* 267–286.

Castonguay, L. G. (2000). A common factors approach to psychotherapy training. *Journal of Psychotherapy Integration, 10,* 263–282.

Castonguay, L. G. (2000). Training in psychotherapy integration: Introduction to current efforts and future visions. *Journal of Psychotherapy Integration, 10,* 229–231.

Castonguay, L. G. (2005). Training issues in psychotherapy integration: A commentary. *Journal of Psychotherapy Integration, 15*(4), 384–391.

Castonguay, L. G. (2006). Personal pathways in psychotherapy integration. *Journal of Psychotherapy Integration, 16,* 36–58.

Castonguay, L. G. (2011). Psychotherapy, psychopathology, research and practice: pathways of connection and integration. *Psychotherapy Research, 21,* 125–140.

Castonguay, L. G., Barkham, M., Lutz, W., & McAleavey, A. A. (2013). Practice-oriented research: Approaches and applications. In M. J. Lambert (ed.), *Bergin and Garfield's handbook of psychotherapy and behaviour change.* New York: Wiley.

Castonguay, L. G., & Beutler, L. E. (2005a). *Principles of therapeutic change that work.* New York: Oxford University Press.

Castonguay, L. G., & Beutler, L. E. (2005b). Common and unique principles of therapeutic change: What do we know and what do we need to know? In L. G. Castionguay & L. E. Beutler (Eds.), *Principles of therapeutic change that work* (pp. 353–369). New York: Oxford University Press.

Castonguay, L. G., Boswell, J. F., Constantino, M. J., Goldfried, M. R., & Hill, C. E. (2010). Training implications of harmful effects of psychological treatments. *American Psychologist, 65,* 34–49.

Castonguay, L. G., Boswell, J. F., Zack, S., Baker, S., Boutselis, M., Chiswick, N., et al. (2010). Helpful and hindering events in psychotherapy: A practice research network study. *Psychotherapy: Theory, Research, Practice and Training, 47,* 327–344.

Castonguay, L. G., & Goldfried, M. R. (1994). Psychotherapy integration: An idea whose time has come. *Applied and Preventive Psychology, 3,* 159–172.

Castonguay, L. G., Goldfried, M. R., Wiser, S., Raue, P. J., & Hayes, A. H. (1996). Predicting outcome in cognitive therapy for depression: A comparison of unique and common factors. *Journal of Consulting and Clinical Psychology, 64,* 497–504.

Castonguay, L. G., & Hill, C. E. (2006). *Insight in psychotherapy.* Washington, DC: American Psychological Association Press.

Castonguay, L. G., Locke, B. D., & Hayes, J. A. (2011). The Center for Collegiate Mental Health: An example of a practice-research network in university counseling centers. *Journal of College Student Psychotherapy, 25,* 105–119.

Castonguay, L., Muran, C., Angus, L., Hayes, J., Ladany, N., & Anderson, T. (2010), *Bringing psychotherapy research to life.* Washington, DC: American Psychological Association.

Castonguay, L., Nelson, D., Boutselis, M, Chiswick, N., Damer, D., Hemmelstein, N., et al. (2010). Clinicians and/or researchers? A qualitative analysis of therapists' experiences in a practice research network. *Psychotherapy: Theory, Research, Practice and Training, 47,* 345–354.

Castonguay, L. G., Newman, M. G., Borkovec, T. D., Grosse Holtforth, M., & Maramba, G. G. (2005). Cognitive-behavior assimilative integration. In J. C. Norcross & M. R. Goldfried (Eds.), *The handbook of psychotherapy integration* (2nd ed., pp. 241–260). New York: Oxford University Press.

Castonguay, L. G., & Oltmanns, T. F. (2013). *Psychopathology: Bridging the gap between basic empirical findings and clinical practice.* New York: Guilford Press.

Castonguay, L. G., Reid, J. J., Halperin, G. S., & Goldfried, M. R. (2003). Psychotherapy integration . In G. Stricker & T.A. Widiger (Eds.), *Comprehensive handbook of Psychology,* Vol. 8, *Clinical Psychology* (pp. 327–345). New York: Wiley.

Castonguay, L. G., Schut, A. J., Aikins, D., Constantino, M. J., Laurenceau, J. P., Bologh, L., et al. (2004). Integrative cognitive therapy: A preliminary investigation. *Journal of Psychotherapy Integration, 14,* 4–20.

Chambless, D. L., & Ollendick, T. H. (2001). Empirically supported psychological interventions: Controversies and evidence. *Annual Review of Psychology, 52,* 685–716.

Chekhov, A. (2001). The death of a civil servant. In G. McVay (Ed.), *Anton Chekhov. Short stories* (pp. 1–3). London: Folio Society.

Chen, E. C., & Mallinckrodt, B. (2002). Attachment, group attraction and self-other agreement in interpersonal circumplex problems and perceptions of group members. *Group Dynamics, 6,* 311–324.

Cheston, R. (2013). Dementia as a problematic experience: The assimilation of problematic voices within psychotherapeutic work with people with dementia. *Neuro-disability and Psychotherapy, 1,* 70–95.

Cicchetti, D., Beeghly, M., Carlson, V., & Toth, S. (1990). The emergence of the self in atypical populations. In D. Cicchetti & M. Beeghly (Eds.), *The self in transition: Infancy to childhood* (pp. 309–344). Chicago: University of Chicago Press.

Cizza, G., Ravin, P., Chrousos, G. P., & Gold, P. W. (2001). Depression: A major, unrecognized risk factor for osteoporosis. *Trends in Endocrinology & Metabolism, 12,* 198–203.

Clark, D. M. (2011). Implementing NICE guidelines for the psychological treatment of depression and anxiety disorderes: The IAPT experience. *International Review of Psychiatry, 23,* 375–384.

Clark, D. M., Fairburn, C. G., & Wessely, S. (2008). Psychological treatment outcomes in routine NHS services: A commentary on Stiles et al. (2007). *Psychological Medicine, 38*(5), 629–634.

Clark, L. A. (2007). Assessment and diagnosis of personality disorder: Perennial issues and an emerging reconceptualization. *Annual Review of Psychology, 58,* 227–257.

Clarkin, J. F., Critchfield, K., & Levy, K. N. (2005). An approach to the heterogeneity of the borderline patient. Manuscript in preparation.

Clarkin, J. F., & De Panfilis, C. (2013). Developing conceptualization of borderline personality disorder. *Journal of Nervous and Mental Disease, 201,* 88–93.

Clarkin, J. F., Hull, J. W., & Hurt, S. W. (1993). Factor structure of borderline personality disorder criteria. *Journal of Personality Disorders, 7,* 137–143.

Clarkin, J. F., & Levy, K. N. (2004). The influence of client variables on psychotherapy. In M. J. Lambert (Ed.), *Bergin & Garfield's handbook of psychotherapy and behavior change* (pp. 194–226). New York: Wiley.

Clarkin, J. F., Levy, K. N., Lenzenweger, M. F., & Kernberg, O. F. (2007). Evaluating three treatments for borderline personality disorder: A multiwave study. *American Journal of Psychiatry, 164,* 922–928.

Clarkin, J. F., Marziali, E., & Monroe-Blum, H. (1992). *Borderline personality disorder: Clinical and empirical perspectives.* New York: Guilford Press.

Clarkin, J. F., Widiger, T. A., Frances, A., Hurt, S. W., & Gilmore, M. (1983). Prototypic typology and the borderline personality disorder. *Journal of Abnormal Psychology, 92,* 263–275.

Clarkin, J. F., Yeomans, F. E., & Kernberg, O. F. (2006). *Psychotherapy for borderline personality: Focusing on object relations.* Washington, DC: American Psychiatric Publishing.

Clementz, B. A., & Sweeney, J. A. (1990). Is eye movement dysfunction a biological marker for schizophrenia? A methodological review. *Psychological Bulletin, 108,* 77–92.

Coccaro, E. F., Siever, L. J., Klar, H. M., Maurer, G., Cochrane, K., Cooper, T. B., et al. (1989). Serotonergic studies in patients with affective and personality disorders: Correlates with suicidal impulsive aggressive behavior. *Archives of General Psychiatry, 46,* 587–599.

Cogar, M., & Hill, C. E. (1992). Examining the effects of brief individual dream interpretation. *Dreaming, 2,* 239–248.

Cole, S. (1992). *Making science: Between nature and society.* Cambridge, MA: Harvard University Press.

Compton, A. (1990). Psychoanalytic process. *Psychoanalytic Quarterly, 59,* 585–598.

Connelly, J. L., & Piper, W. E. (1989). An analysis of pretraining work behavior as a composition variable in group psychotherapy. *International Journal of Group Psychotherapy, 39,* 173–189.

Connolly, M. B., Crits-Christoph, P., Barber, J. P., & Luborsky, L. (1997). *Interpersonal themes before therapy compared to themes in the relationship with the therapist.* Unpublished manuscript.

Connolly, M. B., Crits-Christoph, P., Demorest, A., Azarian, K., Muenz, L., & Chittams, J. (1996). Varieties of transference patterns in psychotherapy. *Journal of Consulting and Clinical Psychology, 64,* 1213–1221.

Connolly, M. B., Crits-Christoph, P., Shappell, S., Barber, J. P., & Luborsky, L. (1997). The role of transference interpretations in brief supportive-expressivepsychotherapy for depression. Paper presented at the meeting of the Society for Psychotherapy Research, Geilo, Norway, June.

Connolly Gibbons, M. B., Crits-Christoph, P., de la Cruz, C., Barber, J. P., Siqueland, L., & Gladis, M. (2003). Pretreatment expectations, interpersonal functioning, and symptoms in the prediction of the therapeutic alliance across supportive-expressive psychotherapy and cognitive therapy. *Psychotherapy Research, 13,* 59–76.

Constantino, M. J., & Castonguay, L. G. (2003). Learning from the basics: Clinical implications of social, developmental, and cross-cultural study of the self. *Journal of Psychotherapy Integration, 13,* 3–8.

Constantino, M. J., Klein R., Smith-Hansen, L., & Greenberg, R. P. (2009). Augmenting cognitive therapy for depression with an Expectancy Enhancement module: Preliminary efficacy. Paper presented at the meeting of the Canadian Chapter of the Society for Psychotherapy Research, Montreal, Canada, October.

Constantino, M. J., Marnell, M., Haile, A. J., Kanther-Sista, S. N., Wolman, K., Zappert, L., & Arnow, B. A. (2008). Integrative cognitive therapy for depression: A randomized pilot comparison. *Psychotherapy: Theory, Research, Practice, Training, 45,* 122–134.

Cook, T. D., & Campbell, D.T. (1979). *Quasi-experimentation: Design and analysis issues for field settings.* Chicago: Rand McNally.

Cooper, M., & McLeod, J. (2010). *Pluralistic counselling and psychotherapy.* London: Sage.

Cooper, P., Osborn, M., Gath, D., & Fegetter, G. (1982). Evaluation of a modified self-report measure of social adjustment. *British Journal of Psychiatry, 141,* 68–75.

Cotter, D., Mackay, D., Landau, S., Kerwin, R., & Everall, I. (2001). Reduced glial cell density and neuronal size in the anterior cingulate cortex in major depressive disorder. *Archives of General Psychiatry, 58,* 545–553.

Crick, F., & Mitchison, G. (1983). The function of dream sleep. *Nature, 304,* 111–114.

Critchfield, K. L., & Benjamin, L. S. (2008). Internalized representations of early interpersonal experience and adult relationships: a test of copy process theory in clinical and nonclinical populations. *Psychiatry: interpersonal and biological processes, 71,* 71–92.

Critchfield, K. L., & Benjamin, L. S. (2010). Assessment of repeated relational patterns for individual cases using the SASB-based Intrex questionnaire. *Journal of Personality Assessment, 92,* 480–489.

Critchfield, K. L., Levy, K. N., & Clarkin, J. F. (2004). The relationship between impulsivity, aggression, and impulsive aggression in borderline personality disorder: An empirical analysis of self-report measures. *Journal of Personality Disorders, 18,* 555–570.

Crits-Christoph, P. (1991). When therapists miss the mark. Paper presented at the meeting of the Society for Psychotherapy Research, Lyons, France, July.

Crits-Christoph, P. (1998). The interpersonal interior of psychotherapy. *Psychotherapy Research, 8,* 1–16.

Crits-Christoph, P., & Baranackie, K. (1991). The process of cognitive and dynamic psychotherapies for substance abusers. Paper presented at the meeting of the North American Society for Psychotherapy Research. Panama City, FL, November.

Crits-Christoph, P., Barber, J. P., & Kurcias, J. S. (1993). The accuracy of therapists' interpretations and the development of the therapeutic alliance. *Psychotherapy Research, 3,* 25–35.

Crits-Christoph, P., & Connolly, M. B. (1999). Alliance and technique in short-term dynamic therapy. *Clinical Psychology Review, 19,* 687–704.

Crits-Christoph, P., Connolly Gibbons, M. B., Crits-Christoph, K., Narducci, J., Schamberger, M., & Gallop, R. (2006). Can therapists be trained to improve their alliances? A preliminary study of alliance-fostering psychotherapy. *Psychotherapy Research, 16,* 268–281.

Crits-Christoph, P., Cooper, A., & Luborsky, L. (1988). The accuracy of therapists' interpretations and the outcome of dynamic psychotherapy. *Journal of Consulting and Clinical Psychology, 56,* 490–495.

Crits-Christoph, P., Demorest, A., & Connolly, M. B. (1990). Quantitative assessment of interpersonal themes over the course of psychotherapy. *Psychotherapy, 27,* 513–521.

Crits-Christoph, P., Demorest, A., Muenz, L. R., & Baranackie, K. (1994). Consistency of interpersonal themes for patients in psychotherapy. *Journal of Personality, 62,* 499–526.

Crits-Christoph, P., Gibbons, M. B., Temes, C., Elkin, I., & Gallop, R. (2010). Interpersonal accuracy of interventions and the outcome of cognitive and interpersonal therapies for depression. *Journal of Consulting and Clinical Psychology, 78,* 420–428.

Crits-Christoph, P., & Luborsky, L. (1990). The changes in CCRT pervasiveness during psychotherapy. In L. Luborsky, & P. Crits-Christoph (Eds.), *Understanding Transference: The CCRT Method.* New York: Basic Books.

Crits-Christoph, P., Luborsky, L., Dahl, L., Popp, C., Mellon, J., & Mark, D. (1988). Clinicians can agree in assessing relationship patterns in psychotherapy: The core conflictual relationship theme method. *Archives of General Psychiatry, 45,* 1001–1004.

Crits-Christoph, P., Ring-Kurtz, S., Hamilton, J., Lambert, M. J., Gallop, R., McClure, B., et al. (2011). Preliminary study of the effects of individual patient-level feedback in outpatient substance abuse treatment programs. *Journal of Substance Abuse Treatment, 42*(3), 301–309.

Crits-Christoph, P., Siqueland, L., Blaine, J., Frank, A., Luborsky, L., Onken, L. S., et al. (1999). Psychosocial treatments for cocaine dependence: Results of the National Institute on Drug Abuse Collaborative Cocaine Treatment Study. *Archives of General Psychiatry, 56,* 493–502.

Cronbach, L. (1975). Beyond the two disciplines of scientific psychology. *American Psychologist, 30,* 116–127.

Cronbach, L. (1982). *Design, evaluations of educational and social programs.* San Francisco: Jossey-Bass.

Dahl, H. (1972). A quantitative study of psychoanalysis. *Psychoanalysis and Contemporary Science, 1,* 237–257.

Dahl, H. (1974). The measurement of meaning in psychoanalysis by computer analysis of verbal context. *Journal of the American Psychoanalytic Association, 22,* 37–57.

Dalal, F. (1998). *Taking the group seriously.* London: Jessica Kingsley.

Daldrup, R., Beutler, L., Engle D., & Greenberg, L. (1988). *Focused expressive psychotherapy.* New York: Guilford Press.

Damasio, A. R., Grabowski, T. J., Bechara, A., Damasio, H., Ponto, L. L. B., Parvizi J., & Hichwa, R. D. (2000). Subcortical and cortical brain activity during the feeling of self-generated emotions. *Nature Neurosciences, 3,* 1049–1124.

Davidson, R. J. (1993). Cerebral asymmetry and emotion: Conceptual and methodological conundrums. *Cognition and Emotion, 7,* 115–138.

Davidson, R. J. (1998). Affective style and affective disorders: Perspectives from affective neuroscience. *Cognition and Emotion, 12*(3), 307–330.

Davidson, R. J., Pizzagalli, D., Nitschke, J. B., & Putnam, K. (2002). Computational perspectives on dopamine function in prefrontal cortex. *Current Opinion in Neurobiology, 12,* 223–229.

Davies-Osterkamp, S., Strauss, B. M., & Schmitz, N. (1996). Interpersonal problems as predictors of symptom related treatment outcome in long term psychotherapy. *Psychotherapy Research, 6,* 164–176.

de Jong, K., Nugter, M. A., Polak, M. G., Wagenborg, J. E. A., Spinhoven, P., & Heiser, W. J. (2007). The Outcome Questionnaire (OQ-45) in a Dutch population: A cross-cultural validation. *Clinical Psychology and Psychotherapy, 14,* 28–301.

de Roten, Y., Drapeau, M., Stigler, M., & Despland, J. (2004). Yet another look at the CCRT: The relation between core conflictual relationship themes and defensive functioning. *Psychotherapy Research, 14*(2), 252–260.

Derogatis, L. B. (1977). *SCL-90 administration, scoring and procedures manuals for the revised version.* Baltimore: Clinical Psychometric Research.

Derogatis, L. R. (1983). *SCL-90R. Administration, scoring and procedures-Manual 11.* Towson, MD: Clinical Psychometric Research.

DeRubeis, R. J., Brotman, M. A., & Gibbons, C. J. (2005). A conceptual and methodological analysis of the nonspecifics argument. *Clinical Psychology: Science and Practice, 12,* 174–183.

DeRubeis, R. J., & Feeley, M. (1990). Determinants of change in cognitive therapy for depression. *Cognitive Therapy and Research, 14,* 469–482.

DeRubeis, R. J., Hollon, S., Evans, M., & Bemis, K. (1982). Can psychotherapies for depression be discriminated? A systematic investigation of cognitive therapy and interpersonal therapy. *Journal of Consulting and Clinical Psychology, 50,* 744–756.

DeRubeis, R. J., Siegle, G. J., & Hollon, S. D. (2008). Cognitive therapy versus medication for depression: Treatment outcomes and neural mechanisms. *Nature Reviews Neuroscience, 9,* 788–796.

Detert, N. B., Llewelyn, S. P., Hardy, G. E., Barkham, M., & Stiles, W. B. (2006). Assimilation in good- and poor-outcome cases of very brief psychotherapy for mild depression: An initial comparison. *Psychotherapy Research, 16,* 393–407.

di Marino, L., & Mergenthaler, E. (2003). Stati mentali e processi di cambiamento in una terapia sistemica [States of mind and change processes in a systemic therapy]. *Psicoterapia, 27,* 45–52.

Diamond, D., Clarkin, J. F., Stovall-McClough, K. C., Levy, K. N., Foelsch, P., Levine, H., & Yeomans, F. (2003). Patient-therapist attachment: Impact on therapeutic process and outcome. In M. Cortina & M. Marrone (Eds.), *Attachment theory and the psychoanalytic process* (pp. 179–203). London: Whurr Press.

Diemer, R., Hill, C. E., Lobell, L., & Vivino, B. (1996). A comparison of dream interpretation, event interpretation, and therapy-as-usual in brief psychotherapy. *Journal of Counseling Psychology, 43,* 93–112.

Diguer, L., Barber, J. P., & Luborsky, L. (1993). Three concomitants: Personality disorder, psychiatric severity, and outcome of dynamic psychotherapy of major depression. *American Journal of Psychiatry, 150,* 1246–1248.

Donegan, N. H., Sanislow, C. A., Blumberg, H. P., Fulbright, R. K., Lacadie, C., Skudlarski, P., et al. (2003). Amygdala hyperactivity in borderline personality disorder: Implications for emotional dysregulation. *Biological Psychiatry, 54,* 1284–1293.

Donenberg, G. R., Lyons, J. S., & Howard, K. I. (1999). Clinical trials versus mental health Ser-vices research: Contributions and connections. *Journal of Clinical Psychology, 55,* 1135–1146.

Doss, B. D., Rowe, L. S., Carhartt, K., Madsen, J. W., Georgia, E. J. (2011). Sudden gains in treatment-as-usual couple therapy for military veterans. *Behavior Therapy, 42,* 509–520.

Dreher, A. U. (2005). Conceptual research. In Person, E. S., Cooper, A. M., & Gabbard, G. O. (Eds.), *Textbook of Psychoanalysis* (pp. 361–372). Washington, DC & London: American Psychiatric Press.

Drevets, W. C. (2001). Neuroimaging and neuropathological studies of depression: Implications for the cognitive-emotional features of mood disorders. *Current Opinions in Neurobiology, 11,* 240–249.

Dunbar, G. C., & Lishman, W. A. (1984). Depression, recognition-memory, and hedonic tone: A signal detection analysis. *British Journal of Psychiatry, 144,* 376–382.

Durham, C. J., McGrath, L. D., Burlingame, G. M., Schaalje, G. B., Lambert, M. J., & Davies, D. R. (2002). The effects of repeated administrations on self report and parent report scales. *Journal of Psychoeducational Assessment, 20,* 240–257.

Eddington, K. M., Dolcos, F., Cabeza, R., R Krishnan, K. R., & Strauman, T. J. (2007). Neural correlates of promotion and prevention goal activation: An fMRI study using an idiographic approach. *Journal of Cognitive Neuroscience, 19*(7), 1152–1162.

Egenolf, Y. (2011). Das implizite Selbst—Ein möglicher neuronaler Biomarker der Depression. [The implicit self—A possible neural biomarker of depression]. Doctoral dissertation, University of Bern.

Eisenberg, N., Smith, C. L., Sadovsky, A., & Spinrad, T. (2004). Effortful control: Relations with emotional regulation, adjustment, and socialization in childhood. In R. F. Baumeister & K. D. Vohs (Eds.), *Handbook of self-regulation: Research, theory, and applications* (pp. 259–282). New York: Guilford Press.

Elkin, I. (1988). Relationship of therapists' adherence to treatment outcome in the Treatment of Depression Collaborative Research Program. Paper presented at the annual meeting of the Society for Psychotherapy Research, Santa Fe, NM, June.

Elkin, I. (1999). A major dilemma in psychotherapy outcome research: Disentangling therapists from therapies. *Clinical Psychology: Science and Practice, 6,* 10–32.

Elkin, I., Parloff, M. B., Hadley, S. W., & Autry, J. H. (1985). NIMH Treatment of Depression Collaborative Research Program: Background and research plan. *Archives of General Psychiatry, 42*(3), 305–316.

Elkin, I., Shea, M. T., Watkins, J. T., Imber, S. D., Sotsky, S. M., Collins, J. F., et al. (1989). NIMH Treatment of Depression Collaborative Research Program: I. General effectiveness of treatments. *Archives of General Psychiatry, 46,* 971–982.

Elliott, R. (1983). Fitting process research to the practicing psychotherapist. *Psychotherapy: Theory, Research & Practice, 20,* 47–55.

Elliott, R. (1986). Interpersonal process recall (IPR) as a psychotherapy process research method. In L. Greenberg & W. Pinsof (Eds.). *The psychotherapeutic process: A research handbook* (pp. 503–528). New York: Guilford Press.

Elliott, R. (1998). A guide to the empirically supported treatments controversy. *Psychotherapy Research, 8,* 115–125.

Elliott, R. (2000). Features of a good therapist. Paper presented at the 31st Annual Meeting of the SPR. Bloomingdale, Illinois.

Elliott, R. (2001). Hermeneutic single case efficacy design (HSCED): An overview. In K. J. Schneider, J. F. T. Bugental, & J. F. Fraser (Eds.), *Handbook of Humanistic Psychology* (pp. 315–324), Thousand Oaks, CA: Sage.

Elliott, R. (2002). Hermeneutic single-case efficacy design. *Psychotherapy Research, 12,* 1–21.

Elliott, R. (2010). Psychotherapy change process research: Realizing the promise. *Psychotherapy Research, 20,* 123–135.

Elliott, R., & Anderson, C. (1994). Simplicity and complexity in psychotherapy research. In R. L. Russell (Ed.), *Reassessing psychotherapy research* (pp. 65–113). New York: Guilford Press.

Elliott, R., Fischer, C. T., & Rennie, D. L. (1999). Evolving guidelines for publication of qualitative research studies in psychology and related fields. *British Journal of Clinical Psychology, 38*(3), 215–229.

Elliott, R., Hill, C. E., Stiles, W. B., Friedlander, M. L., Mahrer, A. R., & Margison, F. R. (1987). Primary therapist response modes: Comparison of six rating systems. *Journal of consulting and Clinical Psychology, 55,* 218–223.

Elliott, R., Partyka, R., Wagner, J., Alperin, R. & Dobrenski. R., Messer, S. B., et al. (2009). An adjudicated hermeneutic single-case efficacy design of experiential therapy for panic/phobia. *Psychotherapy Research, 19,* 543–557.

Elliott, R., Shapiro, D. A., Firth-Cozens, J., Stiles, W. B., Hardy, G. E., Llewelyn, S. P., et al. (1994). Comprehensive process analysis of insight events in cognitive-behavioral and psychodynamic-interpersonal psychotherapies. *Journal of Counseling Psychology, 41,* 444–463.

Elliott, R., Shapiro, D. A, & Mack, C. (1999). *Simplified personal questionnaire procedure manual.* Department of Psychology, University of Toledo.

Elliott, R., Slatick, E., & Urman, M. (2006). Qualitative change process research on psychotherapy: Alternative strategies. In J. Frommer and D. L. Rennie (Eds.), *Qualitative psychotherapy research: Methods and methodology* (pp. 69–111). Lengerich, Germany: Pabst Science Publishers.

Elliott, R., Stiles, W. B., & Shapiro, D. A. (1993). Are some psychotherapies more equivalent than others? In T. R. Giles (Ed.), *Handbook of effective psychotherapy* (pp. 455–479). New York: Plenum.

Ellis, A. (1973). *Humanistic psychotherapy, the rational emotive approach.* New York: Julian Press.

Ellsworth, J. R., Lambert, M. J., & Johnson, J. (2006). A comparison of the Outcome Questionnaire-45 and Outcome Questionnaire-30 in classification and prediction of treatment outcome. *Clinical Psychology and Psychotherapy, 13*(6), 380–391.

Erikson, E. (1954). The dream specimen of psychoanalysis. In R. Knight & C. Friedman (Eds.), *Psychoanalytic psychiatry and psychology* (pp. 131–170). New York: International Universities Press.

Eubanks-Carter, C., Muran, J. C., Safran, J. D., & Hayes, J. A. (2010). Interpersonal interventions for maintaining an alliance. In L. M. Horowitz & Strack, S. (Eds.), *Handbook of interpersonal psychology: Theory, research, assessment, and therapeutic interventions* (pp. 519–531). New York: Wiley.

Eysenck, H. J. (1952). The effects of psychotherapy: An evaluation. *Journal of Consulting Psychology, 16*(5), 319–324.

Fabi, G., & Mergenthaler, E. (2004). Therapist's interventions and their effect on emotional and cognitive regulation in individual psychotherapy. In Society for Psychotherapy Research (Ed.), *Book of abstracts, 35th annual meeting* (p. 95). Ulm, Germany: Ulmer Textbank.

Falk, D. R., & Hill, C. E. (1995). The effectiveness of dream interpretation groups for women in a divorce transition. *Dreaming, 5,* 29–42.

Feeley, M., DeRubeis, R. J., & Gelfand, L. A. (1999). The temporal relation of adherence and alliance to symptom change in cognitive therapy for depression. *Journal of Consulting and Clinical Psychology, 67,* 578–582.

Feldstein S., & Jaffe, J. (1963). An IBM 650 program written in SOAP for the computation of speech disturbances per time, speaker, and group. *Behavioral Science, 8,* 86.

Fenichel, O. (1941). *Problems of psychoanalytic technique.* Albany, NY: Psychoanalytic Quarterly.

Fennel, M. J. V., & Teasdale, J. D. (1987). Cognitive therapy for depression: Individual differences and the process of change. *Cognitive Therapy and Research, 11,* 253–271.

Fensterheim, H., & Raw, S. D. (1996). Psychotherapy research is not psychotherapy practice. *Clinical Psychology: Science and Practice, 3,* 168–171.

Fertuck, E. A., Lenzenweger, M. F., & Clarkin, J. F. (2005). The association between attentional and executive controls in the expression of borderline personality disorder features: A preliminary study. *Psychopathology, 38,* 75–81.

Fertuck, E. A., Lenzenweger, M. F., Clarkin, J. F., Hoermann, S., & Stanley, B. (2006). Executive neurocognition, memory systems, and borderline personality disorder. *Clinical Psychology Review, 26,* 346–375.

Field, S. D., Barkham, M., Shapiro, D. A., & Stiles, W. B. (1994). Assessment of assimilation in psychotherapy: A quantitative case study of problematic experiences with a significant other. *Journal of Counseling Psychology, 41,* 397–406.

Filipek, P. A. (1999). Neuroimaging in the developmental disorders: The state of the science. *Journal of Child Psychology and Psychiatry, 40,* 113–128.

Finch, A. E., Lambert, M. J., & Schaalje, B. G. (2001). Psychotherapy quality control: The statistical generation of expected recovery curves for integration into an early warning system. *Clinical Psychology and Psychotherapy, 8,* 231–242.

Fink, G. R., Markowitsch, H. J., Reinkemeier, M., Bruckbauer, T., Kessler, J., & Heiss, W. (1996). Cerebral representation of one's own past: Neural networks involved in autobiographical memory. *Journal of Neuroscience, 16,* 4275–4282.

Fishman, D. B. (1999). *The case for pragmatic psychology.* New York: New York University Press.

Fishman, D. B. (2000). Transcending the efficacy versus effectiveness research debate: Proposal for a new, electronic "Journal of Pragmatic Case Studies." *Prevention & Treatment* [online], *3.* Available: http://journals.apa.org./prevention/ volume3/pre0030008a.html

Flor, H. (2002). Phantom limb pain: Characteristics, aetiology and treatment. *Lancet Neurology, 3,* 182–189.

Flor, H., Lutzenberger, W., Knost, B., & Birbaumer, N. (2002). Spouse presence alters cerebral responses to painful stimulation in chronic pain patients. Unpublished manuscript.

Flyvbjerg, B. (2006). Five misunderstandings about case-study research. *Qualitative Inquiry, 12,* 219–245.

Foerster, F. (1990). Refinement and verification of a model of resolution of unfinished business. Unpublished Master's thesis, York University.

Fogel, B. S., Schiffer, R. B., & Rao, S. M. (2002). *Synopsis of neuropsychiatry.* Philadelphia: Lippincott Williams & Wilkins.

Follette, W.C. and Greenberg, L.S. (2005). Techinque factors in treating dysphoric disorders. In L. G. Castonguay, & L. E. Beutler (Eds.), *Principles of therapeutic change that work* (pp. 83–109). New York: Oxford University Press.

Fonagy, P. (2009). Mentalization as a common framework for psychotherapy. Paper presented at the Annual Research Conference of the BACP, Portsmouth, May.

Fonagy, P., Leigh, T., Steele, M., Steele, H., Kennedy, R., Mattoon, G., et al. (1996). The relation of attachment status, psychiatric classification, and response to psychotherapy. *Journal of Consulting and Clinical Psychology, 64*(1), 22–31.

Fonagy, P., Target, M., & Gergely, G. (2000). Attachment and borderline personality disorder: A theory and some evidence. *Psychiatric Clinics of North America, 23,* 103–122.

Fontao, M. I., & Mergenthaler, E. (2002). The therapeutic cycles model: An evaluation in the group psychotherapeutic setting. *Gruppenpsychotherapie und Gruppendynamik, 38,* 349–371.

Fontao, M. I., & Mergenthaler, E. (2005a). Aplicación del Modelo de Ciclo Terapéutico a la Investigación de Microprocesos en la Psicoterapie de Grupo [The application of the therapeutic cycles model in the investigation of microprocesses in group psychotherapy]. *Revista Argentina de Clinica Psicologica, 14,* 53–63.

Fontao, M. I., & Mergenthaler, E. (2005b). Mechanisms of change and language patterns in group therapy with eating disorder. *Gruppenpsychotherapie und Gruppendynamik, 41,* 356–378.

Fontao, M. I., & Mergenthaler, E. (2008). Therapeutic factors and language patterns in group therapy application of computer-assisted text analysis to the examination of microprocesses in group therapy: Preliminary findings. *Psychotherapy Research, 18,* 345–354.

Fontao, M. I., Taborda, R. A., Toranzo, H. E., Mergenthaler, E., Hoffmann, K., & Ross, T. (2011). Gruppenprozesse in einer Fokaltherapie mit Müttern: Eine Pilotstudie über den psychodynamischen Ansatz zu psychotherapeutischen Parallelgruppen von Eltern und Kindern in Argentinien. *Gruppenpsychotherapie und Gruppendynamik, 47,* 38–52.

Frances, A., Kahn, D. A., Carpenter, D., Ross, R., & Docherty, J. P. (1996). The expert consensus practice guideline project: A new method of establishing best practice. *Journal of Practical Psychiatry and Behavioral Health, 2,* 295–306.

Frank, E., Kupfer, D. J., Perel, J. M., & Cornes, C. (1990). Three-year outcomes for maintenance therapies in recurrent depression. *Archives of General Psychiatry, 47,* 1093–1099.

Frank, J. D. (1961). *Persuasion and healing.* Baltimore, MD: Johns Hopkins University Press.

Frank, J. D. (1968). The influence of patients' and therapists' expectations on the outcome of psychotherapy. *British Journal of Medical Psychology, 41,* 349–356.

Frank, J. D. (1973). *Persuasion and healing* (2nd ed.). Baltimore: Johns Hopkins University Press.

Frankel, Z., Levitt, H. M., Murray, D. M., Greenberg, L. S., & Angus, L. (2006). Assessing silent processes in psychotherapy: An empirically derived categorization system and sampling strategy. *Psychotherapy Research, 16,* 627–638.

Fredrickson, B. L. (1998). What good are positive emotions? *Review of General Psychology, 2,* 173–186.

Freitas, C., Pearlman, C., & Pascual-Leone, A. (2012). Treatment of auditory verbal hallucinations with transcranial magnetic stimulation in a patient with psychotic major depression: one-year follow-up. *Neurocase, 18*(1), 57–65.

Freud, S. (1900/1966). *The interpretation of dreams.* New York: Avon.

Freud, S. (1905/1959). Fragment of an analysis of hysteria. In E. Jones (Ed.), *Sigmund Freud collected papers,* Vol. 3. Trans. Mix & James Strachey. New York: Basic Books.

Freud, S. (1912/1958). The dynamics of transference. In J. Strachey (Ed.), *The standard edition of the complete psychological works of Sigmund Freud, 24 volumes* (Vol. 12, pp. 99–108). London: Hogarth Press.

Fried, D., Crits-Christoph, P., & Luborsky, L. (1992). The first empirical demonstration of transference in psychotherapy. *Journal of Nervous and Mental Disease, 180,* 326–331.

Fuchs, T. (2004). Neurobiology and psychotherapy: An emerging dialogue. *Current Opinions in Psychiatry, 17,* 479–485.

Fuchs, T. (2006). Neuromythologien. Mutmassungen über die Bewegkräfte der Hirnforschung. Scheidewege. *Jahresschrift für skeptisches Denken, 36,* 184–202.

Furmark, T., Tillfors, M., Marteinsdottir, I., Fischer, H., Pissiota, A., Langström, B., et al. (2002). Common changes in cerebral blood flow in patients with social phobia treated with citalopram or cognitive-behavioral therapy. *Archives of General Psychiatry, 59,* 425–433.

Gabbard, G. O. (2000). A neurobiologically informed perspective of psychotherapy. *British Journal of Psychiatry, 177,* 117–122.

Garfield, P. (1991). *Women's bodies, women's dreams.* NewYork: Holt, Rinehart, and Witon.

Garfield, S. L. (1994). Research on client variables in psychotherapy. In A. E. Bergin & S. L. Garfield (Eds.), *Handbook of psychotherapy and behavior change.* (4th ed., pp. 190–228). New York: John Wiley.

Garfield, S. L., & Bergin, A. E. (Eds.). (1986). *Handbook of psychotherapy and behavior change* (4th ed.). New York: John Wiley.

Garner, W. P., Hake, H. W., & Eriksen, C. W. (1956). Operationism and the concept of perception. *Psychological Review, 63,* 149–159.

Gaston, L., Thompson, L., Gallagher, D., Cournoyer, L., & Gagnon, R. (1998). Alliance, technique, and their interactions in predicting outcome of behavioral, cognitive, and brief dynamic therapy. *Psychotherapy Research, 8,* 190–209.

Gauggel, S. (2006). Neuropsychotherapie: Anmerkungen eines Neuropsychologen. *Verhaltenstherapie, 16,* 133–138.

Gawande, A. (2004). The bell curve: What happens when patients find out how good their doctors really are? *New Yorker, 12,* 82–91.

Gelo, O. (2008). *Metaphors and emotional-cognitive regulation in psychotherapy: A single-case analysis.* Ulm: Ulmer Textbank.

Gelo, O., & Mergenthaler, E. (2003). Psychotherapy and metaphorical language. *Psicoterapia, 27,* 53–65.

Gelo, O., & Mergenthaler, E. (2012). Unconventional metaphors and emotional-cognitive regulation in a metacognitive interpersonal therapy. *Psychotherapy Research, 22,* 159–175.

Gelso, C. J., & Hayes, J. A. (2002). The management of countertransference. In J. Norcross (Ed.), *Psychotherapy relationships that work: Therapist contributions and responsiveness to patients* (pp. 267–284). New York: Oxford University Press.

Gibbons, J. D. (1985). Pitman tests. In S. Kotz & N. L. Johnson (Eds.), *Encyclopedia of Statistics.* New York: John Wiley.

Gilbert, P. (1984). *Depression: From psychology to brain state.* London: Erlbaum.

Gilboa-Schechtman, E., & Shahar, G. (2006). The sooner, the better: Temporal patterns in brief treatment of depression and their role in long-term outcome. *Psychotherapy Research, 16,* 374–384.

Glaesmer, H., Sonntag, A., Barnow, S., Brähler, E., et al. (2010). Psychotherapy training from the alumnis' perspective. *Psychotherapeut, 54,* 437–453.

Gleick, J. (1987). *Chaos: Making a new science.* New York: Penguin.

Goldapple, K., Segal, Z., Garson, C., Lau, M., Bieling, P., Kennedy, S., et al. (2004). Modulation of cortical-limbic pathways in major depression: Treatment-specific effects of cognitive behavior therapy. *Archives of General Psychiatry, 61*(1), 34–41.

Goldberg, D. P., Hobson, R. F., Maguire, G. P., Margison, F. R., O'Dowd, T., Osborn, M. S., & Moss, S. (1984). The clarification and assessment of a method of psychotherapy. *British Journal of Psychiatry, 114,* 567–575.

Goldfried, M. R. (1980). Toward the delineation of therapeutic change principles. *American Psychologist, 35,* 991–999.

Goldfried, M. R. (1991). Research issues in psychotherapy integration. *Journal of Psychotherapy Integration, 1,* 5–25.

Goldfried, M. R. (1995). *From cognitive-behavior therapy to psychotherapy integration: An evolving view.* New York: Springer.

Goldfried, M. R. (2000). Consensus in psychotherapy research and practice: Where have all the findings gone? *Psychotherapy Research, 10,* 1–16.

Goldfried, M. R., Greenberg, L., & Marmor, C. (1990). Individual psychotherapy: Process and outcome. *Annual Review of Psychology, 41,* 659–688.

Goldfried, M. R., Radin, L. B., & Rachlin, H. (1997). Theoretical jargon and the dynamics of behaviorism. *Clinical Psychologist, 50,* 5–12.

Goldfried, M. R., & Wolfe, B. E. (1996). Psychotherapy practice and research: Repairing a strained alliance. *American Psychologist, 51,* 1007–1016.

Goldfried, M. R., & Wolfe, B. E. (1998). Toward a more clinically valid approach to therapy research. *Journal of Consulting and Clinical Psychology, 66,* 143–150.

Gonçalves, M. M., Ribeiro, A. P., Stiles, W. B., Conde, T., Santos, A., Matos, M., et al. (2011). The role of mutual in-feeding in maintaining problematic self-narratives: Exploring one path to therapeutic failure. *Psychotherapy Research, 21,* 27–40.

Gonçalves, M. M., & Stiles, W. B. (2011). Narrative and psychotherapy: Introduction to the special Section. *Psychotherapy Research, 21,* 1–3.

Goodman, G., & Dooley, D. (1976). A framework for help-intended interpersonal communication. *Psychotherapy: Theory, Research and Practice, 13,* 106–117.

Gotlib, I. H., & McCann, C. D. (1984). Construct accessibiity and depression: An examination of cognitive and affective factors. *Journal of Personality and Social Psychology, 47,* 427–439.

Grande, T., Rudolf, G., Oberbracht, C., & Jakobsen, T. (2001). Therapeutic changes beyond the symptoms: Effects of inpatient treatment in the view of the Heidelberg Structural Change Scale. *Zeitschrift für Psychosomatische Medizin und Psychotherapie, 47,* 213–233.

Grawe, K. (1997). Research-informed psychotherapy. *Psychotherapy Research, 7,* 1–19.

Grawe, K. (2002a). *Psychological psychotherapy*. Seattle, WA: Hogrefe.

Grawe, K. (2002b). How does psychotherapy work?. Paper presented at the conference of the Deutsche Gesellschaft für Psychologie, Berlin, September.

Grawe, K. (2006). *Neuropsychotherapy. How the neurosciences inform effective psychotherapy.* New Jersey: Lawrence Erlbaum.

Grawe, K., & Braun, U. (1994). Quality control in psychotherapy practice. *Zeitschrift für Klinische Psychologie, 23,* 242–267.

Grawe, K., Donati, R., & Bernauer, R. (1994). *Psychotherapy in transition: From confession to profession.* Göttingen, Germany: Hogrefe.

Gray, M. A., & Stiles, W. B. (2011). Employing a case study in building an assimilation theory account of generalized anxiety disorder and its treatment with cognitive-behavioral therapy. *Pragmatic Case Studies in Psychotherapy,* 7, 529–557.

Greenberg, L. S. (1975). Task analysis of psychotherapeutic events. Unpublished doctoral dissertation, York University.

Greenberg, L. S. (1979). Resolving splits: Use of the two chair technique. *Psychotherapy Theory, Research and Practice, 16,* 310–318.

Greenberg, L. S. (1984a). A task analysis of intrapersonal conflict resolution. In L. Rice & L. Greenberg (Eds.), *Patterns of change: Intensive analysis of psychotherapy process* (pp. 67–123). New York: Guilford Press.

Greenberg, L. S. (1984b). Task analysis: The general approach. In L. N. Rice & L. S. Greenberg (Eds.), *Patterns of change* (pp. 124–148). New York: Guilford Press.

Greenberg, L. S. (1986). Change process research. *Journal of Consulting and Clinical Psychology, 54,* 4–9.

Greenberg, L. S. (1991). Research on the process of change. *Psychotherapy Research, 1,* 3–16.

Greenberg, L. S. (2007). A guide to conducting a task analysis of psychotherapeutic change. *Psychotherapy Research, 17,* 15–30.

Greenberg, L. S., Elliott, R., & Foerster, F. (1990). Experiential processes in the psychotherapy of depression. In D. McCann & N. S. Endler (Eds.), *Depression: New directions in research, theory and practice.* Toronto: Wall & Thompson.

Greenberg, L. S., & Pinsof, W. (1986). *The psychotherapeutic process: A research handbook.* New York: Guilford Press.

Grencavage, L. M., & Norcross, J. C. (1990). Where are the commonalties among the therapeutic common factors? *Professional Psychology: Research and Practice, 5,* 372–378.

Gril, S., Altmann, M., & Mergenthaler, E. (2000). From language to change—Psychotherapeutic process research with regard to reliability and narrative. In S. Gril,

A. Ibanez, I. Mosca, & P. L. R. Sousa (Eds.), *Investigación en psicoterapia* (pp. 227–245). Pelotas, Brazil: Universidade Católica de Pelotas.

Gross, J. J., & John, O.P. (2003). Individual differences in two emotion regulation processes: Implications for affect, relationships, and well-being. *Journal of Personality and Social Psychology, 85,* 348–362.

Grosse Holtforth, M., & Castonguay, L. G. (2005). Relationship and techniques in CBT: A motivational approach. *Psychotherapy: Theory, Research, Practice, and Training, 42,* 443–455.

Grünzig, H. (1983). Themes of anxiety as psychotherapeutic process variables. In W. Minsel & W. Herff (Eds.), *Methodology in psychotherapy research* (pp. 135–142). Frankfurt: Peter Lang.

Grünzig, H., & Kächele, H. (1978). Zur Differenzierung psychoanalytischer Angstkonzepte. Ein empirischer Beitrag zur automatischen Klassifikation klinischen Materials. *Zeitschrift für Klinische Psychologie, 7,* 1–17.

Gunderson, J. (1996). The borderline patient's intolerance of aloneness: Insecure attachments and therapist's availability. *American Journal of Psychiatry, 153,* 752–758.

Gurvits, I. G., Koenigsberg, H. W., & Siever, L. J. (2000). Neurotransmitter dysfunction in patients with borderline personality disorder. *Psychiatric Clinics of North America, 23,* 27–40.

Haaga, D. A. F., & Stiles, W. B. (2000). Randomized clinical trials in psychotherapy research: Methodology, design, and evaluation. In C. R. Snyder & R. E. Ingram, *Handbook of psychological change* (pp. 14–39). New York: Wiley.

Haas, E., Hill, R., Lambert, M. J., & Morrell, B. (2002). Do early responders to psychotherapy maintain treatment gains? *Journal of Clinical Psychology, 58,* 1157–1172.

Hamilton, J., & Kivlighan, D. M. (2009). Therapists' projection: The effects of therapists' relationship themes on their formulation of clients relationship episodes. *Psychotherapy Research, 19*(3), 312–322.

Hammen, C., Marks, T., Mayol, A., & deMayo, R. (1985). Depressive self-schemas, life stress, and vulnerability to depression. *Journal of Abnormal Psychology, 49,* 1147–1159.

Hannan, C., Lambert, M. J., Harmon, C., Nielsen, S. L., Smart, D. W., Shimokawa, K., & Sutton, S. W. (2005). A lab test and algorithms for identifying clients at risk for treatment failure. *Journal of Clinical Psychology: In Session, 61,* 155–163.

Hansen, N. B., & Lambert, M. J. (2003). An evaluation of the dose-response relationship in naturalistic treatment settings using survival analysis. *Mental Health Services Research, 5,* 1–12.

Hansen, N. B., Lambert, M. J., & Forman, E. V. (2002). The psychotherapy dose-response effect and its implications for treatment delivery services. *Clinical Psychology: Science and Practice, 9,* 329–343.

Hanson, N. R. (1958). *Patterns of discovery.* Cambridge: Cambridge University Press.

Hardy, G. E., Barkham, M., Shapiro, D. A., Rees, A., Reynolds, S., & Stiles, W. B. (1994). Impact of Cluster C personality disorders on the outcome of contrasting brief psychotherapies for depression. *Journal of Consulting and Clinical Psychology, 63,* 997–1004.

Hardy, G. E., Barkham, M., Shapiro, D. A., Reynolds, S., Rees, & Stiles, W. B. (1995). Credibility and outcome of cognitive-behavioral and psychodynamic-interpersonal psychotherapy. *British Journal of Clinical Psychology, 34,* 555–569.

Hardy, G. E., Stiles, W. B., Barkham, M., & Startup, M. (1998). Therapist responsiveness to client interpersonal styles during time-limited treatments for depression. *Journal of Consulting and Clinical Psychology, 66,* 304–312.

Harlow, H. F., & Harlow, M. K. (1962). Social deprivation in monkeys. *Scientific American, 203,* 136–146.

Harmon, S. C., Lambert, M. J., Smart, D. W., Hawkins, E. J., Nielsen, S. L., Slade K., & Lutz, W. (2007). Methods of enhancing patient outcome for potential treatment failures: The use of therapist/client feedback and Clinical Support Tools. *Psychotherapy Research, 17,* 379–392.

Harrison, P. J. (1999). The neuropathology of schizophrenia. A critical review of the data andtheir interpretation. *Brain, 22,* 593–624.

Harter, S. (1999). *The construction of the self: A developmental perspective.* New York: Guilford Press.

Hatfield, D. R., & Ogles, B. M. (2004). The use of outcome measures use in clinical practice by psychologists. *Research & Practice, 35,* 485–491.

Hattersley, R. (1991). *Goodbye to Yorkshire* (originally published 1976) London: Pan Books.

Hautzinger, M., de Jong-Meyer, R., Treiber, R., Rudolf, G.-A., & Thien, U. (1996). Efficacy of cognitive behavior therapy, pharmacotherapy, and their combination for non-endogenous unipolar depression. *Zeitschrift für Klinische Psychologie, 25,* 130–145.

Hawkins, E. J., Lambert, M. J., Vermeersch, D. A., Slade, K., & Tuttle, K. (2004). The effects of providing patient progress information to therapists and patients. *Psychotherapy Research, 14,* 308–327.

Hayes, A. M., Castonguay, L. G., & Goldfried, M. R. (1996). The effectiveness of targeting the vulnerability factors of depression in cognitive therapy. *Journal of Consulting and Clinical Psychology, 64,* 623–627.

Hayes, A. M., & Harris, M. S. (2000). The development of an integrative treatment for depression. In S. Johnson, A. M., Hayes, T., Field, T. N., Schneiderman, & P. McCabe (Eds.), *Stress, coping, and depression* (pp. 291–306). Mahwah, NJ: Erlbaum.

Hayes, S. C., Barlow, D. H., & Nelson-Gray, R.O. (1999). *The scientist practitioner: Research and accountability in the age of managed care* (2nd ed.). Needham Heights, MA: Allyn & Bacon.

Haynes, S. N., & O'Brien, W. O. (2000). *Principles of behavioral assessment: A functional approach to psychological assessment.* New York: Plenum.

Heffler, B., & Sandell, R. (2009). The role of learning style in choosing one's therapeutic orientation. *Psychotherapy Research, 19,* 283–292.

Heinrichs, M., & Gaab, J. (2007). Neuroendocrine mechanisms of stress and social interaction: Implications for mental disorders. *Current Opinion in Psychiatry, 20*(2), 158–162.

Henry, H. M., & Stiles, W. B. (2012). Contextual influences on acculturation: Psychological assimilation and continuing bonds for two immigrants. In M.-C. Bertau, M. Gonçalves, & P. Raggatt (Eds.), *Dialogic formations: Investigations into the origins and development of the dialogical self* (pp. 289–313). Charlotte, NC: Information Age Publishing.

Henry, H. M., Stiles, W. B., & Biran, M. W. (2005). Loss and mourning in immigration: Using the assimilation model to assess continuing bonds with native culture. *Counselling Psychology Quarterly, 18,* 109–119.

Henry, H. M., Stiles, W. B., Biran, M. W., Mosher, J. K., Brinegar, M. G., & Banerjee, P. (2009). Immigrants' continuing bonds with their native culture: Assimilation analysis of three interviews. *Transcultural Psychiatry, 46,* 257–284.

Henry, W. P., Schacht, T. E., & Strupp, H. H. (1986). Structural analysis of social behavior: Application to a study of interpersonal process in differential psychotherapeutic outcome. *Journal of Consulting and Clinical Psychology, 54,* 27–31.

Henry, W. P., Schacht, T. E., & Strupp, H. H. (1990). Patient and therapist introject, interpersonal process and differential psychotherapy outcome. *Journal of Consulting and Clinical Psychology, 58,* 768–774.

Henry, W. P., Strupp, H. H., Schacht, T. E., & Gaston, L. (1994). Psychodynamic approaches. In A. E. Bergin & S. L. Garfield (Eds.), *Handbook of psychotherapy and behavior change* (pp. 467–508), New York: John Wiley.

Herpertz, S. C. (1995). Self-injurious behavior: Psychopathological and nosological characteristics in subtypes of self-injurers. *Acta Psychiatric Scandinavica, 91,* 57–68.

Herpertz, S. C., Zanarini, M., Schulz, C. S., Siever, L., Lieb, K., & Möller, H. J. (2007). WFSBP Task Force on Personality Disorders; World Federation of Societies of Biological Psychiatry. *World Journal of Biological Psychiatry, 8*(4), 212–44.

Hill, C. E. (1996a). Dreams and therapy. *Psychotherapy Research, 6,* 1–15.

Hill, C. E. (1996b). *Working with dreams in psychotherapy.* New York: Guilford Press.

Hill, C. E. (Ed.) (2004). *Dream work in therapy: Facilitating exploration, insight, and action.* Washington DC: American Psychological Association.

Hill, C. E. (2009). *Helping skills* (3rd ed.). Washington DC: American Psychological Association.

Hill, C. E., Castonguay, L. G., Elliott, R., Gelso, C. J., Goldfried, M. R., Stiles, W. B., et al. (2005). Insight in psychotherapy: Definitions, process, consequences, and research directions. In L. G. Castonguay, & C. E. Hill (Eds.), *Insight in psychotherapy* (pp. 441–454). Washington, DC: American Psychological Press.

Hill, C. E., & Corbett, M. M. (1993). Aperspective on the history of process and outcome research in counseling psychology. *Journal of Counseling Psychology, 40,* 3–28.

Hill, C. E., Diemer, R., Hess, S., Hillyer, A., & Seeman, R. (1993). Are the effects of dream interpretation on session quality, insight, and emotions due to the dream itself, to projection, or to the interpretation process? *Dreaming, 3,* 211–222.

Hill, C. E., Gelso, C. J., Gerstenblith, J., Chui, H., Pudasaini, S., Burgard, J., et al. (2013). The dreamscape of psychodynamic psychotherapy: Dreams, dreamers, dream work, consequences, and case studies. *Dreaming, 23*(1), 1–45.

Hill, C. E., & Knox, S. (2002). Self-disclosure. In J. C. Norcross (Ed.), *Psychotherapy relationships that work: Therapist contributions and responsiveness to patients* (pp. 255–265). New York: Oxford University Press.

Hill, C. E., & Knox, S. (2009). Processing the therapeutic relationship. *Psychotherapy Research, 19*(1), 13–29.

Hill, C. E., & Knox, S. (2010). The use of dreams in modern psychotherapy. In A. Clow & P. McNamara (Eds.), *International Review of Neurobiology* (Vol. 92, pp. 291–317). New York: Academic Press.

Hill, C. E., Knox, S., Crook-Lyon, R. E., Hess, S. A., Miles, J. R., Spangler, P., & Pudasaini, S. (2014). Dreaming of you: Client and therapist dreams about each other during psychodynamic psychotherapy. *Psychotherapy Research, 24,* 523–537.

Hill, C. E., & O'Grady, K. (1985). List of therapist intentions illustrated in a case study and with therapists of varying orientations. *Journal of Counseling Psychology, 32,* 3–22.

Hill, C. E., O'Grady, K. E., & Elkin, I. (1992). Applying the Collaborative Study Psychotherapy Rating Scale to rate therapist adherence in cognitive-behavior therapy, interpersonal therapy, and clinical management. *Journal of Consulting and Clinical Psychology, 60,* 73–79.

Hill, W. F. (1965). Hill Interaction Matrix. Unpublished manuscript. Los Angeles: University of California, Youth Study Center.

Hintzen, B., & Pietrowsky, R. (2001). Cortisol-Response auf emotionalbelastende Stimuli bei Patientinnen mit Borderline-Störung. Paper presented at the DGPs Kongress, Bern, Switzerland, May.

Hobson, J. A., & McCarley, R. W. (1977). The brain as a dream state generator: An activation-synthesis hypothesis of the dream process. *American Journal of Psychiatry, 134,* 1335–1348.

Hobson, R. F. (1985). *Forms of feeling: The heart of psychotherapy.* London: Tavistock.

Hoermann, S., Clarkin, J. F., Hull, J. W., & Levy, K. N. (2005). The construct of effortful control: An approach to borderline personality disorder heterogeneity. *Psychopathology, 38,* 82–86.

Hofmann, S. G., Smits, J. A., Asnaani, A., Gutner, C. A., & Otto, M. W. (2011). Cognitive enhancers for anxiety disorders. *Pharmacology, Biochemistry, and Behavior, 99*(2), 275–284.

Høglend, P. (1993). Transference interpretations and long-term change after dynamic psychotherapy of brief to moderate length. *American Journal of Psychotherapy, 47,* 494–507.

Høglend, P., & Piper, W. E. (1995). Focal adher-ence in brief dynamic psychotherapy: A com-parison of findings from two independent studies. *Psychotherapy, 32,* 618–628.

Hohage, R., & Kubler J. C. (1988). The emotional insight rating scale. In H. Dahl, H. Kächele, & H. Thomä (Eds.), *Psychoanalytic Process Research Strategies* (pp. 243–255). New York: Springer.

Hollon, S. D., Waskow, I. E., Evans, M., & Lowery, H. A. (1984). System for rating therapies for depression. Paper presented at the annual meeting of the American Psychiatric Association, Los Angeles, CA, May.

Holsboer, F. (2000). The corticosteroid receptor hypothesis of depression. *Neuropsychopharmacology, 23,* 477–501.

Holtzheimer, P. E., & Mayberg, H. S. (2011). Deep brain stimulation for psychiatric disorders. *Annual Review of Neuroscience, 34,* 289–307.

Hölzer, M. (2007). Attachment style and emotional cognitive regulatio. Unpublished doctoral dissertation, University of Ulm.

Hölzer, M., Scheytt, N., Pokorny, D., & Kächele, H. (1989). A comparative study of the emotional vocabulary in two cases. Report, 20th Annual Meeting of the Society for Psychotherapy Research. Toronto, June.

Honos-Webb, L. (1998). Development of a manual for rating assimilation of in psychotherapy. Doctoral dissertation, Department of Psychology, Miami University, Oxford, Ohio.

Honos-Webb, L., & Stiles, W. B. (1998). Reformulation of assimilation analysis in terms of voices. *Psychotherapy, 35,* 23–33.

Honos-Webb, L., Stiles, W. B., & Greenberg, L. S. (2003). A method of rating assimilation in psychotherapy based on markers of change. *Journal of Counseling Psychology, 50,* 189–198.

Honos-Webb, L., Stiles, W. B., Greenberg, L. S., & Goldman, R. (1998). Assimilation analysis of process-experiential psychotherapy: A comparison of two cases. *Psychotherapy Research, 8,* 264–286.

Honos-Webb, L., Stiles, W. B., Greenberg, L. S., & Goldman, R. (2006). An assimilation analysis of psychotherapy: Responsibility for "being there." In C. T. Fischer (Ed.), *Qualitative research methods for psychologists: Introduction through empirical studies* (pp. 3–21). New York: Academic Press.

Honos-Webb, L., Surko, M., & Stiles, W. B. (1998). Manual for rating assimilation in psychotherapy: February 1998 version. Unpublished manuscript. Department of Psychology, Miami University, Oxford, Ohio.

Honos-Webb, L., Surko, M., Stiles, W. B., & Greenberg, L. S. (1999). Assimilation of voices in psychotherapy: The case of Jan. *Journal of Counseling Psychology, 46,* 448–460.

Horowitz, L. M. (1994). Pschemas, psychopathology and psychotherapy research. *Psychotherapy Research, 4,* 1–19.

Horowitz, L. M. (2004). *Interpersonal foundations of psychopathology.* Washington, DC: American Psychological Association.

Horowitz, L. M., Rosenberg, S. E., Baer, B. A., Ureño, G., & Villaseñor, V. S. (1988). Inventory of Interpersonal Problems: Psychometric properties and clinical applications. *Journal of Consulting and Clinical Psychology, 56,* 885–892.

Horowitz, L. M., & Turan, B. (2008). Prototypes and personal templates: Collective wisdom and individual differences. *Psychological Review,* 115, 1054–1068.

Horowitz, L. M., & Vitkus, J. (1986). The interpersonal basis of psychiatric symptoms. *Clinical Psychology Review, 6,* 443–469.

Horowitz, L. M., Weckler, D., & Doren, R. (1983). Interpersonal problems and symptoms: A cognitive approach. In P. C. Kendall (Ed.), *Advances in cognitive-behavioral research and therapy* (pp. 82–127). New York: Academic Press.

Horowitz, L. M., Wilson, K. R., Turan, B, Zolotsev, P., Constantino, M. J., & Henderson, L. (2006). How interpersonal motives clarify the meaning of interpersonal behavior: A revised circumplex model. *Personality and Social Psychology Review, 10,* 67–86.

Horowitz, M. J. (1979). *States of mind. Analysis of change in psychotherapy.* New York: Basic Books.

Horowitz, M. J., Ewert, M., & Milbrath, C. (1996). States of emotional control during psychotherapy. *Journal of Psychotherapy Practice and Research, 5,* 20–25.

Horvath, A. O., Del Re, A. C., Flückiger, C., and Symonds, D. (2011) Alliance in individual psychotherapy. In J. C. Norcross (ed.), *Psychotherapy relationships that work: evidence-based Responsiveness* (2nd ed.). New York: Oxford University Press.

Horvath, A. O., & Symonds, D. B. (1991). Relation between working alliance and outcome in psychotherapy: A meta-analysis. *Journal of Counseling Psychology, 38,* 139–149.

Houts, A. C. (2000). Fifty years of psychiatric nomenclature: Reflections on the 1943 War Department Technical Bulletin, Medical 203. *Journal of Clinical Psychology, 56*(7), 935–967.

Howard, K. I., Kopta, S. M., Krause, M. S., & Orlinsky, D. E. (1986). The dose-effect relationship in psychotherapy. *American Psychologist, 41,* 159–164.

Howard, K. I., Orlinsky, D. E., & Lueger, R. J. (1995). The design of clinically relevant outcome research: Some considerations and an example. In M. Aveline & D. A. Shapiro (Eds.), *Research foundations for psychotherapy practice* (pp. 3–47). Chichester: John Wiley.

Hugdahl, K., & Davidson, R. J. (Eds.) (2003). *The asymmetrical brain.* Cambridge, MA: MIT Press.

Humphrey, L. L., & Benjamin, L. S. (1986). Using structural analysis of social behavior to assess critical but elusive family processes: a new solution to an old problem. *American Psychologist, 41,* 979–989.

Humphreys, C. L., Rubin, J. S., Knudson, R. M., & Stiles. W. B. (2005). The assimilation of anger in a case of dissociative identity disorder. *Counselling Psychology Quarterly, 18,* 121–132.

Husserl, E. (1973). *Experience and judgement* (originally published in 1939). Evanston, IL: Northwestern University Press.

Hyman, S. E. (2000). The millennium of mind, brain, and behavior. *Archives of General Psychiatry, 57*(1), 88–89.

Hyman, S. E. (2011). Diagnosis of mental disorders in light of modern genetics. In D. A. Regier, W. E. Narrow, E. A. Kuhl, & D. J. Kupfer (Eds.), *The conceptual evolution of DSM-5* (pp. 3–18). Washington, DC: American Psychiatric Publishing.

Iacoviello, B. M., McCarthy, K. S., Barrett, M. S., Rynn, M., Gallop, R., & Barber, J. P. (2007). Treatment preferences affect the therapeutic alliance: Implications for randomized controlled trials. *Journal of Consulting and Clinical Psychology, 75,* 194–198.

Insel, T. R., & Young, L. J. (2001) The neurobiology of attachment. *Nature Review Neuroscience, 2,* 129–136.

Isen, A. M. (1990). The influence of positive and negative affect on cognitive organization: Some implications for development. In N. L. Stein, B. Leventhal, & T. Trabasso (Eds.), *Conference on the psychological and biological bases of behavior* (pp. 75–94). Hillsdale, NJ: Erlbaum.

Isen, A. M., Daubman, K. A., & Nowicki, G. P. (1987). Positive affect facilitates creative problem solving. *Journal of Personality and Social Psychology, 52,* 1122–1131.

Jacobson, N. S., & Truax, P. (1991). Clinical significance: A statistical approach to defining meaningful change in psychotherapy research. *Journal of Consulting and Clinical Psychology, 59,* 12–19.

Jaffe, J. (1958). Language of the dyad. *Journal for the Study of Interpersonal Processes, 21,* 249–258.

Joffe, R., Segal, Z., & Singer, W. (1996). Change in thyroid hormone levels following response to cognitive behavioral therapy for major depression. *American Journal of Psychiatry, 153,* 411–413.

Johnson, J. E. (2003). Group climate, cohesion, alliance and empathy in group psychotherapy: Multilevel structural equation models. Provo, Brigham Young University (unpublished doctoral dissertation).

Joiner, T. E. (2002). Depression in its interpersonal context. In I. H. Gotlib & C. L. Hammen (Eds.), *Handbook of depression* (pp. 295–313). New York: Guilford Press.

Jones, E. E., & Pulos, S. M. (1993). Comparing the process in psychodynamic and cognitive_behavioral therapies. *Journal of Consulting and Clinical Psychology, 61,* 306–316.

Joormann, J. (2009). Cognitive aspects of depression. In I. H. Gotlib & C. L. Hammen (Eds.), *Handbook of depression* (2nd ed., pp. 298–321). New York: Guilford Press.

Jovev, M., & Jackson, H. J. (2006). The relationship of borderline personality disorder, life events and functioning in a Australian psychiatric same. *Journal of Personality Disorders, 20,* 205–217.

Joyce, A. S., Duncan, S. C., & Piper, W. E. (1995). A task analysis of "working" responses to dy-namic interpretation in short-term individual psychotherapy. *Psychotherapy Research, 5,* 49–62.

Joyce, A. S., Wolfaardt, U., Sribney, C., & Aylwin, A. S. (2006). Psychotherapy research at the start of the 21st century: The persistence of the art versus science controversy. *Canadian Journal of Psychiatry, 51,* 797–809.

Julius Caesar, G. (1960). *War commentaries of Caesar* (trans. R. Warner) (originally published 51 BCE). New York: New American Library.

Junod, O., de Roten, Y., Martinez, E., Drapeau, M., & Despland, J. N. (2005). How to address patients' defenses: A pilot study of the accuracy of defense interpretations and alliance. *Psychology and Psychotherapy: Theory, Research and Practice, 78,* 419–430.

Kächele, H. (1976). *Maschinelle Inhaltsanalyse in der psychoanalytischen Prozessforschung.* Habilitationsschrift. Reprinted PSZ-Verlag, Ulm, 1986.

Kächele, H. (1983). Verbal activity level of therapists in initial interviews and long-term psychoanalysis. In W. H. Minsel & W. Herff (Eds.), *Methodology in psychotherapy research* (pp. 125–129). Frankfurt: Lang.

Kächele, H. (1988). Clinical and scientific aspects of the Ulm process model of psychoanalysis. *International Journal of Psychoanalysis, 69,* 65–73.

Kächele, H. (1990). A computer-based assessment of long-term transference trends. In (abstracts) *21st Annual Meeting of the Society for Psychotherapy Research.* Wintergreen, Virginia, USA.

Kächele, H. (1991). The psychoanalyst's and patient's work with "core conflictual words"—An empirical contribution to the mechanism of psychic change. In IPA (Eds.), International Congress, Buenos Aires. August 1991.

Kächele, H. (1992). Narration and observation in psychotherapy research: Reporting on a 20 year long journey from qualitative case reports to quantitative studies on the psychoanalytic process. *Psychotherapy Research, 2,* 1–15.

Kächele, H., Albani, C., Buchheim, A., Hölzer, M., Hohage, R., Jiménez, J. P., et al. (2009). The German specimen case, Amalia X: Empirical studies. *International Journal of Psychoanalysis, 87,* 809–826.

Kächele, H., & Mergenthaler, E. (1984). Auf dem Wege zur computerunterstützten Textanalyse in der psychotherapeutischen Prozessforschung. In U. Baumann (Ed.), *Psychotherapie: Makro/Mikroperspektive* (pp. 223–239). Göttingen: Verlag für Psychologie Dr. Hogrefe, C. J.

Kächele, H., Schachter, J., Thomä, H., & Ulm Psychoanalytic Process Research Group (2009). *From psychoanalytic narrative to empirical single case research: Implications for psychoanalytic practice.* New York: Analytic Press.

Kächele, H., Thomä, H., & Schaumburg, C. (1975). Veränderungen des Sprachinhaltes in einem psychoanalytischen Prozeß. *Schweizer Archiv für Neurologie: Neurochirurgie und Psychiatrie, 116,* 197–228.

Kadera, S. W., Lambert, M. J., & Andrews, A. A. (1996). A session-by-session analysis of the psychotherapy dose-effect relationship. *Journal of Psychotherapy Practice and Research, 5,* 132–151.

Kandel, E. R. (1998). A new intellectual framework for psychiatry. *American Journal of Psychiatry, 155*(4), 457–469.

Kandel, E. R. (1999). Biology and the future of psychoanalysis: a new intellectual framework for psychiatry revisited. *American Journal of Psychiatry, 156,* 505–524.

Kansaku, K., Yamaura, A., & Kitazawa, S. (2000). Sex differences in lateralization revealed in the posterior language areas. *Cerebral Cortex, 10,* 866–872.

Kaplan, A. (1964). *The conduct of inquiry.* San Francisco: Chandler.

Kazdin, A. E. (1981). Drawing valid inferences from case studies. *Journal of Consulting and Clinical Psychology, 49,* 183–192.

Kazdin, A. E. (1994). Methodology, design, and evaluation in psychotherapy research. In A. E. Bergin & S. L. Garfield (Eds.), *Handbook of psychotherapy and behavior change* (4th ed., pp. 19–71). New York: Wiley.

Kazdin, A. E. (1999). The meaning and measurement of clinical significance. *Journal of Consulting and Clinical Psychology, 67,* 332–339.

Kazdin, A. E. (2002). Mechanisms of change in psychotherapy: Amazing breakthroughs and cutting edge research (do not yet exist). Paper presented at the U.S. National Institute of Mental Health conference, December.

Kazdin, A. E. (2004). Psychotherapy for children and adolescents. In M. J. Lambert (Ed.), *Bergin and Garfield's handbook of psychotherapy and behavior change* (5th ed.). New York: Wiley, pp. 543–589.

Kazdin, A. E. (2007). Mediators and mechanisms of change in psychotherapy research. *Annual Review of Clinical Psychology, 3,* 1–27.

Kazdin, A. E. (2008). Evidence-based treatment and practice: New opportunities to bridge clinical research and practice, enhance the knowledge base, and improve patient care. *American Psychologist, 63,* 146–159.

Kazdin, A. E., & Bass, D. (1989). Power to detect differences between alternative treatments in comparative psychotherapy outcome research. *Journal of Consulting and Clinical Psychology, 57,* 138–147.

Kernberg, O. F., & Caligor, E (2005). A psychoanalytic theory of personality disorders. In M. F. Lenzenweger & J. F. Clarkin (Eds.), *Major theories of personality disorder* (2nd ed., pp. 114–156). New York: Guilford Press.

Kerr, S., Goldfried, M. R., Hayes, A. M., Castonguay, L. G., & Goldsamt, L. A. (1992). Interpersonal and intrapersonal focus in cognitive-behavioral and psychodynamic-interpersonal therapies: A preliminary analysis of the Sheffield Project. *Psychotherapy Research, 2,* 266–276.

Keupp, H. (2009). Mental disturbances and psychotherapy in late modern society. *Psychotherapeut, 54,* 128–128.

Kiesler, D. J. (1966). Some myths of psychotherapy research and the search for a paradigm. *Psychological Bulletin, 65*(2), 110–136.

Kiesler, D. J. (1973). *The process of psychotherapy: Empirical foundations and systems of analysis.* Chicago: Aldine.

Kirchmann, H. (2009). Attachment and depressiveness. Unpublished Philosophical Dissertation, University of Jena, Germany.

Kirchmann, H., Mestel, R., Schreiber-Willnow, K., Mattke, D., et al. (2009). Associations among attachment characteristics, patients' assessment of therapeutic factors, and treatment outcome following inpatient psychodynamic psychotherapy. *Psychotherapy Research, 19,* 234–248.

Kirchmann, H., Steyer, R., Mayer, A., Joraschky, P., Schreiber-Willnow, K., & Strauss, B. (2011). Effects of adult inpatient group psychotherapy on attachment characteristics: An observational study comparing routine care to an untreated comparison group. *Psychotherapy Research, 22,* 95–114.

Kirsch, I., Deacon, B. J., Huedo-Medina, T. B., Scoboria, A., Moore, T. J., Blair, T., et al. (2008). Initial severity and antidepressant benefits: a meta-analysis of data submitted to the food and drug administration. *PLoS Medicine, 5*(2), 260–268.

Kitzmann, A., Kächele, H., & Thomä, H. (1974a). Sprachformale Interaktionsprozesse in psychoanalytischen Erstinterviews. *Zeitschrift für Psychosomatische Medizin und Psychoanalyse, 20,* 25–36.

Kitzmann, A., Kächele, H., & Thomä, H. (1974b). Zur quantitativen Erfassung von Explorationen und Interpretationen in psychoanalytischen Erstinterviews. *Zeitschrift für Psychosomatische Medizin und Psychoanalyse, 20,* 101–115.

Klein, M. H., Mathieu-Coughlan, P., & Kiesler. D. J. (1986). The Experiencing Scales. In L. S. Greenberg & W. M. Pinsoff (Eds.), *The psychotherapeutic process: A research handbook* (pp. 21–71). New York: Guilford Press.

Klein, D. N., Schwartz, J. E., Santiago, N. J., Vivian, D., Voicing, C., Castonguay, L. C., et al. (2003). Therapeutic alliance in depression treatment: Controlling for prior change and patient characteristics. *Journal of Consulting and Clinical Psychology, 71,* 997–1006.

Klein, M. (1948). *Contributions to psycho-analysis, 1921–1945.* London: Hogarth Press.

Klein, M., Mathieu, P., Kiesler, D., & Gendlin, E. (1969). *The experiencing scale.* Madison: Wisconsin Psychiatric Institute.

Klerman, G. L., Weissman, M. M., Rounsaville, B. J., & Chevron, E. S. (1984). *Interpersonal psychotherapy of depression.* New York: Basic Rooks.

Klerman, G. L., & Weissman, M. M. (1986). The interpersonal approach to understanding depression. In T. Millon & G. L. Klerman (Eds.), *Contemporary directions in psychopathology toward the DSM-IV* (pp. 429–456). New York: Guilford Press.

Kochanska, G. (2001). Emotional development in children with different attachment histories: The first three years. *Child Development, 72,* 474–490.

Koenigsberg, H. W., Fan, J., Ochsner, K. N., Liu, X., Guise, K., Pizarello, S., Dorantes, C., Guerreri, S., Tecuta, L., Goodman, M., New, M., & Siever, L. (2009). Neural correlates of the use of psychological distancing to regulate responses to negative social cues: A study of patients with borderline personality disorder. *Biological Psychiatry, 66,* 854–863.

Koenigsberg, H. W., Siever, L. J., Lee, H., Pizzarello, S., New, A., Goodman, M., et al. (2009). Neural correlates of emotion processing in borderline personality disorder. *Psychiatry Research: Neuroimaging, 172,* 192–199.

Kohl, St., Barnow, S., Brähler, E., Fegert, J. M., et al. (2009). Psychotherapy training from the trainers' perspective. *Psychotherapeut, 54,* 445–456.

Kohlberg, L. (1969). State and sequence: The cognitive-developmental approach to socialization. In D. A. Gosh (Ed.), *Handbook of socialization theory and research* (347–480). Chicago: Rand McNally.

Kolb, D. A. (1984). *Experiential learning. Experiences as a source of learning and development.* Englewood Cliffs, NJ: Prentice Hall.

Koren, E. (1979). [Cartoon about metaphors]. *New Yorker,* October 8, 55, 34.

Kounios, J., Frymiare, J. L., Bowden, E. M., Fleck, J. I., Subramaniam, K., Parrish, T. B., et al. (2006). The prepared mind: Neural activity prior to problem presentation predicts subsequent solution by sudden insight. *Psychological Science, 17,* 882–890.

Kraemer, H. C., Wilson, T., Fairburn, C. G., & Agras, W. S. (2002). Mediators and moderators of treatment effects in randomized clinical trials. *Archives of General Psychiatry, 59*(10), 877–883.

Kraemer, S., Lihl, M., & Mergenthaler, E. (2007). Key sessions in the course of cognitive behavior therapy with schizophrenic patients: A contribution to process research. *Verhaltenstherapie, 17,* 90–99.

Kraus, D. R., Castonguay, L. G., Boswell, J. F., Nordberg, S. S., & Hayes, J. A. (2011). Therapist effectiveness: Implications for accountability and patient care. *Psychotherapy Research, 21*(3), 267–276.

Krause, M. S., & Howard, K. I. (1999). "Between-group psychotherapy research and basic science" revisited. *Journal of Clinical Psychology, 55,* 159–170.

Krause, M. S., & Lutz, W. (2009). Process transforms inputs to determine outcomes: Therapists are responsible for managing process. *Clinical Psychology: Science and Practice, 16,* 73–81.

Krogel, J. (2008). The group questionnaire. Unpublished doctoral dissertation, Provo, Brigham Young University.

Krupnick, J. L., Sotsky, S. M., Elkin, I., Simmens, S., Moyer, J., Watkins, J., et al. (1996). The role of the therapeutic alliance in psychotherapy and pharmacotherapy outcome. Findings in the National Institute of Mental Health Depression Collaborative Research Program. *Journal of Consulting and Clinical Psychology, 64,* 532–539.

Kuhn, T. S. (1962). *The structure of scientific revolutions.* Chicago: University of Chicago Press.

Kvale, S. (1997). Psychoanalytic therapy as qualitative research. Unpublished paper presented at the Society for Psychotherapy Research meeting, Geilo, Norway, June.

Ladany, N. (2004). Psychotherapy supervision: What lies beneath. *Psychotherapy Research, 14*(1), 1–19.

Ladany, N., Walker, J. A., Pate-Carolan, L., & Evans, L. G. (2008). *Practising counseling and psychotherapy: Insights from trainees, supervisors.* New York: Routledge.

Laireiter, A. R., & Botermans, J. F. (2005). Training research in psychotherapy. In A. R. Laireiter & U. Willutzki (Eds.), *Training in behaviour therapy]* (pp. 53–101). Göttingen: Hogrefe.

Lakatos, I. (1970). Falsification and the methodology of scientific research programmes. In I. Lakatos & A. Musgrave (Eds.), *Criticism and the growth of knowledge* (pp. 51–58). Cambridge: Cambridge University Press.

Lambert, M. J. (2007). Presidential address: What we have learned from a decade of research aimed at improving psychotherapy outcome in routine care? *Psychotherapy Research, 17,* 1–14.

Lambert, M. J (2013). Outcome in psychotherapy: The past and important advances. *Psychotherapy, 50,* 42–51.

Lambert, M. J., & Anderson, E. M. (1996). Assessment for time limited psychotherapies. *Annual Review of Psychiatry, 15,* 23–47.

Lambert, M. J., & Barley, D. E. (2002). Research summary on the therapeutic relationship and psychotherapy outcome. In J. C. Norcross (Ed.), *Psychotherapeutic relationships that work* (pp. 17–35). New York: Oxford University Press.

Lambert, M. J., & Bergin, A. E. (1994). The effectiveness of psychotherapy. In A. E. Bergin & S. L. Garfield (Eds.), *Handbook of psychotherapy and behavior change* (4th ed., pp. 143–189). New York: Wiley.

Lambert, M. J., Bergin, A. E., & Garfield, S. L. (2004). Introduction and overview. In M. J. Lambert (Ed.), *Bergin & Garfield's handbook of psychotherapy and behavior change* (5th ed., pp. 3–15). New York: Wiley.

Lambert, M. J., Hansen, N. B., & Harmon, S. C. (2010). The OQ-45 system: Development and practical applications in health care settings. In M. Barkham, G. Hardy, & J. Mellor-Clark (Eds.), *Developing and delivering practice-based evidence: A guide for the psychological therapies* (pp. 141–154). New York: Wiley-Blackwell.

Lambert, M. J., Morton, J. J., Hatfield, D., Harmon, C., Hamilton, S., Reid, R. C., et al. (2004). *Administration and scoring manual for the Outcome Questionnaire-45.* Salt Lake City, UT: OQ Measures.

Lambert, M. J., & Ogles, B. M. (2004). The efficacy and effectiveness of psychotherapy. In M. J. Lambert (Ed.), *Bergin and Garfield's handbook of psychotherapy and behavior change* (5th ed., pp. 139–193). New York: Wiley.

Lambert, M. J., Shapiro, D. A., & Bergin, A. E. (1986). The effectiveness of psychotherapy. In S. L. Garfield & A. E. Bergin (Eds.), *Handbook of psychotherapy and behavior change* (3rd ed.). New York: Wiley.

Lambert, M. J., Whipple, J. L., Bishop, M. J., Vermeersch, D. A., Gray, G. V., & Finch, A. E. (2002). Comparison of empirically derived and rationally derived methods for identifying clients at risk for treatment failure. *Clinical Psychology and Psychotherapy, 9,* 149–164.

Lambert, M. J., Whipple, J. L., Harmon, C., Shimokawa, K., Slade, K., & Christofferson, C. (2004). *Clinical support tools manual.* Provo, UT: Department of Psychology, Brigham University.

Lambert, M. J., Whipple, J. L., Hawkins, E. J., Vermeersch, D. A., Nielsen, S. L., & Smart, D. W. (2003). Is it time for clinicians to routinely track patient outcome? A meta-analysis. *Clinical Psychology: Science and Practice, 10,* 288–301.

Lambert, M. J., Whipple, J. L., Smart, D., Vermeersch, D. A., Nielsen, S. L., & Hawkins, E. (2001). The effects of providing therapists with feedback on patient progress during psychotherapy. Are outcomes enhanced? *Psychotherapy Research, 11,* 49–68.

Lambert, M. J., Whipple, J. L., Vermeersch, D. A., Smart, D. W., Hawkins, E. J., Nielsen, S. L., et al. (2002). Enhancing psychotherapy outcomes via providing feedback on client progress: A replication. *Clinical Psychology and Psychotherapy, 9,* 91–103.

Lampropoulos, G. K., Goldfried, M. R., Castonguay, L. G., Lambert, M. J., Stiles, W. B., & Nestoros, J. N. (2002). What kind of research can we realistically expect from the practitioner? *Journal of Clinical Psychology, 58,* 1241–1264.

Latour, B. (1987). *Science in action: How to follow scientists and engineers through society.* Cambridge, MA: Harvard University Press.

Leach, C., Lucock, M., Barkham, M., Stiles, W. B., Noble, R., & Iveson, S. (2006). Transforming between Beck Depression Inventory and CORE-OM scores in routine clinical practice. *British Journal of Clinical Psychology, 45,* 153–166.

Leahy, R. (2001). *Overcoming resistance in cognitive therapy.* New York: Guilford Press.

LeDoux, J. (2002). *The synaptic self: How our brains become who we are.* New York: Viking.

Leichsenring, F., & Leibing, E. (2003). The effectiveness of psychodynamic theory and cognitive behavior therapy in the treatment of personality disorders: A meta-analysis. *American Journal of Psychiatry, 160,* 1223–1232.

Leichsenring, F., & Rabung, S. (2008). Effectiveness of long-term psychodynamic psychotherapy: A meta-analysis. *JAMA: Journal of the American Medical Association, 300,* 1551–1565.

Leiman, M. (1992). The concept of sign in the work of Vygotsky, Winnicott and Bakhtin: Further integration of object relations theory and activity theory. *British Journal of Medical Psychology, 65,* 209–221.

Leiman, M. (1997). Procedures as dialogical sequences: A revised version of the fundamental concept in cognitive analytic therapy. *British Journal of Medical Psychology, 70,* 193–207.

Leiman, M. (2011). Mikhail Bakhtin's contribution to psychotherapy research. *Culture & Psychology, 17,* 441–461.

Leiman, M., & Stiles, W. B. (2001). Dialogical sequence analysis and the zone of proximal development as conceptual enhancements to the assimilation model: The case of Jan revisited. *Psychotherapy Research, 11,* 311–330.

Lenzenweger, M. F. (2010). Current status of the scientific study of the personality disorders: An overview of epidemiological, longitudinal, experimental psychopathology, and neurobehavioral perspectives. *Journal of the American Psychoanalytic Association, 58,* 741–748.

Lenzenweger, M. F., & Clarkin, J. F. (Eds.). (2005). *Major theories of personality disorder* (2nd ed.). New York: Guilford Press.

Lenzenweger, M. F., Clarkin, J. F., Fertuck, E. A., & Kernberg, O. F. (2004). Executive neurocognitive functioning and neurobehavioral systems indicators in borderline personality disorder: A preliminary study. *Journal of Personality Disorders, 18,* 421–438.

Lenzenweger, M. F., Clarkin, J. F., Yeomans, F. E., Kernberg, O. F., & Levy, K. N. (2008). Refining the borderline personality disorder phenotype through finite mixture modeling: Implications for classification. *Journal of Personality Disorders, 22,* 313–331.

Lepper, G., & Mergenthaler, E. (2005). Exploring group process. *Psychotherapy Research, 15,* 433–444.

Lepper, G., & Mergenthaler, E. (2007). Therapeutic collaboration: How does it work? *Psychotherapy Research, 17,* 576–587.

Lepper, G., & Mergenthaler, E. (2008). Observing therapeutic interaction in the "Lisa Case." *Psychotherapy Research, 18,* 634–644.

Leszcz, M., & Kobos, J. S. (2008). Evidence-based group psychotherapy: using AGPA's practice guidelines to enhance clinical effectiveness. *Journal of Clinical Psychology, 64,* 1238–1260.

Leuzinger-Bohleber, M., & Kächele, H. (1988). From Calvin to Freud: Using an artificial intelligence model to investigate cognitive changes during psychoanalysis. In H. Dahl, H. Kächele, & H. Thomä (Eds.), *Psychoanalytic Process Research Strategies* (pp. 291–306). New York: Springer.

Levins, R. (1968). *Evolution in changing environments: Some theoretical explorations.* Princeton, NJ: Princeton University Press.

Levy, K. N., Meehan, K. B., Kelly, K., Reynoso, J. S., Weber, M., Clarkin, J. F., & Kernberg, O. F. (2006). Change in attachment patterns and reflective function in a randomized control trial of transference-focused psychotherapy for borderline personality disorder. *Journal of Consulting and Clinical Psychology, 74,* 1027–1040.

Levy, K. N., Meehan, K. B., Weber, M., Reynoso, J., & Clarkin, J. F. (2005). Attachment and borderline personality disorder: Implications for psychotherapy. *Psychopathology, 38,* 64–74.

Lieblich, A., McAdams, D., & Josselson, R. (Eds.) (2004). *Healing plots: The narrative basis of psychotherapy.* Washington, DC: APA Books.

Liepert, J., Bauder, H., Miltner, W. H. R., Taub, E., & Weiller, C. (2000). Massive cortical reorganization resulting from treatment-induced rehabilitation of movement after stroke in humans. *Stroke, 31,* 1210–1216.

Liggan, D. Y., & Kay, J. (1999). Some neurobiological aspects of psychotherapy: A review. *Journal of Psychotherapy Practice and Research, 8,* 103–114.

Limberg, C. O. (2008). Psychotherapist's language tools leading to connecting in the patient. Unpublished doctoral dissertation, University of Ulm.

Linehan, M. M. (1993). *Cognitive-behavioral treatment of borderline personality disorder.* New York: Guilford Press.

Linehan, M. M., Armstrong, H. E., Suarez, A., Allmon, D., & Heard, H. L. (1991). Cognitive- behavioral treatment of chronically parasuicidal borderline patients. *Archives of General Psychiatry, 48,* 1060–1064.

Links, P. S., Heslegrave, R., & van Reekum, R. (1999). Impulsivity: Core aspect of borderline personality disorder. *Journal of Personality Disorders, 13,* 1–9.

Linton, S. J., Melin, L., & Götestam, G. (1985). Behavioral analysis of chronic pain and itsmanagement. *Progress in Behavior Modification,* Vol. 18. New York: Academic Press.

Lishman, E., & Cheston, R. (2012). The markers of assimilation in dementia coding frame. Unpublished manuscript, Clinical Psychology Department, University of Exeter, UK.

Livesley, W. J. (2001). Conceptual and taxonomic issues. In J. Livesley (Ed.), *Handbook of personality disorders* (pp. 3–36). New York: Guilford Press.

Llewelyn, S. (1988). Psychological therapy as viewed by clients and therapists. *British Journal of Clinical Psychology, 27,* 223–238.

Locke, B., Crane, A., Chun-Kennedy, C., & Edens, A. (2010). The center for the study of collegial mental health: A novel practice research network with national reach and a pilot study to match. *Psychotherapy Bulletin, 44,* 17–21.

Löffler, J., Bormann, B., Burlingame, G.M., & Strauss, B. (2007). Auswahl von Patient(inn) en für Gruppenpsychotherapien—Validierung der deutschen Version des Group Selection Questionnaire (GSQ) [Selection of patients for group treatments—Validity of the German version of the GSQ]. *Zeitschrift für Psychiatrie, Psychologie und Psychotherapie, 55,* 75–86.

Lomas, P. (1981). *The case for a personal psychotherapy.* Oxford: Oxford University Press.

Lopata, H. Z. (1969). Loneliness: Forms and components. *Social Problems, 17,* 248–262.

Loranger, A. W., Lenzeweger, M. F., Gartner, A. F., Susman, V. L., Herzig, J., Zammit, G. K., Gartner, J. D., Abrams, R. C., & Young, R. C. (1991). Trait-state artefacts and the diagnosis of personality disorders. *Archives of General Psychiatry, 48,* 720–728.

Luborsky, L. (1977). Measuring a pervasive psychic structure in psychotherapy: The core conflictual relationship theme. In N. Freedman & S. Grand (Eds.), *Communicative structures and psychic structures* (pp. 367–395). New York: Plenum Press.

Luborsky, L. (1984). *Principles of psychoanalytic psychotherapy: A manual for supportive-expressive treatment.* New York: Basic Books.

Luborsky, L., & Crits-Christoph, P. (1990). *Understanding transference: The Core Conflictual Relationship Theme method.* New York: Basic Books.

Luborsky, L., & Crits-Christoph, P. (1998). *Understanding transference: The Core Conflictual Relationship Theme method* (2nd ed.). Washington, DC: APA Books.

Luborsky, E., Crits-Christoph, P., McLellan, A. T., Woody, G. E., Piper, W. E., Lieberman, D. M., et al. (1986). Do therapists vary much in their success? Findings from four outcome studies. *American Journal of Orthopsychiatry, 51,* 501–512.

Luborsky, L., Crits-Christoph, P., Mintz, J., & Auerbach, A. (1988). *Who will benefit from psychotherapy: Predicting therapeutic outcomes.* New York: Basic Books.

Luborsky, L., Diguer, L., Seligman, D. A., Rosenthal, R., Krause, E. D., Johnson, S., et al. (1999). The researcher's own therapy allegiances: A "wild card" in comparisons of treatment efficacy. *Clinical Psychology: Science and Practice, 6,* 95–106.

Luborsky, L., & Mark, D. (1991). Short-term supportive-expressive psychoanalytic psychotherapy. In P. Crits-Christoph & J. P. Berber (Eds.), *Handbook of short-term dynamic psychotherapy* (pp. 110–136). New York: Basic Books.

Luborsky, E., McLellan, A. T., Diguer, L., Woody, G. E., & Seligman, D. A. (1997). The psychotherapist matters: Comparison of outcome across twenty-two therapists and seven patient samples. *Clinical Psychology: Science and Practice, 4,* 53–65.

Luborsky, L., Rosenthal, R., Andrusyna, T., Berman, J., Shapiro, D. A., & Seligman, D. (2001). *Recommendations for improving psychotherapy outcome studies.* Paper presented at the European and UK meeting of the Society for Psychotherapy Research, Leiden, the Netherlands, March.

Luborsky, L., Rosenthal, R., Diguer, L., Andrusyna, T. P., Berman, J. S., Levitt, J. T., et al. (2002). The dodo bird verdict is alive and well mostly. *Clinical Psychology: Science and Practice, 9,* 2–12.

Luborsky, L., Singer, B., & Luborsky, L. (1975). Comparative studies of psychotherapies: Is it true that "Everyone has won and all must have prizes?" *Archives of General Psychiatry, 32,* 995–1008.

Luborsky, L., & Spence, D. P. (1971). Quantitative research on psychoanalytic therapy. In A. E. Bergin & S. L. Garfield (Eds.), *Handbook of psychotherapy and behaviour change* (pp. 408–437). New York: Wiley.

Lunnen, K. M., & Ogles, B. M. (1998). A multiperspective, multivariable evaluation of reliable change. *Journal of Consulting and Clinical Psychology, 66,* 400–410.

Lunnen, K. M., Ogles, B. M., Anderson, T. M., & Barnes, D. L. (2006). A comparison of CCRT pervasiveness and symptomatic improvement in brief therapy. *Psychology and Psychotherapy: Theory, Research and Practice, 79,* 289–302.

Lutz, W., Lambert, M. J., Harmon, S. C., Stulz, N., Tschitsaz, A., & Schürch, E. (2006). The probability of treatment success, failure and duration: What can be learned from empirical data to support decision making in clinical practice? *Clinical Psychology and Psychotherapy, 13,* 223–232.

Lutz, W., Stulz, D., Smart, D., & Lambert, M. J. (2007). Patterns of early change in outpatient psychotherapy. *Zeitschrift für Klinische Psychologie und Psychotherapie, 36*(2), 93–104.

Machado, P. P. P., & Gonçalves, O. F. (Eds.) (1999). Special section on narrative in psychotherapy: The emerging metaphor. *Journal of Clinical Psychology, 55,* 1175–1270.

MacLean, P. D. (1985). Brain evolution, relating to family, play, and the separation call. *Archives of General Psychiatry, 42,* 405–417.

MacLeod, R., & Elliott, R. (2012). Emotion-focused therapy for social anxiety: A hermeneutic single-case efficacy design study of a low-outcome case. *Counselling Psychology Review, 27,* 7–22.

MacLeod, R., Elliott, R., & Rodgers, B. (2012). Process-experiential/emotion-focused therapy for social anxiety: A hermeneutic single-case efficacy design study. *Psychotherapy Research, 22,* 67–81.

Magnavita, J. J. (2008). Toward unification of clinical science: The next phase in the evolution of psychotherapy? *Journal of Psychotherapy integration, 18,* 264–291.

Mahoney, M. J. (1976). *Scientist as subject: The psychological imperative.* Cambridge, MA: Ballinger.

Mahrer, A. R. (1990). *Dream work in psychotherapy and self-change.* New York: Norton.

Maier, D. (2008). Negation and valence of emotional tone. Unpublished doctoral dissertation, University of Ulm.

Mallinckrodt, B. (2000). Attachment, social competencies, social support and interpersonal process in psychotherapy. *Psychotherapy Research, 10,* 239–266.

Marks, I. M. (2002). The maturing of therapy: Some brief psychotherapies help anxiety/depressive disorders but mechanisms of action are unclear. *British Journal of Psychiatry, 180,* 200–204.

Martin, A., Buchheim, A., Berger, U., & Strauss, B. (2006). The Impact of attachment organization on potential countertransference reactions. *Psychotherapy Research, 17,* 46–58.

Martin, D. J., Garske, J. P., & Davis, M. K. (2000). Relation of the therapeutic alliance with outcome and other variables: A metaanalytic review. *Journal of Consulting and Clinical Psychology, 68,* 438–450.

Martin, S. D., Martin, E., Rai, S. S., Richardson, M. A., Royall, R., & Eng, C. (2001). Brain blood brain flow changes in depressed patients treated with interpersonal psychotherapy or venlafaxine hydrochloride. *Archives of General Psychiatry, 139,* 565–570.

Maser, J. D., & Cloninger, C. R. (Eds.). (1990). *Comorbidity of mood and anxiety disorders.* Washington, DC: American Psychiatric Press.

Maslove, V. (1990). The differential effects and depth of experiencing of empty chair dialogue and empathic reflection. Unpublished manuscript. University of British Columbia, Vancouver.

Matarazzo, R. G., & Patterson, D. R. (1986). Methods of teaching therapeutic skills. In S. L. Garfield & A. E. Bergin, (Eds.), *Handbook of psychotherapy and behaviour change* (3rd ed.) (pp. 821–843). New York: Wiley.

May, A., Hajak, G., Gänßbauer, S., Steffens, T., Langguth, B., Kleinjung, T., et al. (2007). Structural brain alterations following 5 days of intervention: Dynamic aspects of neuroplasticity. *Cerebral Cortex, 17,* 205–210.

Mayberg, H. S., Silva, J. A., Brannan, S. K., Tekell, J. L., McGinnis, S., Manhurin, R. K., et al. (2002). The functional neuroanatomy of the placebo effect, *American Journal of Psychiatry, 159*(5), 728–737.

McCallum, M., & Piper, W. E. (Eds.). (1997). *Psychological mindedness: A contemporary understanding.* Mahwah, NJ: Lawrence Erlbaum Associates.

McCallum, M., Piper, W. E., & O'Kelly, J. (1997). Predicting patient benefit from a group oriented, evening treatment program. *International Journal of Group Psychotherapy, 47,* 291–314.

McCarthy, K. L., Mergenthaler, E., Schneider, S., & Grenyer, B. F. S. (2011). Psychodynamic change in psychotherapy: Cycles of patient-therapist linguistic interactions and interventions. *Psychotherapy Research, 21,* 722–731.

McCarthy, K. S., & Barber, J. P. (2009). The Multitheoretical List of Therapeutic Interventions (MULTI): Initial report. *Psychotherapy Research, 19,* 96–113.

McClelland, J. L., Rummelhardt, D. E., & the PDP Research Group. (1986). *Parallel distributed processing: Explorations in the microstructure of the cognition,* Vol. 2, *Psychological and biological models.* Cambridge, MA: MIT Press.

McClure, E. B., Adler, A., Monk, C. S., Cameron, J., Smith, S., Nelson, E. E., et al. (2007). fMRI predictors of treatment outcome in pediatric anxiety disorders. *Psychoparmacology, 191,* 97–105.

McCullough, J. P. (2000). *Treatment for chronic depression: Cognitive Behavioral Analysis System of Psychotherapy (CBASP).* New York: Guilford Press.

McGuire, W. J. (1986). A perspectivist looks at contextualism and the future of behavioral science. In R. Rosnow and M. Georgoudi (Eds.), *Contextualism and understanding in behavioural science* (pp. 271–301). New York: Praeger.

McHugh, R. K., Murray, H. W., & Barlow D. H. (2009). Balancing fidelity and adaptation in the dissemination of empirically-supported treatments: The promise of transdiagnostic interventions. *Behavior Research and Therapy, 47,* 946–953.

McLeod, J. (2010). *Case study research in counselling and psychotherapy.* London: Sage.

McLeod, J., & Balamoutsou, S. (1996). Representing narrative process in therapy: Qualitative analysis of a single case. *Counselling Psychology Quarterly, 9,* 61–76.

Meares, R. (1976). The secret. *Psychiatry, 39,* 258–265.

Meares, R. (2001). *Intimacy and alienation: Memory, trauma and personal being.* Hove, UK: Brunner-Routledge.

Meares, R., & Hobson, R. F. (1977). The persecutory therapist. *British Journal of Medical Psychology, 50,* 349–359.

Meehl, P. E. (1954). *Clinical versus statistical prediction.* Minneapolis: University of Minnesota Press.

Meehl, P. E. (1978). Theoretical risks and tabular asterisks: Sir Karl, Sir Ronald, and the slow progress of soft psychology. *Journal of Consulting and Clinical Psychology, 46,* 806–834.

Mergenthaler, E. (1985). *Textbank systems. Computer science applied in the field of psychoanalysis.* New York: Springer.

Mergenthaler, E. (1990). Parts of speech: A measure of therapeutic alliance. In *Abstracts of the 21st Annual Meeting SPR.* Wintergreen, Virginia, USA.
Mergenthaler, E. (1996). Emotion-abstraction patterns in verbatim protocols: A new way of describing psychotherapeutic processes. *Journal of Consulting and Clinical Psychology, 64,* 1306–1315.
Mergenthaler, E. (1999). The word as a mediator between body and psyche: Can psychotherapeutic processes be measured? In S. Hawighorst- Knapstein, G. Schönefuß, P. G. Knapstein, & H. Kentenich (Eds.), *Psychosomatic gynecology and obstetrics* (pp. 57–63). Gießen, Germany: Psychosozial-Verlag.
Mergenthaler, E. (2002). The cycles model–A way towards training oriented research? *Psychologische Medizin, 13,* 3–10.
Mergenthaler, E. (2003). Shifts from negative to positive emotional tone: Facilitators of therapeutic change? In Society for Psychotherapy Research (Ed.), *Book of abstracts, 34th annual meeting* (p. 45). Ulm, Germany: Ulmer Textbank. Unpublished.
Mergenthaler, E. (2004). Emotional cognitive and behavioral changes in a single case study: An application of the therapeutic cycle model. In Society for Psychotherapy Research (Ed.), *Book of abstracts, 35th annual meeting* (p. 55). Ulm, Germany: Ulmer Textbank.
Mergenthaler, E., & Bucci, W. (1999). Linking verbal and nonverbal representations: Computer analysis of referential activity. *British Journal of Medical Psychology, 72,* 339–354.
Mergenthaler, E., & Casonato, M. (2009). *Trattato del ciclo terapeutico.* Bologna: CLUEB.
Mergenthaler, E., & Gelo, O. (2009). Il Modello dei Cicli Terapeutici. In M. Vigorelli (Ed.), *Laboratorio didattico per la ricerca in psicoterapia* (pp. 67–87). Milano: Edizioni libreria Cortina.
Mergenthaler, E., & Horowitz, M. J. (1994). Linking computer aided text analysis with variables scored from video tape. In F. Faulbaum (Ed.), SoftStat '93. *Advances in statistical software 4. The 7th Conference on the Scientific Use of Statistical Software, Heidelberg* (Proceedings) (pp. 385–393). Stuttgart, Germany: Fischer.
Mergenthaler, E., & Kächele, H. (1985). Changes of latent meaning structures in psychoanalysis. *Sprache und Datenverarbeitung, 9,* 21–28.
Mergenthaler, E., & Kächele, H. (1988). The Ulm textbank management system: A tool for psychotherapy research. In H. Dahl, H. Kächele, & H. Thomä (Eds.), *Psvchoanalytic process research strategies* (pp. 195–212). New York: Springer.
Mergenthaler, E., & Kächele, H. (1991). The Ulm textbank research program. In L. Beutler (Ed.), *International psychotherapy research programs.* New York: Pergamon.
Mergenthaler, E., & Levitt, H. (2005). Pausing experiences and the therapeutic cycles model. In Society for Psychotherapy Research (Ed.), *Book of abstracts, 36th annual meeting* (p. 93). Ulm, Germany: Ulmer Textbank.
Merton, R. K. (1942). Science and technology in a democratic order. *Journal of Legal and Political Sociology, 7,* 115–126.
Merton, R. K. (1957). Priorities in scientific discovery: A chapter in the sociology of science. *American Sociological Review, 22,* 635–659.
Messer, S. B. (1986). Behavioral and psychoanalytic perspectives at therapeutic choice points. *American Psychologist, 41,* 1261–1272.
Messer, S. B. (2001). Introduction to the special issue on assimilative integration. *Journal of Psychotherapy Integration, 11,* 1–4.

Meystre, C., Kramer, U., De Roten, Y., Despland, J.-N., & Stiles, W. B. (2014). How psychotherapeutic exchanges become responsive: A theory-building case study in the framework of the assimilation model. *Counselling and Psychotherapy Research, 14,* 29-41.

Michal, M., Overbeck, G., Grabhorn, R., Stirn, A., Mergenthaler, E., & Jordan, J. (2001). Representing relationship, resistance and insight using formal and substantial discourse Marker. Zeitschrift für *Psychosomatische Medizin und Psychotherapie, 47,* 348–365.

Michels-Lucht, F., Freyberger, H. J., von Rad, K., Schulz, A., Glaesmer, H., Kohl, St., et al. (2009). Results of a Delphi-suvey related to the research expertise on the training of psychological psychotherapists and child and adolescent psychotherapists. *Psychodynamische Psychotherapie, 8,* 178–232.

Miklowitz, D. J., & Clarkin, J. F. (1999). Balancing internal and external validity. *Prevention & Treatment* [Online], *2.*

Miller, F. G., Rosenstein, G. L., & DeRenzo, E. G. (1998). Professional Integity in clinical research. *Journal of the American Medical Association, 280*(16), 1449–1454.

Millon, T. (1982). *Millon Clinical Multiaxial Inventory Manual* (2nd ed.). Minneapolis: Nationa Computer Systems.

Millon, T. (1991). Classification in psychopathology: Rationale, alternatives, and standards *Journal of Abnormal Psychology, 100,* 245–261.

Miranda, J., & Persons, J. B. (1988). Dysfunctional attitudes are mood-state dependent. *Journal of Abnormal Psychology, 97,* 76–79.

Misch, D.A. (2000). Psychosocial formulation training using commercial films. *Academic Psychiatry, 24,* 99–104.

Mischel, W., & Shoda, Y. (1999). Integrating dispositions and processing dynamics within a unified theory of personality: The cognitive-affective personality system. In L. A. Pervin & O. P. John (Eds.), *Handbook of personality* (2nd ed., pp. 197–218). New York: Guilford Press.

Mitroff, I. I. (1974). *The subjective side of science: A philosophical inquiry into the psychology of the Apollo moon scientists.* Amsterdam: Elsevier.

Mohr, L. B. (1999). The qualitative method of impact analysis. *American Journal of Evaluation, 20,* 69–84.

Mohr, L. B. (1993). Causation and the case study. Paper presented at meeting of the National Public Management Research Conference, University of Wisconsin, Madison, WI, October.

Mohr, P., Rodriguez, M., Slavíčková, A., & Hanka, J. (2011). The application of vagus nerve stimulation and deep brain stimulation in depression. *Neuropsychobiology, 64*(3), 170–181.

Moras, K. (2002). Research in psychotherapy. In M. Hersen, & W. Sledge (Eds.), *Encyclopedia of psychotherapy* (Vol. 3, pp. 525–545). New York: Elsevier Science.

Moras, K. (2006). The value of neuroscience strategies to accelerate progress in psychological treatment research, *Canadian Journal of Psychiatry, 51*(13), 810–822.

Morey, L. C. (1991). Classification of mental disorder as a collection of hypothetical constructs. *Journal of Abnormal Psychology, 100,* 289–293.

Morgan, D. L., & Morgan, R. K. (2001). Single-participant research design. *American Psychologist, 56,* 119–127.

Morrow-Bradley, C., & Elliott R. (1986). Utilization of psychotherapy research by practicing psychotherapists. *American Psychologist, 41,* 188–197.

Mosher, J. K., & Stiles, W. B. (2009). Clients' assimilation of experiences of their therapists. *Psychotherapy, 46,* 432–447.

Moyers, T. B., Miller, W. R., & Hendrickson, S. M. L. (2005). How does motivational interviewing work? Therapist interpersonal skill predicts client involvement within motivational interviewing sessions. *Journal of Consulting and Clinical Psychology, 73,* 590–598.

Moynihan, R. (2011). It's time to rebuild the evidence base. *British Medical Journal, 342,* d3004. doi: 10.1136/bmj.d3004

Mueller, R. M., Lambert, M. J., & Burlingame, G. M. (1998). Construct validity of the Outcome Questionnaire: A confirmatory factor analysis. *Journal of Personality Assessment, 70,* 248–262.

Muran, J., Safran, J., Samstag, L., & Winston, A. (2005). Evaluating an alliance-focused treatment for personality disorders. *Psychotherapy Theory, Research, Practice, Training, 42,* 532–545.

Murray, E. J., & Jacobson, L. E. (1971). The nature of learning in traditional and behavioral psychotherapy. In A. E. Bergin & S. L. Garfield (Eds.), *Handbook of psychotherapy and behavior change* (pp. 709–747). New York: John Wiley.

Murray, H. A. (1938). *Explorations in personality.* New York: Oxford Press.

Nemeroff, C. B., Heim, C. M., Thase, M. E., Klein, D. N., Rush, A. J., Schatzberg, A. F., et al. (2003). Differential responses to psychotherapy versus pharmacotherapy in patients with chronic forms of major depression and childhood trauma. *Proceedings of the National Academy of Sciences of the United States of America, 100,* 14293–14296.

Neudert, L., Grünzig, H. J., & Thomä, H. (1987). Change in self-esteem during psychoanalysis: a single case study. In: N. M. Cheshire, & H. Thomä (Eds.), *Self, symptoms and psychotherapy* (pp. 243–265). New York: Wiley.

Neudert, L., & Hohage, R. (1988). Different types of suffering during a psychoanalysis. In H. Dahl, H. Kächele, & H. Thomä (Eds.), *Psychoanalytic process research strategies.* New York: Springer.

Newell, A., & Simon, H. (1972). *Human problem solving.* New York: Wiley.

Newman, D. W., & Beail, N. (2002). Monitoring change in psychotherapy with people with intellectual disabilities: the application of the assimilation of problematic experiences scale. *Journal of Applied Research in Intellectual Disabilities, 15,* 48–60.

Newman, D. W., & Beail, N. (2005). Analysis of assimilation during psychotherapy with people who have mental retardation. *American Journal on Mental Retardation, 110,* 359–365.

Newman, M. G., Castonguay, L. G., Borkovec, T. D., Fisher, A. J., & Nordberg, S. (2008). An open trial of integrative therapy for generalized anxiety disorder. *Psychotherapy: Theory, Research, Practice, and Training, 45,* 135–147.

Newman, M. G., Castonguay, L. G., Borkovec, T. D., Fisher, A. J., Boswell, J. F., Szkodny, L., et al. (2011). A randomized controlled trial of cognitive-behavioral therapy for generalized anxiety disorder with integrated techniques from emotion-focused and interpersonal therapies. *Journal of Consulting and Clinical Psychology, 79,* 171–181.

Newman, M. G., Castonguay, L. G., Borkovec, T. D., & Molnar, C. (2004). Integrative therapy for generalized anxiety disorder. In R. G. Heimberg, C. L. Turk, & D. S. Mennin (Eds.), *Generalized anxiety disorder: Advances in research and practice* (pp. 320–350). New York: Guilford Press.

Newman, M. G., & Erickson, T. M. (2010). Generalized anxiety disorder. In J. G. Beck (Ed.), *Interpersonal processes in the anxiety disorders: Implications for understanding psychopathology and treatment* (pp. 235–259). Washington, DC: American Psychological Association.

Nicolò, G., Mergenthaler, E., Pontalti, I., Semerari, A., & Catania, D. (2000). The analysis of emotion-abstraction patterns in a cognitive therapy: Preliminary results. *Psicoterapia, 21,* 67–72.

Nielsen, S. L., & Lambert, M. J. (2006). Psychotherapeutic treatment as usual at a large university counseling center: Dose effect or Goldilocks response? Manuscript submitted for publication.

Norcross, J. C., & Rossi, J. S. (1994). Looking weakly in all the wrong places? Comment on Shapiro et al. (1994). *Journal of Consulting and Clinical Psychology, 62,* 535–538.

Norcross, J. C. (Ed.) (2002) *Psychotherapy relationships that work: Therapist contributions and responsiveness to patient need.* New York: Oxford University Press.

Norcross, J. C. (Ed.) (2011) P*sychotherapy relationships that work: Evidence-based responsiveness* (2nd ed.). New York: Oxford University Press.

Nordberg, S., Boswell, J. F., Castonguay, L. G., & Kraus, D. (2008). Measuring the shape of change: Results from three years of repeated assessment in a university clinic. Paper presented at the Annual Meeting of the Society for Psychotherapy Research. Barcelona, Spain (June).

Norquist, G., Lebowitz, B., & Hyman, S. (1999). Expanding the frontier of treatment research. *Prevention & Treatment, 2*(1), 1–10.

Norville, R., Sampson, H., & Weiss, J. (1996). Accurate interpretations and brief psychotherapy outcome. *Psychotherapy Research, 6,* 16–29.

Nutt, D., & Goodwin, G. (2011). ECNP Summit on the future of CNS drug research in Europe 2011: Report prepared for ECNP by David Nutt and Guy Goodwin. *European Neuropsychopharmacology, 21,* 495–499.

Ogles, B. M., Lambert, M. J., & Sawyer, J. D. (1995). Clinical significance of the National Institute of Mental Health Treatment of Depression Collaborative Research Program data. *Journal of Consulting and Clinical Psychology, 63,* 321–326.

Ogrodniczuk, J. S. (2006). Men, women, and their outcome in psychotherapy. *Psychotherapy Research, 16,* 453–462.

Okiishi, J. C., Lambert, M. J., Eggett, D., Nielsen, S. L., Dayton, D. D., & Vermeersch, D. A. (2006). An analysis of therapist treatment effects: Toward providing feedback to individual therapists on their patients' psychotherapy outcome. *Journal of Clinical Psychology, 62,* 1157–1172.

Okiishi, J. C., Lambert, M. J., Nielsen, S. L., et al. (2003). Waiting for supershrink: An empirical analysis of therapists´ effects. *Clinical Psychology and Psychotherapy, 10,* 361–373.

Olko, C. (2002). Cerebral asymmetry of emotions. *Advances in Psychology Research, 10,* 166–181.

OPD Task Force (2008). Operationalized psychodynamic Assessment. Bern: Huber.

Orlinsky, D. E. (1994). Learning from many masters. *Psychotherapeut, 39,* 2–9.

Orlinsky, D. E. (1995). The graying and greening of SPR: A personal memoir on forming the Society for Psychotherapy Research. *Psychotherapy Research, 5*(4), 343–350.

Orlinsky, D. E. (2008). What would I like to read in the next 10 years of psychotherapy research? *Psychotherapie, Psychosomatik, Medizinische Psychologie, 58,* 345–354.

Orlinsky, D. E., Grawe, K., & Parks, B. K (1994). Process and outcome in psychotherapy—Noch einmal. In A. E. Bergin & S. L. Garfield (Eds.), *Handbook of psychotherapy and behaviour change.* (4th ed., pp. 270–376). New York: John Wiley.

Orlinsky, D. E., & Howard, I. C. I. (1986). Process and outcome in psychotherapy. In Orlinsky, D. E., & Ronnestad, M. H. (2002). *The psychotherapist's perspective: Therapeutic work, professional development, and personal life.* Washington, DC: APA.

Orlinsky, D. E., & Howard, K. I. (1987). A generic model of psychotherapy. *Journal of Integrative & Eclectic Psychotherapy, 6,* 6–27.

Orlinsky, D. E., & Ronnestad, M. H. (2002). *The psychotherapist's perspective: Therapeutic work, professional development, and personal life.* Washington, DC: APA.

Orlinsky, D. E., & Ronnestad, M. H. (2005). *How psychotherapists develop: A study of therapeutic work and professional growth.* Washington, DC: American Psychological Association.

Osatuke, K., Moore, S. C., & Stiles, W. B. (2011). Assimilation of shared problematic experiences in organizational settings. Panel presented at the Society for Psychotherapy Research meeting, Bern, Switzerland, June.

Osatuke, K., Mosher, J. K., Goldsmith, J. Z., Stiles, W. B., Shapiro, D. A., Hardy, G. E., & Barkham, M. (2007). Submissive voices dominate in depression: Assimilation analysis of a helpful session. *Journal of Clinical Psychology, 63,* 153–164.

Osatuke, K., Reid, M., Stiles, W. B., Zisook, S., & Mohamed, S. (2011). Narrative evolution and assimilation of problematic experiences in a case of pharmacotherapy for schizophrenia. *Psychotherapy Research, 21,* 41–53.

Osatuke, K., & Stiles, W. B. (2006). Problematic internal voices in clients with borderline features: An elaboration of the assimilation model. *Journal of Constructivist Psychology, 19,* 287–319.

Osatuke, K., & Stiles, W. B. (2010). Change in PTSD: An assimilation model account. In G. Dimaggio & P. H. Lysaker (Eds.), *Metacognition and severe adult mental disorders: From research to treatment* (pp. 283–300). New York: Brunner-Routledge.

Osatuke, K., & Stiles, W. B. (2011). Numbers in assimilation research. *Theory & Psychology, 21,* 200–219.

Osatuke, K., & Stiles, W. B. (2012). Supervision as a conversation among developing voices: An assimilation model perspective. In M.-C. Bertau, M. Gonçalves, & P. Raggatt (Eds.), *Dialogic formations: Investigations into the origins and development of the dialogical self* (pp. 259–287). Charlotte, NC: Information Age Publishing.

Osatuke, K., Stiles, W. B., Barkham, M., Hardy, G. E., & Shapiro, D. A. (2011). Relationship between mental states in depression: The assimilation model perspective. *Psychiatry Research, 190,* 52–59.

Ostwald, P. (1985). *Schumann: The inner voices of a musical genius.* Boston: Northeastern University Press.

Otto, M. W., Pollack, M. H., & Maki, K. M. (2000). Empirically supported treatments for panic disorder: Costs, benefits, and stepped care. *Journal of Consulting and Clinical Psychology, 68,* 556–563.

Panksepp, J. (1998). *Affective neuroscience: The foundations of human and animal emotions.* New York: Oxford University Press.

Parloff, M. (1984). Psychotherapy research and its incredible credibility crisis. *Clinical Psychology Review, 4*(1), 95–109.

Parra, G., Mergenthaler, E., & Kächele, H. (1988). Analisis computerizado de la conducta verbal de pacientes y terapeutas en la primera entrevista diagnostica. *Acta Psiquiatrica y Psicologica de America Latina, 34,* 309–320.

Parsons, L. M., & Osherson, D. (2001). New evidence for distinct right and left brain systems for deductive versus probabilistic reasoning. *Cerebral Cortex, 11,* 954–965.

Pascual-Leone, A., & Greenberg, L. S. (2007). Emotional processing in experiential therapy: Why "the only way out is through." *Journal of Consulting and Clinical Psychology, 75*(6), 875–887.

Pascual-Leone, A. (2009). Dynamic emotional processing in experiential therapy: Two steps forward, one step back. *Journal of Consulting and Clinical Psychology, 77,* 113–126.

Pascual-Leone, J. (1984). Attentional, dialectic, and mental effort: Toward an organismic theory of life stages. In M. L. Commons, A. Richards, & C. Armons (Eds.), *Beyond formal operations: Late adolescent and adult cognitive development.* New York: Praeger.

Pascual-Leone, J., & Goodman, D. (1979). Intelligence and experience: A neo-Piagetian approach. *Instructional Science, 8,* 301–367.

Patrick, M., Hobson, R. P., Castle, D., Howard, R., & Maugham, B. (1994). Personality disorder and the mental representation of early social experience. *Developmental Psychopathology, 6,* 375–388.

Peirce, C. S. (1931–1958). *The collected papers of Charles Sanders Peirce,* vols. 1–8 (ed. C. Hartshorne, P. Weiss, & A. Burks). Cambridge, MA: Harvard University Press.

Pekkola, J., Ojanen, V., Autti, T., Jääskeläinen, I. P., Möttönen, R., & Sams, M. (2006). Attention to visual speech gestures enhances hemodynamic activity in the left planum temporale. *Human Brain Mapping, 27,* 471–477.

Perani, D., Cappa, S. F., Schnur, T., Tettamanti, M., Collina, S., Rosa, M. M., et al. (1999). The neural correlates of verb and noun processing A PET study. *Brain, 122,* 2337–2344.

Percevic, R., Lambert, M. J., & Kordy, H. (2006). What is the predictive value of responses to psychotherapy for its future course? Empirical explorations and consequences for outcome monitoring. *Psychotherapy Research, 16,* 364–373.

Perls, F. S. (1969). *Gestalt therapy verbatim.* Lafayette, CA: Real People Press.

Peterson, D. R. (1968). *The clinical study of social behavior.* New York: Appleton-Century-Crofts.

Pfäfflin, F., & Mergenthaler, E. (1998). What happens in psychotherapies? Definition, operationalization and measurement of insight. *Forensische Psychiatrie und Psychotherapie, 5,* 21–40.

Pfäfflin, F., Böhmer, M., Cornehl, S., & Mergenthaler, E. (2005). What happens in therapy with sexual offenders? A model of process research. *Sexual Abuse: A Journal of Research and Treatment, 17,* 141–151.

Pfeiffer, K. J. (2006). Kognitive Leistungsunterschiede nach expressivem Schreiben versus Sprechen [Difference in cognitive performance after expressive writing vs. speaking]. Unpublished doctoral dissertation, University of Ulm.

Piaget, J. (1970). Piaget's theory (trans. G. Gellerier & J. Langer). In P. H. Mussen (Ed.), *Carmichael's manual of child psychology,* (3rd ed., Vol. 1, pp. 703–732). New York: John Wiley.

Piefke, M., Weiss, P. H., Zilles, K., Markowitsch, H. J., & Fink, G. R. (2003). Differential remoteness and emotional tone modulate the neural correlates of autobiographical memory. *Brain, 126,* 650–668.

Pincus, A. L. (2005). A contemporary integrative interpersonal theory of personality disorders. In M. F. Lenzenweger & J. F. Clarkin (Eds.), *Major theories of personality disorder* (2nd ed., pp. 282–231). New York: Guilford Press.

Piper, W. E., & Duncan, S. C. (1999). Object relations theory and short-term dynamic psychotherapy: Findings from the Quality of Object Relations Scale. *Clinical Psychology Review, 19,* 669–686.

Piper, W. E., Azim, H. F. A., McCallum, M., & Joyce, A. S. (1990). Patient suitability and outcome in short-term individual psychotherapy. *Journal of Consulting and Clinical Psychology, 58,* 475–481.

Piper, W. E., Debbane, E. G., Bienvenu, J. P., Garant, J. (1984). A comparative study of four forms of psychotherapy. *Journal of Consulting and Clinical Psychology, 52,* 268–279.

Piper, W. E., Debbane, E. G, de Carufel, F. L., & Bienvenu, J. P. (1987). A system for differentiating therapist interpretations and other interventions. *Bulletin of the Menninger Clinic, 57,* 532–550.

Piper, W. E., Debbane, E. G., & Garant, J. (1977). An outcome study of group therapy. *Archives of General Psychiatry, 34,* 1027–1032.

Piper, W. E., Debbane, E. G., Garant, J., & Bienvenu, J. P. (1979). Pretraining for group psychotherapy: A cognitive-experiential approach. *Archives of General Psychiatry, 36,* 1250–1256.

Piper, W. E., Doan, B. D., Edwards, E. M., & Jones, B. D. (1979). Cotherapy behavior, group therapy process and treatment outcome. *Journal of Consulting and Clinical Psychology, 47,* 1081–1089.

Piper, W. E., Joyce, A. S., McCallum, M., & Azim, H. F. A. (1993). Concentration and correspondence of transference interpretations in shortterm psychotherapy. *Journal of Consulting and Clinical Psychology, 61,* 586–595.

Piper, W. E., Joyce, A. S., McCallum, M., & Azim, H. F. A. (1998). Interpretive and supportive forms of psychotherapy and patient personality variables. *Journal of Consulting and Clinical Psychology, 66,* 558–567.

Piper, W. E., Joyce, A. S., Rosie, J. S., Ogrodniczuk, J. S., McCallum, M., O'Kelly, J. G., & Steinberg, P. I. (1999). Prediction of dropping out in time-limited interpretive individual psychotherapy. *Psychotherapy, 36,* 114–122.

Piper, W. E., McCallum, M., & Azim, H. F. A. (1992). *Adaptation to loss through short-term group psychotherapy.* New York: Guilford Press.

Piper, W. E., McCallum, M., Joyce, A. S., Azim, H. F., & Ogrodniczuk, J. S. (1999). Follow-up findings for interpretive and supportive forms of psychotherapy and patient personality variables. *Journal of Consulting and Clinical Psychology, 67,* 267–273.

Piper, W. E., Ogrodniczuk, J. S., Joyce, A. S., Weideman, R., & Rosie, J. S. (2007). Group composition and group therapy for complicated grief. *Journal of Consulting and Clinical, Psychology, 75,* 116–125.

Piper, W. E., Rosie, J. S., Joyce, A. S., & Azim, H. F. A. (1996). *Time-limited day treatment for Personality disorders: Integration of research and practice in a group program.* Washington, DC: American Psychological Association.

Platt, J. D. (1964). Strong inference: Certain systematic methods of scientific thinking may produce much more rapid progress than others. *Science, 146*(3642), 347–353.

Popp, C. A., Diguer. L., Luborsky, L., & Faude, J. (1996). Repetitive relationship themes in waking narratives and dreams. *Journal of Consulting and Clinical Psychology, 64,* 1073–1078.

Posner, M. K., & Rothbart, M. K. (2000). Developing mechanisms of self-regulation. *Developmental Psychopathology, 12,* 427–441.

Posner, M. I., Rothbart M. K., Vizueta, N., Levy, K., Thomas, K. M., & Clarkin, J. (2002). Attentional mechanisms of borderline personality disorder. *Proceedings of the National Academy of Sciences, USA, 99,* 16366–16370.

Posner, M. I., Rothbart, M. K., Vizueta, N., Thomas, K. M., Levy, K. N., Fossella, J., Silbersweig, D., Stern, E., Clarkin, J. F., Kernberg, O. F. (2003). An approach to the psychobiology of personality disorders. *Development and Psychopathology, 15,* 1093–1106.

Powers, W. T. (2005). *Behavior: The control of perception* (2nd ed.). New Canaan, CT: Benchmark.

Prochaska, J. O., Rossi, J. S., & Wilcox, N. S. (1991). Change processes and psychotherapy outcome in integrative case research. *Journal of Psychotherapy Integration, 1,* 103–119.

Rajkowska, G. (2000). Postmortem studies in mood disorders indicate altered numbers ofneurons and glial cells. *Biological Psychiatry, 48,* 766–777.

Rawlins, M. (2008). De Testimonio: on the evidence for decisions about the use of therapeutic interventions. *Clinical Medicine, 8*(6), 579–588.

Reid, M., & Osatuke, K. (2006) Acknowledging problematic voices: Processes occurring at early stages of conflict assimilation in patients with functional somatic disorder. *Psychology and Psychotherapy: Theory, Research and Practice, 79,* 539–555.

Rennie, D. L., (1999). Qualitative research: A matter of hermeneutics and the sociology of knowledge. In M. Kopala & L.A. Suzuki (Eds.), *Using qualitative methods in psychology* (pp. 3–13). Thousand Oaks, CA: Sage Publications.

Rennie, D. L. (2000). Grounded theory methodology as methodological hermeneutics: Reconciling realism and relativism. *Theory & Psychology, 10,* 481–502.

Reynolds, S., Stiles, W. B., Barkham, M., Shapiro, D. A., Hardy, G. E., & Rees, A. (1993). *Acceleration* of *affective change in contrasting time-limited psychotherapies.* University of Sheffield: SAPU Memo 1434.

Reynolds, S., Stiles, W. B., Barkham, M., Shapiro, D. A., Hardy, G. E., & Rees, A. (1996). Acceleration of changes in session impact during contrasting time-limited psychotherapies. *Journal of Consulting and Clinical Psychology, 64,* 577–586.

Ribeiro, A. P., Ribeiro, E., Loura, J., Gonçalves, M. M., Stiles, W. B., Horvath, A. O., & Sousa, I. (2014). Therapeutic collaboration and resistance: Describing the nature and quality of the therapeutic relationship within ambivalence events using the Therapeutic Collaboration Coding System. *Psychotherapy Research, 24,* 346–359.

Rice, L. N., & Greenberg, L. (1984). *Patterns of change: Intensive analysis of psychotherapeutic process.* New York: Guilford Press.

Rice, L. N., & Saperia, E. P. (1984). Task analysis and the resolution of problematic reactions. In L. N. Rice & L. S. Greenberg (Eds.), *Patterns of change* (pp. 29–66). New York: Guilford Press.

Rief, W., & Hofmann, S. G. (2009). Die Psychoanalyse soll gerettet werden. Mit allen Mitteln? [Psychoanalysis shall be saved. By all means?] *Nervenarzt, 80*(5), 593–597.

Riemann, D., Berger, M., & Voderholzer, U. (2001). Sleep and depression—Results frompsychobiological studies: An overview. *Biological Psychology, 57,* 67–103.

Ritchey, M., Dolcos, F., Eddington, K. M., Strauman, T. J., & Cabeza, R. (2011). Neural correlates of emotional processing in depression: Changes with cognitive behavioral therapy and predictors of treatment response. *Journal of Psychiatric Research, 45*(5), 577–587.

Rizvi, S. J., Donovan, M., Giacobbe, P., Placenza, F., Rotzinger, S., & Kennedy, S. H. (2011). Neurostimulation therapies for treatment resistant depression: A focus on vagus nerve stimulation and deep brain stimulation. *International Review of Psychiatry, 23*(5), 424–436.

Robins, C. J., Block, P., Peselow, E. D., & Klein, R. (1986). Relationship of sociotropic and autonomous personality styles to specific symptoms in depressed patien*ts*. Paper presented at the annual meeting of the Eastern Psychology Association, New York, April.

Roffman, J. L., Marci, C. D., Glick, D. M., Dougherty, D. D., & Rauch, S. L. (2005). Neuroimaging and the functional neuroanatomy of psychotherapy. *Psychological Medicine, 35,* 1–14.

Rogers, C. R. (1951). *Client-centered therapy.* Boston, MA: Houghton-Mifflin.

Romano, V., Fitzpatrick, M., & Janzen, J. (2008). The secure-base hypothesis: Global attachment, attachment to counselor, and session exploration in psychotherapy. *Journal of Counseling Psychology, 55*(4), 495–504.

Rosen, G. M., & Davison, G. C. (2003). Psychology should list empirically supported principles of change (ESPs) and not credential trademarked therapies or other treatment packages. *Behavior Modification, 27*(3), 300–312.

Rosenstein, D. S., & Horowitz, H. A. (1996). Adolescent attachment and psychopathology. *Journal of Consulting and Clinical Psychology, 64,* 244–253.

Rosenthal, H. R. (1980). *The discovery of the subunconscious in a new approach to dream analysis.* South Miami, FL: Banyan Books.

Rosenwald, G. C. (1986). Why operationism doesn't go away: Extrascientific incentives of social-psychological research. *Philosophy of the Social Sciences, 16,* 303–330.

Rosenzweig, S. (1936). Some implicit common factors in diverse methods of psychotherapy. *American Journal of Orthopsychiatry, 6,* 412–415.

Rosnow, K., & Georgoudi, M. (1986). *Contextualism and understanding in behavioral science.* New York: Praeger.

Roth, A., & Fonagy, P. (1996). *What works for w whom?* New York: Guilford Press.

Roth, A., & Fonagy, P. (2005). *What works for w whom?* (2nd ed.). New York: Guilford Press.

Rothbart, M. K., & Bates, J. E. (1998). Temperament. In W. Damon & N. Eisenberg (Eds.), *Handbook of child psychology* (Vol. 3, pp. 105–176). New York: Wiley.

Rothbart, M. K., Ahadi, S. A., & Evans, D. E. (2000). Temperament and personality: Origins and outcomes. *Journal of Personality and Social Psychology, 78,* 122–135.

Rothbart, M. K., Ahadi, S. A., & Hershey, K. (1994). Temperament and social behavior in children. *Merrill-Palmer Quarterly, 40,* 21–39.

Roussos, A. J., Acosta, S., Juárez, C., & Mergenthaler, E. (2001). Introduction to the techniques for computer assisted investigation of therapeutic processes: Models for therapeutic cycles. *Interamerican Journal of Psychology, 35,* 53–77.

Rudolf, G., Grande, T., & Oberbracht, C. (2000). The Heidelberg restructuring scale. A model of changes in psychoanalytic therapies and its operationalization on an estimating scale. *Psychotherapeut, 45,* 237–246.

Russell, J. A., & Carroll, J. M. (1999). On the bipolarity of positive and negative affect. *Psychological Bulletin, 125,* 3–30.

Russell, J., Moskowitz, D. S., Zuroff, D., Sookman, D., & Paris, J. (2007). Stability and variability of affective experience and interpersonal behavior in borderline personality disorder. *Journal of Abnormal Psychology, 116,* 578–588.

Ryle, A. (1990). *Cognitive-analytic therapy: Active participation in change.* Chichester: John Wiley.

Ryle, A. (1997). *Cognitive analytic therapy and borderline personality disorder. The model and the method.* Chichester: Wiley.

Sabel, E. (2007). Efficacy and efficiency of therapeutic processes of a psychoanalytic group psychotherapy in a day care clinic with special regard to processes of mentalization] Unpublished doctoral dissertation, University of Bremen.

Safran, J. D., & Muran, J. C. (2000). *Negotiating the therapeutic alliance: A relational treatment guide.* New York: Guilford Press.

Safran, J. D., & Segal, Z. V. (1990). *Interpersonal process in cognitive therapy.* New York: Basic Books.

Sandell, R. (2007). *Die Menschen sind verschieden—Auch als Patienten und Therapeuten* [People are different—Also as patients and therapists]. In A. I. Springer, K. Muench, &

D. Munz (Eds.), *Psychoanalyse heute* [*Psychoanalysis today*] (pp. 461–481). Giessen: Psychosozial.

Sanislow, C. A., Grilo, C. M., & McGlashan, T. H. (2000). Factor analysis of the DSM-III-R borderline personality disorder criteria in psychiatric patients. *American Journal of Psychiatry, 159,* 1629–1633.

Sanislow, C. A., Pine, D. S., Quinn, K. J., Kozak, M. J., Garvey, M., Heinssen, R. K., et al. (2010). Developing constructs for psychopathology research: Research domain criteria. *Journal of Abnormal Psychology, 119,* 631–639.

Santayana, G. (1905/1998). *The life of reason: I—Reason in common sense.* Amherst, NY: Prometheus Books.

Sappington, A. A. (1990). Recent psychological approaches to the free will versus Determinism issue. *Psychological Bulletin, 108,* 19–29.

Sarason, B. R., Shearin, E. N., Pierce, G. R., & Sarason, I. G. (1987). Interrelations of social support measures: Theoretical and practical implications. *Journal of Personality and Social Psychology, 52,* 813–832.

Schaumburg, C. (1980). Personalpronomina im psychoanalytischen Prozess. PhD dissertation, Universität Ulm.

Scheel, K. R. (2000). The empirical basis of dialectical behaviour therapy: Summary, critique and implication. *Clinical Psychology: Science and Practice, 7,* 68–86.

Schielke, H. J., Stiles, W. B., Cuellar, R. E., Fishman, J. L., Hoener, C., Del Castillo, D., et al. (2011). A case investigating whether the process of resolving interpersonal problems in couple therapy is isomorphic to the process of resolving problems in individual therapy. *Pragmatic Case Studies in Psychotherapy, 7,* 477–528.

Schiepek, G. (2003). *Neurobiologie der Psychotherapie.* Stuttgart: Schattauer.

Schiffer, F., Teicher, M. H., & Papanicolaou, A. C. (1995). Evoked potential evidence for right brain activity during the recall of traumatic memories. *Journal of Neuropsychiatry and Clinical Neuroscience, 7,* 169–175.

Schlaepfer, T. E., Lisanby, S. H., & Pallanti, S. (2010). Separating hope from hype: Some ethical implications of the development of deep brain stimulation in psychiatric research and treatment. *CNS Spectrums, 15*(5), 285–287.

Schneider, K. J. (1999). Multiple-case depth research. *Journal of Clinical Psychology, 55,* 1531–1540.

Schön, D. A. (1983). *The reflective practitioner: How professionals think in action.* New York: Basic Books.

Schore, A. (2000). Attachment and the regulation of the right brain. *Attachment & Human Development, 2,* 23–47.

Schors, R., & Kächele, H. (1982). *Computer-aided content analysis in the study of body concepts.* Noorwijkerhout, Holland: European Congress of Psychosomatic Research.

Schut, A. J., Castonguay, L. G., Bedics, J. D., Smith, T. L., Barber, J. P., Flanagan, K. M., & Yamasaki, A. S. (2005). Therapist interpretation, patient-therapist interpersonal process, and outcome in psychodynamic psychotherapy for avoidant personality disorder. *Psychotherapy: Theory, Research, Practice, and Training, 42,* 494–511.

Schwartz, J. M. (1998). Neuroanatomical aspects of cognitive-behavioural therapy response in obsessive-compulsive disorder. *British Journal of Psychiatry, 173*(Suppl. 35), 38–44.

Schwartz, J. M., Stoessel, P. W., Baxter, L. J., Martin, K. M., & Phelps, M. E. (1996). Systematic changes in cerebral glucose metabolic rate after successful behavior modification treatment of obsessive-compulsive disorder. *Archives of General Psychiatry, 53,* 109–113.

Seligman, M. E. P. (1989). Research in clinical psychology: Why is there so much depression today? In I. S. Cohen (Ed.), *The G. Stanley Hall Lecture Series* (pp. 79–96). Washington, DC: American Psychological Association Press.

Semerari, A., Carcione, A., Dimaggio, G., Nicolò, G., & Procacci, M. (2007). Understanding minds: Different functions and different disorders? The contribution of psychotherapy research. *Psychotherapy Research, 17,* 106–119.

Shapiro, A. K., & Morris, L. A. (1978). The placebo effect in medical and psychological therapies. In S. L. Garfield & A. E. Bergin (Eds.), *Handbook of psychotherapy and behavior change: An empirical analysis* (2nd ed., pp. 369–410). New York: Wiley.

Shapiro, D. A. (1995). Finding out how psycho-therapies help people change. *Psychotherapy Research, 5,* 1–21.

Shapiro, D. A., & Startup, M. J. (1992). Measuring therapist adherence in exploratory psychotherapy. *Psychotherapy Research, 2,* 193–203.

Shapiro, D. A., Barkham, M., Rees, A., Hardy, G. E., Reynolds, S., & Startup, M. (1994a). Effects of treatment duration and severity of depression on the effectiveness of cognitive-behavioral and psychodynamic-interpersonal psychotherapy. *Journal of Consulting and Clinical Psychology, 62,* 522–534.

Shapiro, D. A., Barkham, M., Rees, A., Hardy, G. E., Reynolds, S., & Startup, M. (1994b). Looking as strongly as we should in the right places in psychotherapy research. *Journal of Consulting and Clinical Psychology, 62,* 539–542.

Shapiro, D. A., Barkham, M., Rees, A., Hardy, G. E., Reynolds, S., & Startup, M. (1995). Decisions, decisions, decisions: Determining the effects of treatment method and duration on the outcome of psychotherapy for depression. In M. Aveline & D. A. Shapiro (Eds.), *Research foundations for psychotherapy practice* (pp. 151–174). Chichester: John Wiley.

Shapiro, D. A., Barkham, M., Reynolds, S., Hardy, G., & Stiles, W. B. (1992). Prescriptive and Exploratory psychotherapies: Toward an integration based on the assimilation model. *Journal of Psychotherapy Integration, 2,* 253–272.

Shapiro, D. A., & Firth, J. A. (1987). Prescriptive vs. exploratory psychotherapy: Outcomes of the Sheffield Psychotherapy Project. *British Journal of Psychiatry, 252,* 790–799.

Shapiro, D. A., Harper, H., Startup, M., Reynolds, S., Bird, D. & Suokas, A. (1994). The high-water mark of the drug metaphor: A meta-analytic critique of process-outcome research. In R. L. Russell (Ed.), *Reassessing psychotherapy research* (pp. 1–35). New York: Guilford Press.

Shapiro, F. (1995). *Eye movement desensitization and reprocessing: Basic principles, protocols, and procedures.* New York: Guilford Press.

Sharpless, B. A., & Barber, J. P. (2009). A conceptual and empirical review of the meaning, measurement, development, and teaching of intervention competence. *Clinical Psychology Review, 29,* 47–56.

Shaw, B. F., Elkin, I., Yamaguchi, J., Olmsted, M., Vallis, T. M., Dobson, K. S., et al. (1999). Therapist competence ratings in relation to clinical outcome in cognitive therapy of depression. *Journal of Consulting and Clinical Psychology, 67,* 837–846.

Shea, M. T., Elkin, I., Imber, S. D., Sotsky, S. M., Watkins, J. T., Collins, J. F., et al. (1992). Course of depressive symptoms over follow-up: Findings from the National Institute of Mental Health Treatment of Depression Collaborative Research Program. *Archives of General Psychiatry, 49,* 782–787.

Shedler, J., & Westen, D. (2010). The Shedler-Westen assessment procedure: Making personality diagnosis clinically meaningful. In J. F. Clarkin, P. Fonagy, & G. O. Gabbard

(Eds.), *Psychodynamic psychotherapy for personality disorders: A clinical handbook* (pp. 125–164). Washington, DC: American Psychiatric Publishing.

Shimokawa, K., Lambert, M. J., & Smart, D. W. (2010). Enhancing treatment outcome of patients at risk of treatment failure: Meta-analytic and mega-analytic review of a psychotherapy quality assurance system. *Journal of Consulting & Clinical Psychology, 78,* 298–311.

Shriver, L. (2005). *We need to talk about Kevin.* London: Serpent's Tail.

Sidman, M. (1960). *Tactics of scientific research.* New York: Basic.

Siegle, G. J., Carter, C. S., & Thase, M. E. (2006). Use of fMRI to predict recovery from unipolar depression with Cognitive Behavior Therapy. *American Journal of Psychiatry, 163,* 735–738.

Siegle, G. J., Ghinassi, F., & Thase, M. E. (2007). Neurobehavioral therapies in the 21st century: Summary of an emerging field and an extended example of Cognitive Control Training for depression. *Cognitive Therapy and Research, 31,* 235–262.

Siever, L. J., & Davis, K. L. (1991). A psychobiological perspective on the personality disorders. *American Journal of Psychiatry, 148,* 1647–1658.

Silberschatz, G., Curtis, J. T., & Fretter, P. B. (1985). Testing hypotheses of psychotherapeutic change processes. In H. Dahl, H. Kaechele, & H. Thomae (Eds.), *Psychoanalytic process research strategies.* Berlin: Springer-Verlag.

Silberschatz, G., Curtis, J. T., & Nathan, S. (1989). Using the patient's plan to assess progress in psychotherapy. *Psychotherapy, 26,* 40–46.

Silberschatz. G., Fretter. P., & Curtis, J. (1986). How do interpretations influence the process of psychotherapy? *Journal of Consulting and Clinical Psychology, 54,* 646–652.

Silbersweig, D., Clarkin, J., Goldstein, M., Kernberg, O., Tuescher, O., Levy, K., et al. (2007). Failure of fronto-limbic inhibitory function in the context of negative emotion in borderline personality disorder. *American Journal of Psychiatry, 164,* 1832–1841.

Silverman, J. M., Pinkham, L., Horvath, T. P., Coccaro, E. F., Klar, H., Schear, S., et al. (1991). Affective and impulsive personality disorder traits in the relatives of patients with borderline personality disorder. *American Journal of Psychiatry, 148,* 1378–1385.

Simon, J., Fink, G., Endicott, N. A., & Gill, M. (1968). Psychoanalytic research and the concept of analytic work. Draft of a paper, Department of Psychiatry, Brookdale Hospital Center, Brooklyn, New York, December.

Simon, W., Lambert, M. J., Busath, G., Vazquez, A., Berkeljon, A., Hyer, K., et al. (2013). Effects of providing patient progress feedback and clinical support tools to psychotherapists in an inpatient eating disorders treatment program: A randomized controlled study. *Psychotherapy Research, 23*(3), 287–300.

Simon, W., Lambert, M. J., Harris, M. W., Busath, G., & Vazquez, A. (2012). Providing patient progress information and clinical support tools to therapists: Effects on patients at risk for treatment failure. *Psychotherapy Research, 22,* 638– 647.

Simons, A. D., Garfield, S. L., & Murphy, G. E. (1984). The process of change in cognitive therapy and pharmacotherapy for depression: Changes in mood and cognition. *Archives of General Psychiatry, 41*(1), 45–51.

Singer, J, L., & Salovey. P. (1991). Organized knowledge structures and personality. In M. J. Horowitz (Ed.), *Person schemas and maladaptive interpersonal patterns* (pp. 33–80). Chicago: University of Chicago Press.

Skinner, B. F. (1950). Are theories of learning necessary? *Psychological Review, 57,* 193–216.

Skinner, H. A. (1981). Toward the integration of classification theory and methods. Perspectives from psychology. *Journal of Abnormal Psychology, 90,* 68–87.

Slade, K., Lambert, M. J., Harmon, S. C., Smart, D. W., & Bailey, R. (2008). Improving psychotherapy outcome: The use of immediate electronic feedback and revised clinical support tools. *Clinical Psychology & Psychotherapy, 15,* 287–303.

Smith, M. L., & Glass, G. V. (1977). Meta-analysis of psychotherapy outcome studies. *American Psychologist, 32*(9), 752–760.

Smith, M. L., Glass, G. V., & Miller, T. I. (1980). *The benefits of psychotherapy.* Baltimore, MD: Johns Hopkins University Press.

Smolensky, P. (1986). Information processing in dynamical systems: Foundations of harmony theory. In D. E. Rumelhart, J. L. McClelland, & PDP Research Group (Eds.), *Parallel distributed processing: Explorations in the microstructure of cognition* (pp. 194–281). Cambridge, MA: MIT Press.

Snell, M. N., Mallinckrodt, B., Hill, R. D., & Lambert, M. J. (2001). Predicting counseling center clients' response to counseling: A 1-year follow-up. *Journal of Counseling Psychology, 48,* 463–473.

Soloff, P. H., Meltzer, C. C., Greer, P. J., Constantine, D., & Kelly, T. M. (2000). Afenfluramin eactivated FDG-PET study of borderline personality disorder. *BiologicalPsychiatry, 47,* 540–547.

Sommerfeld, E., Orbach, I., Zim, S., & Mikulincer, M. (2008). An in-session exploration of ruptures in working alliance and their associations with clients core conflictual relationship themes, alliance-related discourse, and clients' postsession evaluations. *Psychotherapy Research, 18*(4), 377–388.

Sonntag, A., Glaesmer, H., Barnow, S., Brähler, E., et al. (2009). Psychotherapy training from the trainees' perspective. *Psychotherapeut, 54,* 427–434.

Spence, D. (1969). Computer measurement of process and content in psychoanalysis. *Transactions of the New York Academy of Science, 31,* 828–841.

Spence, D. (1968). The processing of meaning in psychotherapy: Some links with psycholinguistics and information theory. *Behavioral Sciences, 13,* 349–361.

Spence, D., & Lugo, M. (1972). The role of verbal clues in clinical listening. *Psychoanalysis & Contemporary Society, 1,* 109–131.

Spering, M., Wagener, D., & Funke, J. (2005). The role of emotions in complex problem-solving. *Cognition and Emotion, 19,* 1252–1261.

Spielmans, G. I., Masters, K. S., & Lambert, M. J. (2006). A comparison of rational versus empirical methods in prediction of negative psychotherapy outcome. *Clinical Psychology and Psychotherapy, 13,* 202–214.

Staats, A. W. (1983). *Psychology's crisis of disunity: Philosophy and method for a unified science.* New York: Praeger.

Staats, A. W. (1991). Unified positivism and unification in psychology: Fad or new field? *American Psychologist, 46,* 899–912.

Stalker, C. A., & Davies, F. (1995). Attachment organization and adaptation in sexually-abused women. *Canadian Journal of Psychiatry, 40,* 234–240.

Startup, M. J., & Shapiro, D. A. (1993a). Dimensions of cognitive therapy for depression: A confirmatory factor analysis. *Cognitive Therapy and Research, 17,* 139–151.

Startup, M. J., & Shapiro, D. A. (1993b). Therapist treatment fidelity in prescriptive vs. exploratory psychotherapy. *British Journal of Clinical Psychology, 32,* 443–456.

Steinbeck, J. (1958). *Of mice and men.* New York: Bantam.

Steinberg, S., & Weiss, J. (1954). The art of Edvard Munch and its function in his mental life. *Psychoanalytic Quarterly, 23,* 409–423.

Stephen, S., Elliott, R., & Macleod, R. (2011). Person-centred therapy with a client experiencing social anxiety difficulties: a hermeneutic single case efficacy design. *Counselling and Psychotherapy Research, 11,* 55–66.

Sterling, B. (2003). *Tomorrow now: Envisioning the next 50 years.* New York: Random House.

Stigler, M., de Roten, Y., Drapeau, M., & Despland, J. N. (2007). Process research in psychodynamic psychotherapy: A combined measure for accuracy and conflictuality of interpretations. *Schweizer Archiv für Neurologie und Psychiatrie, 158*(5), 225–232.

Stiglmayr, C., Shapiro, D. A., Stieglitz, R. D., Limberger, M., & Bohus, M. (2001). Experience of aversive tension and dissociation in female patients with borderline personality disorder: A controlled study. *Journal of Psychiatric Research, 35,* 111–118.

Stiles, W. B. (1979). Verbal response modes and psychotherapeutic technique. *Psychiatry, 42,* 49–62.

Stiles, W. B. (1988). Psychotherapy process-outcome correlations may be misleading. *Psychotherapy, 25,* 27–35.

Stiles, W. B. (1992a). *Describing talk: A taxonomy of verbal response modes.* Newbury Park, CA: Sage.

Stiles, W. B. (1992b). The assimilation model's approach to the metamorphosis problem. In W. B. Stiles (moderator), The metamorphosis problem Assessing qualitative change in psychotherapy. Panel presented at the Society for Psychotherapy Research meeting, Berkeley, California, June.

Stiles, W. B. (1993). Quality control in qualitative research. *Clinical Psychology Review, 13,* 593–618.

Stiles, W. B. (1997a). Multiple voices in psychotherapy clients. *Journal of Psychotherapy Integration.*

Stiles, W. B. (1997b). Signs and voices: Joining a conversation in progress. *British Journal of Medical Psychology, 70,* 169–176.

Stiles, W. B. (1999a). Signs and voices in psychotherapy. *Psychotherapy Research, 9,* 1–21.

Stiles, W. B. (1999b). *Signs, voices, meaning bridges, and shared experience: How talking helps.* Visiting Scholar Series No. 10 (ISSN 1173–9940). Palmerston North, NZ: School of Psychology, Massey University.

Stiles, W. B. (2003). Qualitative research: Evaluating the process and the product. In S. P. Llewelyn & P. Kennedy (Eds.), *Handbook of Clinical Health Psychology* (pp. 477–499). London: Wiley.

Stiles, W. B. (2005). Case studies. In J. C. Norcross, L. E. Beutler, & R. F. Levant (Eds.), *Evidence-based practices in mental health: Debate and dialogue on the fundamental questions* (pp. 57–64). Washington, DC: American Psychological Association.

Stiles, W. B. (2006). Numbers can be enriching. *New Ideas in Psychology, 24,* 252–262.

Stiles, W. B. (2007). Theory-building case studies of counselling and psychotherapy. *Counselling and Psychotherapy Research, 7,* 122–127.

Stiles, W. B. (2009a). Logical operations in theory-building case studies. *Pragmatic Case Studies in Psychotherapy, 5*(3), 9–22. Available at: http://jrul.libraries.rutgers.edu/index.php/pcsp/article/view/973/2384

Stiles, W. B. (2009b). Responsiveness as an obstacle for psychotherapy outcome research: It's worse than you think. *Clinical Psychology: Science and Practice, 16,* 86–91.

Stiles, W. B. (2010). Theory-building case studies as practice-based evidence. In M. Barkham, G. Hardy, & J. Mellor-Clark (Eds.), *Developing and delivering practice-based evidence: A guide for the psychological therapies* (pp. 91–108). Chichester, UK: Wiley-Blackwell.

Stiles, W. B. (2011). Coming to terms. *Psychotherapy Research, 21,* 367–384.

Stiles, W. B., Barkham, M., Connell, J., & Mellor-Clark, J. (2008). Responsive regulation of treatment duration in routine practice in United Kingdom primary care settings: Replication in a larger sample. *Journal of Consulting and Clinical Psychology, 76,* 298–305.

Stiles, W. B., Barkham, M., Mellor-Clark, J., & Connell, J. (2008). Effectiveness of cognitive-behavioural, person-centred, and psychodynamic therapies in UK primary care routine practice: Replication in a larger sample. *Psychological Medicine, 38*(5), 677–688.

Stiles, W. B., Barkham, M., & Shapiro, D. A. (1993). Lack of synchronised seasonal variation in intensity of psychological problems. *Journal of Abnormal Psychology, 102,* 388–394.

Stiles, W. B., Barkham, M., Shapiro, D. A., & Firth-Cozens, J. (1992). Treatment order and thematic continuity between contrasting psychotherapies: Exploring an implication of the assimilation model. *Psychotherapy Research, 2,* 112–124.

Stiles, W. B., Barkham, M., Twigg, E., Mellor-Clark, J., & Cooper, M. (2006). Effectiveness of cognitive-behavioural, person-centred, and psychodynamic therapies as practiced in UK National Health Service settings. *Psychological Medicine, 36,* 555–566.

Stiles, W. B., Elliott, R., Llewelyn, S. P., Firth-Cozens, J. A., Margison, F. R., Shapiro, D. A., & Hardy, G. (1990). Assimilation of problematic experiences by clients in psychotherapy. *Psychotherapy, 27,* 411–420.

Stiles, W. B., & Goldsmith, J. Z. (2010). The alliance over time. In J. Muran, J. P. Barber, J. Muran, & J. P. Barber (Eds.), *The therapeutic alliance: An evidence-based guide to practice* (pp. 44–62). New York: Guilford Press.

Stiles, W. B., Honos-Webb, L., & Surko, M. (1998). Responsiveness in psychotherapy. *Clinical Psychology: Science and Practice, 5,* 439–458.

Stiles, W. B., Meshot, C. M., Anderson, T. M., & Sloan, W. W., Jr. (1992). Assimilation of problematic experiences: The case of John Jones. *Psychotherapy Research, 2,* 81–101.

Stiles, W. B., Morrison, L. A., Haw, S. K., Harper, H., Shapiro, D. A., & Firth-Cozens, J. (1991). Longitudinal study of assimilation in exploratory psychotherapy. *Psychotherapy, 28,* 195–206.

Stiles, W. B., Reynolds, S., Hardy, G. E., Rees, A., Barkham, M., & Shapiro, D. A. (1994). Evaluation and description of psychotherapy sessions by clients using the Session Evaluation Questionnaire and the Session Impacts Scale. *Journal of Counseling Psychology, 41,* 175–185.

Stiles, W. B., Shankland, M. C., Wright, J., & Field, S. D. (1997a). Aptitude-treatment interactions based on clients' assimilation of their presenting problems. *Journal of Consulting and Clinical Psychology, 65,* 889–893.

Stiles, W. B., Shankland, M. C., Wright, J., & Field, S. D. (1997b). Dimensions of clients' initial presentation of problems in psychotherapy: The Early Assimilation Research Scale. *Psychotherapy Research, 7,* 155–171.

Stiles, W. B., & Shapiro, D. A. (1989). Abuse of the drug metaphor in psychotherapy process-outcome research. *Clinical Psychology Review, 9,* 521–543.

Stiles, W. B., & Shapiro, D. A. (1994). Disabuse of the drug metaphor: Psychotherapy process-outcome correlations. *Journal of Consulting and Clinical Psychology, 62,* 942–948.

Stiles, W. B., & Shapiro, D. A. (1995). Verbal exchange structure of brief psychodynamic-interpersonal and cognitive-behavioral psychotherapy. *Journal of Consulting and Clinical Psychology, 63,* 15–27.

Stiles, W. B., Shapiro, D. A., & Barkham, M. (1993). Research directions for psychotherapy integration. In J. Norcross (Ed.), Research directions for psychotherapy integration: A roundtable. *Journal of Psychotherapy Integration, 3,* 91–131.

Stiles, W. B., Shapiro, D. A., & Elliott, R. (1986). Are all psychotherapies equivalent? *American Psychologist, 41,* 165–180.

Stiles, W. B., Shapiro, D. A., & Firth-Cozens, J. A. (1988). Verbal response mode use in contrasting psychotherapies: A within-subjects comparison. *Journal of Consulting and Clinical Psychology, 56,* 727–733.

Stiles, W. B., Shapiro, D. A., & Harper, H. (1994). Finding the way from process to outcome: Blind alleys and unmarked trails. In R. L. Russell (Ed.), *Reassessing psychotherapy research* (pp. 36–64). New York: Guilford Press.

Stiles, W. B., Shapiro, D. A., Harper, H., & Morrison, L. A. (1995). Therapist contributions to psychotherapeutic assimilation: An alternative to the drug metaphor. *British Journal of Medical Psychology, 68,* 1–13.

Stiles, W. B., & Sultan, F. E. (1979). Verbal response mode use by clients in psychotherapy. *Journal of Consulting and Clinical Psychology, 47,* 611–613.

Stiles, W. B., & Wolfe, B. E. (2006). Relationship factors in treating anxiety disorders. In L. G. Castonguay & L. E. Beutler (Eds.), *Principles of therapeutic change that work* (pp. 155–165). New York: Oxford University Press.

Stinson, C. H., & Palmer, S. E. (1991). Parallel distributed processing models of person schemas and psychopathologies. In M. J. Horowitz (Ed.), *Person schemas and maladaptive interpersonal patterns* (pp. 334–378). Chicago: University of Chicago Press.

Stirman, S., DeRubeis, R. J., Crits-Christoph, P., & Brody, P. (2003). Are samples in randomized controlled trials of psychotherapy representative of community outpatients? A new methodology and initial findings. *Journal of Consulting and Clinical Psychology, 71,* 963–972.

Stoffers, J., Völlm, B. A, Rücker, G., Timmer, A., Huband, N., & Lieb, K. (2010). Pharmacological interventions for borderline personality disorder. *Cochrane Database Systematic Reviews*, CD005653.

Stone, A. R. (1978). The inter-disciplinary research team: A case study. In J. D. Frank, R. Hoehn-Saric, S. D. Imber, B. L. Liberman, & A. R. Stone (Eds.), *Effective ingredients of successful psychotherapy*. New York: Brunner-Mazel.

Stone, G. L., & McMichael, J. (1996). Thinking about mental health policy in university and college counseling centers. *Journal of College Student Psychotherapy, 10,* 3–27.

Strauman, T. J., & Wilson, W. A. (2010). Individual differences in approach and avoidance behavioral activation/inhibition and regulatory focus as distinct levels of analysis. In R. H. Hoyle (Ed.), *Handbook of personality and self-regulation* (pp. 447–473). New York: Wiley-Blackwell.

Strauss, B. (2007). Attachment, empathy and intersubjectivity. In S. Herpertz, H. Mundt, & F. Caspar (Eds.), *Disorder oriented psychotherapy*. München: Elsevier.

Strauss, B. (2008) (Ed.) *Attachment and psychop*athology. Stuttgart: Klett-Cotta.

Strauss, B. (2009). Patterns of psychotherapeutic practice and professionalisation in Germany. *European Journal of Psychotherapy and Counselling, 11,* 141–150.

Strauss, B., Barnow, S., Brähler, E., Fegert, J., Fliegel, S., Freyberger, H. J., et al. (2009). Research expertise related to the training of psychological psychotherapists and child- and adolescent psychotherapists. Available at: www.med.uni-jena.de/mpsy/forschungsgutachten/Endfassung_Forschungsgutachten_Psychotherapieausbildung.pdf

Strauss, B., Burlingame, G. M., Bormann, B. (2008). Using the CORE Battery-R in Group Psychotherapy. *Journal of Clinical Psychology, 64,* 1225–1237.

Strauss, B., Kirchmann, H., Eckert, J., et al. (2006). Attachment characteristics and treatment outcome following inpatient psychotherapy: Results of a multisite study. *Psychotherapy Research, 16,* 579–594.

Strauss, B., Spangenberg, L., Brähler, E., & Bormann, B. (2014). Attitudes towards (psychotherapy) groups: Results of a survey in a representative sample. *International Journal of Group Psychotherapy.* doi: 10.1521/ijgp_2014_64_001.

Strauss, B., & Kohl, St. (2009). Development of psychotherapy and psychotherapy training in European countries—Results of an expert survey. *Psychotherapeut, 54,* 457–462.

Strauss, B., Lobo-Drost, A., & Pilkonis, P. A. (1999). Rating of attachment styles among adults. *Zeitschrift für Klinische Pychologie, Psychiatrie und Psychotherapie, 47,* 347–364.

Strauss, B., Mestel, R., & Kirchmann, H. (2011). Changes of attachment status among women with personality disorders undergoing inpatient treatment. *Counselling and Psychotherapy Research, 11,* 275–283.

Strauss, B., & Schwark, B. (2007). Attachment theory and its relevance for psychotherapy—Ten years later. *Psychotherapeut, 52,* 405–425.

Strian, F., Klicpera, C., & Caspar, F. (1977). Autonomic activation and endogenous depression. *Archiv für Psychiatrie und Nervenkrankheiten, 23,* 203–218.

Stroop, J. R. (1935). Studies of interference in serial verbal reactions. *Journal of Experimental Psychology, 18,* 643–662.

Strunk, D. R., Brotman, M. A., & DeRubeis, R. J. (2008). The process of change in cognitive therapy for depression: Predictors ofearly inter-session symptom gains and continued response to treatment. Unpublished manuscript, Department of Psychology, Ohio State University.

Strupp, H. H. (1955). An objective comparison of Rogerian and psychoanalytic techniques. *Journal of Consulting Psychology, 19,* 1–7.

Strupp, H. H. (1957). A multidimensional comparison of therapists in analytic and client-centered therapy. *Journal* of *Consulting Psychology, 21,* 301–308.

Strupp, H. H. (1993). The Vanderbilt psychotherapy studies: Synopsis. *Journal of Consulting and Clinical Psychology, 61,* 431–433.

Strupp, H. H., & Binder, J. L. (1984). *Psychotherapy in a new key.* New York: Basic Books.

Strupp, H. H., Hadley, S. W., & Gomes-Schwartz, B. (1977). *Psychotherapy for better of worse: An analysis of the problem of negative effects.* New York: Jason Aronson.

Strupp, H. H., Horowitz, L. M., & Lambert, M. J. (Eds.) (1997). *Measuring patient changes in mood, anxiety and personality disorders: Toward a core battery.* Washington, DC: American Psychiatric Association.

Stuckler, D., & Basu, S. (2013). *The body economic: Why austerity kills.* London: Allen Lane.

Sullivan, H. S. (1953). *The interpersonal theory of psychiatry.* New York: Norton.

Svartberg, M., & Stiles, T. C. (1994). Therapeutic alliance, therapist competence, and client change in short-term anxiety-provoking psychotherapy. *Psychotherapy Research, 4,* 20–33.

Talley, P. F., Strupp, H. H., & Butler, S. F. (Eds.) (1994). *Research findings and clinical practice: Bridging the gap.* New York: Basic Books.

Tang, T. Z., & DeRubeis, R. J. (1999). Sudden gains and critical sessions in cognitive-behavioral psychotherapy for depression. *Journal of Consulting and Clinical Psychology, 67,* 894–904.

Taub, E., Crago, J. E., & Uswatte, G. (1998). Constraint-induced movement therapy: A new approach to treatment in physical rehabilitation. *Rehabilitation Psychology, 43,* 152–170.

Tavare, A. (2012). Scientific misconduct is worryingly prevalent in the UK, shows BMJ survey [News]. *British Journal of Medicine, 344*, e377. doi: 10.1136/bmj.e377

Teasdale, J. D., Howard, R. J., Cox, S. G., Ha, Y., Brammer, M. J., Williams, S. C. R., et al. (1999). Functional MRI study of the cognitive generation of affect. *American Journal of Psychiatry, 156*(2), 209–215.

Tellegen, A. (1982). Brief manual of the multidimensional personality questionnaire. Unpublished manuscript.

Tellides, C., Fitzpatrick, M., Drapeau, M., Bracewell, R., Janzen, J., & Jaouich, A. (2008). The manifestation of transference during early psychotherapy sessions. *Counselling & Psychotherapy Research, 8*(2), 85–92.

Teusch, L., Böhme, H., Finke, J., Gastpar, M., & Skerra, B. (2003). Antidepressant medication and the assimilation of problematic experiences in psychotherapy. *Psychotherapy Research, 13,* 307–322.

Thase, M. E., Buysse, D. J., Frank, E., Cherry, C. R., Cornes, C. L., Mallinger, A. G., et al. (1997). Which depressed patients will respond to interpersonal psychotherapy? The role of abnormal EEG sleep profiles. *American Journal of Psychiatry, 154,* 502–509.

Thomä, H., & Kächele, H. (1994). *Psychoanalytic Practice.* Vol. 1, *Principles.* New York: Jason Aronson.

Thompson, J. R. (1987). *The process of psychotherapy: An interpretation of clinical experience and empirical research.* Lanham, MD: University Press of America.

Tikkanen, S., Stiles, W. B., & Leiman, M. (2011). Parent development in clinical child neurological assessment process: Encounters with the assimilation model. *Psychotherapy Research, 21,* 593–607.

Tikkanen, S., Stiles, W. B., & Leiman, M. (2013). Achieving an empathic stance: Dialogical sequence analysis of a change episode. *Psychotherapy Research, 23,* 178–189.

Tonti, M. (2006). A computational approach to the psychotherapeutic process. Unpublished master's thesis, University of Bologna.

Toranzo, E., Taborda, A., Ross, T., Mergenthaler, E., & Fontao, M. I. (2008). Foco, interacción grupal y patrones verbales en grupos de padres: Primeros resultados de un estudio piloto. *Revista Argentina de Clínica Psicológica, 17,* 49–55.

Torgersen, S., Lygren, S., Oien, P. A., Skre, I., Onstad, S., Evardsen, J., et al. (2000). A twin study of personality disorders. *Comprehensive Psychiatry, 41,* 416–425.

Toulmin, S. (1961). *Foresight and understanding.* Watford, IN: Indiana University Press.

Tukey, J. W. (1977). *Exploratory data analysis.* Reading, MA: Addison Wesley.

Turan, B., & Horowitz, L. M. (2007). Can I count on you to be there for me? Individual differences in a knowledge structure. *Journal of Personality and Social Psychology, 93,* 447–465.

Turner, E. H., Matthews, A. M., Linardatos, E., Tell, R. A., & Rosenthal, R. (2008). Selective publication of antidepressant trials and its influence on apparent efficacy. *New England Journal of Medicine, 358*(3), 252–260.

Turner, R. A., Altemus, M., Enos, T., Cooper, B., & McGuinness, T. (1999). Preliminary research on plasma oxytocin in normal women: Investigating emotion and interpersonal distress. *Psychiatry, 62,* 97–113.

Varvin, S. (2003). *Mental survival strategies after extreme traumatisation.* Copenhagen, Denmark: Multivers APS Publishers.

Varvin, S., & Stiles, W. B. (1999). Emergence of severe traumatic experiences: An assimilation analysis of psychoanalytic therapy with a political refugee. *Psychotherapy Research, 9,* 381–404.

Velten, E. (1968). A laboratory task for induction of mood states. *Behaviour Reearch and Therapy, 6,* 473–482.

Vermeersch, D. A., Lambert, M. J., & Burlingame, G. M. (2002). Outcome Questionnaire: Item sensitivity to change. *Journal of Personality Assessment, 74,* 242–261.

Vermeersch, D. A., Whipple, J. L., Lambert, M. J., Hawkins, E. J., Burchfield, C. M., & Okiishi, J. C. (2004). Outcome Questionnaire: Is it sensitive to changes in counseling center clients? *Journal of Counseling Psychology, 51,* 38–49.

Volkow, N. D. (2003). Imaging the addicted brain: Predisposition or environment. In National Institutes of Health symposium, Stress and the brain: Developmental, neurobiological, and clinical implications. Bethesda, MD, March. Available at: http://videocast.nih.gov/launch.asp?9928

Volkow, N. D., Hitzemann, R., Wang, G.-J., Fowler, J. S., Wolf, A. P., & Dewey, S. L. (1992). Long-term frontal brain metabolic changes in cocaine abusers. *Synapse, 11*(3), 184–190.

Vygotsky, L. (1978). *Mind in society: The development of higher psychological processes* (ed. M. Cole, V. John-Steiner, S. Scribner, & E. Souberman). Cambridge, MA: Harvard University Press.

Wagner, J., & Elliott, R. (2001). The Simplified Personal Questionnaire. Unpublished manuscript, Department of Psychology, University of Toledo.

Wagner, T. D., Phan, K. L., Liberzon, I., & Taylor, S. F. (2003). Valence, gender, and lateralization of functional brain anatomy in emotion: A meta-analysis of findings from neuroimaging. *NeuroImage, 19,* 513–531.

Wallerstein, R. S. (1986). *Forty-two lives in treatment: A study of psychoanalysis and psychotherapy.* New York: Guilford Press.

Wallerstein, R. S. (1989). The Psychotherapy Research Project of the Menninger Foundation: An overview. *Journal of Consulting and Clinical Psychology, 57,* 195–205.

Walter, S. (2008). *Therapeutische Gesprächsführung und Emotions-Abstraktionsmuster des Patienten.* Ulm: Ulmer Textbank.

Walter, S., Gelo, O. C. G., Carrozzi, S., & Mergenthaler, E. (2009). Attivazione emotiva e insight terapeutico: Risultati preliminari di uno studio empirico. *Psichiatriea e Psicoterapia, 28,* 239–259.

Walter, S., Schiepek, G. K., Schneider, S., Strunk, G., Kaimer, P., & Mergenthaler, E. (2010). The synchronization of plan activations and emotion-abstraction patterns in the psychotherapeutic process: A single-case study. *Psychotherapy Research, 20,* 214–223.

Waltz, J., Addis, M. E., Koerner, K, & Jacobson, N. S. (1993). Testing the integrity of a psychotherapy protocol. Assessment of adherence and competence. *Journal of Consulting and Clinical Psychology, 61,* 620–630.

Wampold, B. E. (2001). *The great psychotherapy debate: Models, methods, and findings.* Mahwah, NJ: Erlbaum.

Wampold, B. E., Mondin, G. W., Moody, M., Stich, F., Benson, K., & Ahn, H. N. (1997). A metaanalysis of outcome studies comparing bona fide psychotherapies: Empirically, "all must have prizes." *Psychological Bulletin, 122,* 203–215.

Wang, X. (2003). Persistent neural activity: Experiments and theory. *Cerebral Cortex, 13,* 1123.

Waskow, I. E., & Parloff, M. B. (1975). *Psychotherapy change measures.* Rockville, MD: National Institute of Mental Health, No. 74–120.

Wassermann, E. M., & Zimmermann, T. (2012). Transcranial magnetic brain stimulation: Therapeutic promises and scientific gaps. *Pharmacology Therapeutics, 133*(1), 98–107.

Watkins, R., Cheston, R., Jones, K., & Gilliard, J. (2006). "Coming out" with Alzheimer's disease: Changes in awareness during a psychotherapy group for people with dementia. *Aging & Mental Health, 10,* 166–176.

Watson, D. L. (1938). *Scientists are human.* London: Watts and Co.

Watson, J. (1968). *The double helix.* New York: Mentor Books.

Weiss, J., & Sampson, H. (1986). *The psychoanalytic process. Theory, clinical observation and empirical research.* New York: Guilford Press.

Weiss, L. (1986). *Dream analysis in psychotherapy.* New York: Pergamon.

Weissman, A. (1979). The Dysfunctional Attitude Scale: A validation study (University Microfilm No. 79–19, 533). Dissertation Abstracts International, 40.

Westen, D. (1993). The impact of sexual abuse on self structure. In *Rochester Symposium on Developmental Psychopathology: Disorders and dysfunctions of the self* (Vol. 5, pp. 223–250). Rochester, NY: University of Rochester Press.

Westen, D. (2000). The efficacy of dialectical behavior therapy for borderline personality disorder. *Clinical Psychology: Science and Practice, 7,* 92–94.

Westen, D. (2006). Commentary on Trull: Drizzling on the 5+- 3 factor parade. In T. A. Widiger, E. Simonsen, P. J. Sirovatka, & D. A. Regier (Eds.), *Dimensional models of personality disorders: Refining the research agenda for DSM-V* (pp. 189–194). Washington, DC: American Psychiatric Association.

Wheeler, S., Aveline, M., & Barkham, M. (2011). Practice-based supervision research: A network of researchers using a comon toolkit. *Counselling and Psychotherapy Research, 11*(2), 88–96.

Whipple, J. L., Lambert, M. J., Vermeersch, D. A., Smart, D. W., Nielsen, S. L., & Hawkins, E. J. (2003). Improving the effects of psychotherapy: The use of early identification of treatment failure and problem solving strategies in routine practice. *Journal of Counseling Psychology, 58,* 59–68.

Widiger, T. A., & Clark, L. A. (2000). Toward DSM-V and the classification of psychopathology. *Psychological Bulletin, 126*(9), 946–963.

Wilkinson, R. G., & Pickett, K. (2010). *The spirit level: Why equality is better for everyone.* London: Penguin.

Williams, J. B. W., Gibbon, M., First, M. B., Spitzer, R. L., Davis, M., Borus, J., et al. (1992). Structured Clinical Interview for DSM-III-R (SCID): II. Multi-site test-retest reliability. *Archives of General Psychiatry, 49*(8), 630–636.

Williams, J. M. G. (1992). *The psychological treatment of depression: A guide to the theory and practice of cognitive behaviour therapy.* London & New York: Routledge.

Wing, J. K., Cooper, J. E., & Sartorius, N. (1974). *The measurement and classification of psychiatric symptoms.* Cambridge: Cambridge University Press.

Winnicott, D. (1958). *Col1ected papers.* New York: Basic Books.

Wirtz, E. M., & Kächele, H. (1983). Emotive aspects of therapeutic language: a pilot study on ver-adjective-ratio. In W. R. Minsel, & W. Herff (Eds.), *Methodology in psychotherapy research* (pp. 130– 135). Frankfurt am Main: Lang.

Wiser, S. L., & Goldfried, M. R. (1993). A comparative study of emotional experiencing in pyschodynamic-interpersonal and cognitive-behavioral therapies. *Journal of Consulting and Clinical Psychology, 61,* 892–895.

Wolgast, B. M., Lambert, M. J., & Puschner, B. (2003). The dose-response relationship in a college counseling center: Implications for setting session limits. *Journal of College Student Psychotherapy, 8,* 15–29.

Woody. G. E., Luborsky, L., McLellan, A. T., O'Brien, C. P., Beck, A. T., Blaine, J., et al. (1983). Psychotherapy for opiate addicts: Does it help? *Archives of General Psychiatry, 40,* 639–645.

Wulsin, L. R., Vaillant, G. E., & Wells, V. E. (1999). A systematic review of the mortality of depression. *Psychosomatic Medicine, 61,* 6–17.

Wündrich, M., Peters, J., Philipsen, A., Kopasz, M., et al. (2008). Clinical teaching with simulated patients in psychiatry and psychotherapy. *Nervenarzt, 79,* 1273–1281.

Yalom, I. D. (1995). *The theory and practice of group psychotherapy* (4th ed.). New York: Basic Books.

Yalom, I. D., & Lieberman, M. A. (1971). A study of encounter group casualties. *Archives of General Psychiatry, 25,* 16–30.

Yeaton, W. H., & Sechrest, L. (1981). Critical dimensions in the choice and maintenance of successful treatments: Strength, integrity, and effectiveness. *Journal of Consulting and Clinical Psychology, 49,* 156–167.

Yomogida, Y., Sugiura, M., Watanbe, J., Akitsuki, Y., Sassa, Y., Sato, T., et al. (2004). Mental visual synthesis is originated in the fronto-temporal network of the left hemisphere. *Cerebral Cortex, 14,* 1376–1383.

Zanarini, M. C. (1993). BPD as an impulse spectrum disorder. In J. Paris (Ed.), *Borderline personality disorder: Etiology and treatment* (pp. 67–85). Washington, DC: American Psychiatric Press.

Zarbock, G., Drews, M., Bodansky, A., & Dahme, B. (2009). The evaluation of supervision: Construction of brief questionnaires for the supervisor and the supervisee. *Psychotherapy Research, 19,* 194–204.

Zinbarg, R. E., Barlow, D. H., Brown, T. A., & Hertz, R. M. (1992). Cognitive-behavioral approaches to the nature and treatment of anxiety disorders. *Annual Review of Psychology, 43,* 235–267.

Zuroff, D. C., Colussy, S. A., & Wielgus, M. S. (1983). Selective memory and depression: A cautionary note concerning response bias. *Cognitive Therapy and Research, 7,* 223–232.

Zuroff, D. C., & Mongrain, M. (1987). Dependency and self-criticism: Vulnerability factors for depressive affective states. *Journal of Abnormal Psychology, 94,* 14–22.

INDEX